The Real Business of Ancient Maya Economies

Maya Studies

UNIVERSITY PRESS OF FLORIDA

Florida A&M University, Tallahassee
Florida Atlantic University, Boca Raton
Florida Gulf Coast University, Ft. Myers
Florida International University, Miami
Florida State University, Tallahassee
New College of Florida, Sarasota
University of Central Florida, Orlando
University of Florida, Gainesville
University of North Florida, Jacksonville
University of South Florida, Tampa
University of West Florida, Pensacola

The Real Business
of Ancient Maya Economies

From Farmers' Fields to Rulers' Realms

EDITED BY

Marilyn A. Masson,

David A. Freidel,

and Arthur A. Demarest

Foreword by Arlen F. Chase and Diane Z. Chase

UNIVERSITY PRESS OF FLORIDA

Gainesville / Tallahassee / Tampa / Boca Raton

Pensacola / Orlando / Miami / Jacksonville / Ft. Myers / Sarasota

25 24 23 22 21 20   6 5 4 3 2 1

Library of Congress Cataloging-in-Publication Data
Names: Masson, Marilyn A., editor. | Freidel, David A., editor. | Demarest,
    Arthur Andrew, editor.
Title: The real business of ancient Maya economies : from farmers' fields
    to rulers' realms / edited by Marilyn A. Masson, David A. Freidel, and
    Arthur A. Demarest ; foreword by Arlen F. Chase and Diane Z. Chase.
Description: Gainesville, FL : University Press of Florida, 2020. | Series:
    Maya studies | Includes bibliographical references and index.
Identifiers: LCCN 2019024403 (print) | LCCN 2019024404 (ebook) | ISBN
    9780813066295 (hardback) | ISBN 9780813057408 (pdf)
Subjects: LCSH: Mayas—Economic conditions. | Mayas—Antiquities. |
    Mayas—History.
Classification: LCC F1435.3.E27 R45 2020 (print) | LCC F1435.3.E27
    (ebook) | DDC 972.81—dc23
LC record available at https://lccn.loc.gov/2019024403
LC ebook record available at https://lccn.loc.gov/2019024404

The University Press of Florida is the scholarly publishing agency for the State University
System of Florida, comprising Florida A&M University, Florida Atlantic University, Florida
Gulf Coast University, Florida International University, Florida State University, New
College of Florida, University of Central Florida, University of Florida, University
of North Florida, University of South Florida, and University of West Florida.

University Press of Florida
2046 NE Waldo Road
Suite 2100
Gainesville, FL 32609
http://upress.ufl.edu

Contents

Figures

Tables

Foreword

Over the course of the last two decades there has been a dramatic change in our understanding of the complexity of ancient Maya civilization. This has been possible for several reasons: (1) LiDAR (Light Detection and Ranging) has permitted a much more nuanced and broader understanding of the ancient Maya landscapes; (2) acknowledgment that markets and market exchange existed in the past has led to a different view of the ancient Maya economy; (3) new interpretations of hieroglyphic texts have confirmed both broader political ties and complexity; and (4) a major expansion of archaeological projects within the Maya area has provided a greater understanding of site patterns and variability.

A primary catalyst for revolutionizing our understanding of the Maya past has been the application of LiDAR to the Maya region. This technology has finally permitted Maya archaeologists to gain spatial data on ancient Maya land use in large swaths of jungle landscape. Researchers are no longer constrained by limited site maps and budgets that only permit mapping work in small restricted areas. LiDAR data have demonstrated how large and densely settled some Maya cities were; these data have also revealed road systems that integrated cities and polities as well as recovered evidence for constructed defenses, indicating more widespread warfare than had once been suspected. Importantly, the LiDAR data confirmed that Classic Period Maya civilization was exceedingly complex and that sites were diverse in their layouts. Importantly, models portraying the ancient Maya at their height as being small isolated settlements engaging in less complex forms of sociopolitical organization (chiefdoms) could no longer be supported by spatial data.

A second reason for our new understanding of the ancient Maya is the acknowledgment of the existence of markets and market systems, leading archaeological discussion of ancient economic systems to break away from conceptions that formal market systems were relatively recent and only associated with monetary systems. The recognition that ancient New World societies used both marketplaces and market systems is still relatively new in its application in archaeology. In the Maya area, it was initially especially difficult to reconcile this economic revisionism with hieroglyphic texts that contained almost no economic information—and we are still contemplating this conundrum. Thus, this volume is a timely attempt by Maya archaeologists to understand how ancient Maya economic systems operated in archaeological data recovered on the ground and to come to terms with what the implications of a market-based society might mean for our interpretations of the past.

Hieroglyphic interpretation has been key in driving forward the field of Maya Studies. Yet, before LiDAR and without the acceptance of market-based economic systems, it also served to promote a less complex model of ancient Maya society at its height that was largely devoid of economics other than gifting and developed political models based more on a cult of personality than on any recognition of large populations and bureaucracies. Hieroglyphic transcriptions undoubtedly are currently driving our understanding of larger political units, warfare, and secondary elites. But revisions in our view of ancient economics and the data provided by LiDAR "surveys" have resulted in a broader recognition that the detailed organization of ancient Maya society was only partially represented within these texts. Thus, the conjunction of Maya hieroglyphic texts with archaeological data and spatial data are yielding new insights into the past.

A final reason for our new understanding of the ancient Maya also comes from the expansion of archaeological research in the Maya area—and this is well represented within this volume. This expansion not only has produced sizable amounts of new data at varied sites and regions over the last two decades but has also permitted new researchers with diverse and alternative interpretations to have a voice. Yet, without the advances in our spatial and economic understandings of the Maya, these new data were (and are) difficult to process in a coherent theoretical fashion. Past training, preconceptions, and indoctrination in traditional anthropological theory based on smaller and simpler societies have created barriers for recognizing and interpreting the complexity that we now embrace in Maya Studies. This may mean that some of the changes caused by our new understanding of ancient Maya society will be slow in their application. However, we have no doubt that the new syntheses that will evolve will be substantially different from those followed in the nineteenth and twentieth centuries. Archaeologist J. O. Brew (1946:65) famously said of typologies: "We need more rather than fewer classifications, classifications, always new classifications, to meet new needs." This same sentiment is applicable to Maya Studies; we also need new and better theory than what we have traditionally been using. This volume represents a strong move in this direction.

Arlen F. Chase and Diane Z. Chase
Series Editors

Abbreviations

AMS	accelerator mass spectrometry
APG	Angiosperm Phylogeny Group
CAM	Crassulacean Acid Metabolism
CCQ	Callar Creek Quarry
CONANP	Comisión Nacional de Áreas Naturales Protegidas
EIR	Elevated Interior Region
FAMSI	Foundation for Advancement of Mesoamerican Studies
GIS	geographic information system
GRIN	Germplasm Resources Information Network
GUBs	General Utility Bifaces
INAA	Instrumental Neutron Activation Analysis
INAH	Instituto Nacional de Antropología e Historia
JBG	Jato Black-on-Gray
LiDAR	Light Detection and Ranging
LMHP	Lake Mensabak Homegarden Project
MBR	Maya Biosphere Reserve
MNV	minimum number of vessels
NAA	neutron activation analysis
NCALM	National Center for Airborne Laser Mapping
NGO	nongovernmental organization
NSF	National Science Foundation
PRALC	Proyecto Regional La Corona
pXRF	Portable X-ray Florescence
SAA	Society for American Archaeology
SMJ	San Martín Jilotepeque
TBJ	Tierra Blanca Joven
UBRV	upper Belize River valley

I

Theoretical Approaches

1

Nuts, Bolts, and Bridges

Some Reflections

DAVID A. FREIDEL

This has been a long time coming. I thought I had seen the last of paradigm shifts in our discipline's local knowledge with the acceptance of the decipherment of Maya texts and the integration of history into our archaeological thinking, but I was wrong. Paradigm shifts, as Thomas Kuhn (1962) showed more than fifty years ago, are not reasoned, rational, dry, or quiet. They are exuberant, celebratory, hopeful, and potentially fragile (Lakatos and Musgrave 1970) and therefore worthy of defense and substantiation with the nuts and bolts of our efforts. With discovery in the field and in the lab, serious attention to detail and privileged information like that from Cerén, the prospect of complex variation, and the patient compilation of evidence patterns years in the making like those at Caracol, the contributors to this book show what makes archaeological science truly worth doing. We know better now and we will know much better in the future: nuts, bolts, and the interpretive bridges to a new understanding of Maya political economy that we build with them are here. Important recent books underscore the trends represented in our collective work (Hirth and Pillsbury, ed. 2013; King, ed. 2015). Friends and colleagues no longer with us like Bruce Dahlin (Dahlin et al. 2007) and Leslie Shaw—who declared: "It really does matter for the larger understanding of Maya economy how goods were moved from producer to consumer, as this exposes the power and decision-making retained by various segments of society" (Shaw 2012:118)—recently synthesized the state of this inquiry and helped pioneer the way forward. We acknowledge their foresight and intellectual courage. I am happy to say that many of the authors address Shaw's elementary concern in concrete ways. We have all been teaching each other in the preparation of this book, and it is a great privilege for me to be able to comment on some of the major trends outlined.

Paradigms are made of paradigms, great examples of imaginative method linked compellingly to good theory. Arthur Demarest, Bart Victor, Chloé Andrieu, and Paola Torres (Chapter 3) and Eleanor King (Chapter 2) review theory and a lot of the literature for us, including reference to chapters in this book, to show that we have some ways to go before consensus on the bridges. Everyone who opens this book should study these innovative, challenging, and enthusiastic theory papers. Both King and Demarest and his collaborators argue that we need to abandon dichotomous positions such as market versus nonmarket and recognize spectrums of institutional variability. Both these chapters underscore the agency of traders and those involved in commercial enterprise. Demarest and his colleagues call on us to embrace the polythetic nature of the terms that we use to discuss political economic institutions as now core to the discipline of applied economics. They draw on more than a decade of intensive research at the site of Cancuén and applied economics as practiced by Bart Victor and others at the Owen School of Business at Vanderbilt to frame what they clearly view as a new programmatic approach to the Maya past to gain a better understanding of economic variability and agency. They suggest that we turn to applied economics as a source of new models and require ourselves to refine our chronological controls significantly, especially our ceramic chronologies, to allow for the application of such contemporary modeling. Distributional dynamics are volatile and variable in this view and hold the key to transcending a focus of marketplaces as such and discerning the presence and nature of market economics that do not even require the existence of such places—Cancuén, they declare, did not have a marketplace despite its extraordinary and innovative commercial enterprises.

Demarest and his colleagues critique the chronological and contextual controls in Masson and Freidel's collaborative work on artifact distributions and concomitant economic organization at Mayapán and Tikal suggesting the existence of marketplace exchange in both places (Masson and Freidel 2012, 2013). It is true that Classic Tikal's record spans a much longer period than Mayapán's Postclassic record. The distributional studies reflect this, so are these apples and oranges (nuts and bolts)? Andrieu (Chapter 24) suggests that the Early and Late Classic economies of Tikal were quite different in the use of jade and obsidian, so perhaps Demarest and his collaborators have a point. They would argue that in some other cases, such as at Caracol in the Late Classic Period, evident stability in the economic institutions allows the use of longer spans to compose distributional patterns (Chase and Chase, Chapter 8). Still, Demarest and his colleagues do acknowledge that Tikal likely did have a marketplace: they just do not think that such places matter all that much when determining political economies and their development over time. What matters is getting much more clarity on distributional patterns over wider ranges of context and shorter spans of time and then using more sophisticated modeling facilitated by the use of applied economics.

But marketplaces are likely to remain of interest to many contributors to this book, including me, even as we strive to refine our other approaches to Maya political economy. Christopher Jones (1996), of course, identified the central market at Tikal decades ago, a distinctive masonry complex. Recently Ruhl, Dunning, and Carr (2018) used LiDAR imagery to detect other likely masonry marketplaces with designs similar to the Tikal market in southwestern Campeche. Bernadette Cap (Chapter 22) shows how archaeologists can forensically identify marketplaces in what Marilyn Masson and I dubbed "wide open spaces" (Masson and Freidel 2013). If Cancuén did not have a marketplace, that may have been due to its exceptional economic organization as now being published by Demarest and his colleagues in many new articles and chapters (as summarized in Chapter 3). They make the intriguing observation that eighth-century Cancuén's economic strategies were quite distinct from those used at coeval Classic cities to the north in the southern Maya lowlands. They argue that such dynastic Classic Maya polities evince a hypercoherent pattern of settlement and political economic interaction. I am reminded of the great excitement surrounding the adoption of theory from the New Geography and the application of Central Place Theory to the Maya lowland polities.

Eleanor King, along with Leslie Shaw, has been working on marketplaces and their denizens. She points out that we need more refined ways to access the institutions of exchange themselves, the kinds of traders, their class status, and their organizations. In ethnohistorical literature she discerns levels within the institutionalization of Ppolom (or p'olom) merchants, pointing to specialists in local trade as well as specialists in long-distance trade. On the nitty-gritty side, Kenneth Hirth's (1998) exemplary study of the economy of Xochicalco has gained traction among us. We learned from Hirth that we can potentially discern the economic agents in a marketplace economy if we pay close attention to the distribution patterns of the things people made, used, and discarded: those lively social things described by Appadurai (1988), chirping quietly in our lab drawers and boxes and waiting as in *Toy Story* for us to get with the program.

Marilyn Masson (Masson and Freidel 2012, 2013) used this distributional analysis technique to show that the people of Classic Period Tikal, like those of Mayapán, worked with market places as registered in the kinds and amounts of trade goods found in households of the city. In another close-grained study of contextual distribution (Chapter 4), Scott Hutson, a collaborator in Bruce Dahlin's (2009) marketplace hypothesis, shows how the obsidian consumers of Chunchucmil are not like those of Tikal. Keying into obsidian, a commodity of focus for many scholars looking at Maya exchange, Hutson uses statistical analyses comparing Tikal and Chunchucmil household samples to conclude that, while frequency of this import at Tikal seemingly varies with overall prosperity or wealth of households and proximity to the central market, at Chunchucmil such correlations remain more obscure and problematic. He concludes that marketplace exchange exists in both places, but it was no doubt institutionally part of larger and distinct political and social arrangements—dynastic rulers and their courts at Tikal, more likely peer associations of great merchant houses at Chunchucmil for starters. Personally, I am intrigued by the Chunchucmil household with high access to obsidian and evidence of processing rough textiles. Bulk commodities require bulk containment, and bags of cactus fiber cloth would have been at a premium in the salt trade of Chunchucmil. Perhaps the obsidian tools were important to such production.

Once we have the perspective and the methodology, we can start to discern and study the variability. We see the choices made by people operating within institutional parameters, defining their social relationships and undertaking daily business. The Terminal Classic rural households studied by Masson and her colleagues (Chapter 5) had access to a wide array of nonlocal goods, suggesting that they had options for trading opportunities to supply basic household inventories. But what could be more commonsensical than those Postclassic rural farmers and craftswomen who found themselves drawn to the urban marketplace of Mayapán, the last standard of the north? The Maya got into the towns and cities. Marketplaces were socializing places, good for exchanging glances as well as goods and setting up family negotiations that resulted in reproduction. And they got around a lot: bioarchaeologists Andrew Scherer and Lori Wright (2015; see also Cucina 2015) show us that there is really only one genetic pool in the Maya lowlands.

When people were in their places, they very likely owned them. Iván

Batún, Patricia McAnany, and Maia Dedrick (Chapter 12), through their fine ethnohistorical exegesis, draw the scales from our eyes and show that the ordinary people of the Contact Period Maya of the north owned land. As part of Jeremy Sabloff and William Rathje's Harvard-Arizona Cozumel Project in 1972, I could monitor Postclassic households through accumulative stone wall construction, gradually dividing up houselots to accommodate expanding families at the small town of La Expedición. This place with its modest center and massive "agglutinated" platforms was evidently one of several given to warehousing long-distance trade goods on the island (Freidel and Sabloff 1984). Living in the center of the community may have given privileged access to the warehouse business.

The low-density urbanism of the Maya was a deeply ancient strategy and a prevalent one, with exceptions such as the astonishing Middle Preclassic town of Nixtún Ch'ich' (Rice and Pugh 2017). Preclassic El Mirador and its satellite cities were truly enormous (Hansen 1998), but the people of the area were spread out and willing to walk or canoe over significant distances. Richard Hansen and his colleagues (Chapter 18) propose a Dendritic Model for the Mirador region, based on Robert Santley's study of Tenochtitlán and its hinterland in the Basin of Mexico (see his Matacapan work, 1994). El Mirador has terraced intensively cultivated lands around it and a causeway system denoting effective integration of these lands. A Dendritic system is an extractive one (C. Smith 1976). Was El Mirador a tributary state? This is plausible, but we need more fine-grained analyses of contextualized artifacts from the site and architectural evidence of elites and their palaces. Looking at the Central Karstic Uplands, Beniamino Volta, Joel Gunn, Lynda and William Folan, and Geoffrey Braswell (Chapter 20) survey the likely walking and canoeing routes east-west across the peninsula. One of these goes through El Mirador. Their GIS (geographic information system) models make a plausible case for such routes passing through Classic Period Calakmul, seventh and early eighth century capital of the Kaanul regime. Looking at this geography from Chetumal Bay, Debra Walker (2016) shows how canoe trade converging there could well have moved goods overland to Campeche. Volta and Gunn (2012) affirm the existence of this cross-peninsular route. Would Calakmul and Tikal have been Late Classic rivals in cross-peninsular trade? In 1979 at the International Congress of Americanists in Vancouver, Chris Jones (1996) gave a presentation on the Tikal Central Market, suggesting that Tikal's economic power derived from its location on a reasonable portage from the eastern to the western river systems in the southern lowlands. Volta and his colleagues (Chapter 20) describe the exchange networks and routes with lithic distributions. Rocks, as we have already seen, make great bolts.

Shifting back to marketplace exchange, Keith Eppich (Chapter 9), who embraced Hirth's marketplace paradigm long ago (Eppich and Freidel 2015), lucidly describes how the entangled means of making and moving things works within and around markets at El Perú–Waka'. Such institutional dances of politics and their economic foundations represent key relationships that we all strive to elucidate in our contemplation of Classic courts and those who lived within them and outside them.

Diane and Arlen Chase, who grew up with the reality of the Tikal market, have always favored a marketplace economy. Their prodigious database from metropolitan Caracol allows them to demonstrate, again through fine-grained patterns in the production and consumption of goods, that a marketplace economy worked for a great metropolis in the Late Classic Period but started to fail there in the Terminal Classic Period. Yes, drought occurred in the ninth century, but there had always been drought periodically. The Maya region evolved over millennia as a world, an interconnected and ultimately mutually reliant array of economic agents and institutions. When politicians started to mess with the transport and trade of goods in the Late Classic wars in the southern lowlands, many traders slowed or diverted their caravans: marketplaces diminished in scale and reliability.

Weighing in on the theory side, Chase and Chase outline the scales of political economy from household to regional civilization (Chapter 8). They have an enduring conception of the distinctive role of Caracol in the history of Classic Maya civilization. Whether or not one agrees with this conception, Caracol was a city to be reckoned with by all contemporaries: of necessity, events and interaction at the regional level impacted all the scales below. To be sure, as several contributors make clear and as discussed below, economics, like politics, are local. In some instances local economics owed little or nothing to what was going on in wider spheres. But it would be a mistake to retreat to an earlier conception of Maya villagers and townsfolk as predominantly independent economically (see Masson and Peraza 2004). As Chase and Chase have documented over decades of work, when Caracol as a state failed, its people suffered and ultimately left for viable social networks elsewhere. The same can be said generally about the Maya lowlands: states and elites on the one hand and ordinary peoples on the other reciprocally served common interests by means of common economic institutions. That is, in essence, the new Maya political economics.

Economic scales were institutionally integrated because the Maya, like everyone else who farms on the planet, figured out that they had to mitigate environmental risks by sharing them across real or potential exchange networks. The basic alternatives are migration, a fraught undertaking at best, as we see in our modern world, or famine, which indeed plagued the late Protohistoric Maya as well as postconquest populations when the Spanish dismantled their political economies. So our economic models must also be complex and mutable. If food moved, it did so in response to risk (Freidel and Shaw 2000). As Prudence Rice (Chapter 25) shows in her study of Jato Black-on-Gray ware, some communities and commerce survived the ninth-century chaos in the southern lowlands: the trade routes through the Lakes District and across the Petén, never completely abandoned, never completely failed.

But when this world worked, the people in it moved a lot of stuff. Arthur Demarest, Chloé Andrieu, and their colleagues (2014) have demonstrated that the elite of Cancuén on the Pasión River were moving jade and obsidian in the Late Classic Period as bulk commodities. They would argue that this is a very late development, but that may be because their Cancuén data are from the end of the Classic. Brent Woodfill (Chapter 10) in his fine-grained studies of the industrial production of salt at Salinas de los Nueve Cerros on the Chixoy River has good reason to suggest that bulk commodity production and distribution extends back into the Preclassic Period. What these two important arenas have in common is canoe transport. A distinctive concentration of obsidian scrapers is present at one locality in the settlement of Salinas that is otherwise not particularly distinctive. I wonder if the people there were crafting cactus cloth, which would require much scraping to prepare the fiber, for bagging the salt that Salinas clearly was producing in great quantities. We need to start looking more closely at bulk commodity storage and shipment as an area of economic activity (e.g., Kepecs 2003). Edge-damage microscopic investigation could test the idea of a complementary industry of salt bag-making. Guatemalans make fine cactus-cloth bags nowadays, which they probably made for overland hauling and canoe transport of goods in Pre-Columbian times as well.

Canoe transport has even greater importance, as reflected in the discovery of the Intracoastal Waterway on the western and northern coast of Yucatán by Fernando Robles Castellanos, Anthony Andrews, and Rubén Chuc Aguilar (Chapter 21). The benchmark monograph on the Maya salt trade (Andrews 1983) really established bulk commodity production and distribution as a working hypothesis. There is now more reason than ever to see the lowland Maya economy as one that moved enormous quantities of salt along with other perishable bulk commodities like maize, fine lime for nixtamal and cotton, and both raw and woven textiles. Dorie Reents-Budet and Ronald Bishop (Chapter 19) outline potential cotton textile production and exchange networks in the lowlands as political economic organizations, drawing on evidence from textile representations in Maya vase art and other media. Certainly the idea that the great rival states of Tikal and its allies on the one side and Calakmul as the seat of the Kaanul Empire on the other had well-organized supply networks for textiles makes good sense of the geopolitics of the southern lowland Classic Period. Reents-Budet and Bishop underscore the evidence for textile tribute, but they are mindful of textiles as currency as well. The economic anthropologist David Graeber (2014) shows that tribute and currency are inextricably entwined phenomena.

Kenichiro Tsukamoto at El Palmar in Campeche (Chapter 15) shows that *lakam* "banner bearing" ambassadors from the Kaanul regime (under Yuknoom Ch'een the Great) to Copán's court of Waxaklajuun Ubah K'awiil were privileged to commission hieroglyphic stairways and carry out lavish feasts in their own ceremonial center near those of their local rulers, Kaanul vassal lords of the ajaw status. The fine ceramics of the Lakam included small tobacco containers. A distinctive white ware tobacco container of a kind made in Copán was discovered as a prized possession of Queen K'abel, a Kaanul royal woman and likely the daughter of Yuknoom Ch'een the Great, who married into the Wak dynasty at El Perú–Waka' (Eppich 2011). It would be more plausible to see this souvenir arriving by way of El Palmar and Calakmul than across enemy territory held by Tikal and its allies. Gift-giving and tribute are clearly still vital features of Maya political economy, even as we study marketplace exchange and other nuts and bolts features of it. Tsukamoto's discovery of this official status makes sense to me in terms of the ethnohistorical descriptions of the gathering of the banners at the Temple of Kukulcán in Mayapán during the heyday of that trade-anchored confederacy. Alexandre Tokovinine, in his intriguing epigraphic investigation of tallies and tally sticks, counting, and accounting (Chapter 16), observes that Classic Maya bean counters were likely counting tens of thousands of cacao beans, a bulk commodity that moved over very significant distances. Again, who is studying cactus fiber production and the sacks? Scott Hutson identifies at least one family, using obsidian to make sacks, at Chunchucmil (Chapter 4). Everything from maize to rocks would have required these sacks for shipment.

That brings me back to rocks. It may be surprising to think of obsidian as a lowland bulk commodity—note the large bullet cores from near Cancuén as far as the eye can see cited in Chapter 3—but the existence of large-scale production of chert at Río Azul, Colhá, and other sites has been established for a generation. Eleanor King (Chapter 2) explores the different scales of trade and marketplace distribution that Colhá chert patterns imply in different periods of the site's history. Chert can be found in several parts of the lowlands, so its movement was as much a matter of taste as of necessity for many people: still, it did move and its manner of moving can elucidate both craft and trade dynamics.

Chloé Andrieu (Chapter 24) ingeniously looks at flake deposits from ritually charged contexts like royal tombs to discern indirectly that more workshops indeed existed than we have as yet discovered. She argues that we need to study these special deposits in conjunction with workshops, which means finding more workshops in our settlement pattern excavations. This is a matter of luck and expense, which is to say, a priority in research. Rachel Horowitz, Marcello Canuto, and Chloé Andrieu (Chapter 7) are also investigating the nuances of crafting and distribution from the vantage point of chert, sustaining the plausible inference that when chert is an import, as it is at La Corona in western Petén, its production, use, and disposal patterns show it to be a different economic medium than when it is locally available in abundance as in northwestern Belize. Chert may well have been a bulk commodity, but it was also heavy and expensive to move unless the people could use rivers, coasts, and flooded places.

But the rock stars in this book are the masons elucidated by William Ringle, Tomás Gallareta Negrón, and George Bey (Chapter 6), based on their long-term research in the Puuc region of Yucatán. This is the most illuminating discussion of how, and more importantly why, Puuc region families constructed so many masonry stone houses and palaces, of the kind that Frank Lloyd Wright called the finest in the Western Hemisphere, bar none. We all need to attend to this important housing *chaîne opératoire* elsewhere in the Maya world. Ringle and his colleagues make a compelling case for the idea that such beautifully made homes were gifts from rulers to vassals, involving vital and successful mobilization of expert craftspeople to sustain polities. We are used to arguing for the consolidation of control over redistribution of goods and services through central monumental construction projects, but turning centrally controlled talent and effort back into the hinterland communities is a novel and refreshing perspective.

Speaking of houses, Daniela Triadan and Takeshi Inomata (Chapter 17) review the wonderfully preserved evidence of crafting, food preparation, and quotidian consumption in the elite houses of Aguateca, preserved by sudden attack and abandonment. They arrive at the arresting conclusion that these prosperous and skilled folk were quite independent of any governing court in their access to things and their production of daily consumables. Such a perspective, of course, raises the question of just what the institutions of exchange might have been if the court played no central role. Others in this book have been pointing to marketplaces as an alternative to court transactions, as discussed below. Payson Sheets (Chapter 14) offers another example of superb preservation from Cerén and residents taking care of many of their own needs in a small community. Both of these contributions remind us that we are working, for the most part, with very difficult and incomplete data sets in Maya archaeology. Still, I don't think that lots of household crafting, gardening, and food preparation necessarily means that the Maya did not also participate in the trade and marketing activities. Indeed, Andrew Wyatt (Chapter 11) offers a perspective from the ordinary matters of gardening at Chan. How might we discern the degree to which the cultivation of one's own garden still implicates the larger economic world of trade and markets of which Maya villages were a key component? We return full circle in this regard to the lands of Yucatec farmers and their property rights.

So, did Pre-Columbian Maya marketplaces exist into the Classic Period or earlier? The consensus seems to be yes. Variability is anticipated as more concerted investigations are added to the literature from sites situated differently in space and time. Bernadette Cap at Buenavista del Cayo (Chapter 22), along with the research team at Chunchucmil (see Dahlin et al. 2010; Hutson 2016, 2017), has really shown us how to put together a convincing forensic investigation of a potential marketplace. Her methodological approaches are exemplary. Eleanor King (Chapter 2) is reviewing marketplaces and paralleling such efforts at Maax Na, also in Belize. The more forensic studies we have, the stronger the case for marketplaces.

Charles Golden, Andrew Scherer, and their colleagues (Chapter 23) in their multidisciplinary long-term work in the Usumacinta region, have markets firmly in mind as they deeply consider the impacts of Late Classic Maya polity dynamics. The Piedras Negras market system is coming into focus: perhaps the central market gradually gave way to more local markets in the surrounding towns as political bonds loosened within the polity. The governing elite of the capital relied on the steadfast participation of their towns and villages to maintain control of the Usumacinta region trade pathways, not only for internal integrity but as a bulwark against neighboring adversaries and their allies.

The theme of "nuts and bolts," the practical inner workings of what we know and what we hope to know through future work, in terms of the ancient Maya political economy has inspired the contributors to show how their research contributes to a common project. That project may never yield a singular "mainstream" reconstruction, for there were undoubtedly many political and economic institutional configurations in the ancient Maya world. A sharpened focus on such diversity is emerging. That said, I am encouraged to think that we will continue to find that the Maya world as a whole did thrive. From the beginning of their civilization and throughout its ups and downs, Maya people interacted politically and economically with larger regional societies and obtained access to localized, desirable resources available in a heterogeneous landscape. Their world is an aspect of the larger Mesoamerican one. Interaction was anchored in material things that people grew, crafted, used, and consumed, identified culturally as Maya. I believe the ancient Maya quite deliberately sustained and reproduced that world identity and thus regarded their political economies, for all their diversity, as a common project as well.

2

Modeling Maya Markets

ELEANOR M. KING

As this book demonstrates, recent advances in research have begun to redefine our views of Prehispanic Maya economic systems, a topic that has long eluded scholars (King 2016). Among the most significant conceptual breakthroughs are the ideas that Maya economies were plural in nature, rather than a single, common entity, and that markets played a more important and earlier role than previously thought (Dahlin et al. 2007; King and Shaw 2015; Tokovinine and Beliaev 2013). Methodological advances such as the distributional approach pioneered by Kenneth Hirth (1998), now widely applied in the Maya area (e.g., Eppich and Freidel 2015), also have been important. These developments enable us to examine specific sectors of the economy in greater detail and look at how they interrelated with other sectors. To date, however, we still lack working models of how Maya economies functioned.

With that in mind, this chapter focuses on developing a model of Maya markets based on current information and applying it to a specific test case: the site of Colhá, Belize, a center for lithic production. Before proceeding to these nuts and bolts, however, it is necessary to look back at the intellectual space from which we have just emerged. Several articles have already comprehensively reviewed the history of the archaeological concepts of markets and trade (e.g., Feinman and Garraty 2010; Oka and Kusimba 2008). Rather than repeat that information here, this chapter contextualizes what we now know and identifies lingering assumptions that may continue to infect our views.

A Brief Review of Assumptions

Archaeological views of trade, markets, and exchange in general come straight from anthropology, archaeology's parent discipline in the United States. Marcel Mauss irrevocably changed anthropological views of exchange in the 1920s when he posited that it was more of a social than an economic interaction, especially among non-Western peoples (Oka and Kusimba 2008). Despite this early revelation, economic anthropology had a slow start as an analytical focus within the profession (Firth 1967). Mauss's work led to an initial debate between primitivists, who viewed trade as marginal in early and non-Western societies because they relied primarily on agriculture, and modernists, who "saw no difference between contemporary and past human economic strategies" (Oka and Kusimba 2008:344). By the mid-twentieth century this discussion had morphed into the now famous substantivist versus formalist debate (Oka and Kusimba 2008). Based on Karl Polanyi's (1944, ed. 1957) work, the substantivists argued that markets could not exist outside of a capitalist system (Garraty 2010). Formalists, in contrast, thought that economic rationality—embodied in the term *Homo economicus*—was constant across time and cultures (Oka and Kusimba 2008). Formalists thus believed that trade was a natural human activity, which would evolve wherever resources were differentiated and the population was dense enough to support it (C. Smith 1976a; King and Shaw 2015). In the past few decades, this debate in anthropology has been muted by the rise of Marxism (Dalton 1990), political economy, world systems theory, and other approaches geared toward understanding the tangled relationships between the communities that anthropologists study and the ever-encroaching, increasingly international and capitalist world in which everyone lives. While the classic debate has been declared dead (Halperin 1984; Isaac 1993, cited in Feinman and Garraty 2010), crucial issues underlying it persist. Anthropologists still wrestle, for example, over whether theories that have universal explanatory power trump those of more specific cultural scope (Dalton 1990). They also continue to explore the role that different types of anthropological exchange—reciprocity, redistribution, and market—play in economies, especially those of non-Western societies.

This intellectual trajectory is familiar to many scholars, but its legacy in archaeology is less well understood. Because archaeologists deal primarily with premodern, precapitalist, and non-Western societies, the substantivist perspective cast a long shadow. Focusing on the social context of trade and exchange, archaeologists have tended to dismiss "profit, commerce, and other such motivations" as "absent, or, at best, negligible in early and non-Western societies" (Oka and Kusimba 2008:344). Where trade existed, it was viewed as being regulated by elites (Oka and Kusimba 2008). When long-distance trade became an analytical focus in the 1960s and 1970s, it fit neatly into this scenario, because elite control of exotic resources served to explain the development of socio-political complexity, especially in the New World (King 2000, 2016; Oka and Kusimba 2008). The advent of political economy in archaeology bolstered this view, as trade was subjugated to top-down social and cultural decision-making (Oka and Kusimba 2008).

Archaeologists have recently begun challenging substantivist views on pre-capitalist markets, especially in Prehispanic Mexico (e.g., Hirth 2010; Smith 2004), where Aztec markets were well documented. Accordingly, central Mexicanists leaned more toward formalism (Smith 1976; King and Shaw 2015). Their central research question, then, was never whether markets existed, but when they first emerged and what their presence signified (King and Shaw 2015). Yet the substantivist perspective influenced archaeologists to view precapitalist market systems, where they could be recognized, as largely controlled by the elite (Feinman and Garraty 2010). One result was the unexamined tautology that "the definition of a state is a polity that successfully controls a market economy and . . . the definition of a market economy is one centralized and regulated by the state" (Hartnett and Dawdy 2013:46–47). Equally insidious were the binary oppositions that implicitly framed all discussions of trade and exchange. While terms varied according to researchers, some examples include Western/non-Western, presence/absence of markets, *Homo economicus*/elite control, commercial or market economy/political economy, free market/command market, and market exchange/redistributive exchange (Feinman and Garraty 2010; Oka and Kusimba 2008). The dichotomy between precapitalism and capitalism could be added to that list. This binary mentality has made it difficult to view ancient and modern economies within the same framework (Feinman and Garraty 2010).

That prevailing attitude was particularly harmful in the Maya area, which suffered from a pair of additional handicaps not found elsewhere. First, initial misperceptions of the rainforest as a uniform habitat rather than a diverse one (Potter and King 1995) led to the idea that trade would be both unnecessary and difficult to conduct, given the dense vegetation (Bell 1956, cited in King and Shaw 2015). Accordingly, the only beneficial trade would be long-distance trade to import nonlocal necessities or luxuries, which the elite, as noted, could comfortably control. Second, the brand of tropical urbanism particular to the Maya consisted of dispersed settlement patterns. This configuration led many researchers to view Maya cities—and, by extension, their society—as less complex than those in more temperate areas (e.g., Sanders and Webster 1988; Webster and Sanders 2001:36–90). While scholars recognized the Maya as a civilization, it was either an "intractable exception" to generalizations about complexity (Bell 1956:433) or a society not quite as developed as its highland Mesoamerican counterparts (King 2000:1–90; King and Shaw 2015). These views prolonged and accentuated substantivism's hold on Maya studies, leading scholars to lean heavily on political and other top-down economic models and to continue debating the existence and relative importance of markets rather than focusing on their origins, as in the highlands. To this day, we struggle to break from the binary mind-set and to envision economic systems that can encompass elite control (or degrees of commoner control); ritual, political, and social purpose; *and* commercial activity by elite and nonelite alike.

Recent theoretical developments within economics and anthropology promise to help us out of this quagmire. They have shown that trade itself can be traced back to the Neolithic at least (Bar-Yosef 2002, cited in Oka and Kusimba 2008). It therefore predates—and may even be a precondition for—social complexity (Oka and Kusimba 2008). Even more important is the growing realization that all trade, even modern Western trade, is to some degree embedded (Feinman and Garraty 2010; cf. Polanyi 1944). In other words, all forms of trade combine political, social, economic, and other elements and motivations (Oka and Kusimba 2008). Among scholars of contemporary communities, this recognition has led to a resurgence of Polanyi's views as a way to critique neoliberalism (e.g., Bibeau 2008; Maya Ambía 2014). Among archaeologists, it has led to a reconceptualization of premodern economies as part of a continuum rather than as a binary opposition (Feinman and Garraty 2010; King and Shaw 2015). While not denying historical context or analytically important differences, researchers can now compare modern economies and their predecessors within a consistent theoretical framework (Feinman and Garraty 2010; Oka and Kusimba 2008). Specifically, we can examine markets in terms of characteristics that differ more by degree than by kind. While we are still developing strategies to do so, the following section reviews some issues to consider in the process.

Conceptualizing Markets

First, we need to be multiscalar in our approach (Feinman and Garraty 2010; Feinman and Nicholas 2010; King and Shaw 2015). Market systems operate on local, regional, and long-distance scales. While archaeologists have already proposed methods for considering multiple scales at once (e.g., Feinman and Nicholas 2010, cited in Feinman and Garraty 2010:178), problems remain. We need to question how well integrated were the markets that operated at different scales, rather than assume that they were part of an overarching network. We also need to agree on definitions for the different scales, which have been subject to a proliferation of varied descriptions and vocabulary (King and Shaw 2015). These definitions might need to be tailored to specific areas, as distances calculated for product travel in central Mexico (Hirth 2013), for example, do not necessarily match the range for comparable products in the Maya lowlands (Masson and Freidel 2013). We also need to consider issues of control, if any, that may have varied at each level. Our substantivist legacy leads us to want to see elite control at least at the regional and long-distance levels (e.g., Blanton 2013), if not at the local level, which some concede may have been in the hands of the producers (King 2000; Scarborough and Valdez 2009). Rather than look for indices of control, though, we should question whether it was present at all and be open to the idea that control could have varied in degree, rather than view it like other traditional dichotomies in stark terms of presence/absence.

Second, we need to figure out how markets interacted with other types of exchange, specifically, reciprocity and redistribution. For example, barter is often taken to be synonymous with or at least equivalent to market transactions (e.g., Dahlin 2009:356; Hirth and Pillsbury 2013:7). As argued elsewhere (King and Shaw 2015), however, barter is more properly defined as a type of reciprocity, because it involves the exchange of two things of an approximately equal value that is set by social consensus (Stanish and Coben 2013; but see Graeber 2012). Barter coexists with market transactions to this day, with neighboring vendors swapping products. Its prevalence in premodern markets (Stark and Garraty 2010), though, suggests that exchange systems then were even more mixed. Similarly, we should reexamine redistribution, the lynchpin of Polanyi's vision of ancient economies (Feinman and Garraty 2010). While some goods moved through redistributive networks (King 2016; King and Shaw 2015), many scholars agree that redistribution has never been used historically for large-scale provisioning except in times of crisis (Feinman and Garraty 2010). When and how, then, did it occur and what was its relationship to tribute and other forms of exchange? These are questions to pose rather than answers to presume.

In the same vein, we should remember, as Barry Isaac (2013) has pointed out, that the bulk of premodern economic activities probably took place outside of markets at the domestic level (King and Shaw 2015). These form part of the informal economy (Hartnett and Dawdy 2013; Oka and Kusimba 2008), which extends also to illicit activities that counter government control (Hartnett and Dawdy 2013). We need to integrate all these transactions into the larger economic picture, or we will have only a partial view of how premodern economies worked (Hirth 2013; Hirth and Pillsbury 2013; Isaac 2013; Masson and Freidel 2013). We also need to be prepared to find that relationships between formal and informal economies varied over time and space.

The common thread that runs through these different issues is one of agency: what did different actors do in different sectors and at different levels of the economy? Focusing anew on agency might help us reframe some of the issues just discussed. While this postmodern concept has worked its way into the Mayanist literature, it has not been applied evenly. Too often, again as a legacy of substantivism, we only look at the agency of elites. Political economic discussions are rife with the actions of rulers and their representatives but infrequently discuss anyone below that rarefied level. Commoners tend to be viewed more as pawns in a larger political end-game than as autonomous actors in their own right (Dahlin et al. 2010; King 2016). This perspective is aided and abetted by Prehispanic Maya texts and images, which focus on the rulers and rarely refer to anyone of a lesser status (Tokovinine and Beliaev 2013). Yet commoners, like the elite, made decisions and participated in the wider economic system (Lohse and Valdez 2004; Scarborough and Valdez 2009). We should therefore examine the strategies and choices of individuals of all ranks as well as their interactions (King 2016).

Focusing on agency allows us to do a couple of things. First, it forces us to concentrate on human behavior and decision-making, which are otherwise largely missing from our economic models (Shaw 2012) but absolutely critical to any true understanding of economies. Second, by investigating the conditions that motivated consumers and producers to accept and engage in market institutions (Garraty 2010:27), we can follow different threads of decision-making and see how they interconnect. We can also make allowances for the different types of motivation—commercial, social, religious, and/or political—that are part of all economies (Oka and Kusimba 2008). In this way, it might be possible to uncover the links among the formal and informal economies, different types of exchange, and different scales of marketing.

What I propose is no easy task; human behavior is notoriously hard to get at in the archaeological record. In economic research, problems of equifinality (e.g., Stark and Garraty 2010), in particular, obstruct attempts to reconstruct past processes and decision-making. There are nevertheless a few places where we can look at behavior. One is in the actual physical location of the market-place, which is where "behavior meets space" (Shaw and King 2015:169). We are now well on the way to identifying such locations in the Maya area and figuring out how they were organized (King 2015a). What we lack, however, is a concrete sense of how they functioned within the larger sphere of Maya affairs. In addition to the conceptual problems already enumerated, efforts in this direction have been hampered by the poverty of the lowland ethnohistorical record and the traditional reluctance of archaeologists to look to modern ethnographic examples (King 2015b). It is critical that we develop models that contextualize Maya market systems in ways that conform to how they organized the social, political, and religious aspects of their lives. Even if we now conceptualize ancient and modern markets on a continuum (Feinman and Garraty 2010), we still need to understand specific historical contexts (Feinman and Garraty 2010; Oka and Kusimba 2008) in order to place Maya market institutions through space and time within that framework. Cross-cultural frameworks, to date largely drawn from Western or highland Mexican models, should supplement rather than substitute for direct evidence from Maya archaeology.

The following section sketches a model of Maya marketing drawn from epigraphic, iconographic, ethnohistorical, and ethnographic sources detailed elsewhere (King 2015b, 2018). My intent is not to suggest that only one model fits the whole Maya area but rather to repeople the Maya world with actors as a basis for ongoing discussions. I then use information from the well-documented lithic production site of Colhá, Belize, to show how the model can be linked to archaeological data.

An Agent-Centered Model of the Maya Market System

Based on ethnohistorical sources, the Maya trading system seems to have been populated by many agents, who operated at different levels. Best known are the *p'olom*, the professional traveling merchants. They appear to have been long-distance traders, who went to the far reaches of the Maya area and beyond. While the *p'olom* have been compared to the Aztec *pochteca*, the two groups were not equivalent, as the *p'olom* did not carry the same kind of official status (Feldman 1985:15). Also, the *pochteca* were commoners, albeit ones with great influence (Calnek 1974; Hirth 2013; Léon-Portilla 1962), while the status of the *p'olom* is unclear. The most famous of the *p'olom* was a son of the Cocom noble house who was away on business when Mayapán was sacked (Roys 1962). Merchants are conspicuously absent from most Maya glyphs and pictorial representations (Tokovinine and Beliaev 2013), so it is unlikely that many were from the ruling elite. They may well therefore have been of lower elite or high commoner status. They would have owed fealty to the ruler and likely paid tax or tribute that was levied in the marketplace (King 2015b).

Another group of traveling traders were the *ah p'olom yokob* (singular: *ah p'olom yok*). Their range seems to have been less extended, though, as *yok* is a term often combined with a place designation to indicate a particular type of merchant. While interpretations of this term differ (cf. Tokovinine and Beliaev 2013), one likely explanation is that it designates merchants specializing in the goods of particular regions. *Ah kampech yok*, for example, would then indicate someone who traveled to Campeche for merchandise (King 2015b). In any case, the *p'olom yok* seem to have had a lesser scope than the *p'olom* and could be considered regional-level traders.

Beneath these two professional groups was an assortment of peddlers. Some, like the *ah k'aay*, seem to have traveled locally from town to town selling their wares. Others appear to have stayed put—or at least stayed in one town, though they may have traveled within it. Still other terms designate wholesale or bulk merchants and people who seem to have bought from local producers for re-sale in the market. There is also a term that refers to people who traded in the marketplace specifically, the *ah k'iwik yah* (King 2015b). Iconographic evidence from Calakmul supports the idea that many of these sellers specialized in particular goods, especially foods of different kinds. In fact, the evidence indicates that most goods sold were perishable (Dahlin 2009:354), a factor that has increased the difficulty of recovering marketplaces (King and Shaw 2015). Added to these specialized sellers in the marketplace were likely occasional vendors such as farmers and craftspeople who produced a surplus to share—what Frederic Hicks (1987:91, cited in Garraty 2010:18) calls "target marketers" (King 2015b). They would do so, presumably, only when they had more than they could exchange reciprocally with their immediate neighbors for other goods that they themselves required. As both ethnographic and ethnohistoric sources record their presence, women could have sold in the marketplaces as well as men. The acceptability of this profession varies in contemporary communities (Wurtzburg 2015), however, and probably did in the past as well. Whether women could be *p'olom*, *p'olom yok*, or other kinds of longer-range traders, for example, remains an open question.

In summary, then, the lowland Maya had professional long-distance and regional traders, as well as other, less formal types of vendors. Some of the latter traveled locally within a small group of towns, like the tinkers of Europe; others had a more fixed, permanent base. Some, too, likely traded full-time, like the *ah k'aay* or peddlers; others may have been part-timers. All these groups met at different times in the marketplace, the physical space where much of the trading happened. This space was generally in the center of a town or city, near the temples and secular administrative buildings. This pattern is common in Mesoamerica today, most likely because it allows both buyers and sellers to conduct other business while attending the market (Shaw and King 2015). Based on contemporary ethnographic data, it is likely that most Prehispanic markets were periodic, occurring at regular intervals over the course of the calendar, but cycled from town to town. Some of the largest cities, though, such as Tikal and Calakmul, probably had markets day-in, day-out, and year-round, judging by the permanence of their architecture.

The degree to which the elite controlled these markets remains moot. In the Maya highlands, a judge or arbiter adjudicated disputes and oversaw market operations. This person does not seem to have been of elite status or to have worked directly for elites. Rather, his social position was most likely on a par with that of the professional merchants, the group to which he was primarily responsible, which may even have selected him. As for the elite, they could have controlled access to the market itself (Shaw 2012), probably in the form of a tax or tribute, as is recorded for the *p'olom* (King 2015b). Elite control over market activities, however, seems unlikely.

Finally, it is worth recalling here that the marketing system was not the only way that goods circulated among the Maya. Not only were there reciprocal exchanges among neighbors, as noted above, but scholars have also long noted the presence of a dual exchange system ethnohistorically: one through the markets, the other through the "special exchange of the lords" (Feldman 1985:21, cited in Foias 2002:228). While the latter can be considered "wealth finance" (D'Altroy and Earle 1985) or part of the political economy (Foias 2002), the goods did not necessarily circulate hierarchically as tribute and redistribution. Many were also traded laterally, from one peer group to another (Potter and King 1995), as part of a balanced reciprocal exchange aimed at cementing alliances. Since the same goods could assume different values depending on how they were traded (Graham 2002; Lesure 1999; Speal 2009), we need to keep these different mechanisms in mind when examining their traces in the archaeological record.

Colhá Lithics and the Maya Marketing System: A Brief Overview

Colhá, Belize, has been well documented as an important manufacturing center for high-quality lithics from the Preclassic through the Postclassic Periods (Figure 2.1; Hester 1985; Hester and Shafer 1984; Shafer and Hester 1983, 1991). Chert bifaces and blades from the site circulated widely both regionally and interregionally (Hester and Shafer 1994; Shafer and Hester 1983, 1991). It is thus an ideal test case for the model sketched above. I focus here on the Classic, a period when marketing systems have been established to exist among the Maya (e.g., King 2015a).

While Colhá was an important regional center in the Preclassic, by the Late Classic it was a small community in comparison to other Maya sites (King 2000). The site center did not grow appreciably during this period, and lithic production moved away from the vicinity of the center, in part because stone resources were probably depleted there and in part because production was no longer centralized. Each workshop produced its own distinctive mix of tool types, ranging from oval bifaces to blades and tranchet-bit tools (King 2000). These types were standardized in form but idiosyncratically produced according to slightly different manufacturing techniques (King 2000). Though there are tantalizing hints that some chertworkers might have been women (King 2000:130), most of them are presumed to have been men, as it takes considerable physical strength to work the tough Colhá chert.

While Harry Shafer and Thomas Hester (1983) initially suggested that Altun Ha, a large site to the south, controlled Colhá and its production during this period, their proposal now seems unlikely. Altun Ha had its own workshops, with no evidence to support its direct meddling in Colhá's production, though it may have commanded political allegiance from the smaller site. Instead, as I have argued elsewhere (King 2000, 2012), it seems likely that the Colhá chertworkers themselves were in charge of both production and distribution. How they moved products from site to site has remained unspecified, however. So, the question before us now is: how might this data fit into the economic model just sketched? Also, how might market exchange in this case articulate with redistributive and reciprocal exchange?

Beginning with the local level, chert within Colhá almost certainly followed the reciprocal pathways of the informal economy. Since not everyone was a chertworker at the site, and since the chertworkers seem to have been full-time craftspeople (King 2000, 2012), neighbors with differing occupations

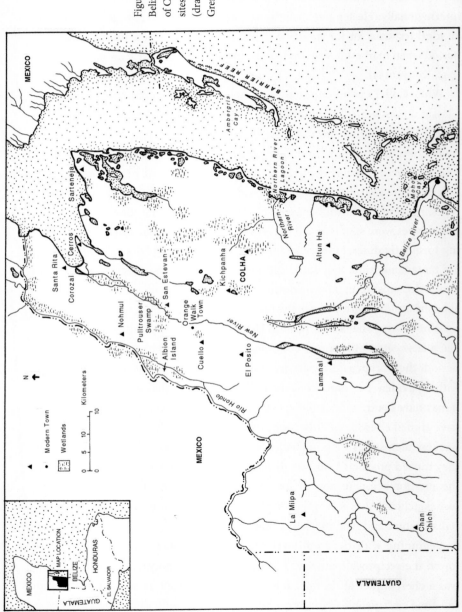

Figure 2.1. Map of Northern Belize showing the location of Colhá and some of the sites with which it traded (drawing by Georgianna Grentzenberg, 2000).

would have benefited from exchanging goods, much as Payson Sheets (2000) has documented for the site of Joya de Cerén in El Salvador. However, it is clear that not everyone at Colhá was plugged into the same networks. There is good evidence that the members of at least one household, more humble in material goods than its neighbors, did not receive all their tools from nearby workshops. Instead, they seem to have made a number of their own informal tools; what formal tools they had were not of the highest quality (King 2000, 2012). Reciprocal exchange might also have extended from the Colhá chert-workers to relatives and associates at other nearby sites. However, it also seems likely that the Colhá lithic specialists occasionally took their excess tools to market themselves, as target marketers. Whether there was ever a small market at Colhá itself remains a moot point, but there were likely markets at Altun Ha and Nohmul, large sites within a day's easy travel from Colhá. Wholesalers and other types of merchants, who specialized in obtaining goods from producers and reselling them in the marketplace, also might have helped to circulate Colhá goods at a local level (King 2015b).

On a regional and long-distance level the picture becomes more complicated. Shafer and Hester (1991) identified two distinct spheres of exchange for Colhá products: a "primary consumer area" of about 75 km in radius from the site that encompassed mostly northern Belize and a "peripheral consumer area" that reached places as far away as the central Petén. These types of distances suggest that the goods were largely in the hands of professional traders. At the regional level, the p'olom yok could have procured the lithics directly from the producers and sold them in various markets, from which they were then disseminated farther out into the area via consumers and/or local wholesalers and peddlers. In fact, some p'olom yok probably specialized specifically in northern Belize or parts of it, based on what we know of similarities in other types of goods, such as ceramics (King 2016). The farther-ranging p'olom, too, could have visited Colhá from time to time to acquire lithics. It seems even more likely, though, that neither group needed to have gone to the site. Instead, they could have obtained their supplies from target marketers or wholesalers in the regional markets.

While the evidence supporting the role of the p'olom yok is persuasive, given the widespread distribution of Colhá lithics in northern Belize, the part the p'olom played remains murkier. The goods recovered in the more far-flung sites that are tentatively or strongly associated with Colhá are mostly stemmed bifaces, a tool with both a utilitarian and a ritual function. Though many stemmed blades in the Late Classic were apparently used as spearpoints, others appear to have had a ritual function as well, as they are found in elite caches and burials (King 2000:162). It seems likely, then, that many of the blades found at distant sites entered the hands of the elite and the archaeological record in a variety of ways. While some could have been sold to elites by the *p'olom* at markets, it is more likely that they were part of the "special exchange of the lords" during at least part of their lifecycle. This exchange could have taken many forms. Northern Belizean elites could have purchased the blades in city markets and gifted them to peers, superiors, or subordinates at other sites within the region and beyond. These same elites could have acquired the tools as part of a tax or tribute from the *p'olom* or *p'olom yok*, paid as part of either the merchants' fees for participating in a market or the goods owed to a ruler upon return from travel, a practice documented ethnohistorically for the Maya highlands (King 2015b). Finally, the *p'olom*, some of whom operated from bases outside northern Belize, could have given the rulers of their own home cities stemmed blades as a part of the goods that *they* were obligated to pay. Disentangling which of these processes was at work requires finer-grained information than is currently available. However, all these different avenues and their intersections are important to keep in mind as we try to decipher how the system worked.

Conclusions

The market model presented here and its links to the known Colhá production and distribution network remain open for discussion. Much more work will need to be done before we really understand how Maya marketing systems worked. Two points should be clear, however. First, it is going to take us a while to divest ourselves of the lingering effects of prior assumptions, especially if we do not question and challenge those assumptions in the first place. Second, even if we do now allow for more commercial motivations in premodern societies, we still need to take local historical and cultural circumstances into account. It is important, then, that we begin constructing specifically *Maya* models for the Maya area. While comparisons from other parts of the world can be productive, they need to be controlled rather than imported wholesale to explain weak or absent phenomena, as has too often been the case in the past (e.g., Adams and Smith 1981; see also Becker 1979).

We are now in a better position than ever to begin constructing a more realistic picture of Prehispanic Maya economies, as they varied over time and space. By using models like the one proposed and building on past research, we can examine different exchange processes at different scales. For example, both Geoffrey Braswell (2010) and Masson and Freidel (2013) have used product distribution to emphasize the importance of polity-driven, regional exchange, albeit differently configured. However, how did those exchanges actually happen? Which agents carried those products to their final destinations? Were they professional or informal traders or a combination of both? Among the professionals, were they *p'olom* or *p'olom yok*? Which products moved through reciprocity and redistribution and which through markets? These and other questions can help us focus anew on the people behind the behaviors, who were, after all, at the center of the system.

By establishing the particular marketing system that characterized the Maya, we can also begin to distinguish behaviors that might be due to cultural factors from those that might be more universal. Oka and Kusimba (2008) have suggested that some attitudes and behaviors may be common to traders across cultures. Often, for example, professional traders keep to themselves as a community and develop separate networks because they are viewed with suspicion and even hostility by the political and intellectual elite (Oka and Kusimba 2008:357). Certainly, there are signs that this was the case among the Maya (King 2015b). What characteristics of this group, then, are near universal and which ones are culturally specific? These and other issues are before us as we take these first steps toward a better understanding of *Homo economicus maya*.

3

A New Direction in the Study of Ancient Maya Economics

Language, Logic, and Models from Strategic Management Studies

ARTHUR A. DEMAREST, BART VICTOR,
CHLOÉ ANDRIEU, AND PAOLA TORRES

Here we try to address the central question of this volume: How can we discover and understand the specific mechanisms and structures of the ancient Maya economy? The volume goal is to leave behind futile debates about overarching theories and "types" of economies and take a new direction by investigating how different Maya economies functioned from day to day and how and why economic mechanisms changed.

Overview

Following that general mandate, in this chapter we seek to accomplish several more specific goals, addressed more or less in the following order. First, this chapter invites Mayanist archaeologists to look at a new source of very specific, nondichotomous methodologies and case studies from contemporary to ancient, Western and non-Western, indigenous and colonial, using relativistic frameworks for interpretation and very specific elements or patterns that have been identified in all manner of societies—not just Western or "modern." Some of these are selected from the vast literature, debates, and ideas used in strategic management studies. For that reason they identify evaluate and use *very specific* aspects and tools, "nuts and bolts," of all manner of economies. Collaboration with strategic management experts (not academics) allows identification and interpretation of such specific elements as they are applied to advising development programs, business strategy, and other activities. Because they are applied, these specific observations usually avoid dichotomies or even broad characterizations and labels, as such titles are not analytical and don't really describe economies well or how they function. Note that generally unproductive use or studies of labels or "types" are common in archaeological literature. Many other studies, however, like those in this volume, are more focused on specific aspects of economy.

Second, in one subsection of the chapter we recommend that we *always* address "concepts" not in terms of labels or "types" of economies or dichotomies but in the framework used in the sciences and quantifiable social science: approaching aspects of the economy as a polythetic set composed of somewhat variable *individual elements* that can be evaluated on a relative scale. We argue that this has proven to be a more productive approach in most disciplines than seeking to justify global labels such as "market," "nonmarket," "Pre-Columbian," "Western," or "modern," "ancient," "capitalist," generally based on dichotomizing what are actually inherently relative scales on clusters of relative elements.

Third, such logic and some specific elements are used here to discuss a few recent examples. These show the utility of the use of the normal conceptual and methodological frameworks of science, forensic debate, and the social sciences that do sometimes use quantification. A core part of that approach is breaking down objects of study that are polythetic sets into elements that can be studied individually on relative scales. Such approaches or conceptions are often implicitly used in our field but often not used, losing great opportunities. Also, our examples show that, while conclusions can be clearly correct, the arguments for them may not be valid. Nonetheless, most applications come to convincing conclusions.

Our fourth goal is advanced at a few points this chapter where we call for giving a greater *relative weight* to some arguments or investigation that *should* be *presented* but have less precise chronologies or use *pars pro toto* and other logical flaws. Thus, "course corrections" are suggested in some uses of language that have drifted away from some basic rules of logical discourse. Such fallacies lead to some disagreements that are simply created by language.

Fifth, and finally, we provide short synopses of a number of recent (we believe successful) applications of very specific economic practices and/or strategies that we selected from a broad menu of such elements identified elsewhere in strategic management studies. Most of the items in that general menu don't work for Cancuén or for most of the other Classic Period lowland Maya economies, but some of the ones recently used have proven be very helpful. We summarize these applications then refer the reader to more extensive presentations, specifically comparisons that have helped us to understand some of the economic devices involved in the rise and collapse of the late eighth-century southwestern innovative economic network and of Cancuén.

Mayanists are invited to avail themselves of what they themselves believe to be examples, methods, or ideas that they find useful for their own work, adding new elements to the inventory of research tools, concepts, and case studies in the fields of organizational and management studies. Some aspects of the model seem complex, though they are really simple applications of logical language that offer the use of comparative elements in management research that might be helpful.

Here we focus on the polythetic/relativist approach and specific elements that might be useful to Mayanists and some critique of problems when they are not used. Be assured that in journals on management and administrative theory we are being just as critical of their misconceptions. We suggest new possibilities, case studies, and lessons from Pre-Columbian economies, especially Maya archaeology (e.g., Demarest and Victor 2018).

A New World of Ideas from Management Studies

Archaeologists, including the first co-author, have generally not looked at scholarship in the best university business and management schools. Research and teaching there now cover non-Western and ancient Western economies (e.g. Hudson 2010; Landes et al. 2010; Wunsch 2010), contemporary indigenous and "developing" economies (Fischer and Victor 2014), morality in Western/indigenous exchange (Victor et al. 2013), the sociological embeddedness of "economic cultures" (Dutton and Baum 1996; Granovetter 1985; Oliver 1996; Uzzi 1996), variability in the impact of symbolic factors on elements of market systems (Friedland and Alford 1991), economic ideologies (Meyer and Brian 1991), "trust" between economic systems to form and maintain new partnerships and networks (Suchman 1995; Zaheer et al. 1998; Zucker 1986), legitimation of innovations and exchange outside of preexisting stable exchange relationships (Doz 1996; Hamman and Provan 2000), merchant agency in practices and exchange networks (Hudson 2010), and many other elements from different societies worldwide that could be useful to our own research and interpretations of Maya economies.

In our opinion, management studies are far more useful than general economic theory or collaboration with economists precisely because they are *applied*, which moves away from grand overarching theory to specific mechanisms and elements used in economies: the far more realistic and we believe
more important goal of this volume.

Archaeologists would be surprised to see the degree to which management
studies draw on sociology and anthropology. The work of Kopytoff (1986),
Appadurai (e.g., 1986), and others on "the cultural biography of things" is
important to many scholars of management, because the manipulation of key
points in that "biography" is one goal of strategic management. Researchers
study culturally embedded economic practices and how they can lead to conflict or can be altered and manipulated for gain by multiple levels of agents in
those systems (e.g., Dutton and Baum 1996). This is essentially the analysis of
structure and agency, as in *doxa*, *habitus*, cultural capital, field, and so forth,
but in very specific applications and without pretentious citations of Conti-
nental sociology.

The most important benefit of such collaborations may be the vast and
comprehensive literature available in administration, organization, and management theory that is relevant to our studies. The size of this corpus reflects
the involvement of many thousands of scholars in these fields. Of course, it is
demanding for archaeologists to research a very dissimilar literature, most of
it narrow presentations or quantifications in a very different jargon (and most
of it turgid to archaeologists!). For that and other reasons it is preferable to col-
laborate directly with strategic management experts and get their help on this
literature (and vice versa).

Useful Conceptual Approaches to the Maya Economy and Research Tools That Could Be More Productive

Cowgill (1988) pointed out that many difficulties in the study of collapses were
due to miscommunication, differing implicit definitions of terms and concepts,
different "levels" in spatial or chronological units of interpretation, and other
issues of language and logic. Similarly, we believe that one stumbling block to
our economic research is not taking advantage of Cowgill's advice on this in
our debates.

First, while it may seem obvious, we can miss insights and opportunities by
overlooking the *relative* nature of many words, phrases, concepts, or elements

that define those broader concepts, including "diverse," "wealth," "integrated," "market," "marketplace," and so on.

It is generally accepted that such concepts or norms are actually polythetic sets of traits or elements, not single absolute entities. Words or phrases like "barter," "market," "money," and "market economy" can best be understood as polythetic sets of elements or traits in which one or two elements might be required but any other two out of four or three out of six elements, for example, are sufficient to use that term or concept. Then the elements in such polythetic sets can each be studied as variables on a *relative* scale, making analysis easier.

One unexpected benefit of this collaboration with management experts is this analytical clarity. In management and organizational assessments they normally utilize the relative and polythetic nature of concepts like "social benefit," "open distribution," "reciprocal exchange," and "market economy" to make research more productive and applicable. They use the elements within these polythetic sets on relative scales to study variability or change. Thus, relative and polythetic perspectives provide useful tools for analyzing specific economic practices, the goal of this volume.

One way in which polythetic and relativistic approaches can lead to new perspectives is by simply using the logic discussed above. As an example, it is frequently stated that now we recognize that the tropical forest is a "diverse" environment with significant environmental variability (e.g., Demarest 2004; King, Chapter 2; Potter and King 1995). It has been hypothesized that this diversity might necessitate high-volume exchange of foodstuffs for subsistence or as a hedge against drought via energy averaging. Here we agree completely with the main hypothesis but not with the argument as to why. We see merchant agency as pushing exchange of redundant resources as observed in economies, including Pre-Columbian ones, around the world.

Of course, the words "diverse" and "variability," like the word "tall," require that we always include or understand the implicit key question "Compared to what?!" (McDaniels 1969) in order to give such words meaning. Both "diversity" and "variability" are always present because both are relative terms. The real utility of concepts like "tropical forest" and "market economy" is to study individual elements in their *polythetic* set of traits that can be studied on *relative* scales (e.g., Masson and Freidel 2012, 2013; Hutson, Chapter 4; and other chapters in this volume). In this case, diversity in species per unit area is at a very high relative scale for "tropical forests" in terms of species and diversity compared to most environments. However, other elements of the polythetic set "environmental diversity" include diversity in geomorphology, mineral deposits, rock forms, elevations, temperatures, soil types, potential for different agricultural systems, range of possible food products, and other such relative elements. Overall, the tropical forest is less "diverse" *in comparison to some other Maya environments* in several of those other critical elements that together form the polythetic set called "tropical forest." If we compare the area most studied, the northern Petén lowlands, to an area of the same square kilometers in most highland zones or the actual functioning highland to coast systems, the Petén tropical forest is comparatively less "diverse" in the elements of elevations, diversity in geomorphology, mineral resources, temperatures, hydraulics, soil types, and thus the required or possible agricultural practices, resulting crop diversity, and hence both the pressures and the possibilities for exchange in food or anything else. So energy-averaging is a possible motive for some large-scale food exchange, but we suggest an alternative that we believe is more likely as a pressure for food exchange.

This is not a negative observation on current dialogue: rather, such logical clarifications of the relative nature of elements within polythetic sets can guide us toward new possibilities in explaining the clearly visible bulk exchange of some foodstuffs as found in all periods all along the Pasión River Valley, at Caracol, and elsewhere. For example, while some environments require considerable exchange to obtain needed subsistence goods, intensified but "redundant" interregional exchange systems involving widely or locally available foodstuffs are frequently not due to environmental resource diversity or agricultural deficiencies. More often the use of such exchange arrangements is to increase efficiency through specialization and is generally the result of strategies and agency by the intermediaries in exchange and production. This agency can be from the state or from merchants and managers (often a combined role). This alternative explanation for a higher level of exchange even in redundant resources including foodstuffs would be immediately recognized in strategic management studies. Merchants are not just intermediaries operating in the existing economic system and fulfilling the needs of consumers: they are also major agents of change in those economies, so we need to look at the opportunities for possible agency in the nature of the changes.

Merchant agency for self-interest might be seen in two well-documented examples of a shift to mass overproduction and intensification of exchange: Caracol with its sprawling landscape of underpopulated terraces for overproduction of agricultural products (A. Chase and D. Chase 2001; D. Chase and A. Chase 2014a, 2016; A. Chase et al. 2012) and Cancuén with an extremely high level of overproduction of obsidian blades and later jade preforms and we believe bulk importation and trade in a number of subsistence goods from the zone to its south (Andrieu, Chapter 24; Andrieu et al. 2011, 2014; Demarest et al. 2014, 2017a, 2017b).

It is not coincidental that in both of these cases, in different periods and for different reasons, such changes and intensifications of exchange as well as other radical shifts in economic practices occurred in times of great reduction in the centralized power of divine kingships and thus reduction of the ruler's political and ideological restraints on agents and less state distortion of purely economically determined equivalencies (e.g., A. Chase and D. Chase 2021; Demarest 2013; Demarest et al. 2014; Demarest, Victor, and Torres 2019). During such periods economic agents can enhance their role, benefits, and power (see the Venetian example below) through more commercialization, vertical integration, increased interregional exchange, and other aspects of economy that require more management and agents with more economic power.

We know that a rising class of merchants was present from the beginning in Maya societies from the Middle Preclassic on. For example, the population of Nakbe and Mirador could not be fully supported without large-scale exchange of food stuffs despite local intensive systems of agriculture (Hansen 2001). In turn that indicates a major role for exchange agents (merchants). In general the role of merchants probably declined at most sites due to the Terminal Preclassic crisis at the largest sites, but it recovered rapidly in the Early Classic. That is very notable in Tikal's control of the Pasión River route that we have hypothesized since the early 1990s, which would have included cacao, salt, cotton, and perhaps vanilla in addition to obsidian and jade that continued under other polities up to the collapse of most Pasión River sites (McAnany 2010, 2013). At many sites the merchant class had already promoted major changes in economic practices for their gain. This seems to have been growing and intensifying in the Classic Period and greatly increased (relative to some previous centuries) in the eighth century, ninth century, and Postclassic, especially in the northern lowlands and, of course, the highlands to the south.

Thus, using the polythetic nature and the relative scale of elements in concepts like "environmental diversity," "tropical forest," and "market economy" strategic management theory can provide alternative hypotheses on economic configurations and more importantly explain in different ways the reasons and devices utilized in their implementation. Another advantage of collaborations with management experts is that their prime business objective concerns the agency of merchants: many of them are economic advisers on decision-making by active merchants or development agencies that are interested in agency and specific tools to increase the profits or success of those that they advise.

Classic Maya Exchange, Marketplaces, and Market Economies

As archaeologists we seek physical evidence to generate and support hypotheses about marketplaces and are frustrated at the difficulty of their identification, as they are indeed "elusive" (Shaw 2012) and "transient" (King, ed. 2015). Some efforts have actually physically identified marketplaces (e.g., Dahlin et al. 2007), but in most cases they must be inferred from indirect measures like architecture forms or plaza placement, but especially from more open distribution of types of artifacts and materials (Hirth 1998, 2010; Hirth and Pillsbury, eds. 2013). Yet archaeologists are also becoming aware of the difference between "marketplace" and "market economy" and that market exchange can exist without large-scale marketplaces in the physical sense (e.g., Feinman and Nicholas 2010; Isaac 2013; Stanish and Coben 2013; Stark and Garraty, eds. 2010).

Market economies are not primarily about physical marketplaces, as seen in the Cancuén case below (where its general role was specialized as one node in an interregional long-distance exchange system). Local markets had to be present for local exchange but were a less important element in the economy and its radically growing wealth. Isaac points out that a more limited role for physical marketplaces, even in the most commercialized Mesoamerican economies of the Aztecs and the highland Postclassic regions and even though they were to a larger degree involved in some elements of "market economies": "Thus, instead of saying that 'the marketplace was the center of economic life in ancient Mesoamerica' (Hirth 1998:451), I suggest we speak more modestly of marketplaces as simply the principal urban exchange venues in the Mexican Central Highlands during the Late Postclassic period" (Isaac 2013:435).

Regarding the Aztec/Maya comparisons, however, we believe that contrary to most thinking a comparative perspective suggests that marketplaces were probably a *more* important element in earlier, less "international" economies and thus more, not less, central to Maya economics, if compared to the Aztec or to the variable complex economies today. That relative importance later may have declined even locally at some sites that became specialized centers in larger exchange networks like Caracol, Cancuén, Colhá, and some other southern lowland sites and much more in the northern lowlands. A more accurate and positive approach than Isaac's critique of Hirth's application and other distributional studies is to realize that those distributions are in fact much *more* informative for some evaluations than finding and studying the marketplaces themselves. Adjusting for the degree of chronological resolution and the various types of distributions of different kinds of products, material distributions tell us much more about the overall nature of an economy than any physical marketplace can. That perspective reflects part of Hirth's original intent (e.g., Hirth 2010).

Markets are actually implicit or explicit contracts about "prices," "values," or "equivalencies." "Market economy" is a classical polythetic set of elements. In all societies many of those elements are present: the question is not presence/absence but the *relative degree* or level of presence or importance of each of those characteristic elements. In some definitions of market economy or market exchange elements can include the degree of "openness" in distribution, level of restrictions on participation, degree of differentiation of commodities into products, degree of vertical integration of production and exchange, degree and nature of monetization, degree of freedom of choice of buyers and sellers, degree of commercialization in organization, level of use of factor markets, degree of breadth in access to economic information, and, above all, degree to which equivalencies are set by purely economic factors—such as "supply and demand" (itself defined by relative variable traits). The degree of economic determination of equivalences in turn reflects the degree of noneconomic influences and restraints by political or ideological institutions or norms or personal or community relationships. One goal of strategic management studies is to seek points and positions among the elements or in the relative ranges of those elements that are vulnerable to manipulation.

In practice, because the individual elements and their ranges can accurately describe an economy, labels based on some "cut-off point" or dichotomy in those variables needed to call it "a market economy" or "barter" are no longer of much utility. The debate over use of those labels and many others has in general ceased in management and administration theory and applied economics. Though not using those terms, King (Chapter 2, 2015; see also G. Braswell 2010) has been explicit, insightful, and we feel correct in implicitly emphasizing the polythetic and relative nature of factors in an economy, though we would not emphasize "premodern" itself, a term creating a "binary" modern/premodern opposition: "Among archaeologists, it [economic research] has led to a reconceptualization of premodern economies as part of a continuum rather than as a binary opposition" (King, Chapter 2).

There is a stylistic difference in the more explicit expression of this here in that the "continuum" applies not to systems but to specific elements in those systems that can be more easily studied and be of greater insight. While King understands this, some archaeologists see major disjunctions in the more visible presence of features in economic systems. Many others often refer to concepts like "market," "marketplace," or "commodity" in less relativistic terms and don't fully understand the polythetic and relative degree of *elements* in King's "continuum." Nonetheless, her comments suggest that it would not be such a radical change to begin to use the more formal analytical language and some of the menu of methods, concepts, and case studies already available in management research. King may have been generous in using the collective term "archaeologists": "some archaeologists" would be more correct.

Also, stated or implicit use of the (admittedly somewhat obnoxious) formal language of logic gives us a constant awareness of the relative/polythetic framework. Otherwise all of us tend to slip back into dichotomous thinking and labels: many of the relative elements are not specified but are conceptually lumped under the rubrics of "modern economies," "Western economies," "capitalism," or "market economy" though they are found to varying degrees in "nonmodern," "non-Western" societies and identifiable in ancient economies. For example, Mesopotamian economies, since 4000–5000 BC, had most of the elements of current "Western" modern economies, including even forms of corporations and the active presence of agents who were essentially corporate lawyers (who, of course, may lead to the disintegration of all social systems!). Indigenous, non-Western, ancient, and contemporary economic practices are studied in detail by business management scholars (e.g., Hudson 2010; Landes et al. 2010; Victor et al. 2013; Victor et al. 2014, Demarest and Victor 2018; Wunsch 2010; also see Yoffee, Chapter 26 in this volume; and Wright 2013). In most societies, study labels, like "reciprocal exchange," "barter," and "market," are not absolute unitary terms but are defined by elements on a relative scale, often growing in scale over time. Still, Mayanists do often continue to use earlier conceptions and statements (e.g., Demarest 2004), especially common in syntheses like "the Maya had a well-developed market economy," which incorporates several of the logical errors noted above. Mesoamerican economies had a *relatively* less commercialized "market system" in many elements *when compared to* some other ancient, historic, and recent economies (see Landes et al. 2010), because Maya factor markets were of very little importance (Isaac 2013). Though we differ from Isaac in that some of their elements are at least present at a lower level than in many comparable scale ancient economies, Isaac (2013) also points out that most exchange was outside of commercialized contexts. Nonetheless, the Classic Period southern lowland Maya economies had higher relative "scores" on many other elements associated with economic "markets" when compared to some other ancient economies given their initial, but developing, "monetization," accounting devices, and possibly even stored capital (e.g. . Freidel et al. 2002; Freidel et al. 2016; Freidel and Reilly 2010). Note that all of these descriptions are a matter of degree, not kind.

One critical factor emphasized more in management and organization analyses is that relative variation in economies also relates to the exchange of information. Sometimes these analyses add as a variable the degree of efficiency in communication of values and equivalencies. Indeed, the principal importance of physical marketplaces in Maya economies may have been the ability for people directly to observe other negotiations around them and thus have more information on the range of values for a given material or product.

Overall, Classic Maya economies appear to have had a lower relative efficiency in communication of values and economic data than some ancient societies of comparable scale. There was less writing for transmission of economic data, in contrast to the tens of thousands of tablets at most large sites in early Mesopotamia, most of which conveyed economic information (e.g., Hudson 2010; Wright 2013; Wunsch 2010). Recent LiDAR findings (Wootson 2018), however, show many more sacbes in some Classic Period Maya regions, particularly the northern Petén and Campeche economic "community network" (see below). These would have more closely linked the centers there, potentially providing more rapid information flow, but still less efficient than the detailed writing of invoices, written negotiations, and contracts of the Mesopotamian "community network" of cities.

Time, Problematics, and Possibilities in Distributional Approaches to Maya Marketplaces and Markets

The "distributional approach" introduced to archaeology by Hirth (1998, 2010; Hirth and Pillsbury 2013) is a good example of the type of very specific analytical tool used in market and management studies. There it has been refined to assess distributions of all kinds, from distributions of specific products or types of products to specific distributions of social, political, psychological, or health benefits (e.g. Fischer 2014; Fischer, ed. 2014; Victor et al. 2013, 2014), as well as the factors and agents involved in creating those distributions. With a sound ceramic chronology concepts and caution about problems, contemporary studies of distributions can be used in archaeology.

In many recent economic studies, general distributions of products, artifacts, or materials are distinct or equivalent to varying degrees with distribution of social benefits that can be more subject to a wide range of economic, political, social, and ideological factors. In archaeologists' studies this aspect of social benefit is underemphasized due to the focus on artifact distributions. Distribution of benefits could take into account architecture volume, forms, quality, placement, diet, and health (Victor et al. 2013, 2014). It also can include elite markers such as the nature and symbolic significance of specific types of grave goods, benches, inscriptions, murals, and so forth and the degree of clustering of valuable artifacts in nonepicenter, local elite complexes, as seen in "middle and lower elite" family groups and tombs at Caracol (e.g., A. Chase and D. Chase 2001; D. Chase and A. Chase 1994, 2014b, 2016).

However, distributional studies in archaeology entail a methodological danger: patterns of distribution are among the most volatile indicators in economic systems, subject to the possibility of rapid change by management agency or in any other aspect of political, ideological, or social institutions into which the economy is embedded as well as external factors. This time-sensitive variability makes distributional studies clear in study of contemporary and historical systems but very tricky for archaeology or sometimes just for particular ancient material distributions. Though less high-resolution distribution studies can be used and should be presented, they must be assessed and "weighed" in terms of the probable degree of reliability by other studies and syntheses.

Given their volatility, distributional studies are most successful when their dating is well controlled and ceramic complex periods are short. Yet distributions can remain similar for long (even a century or two) or short periods (ten years), depending upon total system stability. Therefore, both chronological resolution and system stability together determine the reliability of archaeological distribution studies. For southern lowland sites measures of economy using distributions are often unreliable due to low-resolution ceramic chronologies for dating artifact contexts. This factor, however, could be improved by emphasizing laboratory ceramic studies and midden excavation targeting opportunities for better ceramic chronologies. High-resolution chronologies of ceramics are more reliable for assessments and dating of distributions than epicenter inscriptions or AMS (accelerator mass spectrometry). Those are absolute dates of only their specific contexts, while ceramic chronologies are applicable to the entire site, its region, and even to cross-date and/or identify relations with sites beyond the region.

At Cancuén and a number of other sites (Caracol, Copán, Tikal, etc.), decades of widely distributed excavations including many domestic middens and great investment in ceramic lab work have made it possible to date some artifact distributions by very narrow periods. At Cancuén its late apogee ceramic chronology is now down to periods of less than ten to twenty years to define changes and then relate them to other aspects of material culture (e.g., Forné et al. 2010; Torres, Demarest, et al. 2017; Torres, Forné, et al. 2017; Torres et al. 2018). As the ceramic chronology improved, interpretations changed or were even reversed and revealed very new important events and patterns. That degree of precision is desirable but not usually necessary, as most sites appear to have had relatively more stable economies for longer periods. For example, extensive excavations and thorough lab analyses have shown that sites like Xochicalco (Hirth 2000), Mayapán (Masson and Peraza 2014a), Chunchucmil (Hutson 2017), and Caracol (D. Chase and A. Chase 1994, 2012, 2016), and others had long apogees during which most elements of material culture and site structure appear to have been relatively stable, so distributional studies there are more reliable, despite longer ceramic periods.

However, when distributions at sites can only be reported for very long periods or when the study combines artifact contexts from two or more periods—during which there was significant change—the methodology can create a single mixed, homogenized, and blurred pattern from different superimposed sequential distributions that look less clustered, implying a more open economy. Possible examples of this problem might be present in two recent uses of the Tikal artifact data set. One is a well-presented, careful, and very specific statistical comparison of the large corpus of Mayapán and Tikal artifact distribution data (Masson and Freidel 2012, 2013). This study of very specific nuts and bolts of artifact distributions found similar "open" distributions indicating important marketplaces and broadly similar economies at the two sites.

The flaw in the argument is again one of differing degrees of chronological control of the distributions cited. Mayapán has only a very small percentage of ceramics from earlier periods, so almost all of the sample is from its well-dated apogee occupation, showing little indication of significant change in most elements of the site. In contrast, the Tikal distribution data to which Mayapán distributions are compared combines as much as 350 years in the use

Arthur A. Demarest, Bart Victor, Chloé Andrieu, and Paola Torres

of William Haviland's data, but potentially combined for as much as 600 years for the far larger and more utilized Hattula Moholy-Nagy's data (Masson and Freidel 2012; but see Masson and Freidel 2013). These chronologically combined Tikal distributions from different periods could create a single more "blurred" pattern and a mirage of a more uniform distribution. One factor is that Tikal experienced significant economic change between the Early Classic, when it was a large-scale producer and regional distributor of obsidian, jade, and other products, and the Late Classic, when it was primarily a consumer of those and presumably many other commodities, probably due to its much larger size and population by the Late Classic Period. For Masson and Freidel this problem of using combined Tikal distributions was unavoidable due to the limitations of Moholy-Nagy's enormous, well-analyzed, and beautifully presented data set (Moholy-Nagy 2003a, 2008a, 2008b). That impressive corpus of artifact analysis is extremely useful for most purposes but is falsely seductive for many distributional studies, since it records artifacts by periods but *separately* records artifacts by structure. Thus, distribution patterns by *both* context and period cannot be generated from that corpus.

However, in logic and dialectics the rejection of an argument for a hypothesis does *not* invalidate the hypothesis itself but only that particular argument for the hypothesis. Thus, Tikal no doubt would have had a large central major marketplace and several more localized marketplaces. However, regarding overall comparability in the general natures of the two economies (relative "scores" on defining elements such as architecture forms, standard deviation in structure volumes, structure and monument distributions, and so on), it seems unlikely that the economic elements, their relative levels, and the distributions of social benefits were similar between Tikal and Mayapán. Distributions of other materials and features in a site should also be included in a broader study of economic elements. This more inclusive approach to distributions suggests that in comparison to Tikal there was *relatively* much less variability in the "wealth" of rulers, "nobles," subroyal, and local elite groups at Mayapán, Chunchucmil, and Caracol during their own apogee periods.

Hutson (Chapter 4) in his similar comparisons of Chunchucmil and Tikal artifact distributions tries to correct the problematics of the Tikal data set by analyzing artifact distributions by volume in cubic meters. While his approach to distributions does solve some proportionality and sampling issues, it is a very weak argument for his hypothesis because of the same problem found in the Tikal data. Note again, however, that negation of an argument for a hypothesis does not negate the hypothesis itself. For other reasons concerning different elements cited above, we agree with Hutson's conclusion itself: a greater concentration of valued materials, specifically obsidian, in elite contexts and a more asymmetrical distribution of "social benefit" at Tikal, despite the problems with his different analysis of the Moholy-Nagy studies. Our own realizations about such applications of distributional approaches did not come only from our analytical thinking and the Cancuén sequence of changes but from the normal uses of distributions in marketing, managerial strategy, and applied economics—another example of learning from their implicit logical framework, but more from their uses of relative elements in analysis and interpretation.

The early 2000 to 2006 interpretations at Cancuén are another example of error due to chronological control. Prior to developing a high-resolution ceramic chronology we believed that we had a single apogee period and distribution (Barrientos et al. 2001; Demarest 2002; cf. Demarest 2012b), which was believed to indicate the presence of a large central marketplace, multiple jade workshops, nonelite craftspeople, who had some special ceramics, and so on (e.g., Kovacevich 2006, 2013a). Later, with hundreds of thousands more sherds and data and years of lab work leading to a high-resolution ceramic chronology, the more precisely dated and segregated Cancuén patterns demonstrated almost the opposite for the late eighth-century apogee: highly centrally clustered distributions, no evidence of a large central marketplace, no identified crafting workshops, no special craftspeople ceramics, and only the one large and very late (786/790 to 800/810) centralized "mass production" preform workshop (see, for example, Andrieu et al. 2014; Demarest 2012a; Demarest et al. 2014), and also the complete disappearance of our hypothesized ninth-century occupation! We assume that smaller local marketplaces existed for basic subsistence goods, but almost all of the economy was based on centralized import/export exchange at its ports, including bulk import of salt and probably large-scale exchange of agriculture products (e.g., Barrientos 2014; Demarest 2012b; Demarest et al. 2014; Demarest, Andrieu, Victor, Torres, and Forné 2019; Demarest, Victor, and Torres 2020; Woodfill 2010; Woodfill et al. 2015) and then later based more on the mass production of obsidian and jade. Also, the population of Cancuén could not possibly feed itself, since it is almost an island in lakes and swamps with variable and unpredictable water levels and thus limited cultivable land. Foodstuffs would have had to be imported in considerable scale from the fertile Transversal piedmont route to the south.

That refinement of ceramic dating then allowed applications of management

Arthur A. Demarest, Bart Victor, Chloé Andrieu, and Paola Torres

models leading to insights into economic patterns (Demarest, Andrieu, Victor, Torres, and Forné 2019, 2020; Demarest and Victor 2018; Demarest, Victor, et al. 2018; Torres, Demarest, et al. 2017a). These examples from Cancuén and its region, positive and negative, demonstrate that close control of ceramic chronology is important for meaningful distributional studies or, alternatively, often (not always) the weight given to an interpretation of distribution patterns should correlate with the degree of resolution of the dating of those patterns.

Pars Pro Toto and the Study of Change in Ancient Maya Economy

For developing understandings of ancient Maya economies, we can use contemporary models of management agency to look at the differences and economic histories. In order to do that we will need to move beyond some current practices that tend to underemphasize change and agency.

One is the frequent use of very large spatial and temporal parameters for our generalizations, especially in syntheses about characteristics, mechanisms, and variability of elements or institutions in ancient Maya economies, sometimes combining traits from the Preclassic to Postclassic Periods and from many Maya regions: southern lowlands and far northern lowlands and sometimes even the highlands of eastern Mesoamerica (e.g., Demarest 2004; Masson and Freidel 2013). Secondly, that weakness is sometimes compounded and reified by a *pars pro toto* logic that can often add unusual features or elements at a specific site into general all-inclusive definitions of the "Maya economy." Occasionally scholars avoid this mistake by just noting the "great variability" in Maya economies, which is certainly true but somewhat unenlightening. Yet sometimes almost universalizing variant features or the different relative levels of elements from sites and regions can inadvertently create a nearly timeless Maya economy, methodologically minimizing change and so often failing to explain it.

Instead, it can be argued that it can be more useful to study sites in approximately coeval periods and then also compare sites from different periods that have differing relative "scores" on economic elements and/or structural features in order to contrast variants and discover the reasons for their differences. From that we can examine change in their economic systems and variability between regions or sites and seek to explain the reasons for those changes and differences. The search for differences and change, rather than just increasing inventories of Preclassic to Postclassic ancient Maya economic features, sometimes reveals the impact of external factors or pan-Mesoamerican trends. It can also lead us to discover local agency and changes in economic strategies and sometimes suggest how agents, especially merchants, might have created some of the observed shifts in economic features or strategies.

For example, Caracol during its apogee had a strikingly different economy from its earlier and its later periods in terms of the elements of degree of commercialization, integration, and wider distribution of both artifacts and social benefits. During its seventh and early eighth-century apogee Caracol had very extensive terraces for food production for export, a centralized causeway network, a connected hierarchy of probable market loci, what appears to be orchestrated heterarchy in community production, wider distribution and relatively less variable elite family architecture and tombs, and a very "open" distribution of artifacts. Together these features suggest an economy that was more commercialized, more open, and strategically managed than the economies indicated for most large Late Classic southern lowland centers as well as for earlier and later periods at Caracol itself (e.g., A. Chase and D. Chase 1996; D. Chase et al. 1990).

In some earlier publications the Caracol project directors and others added Caracol's features to the growing ever more amorphous inventory of traits of the "Maya economy" and general "Classic Maya urbanism" (e.g., A. Chase and D. Chase 1996, 2016; D. Chase et al. 1990). More recently, however, the excavators have emphasized more the differences at Caracol during its late seventh and eighth century apogee from most Classic Maya divine kingship forms of political economy and from its own economy before and after that apogee (D. Chase and A. Chase 2016, 2020). The latter interpretation is far more useful, because it can explain what is behind this change. This more time-sensitive view of Caracol reveals a radical shift in political structure from the divine kingship system, raising the question for future research as to why this occurred, a fascinating problem about causes of radical change there (e.g., A. Chase and D. Chase 2021).

Cancuén and the southwestern exchange network (Figures 3.1, 3.2, 3.3) also present some puzzling differences from most Classic Maya economies. Cancuén was a state dominated by economic functions and a major participant in a more extensive "interregional" Mesoamerican market system. Its economy had more intensive applications ("higher scores") on many of the features (elements, variables) of what could be referred to as the polythetic concept of a specialized node in a "international market economic system." Furthermore, while it is definitely easier for high elites to control distribution than production, (Freidel 1981; Masson and Freidel 2013), Cancuén's subroyal elites controlled *both* mass production and local as well as interregional distribution of many products, though probably not most foodstuffs or low-value items. Despite all of these indications of "higher scores" on many elements in a more interregional market economy, Cancuén has no indications of a relatively large internal central marketplace: distribution of artifacts was very centralized, not disbursed, and this more "wealthy" center had an extremely iniquitous distribution of social benefit. Also, all large apparently open areas in the epicenter peninsula have

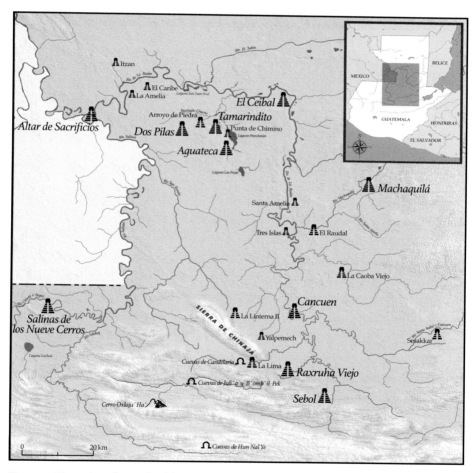

Figure 3.1. The region of research of the Petexbatún and Cancuén Regional Archaeological Projects and nearby western Petén neighbors.

Figure 3.2. The specific exchange partners and routes of the southwestern community networks discovered by 2018. This is greatly modified from previous versions due to 2017–2018 discoveries.

been intensively excavated and contained buried structures, ritual water channels, and so on. It would appear that this pattern of only small local markets probably was due to the centralization and elite merchant control of ports and jade production workshops and the tight control of obsidian distribution, a pattern common in a specialized import/export centers with mass production as at Cancuén (see below). Furthermore, high elite architecture is only in the epicenter: almost all such construction was in the central area of that epicenter peninsula, and the palace became a huge administrative complex.

These are very different distributions from many current, and correct, expectations of a Maya city economy with a marketplace as its central economic feature. Yet Cancuén's economic evidence is a clear indication and confirmation of a growing Maya "market economy." Surely, some other centers in the late eighth to ninth centuries and earlier have broadly similar economic patterns.

Arthur A. Demarest, Bart Victor, Chloé Andrieu, and Paola Torres

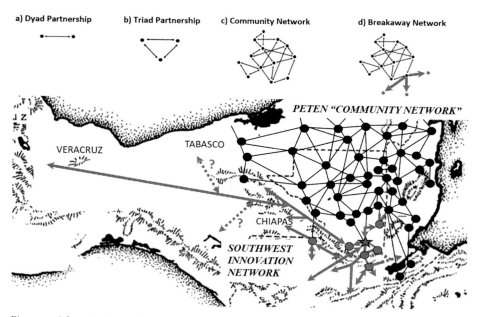

Figure 3.3. Schematic Network Diagrams of (*a*) a dyadic relationship, (*b*) a triadic shared-partner network, (*c*) a "community network" of partners, and (*d*) an "innovative breakaway network." The bottom image is a schematic estimation of the southwest long-distance innovation partnership network as determined by both excavations and compositional studies in Guatemala and primarily by compositional studies for Mexican regions. Again due to recent discoveries in the previously unexplored Sierra de Chinaja and eastern Transversal regions, this is also greatly modified from previous versions.

Rather than somehow adding the unusual features of Cancuén to the general inventory of traits in the "Maya economy," we turned to strategic management and organizational network theory to try to explain these puzzling patterns.

Some Recent Applications of Strategic Management Approaches to the Study of Elements of Classic Maya Economies

The potential of collaborations between archaeologists and scholars of business management strategy is demonstrated by recent successful applications that identified mechanisms, changes, and innovations in key elements and their significance. Here we can only provide a summary list of a few of our applications of management theory and case studies and most recent relevant data from Cancuén and a dozen other sites in the southwest highland/lowland/Gulf Coast exchange system (Figures 3.1, 3.2, 3.3; see Cancuén data summaries in Andrieu et al. 2011, 2014; Bishop et al. 2005; Demarest 2012a, 2012b, 2013; Demarest et al. 2014; Sears 2016; Torres, Demarest, et al. 2017; Torres, Forné, et al. 2017; Woodfill 2010; Woodfill et al. 2015). The collaborations sketched below are presented elsewhere in more detail (Demarest et al. 2017a, 2017b; Demarest et al. 2020; Demarest and Victor 2018; Demarest, Victor, Andrieu, and Torres 2020; Torres, Demarest et al. 2017; Torres, Forné, et al. 2017b; Torres et al. 2018).

Overall, we have been able to explain many of the reasons for the meteoric trajectory of Cancuén with its very rapidly growing wealth followed by sudden collapse. Here, among other tools, we have drawn on economic network theories, studies of components in legitimation of new partnerships and new strategies, and analyses of the elements in "network failure." Some specific applications of strategic management approaches to Maya economy are summarized in the paragraphs below.

The nature of Cancuén's very rapid creation of extreme wealth is typical of the breaking off of one partner from a "community network" (Figure 3.3c) of exchange partners (Figure 3.3d) in order to try to create new dyadic partnerships outside of those familiar systems (e.g., Ahuja 2000; Larson 1992; Sytch and Tatarynowicz 2014). Sometimes these new dyadic partnerships can begin (Figure 3.2, 3.3b, d) to form an "innovation ecosystem network" that can have immediate very high yields. In addition to greater "yields" through trade, both sides of the new exchange relationships benefit by communicating differing ideas on management and production strategies (e.g., Cowan and Jonard 2004; Davis 2016; Sytch et al. 2012). Such attempts by an economic entity to look beyond its "community network" of exchange partners have great advantages and "profits." On the downside, because they are initially constructs of new unstable dyadic partnerships they also have high risks (see below) as compared with more stable, but lower-yield "community networks" of long-known partners and established routes like those of most of the Late Classic Maya southern lowlands. Again, this is a common pattern in ancient and contemporary economies.

Management network models (e.g., Breschi and Malerba 2007) helped to explain the inverse in the of expectations in the southwestern network of some models of "border zones" such as "World System Theory," "frontier" models, and so on, which expect dominance of more complex core societies over the "periphery" societies in economic, political, or cultural terms (see also the total contradiction of this in Schortman and Urban 2011, 2012, etc.).

The non-Classic Maya partner sites of Cancuén (Figure 3.2) in the transversal piedmont, the highlands, and along the route to the Gulf Coast have varying but limited presences of southern lowland Classic Maya ritual settings. Only two have Cancuén stelae or altar forms, each with only a small percentage of Cancuén ceramics. These Maya lowland ritual forms and artifacts were embedded in non-Classic Maya local ritual settings, material culture, and ceramic assemblages (e.g., Demarest 2013). There are no indications of defensive features, except an incomplete one at Cancuén at its very end ca. 800/810, and all but one of these exchange partner sites are located in open indefensible positions. Thus, neither conquest nor political control is indicated at these southwest network sites. Nonetheless, the situation is far different in the southeastern region, since there was very high-scale exchange of both basic resources and high-value materials in the southwestern exchange network between the southwestern Classic Maya and piedmont/highland cities.

Conversely, Cancuén itself had far more material culture, ritual forms, and architectural settings borrowed from its piedmont and highland non-Classic Maya exchange partners (Demarest 2013). Analysis of these patterns at Cancuén benefited from the literature on legitimation and building trust in new contracts and partnerships (see below).

Also useful were the many historical and contemporary management case studies regarding the creation, growth, and problems of innovative business or mercantile hegemonies and their impact. For example, the Venetian exchange "empire" without significant physical territory was unusual for Renaissance Europe, yet in a number of studies it parallels some elements of the Cancuén and interregional southwestern network. This helps and informs our own investigations by providing some traits in the richer and more detailed historical evidence of Venice. Many important elements in a recent investigation by business management and finance experts on the Venetian exchange system parallel the culture-history of Cancuén and the agency of its merchants:

International trade can have profound effects on domestic institutions . . . We show that initially exogenous increases in long-distance trade enriched a large group of merchants and these merchants used their newfound muscle to push for constraints on the executive i.e., for the end of a de facto hereditary Doge. . . . The merchants also pushed for remarkably modern innovations in contracting institutions (such as the colleganza) that facilitated large-scale mobilization of capital for risky long-distance trade. (Puga and Trefler 2012; see also Formica 2017)

Cancuén's economic history is parallel overall and in many specific features and is also similar to contemporary extensions of exchange networks that were assisted by governments primarily in legitimating activities for partner formation.

Management theory and case studies helped to explain specific details of the Cancuén/highland links (Figure 3.2). We drew on the literature cited above and also the many current and historical studies in strategic management on "trust" and "legitimation" in creating and maintaining contracts, existing exchange relationships, and especially new exchange relationships with partners from different "economic cultures" embedded in differing ideologies and with differing economic rules or ethics (e.g., Das and Teng 1998, 2001; Davis 2016; Doz 1996; Suchman 1995; Zucker 1986). Recent studies on the role of trust in holding Maya polities together parallel these studies (e.g., Golden and Scherer 2013; Golden et al., Chapter 23) and could benefit from comparative use of the large corpus of strategic management literature on the role of trust in economic exchange partnerships and contracts.

In this regard, business case studies helped to explain the enigma of Cancuén's puzzling variety of unusual built settings for different rituals. The settings and rituals were in the forms of each specific new trading partner, who were always located in source areas for commodities or in key locations in the southwestern Petén and highland trade routes (Figure 3.2) (Demarest 2013; Demarest and Victor 2018; Demarest, Victor, and Torres 2018; Demarest, Victor, Andrieu, and Torres 2020).

Business legitimation and administration models and examples helped evaluate the changing details of the six sequential reconstructions of Cancuén's royal palace (Barrientos 2014; Barrientos and Demarest 2012) that in stages slowly turned it from a palace with primarily a residential and some elite gathering functions into a huge economic administrative complex of offices for elites with specific functions, with the ruler pushed into only a small, off-axis royal residence. Studies of management administrative growth and specialization as well as strategic settings in contemporary and historical business architecture helped to evaluate area functions for day-to-day administration and others as settings for visits to form and maintain ritualized economic relationships. At Cancuén room forms, courtyards, gathering structures, and interior pathways were each directed at economic relations with specific local, regional, or interregional elites (Barrientos 2014; Barrientos and Demarest 2012; Demarest 2013; Demarest, Victor, Andrieu, and Torres 2020).

Vertical integration models for management of commodity production

Arthur A. Demarest, Bart Victor, Chloé Andrieu, and Paola Torres

chains (Arrow 1975; Dickson and Ginter 1987; Harrigan 1985; Porter 1998) fit the 760–800 shifts in Cancuén functions from transport to transport and production of obsidian blades, adding later production for export of jade preforms. Obsidian production increased in scale to levels higher than at any Late Classic Maya site, with more bullet cores than even at Tikal! There is, however, also a specialized economy with large-scale salt processing at Salinas de Nueve Cerros (Woodfill et al. 2015), massive agricultural production at Caracol, Colhá mass production and trade in chert, and possibly production and exchange at a few yet unexcavated sites. Yet in the southern lowland Classic Period that was an usual pattern; even more unusual is the fact that at Cancuén and in the southwest import/export was primarily (later almost exclusively) long distance and reaching far beyond the Classic Maya lowlands. The "added value" of these exports through this vertical integration and intensification was a major factor in Cancuén's meteoric increase in wealth.

The timing of the introduction of these changes in management strategy and production corresponds to the known impacts of a breakaway from a "community network" of a network partner to a series of dyadic innovation partnerships that stimulate strategic economic changes (Cowan and Jonard 2004; Davis 2016; Tatarynowicz et al. 2016; Whittington et al. 2009). The sequence, timing, and reasons for each economic change align with the formations of each new dyadic partnership outside of the Petén "community network" of partners. New exchange relationships outside of familiar networks bring new ideas on economic strategy and tools (Cowan and Jonard 2004).

To the surprise of Cancuén archaeologists, models of production chains of commodities, especially examples from the nineteenth and early twentieth century, correspond to the counterintuitive pattern of Cancuén having mass production of obsidian and later of jade, yet with extreme obsidian scarcity outside of the epicenter and scarcity of jade everywhere in the site, even within the elite areas and burials in its epicenter. It turns out that this is a typical pattern in ancient, historic, and contemporary source centers or initial transport or production centers and their regions. The production is for export, not consumption, because the exported product can increase geometrically in value. Specific comparisons have been very useful, such as looking at the nineteenth-century and to some degree current South African trade in diamonds and comparing it to the current Maya highland family and Maya community participation in high-quality arabica coffee production for export (Demarest, Andrieu, Victor, Torres, and Forné 2019; Demarest and Victor 2020; Fischer, ed. 2014; Fischer and Victor 2014).

Using historical and present examples we have been able to explain why one of the richest Classic Maya centers in its "economic output" has extreme nonelite poverty in artifacts and architecture even for the laborers in the jade preform workshop and at the ports, both economic engines of the site and state (Fischer, ed. 2014; Goodenough and Cheney 2007; Victor et al. 2013, 2014; Victor and Stephens 1994). In present and historical innovation networks, the new ideas and practices often lead to rapid success for elite participants on both sides, but such networks can also lead to much greater inequality in the social benefits (Fischer, ed. 2014; Victor and Stephens 1994; Victor et al. 2013). That iniquitous social pattern can potentially precipitate local or regional failure of trust if the general population perceives a political or ideological "contract violation" with rival elites or the populace.

Drawing on such theories, but also on sociology and some anthropology (e.g. Harrigan 1985; Kopytoff 1988; Porter 1988) and nineteenth-century examples, we can better understand the steps in the complex cultural biography of things for Cancuén's jade: first delivered to Cancuén through a ritualized form of exchange (Wells and McAnany 2008), as more than a simple commodity in ideological terms, but then received and processed at Cancuén as simply a high-value commodity for large-scale initial production and then differentiated into more valuable initially processed products, preforms, at Cancuén's single very large and late (circa AD 790) workshop (e.g. Andrieu et al. 2011, 2014; Demarest et al. 2014). Such high-value products would have come under much more strict sumptuary rules on arrival at consumer sites and much more. Then values increase greatly with artisan carving at those recipient sites, where the jade preforms were differentiated into either a much higher value artifact with even more sumptuary restrictions. Then some even became "inalienable property" of high elites or royals. Jade objects, like most designated inalienable objects, were sometimes "alienated" later to continue their histories as booty, tribute, recycled heirlooms, and so on. Today analyses of such histories of commodities and processed products (influenced by both Kopytoff and Appadurai) allow manipulation of their rises and falls in value. At Cancuén there is ample evidence of such manipulation with changing levels of "vertical integration" (Demarest, Victor, and Torres 2020; Demarest and Victor 2018).

Exchange and management network models and specific examples show that some of the general southern lowland Classic Maya exchange systems to the north and northeast had more long-term, more stable, and lower-risk "community networks" of known multiple shared partners with more shared elements

Arthur A. Demarest, Bart Victor, Chloé Andrieu, and Paola Torres

in common economic culture and a higher proportion of internal exchange. The downside of that stability is that community networks have a higher level of in-network exchange, so they can be slower in innovation or adjustment to outside changes (Cowan and Jonard 2004; Davis 2016; Tatarynowicz et al. 2016). In the Classic Maya case the intensity and the proportion of their *internal* community network exchange may have even become hypercoherent, given recent LiDAR findings (Wootson 2018).

Perhaps the most useful applications of business management models were identifications of both general and specific economic factors in the Cancuén and southwestern network collapse as well as some insights into the general southern lowland wave of "dynastic disasters" between 750 and 822 (Demarest, Andrieu, Victor, and Torres 2021; Iannone et al. 2016).

Various aspects of economic change in the Cancuén and southwest network collapse were elucidated using business and sociological models of partnership "network failure" and the above-cited business literature on "trust" and "legitimation" of innovations, all embedded in differing "economic cultures." The sudden, violent, and ritualized collapse of Cancuén and simultaneous collapse of all of the centers in the new highland/lowland southwestern exchange network is typical of the risks of network failure (Eggers 2012; McMillan and Overall 2017; Schrank and Whitford 2011) of breakaway innovative networks of dyadic partnerships (Davis 2016; Freeman et al. 1983; Sytch and Tatarynowicz 2014).

It would have been very challenging for Cancuén and its partners to create new, and vulnerable, economic and political links with southern highland and Mexican economies, which were unusually fragile. They faced significant challenges in legitimation of new partnerships. Management case studies suggest that the timing and form of the region's manifestation of "network failure" may have been due to overreach in attempts at rapid legitimation of its new external relationships, pulling together unfamiliar economic cultures and alien ideologies and attempting to enhance trust (Demarest 2013; Demarest, Andrieu, Victor, and Torres 2020; Demarest, Victor, Andrieu, and Torres 2020). In Cancuén's case the population, rival elites, and/or regional partners may have perceived a violation of the ruler's sacred contract in the probably too rapid introduction of new highland ritual settings at Cancuén for alien non-Classic Maya ritual events.

Other economic determinants in collapse or "nonrecovery" of the southwest network surely included the shift in trade routes to more coastal exchange. For the southwestern network the specifics of Venetian and also major historic southeast Asian business histories and network failures have guided new hypotheses and their testing. This factor of changing routes of exchange and access to valued commodities would also have had a negative impact on the interior Petén economic network in addition to the southwestern and Cancuén exchange systems.

New Directions for Maya Economic Research

Use of the greater inventory of methodologies and mechanisms in strategic management studies gives us warnings about some flaws in some applications of methodologies, language, and paradigms in some studies of Maya economies but also corrective measures. Yet, to a greater degree, applied economics and various facets of managerial and organizational studies provide potential solutions through examples of "tools" used in some other economies. The efficacy of these has been confirmed by applications to Cancuén and the southwestern exchange network with some implications for the Classic Maya southern lowlands in general.

Collaborations with experts in strategic management studies and organization and administration research could refine and advance our studies of ancient Maya economies. Such collaborations can incorporate into our work a new large menu of potential insights, more logical conceptual frameworks, new methodologies, case studies, and a huge volume of literature. Study of the southwest region has even drawn heavily on the most recent developments on innovation networks and exchange with "alien" partners outside of our western community networks, both of which have become far more common, and more analyzed, with "hyperglobalization" and the "boom and bust" histories of enterprises with partners outside of Western networks and/or in the high-tech fields.

Overall, economic management approaches would not import models of "economic systems," but they could help us improve some aspects of our analytical frameworks and perceive new patterns in *specific* aspects of economies or better explain familiar ones. Above all, these collaborations could facilitate our efforts to identify some of the actual elements the "nuts and bolts" that made Maya economies work yet also left open possibilities for agency and change.

II

Household and Community
Economies and Resources

4

Similar Markets, Different Economies

Comparing Small Households at Tikal and Chunchucmil

SCOTT R. HUTSON

The editors of this book have asked the contributors to consider the "nuts and bolts of ancient Maya exchange," encouraging us to build economic frameworks based not on "ideal types" but on "sound empirical data." This chapter uses many different kinds of data to explore variation in the consumption of obsidian among modest households at a pair of Classic Period cities with markets: Tikal and Chunchucmil. The analysis at the core of this chapter reveals major differences in patterns of obsidian consumption at these two sites. These differences suggest that exchange is indeed more complex than ideal types would predict. Both cities had large permanent marketplaces. In both cities small households—the bulk of the population—acquired a lot of blades, but the finer details of obsidian consumption suggest that marketing is only part of the story. Nevertheless, I retain a sanguine view of ideal types. As models, they guide the generation of test expectations and organize the research designs whose implementation yields sound empirical data. Indeed, the central question of this chapter—why one small household might consume so much more obsidian than another small household—grew from testing two ideal types: redistribution versus market-based exchange. Before fleshing out the question of variation in consumption, I provide background on how my colleagues and I came to this question in the first place.

In his landmark paper on the distributional approach, Hirth (1998) posited archaeological expectations for the two ideal types mentioned above: market exchange and redistribution. In short, presuming that a good was not outrageously expensive, it should be evenly distributed throughout the city if it was traded at a central market. An "even distribution" means it should be found in households located all across the space of the site but also in households located all across the status spectrum. If a good circulated through redistribution, we should find more of it in higher-status households: particularly items that are more closely related to or at least more strategically important to the authorities that control distribution. At Chunchucmil, a densely populated, northern Maya lowland city with over 30,000 people within about 15 km^2 (Hutson, Magnoni, Ardren, et al. 2017), we evaluated whether or not two commodities (obsidian and fancy pottery) exhibited distributions compatible with marketing or with redistribution (Hutson et al. 2010). Several other archaeologists have used this same approach at other Maya sites, such as El Perú–Waka' (Eppich and Freidel 2015), Chichén Itzá (Braswell and Glascock 2003), Caracol (D. Chase and A. Chase 2014a), and comparisons of Mayapán and Tikal (Masson and Freidel 2012). For the Chunchucmil data, analysis of Variance showed that, on average, small households, medium-sized households, and large households (see below for definitions and consideration of how these units correlate with status) all had access to about the same amount of obsidian and fancy pottery (Figure 4.1, Table 4.1, Hutson et al. 2010). The lack of significant differences suggested market-based distribution and corroborated contextual and configurational evidence for the existence of a major marketplace (Hutson, Terry, and Dahlin 2017). Regarding contextual factors, settlement pattern research and household excavations showed that Chunchucmil was a huge site with some degree of occupational specialization and limited agricultural prospects. Regarding configurational factors, excavations, soil chemistry, and mapping at the site core suggested that Area D contained precisely the kind of architecture, accessibility, and residues expected of a marketplace (Dahlin et al. 2007, 2010).

When we published our analysis of the distribution of obsidian and fancy pottery, we did not comment on the seemingly large standard deviations (see Table 4.1). These large standard deviations indicate that even if the average small household and the average medium-sized household, for example, had relatively equal access to obsidian and fancy pottery, any two households in the small households category could have consumed very different amounts of these goods. Indeed, small households exhibit the largest variation in the amount of obsidian and pottery consumed: some small households consumed very little obsidian, while others consumed lots. Thus, the similarities in consumption between categories of households (small versus medium versus large) stand in stark contrast to the substantial disparities within categories.

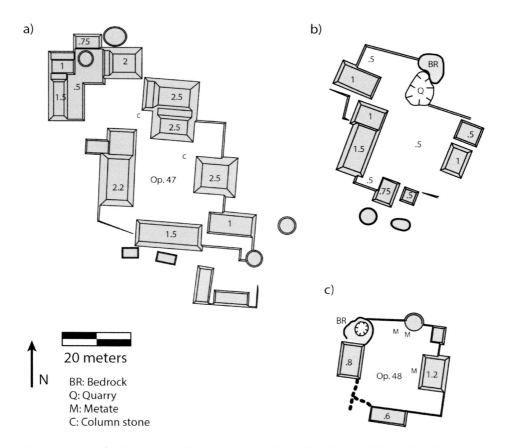

Figure 4.1. Maps showing representative examples of (a) large, (b) medium, and (c) small residential groups at Chunchucmil. Numbers indicate building heights.

Table 4.1. Consumption of obsidian and fancy pottery at residential groups of different sizes at Chunchucmil

	Large groups (n = 13)	Medium groups (n = 38)	Small groups (n = 64)	F value	P value
Mean grams obsidian per kg ceramics	0.95	1.27	1.7	0.83	0.44
Standard deviation	0.72	1.61	2.72		
Mean % fine pottery by mass	0.87	0.89	0.96	0.05	0.95
Standard deviation	0.48	0.69	1.47		

The goal of this chapter is to learn more about the variation in the consumption of obsidian at Chunchucmil by putting it in broader context and to explore the factors that contribute to this variation. The hope is that investigating this single good can tell us about consumption patterns more broadly. I have chosen obsidian as opposed to fancy pottery because we know a bit more about obsidian. Whereas we have not located any producers of fancy pottery and do not know how many producers there were, we know that 98% of the obsidian at Chunchucmil came from a single source (El Chayal, 640 km away as the crow flies), which also accounts for most of Tikal's assemblage (Moholy-Nagy 1989).

The Data Sets

To put variation in consumption of obsidian in broader context, I compared it with variation observable at Tikal. This section compares the two sites and summarizes the data from each. Tikal differs from Chunchucmil in many ways (which I address later, as they might help explain variation in consumption at the two sites), but they share several key traits. First, though Chunchucmil had significantly higher settlement density than Tikal, they were both large cities. Culbert et al. (1990) estimated that Tikal had a population of 13,275 in the central 16 km². Based on Puleston's (1983) conclusion that Tikal extended an additional 104 km² beyond the central 16 km², Culbert et al. (1990) estimate that Tikal's total population was 62,000. However, newer fieldwork on the periphery of Tikal suggests that the figure of 120 km² is unfounded (Webster et al. 2007). Haviland (1970:193, 1972:138, 2003:129) has consistently provided lower population estimates for Tikal, from 40,000 to 45,000, falling within the range for the population estimate of Chunchucmil (between 31,000 and 47,000).

Second, both Tikal and Chunchucmil reached these populations in the Classic Period. At Tikal, the occupation of small structures may have plateaued as early as 550 CE and remained at this level until about 770 CE, spanning the Ik and early Imix ceramic phases (Haviland 2003:124–129, 2014a:131). Chunchucmil reached its peak population toward the end of the Late Aak phase, which runs from 400 to 630 CE (Jiménez et al. 2017).

Third, and perhaps most importantly, both Tikal and Chunchucmil feature market-based systems of distribution. Edwin Shook and William Coe, directors of the University of Pennsylvania Tikal project, both thought that a complex of gallery-like structures in the East Plaza looked like a marketplace (Coe 1965) and had Christopher Jones excavate a portion of it in 1964. His results (Jones 1996,

2015) showed that the architecture and accessibility of the space meet the expectations for a marketplace. Tikal's marketplace is one of the few ancient urban Maya marketplaces (along with those at Chunchucmil and Calakmul) with extensive permanent architecture in a large (>1 ha) space at the very core of the city.

Furthermore, comparisons of artifacts from small structures at Tikal as opposed to civic ceremonial groups and range structures provide distributional support for marketing at Tikal (Masson and Freidel 2012, 2013; Moholy-Nagy 1997:296, 2008a). The introduction to this chapter summarizes the argument for the existence of marketing at Chunchucmil and contains references to supporting literature. As noted, both sites got the vast majority of obsidian from the same source. In fact, Chunchucmil and Tikal may have been trade partners: Tikal controlled the flow of obsidian from El Chayal down the Pasión River (Woodfill and Andrieu 2012), part of the route by which obsidian eventually arrived at Chunchucmil. Though Chunchucmil's pottery lacks strong Tikal connections, its domestic architecture is anomalous in northwest Yucatán, instead resembling that from central Petén sites such as Tikal (see below).

The final similarity worth highlighting is that both Tikal and Chunchucmil received the kind of excavations that permit site-wide generalizations and make possible a comparison between the two cities. My discussion focuses on small, nonelite households at both sites for several reasons. First, such households are the most common kind of household at the two sites, so focusing on them ensures that we are learning about patterns that affected the broadest swath of the site's residents. Second, more small households have been excavated than any other kind of architectural compounds (temple complexes, palaces, large households, etc.) at the two sites. Third, at Chunchucmil the variation is largest among small households, therefore calling for more attention.

For Chunchucmil, my colleagues and I define a small architectural compound as one with five or fewer structures (Hutson, Magnoni, and Dahlin 2017). The category of "structure" does not include *chi'ich* mounds, which are low, oval piles of 10 cm–long limestone cobbles with no wall lines. Within a 9.3 km^2 mapped polygon, we documented approximately 900 compounds of this size with relatively clear spatial boundaries (usually delimited by *albarradas*). Typically, the structures in such compounds open onto a shared patio. Extensive excavations in such compounds reveal that they contain houses as well as auxiliary buildings (kitchens, small shrines) and the normal suite of domestic artifacts. We therefore use the term "household" to refer to the social group that occupied a compound. The current analysis draws on a sample of 60 small compounds. Excavations at most of these compounds were minor, usually consisting of between six and eight test pits, but usually yielded appreciable amounts of artifacts. The sampling strategy prioritized an even spatial distribution across the central 9.3 km^2 polygon of Chunchucmil (Figure 4.2). In general, small households at Chunchucmil are less wealthy than larger households because they have access to less labor (fewer people live in them) and fewer construction resources (architectural compounds with more structures at Chunchucmil have larger structures, in terms of both surface area and platform height, equating to greater volume of construction material). Nevertheless, wealth can vary substantially among small households at Chunchucmil. The introduction to this chapter implies that small households are of lower social status than larger households, because wealth and status overlapped to a large degree among the Classic Period Maya (many small, less wealthy households were probably also of lower status), but there are of course caveats (McAnany 1993a). At least one small household (Group S2E2-F/Aak) had significant access to jade and a pot with a carved PSS (Primary Standard Sequence) text, indicating high status in the form of symbolic capital and a close relation with the elites who likely gave them the pot (LeCount 1999).

Tikal Reports (hereafter "TR") 19 and 20 (Haviland 1985, 2014a, 2014b) make available excavation data from nonelite architectural groups without shrines. Several other residential groups were also excavated at Tikal (see Haviland 2003:Table 4.1) but these are not included in TR 19 or 20 or in the current chapter, because several are unquestionably elite, such as group 7f-1 (see Haviland 2015). TR 19 reports on major excavations at groups 4F-1 and 4F-2 (over 700 m^2 of excavation at each group) while TR 20 reports on 119 smaller excavation operations (none with over 300 m^2). Most excavations reported in TR 20 consist of test pits that did not yield a large sample of artifacts for analysis. Of the 33 compounds that received more substantial excavations, two consisted of *chultun* excavations that did not yield data on the associated architecture. The analysis in the current chapter includes 31 of the substantially excavated compounds and one test-pitted compound from TR 20 (6B3) as well as Groups 4f-1 and 4F-2 from TR 19. Figure 4.3 shows the spatial distribution of Tikal's 34 compounds across the central 9 km^2 of the site. Haviland identifies two groupings of ordinary artifact types: basic and common. Basic artifact types are those artifact types that all households possess, which count as the signature of a domestic occupation. Haviland identifies nine basic artifact types: figurines, cores, ovate bifaces, irregularly retouched flakes, prismatic blades, used and unused flakes, and manos and metates. Common artifact types are possessed by many but not all of Tikal's

Figure 4.2. Map of the central 9.3 km² of Chunchucmil, showing the locations of the 60 excavated small residential groups.

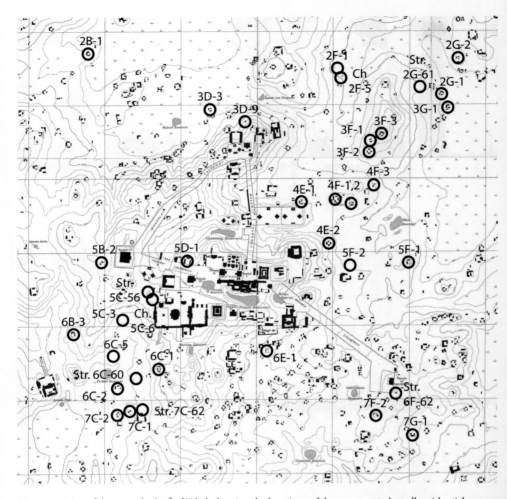

Figure 4.3. Map of the central 9 km² of Tikal, showing the locations of the 34 excavated small residential groups (from Carr and Hazard 1961).

households and consist of censers/braziers, centrally perforated sherds, thin bi-faces, point-retouched flakes, hammer stones, and rubbing stones.

The samples of 60 compounds from Chunchucmil and 34 from Tikal and are broadly comparable (Tables 4.2, 4.3). The small architectural compounds at both sites qualify as patio groups (Ashmore 1981:49). This similarity is no-table because most small residential compounds at Classic Period sites on the northern plains (e.g., Dzibilchaltún, Yaxuná, Izamal area sites) of Yucatán

Table 4.2. Data from the 60 small residential groups at Chunchucmil

Op. #	Obsidian blades	Obs. grams per kg pottery	Sq m of exc.	Metate #	Sascabera #	Quarry #	Surface area of residences	Total building volume	Fancy pottery as % of total pottery	Shell g per kg pottery	Distance from market
10	40	0.67	249	6	0	0	124	530	0.00	0.00	553
18	10	1.28	4	4	0	0	151	601	2.19	0.00	227
22	12	1.31	4	2	0	0	30	381	0.42	0.00	548
23	9	1.47	8	2	0	0	41	420	0.61	0.00	532
33	4	1.04	26	0	1	0	422	1107	0.00	0.00	2164
37	9	0.44	2	4	0	2	65	415	1.44	0.56	512
39	21	1.77	2	2	0	0	305	1709	2.99	3.02	415
40	13	2.71	7.5	3	0	0	193	170	0.36	0.46	357
41	6	0.56	7.5	7	0	0	208	235	0.64	0.00	350
42	10	1.46	5	1	0	0	240	510	1.01	1.76	1003
48	9	2.48	9	3	0	0	170	357	0.35	0.00	1020
49	2	1.03	6	0	0	0	117	446	0.94	0.45	959
50	2	0.24	6	2	0	0	105	556	1.06	0.09	1352
53	10	1.37	10	0	0	1	139	547	3.26	0.21	1716
58	1	2.93	9	0	0	0	26	61	0.73	0.00	1767
64	7	2.77	8	1	0	0	96	201	0.13	0.00	776
65	2	0.22	7	5	1	0	170	127	2.22	0.00	716
67	2	0.13	6	1	0	0	127	617	10.48	0.33	688
69	3	0.90	9	0	0	0	182	224	1.70	0.95	868

(continued)

Table 4.2.—*continued*

Op. #	Obsidian blades	Obs. grams per kg pottery	Sq m of exc.	Metate #	Sascabera #	Quarry #	Surface area of residences	Total building volume	Fancy pottery as % of total pottery	Shell g per kg pottery	Distance from market
71	11	1.60	8	0	1	0	233	875	1.57	0.28	1068
72	4	0.72	7	4	0	0	179	446	1.20	0.00	765
73	4	0.44	7	3	0	0	89	520	1.84	0.21	748
74	4	0.46	6	2	0	0	127	516	0.76	0.82	724
76	7	0.53	5	1	0	0	114	140	1.10	0.00	680
85	1	0.11	6	0	0	0	55	131	0.44	0.27	1532
90	6	1.22	8	0	0	0	105	205	0.24	0.30	936
91	6	0.39	6	2	0	0	190	185	0.38	0.40	463
92	2	0.69	5	2	0	0	161	341	0.48	0.00	415
94	3	2.07	8	1	0	0	64	16	0.00	0.00	1091
96	1	0.07	8	1	0	0	48	60	0.00	0.00	1678
97	3	0.26	8	2	0	0	39	461	0.12	1.77	1190
101	3	0.46	10	2	0	1	182	466	0.29	0.00	1460
103	1	1.79	8	0	0	0	142	677	0.00	0.00	1890
104	4	10.48	8	0	0	0	98	35	0.00	0.00	2063
106	6	2.24	8	1	0	0	90	229	0.31	0.00	1811
108	6	0.63	8	3	0	0	370	609	0.56	0.00	1742
109	6	1.09	8	0	0	0	202	474	0.31	0.28	1611
110	0	0.00	8	0	0	0	300	293	0.25	0.00	1650

111	0	0.00	8	0	0	100	213	0.00	0.00	1539
115	6	1.39	8	0	0	220	283	0.22	0.31	1825
116	2	18.86	8	0	0	326	299	0.00	0.00	1739
117	5	4.83	8	3	0	240	281	0.67	0.00	973
121	1	0.42	8	0	0	0	264	0.00	4.84	1930
122	3	1.46	10	0	0	225	286	0.70	0.00	1365
127	1	0.82	8	0	0	111	28	0.16	0.00	1153
129	7	0.97	5	1	0	222	750	0.87	0.00	1222
130	11	2.37	12	1	0	148	561	1.86	0.21	1611
131	1	1.81	12	0	0	105	639	0.00	0.00	1696
133	29	1.61	16	1	0	92	341	2.18	0.00	1299
134	25	0.85	12	2	0	303	1589	0.83	2.79	1779
137	14	1.66	4	6	0	181	303	1.08	0.31	851
140	0	0.00	8	4	0	68	523	1.69	0.50	1626
141	11	1.34	7	2	0	282	602	1.14	0.74	1211
145	7	5.45	7	2	0	20	376	1.15	0.00	1716
146	8	5.12	8	1	1	51	300	0.63	0.82	1261
149	2	0.00	8	1	0	127	56	0.32	3.84	902
156	6	2.00	4	1	0	183	474	0.52	0.58	1385
153 + 4A	4	1.81	8	1	0	202	691	0.27	1.03	909
9c Aak	670	2.52	369	12	0	203	579	0.00	0.49	559
9f	46	0.62	70	0	1	200	458	0.00	1.02	647
Chiwool										

Table 4.3. Data from the 34 small residential groups in the sample from Tikal

Grp	Quadrangle	Periods occupied	Other artifact types	Surface area of arch. excav.	Obsidian prismatic blades	Blades/ m² of excavation	Shell artifacts	Crafting?	Structure surface area	# of structures	Distance from market
2B-1	Bejucal	4	0	28	1	0.04	0	no	218	4	1789
4F-1	Camp	6	29	1127	1105	0.98	68	yes	454	6	632
4F-2	Camp	4	32	740	1662	2.25	73	yes	275	7	700
4F-3	Camp	5	6	100	66	0.66	2	no	65.5	4	868
5F-1	Camp	6	7	60	31	0.52	31	no	145	2	905
5F-2	Camp	1	1	175	35	0.20	3	no	173.7	6	526
6E-1	Corriental	5	29	150	172	1.15	53	yes	117	4	474
2F-1	Encanto	3	2	224	4	0.02	1	no	308	1	1421
2G-1	Encanto	2.5	8	230	89	0.39	8	no	239.5	5	1621
2G-2	Encanto	2	6	134	11	0.08	0	no	125	3	1842
3F-1	Encanto	3	3	66	26	0.39	0	no	108.5	2	1079
3F-2	Encanto	2.5	4	90	12	0.13	1	no	114.75	4	1016
3F-3	Encanto	4	1	30	1	0.03	0	no	231.5	5	1158
3G-1	Encanto	3	2	24	7	0.29	1	no	485	5	1579
Str 2G-61	Encanto	2.5	4	250	45	0.18	8	yes	135.5	1	1537
4E-1	Great Plaza	1	1	48	3	0.06	0	no	430	5	484

4E-2	Great Plaza	1	2	89	4	0.04	0	no	230	4	421
5D-1	Great Plaza	4	4	96	74	0.77	6	no	960	4	474
Dtr 6F-62	Inscriptions	5	0	21	0	0.00	0	no	30	1	1132
7F-2	Inscriptions	4	0	16	1	0.06	0	no	152	7	1168
7G-1	Inscriptions	3	1	14	4	0.29	1	no	110	3	1421
3D-3	North zone	2	0	49	0	0.00	0	no	113	3	1105
3D-9	North zone	2	2	54	17	0.31	3	no	40	2	974
6B-3	Perdido	1	0	4	1	0.25	0	no	166	4	1263
6C-1	Perdido	2.5	13	114	163	1.43	48	yes	276	4	895
6C-2	Perdido	3	2	12	3	0.25	1	no	338	3	1184
6C-5	Perdido	2.5	0	63	0	0.00	0	no	2	2	1084
7C-1	Perdido	3	2	54	17	0.31	1	no	56.75	2	1232
7C-2	Perdido	3	1	12	7	0.58	0	no	246.75	4	1316
Str 6C-60	Perdido	3.5	0	70	1	0.01	0	no	71.6	2	1053
Str 7C-62	Perdido	0.5	6	35	22	0.63	6	no	7.5	1	1163
5B-2	Temple IV	2	0	39	2	0.05	0	no	80	2	1026
5C-3	Temple IV	2	0	100	5	0.05	0	no	100	1	921
Str 5C-56	Temple IV	3	13	70	81	1.16	30	no	51	2	721

are not patio groups. The 34 Tikal compounds have an average of 3.3 structures in them, while the average number of structures in the 60 Chunchucmil compounds is 3.5. Based on estimates derived from Haviland's maps of each compound, the mean surface area of architecture per compound is 196 m^2 (not counting patio platforms). The corresponding mean for Chunchucmil is 164 m^2. At both sites there is diversity in the scale of architecture within these small groups. Some compounds at each site had vaulted buildings standing up to 3.5 m high today, and some buildings at each site had very little architectural volume. The mound volumes at Chunchucmil range from 16 m^3 to 1,709 m^3 (mean = 430, SD = 316). Quantifying the range of variation in mound volume is not possible for Tikal because the Tikal map lacks height estimates for buildings. The sampled compounds of both sites spread across areas of very similar size (9 km^2 at Tikal, 9.3 km^2 at Chunchucmil), though the Chunchucmil sample is spread more evenly across its respective area (compare Figures 4.2 and 4.3). The amount of excavation per compound at Tikal is larger than the amount for Chunchucmil.

Results

Do small structure groups at Tikal and Chunchucmil exhibit as much variation in the amount of obsidian per group? The average number of obsidian artifacts per square meter of excavation in small groups at Tikal is 0.4, and the standard deviation is 0.5, giving a coefficient of variation of 1.25. This indicates a rather large amount of variation. For comparison, the average number of obsidian artifacts per square meter of excavation in small groups at Chunchucmil is 1.04 and the standard deviation is 1.52 (this differs from the standard deviation of 2.72 given in Table 4.1 because the value in Table 4.1 is grams obsidian per kg of pottery), giving a coefficient of variation of 1.47, very similar to the coefficient of variation at Tikal. To help understand the sizable and comparable variation in access to obsidian at Tikal and Chunchucmil, I propose a series of hypotheses:.

> Hypothesis #1: amount of obsidian correlates with length of occupation.
> Hypothesis #2: amount of obsidian correlates with wealth.
> Hypothesis #3: amount of obsidian correlates with size of household.
> Hypothesis #4: amount of obsidian correlates with distance to the main market.
> Hypothesis #5: amount of obsidian correlates with degree of craft specialization.

This section explores each of these hypotheses and then considers how much of the variation in obsidian can be accounted for by a suite of measurable independent variables.

Hypothesis #1: Amount of Obsidian Correlates with Length of Occupation

For Chunchucmil we know that most of the households at the site had a robust occupation during only one chronological phase, the Late Aak phase (400 to 630 CE). Within that phase, some households were occupied longer than others. For example, Group S2E2-F/Aak appears to have been occupied for a few generations longer than its next-door neighbor, S2E2-C/Muuch (Hutson 2010:109). Nevertheless, in most cases we cannot determine whether a household had a short or long occupation within the Late Aak phase. There is a rather simple way, however, to filter out the effect of differences in length of occupation. Assuming that households with longer Late Aak phase occupations consumed more pottery, variation in the consumption of obsidian caused by length of occupation can be standardized by quantifying obsidian as a ratio with ceramics (grams obsidian per kg of pottery). We cannot standardize the sample for length of occupation at Tikal because exact quantities of pottery per excavation are not reported. Furthermore, Tikal's households had much more varied occupational histories than those at Chunchucmil. Though nearly all were occupied in the Late Classic Period, many were also occupied in the Early Classic and Late Preclassic. In other words, some groups (6E-1, 4F-1, 4F-3, and 5F-1) in the 34 group sample at Tikal show over 1,000 years of occupation (though not necessarily 100% continuous) while others (4E-1, 4E-2, and 6B-3) were occupied for less than 200 years. Despite these differences, length of occupation (quantified as number of ceramic phases) has only a weak positive correlation with amount of obsidian ($r = 0.315$, $p = 0.070$) at Tikal. Thus, for the analyses below, I quantify obsidian at Tikal as number of artifacts per square meter of excavation as opposed to number of artifacts per ceramic phase.

Hypothesis #2: Amount of Obsidian correlates with Wealth

Wealth can be measured in many ways, two of which are operationalized here: portable goods and architecture. In terms of portable goods, Michael Smith

(1987:312) notes that fancy pottery for serving food "appears to represent the most useful class of archaeological artifact for assessing wealth." For Chunchucmil, we have data on fancy pottery as a percentage of the total ceramic assemblage by mass, though we lack these data for Tikal. Beyond simple quantity of fancy pottery, higher wealth has also been correlated with greater diversity of household goods (Haviland 2014a:116; Smith 2015; cf. Smith 1987:309). Haviland presents good data on this for Tikal, where a wide variety of lithic tools were found in small households. Though lithic artifacts are much less abundant at Chunchucmil (Dahlin et al. 2011), assemblage diversity could be assessed by the quantities of metates (grinding basins) and shell artifacts. I can also test to see if possession of other resources, such as a stone quarry or *sascab* mine, correlates positively with obsidian at Chunchucmil.

Architecture stands as a proxy for wealth to the extent that larger buildings index greater control of labor and material resources (Sewell 1940; Smith 1987, 2015; Smith et al. 2014; Wilk 1983). In many agrarian societies, house size communicates wealth (Blanton 1994). Since energetics calculations (Abrams 1994) have not been performed at Chunchucmil or Tikal, we rely on measurements of the volume of construction in the case of Chunchucmil and surface area of structures for Tikal.

Statistical analyses show that wealth and consumption of obsidian are not strongly correlated at Chunchucmil. A very weak negative correlation exists between obsidian and portable wealth as measured by fancy pottery ($r = -0.137$, $p = 0.301$). Equally insignificant correlations exist between obsidian and shell ($r = -0.146$, $p = 0.264$), grinding basins ($r = -0.114$, $p = 0.388$), quarries ($r = -0.084$, $p = 0.521$), and *sascab* mines ($r = -0.005$, $p = 0.969$). Looking now at wealth as measured by architecture, obsidian is essentially uncorrelated with volume of architecture at Chunchucmil ($r = -0.119$, $p = 0.363$). At Tikal, in contrast, wealth in terms of assemblage diversity (as measured by the number of nonordinary artifact types) has a very strong positive correlation with obsidian artifacts per m^2 of excavation ($r = 0.849$, $p < 0.001$). The correlation is still strong if we measure assemblage diversity as the number of nonordinary artifact types per m^2 of excavation ($r = 0.514$, $p = 0.002$). In particular, the five architectural groups with the most obsidian per m^2 of excavation at Tikal are also the five architectural groups with the most diverse artifact assemblages. The amount of shell per m^2 of excavation also correlates positively with obsidian ($r = 0.578$, $p < 0.001$). In sum, obsidian correlates more closely with wealth at Tikal than at Chunchucmil (see also P. Rice 1987a).

Hypothesis #3: Amount of Obsidian Correlates with Size of Household

The logic here is that larger social groups may either have a higher demand for a foreign good like obsidian or have more laborers present, who can produce more goods and therefore afford to purchase more obsidian. Household size could be quantified by surface area of residences or number of residences. At Tikal obsidian exhibits weak positive correlations with household size, quantified as the number of structures per group ($r = 0.341$, $p = 0.049$) or the surface area per group ($r = 0.207$, $p = 0.239$). At Chunchucmil there is no significant correlation between residential surface area and access to obsidian ($r = 0.129$, $p = 0.330$).

Hypothesis #4: Amount of Obsidian Correlates with Distance to Main Market

Excavations conducted by myself, Daniel Mazeau, and David Hixson in Chunchucmil's hinterlands have found that households just beyond the site have about a third as much obsidian as households within the site and households over 5 km away from the site core have about one-twentieth the amount (Hutson et al. 2008; see also Aoyama 2001; Garraty 2009:168–169). Did distance from the central marketplaces at Chunchucmil and Tikal affect access to obsidian *within* these sites? At Chunchucmil there is a weak *positive* correlation between obsidian and distance from Plaza D, the central marketplace ($r = 0.249$, $p = 0.055$); people living farther away from the market tended to have more obsidian. At Tikal we find the reverse: people living closer to the central market (the East Plaza; Jones 2015) have more obsidian ($r = -0.393$, p = 0.021). Given that there is also a positive correlation between wealth and obsidian at Tikal, this finding is consistent with Haviland's (1982) argument that households located closer to the site center were wealthier and more powerful (cf. Arnold and Ford 1980; Hutson 2016).

Hypothesis #5: Amount of Obsidian Correlates with Degree of Craft Specialization

Tikal gives strong support to this hypothesis. Four of the five households that engaged in craft specialization (4F-1, which made figurines and shell adornments; 4-F2, which made obsidian tools and textiles; 6C-1, which worked shell;

and 6E-1, which specialized in textiles) are among the five with the highest access to obsidian. These four households also have the highest scores for assemblage diversity, which, as noted above, can be treated as a proxy for wealth. Thus, there seems to be an important overlap between wealth and craft specialization, a point noted by Haviland as well (2014a:123). Rather than asking whether people get lots of obsidian because they can afford it or whether people get lots of obsidian because they need it for crafting, it seems that both are correct. This conclusion dovetails with the idea that crafting can be a means for amplifying household wealth, particularly in contexts (such as Tikal) where the existence of a market incentivizes craft production by simplifying access to buyers (Hirth 2009a). At Chunchucmil the small household with the strongest evidence for craft specialization—group S2E2-F/Aak, which specialized in processing coarse fibers (Hutson et al. 2007)—has the second highest amount of fancy pottery and the thirteenth highest architectural volume (among residential groups with five or fewer structures). Thus, Chunchucmil also lends support to the idea that crafting households were better off.

Accounting for Total Variation

At Tikal crafting and household wealth are heavily correlated with the amount of obsidian consumed by small households, while length of occupation and distance from market are lightly correlated. How much of the total variation do these variables account for? A multiple regression shows that seven variables considered thus far (number of ceramic phases, assemblage diversity, distance from marketplace, access to shell, surface area of architecture, number of structures, presence/absence of crafting) account for 78.3% of the variation in the amount of obsidian (per m^2 of excavation) consumed by small households. Vagaries of excavation sampling probably account for additional variation. The number of square meters of excavation among the 34 groups ranged from 4 m^2 (group 6B-3) to 1,127 m^2 (Group 4F-1), with a significant correlation between the amount of excavation and the amount of obsidian recovered per m^2 of excavation ($r = 0.532$, $p < 0.001$). The seven variables mentioned above and the amount of excavation per group accounts for 82.7% of the variation.

At Chunchucmil there is probably a correlation between access to obsidian and craft production but no correlation between obsidian and wealth. In general, only 15% of the variation in access to obsidian is accounted for by the variables presented here. If I add another dozen variables to the mix, such as patio surface area, shrine volume, and number of *chi'ich* mounds, the amount of variation explained is still below one third. Furthermore, unlike Tikal, excavation sampling does not seem to play any role in the analysis: the amount of excavation per residential group exhibits no correlation with access to obsidian ($r = -0.048$, $p = 0.713$).

Discussion

The comparison of the variation in the amounts of obsidian consumed by small households at Tikal and Chunchucmil as well as the sources of this variation exposes two unresolved questions. First, at both sites there is quite a bit of variation in obsidian consumed. Unlike at Tikal, however, the factors that account for this variation at Chunchucmil remain obscure. Additional sources of variation must be considered. Though I lack the tools to explore these sources of variation systematically, several can be mentioned. First, as noted above, Tikal and Chunchucmil share much in common but also differ in at least two important ways. Tikal is an exemplar of dynastic rulership with major geopolitical ambitions. Data from Chunchucmil suggest corporate, as opposed to dynastic, leadership. Also, whereas Chunchucmil was a short-lived, agriculturally unsustainable commercial center, Tikal exhibited long-term stability and a livelihood much more strongly grounded in local agricultural resources (Lentz, Dunning, and Scarborough 2015).

Another possible explanation of the variation at Chunchucmil is that many of the excavations there might not have recovered a representative sample of debris. As mentioned above, most of the 60 households in the sample at Chunchucmil only received a small amount of test pits. Following the results of several houselot studies and our own pilot studies (Becker 2003a; Hayden and Cannon 1983; Hutson et al. 2007), my colleagues and I placed these test pits off the corners of patios and behind buildings. However, some important debris, such as that from shellmaking at a Mayapán household (Masson and Peraza 2014a:336), is occasionally found in patios.

An alternative explanation for the variation at Chunchucmil concerns distribution systems. Studies of obsidian from the San Lorenzo B phase (1200 to 1000 BCE) at the Olmec center of San Lorenzo show that some households got their obsidian from entirely different obsidian sources than other households. According to Hirth et al. (2013:2796), these data suggest that obsidian "moved through a network of decentralized domestic exchanges." Rather than depending on centralized and homogenized supply chains, each household may have had its own trade partnerships. These independent connections resulted in the consumption of obsidian from an appreciable diversity of obsidian sources, ten in total. The vast majority of obsidian at Chunchucmil came from El Chayal. Is it possible, however, that independent trade partnerships supplemented market exchange and might help explain the variation in quantities of obsidian consumed by each of Chunchucmil's small households? In previous publications my colleagues and I have suggested that nearly all obsidian came from a single source located over 600 km away (as the crow flies) and Chunchucmil as a whole was heavily engaged in commerce of various kinds, so there would have been a dozen or so trade cooperatives, each headquartered in one of the large architectural compounds at the site core, that coordinated the production of local surpluses (such as salt) and the exchange of these surpluses for long-distance goods from the south, such as obsidian. These cooperatives do not represent absolute centralization of the obsidian trade (e.g., Santley 1983) but are more centralized than the potpourri of procurement strategies at San Lorenzo. Since we lack nodule cortex or waste products from the reduction of polyhedral macrocores, Chunchucmil's trade cooperatives were most likely not traveling all the way to El Chayal. Obsidian procurement was therefore complex, involving people from Chunchucmil as well as independent agents further away (Hirth 2008).

Unfortunately, our failure to locate any local obsidian workshops prevents us from discussing obsidian technology in great detail. We have always assumed that households procured prismatic blades from the marketplace and that the trade cooperatives supplied the market. No economies with market places, however, are exclusively market economies (Garraty 2010; Hirth and Pillsbury 2013). A place like Chunchucmil surely featured reciprocity and redistribution alongside marketing. I suggest, admittedly without any direct support, that some of the variation in the amounts of obsidian consumed by small households at Chunchucmil is due to the existence of a variety of independent trade partnerships not completely tied to Chunchucmil's marketplace. Such trade partnerships may have been less reliable than the central marketplace. On the other hand, the supply of obsidian at the central marketplace may have fluctuated over time such that households whose most intensive occupations occurred at different times during the Late Aak phase may have had differential access to market-distributed obsidian.

The very strong correlation between wealth and consumption of obsidian in Tikal's small households raises the second unresolved question. If obsidian does correlate with wealth, we might expect larger, elite groups to have more obsidian than the small, nonelite groups discussed in this chapter. Yet Moholy-Nagy (1989:385) shows that the amount of obsidian blades found in small structure groups is three to five times as large as the amount found in higher-status residential contexts such as Intermediate Structure Groups and Range Structure Groups (see also Masson and Freidel 2012:Table 4). Moholy-Nagy notes that these numbers have not been controlled for the quantity of excavation (for example, the Tikal project dug more in small structures than intermediate structures). It should also be noted that volumes of excavation were not always recorded at Tikal, and not all dirt was screened (Moholy-Nagy 1997:296). Furthermore, massive deposits of obsidian were found above burial chambers in the site core, but only about a tenth of this obsidian was tabulated and kept (Moholy-Nagy 1997:296). The unrecorded pieces of obsidian, numbering in the hundreds of thousands, are said to be debitage/workshop debris. If even a small portion of these unrecorded fragments were blades, and if they originated in higher-status contexts, this might explain the unexpected shortage of blades in higher-status contexts. Alternatively, in wealthier households at Tikal, a portion of the tasks requiring obsidian blades may have been completed by people in smaller households. This could indicate relations of servitude across households at Tikal. This situation differs from the idea that elite households had "live-in" servants, occupying the small houses within otherwise impressive residential compounds (Haviland 2015:118).

Conclusion

This chapter shows substantial variation in obsidian consumption among small, nonelite residential groups at both Tikal and Chunchucmil. At Tikal about four-fifths of this variation can be accounted for by factors such as wealth, craft specialization, and distance from the marketplace. At Chunchucmil consumption of obsidian does not correlate strongly with wealth or any other variables: over two-thirds of the variation in household consumption remains unaccounted for. The gulf between the explanations for variation in consumption between Tikal and Chunchucmil shows that large, Classic Period Maya cities with central marketplaces can still be quite different from each other in terms of economic processes (not to mention other processes; D. Chase et al. 1990). Perhaps these differences reflect discrepancies in the core of Tikal's economy, which relied heavily on upland farming, and Chunchucmil's economy, which relied heavily on long-distance trade of salt. Alternatively, different forms of political organization may also impact consumption: Tikal was led by strong, centralized dynasties, whereas leadership at Chunchucmil was more heavily factionalized and decentralized. Finally, I propose that the variation in amounts of obsidian available to small households at Chunchucmil may have been due to fluctuating supply at the marketplace and the possibility that some households relied on nonmarket-based exchange networks to get access to obsidian. Nowadays, more and more evidence for market-based exchange among the ancient Maya has come to light. The existence of a marketplace, however, does not necessarily entail other conclusions. The data presented in this chapter highlight the point that market-based exchange can result in quite different outcomes at two sites that otherwise share many similarities.

5

Rural Economies of Agrarian Houselots before and after the Rise of Urban Mayapán

MARILYN A. MASSON, CARLOS PERAZA LOPE,
TIMOTHY S. HARE, BRADLEY W. RUSSELL,
PEDRO DELGADO KÚ, BÁRBARA ESCAMILLA OJEDA,
AND LUIS FLORES COBÁ

The nuts and bolts of Maya economies have been studied using various approaches to household archaeology, given that dwelling groups represented the primary and most ubiquitous units for production and consumption of the majority of goods in use for premodern Mesoamerican states (e.g., Feinman and Nicholas 2004; Hirth 2009a; Wilk 1989; Wilk and Ashmore 1988). Obtaining a robust understanding of comparative domestic economies is an essential component of reconstructing regional political economies (Feinman and Nicholas 2000, 2012; Kowalewski 1990; Pyburn 1997; M. Smith 2004). Studies of activities at dwellings in the Maya area provide valuable insight into many dimensions of social organization and daily life (e.g., Haviland 1985; King 2000; Lohse and Valdez 2004; McAnany 1995, 2004; Masson and Freidel 2012; Masson and Peraza, eds. 2014; Robin 2012; Scarborough et al. 2003). Three key questions have guided recent investigations at Mayapán that focus on rural domestic economies in order to complement what is known from urban houselots at this site. First, to what degree were rural households dependent on others at the local or regional levels for basic goods deemed essential to daily existence? Second, by what means were these needs met via exchange for products derived from surplus crafting or agrarian production (or other occupational niches)? Third, how did rural commoner affluence compare to the affluence of their urban counterparts? In this chapter we consider new data from eight rural dwellings excavated outside of Mayapán's city wall in 2015, under the auspices of a National

Science Foundation (NSF) grant for a project entitled "Agrarian Foundations of Urban Life at Mayapán" (NSF-BCS-1406233).

Although rural houses sprawl across vast tracts of territory intermediate to minor (and major) centers in portions of the Maya lowlands, especially for the Late or Terminal Classic in the state of Yucatán, Mexico, this category of settlement is primarily understood from surface mapping (C. Brown et al. 2006; Dunning 2004; Houck 2004:52; Hutson et al. 2008; Johnson 2000; Pyburn et al. 1998; D. Rice 2006; J. Smith 2000; Zetina 2004). Where dwellings have been excavated, they are often well within the settlement boundaries of central places or secondary towns in the Maya area, with some exceptions (e.g., Hanson 2008; Robin 2012; Sheets 2000). Less is known about the economies of families living in the countryside, at the margins of towns, or in low-density settlement zones between them.

A Brief Summary of Household Economy Studies at Mayapán

Research at Mayapán from 2001 to 2009 focused on the economic organization of dwellings within the city wall (an enclosure with a circumference of 9.1 km), a zone referred to as "urban" in this chapter. This work identified diverse surplus craft economies at houses across the urban zone as well as houselots with more generalized (nonsurplus crafting) activities whose residents may have held service occupations or were primarily engaged in cultivation (Masson and Peraza 2014a; Masson et al. 2016). Mayapán commoners undertook a range of activities besides crafting, such as maintaining gardens and infield plots, raising deer and turkeys, hunting, making some of their own goods, and trading for many more. Most residents possessed obsidian blades, at least one pottery vessel made of nonlocal (Matillas Fine Orange) pottery, and raw materials or finished products of marine shell debris and chert or chalcedony from elsewhere in Yucatán. None of these goods were available at the city or within a day's walk from it. Our excavations of urban dwellings have tended to be biased toward surplus crafting affluent houselots. Despite efforts to investigate nonsurplus-generating houselots, significant craft industries at some contexts were revealed after extensive excavations had begun. The economies of more peripheral Mayapán houselots are not as well understood. To what degree were rural contexts integrated into the regional political economy, based on evidence for consumption of regional goods? Although relatively equitable distributions of nonlocal or fancy goods reflect well-developed market exchange in Hirth's (1998) model, we know little of such patterns for Maya contexts in more remote locations outside of towns or cities. Furthermore, in the absence of local, ordinary goods production at the houselot or community level, even the basic inventories of rural dwellings in our sample reflect dependence on regional exchange, without large quantities of long-distance or fancy goods.

Russell (2008) analyzed results of a surface survey and test pitting program within transects (1,000 × 250 m) extending outward from the city wall. This study and subsequent efforts found no evidence for surplus crafting outside of the wall (referred to as the "rural" zone in this chapter). Russell was the first to determine that artifact densities tend to be lower in the periphery than at downtown Mayapán houselots. The study of settlement patterns in "greater" Mayapán was expanded in 2013 by Hare, Masson, Peraza, and Russell, aided by a LiDAR survey of a 40 sq km area, including the walled city and adjacent areas (Hare, Masson, and Peraza 2014, funded by NSF, BCS-1144511). Image analysis and ground checking revealed that houselots extend across most of this area. Temporal components range from the Middle Preclassic through the colonial era, but the majority were of Terminal Classic or Postclassic date (as indicated by ground checking and surface pottery collections). Four Terminal Classic and four Postclassic houselots were extensively excavated in 2015, with the explicit goal of comparing rural domestic assemblages and activities to each other and to patterns of urban Mayapán. This chapter offers a preliminary assessment of rural household economies with respect to degrees of dependence on regional (northern Yucatán) trade, affluence, activity differentiation, and occupational longevity.

The full impacts of a regional political economy are best measured from a representative sample of the humblest houselots in the realm (e.g., Masson and Peraza 2004; Sheets 2000). Such contexts reflect the degree to which urban centers and minor centers depended on rural householders for provisions and surpluses essential to fund public works. McAnany et al. (2002) propose that heavy tribute burdens correlate with suppressed household wealth compared to cases where householders retain more of the surplus fruits of their labor. Both the quantity and the diversity of certain goods are indicators of household wealth (M. Smith 1987).

The notion of the self-sufficient houselot once carried weight for the Maya area and other premodern states (Webster and Sanders 1998), although this condition is unduly laborious and rarely witnessed in comparative cases (Hirth 2009a; Wolf 1982). To what degree did households and cities strive for self-sufficiency? While risk-reduction justifies significant efforts in this regard cross-culturally (Dunning et al. 2003; Pounds 1973), regularly occurring localized catastrophes (hurricanes, pests, droughts) are mitigated by options to trade with unaffected regions (e.g., Masson and Freidel 2013), especially given problems in long-term food storage in the tropics (Freidel and Shaw 2000). Fluctuating degrees of production heterogeneity and relative autonomy can be compared through the study of houselot assemblages, including the rural contexts evaluated in this chapter.

Comparing Postclassic houselots to Terminal Classic ones provides a longer view of countryside economies in the Mayapán vicinity, before and after the rise of the Postclassic urban capital. What was rural life like in the outback represented by Terminal Classic settlement in the study area, distant from Tier 1 capitals such as Chichén Itzá and Uxmal? How did Terminal Classic household economies in this area compare to those of Postclassic residents living within a 30-minute walk from Mayapán? Prior to the foundation of Mayapán in the twelfth century AD, the area was particularly remote. The ubiquitous Terminal Classic dwellings documented via LiDAR and ground survey sprawled in regular if low densities (roughly 6–10 people per hectare) beyond a Rank IV minor center, Tichac (modern pueblo of Telchaquillo). Minor centers smaller than Tichac dot the 40 sq km study area, marked mostly by public buildings of 5 m (or less) in elevation (Figure 5.1). The nearest Terminal Classic Rank III center, Yaxcopoíl, lies 30 km to the northeast (Garza Tarazona de González and Kurjack Bacso 1980). Houselots were recognized in the LiDAR images in the form of modified (rectangular) hill platforms that represent natural knolls to which tons of rock fill and retaining walls were added; outlines of dwellings can sometimes also be discerned.

Most rural dwellings of the eight excavated contexts discussed here were probably the homes of agriculturalists, given their relatively distant location from town or city settings, generalized artifact assemblages, and low densities of materials that are unlike the concentrations that indicate significant surplus crafting in the urban zone. Outbuildings at six of eight rural houselots are inferred to represent agricultural storage features; these are uncommon within walled Mayapán. Did members of rural houselots diversify their income through modest levels of craft production? Preliminary results of this study reveal that most rural houselots of both periods were dependent on exchange for nonlocal basic goods (pottery, stone tools, marine shell, raw materials).

Rural houselots exhibit significant variation within both the Terminal Clas-

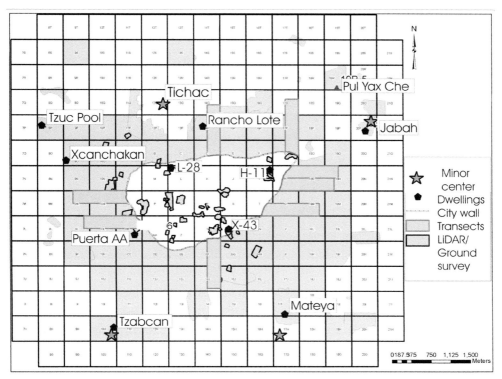

Figure 5.1. Location of rural excavated dwellings of the Terminal Classic and Postclassic Periods outside of the city wall as well as selected excavated dwellings inside of Mayapán's city wall and minor centers mentioned in the text (Tichac, Jabáh, Tzabcán, and Mateyá). More minor centers are present than are shown in the map.

sic and Postclassic Periods, dissimilar in terms of wealth and activity differentiation. Each period has one more affluent dwelling and at least one context that exhibits less wealth than the others. Spatial proximity to one of the more precocious minor centers may have provided enhanced economic opportunities in the Terminal Classic and Postclassic. As for ordinary houselots in urban Mayapán, rural households of both periods engaged in low levels of craft goods manufacture (with no significant surplus), perhaps for their own use or for other social or economic purposes (Masson et al. 2016). Farmers in this study were significantly embedded in regional exchange economies, and surplus agricultural production seems to have afforded a modest degree of affluence. This pattern is relatively similar for both time periods, but lower wealth and artifact densities were observed for the Terminal Classic compared to the Postclassic.

Rural Houses at Mayapán

Most of the houses in our sample were built on modified hill platforms, constructed with the addition of stone fill and retaining or houselot boundary walls. Such platforms are generally characteristic of Yucatán settlement (Carmean 1991). Remnants of circular or square storerooms are present, and most have one principal dwelling; a possible second modest dwelling was mapped for some (Figures 5.2, 5.3). Although most houses within urban Mayapán exhibit a variant of a standard rectangular house form with interior benches (Masson et al. 2014:202, Figure 5.7), different forms appear in our sample outside of the city wall. One of four Terminal Classic houses was apsidal (the other three were rectangular: see Figure 5.2), and one Postclassic house group exhibited two square dwellings, while the other three had a standard Mayapán plan that included benches (Figure 5.3).

The surface features of most houselots suggest considerable longevity of occupation in terms of the functional segmentation houselot space (multiple ancillary buildings), secondary residences or kitchens, and constructed platforms. Some reveal multiple phases of dwelling construction (particularly, Tzabcán and Jabáh) or major components dating to the Terminal and Postclassic Periods (Jabáh). Burials beneath the floors of principal houses at Jabáh and Tzabcán also signify a longer-term occupation. Longevity is an important issue given that rural dwellings in the region have sometimes been interpreted as seasonal farmers' huts (Dunning 2004:108), from which low densities of materials might be expected. Alternatively, low artifact densities at residences occupied year-round may be explained by variations in wealth and economic activities (e.g., M. Smith 1987). Two of the eight rural houselots exhibited lower artifact densities despite significant infrastructural investments; these may have been occupied for less time.

Terminal Classic dwellings in the study include Pul Yax Ché (19R-5), Tzuc Pool (8P-2), Mateyá (17J-2), and Tzabcán (10H-5). They are located to the northeast, northwest, southeast, and southwest portions of the study area, respectively. Postclassic groups include Jabáh (20P-7), Rancho Lote (14P-1), Camino Xcanchakán (9O-2), and Puerta AA (BB-206), present in the east, north, west, and southwest portion of the study area, respectively (Figure 5.1). Puerta AA is located just beyond Gate AA in the city wall. Of the eight houses, three were located within 300–500 m of a minor center, marked by a temple or shrine 2–5 m in height (Figure 5.1). Mateyá (Terminal Classic) and Jabáh (Postclassic) were

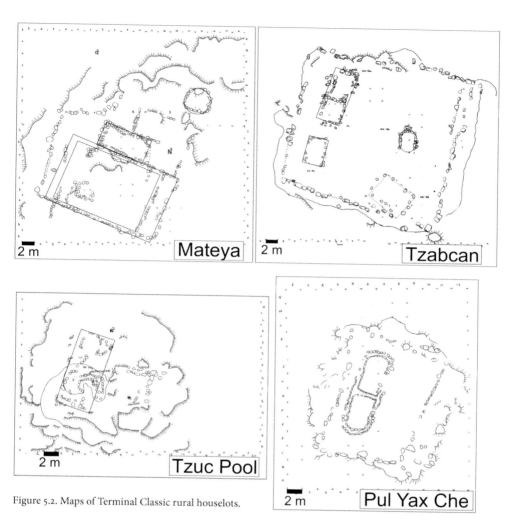

Figure 5.2. Maps of Terminal Classic rural houselots.

located 500 and 250 m (respectively) from two of the more impressive minor centers, while Tzabcán (Terminal Classic) is close (250 m) to a smaller public group. Other minor centers, consisting of small temples or shrines next to cenotes, are present in the area but are not shown on Figure 5.1, as they are distant from the rural dwellings discussed here.

The Jabáh ceremonial group replicates the configuration of the largest Postclassic outlying group within the city wall, Itzmal Ch'en, by the city's eastern Gate H. Like Itzmal Ch'en, it has a broad temple that faces a plaza framed by colonnaded halls and a central round shrine. A serpent sculpture was also lo-

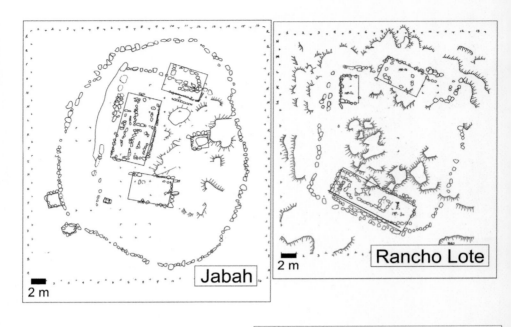

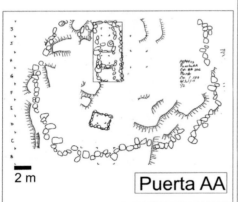

Figure 5.3. Maps of Postclassic rural houselots.

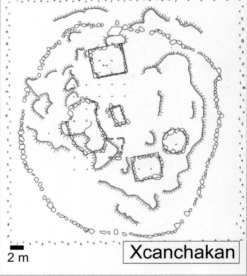

cated atop the temple's surface, and such sculptures are common at Itzmal Ch'en (Peraza and Masson 2014a, 2014b). The Mateyá minor group is formed by a small shrine (2 m in height) and an elongated, hall-like platform. A massive hilltop platform nearby oversees the group. The Tzabcán center is marked by a low, finely built public building that faces a small shrine.

The Terminal Classic dwelling at Tzuc Pool is a single rectangular or C-shaped edifice on a tall hill platform that overlooks the rockshelter-like opening of the Tzuc Pool cenote (Figure 5.2). Part of an outbuilding or terrace demarcation is present in front of this modest edifice. The Pul Yax Ché structure is unlike other Terminal Classic dwellings recorded for the area in terms of its elongated elliptical shape; the interior space is divided in half by a transverse wall (Figure 5.2). No outbuildings are associated with it. Tzabcán is a rectangular dwelling, also divided into two rooms by a transverse wall. Two rectangular outbuildings and one U-shaped outbuilding are present within its patio (Figure 5.2). The Mateyá houselot sample consists of a single dwelling with two round outbuildings on its platform (one of which is shown in Figure 5.2). As for Postclassic groups, Terminal Classic hill platforms have houselot enclosure walls (Tzuc Pool) or retaining walls that partially project from the surface and clearly demarcate the houselot platform.

The principal (Postclassic) Jabáh dwelling is a typical Mayapán-style house of modest construction (5.5 × 10 m), of average commoner dimensions for the site (Masson et al. 2014:238). It is located on the brim of a large *rejollada* depression of the sort long thought to have provided special cultivation opportunities for northern Maya farmers (Kepecs and Boucher 1996). The houselot exhibits one (perhaps two) secondary dwelling(s). Two rectangular, specialized features are present; one is a shrine-like alignment that envelops a large boulder, located directly in front (east) of the principal dwelling. The other is a diminutive box-like enclosure shaped by upright rectangular slabs (south of the principal structure). Two circular alignments or pens are attached to Jabáh's houselot boundary wall (Figure 5.3). All Postclassic rural houselots in this sample exhibited such boundary walls. In the immediate vicinity of the excavated Jabáh house (20P-7), more finely built houses and larger platforms are present, although they also fall into the commoner house size range for Mayapán. We were surprised to discover more than a simple agrarian house at 20P-7, which is the least elaborate of modest groups in the vicinity. Puerta AA (BB-206) features a typical Mayapán commoner house, to which a circular outbuilding is attached (to the rear wall); a small square outbuilding is present within the patio space (Figure 5.3). Postclassic Group Rancho Lote has a principal dwelling with multiple construction phases, a possible secondary dwelling, and a rectangular outbuilding (Figure 5.3). It was of a typical Mayapán style, but with modern disturbances to the interior benches. The Camino Xcanchakán Group exhibits an unusual Postclassic house form, with two square dwellings, along with one large oval pen formed by surface boulders as well as smaller rectangular and circular outbuildings (Figure 5.3).

The selection of rural houses from both periods took into consideration the diverse locations within the study area as well as variation in architectural form. In each case, the principal dwelling was fully excavated, in addition to patio space to the front and sides of the edifices, interior spaces of outbuildings, and refuse zones located within and outside of the enclosure or retaining walls. Artifact assemblages from these excavations, compared below, provide a first opportunity to compare the activities at these rural residences.

Artifact Densities

Certain classes of artifacts provide better measurements of wealth and activity diversification than others (Cyphers and Hirth 2000; Hirth 1998; M. Smith 1987). In this chapter we assess the relative quantities of obsidian, marine shell, chert/chalcedony, and pottery at the eight dwelling groups. Obsidian represents the only long-distance good in this set, deriving primarily from sources in the Guatemalan highlands (Escamilla 2004). Marine shell was imported to the area from various coastal locations in northern Yucatán and as such represents a regional, nonlocal commodity. Similarly, chert/chalcedony sources are not present in the study area or, to our knowledge, near any of the closest modern towns; much of this material likely derives from sources to the south between the modern town of Teabo and the Puuc region. Pottery also represents a regional good, based on typological classifications that indicate close ties to the Puuc region exchange sphere. No evidence for local pottery production is observed from decorative variants or excessively dense concentrations of sherds. The latter, along with molds, are indicative of pottery workshops within Mayapán's city wall (Masson et al. 2016).

Obsidian

The number of obsidian pieces per cubic meter is presented in Table 5.1. For comparative purposes, eight fully excavated dwellings inside of the city wall are also listed. Urban obsidian surplus production localities (I-55, Q-176, and Q-40) exhibit especially high densities (31–50 pieces per cubic meter), but obsidian consumption levels at five fully excavated urban houses where surplus blades were not made range from 0.8 to 19.2/cu m (Q-39, H-11, L-28,

Table 5.1. Obsidian, shell, and chert/chalcedony densities

Context	Obsidian/ cu m	Shell/ cu m	Chert/ cu m
URBAN HOUSES (INSIDE CITY WALL)			
I-55 (affluent multicrafter, obsidian, shell)	49.7	5.4	18.3
Q-176 (affluent multicrafter, obsidian, shell, pottery vessels)	34.5	3.6	9.8
Q-40 (affluent multicrafter, obsidian, pottery effigies, metal)	31.3	1.3	2.5
Q-39 (affluent multicrafter, shell, chert, metal, pottery effigies)	19.2	4.1	184.1
H-11 (ordinary house)	15.1	1.9	7.7
L-28 (ordinary house)	1.8	1.8	3.9
Y-45 (secondary elite house)	1.6	1.3	3.8
X-43 (ordinary house)	0.8		6.9
POSTCLASSIC RURAL HOUSES			
Jabáh	12.6	1.9	11.9
Rancho Lote	4.5		0.9
BB-206	0.6	0.9	6.4
Xcanchakán	0.5	0.1	5.5
TERMINAL CLASSIC RURAL HOUSES			
Mateyá	0.5	0.4	1.7
Tzuc Pool	0.4	0.3	1.6
Tzabcán	0.2		0.2
Pul Yax Ché	0.1	0.1	0.1

Y-45, X-43). Three of four ordinary urban houses have densities ranging from 0.8 to 1.8/cu m, in comparable proportions to two of four Postclassic rural houses (0.5–0.6/cu m). Two Postclassic rural houses (Rancho Lote, Jabáh) have higher obsidian densities (4.5, 12.6) than three ordinary urban contexts, and Jabáh's 12.6/cu m is comparable to that of ordinary urban house H-11 (15.1/cu m). Terminal Classic rural house densities (0.1–0.5/cu m) are lower than the Postclassic urban and rural houses. Only Mateyá equals the density of one rural Postclassic context, where the least obsidian is present (Camino Xcanchakán); both exhibit 0.5/cu m.

But perhaps the most important finding is the presence of obsidian at all rural houses tested. This result suggests a lower level of affluence for six of the rural houses than is found at ordinary residential groups within the city wall, with two rural Postclassic examples obtaining more obsidian than some of their urban counterparts. Ixtepeque was the dominant source for Postclassic contexts, according to Bárbara Escamilla's visual sourcing of the sample, as is also true for urban Mayapán (Escamilla 2004); highland Guatemalan sources of El Chayal and San Martín Jilotepeque were also present at Postclassic rural houselots. Terminal Classic contexts obtained obsidian from the same sources, but significant quantities of the Gulf Coast source of Zaragoza were also represented.

Marine Shell

Marine shell densities indicate a similar pattern. Marine shell debris is present at six of eight rural houses, three each from the Terminal Classic and Postclassic Periods. Two Postclassic contexts stand out for having more than twice as much marine shell per cubic meter than all other rural samples. Jabáh and Puerta AA have densities of 1.9 and 0.9 per cu m, respectively; all other rural houses range from 0.1 to 0.4 (Table 5.1). Ordinary urban houses (H-11, L-28) and another within the city wall (not a shell workshop), Q-40a, exhibit densities (1.3–1.9) similar to extramural contexts at Jabáh and Puerta AA. Higher quantities are evident at surplus shell ornament workshops in the urban zone (3.6–5.4/cu m). These comparisons reveal general parity in low level shell-working at two rural houses and three urban residences. Surplus crafting was identified with the urban zone by an arbitrary metric: where densities exceeded one standard deviation above the mean. But lower-intensity shell-working took place with regularity at ordinary (nonsurplus-generating) dwellings in the urban and rural zones (Masson et al. 2016).

As marine shell represents a nonlocal raw material, it is significant that ornament-making was widespread. Shell artifacts most commonly include debitage, especially percussion flakes. Finished objects or preforms are scarcer. Whether shell-working occurred at houselots or not, some finished ornaments were acquired through exchange, given that finished objects are often of rarer shells (*Oliva*, *Spondylus*) not represented in many houselot debitage samples. In the rural contexts, only Jabáh (*Oliva*) and Tzuc Pool (*Spondylus*) had single examples of these more valuable shells (for a discussion of shell value and shell money, see Freidel et al. 2016; Masson and Peraza 2014a). Debris is most commonly represented by *Dinocardium*, *Melongena corona*, *Pleuroploca gigantea*, *Strombus*, and cockle shells that are available on the beaches closest to Mayapán (north coast); finished objects are also made of these taxa (Masson and Peraza 2014a:Table 6.7). *Oliva* and *Spondylus* were more restricted in peninsular beaches and were more difficult to obtain (Masson and Peraza 2014a:334–336).

Chert and Chalcedony Artifacts

Chert and chalcedony (referred to as "chert" in this chapter) flake densities are variable in the rural zone, ranging from 0.1 to 11.9/cu m, compared to urban Mayapán, where the range is from 2.5 to 18.3/cu m for dwellings not engaged in surplus stone tool production (Table 5.1). Three Postclassic rural houses have densities greater than or equivalent to six urban houselots (5.5–11.9 rural, 2.5–9.8 urban). Remarkably, flakes were scarce at two Terminal Classic and one Postclassic dwelling (Tzabcán, Pul Yax Ché, Rancho Lote), with 0.1–0.9/cu m. More work is needed beyond density comparisons to interpret these results, although five nonworkshop urban houses only exhibit from 2.5 to 9.8 flakes/cu m, not a large quantity. Low-level flake removal for expedient purposes seems to have occurred at six rural houses, in addition to five urban examples, using regional cherts obtained from beyond the Mayapán environs. Material may have been scarcer for rural inhabitants, or cores harder to obtain, resulting in a greater degree of curation of chert resources, with respect to informal tool-making or refurbishing/recycling of tool fragments. As Table 5.1 indicates, urban stone tool workshop Q-39 exhibits much higher densities (184.1), and an urban outbuilding located outside of a houselot (I-57) had 1,008 flakes/cu m (Masson et al. 2016).

Despite the low numbers of flakes, chert tools were present at the rural houses, except for Pul Yax Ché, where none were recovered. Axe-like tools were only found at Postclassic houses in Jabáh and Camino Xcanchakán, but axes are not ubiquitous in Mayapán domestic assemblages, even for presumed farmers' residences (Masson and Peraza 2014a:369, 376, Figure 6.25). They could have been lost in fields or broken and recycled to the point of not being recognizable (beyond a nondescript classification of "biface fragment"). Pointed knives and/or stemmed bifaces were present in six of the eight rural assemblages, forming 11–25%; such tools are useful for a wide range of purposes. Projectile points were present at all rural houses (3.6–39%), and they are also ubiquitous at urban Mayapán houselots (Masson and Peraza 2014a:372, Figure 6.25). Projectiles formed higher proportions of assemblages from Postclassic Puerta AA (39%) and Rancho Lote (29%) and Terminal Classic Tzabcán (25%), compared to other rural contexts. Notably, Puerto AA is located just outside of one of Mayapán's southeast entrance gates, and residents may have been charged with defending the city. However, points were used for hunting as well as warfare (Meissner 2014). Relatively low numbers were present at Jabáh (3.6%).

Informal flake tools (gravers, burins, notches, scrapers, other retouched flakes, and combinations of these) formed much of the stone tool assemblages at the rural houses, representing 50–61% at Postclassic Camino Xcanchakán, Puerta AA, Rancho Lote, and Jabáh and 50–75% at Terminal Classic Tzabcán, Mateyá, and Tzuc Pool. Such tools are valuable for routine tasks of household maintenance, as well as for low-intensity crafting activities. Within urban Mayapán, these flake tools also form nearly 50% of domestic toolkits for surplus crafters and other residents of the city (Masson and Peraza 2014a:372).

Pottery Vessels

The question of occupational longevity is a critical aspect of interpreting artifact densities and their implications for wealth. One relative measure for comparing contexts to one another is the quantity of pottery. For the rural sample, the minimum number of vessels (MNV) was calculated by an analysis of rim sherds of all types and forms represented at each house (Table 5.2). Predominantly Postclassic dwellings ranged from 0.9 (Camino Xcanchakán) to 5.9 (Jabáh) vessels per cubic meter, with Puerta AA and Rancho Lote exhibiting lower densities generally comparable to one another (1.6 and 1.3, respectively). For the Terminal Classic, the MNV/cu m is also relatively high at Jabáh (5.0), followed closely by Mateyá and Tzuc Pool (4.2, 4.0/cu m), with lower quantities at Tzabcán (2.4) and Pul Yax Ché (1.4). The high quantity of pottery vessels at Jabáh in both the Postclassic and Terminal Classic Periods suggests considerable time depth for the two periods, although only Postclassic architecture is preserved on the surface. This measure of occupational intensity, and perhaps indirectly of wealth, is broadly similar for Jabáh and two of the Terminal Classic houses. Fewer relative vessels were possessed by occupants of Postclassic Puerta AA and Rancho Lote and Terminal Classic Tzabcán and Tzuc Pool. For each period, one house stands out with exceptionally low densities: Camino Xcanchakán for the Postclassic and Pul Yax Ché for the Terminal Classic. These data suggest that the presence of multiple outbuildings and dwellings in the case of the Camino Xcanchakán houselot do not necessarily imply more intensive or longer occupation, given the low

Table 5.2. Minimum number of vessels (MNV) per cubic meter at rural house samples

	Jabáh	Xcanchakán	Puerta AA	Rancho Lote	Mateyá	Tzabcán	Tzuc Pool	Pul Yax Ché
Cu m	28.5	29.7	22.8	19.1	26.6	21.6	22.8	19.9
Postclassic MNV	167	28	36	24	12		7	
Postclassic MNV/cu m	5.9	0.9	1.6	1.3	0.5		0.3	
Terminal Classic MNV	142		1	1	112	52	92	27
Terminal Classic MNV/cu m	5.0		0.04	0.1	4.2	2.4	4.0	1.4

pottery density. Pul Yax Ché, although finely built, has no outbuildings; its limited architecture correlates with lower MNVs.

The proportions of different vessel forms upon which the MNV tallies are based are generally similar within each time period, with the principal difference represented by the use of large basins and two (rather than one) forms of serving dishes in the Terminal Classic. This source of variability is reflected statistically, using the Shannon Weaver indices. Diversity (richness values) reveals a range for predominantly Terminal Classic rural contexts of this period of 1.1–1.2, higher than for predominantly Postclassic rural dwellings (0.9–1.1). Evenness (equitability) for mostly Terminal Classic dwellings ranges from 0.8 to 0.9, with Postclassic values exhibiting a greater range, from 0.7 to 1.0. Only Puerto AA and Jabáh have a Postclassic evenness value of 0.7. Each of the four dwellings of each period had a fully functional and diverse vessel inventory, with dishes, bowls, and jars present; some had low numbers of specialized forms. Rancho Lote exhibits the greatest diversity of Postclassic pottery types (type:variety classification), as does Mateyá for the Terminal Classic. All rural contexts acquired a similar basic assemblage of slipped and unslipped vessels that formed the majority of the assemblages. The presence of fancier or imported pottery includes Matillas Fine Orange (at the Postclassic houses of Rancho Lote and Camino Xcanchakán) and incised, thin slate, and appliqué forms for Late/Terminal Classic Mateyá. Low numbers of Gulf Coast Matillas Fine Orange pottery are regularly recovered at urban Mayapán commoner dwellings (Masson and Freidel 2012).

Summary

Within each chronological period, differences are observed in the wealth and activity specialization of rural houselots. Jabáh in particular is distinguished by higher densities most similar to urban commoners who did not engage in surplus crafting. Its proximity to a significant minor center, probably located along a route linking Mayapán to other towns toward the east or northeast, seems to have provided enhanced opportunities for household production and exchange. Table 5.3 summarizes the relative criteria by which rural affluence may be assessed with this chapter's data. These criteria include equivalent or greater densities of (1) obsidian, (2) shell, and (3) chert compared to ordinary (nonsurplus crafter) commoners in the urban zone, (4) relative ranking among other rural contexts within the Postclassic or Terminal Classic periods in terms of density or diversity of materials, (5) the presence of high-value, nonlocal artifacts, and (6) evidence for low-level production of craft products using local materials attesting to diversification of household activities. Jabáh is distinguished from other rural contexts by all six measures. In contrast, other rural houses meet three of these criteria, which vary in each case. Among these three, Rancho Lote expresses the greatest affluence (after Jabáh), having more obsidian than two urban dwellings, and exhibits higher standing according to density and diversity indices. Mateyá is set apart among the Terminal Classic contexts according to artifact densities as well as pottery and obsidian source diversity. Terminal Classic Tzuc Pool is ranked after Mateyá by exhibiting greater artifact density and diversity than the remaining two contexts of this period. Of interest is the evidence for speleothem working in the form of debitage and finished products at many of the rural houselots of both periods (Table 5.3). Residents regularly undertook this small-scale industry using local resources. As Jabáh and Mateyá were located within 250–500 m of impressive minor centers, such localities may have benefited from more diverse and precocious activities hosted at those groups and perhaps from their location along routes more frequently traveled. However, Rancho Lote is located near a small monumental edifice, as is the Tzabcán houselot. Despite the relative distinction of these rural contexts relative to others beyond the city wall, their activity diversification and debris quantities are much lower than those of affluent crafters within the Postclassic city. For example, urban workshop obsidian densities are from 30 to 50 pieces/cu m for fully excavated dwellings, compared to 12.6 at Jabáh. But the mean for urban Postclassic obsidian densities (including workshops and nonworkshops) is 14.6/cu m, close to the value for Jabáh.

Table 5.3. Summary comparisons of rural houselots

	Within 500 m of minor center	≥ densities of obsidian to urban commoners	≥ densities of shell to urban commoners	≥ densities of chert flakes to urban commoners	Higher densities or diversity within time period	Presence of imported or fancy pottery or other nonlocal valuable	Other low-level crafting or local craft goods
		L-28, H-11, and X-43	H-11, L-28	X-43, H-11, L-28			
Postclassic Jabáh	X	> L-28, X-43 = H-11	> L-28, = H-11	>	Density: obsidian, shell, chert, pottery	Copper, *Oliva* shell	Ceramic effigy mold, speleothem products
Postclassic Rancho Lote		> L-28, X-43			Density: obsidian Diversity: obsidian, pottery	Fine Orange	
Postclassic Xcanchakán		= X-43		=		Fine Orange, ground-stone	Speleothem products
Postclassic Puerta AA		= X-43		=	Density: shell		Speleothem products
Term. Classic Mateyá	X	= X-43			Density: shell, chert, pottery Diversity: pottery, obsidian		Speleothem products
Term. Classic Tzuc Pool		= X-43			Density: shell, chert, pottery	*Spondylus* shell	Speleothem products
Term. Classic Tzabcán							Limestone abraders, speleothem products
Term. Classic Pul Yax Ché							

Note: Speleothem products include finished objects and debitage. "=" signifies equal or nearly so.

Comparisons to humble, nonsurplus crafting urban dwellings such as L-28 and X-43 in the urban zone reveal a significant degree of parity between rural contexts and those located near (but within) the city wall. In some cases, rural contexts fared better than these urban counterparts. Within the walled city, houses L-28 and X-43 were peripheral to denser, more interior urban neighborhoods and Mayapán's epicenter and were less affluent, like some of their rural counterparts. Residing outside of the wall was not a uniform predictor of poverty, occupational brevity, or a singular focus on agrarian production, given the variation observed among Postclassic commoners inside of and beyond the city wall. From a diachronic perspective, at least two rural Postclassic houselots were wealthier than all Terminal Classic examples in terms of densities of obsidian, marine shell, and chert flakes. This pattern reflects greater opportunities for commoner prosperity in the Postclassic in the sample, probably explained by the greater distance from large towns or cities during the Terminal Classic. But ceramic densities (MNV) provide contrastive results in that three Terminal Classic dwellings (all but Pul Yax Ché) exhibit greater quantities than three Postclassic rural houses (all but Jabáh). Perhaps regional pottery exchange and household activities calling for ceramic vessels were more important in the Terminal Classic. More research is clearly needed to clarify these results.

Postclassic Camino Xcanchakán and Terminal Classic Pul Yax Ché exhibit much lower pottery (MNV) densities in their respective periods, pointing to the likelihood of shorter occupations, despite the fact that two dwellings and a set of outbuildings imply the intention of longer-term residency at the Camino Xcanchakán houselot. Pul Yax Ché better fits expectations of brief occupations in that a single structure is found in the group, although it is by no means ephemeral. These data suggest that single measures of family growth, such as architecture or segmentation of social space, may not always reflect advantages linked to larger household labor pools and opportunities for stability and wealth (Kent 1990; King 2000; McAnany 1995). Families who built the Camino Xcanchakán and Pul Yax Ché houselots may have planned greater permanence than was ultimately possible.

The preliminary conclusions of these comparisons of rural wealth through time reveal variation within the commoner class indices of occupational longevity, wealth, and activity diversification during both the Postclassic and Terminal Classic Periods. For the Postclassic, some peripheral residents exhibit wealth greater than or equal to the wealth of residents of ordinary (nonsurplus crafting) houselots within urban Mayapán, but they do not approximate the density

Masson, Peraza Lope, Hare, Russell, Delgado Kú, Escamilla Ojeda, and Flores Cobá and diversity of materials found at urban crafter contexts. In general, the more extreme rural position of Terminal Classic houselots in the study area seems to correlate with lower artifact densities (except for pottery) that may reflect more limited means to acquire nonlocal raw materials or finished products or preferences for acquiring more ceramic vessels or other kinds of goods. Evidence also suggests that commoners of both periods were well integrated into regional exchange networks in northwest Yucatán, given the array of nonlocal cherts, marine shell, and pottery (regional, fancy, and/or imported) in their assemblages. All rural houselots also obtained obsidian from more distant sources, although in modest quantities that in some cases were equitable to those of ordinary urban Mayapán houses. The presence of Matillas Fine Orange pottery, exotic groundstone, or copper artifacts also attests to market exchange opportunities that provided Postclassic countryside residents with access to distant goods.

These results suggest that rural household economies were complex and variable phenomena in the study area, as for elsewhere in Maya lowlands (e.g., Iannone and Connell 2003; Lohse and Valdez 2004; Masson 2003; Scarborough et al. 2003; Yaeger and Robin 2004). It is clear that wealth disparities existed within the commoner social sector in urban as well as rural settings. These options for market exchange in the Terminal Classic countryside merit further investigation elsewhere in the peninsula. Although little direct evidence points to an agricultural occupation for residents of the dwellings in this study, their location, the presence of ancillary storage structures, generalized domestic assemblages, and modest levels of crafting debris suggests that these were the homes of farmers (with the possible exception of Jabáh). The producer and consumer assemblages described in this chapter challenge assumptions once held about the peasantry in premodern societies of the Maya area and beyond (for discussion, see Blanton and Fargher 2008:287; Feinman 2013:455; Hirth 2009a:17; Masson and Peraza 2004; Pyburn 2008:253; Sanders and Webster 1988:524–525). These houselots were not autonomous or homogenous; nor were they impoverished; nor were their occupations fleeting, as a rule. Of importance to future research are the demographic implications of populous rural settlement in the region and their agrarian contributions to political economies.

6

Stone for My House

The Economics of Stoneworking and Elite Housing
in the Puuc Hills of Yucatán

WILLIAM RINGLE, TOMÁS GALLARETA NEGRÓN,
AND GEORGE BEY

Ancient Egypt was doubly fortunate, and doubtless owed to this its fabled wealth, in that it possessed two activities, namely, pyramid-building as well as the search for the precious metals, the fruits of which, since they could not serve the needs of man by being consumed, did not stale with abundance. The Middle Ages built cathedrals and sang dirges. Two pyramids, two masses for the dead, are twice as good as one; but not so two railways from London to York.

(Keynes 1936:131, cited in Warburton 2000:174–175)

It also should not be forgotten that in a society whose principal production is food, there is a quantitative and temporal limit to accumulation. The accumulation of food is not in and of itself an incentive. As Max Gluckman (1960) has noted with regard to the Zulu, a leader is not able to eat much more than the common man.

(Valeri 2014:8)

Any attempt to address the economic system of the Puuc region of Yucatán must accommodate two notable features of the archaeological record. First, although recent work has demonstrated a lengthy Formative occupation of the region, it seems clear that there was a marked increase in population during the Late Classic Period, or from about AD 600 onward, with a florescence some 200–300 years later. Late to Terminal Classic occupation is especially significant within the Bolonchén Hill district, where site density was among the highest, if not the highest, in Prehispanic northern Yucatán. Yet, despite the high density of sites in the region, an 11 km² transect in our study zone, surveyed by Gallareta Negrón and colleagues, revealed a generally modest level of intersite occupation, although this needs further corroboration (Figure 6.1).[1] Most of

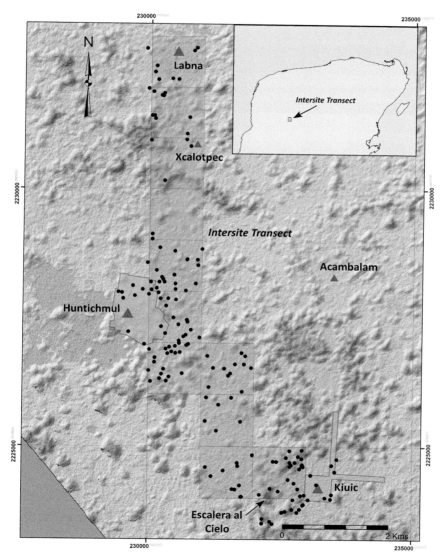

Figure 6.1. The distribution of annular structures in the 11 km² intersite survey (data courtesy of Tomás Gallareta Negrón). Black dots mark the location of annular structures.

the population in this zone was instead concentrated in the centers of Labná, Huntichmul, and Kiuic, plus a few small centers between them. (Intersite settlement densities are as yet unavailable from our survey in the adjacent Valle de Yaxhom, which has so far concentrated on the larger communities.) This same transect demonstrated that there were few if any physical modifications to the landscape to improve agricultural production. Instead the effort was apparently managerial, perhaps by improving labor efficiency, by reserving the best bottomland for cultivation, or both.

The other factor to be explained is the very high incidence of masonry housing in the Puuc, that is, houses with rubble and concrete walls faced with cut veneer stones, either with or without vaulted roofs. This pattern holds true for all of the sites in our survey sample as well as at other Puuc sites that have been adequately mapped. As Table 6.1 demonstrates, this contrasts markedly with the relative scarcity of masonry and vaulted residences at Ek' Balam and Dzibilchaltún on the northern plains. In this chapter we discuss what must have been a substantial component of the Puuc economy, especially if the construction of palaces and civic-ceremonial structures is included. Yet it is a sector that has received little comment in the literature on the Maya economy, although of course palaces once built and households once formed are key elements of recent discussions. The major exceptions are the studies of Elliot Abrams (e.g., 1994, 1995) on the energetics of construction at Copán and those of Kelli Carmean and colleagues with respect to Sayil (Carmean 1991; Carmean et al. 2011). In this chapter we consider evidence for stone quarrying and *cal* (lime) production, followed by a discussion of masonry residences. We conclude with a general model addressing the implications of these activities for the Puuc Terminal Classic economy. We argue that the construction of masonry houses was in fact a force driving economic, political, and demographic expansion but that the failure of this industry at the close of the Classic Period may have been a strong contributing factor to the decline of these centers.

The *Chaîne Opératoire* of House Construction

Evidence for the mining and preparation of construction materials suggests that stoneworking was a major economic activity in the Bolonchén District, possibly involving export to less favored nearby regions but certainly fueling the construction of local residences. The evidence consists of quarry marks, ovens very probably dedicated to the production of *cal* for mortar and plaster, households and possibly workshops dedicated to the production of cut stone, residences probably housing more specialized craftspeople, and evidence of the construction process from buildings both finished and unfinished.

The thin soil cover of the karst *altillos* (bedrock hummocks) and *cerros* (hills) of the Bolonchén District results in the frequent exposure of limestone outcrops, which are subject to intense weathering by heat and moisture. Thus, construction rubble and platform fill could often have been found lying on the surface, reduced to carrying size by a few quick blows. Quarrying took the form of prizing blocks from the edges of exposed outcrops, usually on hill slopes, making it less identifiable than extracting blocks from beds. The usual signature is a relatively straight or lunate ledge unlikely to be the result of weathering. Small pit quarries are also common. Most often these were used for the extraction of *sascab* (limestone marl), but the overlying caprock may also have been used for construction purposes.[2] It is also likely that platform construction provided much of its own construction fill, as their cores were frequently limestone *altillos*. Kiuic Str. P-N1340E1185, near the northern limits of settlement, indicates that an initial step was to quarry along the edges and top of a small *altillo*. The stone quarried could then be used for retaining walls, for fill to level off the surface of the *altillo*, or for other construction projects. The fact that in this case only a single short stretch of retaining wall had been built along one edge of this *altillo* suggests construction had been interrupted.

Cal was necessary for the production of mortar and plaster and appears to have been prepared in annular structures, open rings of rubble and gravel surrounding a central combustion chamber (Figure 6.2). First identified at Sayil (Sabloff and Tourtellot 1991), where twenty-four were noted in the 3.5 km² survey area, annular structures are present throughout our intersite transect and within our urban survey limits, especially toward their peripheries, as was the case at Sayil. Visual inspection of about 41 km² of LiDAR data collected by the National Aeronautics and Space Administration (NASA) in 2013 yielded 157 examples, but intensive pedestrian survey of our 11 km² intersite survey identified over 140 (Gallareta et al. 2014), often at the base of hills (Figure 6.1). Another 10 were identified in the Kiuic urban survey and 12 at Huntichmul. Only one has been found in the Yaxhom area, but importantly, it was along the edge of a Formative acropolis, suggesting the antiquity of the process.[3] Although several functions have been suggested for this type of structure, excavation evidence indicates that they functioned as closed kilns for burning limestone for *cal* production (Ortiz Ruiz 2014; Seligson 2016a, 2016b; Seligson et al. 2017).

Figure 6.2. (*A*) An annular structure cleared prior to excavation (courtesy of Ken Seligson); (*B*) annular structures visible in LiDAR imagery of the secondary site of Acambalám (data courtesy of NASA).

Annular structures are found alone, associated with quarries, or in groups associated with domestic units of varying status. Their proximity to masonry structures and to perishable house foundations suggests that some *cal* may have been produced for the nixtamalization of corn.[4] Clustering of annular structures in close proximity to quarries indicates that some production may have been on a

William Ringle, Tomás Gallareta Negrón, and George Bey

larger scale, perhaps directly monitored by elites. *Chi'ich* piles (low mounds of limestone gravel and small rock) are also often found at the foot of hills marked by quarrying and may be the result of the reduction of larger rocks prior to transport.

An experimental open kiln at Labná (May Ciau and Gallareta 2003; cf. Russell and Dahlin 2007) revealed that not all limestone could be used for producing *cal*. Indeed, local terminology recognizes several types of limestone and limestone by-products, each extracted from different types of quarries: open ones for obtaining stone boulders for fill and cores, others for *sascab* (marl), and probably others for limestone with clear cleavage planes for veneer and specialized carved stones. Others were for the extraction of *cal* for mortar and plaster.[5] The diversity of quarrying techniques and terminology strongly suggests the involvement of specialists, although, because the demand for *cal* for nixtamalization was widespread, more individuals may have been involved in its production. The preparation of mortars, plasters, and cut stones required more skill, however, as was the case until recently.

Stoneworking

At Huntichmul a series of households has been tentatively identified as part of the stoneworking industry. Located on the summits or slopes of the hills surrounding the epicenter, they consist of typical domestic basal platforms, usually supporting perishable structures but occasionally also modest masonry buildings. Above, below, or to their sides are relatively vacant platforms (or, better, *nivelaciones*), which we believe were the loci for stoneworking. Particularly interesting are a set of platforms along the flanks of the Mul Imis hill, at the top of which is what we argue was one of the palace groups of the site. Each of the small households along the sides of this hill had a modest *nivelación* a few meters away. Faced on three sides with roughly cut blocks, their surfaces were featureless except for a rough floor of fist-sized rocks that appear to be debitage from stoneworking. Further evidence of stoneworking includes nearby quarry scars and *chi'ich* mounds. The fact that this was true for all these platforms argues against their being unfinished platforms, although eventually the rock may have been incorporated as subfloor fill as the *nivelaciones* were repurposed for other activities. The alignment of these households below the palace complex makes it likely that they were direct clients of the palace dwellers, but, as we argue later, their labor may have been redirected elsewhere for other construction projects, as may stoneworking households elsewhere at the site.

A possible mason's residence has been excavated in the Escalera al Cielo hilltop group, about 1.5 km from the center of Kiuic (Simms et al. 2012). The evidence consists of several *hachas* (axes) and other lithic tools found in a midden deposit mixed with *chi'ich* alongside S2950E3270, a two-room perishable foundation atop platform P-S2960E3275. Not far away was a substantial *sascabera*, which may have been used for quarrying *sascab* (lime marl). Although the house was not particularly large, the foundation brace of the building partially consisted of cut stones, as might befit a mason (true also of the neighboring frame brace S2955E3280). Another small platform group, as yet unexcavated, lies just to its south and may be another craftsman's residence, given its association with quarries and a *sascabera*. Both lie at the summit of the hill, between two much larger groups of vaulted architecture at either end of the ridge, one probably an administrative/religious structure and the other primarily residential. These two perishable houses thus occupied a prime location but were not incorporated into either plaza group. They also displayed a certain prosperity, though the rooms themselves were not particularly large in comparison to similar houses of perishable materials.

With regard to cut stone, Morris (1931:218) states that at Chichén Itzá: "Obviously, all sculptured columns, pilasters, and door jambs now in original position were carved *in situ*," yet we found that a low platform a few hundred meters southeast of Yaxhom had several capitals and unfinished jambs lying on its surface. Instituto Nacional de Antropología e Historia (INAH) guard Pedro Góngora informed Ringle that this also was where a pair of carved jambs decorated with pseudo-glyphs was also found (now on the grounds of Loltún cave). Thus, at least some carved stonework was transported in final form from the workshop to its final destination. (As note 3 indicates, we found an unfinished stela some distance from the Ek' Balam site center in a pit quarry.)

Morris (1931: 219) did argue that at Chichén Itzá decorative mosaic stonework was not necessarily produced at the building site. At Kiuic survey identified a possible locus of stoneworking associated with Kiuic Str. N1280E1660 and possibly N1270E1700, two featureless platforms, which proved to be the last evidence of settlement along a *brecha* that we extended to the east of the central quadrant. The platform itself was defined along its northern side by impressive bedrock outcrops probably shaped by quarrying and by retaining walls on the others but lacked building foundations on its surface. To the north of the platform was a line of beveled vault and cornice stones. Given the absence of superstructures on the platform and its unprepared surface, this was apparently another platform involved in stoneworking, as supported by several surrounding *chi'ich* piles. A few meters to the east was N1270E1700, a similarly sized platform also with associated *chi'ich* piles. Both platforms may have been placed to take advantage of stone from the low hills a short distance to the west. To the east the landscape flattens out, and thus stone outcrops would have been more difficult to mine. These platforms are thus similar to those from Huntichmul, except that these examples are not closely associated with any vaulted housing.

These platforms could have been construction sites in progress when work prematurely ceased but more probably reflect the standardized production of veneer stones for use elsewhere. Both Morris (1931) and Prem (2003b) note that only a narrow repertoire of forms were used in assembling a façade. This is supported by evidence from the Grupos Chulul and Kuché at Kiuic, where three "pavements" of cut stones lie in front of vaulted structures, consisting of corner, molding, and veneer stones carefully arranged in their proper positions on the ground. In the case of the Grupo Chulul, it seems likely that the two "pavements" were intended for a second story of rooms, the foundations of which survive, but the destination of the Grupo Kuché "pavement" is unclear, as it was laid out in front of Str. N1025E0830, a free-standing range structure. We initially

Figure 6.3. The stone "pavements" in front of Kiuic Str. N1000E0865, consisting of carefully arranged veneer, cornice, and corner stones.

thought these had been arranged by INAH archaeologists for repair of these buildings, but inspection of the earliest photos by Teobert Maler demonstrate that they were present in the 1880s. Whatever the case, the construction process seems to have involved carefully laying out façade veneers prior to incorporating them into the concrete and rubble hearting (Figure 6.3).

Housing

One reason why housing is not often mentioned in considerations of the ancient Maya economy may be an underlying assumption that houses were the product of household labor (that is, those who built them lived in them) or that builders were the immediate clients of those living in masonry structures (Carmean 1991; Carmean et al. 2011). The supposition that houses were inalienable property may also have contributed to the view that they were outside the general circulation of goods and services. Burials in household patios and beneath floors support this notion, as do the importance of the house in iconography (a good case could be made that Puuc communities were "house societies" in Claude Lévi-Strauss's sense), and, for a very few, dedicatory inscriptions naming their owners.

Although houses may have been inalienable and foundational for families, that does not militate against their origin as gifts. In the Puuc region the construction of masonry structures with either perishable or vaulted roofs clearly involved substantial investments in labor and materials. Surveys of Kiuic, Huntichmul, and Yaxhom by Ringle and of Labná by Gallareta Negrón, together with results from Sayil and Xkipché, indicate that between 28 and 40% of the structures were vaulted or had masonry walls, a far higher percentage than at Dzibilchaltún or in the Ek' Balam region, where the values ranged from less than 3% to 11.2%. If room counts are tallied, the disparity is even greater (Tables 6.1 and 6.2). Whether these were the perquisites of the nobility alone is debatable (and if so would suggest a far larger elite stratum than in most archaic states), but they do suggest a high level of prosperity and minimally a significant investment in their construction. Vaulted buildings occur throughout these communities, rather than being clustered in the center, and indeed extend to the fringes of the site and beyond. The Escalera al Cielo, located about 1.5 km from central Kiuic, has already been mentioned, but several other isolated platforms supporting vaulted architecture are known in the hills of the hinterlands.

Here we explore a model arguing that housing, instead of belonging to a closed

Table 6.1. Structure type statistics from four Puuc sites and three sites from the northern plains

Site	Rank	Perishable		Vaulted		Masonry walls		Total
Kiuic	3	101	57.39%	71	40.34%	4	2.27%	176
Huntichmul	3	343	71.91%	112	23.48%	22	4.61%	477
Xkipché	3	136	60.18%	77	34.07%	13	5.75%	226
Sayil	2	384	64.54%	190	31.93%	21	3.53%	595
Ichmul de Morley	3	—	88.60%	—	11.40%	—	—	—
Ek' Balam	1	630	96.33%	24	3.67%	—	—	654
Dzibilchaltún	1	1900	88.79%	240	11.22%	—	—	2140

Data from Kiuic and Huntichmul from the Bolonchén Regional Archaeological Project (BRAP) survey by Ringle. Ek' Balam and Ichmul de Morley from the Ek' Balam project directed by Ringle and Bey. Xkipché data from Prem (2003b). Data on Sayil from Sabloff and Tourtellot (1991). An estimated 55% of the site was surveyed. Data on Dzibilchaltún from Kurjack 1974 (Chapter 3, Tables 3 and 6). Of the 240 vaulted structures, 73 are Pure Florescent. In contrast the vast majority of Puuc buildings are from the same period, increasing the discrepancy. The large number (5,964) of platforms lacking building foundations are not included. Some certainly supported perishable housing, but this would only further depress the relative frequency of vaulted structures. Kurjack included structures with masonry walls and perishable roofs in the nonvaulted category, so they cannot be separated out.

Table 6.2. Statistics on room types from four Puuc sites and Dzibilchaltún

Site	Perishable		Vaulted		Masonry walls		Total
Kiuic	179	45.66%	195	49.74%	18	4.59%	392
Huntichmul	589	68.41%	232	26.95%	40	4.65%	861
Xkipché	256	50.69%	227	44.95%	22	4.36%	505
Sayil	520	48.73%	515	48.27%	32	3.00%	1067
Dzibilchaltún	2300[a]	80.99%	540+	19.01%	—	—	2840

[a] Kurjack (1974) does not break down his multiroom unvaulted structure class by the number of rooms. We estimate the total by assuming an average of three rooms per structure.

economic sphere, was instead part of the tribute economy or, more specifically, an exchange good in the political network of debts and obligations. Given the scarcity of dedicatory texts, the evidence is indirect but compelling. First, Puuc masonry buildings show exceptional craftsmanship and specialized engineering knowledge, especially as the Classic Period advanced. Although we agree with Abrams (1994) that much of the basic labor was unspecialized and could be supplied by individual households, stonemasons responsible for cutting veneer stones, sculptors, artists, and to a lesser extent plasterers had expertise requiring long experience. Since houses were relatively permanent goods, requiring only periodic maintenance, the demand for such skills within a given household would have been limited and sporadic, so it seems unlikely that craftspeople were confined solely to the household or segment in which they were resident. Stonemasons may alternately have formed a relatively free pool of expertise available for hire, but this seems unlikely for most models of the ancient economy.[6]

Instead, it seems more probable that at least the more highly skilled stoneworkers were under the patronage of the central leadership. They may have formed part of the houses or households of nonroyal elites, but their labor may have been requisitioned and redirected by the palace in fulfillment of tribute demands. The advantage of this hypothesis is that it explains how highly skilled craftspeople were kept employed despite relatively sporadic demand, as a relatively small number could have satisfied the needs of communities the size of Labná, Kiuic, or Huntichmul. They may also have formed part of intersite obligations, which would have had the benefit of fostering the exchange of experience and expertise across the region.

Seeing houses less as expressions of individual social pretensions and instead as tokens within a sumptuary system may also explain certain aspects of construction. Sumptuary restrictions may be reflected in the highly formulaic decoration of Puuc façades, which most often consists of little more than simple moldings or at most a frieze or panels of colonnettes. Only very rarely are masks or extensive stone mosaic panels employed. Similarly, only a small minority of masonry buildings have more than three rooms, which would not be expected if houses reflected individual aspirations but is explicable if they were limited by sumptuary rules. Puuc houses were also often built in stages. It is not uncommon to see a single vaulted room with the lateral sides left unfinished for the addition of future rooms (Figure 6.4). The addition of rooms in stages may represent the owner's gradual accumulation of the wherewithal for construction, but it may also reflect a series of favors granted by the palace. Rewards bestowed incrementally over an extended period would thus more lastingly bind the resident to his overlord. Finally, it may also explain the practice of preserving Early Puuc houses, something we have observed repeatedly in our study area.[7] The motivation was probably to commemorate a founding house but perhaps also to reify the original largesse of the overlord.[8]

William Ringle, Tomás Gallareta Negrón, and George Bey

Figure 6.4. An example of buildings intentionally left unfinished. (*Left*) Kiuic Str. N0890E0765 as photographed by Teobert Maler, still standing in 1888–1889 (Maler 1997:Plate 101); (*right*) the right end of the front facade as it exists today. Note that the adjacent side was left without veneer stones for a later addition.

A parallel case of patronage might be the movement of artisans in what was possibly a sister craft, the sculpting of stone monuments, as detailed in several recent studies of scribal signatures (Houston 2016, 2017; S. Martin et al. 2015; M. Miller and Brittenham 2013:162–165). Houston (2016:405–410), who has considered the problem in greatest depth, notes a variety of permutations of the relationship between patron and sculptor, with royal patronage of sculptors internal to a polity being "almost the default category, the basic presumption in the absence of other evidence." Examples of the movement downward and outward of sculptors include the sculptors of Bonampak St. 1 and Lintel 2, who are recorded as the "*anahb* of the Yaxchilán lord," the lords of Yaxchilán and Piedras Negras being particularly prominent as patrons of sculptors lent out to subordinates (M. Miller and Brittenham 2013:162). In the opposite direction, Martin et al. (2015) note that lords from Chatahn and Uxul, two centers subservient to Calakmul, claimed the carving of Calakmul Stelae 51 and 89. Rather than being the actual work of these lords, the strong suggestion is that these were gifts or tribute, as the initial glyph of St. 51 may indicate. The subordinate lords were thus able to either commission their own sculptors to work at Calakmul or commission sculptors residing there and probably beholden to its king. Similarly, Houston (2017) implies that one of the steps from Yaxchilán Hieroglyphic Stairway 3, carved of different stone and bearing the signature of a *sahal*, may actually be the product of a provincial sculptor commissioned by this individual, given the lesser quality of its organization and execution. This sort of patronage from below may be paralleled by contributions of labor and materials to royal palace construction by client elites.

Housing, Palaces, and the Growth of the Puuc Economy

Slow growth and limited demand are characteristic of peasant or feudal societies in which members are largely self-sufficient and markets are undeveloped, especially those without a monetary basis. Although some form of market exchange likely existed in the Puuc, the limited range of nonperishable goods in household inventories of both perishable and masonry structures suggests that external trade may have been less critical than elsewhere in Mesoamerica. Nonlocal pottery, shell items, and obsidian are relatively rare even in elite contexts. If there was significant external trade it must have been for goods as such as cotton, salt, or other perishable commodities. Formal local market exchange would have served to satisfy minor and small-scale needs within the community, while most families probably had access to enough land to support themselves, as our generally modest hinterland population levels indicate, and construction materials were everywhere abundant.

Thus, the stimulants to growth must be sought elsewhere. It seems clear that the palace was a central factor in consumption, leading some to view elites as "parasitic": that is, elites were simply consuming a portion of total wealth or production through tribute exaction. Such an explanation appears insufficient for explaining the situation in the Puuc, where the incidence of palaces and vaulted residences indicates a broad-based prosperity. In the Puuc one likely role for elites was oversight over agricultural production by a group of client families over a particular patch of bottomland "flats" (*planadas*). Such groups were often co-resident on nearby hills, or *cerros residenciales* as Gallareta Negrón has termed them, forming distinct production units.

An increase in tribute demands on these units would have contributed to the prosperity of the palace but is less satisfactory for explaining the broader base of wealth. However, as Warburton (1998, 2000) reminds us, "there is a difference between creating wealth through taxation and acquiring wealth that already exists, although this can also be done through taxation. In ancient Egypt, it would appear that the government created wealth through taxation" (Warburton 2000:172). In other words, taxation, read here as tribute, can be a direct stimulus to growth. This happens, paradoxically, when tribute levels increase, thus raising levels of demand and hence production and employment. Key to differentiating the two forms of taxation is that in the latter case some fraction of tribute revenues are reinvested in ways beneficial to the overall economy, if not to all actors. In a premonetary economy, investment may have assumed the form of support for nonagricultural specialists, patronage of construction or may have involved intangible factors, such as investments in reinforcing patron-client political ties.

It is here that the epigraph to this chapter is relevant, as Keynes's comments, and those of Warburton after him, argue that investment in "useless" inalienable projects, in a strictly economic sense, assumes great significance in precisely this fashion. Being inalienable and thus outside the spheres of supply and demand, the construction of pyramids and cathedrals was capable of being infinitely expanded without danger of sating demand. Thus, investment in such projects provided a direct stimulus to growth without endangering other economic activities (except perhaps to stimulate them as well). This is in some ways akin to deficit spending. These being premonetary economies, patrons do not incur debt, as projects must be financed as they proceed, but like deficit-spending projects, they do stimulate general growth by central expenditures.

If we are correct in arguing that masonry housing was an aspect of royal patronage, these residences would have many points in common with "useless" projects such as temples or palaces. Like them, masonry residences would have been inalienable and relatively permanent; because masonry houses were outside of the realm of exchange, their value never declined with the construction of additional houses. And like the construction of pyramids and cathedrals, the construction of masonry houses would have provided employment for a corps of skilled stoneworkers, architects, masons, and sculptors as well as more localized unskilled labor. Since foodstuffs probably composed a substantial fraction of tribute payments, construction projects and sponsorship of skilled artisans provided one way to convert excess food into useful political capital. Construction meant removal of some fraction of the workforce, however, so additional agricultural workers would have had to have been recruited to meet the increase in demand. Masonry residences would thus directly objectify the web of patronage extended by the palace, a web limited only by the number of client families who could be so honored. That threshold may have been reached at or around the period during which the Puuc went into decline, as discussed below.

The only rival to the building of masonry housing was the construction of palaces, whose sizes expanded enormously during the final period of occupation.[9] Sayil's palace is a famous example, but this trend can be observed at nearly all sites. At Kiuic, the Early Puuc Yaxche Group, excavated by Bey, May Ciau, Gallareta Cervera, and colleagues, was a relatively modest compound of three adjoining quadrangles with a complicated construction history extending back to the Middle Formative. But at the end of the Early Puuc, it was supplanted by a much more ambitious palace complex, perhaps two, to the southwest and with ample plazas for public assembly. At least four architectural styles are evident in the structures, indicating a prolonged series of expansions. An even larger palace arose at Labná, again supplanting an earlier plaza group not unlike Kiuic's Yaxche Group and again with multiple architectural styles in evidence. Multiroom palaces have also been recently reported by Merk and Benavides at the nearby site of Sabana Piletas (Benavides et al. 2009; Merk 2016). For reasons that are unclear, sprawling palaces were never built at Huntichmul, the largest site in our study area, though it had several groups that stood out significantly in terms of size and room count.

The investment in ever-larger palaces was probably also an expression of the dynamic outlined above. The modest domestic accommodations of most palaces (few cisterns for water, few retainer houses, limited food preparation facilities) suggest that palaces had only a relatively small number of full-time residents. The other rooms may have been dedicated to storage (since no other permanent storage facilities have been identified) but, more importantly, probably housed a burgeoning stratum of nonroyal courtiers on occasions of state, precisely the individuals who had been granted license to live in masonry buildings (or at least some subset of them). Other lines of evidence, such as masonry quadrangles and sculptures, also suggest that councils were increasingly able to share in representations of rule during the Terminal Classic Period (Bey and May 2014; Ringle 2012, 2014). Palaces too were "useless" in the above sense, and their expansion would have only increased demand on the tribute system generally. Most palaces investigated in any detail show that additions, repairs, and refurbishments were never ending, always capable of accommodating labor obligations. And to the extent that they were storehouses (currently unknown), they would have further stimulated production by removing foodstuffs from circulation.

William Ringle, Tomás Gallareta Negrón, and George Bey

The Collapse of Puuc Communities

In the Puuc Hills the stimulus of masonry construction seems to have flagged at the conclusion of the Terminal Classic. Most archaeologists working in the Puuc have noticed that buildings are frequently unfinished. In some cases, as noted above, this may be interpreted as the withholding of further "building permits" from the overlord for political reasons. Such structures are characterized as having fully completed rooms with preparations for additional rooms never added, and some reflect early architectural styles. Other unfinished structures seem to have been stopped during the process of construction. These often reflect the latest stage of stoneworking techniques, suggesting that they are reflections of the general social decline commencing somewhere between AD 850 and 900. The work of Bey and colleagues on the Escalera al Cielo outside Kiuic demonstrates that abandonment of this *cerro residencial* was indeed rapid, resulting in deposits of complete pots, tools, and other items rarely present on house floors (Simms et al. 2012).

Warburton (2000) argues that it was not the construction of the Egyptian pyramids that exhausted the Old Kingdom, but rather that the decline of this central stimulus to the economy led to a more general decline in demand. In the Puuc the decline of a central stimulus may have been due to external factors (agricultural failures due to climatic crises, political instability, and so forth), resulting in a similar inability of the palace to finance further construction. Alternatively, if housing was in fact a primary token of royal largesse, the occasions for rewarding clients may have reached a point of saturation, as the high incidence of masonry structures would argue. The gradual extension of such favors down the social hierarchy may also have led to an unwieldy political system challenging the authority of the central leadership. In such a scenario, demand in effect became elastic as masonry houses lost value as prestige markers. For whatever the reasons, the cessation of royal patronage of construction in this model would have led to a marked slow-down of the economy, contributing to a greater or lesser extent to the final collapse of these communities. The net result would have been the loss of tribute income, a central mode of patronage, and ultimately political allegiance.

Conclusion

Although it would be anachronistic to argue that Maya leaders were self-conscious economic actors, it is not unlikely that they acted within a framework of political economy. That is, Maya leaders reacted to a system of supply and demand and judged according to a scale of values that included both material and nonmaterial considerations, one aspect of which consisted in the favorable balance of political favors. Amassing wealth may have been of far less interest than securing allegiances, or, rather, wealth was primarily important to the degree to which it could advance a given actor's political ambitions. Thus, "investment" should be understood not in a strictly economic sense, with an expectation of increased wealth, but as an action whose benefit for the community happened to coincide with the strategies of rulership. If we are correct in arguing that masonry construction was part of the palace patronage system, it may have provided a relatively long-term stimulus to growth as well as a mechanism for facilitating the exchange of commodities and labor in the absence of more symbolic forms of value. Rather than driving the Puuc economy into bankruptcy, or being an essentially household activity, construction may have been at the very heart of its success and its cessation at the core of its decline.

From a broader perspective, Weiner (1985, 1992) has forcefully argued that inalienable possessions (such as houses) stand at the center of the struggle to subvert loss and change, to disguise the impermanence of social life in the struggle to reproduce it. Inalienable possessions frame the past, creating the memories necessary for social reproduction; but, paradoxically, the "effort to make memory persist, as irrational as the combat against loss can be, is fundamental to change" (Weiner 1992:8). Although ostensibly outside the realm of exchange, inalienable objects such as houses also confer difference and authority upon their possessors. "An individual becomes more than she or he is because the self is enlarged and enhanced by the power of the past" (Weiner 1985:212). Houses are therefore not simply dwellings or status symbols but the very vehicles whereby social identities are reconstituted through time (Weiner 1992:11). We can thus see the premium placed upon the durability of Puuc dwellings, attested by the survival of many of them after the lapse of a thousand years, as grounded in this effort to reify and congeal the flux of political and social relations. Such efforts included the careful preservation of Early Puuc dwellings in the face of newer and more ostentatious styles as the incontrovertible familial stake within the unfolding history of a kingdom. But Keynes may have been incorrect in that ultimately it was possible to build too many monuments and undermine the very relations they were meant to materialize.

Acknowledgments

The doctoral work of project member Dr. Ken Seligson has contributed significantly to our understanding of stone processing. We also wish to thank the National Science Foundation for supporting LiDAR coverage of our region and subsequent fieldwork to verify the imagery. We also thank the editors for the invitation to participate in this volume and for the opportunity to contribute to its publication.

Notes

1. Statements about settlement reflect fieldwork conducted as of 2016, the date when this essay was originally submitted for consideration. Since then a grant from the National Science Foundation funded purchase of LiDAR coverage over a much larger region (237.1 km^2). Analysis of these data is only just beginning but to date supports the statements made herein.

2. At Ek' Balam, on the northern plains, Bey and Ringle found an unfinished stela in a pit quarry.

3. Over 1,100 have now been identified in our LiDAR sample. They are plentiful throughout, though especially so in the region covered by Gallareta's transect.

4. Nixtamalization is the preparation of maize kernels by steeping them in an alkali solution (here slaked lime). This softens the kernels prior to cooking, after which the *nixtamal* is ground into a dough for tamales and other dishes.

5. See Seligson et al. (2017) for a detailed discussion of local limestone classes, incorporating earlier unpublished ethnographic work by Dean Arnold in the 1970s. Seligson also conducted experimental lime burning in a refurbished *altillo*, rather than the open pyres of the other experiments.

6. Carmean (1991:157) accepted a general correlation between residential architecture and social status at Sayil, although noting that it was not "necessarily a straightforward expression." One of the difficulties confronting Carmean (1991:160) was the disparity between her estimates of labor construction costs for several of the platforms, which were high relative to estimates of the number of residents on or near those platforms. Her solution was to posit a large subaltern population residing around Sayil's peripheries on *chi'ich* (gravel) mounds, though she acknowledged that this pushed the population well beyond the proposed carrying capacity. In our experience, *chi'ich* mounds generally lack the two distinguishing traits of domestic occupation: metates and *chultuns*. Another problem is that Carmean considers the elites directing household construction to be free agents, limited only by their personal wealth. It seems likely instead that the paramount family or families would have regarded elaborate houses as material challenges to their authority and so would have limited the elaboration of houses.

7. Carmean (1991) also points to the importance of founding families, though not in regard to early architecture. This "preservationist" attitude toward earlier buildings is reflected in standing buildings that must have been maintained for considerable periods.

In some cases, early masonry residences were encased within later buildings, as is the case at the Yaxche pyramid, the Grupo Góngora at Huntichmul, the Mirador pyramid at Labná, at Kom, and beneath the Adivino and South pyramids at Uxmal.

8. Analysis of hieroglyphic texts associated with structures has yet to be done, but it is interesting that those from the Puuc site of Xcalumkin record that the owner was a *sahal* (second-tier official). It seems unlikely that such a person would have access to skilled scribes and sculptors without the blessings of his (unnamed) overlord.

9. Stepped pyramids are present but often tend to be early and/or are monuments built over earlier houses.

7

Chert Resource Availability, Production, and Economic Logic

Case Studies from the Northwestern Petén, Guatemala, and Western Belize

RACHEL A. HOROWITZ, MARCELLO CANUTO, AND CHLOÉ ANDRIEU

The lowland Classic Maya economy (AD 200–890) was a complex web of prestige exchange, centralized distribution, and local market economies (Dahlin 2009; Demarest 2013; King 2015; Masson and Freidel 2002; McAnany 2010, 2013; Sheets et al. 2015; Wells and McAnany 2008). It is therefore important not to consider the lowland Classic Maya economic system monolithic; rather, it is critical to understand not only how the perceived value of items articulated with their production and distribution but also how that perceived value might have varied throughout the lowland Maya region (see Masson and Freidel 2012). In this light, the idea that separate economic systems existed for different types of goods—such as prestige, utilitarian, and bulk—becomes more important, especially considering that no one type of material necessarily, inalienably, belonged to any one particular system by dint of its intrinsic (lack of) value. In other words, value assigned to a material was contextual and based as much on its culturally assigned relevance as on pragmatic factors such as its accessibility, portability, and appreciated uses. Therefore, as we consider the roles in these specific economic systems, we should avoid assuming that these different economic logics automatically explain the distribution of specific types of materials in all contexts.

In this chapter we address the distribution of chert raw material sources and the economic logic in its extraction, production, and distribution between two areas of the Maya lowlands to consider how different facets of economic organization logics are represented by artifacts of the same material class. Because the Maya area has an uneven distribution of many resources, such as chert (Potter and King 1995), different economic logics were deployed for certain raw materials in regions where the materials are more or less common. While chert is one of the most commonly utilized lithic raw materials in the Maya region, it is generally less studied than its flashier and more easily sourced cousin, obsidian. Obsidian and chert, due to their different qualities and distributions, present an opportunity to study different economic logics among the Maya.

As a nonlocal material in the Maya lowlands, obsidian is found only in highland areas (see G. Braswell 1996; Healan 2002; Pastrana 1998; Suyuc Ley 2011). Thus, long-distance trade of obsidian must have occurred for residents to obtain these goods no matter where in the lowlands they resided. As a result, scholarship has largely assumed that political leaders were in some way involved in the acquisition and distribution of obsidian resources (see Aoyama 1996; Clark 1997; Spence 1981). Alternatively, chert presents a more complicated picture. Although in many areas chert is a local resource, it is not ubiquitous or of equal quality. Therefore, chert implements tend to be interpreted as locally made items and therefore not part of the complex economic and trade dynamics involved with obsidian procurement (but see McAnany 1989). However, this assumption proves inadequate when considering the differential distribution of chert resources throughout the Maya lowlands, especially when comparing chert extraction, production, and distribution patterns between the northwestern Petén and western Belize (Figure 7.1).

To date, studies of chert consumption in the Maya area have tended to focus on materials from Belize due to the large concentrations and high quality of chert available in the region. By adding to this dataset with comparisons from other regions in the Maya area, specifically the northwestern Petén, we attempt to diversify the archaeological perspectives of Maya lithic economies and draw larger conclusions concerning what these exchange systems mean for Maya economies as a whole. Specifically, we focus on addressing the impact of availability and abundance of any raw material on its value and the means devised for its acquisition. In this manner we wish to add nuance to arguments promoting the importance of "inalienable value" of any one type of material within the lowland Maya economic sphere.

By examining variability in chert resource acquisition, we find that the quality and abundance of available materials were more important for ancient Maya

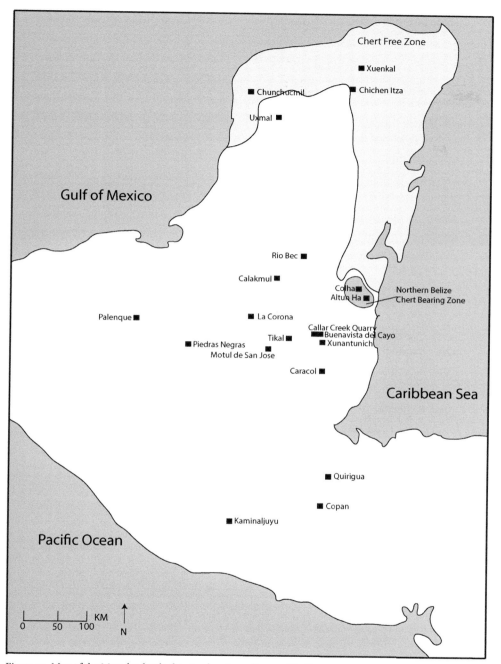

Figure 7.1. Map of the Maya lowlands showing locations discussed in the text.

economies than the particular types of raw material in influencing the perceived value of the item and its distribution mechanism. Long-distance exchange was a medium of exchange utilized not just for the acquisition of prestige or exotic goods but also for securing access to those materials needed for quotidian tasks (see Rathje 1971). The quantity of material and the organization of production help illustrate this economic variability. The acquisition of nonlocal resources for the dual purpose of producing both utilitarian and prestige goods raises questions about the exclusive relationship that prestige and utilitarian economies are implied to have with their goods; this underlying assumption impacts the study of ancient complex economies beyond just the Maya area. We posit that the lowland Maya deployed multiple, overlapping, and intermeshed strategies of exchange to acquire necessary goods that were not locally available or for which local materials were inadequate, irrespective of the assumed notion of the material's "inalienable cultural value."

Regions of Study and Chert Production and Distribution

This chapter examines the relationship between access to chert raw material and lithic production in two areas of the central Maya lowlands: the northwestern Petén and western Belize. Although chert mostly occurs across large swaths of the region, particularly parts of southern Mexico, Belize, and eastern Guatemala (Andrieu 2009a, 2013; Dahlin et al. 2011; Hearth and Fedick 2011; Hester and Shafer 1984; Mejía 2002, 2005), it is important to appreciate how unevenly distributed these chert resources are throughout the Maya lowlands. Regional differences in the production of stone tools are common throughout the Maya lowlands. Such differences in accessibility and the quantities of tools made shed light on variations in lithic economies throughout the lowlands. These data also indicate how value of chert stone tools fluctuated among the ancient Maya.

The northwestern Petén is a relatively understudied region of the Maya area that contained many large settlements, including the site of La Corona. This region lies on the western edge of the riverless central karstic uplands of the Maya Biosphere Reserve (MBR), where rain-fed basins (locally known as *civales*) dot the landscape. The soil in the area is karstic, shallow and dotted with a fragile structure (CONAP 1999). The topography is mostly flat, except for the southeastern part, where there are small rolling hills and sporadic gullies. The area to the west floods seasonally, creating unique environmental niches such as vast savannas and transition forests but also rendering it inimical to permanent human settlement. In fact, the region to the west of La Corona hosted only limited ancient settlement (Leal Rodas and López Aguilar 1993; Leal Rodas et al. 1988).

La Corona is strategically located in an area that drains sufficiently to permit year-long settlement. It is surrounded by a wealth of freshwater seasonal lakes (*civales*) and controlled major riverine routes connecting the central Maya lowlands to the Gulf Coast to the west. To the east of La Corona, the terrain rises steadily in the direction of the central karstic uplands where sites like Tikal, Uaxactún, and El Mirador are located. Finally, a few kilometers to the southwest of La Corona are the headwaters of the Xan and Chocop Rivers that drain into the large westerly drainage of the San Pedro Mártir River that provides access to the lower Usumacinta River and the Gulf of Mexico.

La Corona is a minor regional center occupied from the Early Classic Period to the Terminal Classic Period (ca. AD 300–900; Canuto and Barrientos 2011). Hieroglyphic texts from the site suggest that it played a critical role within the broader political landscape of the lowland Classic Maya as the long-term vassal to the regional kingdom of Kaanul, seated first at Dzibanché and then at Calakmul (Baron 2016; S. Martin 2005; Stuart and Baron 2013:197; Tokovinine 2007; Velásquez García 2004). One of La Corona's most salient characteristics is its location along the western edge of the central karstic uplands of the Petén, where it functioned as an important and safe entrepôt between Campeche and the western and southern lowland centers (such as El Perú–Waka', La Florida, Palenque, Dos Pilas, and Cancuén) while also avoiding unwanted entanglements with the central lowland powers (Canuto and Barrientos 2013b). In that way, La Corona helped anchor a royal road (Canuto and Barrientos 2013a, 2018; Freidel et al. 2013) that facilitated that transmission of information, people, and goods throughout Kaanul's hegemonic kingdom and beyond.

Chert resources are uncommon in northwestern Petén, particularly around La Corona. Although the area around La Corona has not been subject to a full geologic survey, explorations of the region have not recovered any chert source areas. The closest areas to La Corona with quarries and known chert production are in the Motul de San José sphere, a distance of less than 50 km, specifically the sites of Buenavista–Nuevo San José, Trinidad, and Chak Maman Tok'–La Estrella (Emery and Foias 2012; Foias and Emery 2012; Foias et al. 2012; Lawton 2007; Moriarty 2012). Although it remains unclear at the moment what relationships (if any) existed between La Corona and this area of the Petén, the epigraphic data suggest minimal political dialogue between them.

Research farther east in the Petén has shown that chert occurs in pockets at the edge of *bajos* and other low-lying areas (see Kwoka 2014 for the San Bartolo region; also Hansen 2016a:355; King 2016; Woods and Titmus 1996), it is possible that such deposits were sources of chert raw materials around La Corona. In fact, La Corona is surrounded by open rain-fed basins (*civales*) whose edges are often pockmarked by sinkholes where limestone has eroded. Such areas might have provided access to chert nodules embedded in limestone. It is possible that other sites in the eastern Petén with evidence of chert extraction and production (such as Calzado Mopán, Curcuitz, El Chal, El Naranjal, El Pedernal, Ix Ek, Ixcocol, Ixtontón, La Estrella, La Puente, Maringa, Machaquilá, Panorama, Ronrón, Rosario 5, Sayaché, and Suk Che) will provide more evidence for Petén-based strategies for chert extraction. At this point, however, these sites have not been investigated sufficiently (Alonzo 1995; Black 1987; Ciudad Ruiz 1994; Ciudad Ruiz et al. 2003; Doyle 2012; Flores 1994; Laporte et al. 1996, 1999; Mejía 2002, 2005; Mejía et al. 1999; Quezada 1998; Quezada et al. 1998; Ramos et al. 1993; Torres and Laporte 1988; Urbana 1998). At the moment it appears that some of the Petén is a chert-poor region providing few extractive opportunities to its inhabitants.

Consistent with the frequency of chert raw material deposits, chert production areas in the Petén are also not common. Although some have been identified, as discussed above, excavations at La Corona to date have failed to identify any in situ production areas. Over the past decade, excavations at La Corona and surrounding regions have largely focused on civic-ceremonial architecture, surrounding elite households, and special purpose buildings (Baron 2013, 2016; Canuto and Barrientos 2011; Ponce 2013); however, research has also tested surrounding settlement (Bustamante 2011; Cagnato 2013; Guzmán 2012; Patterson et al. 2012; Ponce 2011; Ponce et al. 2013; Pontaza 2011, 2012; Pontaza and González 2013; Roche 2015; Rojas 2011). Despite a research focus on the monumental, administrative, and ceremonial core of La Corona, the sheer lack of lithic materials in the great majority of contexts throughout the site illustrates that stone tools were not produced in any large quantity in the region.

When compared to western Belize, specifically the region around Buenavista, a site of comparable size in western Belize, not only is the quantity of lithics at La Corona much lower but also there are no production areas within 10 km. A comparable area around Buenavista has at least three lithic production areas, including one in the East Plaza of the site (Cap 2015a). Thus, the lack of production areas, combined with the very small quantity of lithic materials, at La Corona leads us to question (1) whether the value of chert materials in these two areas would have been the same and (2) what the difference in value can tell us about the function of past Maya economies. We discuss the production of chert materials below.

As a counterpoint to northwestern Petén, the upper Belize River valley (UBRV) is an area of the lowlands with extensive previous research as well as ancient settlement. Defined by the Macal, Mopán, and Belize Rivers and divided into upper and central valleys, the upper Belize River valley is characterized by hilly terrain to the west of the joining of the Macal and Mopán Rivers. Most of the known Maya settlements lie south of the Belize River, although this may be a result of the areas in which intensive archaeological survey has occurred (Chase and Garber 2004).

The region, known for its close spacing of large sites, has a long history of occupation of both major centers and small settlements. From the Preclassic to the Late/Terminal Classic the political domination of the region cycled through these large sites, especially in relation to their interactions with the major lowland Maya center of Naranjo (see LeCount and Yaeger 2010; Yaeger et al. 2015). In fact, several major UBVR sites, specifically Xunantunich and Buenavista, are thought to have been vassals of Naranjo at various points in time, which in turn was also part of the Kaanul hegemony.

Even though an in-depth discussion of the archaeology of the region is beyond the scope of this chapter (see A. Chase and Garber 2004; Houk 2015; Willey 2004 for overviews), one aspect of research in the region that deserves attention here pertains to regional economic activity. Investigations have suggested a variety of types of economic and lithic reduction activities occurred in the region (see Cap 2015a; Horowitz 2017; VandenBosch 1999; VandenBosch et al. 2010; Yaeger 2000, 2010). Evidence suggests that multiple types of exchange mechanisms—elite prestation, reciprocity, and marketplace exchange—co-existed in the region (Ball and Taschek 2004; Cap 2015a; Reents-Budet et al. 2000).

In addition to variability in exchange mechanisms, the UBRV also presents evidence of a variety of extraction and production mechanisms for lithic materials. Unlike the northwestern Petén, the UBRV contains multiple chert sources and production areas (Horowitz 2017; VandenBosch 1999; VandenBosch et al. 2010; Whittaker et al. 2009; Yaeger 2000). Chert is found in in situ deposits, in secondary deposits resulting from fluvial action, and along riverbeds. The quality of this chert for knapping varies greatly, with both high- and low-quality cherts co-occurring. The UBRV also contains various chert extraction and production areas where local residents managed the extraction and production of these materials (Horowitz 2017; VandenBosch 1999; VandenBosch et al. 2010; Yaeger 2000). For instance, Callar Creek Quarry (CCQ), a chert extraction and production area predominately utilized during the Late to Terminal Classic (AD 670–890), illustrates that local residents produced and extracted materials (Horowitz 2017).

In addition to the extraction and production of materials in quarry areas and specialized production areas such as the marketplaces at Buenavista (Cap 2015a) and Xunantunich (Keller 2006), households in the region all contain evidence of lithic production (see Connell 2000; Peuramaki-Brown 2012; Robin 1999, 2012, 2013; VandenBosch 1999). That is, there is evidence of producers emphasizing cores and preforms at quarries, such as Callar Creek Quarry (Horowitz 2017), and producing bifaces in specialized workshops such as Succotz (VandenBosch 1999) and El Pilar (Whittaker et al. 2009). Stone tool-making also occurred within household contexts. Evidence points to the production of expedient core and flake tools by householders, with more special-purpose implements, such as bifacial axes, produced by more skilled producers in workshop contexts. This is a trend seen elsewhere in the world in other sedentary societies, generally explained as being due to a decrease in skill among the general populace.

This description of the chert raw material access and production areas in the northwestern Petén and western Belize sets up a dichotomy not just in the availability of raw materials but also in the organization of production in the two regions. In western Belize, where chert is fairly ubiquitous, specialized producers and ordinary householders produced different types of materials. In the northwestern Petén, however, it seems as though the majority of materials were brought into the site, although some local materials may have been locally produced. This difference in production organization sets up a question concerning the value of chert materials in the different regions. That is, what can this difference in the production organization tell us about the value of chert materials to the ancient Maya, how did that value change in different regions, and how did it affect the distribution mechanisms of chert materials?

Lithic Extraction and Production Activities

In exploring the use of lithic resources in these two environments, differences in the procurement and production of chert materials are evident. In the UBRV chert production occurs in widespread, diverse households and consists primarily of locally available silicified limestones and other cherts acquired from within the region. In contrast, residents at La Corona made use of locally available silicified limestone; locally available poor, medium, and high-quality chert; and high-quality dark brown and gray chert, thought to come from outside the immediate region (Andrieu and Roche 2015; see Andrieu 2009a, 2013). The nonlocal nature of the superior dark brown and gray material is reflected by the fact that it most commonly appears in the form of finished tools, and occasionally as retouched tools, but is not found in cores or flakes throughout the site. This nonlocal material was brought into the site as preforms or finished tools.

Evidence from Callar Creek Quarry (CCQ), Belize, an extraction and production site surrounded by households, indicates that household residents extracted and produced materials from these areas that were locally distributed (see Horowitz 2017). The majority of this production focused on generalized core reduction, which is a specific mechanism aimed at the production of flakes rather than tools of a specific form. This technique is widely regarded as wasteful, so it is often associated with situations where lithic resources are not scarce (see Parry and Kelly 1987). Chert flakes produced by this method could have been destined for further reduction elsewhere, could have been used for generalized cutting or scraping tasks, or could have served as multifunctional expedient tools. In fact, detailed evidence from households around CCQ illustrate that the chert materials associated with these households are predominately debitage and cores. These data suggest that the residents of CCQ emphasized the production of generalized items rather than formal tools such as bifaces and unifaces, although these formal tools do occur in small quantities (Tables 7.1 and 7.2).

Thus, taken broadly, it would appear that household evidence at CCQ and elsewhere (e.g., Hester and Shafer 1984) in the UBRV suggests that lithic reduction occurred in residential contexts (Table 7.4). That is, householders in the region produced some of their own lithic implements in their own residences. In terms of acquisition of these resources, it seems likely householders acquired raw materials directly from local sources or from individuals who lived around lithic sources, such as from the residents living near the CCQ. As for formal tools, it appears that common householders obtained them from specialized producers, given that several centers of specialized tool production have been found in the valley (Hearth 2012; VandenBosch 1999; VandenBosch et al. 2010), either directly or through market exchange (see Cap 2015a).

Table 7.1. Breakdown of materials from Callar Creek Quarry and households

	Quarry	Household
Debitage	18985 (99.3%)	2701 (98.9%)
Cores	69 (0.4%)	15 (0.5%)
Multidirectional	44	12
Core fragments	12	3
Unidirectional	12	0

Table 7.2. Counts of lithics from Late/Terminal Classic Period at Callar Creek Quarry households

Material	Count
Debitage	3537 (98.8%)
Cores	11 (0.3%)
Biface	15 (0.4%)
Unifaces	14 (0.4%)
Blades	2 (0.06%)
Total	3579

The composition of the lithic assemblage at La Corona presents a markedly and significantly different picture than the UBRV. Chert materials throughout the site are found predominately in the form of finished tools, particularly bifaces, and less frequently cores and production debitage. Chert materials are distributed throughout the site, both within ceremonial structures and in elite and nonelite residences (Table 7.3). The types of finished tools include fine and General Utility Bifaces (GUBs), unifaces, scrapers, drill/gravers, and eccentrics. Bifaces and GUBs were used as cutting and chopping tools, while scrapers were used for scraping tasks, drill/gravers for drilling, engraving, or serving as awls. Other chert objects include cores and debitage, indicative of reduction processes occurring in the vicinity of these structures. Based on the recovered cores and resultant debitage, including some evidence of cortex from early stage core reduction, the production debris largely indicates generalized core reduction. Both high-quality and low-quality raw materials are found throughout the site; higher-quality raw materials were not restricted to wealthier households or ritual contexts.

Table 7.3. Counts of different types of materials from La Corona

	Special	Royal elite households	Other households
Debitage	731 (56.7%)	473 (47.8%)	109 (49.3%)
Biface[a]	146 (11.3%)	114 (11.5%)	23 (10.4%)
Uniface	1 (0.08%)	5 (0.5%)	0 (0%)
Core	6 (0.5%)	7 (0.7%)	0 (0%)
Scraper	2 (0.2%)	1 (0.1%)	0 (0%)
Drill/graver	0 (0%)	1 (0.1%)	0 (0%)
Blade/blade fragments	400 (31%)	388 (39.2%)	89 (40.3%)
Hammerstone	1 (0.08%)	0 (0%)	0 (0%)
Eccentric	1 (0.08%)	0 (0%)	0 (0%)
Other	2 (0.2%)	0 (0%)	0 (0%)
Total	1290	989	221

[a] Totals combine all bifacially flaked material.

In summary, the chert from La Corona points to a few interesting trends in chert use at the site. Overall, chert is not abundant, with only a few thousand pieces from the entire site. Despite a research focus on monumental contexts over residential ones, the overall number of lithics is quite small in comparison to sites in other regions of Mesoamerica. Curiously, its scarcity is more comparable to sites in the northern Yucatán chert-free zone. This observation is salient because La Corona presents both epigraphic and ceramic evidence of strong connections, both political and economic, with areas of plentiful chert, particularly to the north of La Corona. While some of La Corona's chert may come from elsewhere, imported as preforms and finished products, the exact source of these materials cannot be determined at this time.

At La Corona there was evidence for some chert reduction, largely confined to the use of materials accessible nearby; this activity occurred in ceremonial structures as well as in both elite and nonelite residential contexts. Although generalized reduction (of informal tools) is represented by the majority of production activities at La Corona, there was evidence for the production of some formal tools, in the presence of relatively small bifaces that were produced from small chert nodules. It was clear they were derived from small nodules, because cortex was visible on either end of the tool, indicating that the cobbles from which they were made were not any larger than the tool itself. Given the current evidence, it seems clear that the inhabitants of La Corona did not have direct access to better chert raw materials with which to produce tools. Thus, it would seem that La Corona had to import some raw materials to compensate for both the lack of naturally occurring chert in the vicinity and for the poor quality of the little chert that was locally available.

Discussion

In comparisons between the northwestern Petén and western Belize, the first salient point is the large difference in assemblage sizes. The very small number of chert artifacts at La Corona points to the comparative lack of resources or the unsuitability of available raw materials. In western Belize, chert source areas, households, and ritual contexts contain large numbers of lithic materials.

Furthermore, differences between the two regions are observed in terms of the types of lithics found. The most striking difference is the much higher quantity of debitage at CCQ than at La Corona. At La Corona debitage makes up about half of the assemblage (see Table 7.3), while at CCQ almost 99% of the material is debitage (Table 7.2). The remainder of the material at La Corona consists of bifaces and obsidian blades, while those materials are less common at CCQ. These data indicate greater use of formal tools manufactured elsewhere at La Corona, including those produced on obsidian, as opposed to at CCQ, where informal and flake tools were more commonly used.

Greater use of core tools can be a reaction to resource scarcity: generalized core reduction and flake tool production tends to be wasteful, while core tools conserve raw materials (see Parry and Kelly 1987). Residents of La Corona experienced some lithic scarcity, reflected by greater proportions of tools relative to debitage. In contrast, in western Belize informal and flake tools correlate with the greater availability of chert resources. The differences in the tool types utilized suggests a difference in lithic economies of the two areas linked to the relative accessibility of raw materials and the resultant variation in production organization.

Nonlocal chert has greater importance at La Corona than in the UBRV, probably at least in part due to the quality, abundance, and overall suitability of locally available resources. The abundance, widespread distribution, and variable quality of chert in western Belize around Callar Creek Quarry made it unnecessary to import large amounts of chert to the region. Occasionally, however,

Table 7.4. Density of lithics at households in the region

Location	Lithic count	Density (all lithics/m³)	Source
Chaa Creek—CC-1	409	110.84	Connell 2000:553, Table 9.80
Chaa Creek—CC-15	60	240	Connell 2000:555, Table 9.80
Chaa Creek—CC-17	40	111.11	Connell 2000:553, Table 9.80
Chan—CN-1	2479	209.7	Robin 1999:272, Table 14
Chan—CN-4	435	85.9	Robin 1999:272, Table 14
Dos Chambitos—DC-1	29	63.8	Robin 1999:272, Table 14
San Lorenzo—SL-31	19.7	20.3 (lithics/m²)	Yaeger 2000:1087–88, Table III:13
Callar Creek Quarry—CCQ-1	1522	400.5	Horowitz 2017

imported chert is found—mostly from Colhá (northern Belize). Such nonlocal materials were attractive, although some of the chert in western Belize is of high enough quality to make bifaces and other finely made tools.

The differences between western Belize and the La Corona region in availability and quality of local chert resources result in different patterns of chert usage—particularly greater emphasis on formal tools and nonlocal lithic materials from La Corona. The use of some chert resources acquired from nonlocal sources at La Corona suggests a resource acquisition strategy that mediated the scarcity of high-quality chert resources at the site, particularly for large tool production.

Similar patterns of the management of various goods are evident elsewhere in the Maya region for a variety of goods. For instance, studies of obsidian source areas (e.g., G. Braswell 1996) indicated a generalized extraction and production of materials, with local householders extracting materials from source areas. Outside of source areas, however, distribution is more restricted and production is performed by specialists (Aoyama 1996, 1999, 2011). Similarly, studies of jade extraction in the Motaguá Valley suggest that it was performed by neighboring households and that all householders had jade artifacts, indicating access to these raw material resources. Farther away from source areas, and particularly in production contexts, access to these materials becomes more restricted and managed by certain individuals (Andrieu et al. 2014; Demarest et al. 2014; Kovacevich 2011, 2013a). Thus, we see the pattern of locally available resources produced by local residents, with items that were imported having more restricted distributions. The patterns described here for chert distribution allow us to make larger inferences about the functioning of the lowland Late Classic Maya economy as a whole.

Conclusions

The differences in access to chert resources and chert production led us to some important conclusions concerning chert, its usage, the economic organization of various Maya towns concerning chert and their broader economies. First, chert was not inalienable. Its value varied depending on access to material and the demand for it. As a raw material, chert is useful for making durable tools utilized for farming, cutting, other tool production, and ritual/ceremonial objects. While these materials can be, and were, made from other materials, chert represents an obvious choice over obsidian or limestone, due to its durability and workability. Chert was imported into La Corona, presumably along with other items traditionally assigned greater importance and value by archaeologists, and is found there in small quantities. The economic organization pertaining to chert materials at La Corona differed from that of western Belize, where multiple producers exploited local resources to make and distribute chert tools through a variety of mechanisms.

Second, the replicability of chert in certain contexts and its uneven raw material distribution lead to the development of more complex exchange systems and networks for chert than for some other resources. That is, chert exchange networks do not fit neatly into one economic model, as they vary throughout the Maya lowlands. In contrast, for the Petén or Belize, obsidian represented a nonlocal, long-distance good in all of the Maya lowlands, making generalizations easier with respect to its value as an exchange good across these regions. For chert, however, the complex distribution and resultant variation in production organization prohibit such widespread generalizations (see E. Graham 2002).

Third, variation leads us to question the idea of prestige versus household or subsistence (aka utilitarian) exchange networks. If we dichotomize these networks, where would chert fit in? In western Belize chert would seem to fit best in household or subsistence economies as traditionally defined. However, in western Petén, as shown at La Corona, chert seems to fit within patterns of exchange and distribution more typically described as prestige economies.

Given the complexities discussed here regarding Maya lithic economies, it may be difficult to fit these two different patterns into traditional dichotomous labels. La Corona's reliance on imported chert at the minimum suggests that this relatively common good across the Maya lowlands would have been accorded greater value due to its relative scarcity at that site. As it is distributed in non-elite contexts, it is difficult to label it strictly as a prestige or sumptuary good. Thus, we find that the patterns of chert exchange and distribution and the value of chert vary depending on its ubiquity. The relationship between what would generally be considered a subsistence good and patterns of distribution associated with goods of greater value leads us to question the use of the terms and their applicability to Maya economies more broadly.

Acknowledgments

Research at Callar Creek Quarry, Belize, was conducted under the auspices of Mopan Valley Archaeological Project (MVAP) directed by Jason Yaeger, with the permission of the Belize Institute of Archaeology. Funding was provided by a National Science Foundation Doctoral Dissertation Improvement Grant (BCS Grant #1416212), a National Geographic Young Explorer Grant (Grant #9089-12), and the School of Liberal Arts at Tulane University. Research at La Corona, Guatemala, was conducted by the Proyecto Regional La Corona (PRALC) directed by Marcello A. Canuto and Tomás Barrientos, with the permission of the Ministry of Sport and Culture. Funding was provided by the Seaver Foundation, the Alphawood Foundation, National Geographic Society, PACUNAM (Fundación Patrimonio Cultural y Natural Maya), U.S. Department of Interior, and Louisiana Board of Regents. The Middle American Research Institute at Tulane University provided funding for analysis of lithic materials. Comments by Tatsuya Murakami, Jason Nesbitt, Chris Rodning, Luke Auld-Thomas, David Chatelain, Erlend Johnson, Maxime Lamoureaux-St. Hilaire, Jocelyn Ponce, Bobbie Simova, and Dave Watt helped clarify an earlier version of this chapter.

8

The Ancient Maya Economic Landscape of Caracol, Belize

DIANE Z. CHASE AND ARLEN F. CHASE

Although Maya archaeological research has been carried out for well over 150 years, the study of ancient Maya economies remained incomplete until relatively recently. The dilemma faced by Maya researchers was partly fueled by a lack of archaeological data that could be definitively discerned in the archaeological record and that could be distinguished among possible Maya distribution systems (e.g., Hutson and Dahlin 2017:4) as well as by economic theories that underplayed the role of markets and commercialism in the past (see the discussion in Feinman and Garraty 2010 and Garraty and Stark ed., 2010). While Maya archaeologists recognized that nonlocal goods appeared repeatedly in their excavations and were often widely distributed at a site (e.g., A. Chase and D. Chase 1992:5, 13; Willey et al. 1965), they had difficulty establishing the specific mechanisms that led these goods to be located in the various archaeological contexts. Discussions may also have been delayed by a prevalent assumption in the field of economic anthropology that ancient societies could not have had markets (e.g., Polanyi et al. 1957; Sahlins 1972). Expectations that ancient residential groups were generally self-sufficient producers of both subsistence and quotidian items (Sahlins 1972:83–85) may have been a further complication; thus, larger interconnected economic systems would not have been as necessary. Yet another issue has been the unnecessarily dichotomized considerations of distribution systems as being either market or feasting based. While defining the rise of ancient states has been a focus for many researchers (e.g., Clark 2007; Feinman and Marcus 1998; Traxler and Sharer 2016; but see Yoffee 2005), considerations of economy were to a large degree focused on feasting (e.g., Bray 2003; Dietler and Hayden 2001; Hayden and Villeneuve 2011) and prestige goods (e.g., Foias 2013:200; Guderjan et al. 2003:90; Reents-Budet et al. 1994) as primary integrative and distribution mechanisms. Both the anthropological study of urbanism (Hannerz 1980; Low 1999)—especially ancient urbanism (Marcus and Sabloff 2008; Storey 2006; Wheatley 1971)—and globalization (Appadurai 1996, 2001) are relatively recent developments in the field, but both have applications to the Maya archaeological record (A. Chase and D. Chase 2016a, 2016b), as does the current consensus on the existence of markets in ancient Maya societies.

At AD 650 the metropolitan area of Caracol, as opposed to the larger polity of Caracol, covered some 200 square kilometers (A. Chase et al. 2011, 2015; D. Chase and A. Chase 2017). The occupants of this ancient city—over 100,000 of them—lived within a completely anthropogenic landscape filled with housing, monumental architecture, terraced agricultural fields, and a radiating causeway system that permitted communication and economic transactions (Figure 8.1;

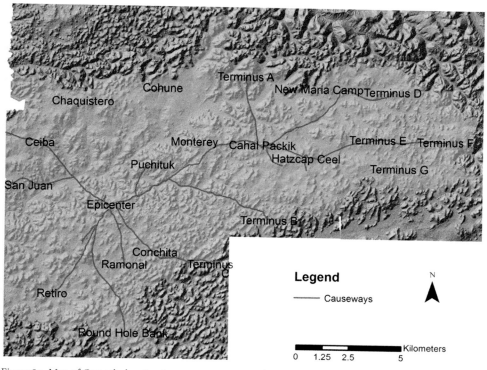

Figure 8.1. Map of Caracol, showing its causeway system and termini groups that functioned as market locales; the boundaries of the city are determined by density of residential groups and agricultural terraces.

see also A. Chase and D. Chase 2016a, 2016b; D. Chase and A. Chase 2017). We have previously described the household economy for Caracol—where the majority of individual household *plazuela* groupings not only were agriculturally sustainable but also created surplus items for exchange, allowing the residents in these groups to participate in the site's market economy (D. Chase and A. Chase 2014a; A. Chase and D. Chase 2015). Virtually every household was within 3 kilometers of their closest local market (A. Chase et al. 2015; A.S.Z. Chase 2016b; D. Chase and A. Chase 2014a;). All of these households were economically interdependent on the structural framework of the site's distributed markets. Economic activities at Caracol took place within this broader system and not within a vacuum. Many items were brought into the site for distribution, with multiple kinds of production and distribution activities taking place within the site itself. In this chapter we first address basic considerations in defining ancient economic activities and then provide the context for considering them through the lens of Late Classic Period Caracol.

The Ancient Maya Economy: Background

Discussion and diverse opinions exist today about the nature of the ancient Maya economy and particularly about systems for distribution of goods. Some researchers focus on market exchange (e.g., King, ed. 2015; L. Shaw 2012). Others focus on feasting and gift exchange (e.g., Foias 2002; LeCount 2001; but see LeCount 2010:153). However, at the onset of this current discussion it is important to note that societies generally use a wide variety of economic transactions. All economic systems include multiple aspects; thus, a market economy can include redistribution and gifting. And economies include activities that have political, social, and religious significance. Contemporary market-based Western economies are no exception. Weddings, birthday parties, potluck dinners, and various kinds of formal and informal gift exchange may be critical to the functioning of our current world; yet few of us would argue that these are the primary drivers of the economy—even though each of these activities may result in economic impact. Weddings, for example, can have both direct and indirect economic impact, involving specialized wedding planners, focused shopping venues, and increased household goods for newlyweds. Weddings, however, are more part of the fabric of society than the hallmark descriptor of the economy. Likewise, the ancient Maya economy was far more than ritual feasting or gift exchange. It is likely that such activities occurred but unlikely that they are omnipresent in the archaeological record or drove the ancient Maya economy, at least at sites like Caracol. In our estimation a focus only on these lower-level economic activities is thus inadvisable. This discussion is focused on the aspects or goods for which we have relatively clear direct or indirect archaeological data related to production and distribution as well as on three specific sectors of the economy (domestic, institutional, and political).

In these discussions, context is of utmost importance, as always. On first glance, and in isolation, an archaeological pattern such as the distribution of one artifact type may have multiple meanings and result from different processes (e.g., Chapters 7, 24). As noted by Carol Smith (1976b; see also A. Chase and D. Chase 2009), the widespread distribution of artifacts across society (especially in situations of small samples) could indicate a market economy, an egalitarian society, or elite payments (or gifting). Hirth (1998) developed this idea further in demonstrating that artifactual distributions in a complex urban setting were almost certainly the result of a market economy. Additional details relative to specific artifacts provide resolution as to how the system worked. For Caracol, this means being able to see how things were distributed over the landscape (D. Chase and A. Chase 2014a).

At the same time, variations among Maya sites are key to determining how the systems worked across sites. It has long been realized that certain sites produced bulk commodities for others, and the known instances have increased in recent years. For example, we know that Colhá produced chert artifacts (Shafer and Hester 1983, 1986) that were widely distributed (Dockall and Shafer 1993) and that the Belize Valley produced red-slipped ash-tempered pottery for a large segment of the eastern Maya area (A. Chase and D. Chase 2012). Cancuén has been demonstrated to have acted as a transshipment point for obsidian and also to have processed jadeite (Demarest et al. 2014; Chapter 3 in this volume), and Salinas de Nueve Cerros is known to have exported salt (Woodfill et al. 2015; Chapter 10, this volume). However, even when the production aspects can be identified, there are differences in distribution and access; sometimes producers at the site had access to the items they produced, as at Colhá, but other times the materials were produced predominantly for export, as at Cancuén, and not utilized internally. Virtually all sites imported some materials—finished or unfinished—from afar, but some sites, like Caracol, were greater consumers than others. Thus, aspects of the ancient Maya economy varied by venue and location. Most sites imported not only exotics like marine shell or jadeite for use in ritual contexts but also materials that

Figure 8.2. Categories of items that would have been available at Caracol's markets: (*a*) finished chert tools; (*b*) *Spondylus* marine shell (in various forms); (*c*) obsidian tools and ritual items; (*d*) imported pottery; (*e*) jadeite artifacts and debris; (*f*) objects made of metamorphic stone.

were used in daily life, like pottery, obsidian, and ground-stone tools (Figure 8.2). Pottery was manufactured by specific producers and not by each individual household; this is evident from the Instrumental Neutron Activation Analysis (INAA) analyses carried out by Ronald Bishop and his colleagues (Rands and Bishop 1980; Halperin et al. 2009). Even basic foodstuffs—as at Chunchucmil (Dahlin et al. 2005; Hutson and Dahlin 2017:9)—could be widely imported and traded.

The distinctions in the supply chain are crucial: a site-by-site, regionwide focus is necessary to understand the economic system as a whole. However, starting with a focus on one site and one period, specifically Late Classic Period Caracol (AD 550–800), can provide a solid building block for investigating the larger economic system. In this case, the units of study are the material goods themselves and the determination of the economic hallmarks found in their systems of production and distribution. Such an analysis is specifically aided by determining: (1) the source of an artifact (and the material from which the artifact was made); (2) the production location of an artifact, meaning whether it was produced wholly or partially finished at the site or was imported as a finished product; (3) a determination of which items were used on site and by whom within the society; and (4) the identification of the degree to which the distribution of artifacts was reflective of both the distribution system and societal wealth.

Other aspects of the economic system also require consideration. How are goods transported within sites and across regions (Chapter 20, this volume)? What evidence remains of preparation for risk due to disruption of production (weather, trade route interruption, warfare, etc.)?

The Economic Framework of Caracol, Belize

The focus here is on the Late Classic Period at Caracol, Belize (AD 550–800), perhaps the best-represented segment of the Caracol archaeological record. This era of widespread prosperity can be compared and contrasted with the situation both before (A. Chase and D. Chase 2005) and after (A. Chase and D. Chase 2007) this well-known period. We feel confident in discussing the economic "nuts and bolts" of the site in part because our long-term project investigations at the site now spans thirty-four archaeological seasons, during which time all of the downtown architectural groups as well as 141 residential groups have been archaeologically sampled, resulting in the recovery of 373 interments containing 753 individuals (associated with 1,375 pottery vessels) and 335 formal caches (associated with 765 pottery vessels). A wide variety of use-related remains have also been recovered in these investigations, including 355 reconstructible pottery vessels found on the floors of plazas and structures as well as numerous other associated materials and wide variety of crafting areas.

For purposes of analysis, the ancient Maya economy at Caracol may be subdivided into three related parts: domestic, institutional, and political. The domestic economy is constituted by land, labor, and capital that is accessed through nonmarket means (A. Chase and D. Chase 2015:15, following a 2013 lecture by Hirth in Chicago). The institutional economy consists of the formalized system for the distribution of goods throughout a society (A. Chase et al. 2015; D. Chase and A. Chase 2014a). The political economy is visible both within and between sites. It was composed of the symbolic capital (or power) amassed and projected by a given state or polity and was sometimes reflected in the distribution of wealth within that society, both directly and symbolically (e.g., D. Chase and A. Chase 2004, 2009, 2017). All of these sectors were interrelated.

Caracol's Domestic Economy

In the Maya area the ancient domestic economy was centered on households and residential groups as the units of production. Subsistence agriculture was practiced at the household level (A. Chase and D. Chase 1998b), and households produced sufficient food on agricultural terraces in the immediate vicinity of each household to sustain themselves (A. Chase and D. Chase 1998b; D. Chase and A. Chase 2017; Murtha 2009, 2015). Similarly, households were invested in the flow of water through these terraces; a majority of them maintained access to their own constructed reservoir for drinking water (A.S.Z. Chase 2016a; A.S.Z. Chase and Weishampel 2016). The majority of these household groups also produced surplus items that gave them access to the institutional economy; thus, various households specialized in the production of shell, lithic, bone, wood, and other finished items that could be sold or exchanged to obtain needed goods from Caracol's markets. The exchange of these goods formed a point of articulation with the site's institutional economy. It is also possible that the households produced surplus crops and goods that were used for export and formed a second point of articulation with the site's institutional economy. A third point of articulation was found in the garbage produced on the household level: while organic waste and nightsoil was likely recycled into the households' agricultural fields as fertilizers, other types of garbage were likely collected and moved about within the site's institutional system as a source of building material.

Production took place in most households at Caracol, with the crafting debris often being buried within structural fills in the residential platforms (A. Chase and D. Chase 1994; Johnson 2014, 2016) or—if made of jadeite, *Spondylus*, pyrite, or obsidian—being placed in ritualized contexts. Thus, the recovery of crafting debris can sometimes be a matter of fortuitous sampling. Thus far, we can identify three areas in the site epicenter (Caana, Barrio, and Northeast Acropolis) and twenty-eight residential groups as having been involved in some form of lithic production. Nine of the residential groups produced evidence of intensive lithic production, and it is suspected that the other nineteen groups were using lithics to craft perishable materials like wood (e.g., C. Pope 1994). Five residential groups produced extensive evidence of having worked conch shell (Cobos 1994), and two residential groups have residues from manufacturing items of bone (A. Chase and D. Chase 2015). Thirty-one residential groups appear to have been involved in textile production (A. Chase et al. 2008). We believe that this focus on specialization and differential crafting in Caracol's residential groups is due to efforts to produce commodities that enabled the residential groups to obtain the quotidian, luxury, and ritual goods found in these residential groups, which would have been available through Caracol's market system. Evidence from Caracol suggests differential production of items among residences. In some cases the products were the focus of the residence as a whole, while in other cases individual residents may have had other occupations.

Caracol's Institutional Economy

The institutional economy at Caracol was market-based. The site's elite controlled the distribution system—the market locations themselves—where the distribution (and taxing) of quotidian, ritual, and prestige goods took place. The institutional economy was physically represented both in the site's transportation system of causeways (A. Chase and D. Chase 2001; D. Chase and A. Chase 2017) and in the structural location of market locales (A. Chase et al. 2015; D. Chase and A. Chase 2014a) throughout the site during the Late Classic Period. The dendritic layout of Caracol's causeway system served to join together a series of public plazas that were used for both economic and administrative purposes (A. Chase 1998; A. Chase and D. Chase 2001, 2004; D. Chase and A. Chase 2004, 2017). In some cases, these large open spaces were purposefully embedded in Caracol's landscape to serve as the contact points for any economic transactions (e.g., Figure 8.3; see A. Chase et al. 2015). The dendritic layout of the site also shows that the public plazas are directly linked to the site epicenter, implying centralized control over what was and was not available at a given location. Imported goods were widely distributed; for instance, jadeite appears in 45% of the investigated groups at Caracol (Figure 8.4; A. Chase et al. 2015:231) and imported Belize Red footed dishes and plates occur in burials in thirty-eight different residential groups at the site, indicating widespread access by a socially diverse population. Yet access to these materials could be skewed; the distribution of Belize Red plates as opposed to Belize Red dishes (both contemporary forms) clearly shows that plates were not available in the northeastern part of the site (D. Chase and A. Chase 2014a:246). Obsidian from the Guatemalan highlands is even more widely distributed at Caracol, occurring in virtually every excavated residential group at the site and presumably available in all the different markets (L. Johnson 2016).

The dense distribution of residential units at Caracol and the anthropogenic landscape that is covered in almost continuous agricultural terraces (A. Chase and D. Chase 1998b; A. Chase and D. Chase 2014) ensured that that causeways were used for transportation and that exchange took place at the market locales. It also ensured elite control over these transactions, as these were the most effective passageways across the metropolitan area. The market locales formed the points of articulation for the domestic economies found in the households. Any goods produced externally to the site would have been brought into these locations, presumably under elite supervision for purposes of taxation (see also M. Smith 2014); these goods included a mix of quotidian, prestige, and ritual items. Based on archaeological contexts, utilitarian, polychrome, and ritual pottery were all available in Caracol's markets as well as other items like obsidian, metamorphic ground stone, jadeite, *Spondylus*, other seashells, and stingray spines (e.g., Figure 8.2). A host of perishable items such as baskets, fibers, wooden objects, and specialized foodstuffs also would have been available. And Caracol's residents would have made their way to these locales with commodities produced in their households to obtain needed items through the market system.

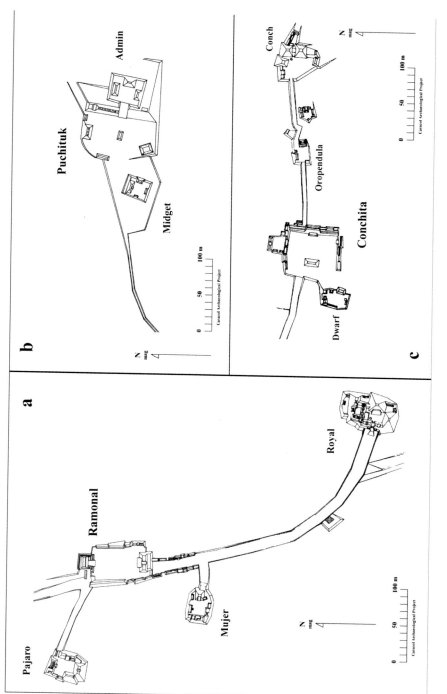

Figure 8.3. Caracol market and administrative locales purposefully constructed at the beginning of the Late Classic Period (see A. Chase et al. 2015).

a

Pajaro

Ramonal

Mujer

Royal

N mag

0   50   100 m

Caracol Archaeological Project

b

Puchituk

Admin

Midget

N mag

0   50   100 m

Caracol Archaeological Project

c

Conch

Oropendula

Conchita

Dwarf

N mag

0   50   100 m

Caracol Archaeological Project

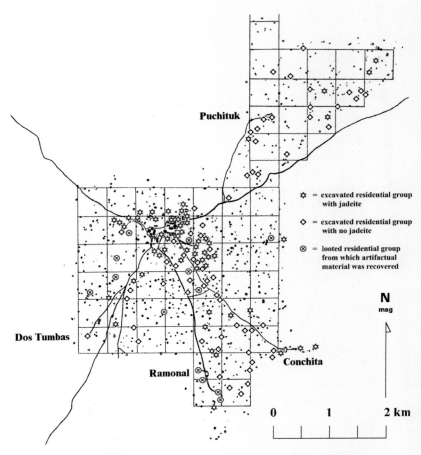

Figure 8.4. Distribution of jadeite recovered in residential groups at Caracol, Belize.

Caracol's Political Economy

Caracol's Late Classic political economy was directly reflected within the site's residential households and indirectly through intersite comparisons. Successful warfare at the beginning of the Classic Period had led to the adoption of a widespread shared identity and shared prosperity. For the majority of Caracol's population, this shared identity was focused on residential shrines that were the loci for household tombs and ritual caches; a good proportion of the individuals within these groups also had teeth inlaid with jadeite and hematite, wore earrings and jewelry made of seashell, and had access to polychrome and imported ceramics (D. Chase and A. Chase 2004). At the same time the site's elite employed a management strategy called "symbolic egalitarianism" (A. Chase and D. Chase 2009), meaning that they did not flaunt their wealth, most likely in life and especially in death. Most of Caracol's elite tombs are not ostentatious, containing relatively plain ceramics in smaller numbers as well as limited amounts of jewelry (in accord with society-wide distributions following the tenets of symbolic egalitarianism), a pattern also found with the two Caracol rulers thought to be interred at Tikal, Guatemala (D. Chase and A. Chase 2017:219). "Burial 23 connotes simplification in most if not every respect, a trend evident in considerably earlier Bu. 195" (W. Coe 1990, 3:843).

Part of Caracol's Late Classic political economy involved the incorporation of other states and polities, presumably as a means of extracting resources and projecting power. The hieroglyphic texts indicate that this was the case for both Tikal and Naranjo in Guatemala during the early part of the Late Classic Period. We have previously argued that the hieroglyphically recorded conquest of Tikal by Caracol in AD 562 was strengthened through the conquest of Naranjo in AD 631 by placing Tikal within direct territorial access and marching distance (A. Chase and D. Chase 1998a). The archaeological data demonstrate that Caracol not only intervened in the politics and economics of Tikal but also used its position of power to symbolically restructure the ritual core of Tikal through the placement of two Caracol rulers there in death (A. Chase and D. Chase 2020). The rebuilding efforts at Tikal associated with these two tombs have been interpreted as "an attempt by usurpers to put their own distinctive stamp on the political and ceremonial heart of the city" (Haviland 1992a:73–74). Thus, Caracol symbolically projected its power over Tikal through the very real appropriation of its central architectural and ritual space. Caracol was also involved in extracting resources from the site, as indicated by the wealth differences that exist between the residential groups of the two sites. Whereas Caracol's wealth, as expressed in the volumetrics of its residential groups (see A.S.Z. Chase 2017 for Gini indices), shows evidence of inequality within a wide range of variability, reported artifactual distributions from Tikal (Moholy-Nagy 2003a, 2008a) suggest that Tikal's degree of inequality is far more pronounced (Kohler et al. 2017)—presumably because of social policies related to an extractive political economy imposed on Tikal's residents by Caracol during the early part of the Late Classic Period. Whereas the Late Classic had a more level playing field, disparity in equality was apparently more common at Caracol in the Early Classic and Terminal Classic Periods, both before and after Caracol's Late Classic Period peak.

Contextually Situating Caracol's Economy

Although seemingly peripheral to the central Maya area in terms of contemporary roads and geography, Caracol is actually situated on a natural corridor forming the easiest transshipment route for the resources found in the Maya Mountains and the central Petén of Guatemala. The site's location provided it with a distinct economic benefit; it was situated relatively close to metamorphic resources that were used for creating ground-stone artifacts like manos and metates that were in demand in the Maya lowlands. The site's causeways span the relatively flat Vaca Plateau, providing a transportation route for the movement of these items through Caracol on their way to sites in the interior of the Petén of Guatemala. Part of Caracol's economic power was certainly derived from this siting and from its control of this trade. Based on the extensive agricultural fields that cover the landscape of Caracol (e.g., A. Chase and D. Chase 1998b; A. Chase and D. Chase 2014, 2017), which easily sustained the projected population (e.g., A. Chase and D. Chase 2015:17; Murtha 2009, 2015:85), it is also possible that Caracol produced surplus crops for export to other parts of the Maya region in conjunction with other items produced within its households. This would match similar arguments regarding the agricultural intensification of wetlands in northern Belize that would have resulted in crop surpluses that could have been exported into the central Petén using canoes that followed riverine and *bajo* routes (Dahlin and Chase 2014; Montgomery 2016).

By the middle of the Late Classic Period the city of Caracol had expanded to encompass some 200 sq km of continuously settled and agriculturally productive landscape that was integrated by its causeway system with its regularly distributed market plazas. Given the site's focus on agricultural terracing, it is unlikely that there was much trade into Caracol of basic subsistence crops, as each residential group had sufficient area to produce its own food. Thus, apart from specialty food items, all agricultural items would have been produced and consumed internally. Animals for consumption—such as rabbits, dogs, deer, pig, armadillos, and agoutis—could have been penned within the city or obtained from outside it. However, the bones of animals were also utilized in internal production areas to make both tools and ornaments (Teeter 2001; Teeter and Chase 2004), and it is likely that leather would also have been made by some residential groups. Perishable items like nets, baskets, and wooden artifacts were also crafted throughout the city. Building materials were obtained internally in the city, largely as a process of expanding the agricultural terraces (A. Chase and D. Chase 2014). Limestone for construction was readily available, and the landscape was terraformed once building materials were removed. Quarries are not in evidence at Caracol because they were covered over and infilled with agricultural terracing (A. Chase and D. Chase 1998b, 2016a, 2016b; D. Chase and A. Chase 2017). Slate from the Macal River area was widely available and was utilized for ritual purposes and for crafting some tools and jewelry. Plaster must have been widely available; even the causeways were plastered. However, the burning of limestone needed to make plaster requires substantial quantities of wood, implying that plaster was likely produced on the edges of the city and then brought back into the urban center.

Some external raw materials were refined through the production process internally. Among these are both obsidian and chert. Obsidian originating from Guatemala and Mexico was widely available to all of Caracol's households and was brought into the site both in finished form and in cores that could be processed by households (Johnson 2016). Poor-quality chert was also widely available at Caracol for household production purposes, but fine-quality finished products of chert were also imported to the site from other areas, like northern Belize, and were available to the people living in the residential groups across the site. Marine shell (obviously nonlocal to this inland city) was widely available to Caracol's inhabitants. Complete conch shells were brought into the site for use as musical instruments and to be utilized by residential groups for crafting smaller items. Other marine items like coral and sea fans were transported to the site to be included as cache contents. Marine items tended to come from the Pacific and Atlantic coasts early in Caracol's history and then almost uniformly from the Caribbean in the Late Classic Period (Cobos 1994). Live sea fish were also among the commodities brought into Caracol, presumably via the Belize River (Cunningham-Smith et al. 2014). While textiles, cloth, and clothing may have been extensively embroidered at Caracol based on the presence of artifacts like needles and spindle whorls, it is suspected that cotton was not grown locally and thus needed to be imported.

Goods not produced by Caracol's households were also brought into the market plazas, where the site's inhabitants could obtain them. Obsidian was certainly available in these locations (Johnson 2016). So, too, were manos and metates made of hard ground stone that came from just east of Caracol in association with the Macal River. Items of jadeite would have also been available, presumably as finished objects, although some processing of jadeite is hinted at by the inclusion of jadeite processing chips within both epicentral and residential caches. In the Early Classic Period jadeite, shell, and pyrite had a more limited distribution outside of the site epicenter; however, in the Late Classic Period these three items were broadly distributed among the site's residential groups. In both periods jadeite, shell, and pyrite tended to be concentrated in symbolic ritual locations.

Importantly, pottery was also likely imported from areas both immediately beyond and well beyond the city boundaries. The pottery that was used for ritual cache vessels (finger bowls and urns) is often crudely made and not slipped; it is likely that these materials were made at the edges of the city, probably by specialized producers, and were available through the market plazas. Many of the site's storage wares, cooking pots, and water jars contain quartzite in their paste as temper, meaning either that the quartzite was traded into the site or, perhaps more likely, that the jars were made to the east along the Macal River, where both water and wood for firing were found and quartzite occurs naturally. Pottery was often fired at the edges of ethnographically known Maya communities (Reina and Hill 1978), which supports the idea that outer Caracol locales such as the Macal River region were production areas. Serving wares were also imported from outside the city boundary; some of the other quotidian pottery vessels were probably made just beyond the western boundary of the city along the Chiquibul River (again, where wood and temper were available for production, similar to the eastern Macal production areas). Others were imported from even greater distances and in standardized forms—as established for Belize Red (A.S.Z. Chase and A.M.Z. Chase 2015; A. Chase and D. Chase 2012), which is widely distributed at Caracol and in southern Belize. Thus, by the Late Classic Period most pottery was likely brought into Caracol from specialized producers located at some distance from the city epicenter, although at least some was potentially produced at the eastern and western edges of the city within the polity itself.

Discussion

When viewed through the lens of production and distribution, the artifactual materials of Caracol add great insight into the Late Classic economic system that was in place. With the exception of agricultural products, Caracol's residential groups were dependent on producers from other Caracol households and from well outside the urban boundaries. The people in these residential groups produced a wide variety of items that permitted their articulation with the site's economic system. Market plazas were located throughout Caracol to facilitate the transfer of goods and, presumably, services to the site's population. The direct connection of these locations to the site epicenter by means of causeways is strong supporting evidence for some kind of central oversight of the economic system.

By the middle part of the Late Classic Period no household was economically self-sufficient in isolation. In addition to locally produced material goods and food items, Caracol's populace was dependent on exterior producers for many of the products that they used. We suspect, given the broader interlinked Late Classic economic landscape, that Caracol was not alone in this situation. Thus, trade and exchange between different Maya regions had come to dominate the economic systems of the ancient Maya, meaning that the economies of many polities were interdependent. Salt, obsidian, cloth, ceramics, exotics, and other goods and raw materials flowed into the Caracol system, and finished products of metamorphic rock and perishable materials, as well as possibly bulk commodities, flowed out. This system of interdependence came to dominate the political economy. However, any imbalance to the interdependent political economies could have had serious repercussions given the institutional system's economic dependence on outside producers. Thus, the economic interconnectedness in the broader Late Classic Maya region at the end of the Late Classic Period would have been vulnerable to outside risk factors.

In marked contrast to the Late Classic situation, Caracol households during the Terminal Classic Period (AD 800–900) show extreme variation in artifact distribution (A. Chase and D. Chase 2007), suggesting changes to the economic system at the site and a potential breakdown of the once-functional market system or, at a minimum, changes in what was available within the markets. The existence of status-linked ceramics at Caracol during the Terminal Classic Period (A. Chase and D. Chase 2004) suggests to us that Caracol had shifted focus to become more of an extractive economy, where prosperity and broader Mesoamerican trade items were no longer shared (A. Chase and D. Chase 2007; D. Chase and A. Chase 2017). Thus, we suspect that the Maya collapse is ultimately at least partially due to the further disruption to this "global" economic system. Rather than climate change or drought, we see disruptions to the interconnectedness of ancient Maya economies and modifications in local distribution systems as leading to the demise of the once successful city and polity of Caracol.

Conclusion

The archaeological data from Caracol, Belize, collected over the last three and a half decades permit insight into a single Maya economic system that has rarely been achieved. These data can be positioned within three very different frames: first, the domestic economy centered on households and residential groups; second, the institutional economy focused on the city itself, its markets, and their administration; and, third, the political economy focused at the polity level and related to the very real acquisition of resources and the symbolic imposition of power. Each of these frames provides a distinctive part of Caracol's economy both over space and over time. Importantly, they suggest that by the middle of the Late Classic Period the economics of many different polities across the southern lowlands were interdependent. This interconnectedness, which had resulted in a reduction in the redundancy in local systems, may have provided a weak link in the overall Maya economic system and surely factored into the final events that led to the heretofore enigmatic Classic Maya collapse.

Acknowledgments

The archaeological work that we have undertaken at Caracol over the past thirty-five years has been performed in conjunction with the Belize Institute of Archaeology and has been sponsored by a host of foundations and funding agencies, including the Alphawood Foundation; the Ahau Foundation; the Dart Foundation; the Foundation for the Advancement of Mesoamerican Studies, Inc.; the Geraldine and Emory Ford Foundation; the Government of Belize; the Harry Frank Guggenheim Foundation; the NASA Space Archaeology Program; the National Science Foundation; the Stans Foundation; UCF-UF Space Research Initiative; the United States Agency for International Development; the Trevor Colbourn Endowment from the University of Central Florida; and private donations to the UCF Foundation, Inc., and the UNLV Foundation, Inc. It is only through the funding and support provided by these various agencies, foundations, and universities that we have been able to garner some semblance of an understanding of Caracol's ancient economic system(s).

9

Commerce, Redistribution, Autarky, and Barter

The Multitiered Urban Economy of El Perú–Waka', Guatemala

KEITH EPPICH

This chapter is an attempt to sketch an outline of Classic Maya economic systems as they existed inside one city. The remains of the Classic economy are to be found among the scattered bits and pieces of ancient mechanisms of production, distribution, and consumption. The Classic world possessed sprawling cities, elaborate political institutions, and an active economy, the scale and complexity of which scholars are only now beginning to appreciate. Maya studies has come a long way from vacant ceremonial centers ruled over by pacifist astronomer-priests. Equally, we have moved away from a vision of the Classic economy as being small, localized systems of vertical redistribution, provisioned only through swidden agriculture, supplemented by gift exchanges of a few high-value items.

A new perspective has emerged over the past two decades. The Classic Maya economy contained a strong commercial element, although no one knows exactly how strong. It contained some degree of elite participation and oversight, although no one knows how much. It involved the production and distribution of bulk commodities over distance, although, again, no one knows how much was moved or how far it traveled. Most likely, these economic exchange systems developed as Classic civilization developed. This was the point made by William Rathje (1972), arguing that the Maya built elaborate exchange networks to obtain basic resources in large quantities acquired over long distances. Such networks fueled the rise of "resource controllers" who expended their newfound wealth in extravagant displays of ritual generosity. In the process of throwing these "Maya potlatches," they transformed themselves into the Classic elite (Rathje 2002:32). Of course, no one knows who these first "resource controllers" were or how far back these economic arrangements extend.

This chapter serves as a part of that new perspective. It models and documents the overlapping patterns of economic exchange present in a single Maya city over the last three hundred years of its existence. It follows the research that David Freidel and I published in 2015, presenting the results of a large-scale statistical analysis of the ceramics recovered from the ruins of El Perú–Waka' (Eppich and Freidel 2015). The research argued strongly for the presence of active marketplaces inside Classic cities, complete with accounting, merchants, vendors, and currencies (see also Freidel et al. 2016; King, ed. 2015; Shaw 2012; Tokovinine and Beliaev 2013). Commercial exchange clearly existed in the Classic centers, but it was unlikely to have been the only mechanism distributing goods and services. Eleanor King and Leslie Shaw (2015:23) stress this, writing that the ancient Maya economy included "the full gamut of exchange—reciprocal, redistributive, and market . . . an interrelated entity that affects all social classes and played out at multiple scales." The numbers from El Perú–Waka' also reflected this. The statistics, as untidy as they were, showed a distributive pattern present for the majority of the city's monochrome ceramics. The households of this ancient Maya city possessed low degrees of variance for domestic ceramic assemblages, a pattern associated with commercial distribution (Garraty 2009; Hirth 1998, 2000, 2010; M. Smith 1999). At El Perú–Waka' we found evidence of marketing activity not in the archaeology of the physical marketplace but in the impact that marketing had on household ceramics.

The numbers also suggested alternatives to commercial distribution. Some ceramics clustered irregularly among the residence compounds and displayed wildly divergent patterns. It is unlikely that such pottery was acquired through marketplace exchange. This chapter addresses those divergent patterns. Different modes of exchange can be modeled in predictive fashions and matched with material recovered from the archaeological record. The modes addressed here include commerce, redistribution, autarky, and barter. The ceramics serve as a proxy for other goods that circulated in the ancient economy. If the ancient Maya were selling, making, and bartering pottery, they were likely doing the same for other goods and services. "Pottery," to quote Sylvanus Morley (1947:382), is the "best guide to cultural development" and the best guide to economic development as well. It serves as one of the better metrics for ancient economic activity, at least in the Maya area. Through its study, it can reveal the patterns of exchange and economic history of at least one Classic city, rendering our perspective on the Classic Maya economy a little less vague.

Multiple Modes of Economic Exchange

An economy is really just a series of relationships. An individual desires an object and is willing to exchange something in order to obtain it. Exactly what is exchanged and how this exchange takes place depends heavily on the social relations surrounding the exchange. Karl Polanyi (1957; see also 1944, 1975a, 1975b) was quite correct when he observed that economic structures function as instituted processes, actions embedded within a particular social and cultural context. What he largely failed to realize is that the reverse is also correct (Garraty 2010; McClosky 1997). Social relations are equally embedded, bounded by the economic structures that allow any particular human society to feed and clothe itself. Studying one necessarily speaks to the nature of the other. Economic relations serve as the means by which a society collectively obtains the goods and services it requires and desires, how it finances its institutions, and how it builds and sustains the mechanisms responsible for making decisions. Different economic structures possess very different managerial elements, the relative success of each leading to very different sorts of societies. This reasoning led Timothy Earle (2002) to his own theories about the development of economy and society. Different political and social arrangements exist in competition. Those arrangements capable of delivering on goods and services succeed; they prosper. Those that cannot do so diminish and fail. Large, centralized social and political institutions develop from large, centralized economic structures. Dispersed, decentralized social and political arrangements develop and develop from dispersed, decentralized economies. Small-scale relations favor small-scale economics. Large-scale institutions favor large ones. Any given society possesses multiple versions of each, different elements of society favoring, and being favored by, different sets of economic exchange. As the needs and desires of a society change, different economies will be favored and the political and social institutions will shift accordingly.

One can model different sets of economic relationships by examining the connections among producers, distributors, and consumers. Objects are produced. They move from one point to another and are exchanged for another set of goods or services. The process is then repeated. The relative social positions of production, distribution, and consumption thus define different modes of economic exchange. These relationships existed as organized, repeated behaviors, and each leaves a distinct pattern in the archaeological record. Such patterns can be predicted and searched for archaeologically.

This has been done before, famously so. Colin Renfrew (1975) described ten "modes of trade" and then modeled the spatial implications of each type of long-distance exchange (see also Renfrew 1977). Thus, the implication of Renfrew's modes could be measured against the archaeological record in order to identify different types of long-distance trade. Renfrew's essay has proven enormously influential, being used in research ranging from Iron Age Phoenicia (Aubet 2001) to medieval Europe (Hodges 1982) to Southeast Asia (Bentley 1986) to the Pre-Columbian Andes (Earle 1994b). In the Maya region, it has proven useful in studying ancient long-distance and regional trade (McKillop 1989, 1996; Sidrys 1976, 1979; see also Kepecs 2003, 2005; Lange and Bishop 1988; West 2002). In any discussion of long-distance exchange, economics, and human cultural development, Renfrew's modes get a nod, even when they do not occupy a central position. Renfrew modeled long-distance exchange across broad areas, offering explanations for the Aegean, Mesopotamia, or Maya region. The present effort has much more modest goals. The "modes of exchange" presented here address short-range movement of goods across the urban landscape of a single Maya center. Renfrew addressed thousands of square kilometers. This chapter confines itself to a half-dozen.

Four different modes of exchange are modeled in Figure 9.1, along with the material pattern expected to be present in the archaeological record of individual households. These modes are not comprehensive or exhaustive. It is very likely that additional sets of social and economic relationships existed in the ancient past, including some that can barely be imagined today. The ones presented here are commerce, redistribution, autarky, and barter. Of these, commerce is the most familiar to modern readers. Producers move objects to the market where they sell them in person or transfer such goods to third-party vendors, who, in turn, sell them to consumers. Prices may be fixed by judges or other authorities, but value itself is determined by the mobile curves of supply and demand. Land, labor, and capital become fungible commodities with different currencies lubricating their transfer (Freidel et al. 2002, 2016; Masson and Freidel 2012, 2013). The debate over the presence of commerce in Classic Maya civilization was lengthy and at times quite bitter (Eppich and Freidel 2015; Hirth and Pillsbury, eds. 2013; King and Shaw 2015). Still, the patient work of archaeologists on the ground confirmed the existence of marketplaces and marketing activity (Cap 2015a; Garraty 2009; Garraty and Stark, eds. 2010; King, ed. 2015; Masson and Freidel 2002; Shaw 2012). Markets themselves are highly efficient exchange systems, allowing for widespread specialization of producers and hence higher-quality goods made with greater efficiency (North 1981, 2005). Markets are volatile, however, being fragile things easily impacted and disrupted by external events and their own internal fluctuations. They possess a degree of "creative destruction" in which older social and economic structures are broken down in favor of newer and more efficient relationships (McCraw 2007; Schumpeter 1942). Thus, markets allow novel arrangements normally not permitted in existing social structures (see Blanton 2013; Wurtzburg 2015).

Archaeologically, scholars have expended much energy in the effort to detect commercial activity (Garraty and Stark, eds. 2010; Scheidel and von Reden 2002). An important part of this has been Kenneth Hirth's distributional approach (Hirth 1984, 1998, 2000, 2010, 2013; see also Cyphers and Hirth 2000; Garraty 2009; Smith 1999), as discussed in Chapters 2–4. This model's expected general uniformity of artifact distributions correlating with well-developed market economies can be detected by using fairly simple statistical techniques (Garraty 2009; Hirth 2000). At El Perú–Waka' these techniques were employed with recovered ceramics, revealing a commercial pattern for most of the site's monochrome ceramics in the seventh to tenth centuries (Eppich and Freidel 2015). For the simple red and black slipped plates and bowls of the Tinaja Rojo and Infierno Negro ceramic types, the most likely explanation for their site-wide distribution is marketing activity. The strongest commercial pattern was discovered for ninth- and tenth-century fine paste ceramics, specifically, Altar Naranjo and Tres Naciones Gris.

Some ceramics, however, did not conform to Hirth's distributional pattern. These include Late and Terminal Classic polychromes and several monochrome types from the ninth to tenth centuries. These particular ceramics began a line of inquiry that led to the current research. If not distribution through marketing, then what?

Key to understanding this is the concept of ceramic "microtraditions." As described by Michael Deal (1998:31–37), microtraditions are the unique stylistic attributes belonging to specific pottery workshops and, in some cases, individual potters. Workshops and even specialist potting communities tend to specialize in a restricted range of ceramic styles and forms. For instance, Deal noted that potters from the town of Chanal manufactured wide-mouthed jars and elliptical single-handle jars, while those from the neighboring village

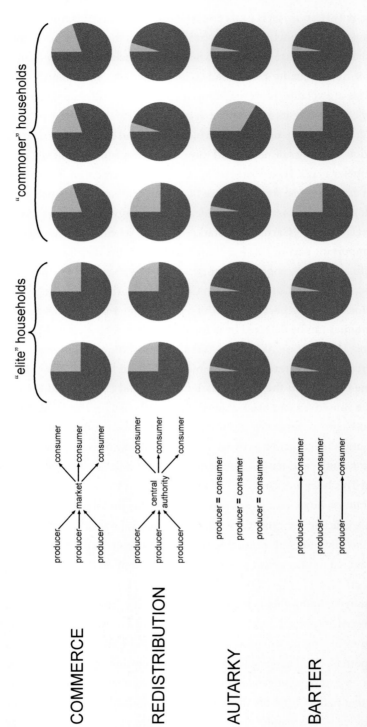

Figure 9.1. Modes of exchange.

of Amatenango fashioned spherical and ovoid vessels. Chanal pottery was un-slipped, while Amatenango pottery sometimes made use of red and white slips (Deal 2007). These distinctions are largely a result of how new potters learn their craft, first apprenticing and then working within established artistic canons (see also Reina and Hill 1978). This is very likely the situation in antiquity, and the archaeology of pottery workshops suggests that individual workshops produced a restricted range of ceramic types and forms (Culbert 2003; Stark 2007). All ceramic producers fed their own microtradition into local exchange systems, making their individual contribution to the considerable diversity of the Classic potting traditions. However, each exchange system would then distribute these microtraditions in different ways.

For market exchange, different pottery styles would mingle in a market setting, resulting in a fairly even distribution across households provisioning themselves from the market. This is again the logic employed in Hirth's distributional approach and should result in low analysis of variance F-statistics from different household assemblages. Thus, any given ceramic freely traded should end up in most households with ceramic assemblages occurring at roughly the same level of frequency, even between "elite" and "commoner" households. The greater buying power of elite households should result in higher frequencies of most commodities, and this should be especially true of finely made or prestige ceramics.

An alternative to market exchange is redistribution. Redistribution is when households collectively contribute goods to a central authority. The central authority, being political or religious elites, then "redistributes" goods to consumers. Value is determined by the governing authority. Societal elites determine the frequency by which goods and service are distributed with the elites keeping a certain percentage for the maintenance of their own households. Redistribution features prominently in the evolutionary theories proposed by Earle (2002), where different political schema flourished or perished based on their ability to collect surplus from one place and redistribute it to another, to store grain after a good harvest and hand it out after a bad one. Centralized political authority developed in accordance with the ability to build and maintain such redistributive structures in a kind of "storage despotism" (see also Sahlins 1972; Service 1962). Redistribution was often assumed rather than demonstrated in archaeology (e.g., Polanyi 1957). This has changed with the new century: numerous scholars have turned their attention to examining the effects of redistributive economic relationships on the archaeological record (Bayman 1995; Feinman and Nicholas 2010; Hirth 1998, 2013; Nakassis et al. 2011; Stark and

Garraty 2010, eds., 2010). By collecting and redistributing, redistributive mechanisms should produce artifactual patterns that mirror existing sets of social and political relationships. "Elite" households would greatly benefit from such a system, possessing high frequencies of valued goods. "Commoner" households locked into social relationships with the elites would also receive these goods. However, those households outside of these social relationships would be largely excluded from the redistributive mechanism. As the central authority decides who gets what, those social units that were most useful to the authority would be favored over those who were not. In terms of ceramics, high-quality vessels would appear in high frequencies in elite household assemblages and in the commoner households attached to them, while other households would be largely excluded from such exchange.

Autarky, economic self-sufficiency, is the simplest and most straightforward of any of the exchange systems presented here. In an autarkic system, households do not exchange goods or services. Rather, they produce materials for their own usage. Producers equal consumers. Nothing is exchanged, so there is little specialization. Hence autarkic systems tend to be very inefficient, producing low-quality goods at high costs (see Common and Stagl 2005; Weddepohl 1990; Yang and Sachs 2003). Autarkic groups can exist within larger economies, being social groups that choose to self-segregate or are pushed to the margins of society (Bernhofen and Brown 2005; Hardin 2000). Excessive poverty in a commercial economy can exclude social units from the market, forcing them into self-sufficiency, as they must make their own goods or do without. The study of autarky has not generally attracted much attention from archaeologists (but see Davies 2005; Watanabe 2007). It should be quite apparent in the archaeological record (compare G. Braswell 2002). In terms of ceramic distribution, it should be represented by a cluster of distinct ceramics. These distinct ceramics should not greatly extend beyond the social unit that produced and consumed them. Whatever microtradition they possessed should cluster largely within a given household assemblage. In other household assemblages, such ceramics should appear in trace amounts, if they appear at all.

The final mode of exchange addressed here is barter, the straightforward trading of one good and service for another. Stark and Garraty (2010:34) define barter as "transactions enacted without media of exchange": trade without currency (see also Dalton 1982; Humphrey and Hugh-Jones 1992). Simply put, a group or individual exchanges one commodity for another. These could equally be goods or services. Exchanging labor for food or status is, in fact, a kind of barter. Reciprocity is itself barter, goods traded for social obligations (Douglas and Isherwood 1996; Sahlins 1972). It is generally considered to be a precursor to market exchange, trade that is waiting for the arrival of currency to allow for more efficient transactions. However, barter frequently exists in tandem with commercial systems, often allowing marginalized groups access to items that they normally lack access to or just cannot afford. As such transactions occur apart from currency or its equivalent, social relations factor heavily in bartered exchange. This is especially true when a trade will be delayed: for instance, exchanging so many days of labor for a portion of a harvest. Kinship or societal ties enforce trust that all sides will act in good faith, so social ties back bartered exchange. Producers possess close and direct ties with consumers. In terms of the archaeological record, this should translate into higher frequencies of a goods occurring between socially allied households. For ceramics, this would be a given microtradition shared between a few households, as one group bartered the pottery to friends and neighbors. This same microtradition should occur in very limited quantities outside of these households.

Economies are additive traditions, not evolutionary ones. As societies become larger in scale and more complex in character, new economic connections tie together disparate parts of a changing social fabric. Older economic connections are not necessarily replaced but can be subsumed beneath newer economic arrangements. Barter and autarky can still exist alongside redistributive or commercial mechanisms, continuing to function and meet the needs of the people who use them. One can buy and sell in a marketplace, barter for something else, collect and redistribute one good, and then simply make and use another. This is true of any economy, from the twenty-first century back to the eighth, and all people make use of different mechanisms over the course of their lives. Multiple types of exchange exist simultaneously and fulfill different functions for the society they serve. As the needs of the society change, so does the reliance on any particular mode of exchange. The goal here is to use archaeological data to identify the ceramic markers for these modes of exchange and then chart changes through time, at least as they existed across the urban landscape of El Perú–Waka'.

El Perú–Waka', a Classic Maya Realm

El Perú–Waka' sits on the western edge of the heart of the Classic Maya world. In modern-day Guatemala it consists of a picturesque collection of ruins in the

Laguna del Tigre National Park, part of the threatened tropical rainforests in the Department of Petén. The core of the city occupies the heights of an 80-meter limestone escarpment that looks down on the junction of the Río San Juan and Río San Pedro Mártir, the more impressive of the two waterways. It one of the main avenues of east-west Classic commerce and exchange, naturally navigable for a good portion of its considerable length. Furthermore, the city was astride the "Great Western Route," a series of north-south overland trails that led from the southern highlands to the northern lowlands (Canuto and Barrientos 2013b; Demarest and Fahsen 2002; Woodfill and Andrieu 2012). The city sat at the center of the one of the great commercial crossroads of the Maya world (see Freidel et al. 2007).

The collaborative efforts of the Proyecto Arqueológico Regional El Perú–Waka' have documented the origin of the city in the third century BC to its final abandonment in the tenth century AD. In the Late Preclassic the site seems to consist largely of a series of small farmsteads scattered across the riverbanks and limestone escarpment. By the first century AD settlement coalesced around a hilltop ritual center. However, our grasp of this early settlement is uncertain, as much of it lies deeply buried under the later Classic city. The city itself took on its current configuration during an apparent surge of urban development in the early portion of the Early Classic, likely in the second or third centuries. During that time, the Maya constructed the city around the broad open space of Plaza 1, leveling the old hilltop ritual center to build Plaza 2. They built the twin 40-meter pyramids of the Mirador Group and the royal palace of the Northwest Palace Group. It was during this period that the site began its monumental history. The first known stela dates to AD 416: Stela 15, a monument celebrating the arrival and royal welcome of Siyaj K'ahk' (Guenter 2014b). The city's emblem glyph first appears in its Early Classic form, a toothed insect head, referring to the giant centipede of the American tropics (Guenter 2007). To the Classic Maya, El Perú–Waka' was simply Wak', the City of the Centipede.

The city reached its apex during the eighth century. The Late Classic city built up from the Early Classic design, raising pyramids and palaces across the urban landscape. The city played a pivotal role in the endemic political conflicts of the day, being a stalwart ally of the Snake dynasty kings of Calakmul. This unequal alliance is demonstrated by the many queens of El Perú–Waka' who were also princesses of Calakmul. All this changed dramatically when the city entered the ninth century. Two major events occurred. The first was the end of Classic kingship. A line of divine shaman-kings had ruled El Perú–Waka' since its founding in the Protoclassic. Yet the line of kings appears to have failed in the early decades of the 800s. The last king is mentioned on a stela-altar pair dating to 801. Both Classic kings and their monumental history cease at this point (Guenter 2014a, 2014b). The second was a major shift in the city's settlement pattern (Marken 2015). Beginning in the 700s, the outlying districts of the city are abandoned, as the population apparently crowded behind the impressive natural defenses of the urban core (see Eppich 2015). The Late Classic city was a sprawling, low-density conurbation spread across both heights of the escarpment and the low-lying riverine plains. The Terminal Classic city was a densely packed and crowded settlement concentrated in the urban core. The outer portions of the city were largely abandoned in favor of the defensible center.

Still, it continued like this for another two hundred years, a dense urban concentration without kings. The end came slowly for El Perú–Waka', with a ragged and patchy abandonment that lasted for most of the tenth century. By AD 1000 the city consisted of deserted ruins, populated only by an apparent handful of hangers-on conducting small-scale rituals in the old heights of the Mirador Complex (Eppich 2011; Rich 2011).

Physically, the city consists of a nucleated mass of residential compounds and ritual precincts clustered around the broad, open spaces of Plaza 1 and Plaza 2 (Figure 9.2). Plaza 1, one of the largest public spaces in the Maya world, runs in a slight diagonal, northwest to southeast along an axis of 285 degrees. This is perpendicular to Maya north, the well-documented orientation of 18 degrees east of north known for Maya architecture and city-planning (Aveni 2001). The royal residence of the Northwest Palace anchors the northwestern corner of this open space. The ritual precinct of Plaza 2 balances its southeast edge with the twin pyramids of the Mirador Complex looming behind. Around this are roughly forty to fifty compounds of various sizes, ranging from sprawling palaces to modest house groups.

Structure density falls away dramatically as one moves away from the site core, especially off the top of the escarpment (see Marken 2015). Scattered across the riverine plains and broken karstic hills surrounding the core are another thirty or more compounds grouped together into irregular clusters. These are likely peripheral neighborhoods, living in the urban hinterland but attached to the city itself. This settlement fades away as one gets farther away from the center until these clusters grow larger and less common, transforming into a combination of satellite communities and rural villages.

The ruins today seem to be a combination of the Late Classic apogee of the

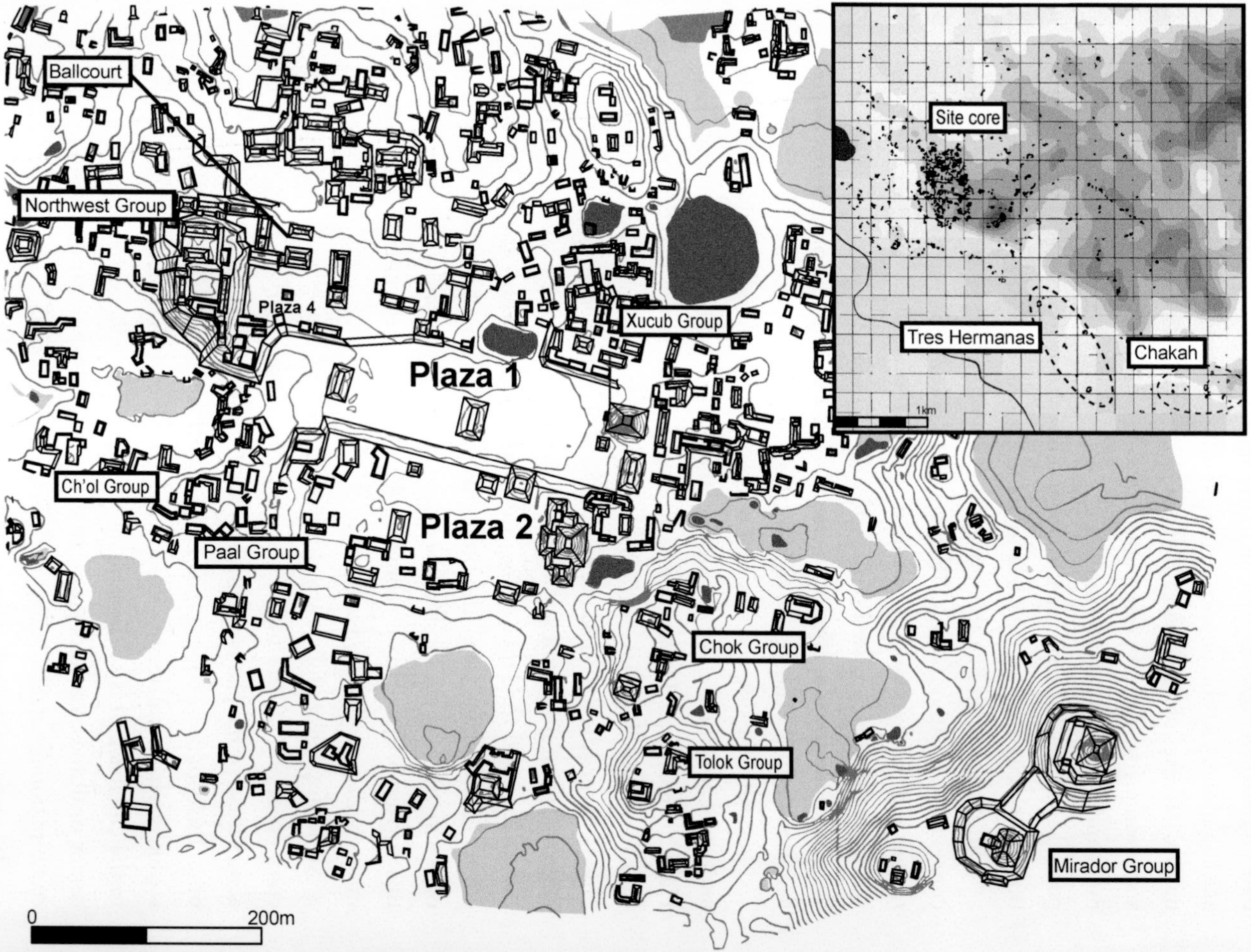

Figure 9.2. Map of El Perú-Waka'.

city itself in the periphery and the Terminal Classic nucleation in the urban core. Earlier settlement continues to be difficult to study, buried beneath large-scale later occupation. Archaeological investigations have generally focused on the site core, on its elite compounds and ritual architecture. More recent studies have expanded beyond the core (Eppich and Austin 2016; Marken and Maxson 2017; Menéndez 2017; Menéndez and Dakos 2017). Two clusters, in particular, have received archaeological attention: the Tres Hermanas Cluster located 0.5 km south of the core and the Chakah Cluster, located 1.5 km to the southeast of the core. Both neighborhoods are below the limestone escarpment, located adjacent to the riverine floodplains of the San Juan and San Pedro Mártir, respectively.

Distribution of Ceramic Types

The current ceramic database contains material from both the elite residences in the core and the commoner residences in the periphery. Total entries currently include 19,666 identifiable sherds recovered from domestic contexts. These contexts include residential middens, architectural fill, ritual deposits, feasting debris, and burials located inside the compounds. This study excludes material recovered from public ritual architecture, test pits, surface collections, and small-scale exploratory excavations. The ceramics themselves range from unslipped utilitarian vessels to high-end, fine polychromes. The ceramic tradition of El Perú–Waka' is especially rich and diverse, even for a Classic Maya city in the Petén (Eppich et al. 2017). The information from this database was used for Eppich and Freidel (2015) and an updated version was used for the current research. The data are limited to large assemblages from good contexts, which unfortunately excludes the Early and Intermediate Classic. Domestic assemblages from earlier periods in the city's history lie too deeply buried for easy access, and the current assemblages are too small, too fragmentary, and come from disturbed contexts.

For the Late and Terminal Classic periods, between AD 700 and 1000, the ceramic tradition at El Perú–Waka' goes through a series of dramatic changes (Figure 9.3; Eppich et al. 2017). Late Classic ceramics consist of co-occurring types and shape-classes termed the Q'eq' Complex, which dates from 600 to 800. The Q'eq' Complex includes a number of common monochrome types such as Tinaja Rojo, Azote Naranja, Infierno Negro, and Maquina Café. This is accompanied by a fairly limited suite of shape-classes: footed dishes and bowls,

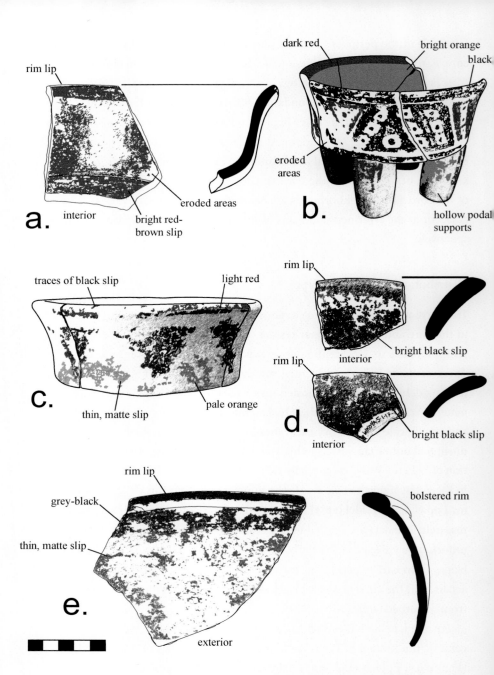

Figure 9.3. Late and Terminal Classic ceramic types: (*a*) Maquina Café rim sherd, (*b*) Late Classic Zacatal Cream Polychrome, (*c*) Terminal Classic Danta Naranja Polychrome, (*d*) Infierno Negro rim sherds, (*e*) Terminal Classic Achotes Negro rim sherd.

flat-bottomed cups and bowls, broad platters, and cylinder vases. Late Classic slips are brighter, glossier, and thinner than the slips that come before and after. They are often applied in a complex multislipping technique that is diagnostic for the Late Classic and produced the spectacular and famous Maya polychrome vessels.

The transitional period between the Late and Terminal Classic produced its own set of unique ceramic types and shape-classes. Termed the Morai Complex and dating from 770 to 820, these transitional ceramics include many of the Late Classic ceramics together with the pottery from the early portion of the Terminal Classic. Indeed, the Maya of the period continue to produce Late Classic types into the early years of the ninth century, a trend not evenly reported at other southern lowland sites. The Morai Complex is distinguished by a general decline in the frequency of the Late Classic monochrome types, accompanied by the rise in the frequency of Terminal Classic monochromes. Unique shapes and forms appear, including small tripod bowls and nearly flat presentation platters. Potters of the era used thin slips with carved and modeled designs appearing in greater frequencies.

This is followed by the ceramics of the Rax Complex, dating from 800 to 1000. Many of the Late Classic monochromes are still present, although in smaller frequencies. To this are added a number of Terminal Classic monochrome types, including Subin Rojo and Achotes Negro. These ceramics are notably lower-quality than their Late Classic counterparts. The surface slips are thin and low-gloss to matte. The slip is not well bonded to the underlying paste and flakes off in large sections, often referred to as "fugitive slips." The slip will even come off during casual handling. Unique forms appear, including rounded barrel forms, flat-bottomed bowls with outflaring sides, *molcajete* grater-bowls, ceiba-spiked censers, and utilitarian pots with thick bolstered rims. The bolstered rim itself is often the only slipped portion of the vessel.

The polychrome tradition continues into the Terminal Classic, but it changes dramatically. The polychrome pottery of the Rax Complex consists of thin, low-gloss and matte slips with simple geometric or curvilinear shapes (Figure 9.3). Compared to the pottery of the previous century, ninth- and tenth-century polychromes are simple, crude things, poorly executed. They do not use the Late Classic tradition of multiple thin slips. The decline in Maya polychromes corresponds to the rise of a new tradition: intricately carved, fine paste ceramics. These ceramics are the fine-gray and fine-orange vessels, possessing a compact and uniform paste with a very finely ground calcite temper. These vessels are both imported and locally manufactured. The introduction of fine paste ceramics indicates a technological shift in ceramic technology, as fine paste material represented a cheaper and higher-quality ceramic. The ceramic paste is compact and uniform enough to resist water, and the pottery does not need a slip to waterproof the surface. It is almost a stoneware ceramic.

These ceramics occur at different times and at different relative frequencies across the ancient city. While part of the same collective ceramic tradition, they are unlikely to have been produced by the same set of people or distributed through the same mechanisms. The distributional approach applied to the recovered ceramics established that most of the monochromes from the Late Classic Period were most likely distributed through marketing activity. This includes Tinaja Rojo and Infierno Negro, the most common Late Classic monochromes. They occur in roughly equivalent frequencies in household assemblages, regardless of the household's social rank. Another of these Late Classic monochromes, Maquina Café (Figure 9.3), is a brown-slipped ceramic with a hard, glossy, and bright slip (Callaghan and de Estrada 2016: 172; R. Smith and Gifford 1966:154). Its name comes from its lustrous red-brown color. Maquina Café is not a prestige ceramic but a pretty, fairly utilitarian piece of serving ware. Its forms include small bowls and large plates. It is not as common as Tinaja Rojo or Infierno Negro, but this type appears across the site and in roughly equivalent frequencies (Figure 9.4). It generally makes up 6% of the assemblage, with a standard deviation of 3.4%. This seems fairly true across the city, from the Northwest Palace (6%) to the humble farmers of Chakah (7.6%). The exception to this appears to be the Chok Group, which currently lacks large eighth-century ceramic assemblages. Still, the most likely explanation for the site-wide distribution of Maquina Café is marketing activity. This makes it similar to most of the Late Classic monochrome ceramics. In fact, the only monochromes that do not show this pattern are those types that occur so rarely as to make any analysis currently impossible.

This pattern, reflective of marketing distribution, does not apply to Late Classic polychromes. The distribution and frequency of polychromes stand in stark contrast to the monochromes. It has long been argued that such polychromes circulated in a prestige-gift economy (Brumfiel and Earle, eds. 1987; Foias and Bishop 2007; Halperin 2014; King and Shaw 2015; Potter and King 1995; Reents-Budet 2008; Reents-Budet et al. 1994; Scarborough and Valdez 2009). Scholars have documented specialized polychrome workshops directly attached to elite residences (Ball and Taschek 1992; Halperin and Foias 2010, 2012; Reents-Budet

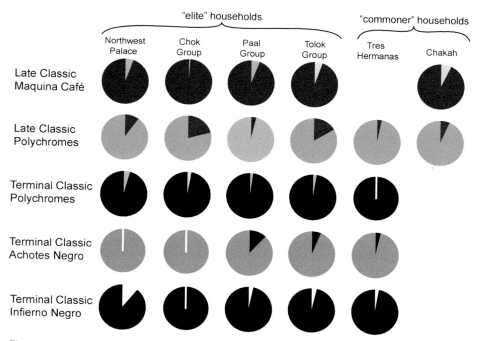

Figure 9.4. Ceramic frequencies.

et al. 2000). Archaeologists have recovered ceramic vessels belonging to rulers in nonroyal contexts (Callaghan 2013; Eppich 2011; Taschek and Ball 1992).

The distribution of Late Classic polychromes appears to support this, matching what one would expect from a redistributive economy. While polychromes are found at all households excavated to date, they occur at much higher frequencies in elite residences. Polychromes range from 11 to 21% of recovered identifiable ceramic assemblages at three elite residences. At "commoner" households, it is a paltry 3 to 6% for Tres Hermanas and Chakah, respectively. Tres Hermanas, in particular, was the home of very poor Maya, people literally at the edge of Late and Terminal Classic society (see Eppich and Austin 2016). These people mattered less to royal authority than did the elites at Chok or Tolok. Curiously, the Paal Group has only 3.7% of its Late Classic assemblage as polychromes. This is more in line with the downscale inhabitants of Tres Hermanas and Chakah than with their fellow elites and might have something to do with the Paal Group's unusual social position. Unlike other groups, the Paal Group seems to have housed a socially mobile group, a social lineage that began as sixth-century commoners and then became eighth-century elites (Eppich 2011). Perhaps they existed as wealthy commoners rather than storied nobles, thus lacking the social connections of their peers. At any rate, they do not appear to be fully integrated into the redistributive mechanisms of a polychrome prestige-gift economy.

The economy appears to go through a series of dramatic changes as it entered the ninth century. Terminal Classic polychromes reveal a very different distribution from the Late Classic antecedents and do not occur often, representing an average of 3% of ninth-century domestic assemblages with a standard deviation of ±3%. Such regularity suggests distribution through marketing activity, not elite redistribution. This shift was suggested during the 2015 statistical analysis, but the low frequencies of Terminal Classic polychromes returned anomalous, unusual ANOVA F-statistics (Eppich and Freidel 2015). The data here imply that polychrome distribution changed: the majority of the ninth-century polychromes circulated through commerce, especially with the households in the site core. The cause for this shift is likely related to the decline of the royal court. Classic kingship ended at the site in the early ninth century, with the abandonment of the Northwest Palace following a generation or two afterward. Perhaps polychromes were both distributed as gifts and sold in the markets, but the end of the prestige-gift economy followed the end of the royal court, leaving only commercial polychromes.

At any rate, the markets are clearly operating at Terminal Classic El Perú–Waka'. The 2015 statistical analysis argued that the fine paste ceramics were being distributed through marketing activity, as were some monochrome ceramics: Tinaja Rojo and Maquina Café (Eppich and Freidel 2015). However, other ceramics appear to diverge from this pattern. One of these is Achotes Negro. The ceramic type itself is typical of Terminal Classic monochromes, possessing a thin, low-gloss to matte slip (Figure 9.3, see Sabloff 1975:181). It is a low-quality ceramic; while never very common, its distribution across the site is decidedly uneven. Achotes Negro is absent from two of the largest elite residences, the Northwest Palace, and the Chok Group and is concentrated in the Paal Group, composing 13% of that compound's identifiable ceramics. Small amounts occur in the Tres Hermanas and Tolok groups: 6.6 and 3.6%, respectively. These results most closely conform to the pattern expected for barter exchange (Figure 9.1) and suggest that this ceramic was manufactured at or near the Paal Group or that the Paal Group possessed preferential access to Achotes Negro (for parallel arguments, see Chapter 17). The elite household may have exchanged ceramics with the inhabitants of the Tres Hermanas and Tolok groups, to the exclusion of Chok and the Northwest Palace. There is of course no way to verify this directional exchange; alternatively, Achotes Negro could have circulated within a limited redistributive pattern. Nevertheless, it suggests simpler mechanisms of exchange than those used for other contemporary ceramics.

Another monochrome black type with unusual distribution is Terminal Classic Infierno Negro. The ceramic type is a fairly high-quality monochrome with a glossy, lustrous black slip (Figure 9.3, see also Sabloff 1975:118). During the Late Classic, this ceramic occurs with a roughly even distribution and similar frequency across the seventh- and eighth-century city. By the ninth century, however, Infierno Negro's distribution shrinks. It appears in frequency only at a single residential compound, the royal Northwest Palace (Figure 9.4). It is completely absent from Chok and appears only in trace amounts elsewhere. This is the pattern expected for autarky, but autarky seems unusual for such a well-made ceramic. One explanation may lie in the Northwest Palace itself. The number of high-quality polychromes found across the site in the Late Classics hints at the presence of a royal ceramic workshop, somewhere in the vicinity of the royal residence (compare C. Halperin and Foias 2010). Test pits placed along the northern side of the Northwest Palace encountered a large number of high-quality polychrome sherds, suggesting a nearby pottery workshop. This workshop would the source of many of the Late Classic polychromes mentioned above and could be the source of the Terminal Classic Infierno Negro sherds. Experienced potters there may have produced vessels for use by the postroyal inhabitants of the palace. Indeed, the potters may have been the postroyal inhabitants of the Northwest Palace. Again, the turn toward autarkic systems suggests a decline in economic complexity for the Terminal Classic city.

Discussion and Conclusion

An economy is a series of relationships between individuals and social units concerning the disposition of goods and services. They make decisions about their respective roles as producers, distributors, and consumers. Collectively, society determines how materials are distributed and how to build a system of material inequality. To do this requires answering a series of questions. Who or what determines value? What, if anything, will function as currency? What are the actual logistics involved in moving goods and services? Who is to be trusted? Who is not to be trusted? The answers to these questions, decided consciously or not, address the actual function of the system, the "nuts and bolts" of the mechanisms of exchange. For the Classic Maya, the ruins of this system left behind a substantial and confusing material culture. It includes lithics found far from their geologic point of origin: basalt metates and obsidian blades from the highlands, found scattered in large quantities across the lowlands. It includes marine shell and oceanic fish recovered hundreds of kilometers from the coast and ceramics chemically sourced to one side of the Maya world yet found on the other. If stones and ceramics crossed the ancient Maya world, then the staples of production did so as well. Corn, salt, cotton, tobacco, and chocolate would not survive in the archaeological record, yet they circulated in substantial quantities. There are considerable field systems documented from northern Belize that seem to have produced agricultural products far in excess of local needs (Guderjan et al. 2017). There are large-scale saltworks that produced enough salt for hundreds of thousands of people (McKillop 1995, 2005; Woodfill et al. 2015; see also Andrews and Mock 2002). The Classic Maya economy was clearly a complex, sizable affair. The challenge posed to archaeology today is to use the remains of this complex system to identify the economic relationships that existed in antiquity.

The distribution of ceramic types across the urban landscape of El Perú–Waka' seems to reflect the complexity of this system. It is an imperfect perspective, to be sure. However, it does show distinct patterns present in the distribution of ceramic types in domestic contexts. It argues for commercial exchange for many of the identifiable ceramics, supplemented by different types of exchange at different points in time. For the Late Classic, there seems to be substantial marketing activity. Alongside this marketing existed a redistributive system moving elaborate polychromes in a prestige-gift exchange. This redistributive system was likely connected to the operation of the royal court and its elite imitators. It ceased to exist as the royal court ceased to exist in the early ninth century. For the remaining centuries of the Terminal Classic, other ceramic elements moved away from marketing, being distributed through barter or autarky. In turn, this suggests that the overall urban economy became less complex as it moved from the eighth century into the ninth.

Out of these ceramic patterns emerges a partial economic history of a Classic Maya city. The data are far from complete and less than fully clear, but these results define complex patterns of significance to scholarship on Pre-Columbian Maya economies. The distribution and frequency of ceramic types at El Perú–Waka' not only reveal the nuts and bolts of this city's ancient economy but reflect various mechanisms of exchange that may have coexisted and/or changed through time. The transition over time seems to move from more complex mechanisms, redistribution and commerce, toward less complex mechanisms, barter and autarky. This would indicate that the economy of the city entered a serious decline in the ninth century, sharp enough to allow the rise of alternative economic relationships.

Such patterns likely occurred on a regional level (see Stark and Garraty 2010). Across the ninth-century Maya lowlands, ceramics reflect a declining, fragmented Terminal Classic regional economy. Ceramic types and shape-classes no longer exhibit the broad and distant distributions observed for those of the Late Classic. Terminal Classic Maya pottery reflects a limited and highly localized distribution (P. Rice 1987a; Masson and Mock 2004). The localization and regionalization of ninth- and tenth-century ceramics has long been noted by Maya scholarship. During the 1965 Guatemala City conference, Gordon Willey and his colleagues noted the "increasing regionalism" and "fragmentation of the ceramic tradition" of Terminal Classic ceramics (Willey et al. 1967:301, 311). This early study proposed the organization of the Maya pottery traditions into "ceramic spheres," labels designed to indicate a high degree of content similarity between the ceramic attributes of contemporaneous sites. For the Late Classic, they called the ceramic sphere Tepeu and noted that this period represented one of "maximum ceramic elaboration and development" (Willey et al. 1967:299–300). In the ninth century the Tepeu sphere divides and fragments. Donald Forsyth (2005) focused on the divisions of the Late Classic patterns, noting how it can be separated into eastern and western groups during the transition into the Terminal Classic (see also P. Rice and Forsyth 2004). Afterward, the spheres completely fragmented into isolated ceramic traditions through the Terminal Classic Petén.

Forsyth suspected that ceramic spheres were the result of economic activity, an idea embraced in the El Perú–Waka' studies. Freidel and I (Eppich and Freidel 2015) proposed that the Classic ceramic spheres were the result of interconnected market systems, the widespread commonalities in potting traditions caused by the circulation of both pottery and potters from market to market. Furthermore, this regional commercial exchange functioned as a key ecological adaptation to sustaining a complex society in a tropical rainforest (see also Freidel and Shaw 2000; Freidel et al. 2002, 2016). The regionalization noted by Willey and detailed by Forsyth thus represents the disintegration of the regional commercial economy and the end of this crucial environmental adaptation. The ties of commerce and communication between Maya communities badly frayed and, in many cases, failed entirely. This is likely a result of endemic warfare and the military violence of the eighth-century lowlands. These combined factors turned the countryside into a "landscape of fear": sites were selected for their defensibility, and unprotected overland travel became a dangerous enterprise (Demarest 2006:85, 147; see also O'Mansky and Dunning 2004). It would be only natural to shift trade routes away from the countryside to the coasts and big rivers (but see Chapter 20). The shift to safer waterborne commerce at this time has long been noticed within subregions of the Maya lowlands (Healy et al. 1984; Jackson and McKillop 1989; McKillop 1989, 2005). As the Great Western Route and Río San Pedro Mártir failed, traders used the Belizean coast to the east and the Usumacinta and Gulf Coast in the west. The crossroads that had sustained El Perú–Waka' through the Classic Period ceased to matter.

The economic pinch felt by El Perú–Waka' seems reflected in the ceramic patterns described above. Behind its 80-meter escarpment, the city might have been protected from any marauding armies, but it was vulnerable as trade routes shifted and interlocked market systems began to fail. While the city's economy still possessed a commercial element, simpler economic mechanisms began to emerge. Ceramics are just proxies for the economic exchange of other goods that did not survive in the archaeological record. If pottery changed from complex to more simple exchange, it is very likely that the distribution mechanisms for key goods such as salt, tobacco, stone, and meat were similarly affected. If simpler economic systems distributed black-slipped bowls, it is likely that simpler, less-efficient systems also distributed the staple crops that sustained Classic society. The ceramic patterns for the Terminal Classic urban landscape hint that it might have gotten harder to buy corn. One might not necessarily have been able to walk into the market and make a purchase. Perhaps to get corn it was necessary to know who had it and who could be trusted to deliver it. Perhaps people just went hungry.

This conclusion is the polar opposite of the one reached by Jeremy Sabloff and William Rathje from their work on Cozumel Island (Sabloff and Rathje 1975, 1980). They argued for the "rise of a Maya merchant class" following the collapse of the southern centers. Viewed from the perspective of the twenty-first century, there was no rise of a Maya merchant class. Rather, it seems likely that Sabloff and Rathje documented the rise of a new commercial center in the north. For the same period, down in the south, we appear to be studying the decline of an old one.

Many issues in the study of the Classic economy remain outstanding, and the ideas raised here require further testing and analysis. To what degree are the ceramic patterns indicative of alternative exchange mechanisms? Were polychromes limited to a single mechanism of exchange? How representative are the ceramic patterns of this single Classic era city? As research continues at El Perú–Waka', will these patterns hold true? Where was the ancient marketplace? Was there a polychrome ceramic workshop north of the royal palace? What mode of local governance replaced the Classic kings in the ninth century? How can we recover sizable samples from the Early Classic? One thing that is certain is that we cannot return to a simplistic view of the Classic Maya economy. The Classic city-states operated according to economic structures comparable to many analogous civilizations of the Old World. To understand what took place inside these cities, Mayanist scholars would benefit from a comparative approach, considering similarities and differences in the economic organization of the great civilizations of ancient Greece and Rome, Iron Age India, Bronze Age China, and even the great trading states of Southeast Asia. Continued research at El Perú–Waka' will focus on the changing urban settlement, the Terminal Classic government, and the ever-changing social landscape of the old city. Accordingly, research will remain focused on the economic systems that were intertwined with these other aspects of society at this center. An improved understanding of Classic era Maya civilization must not only determine how economic mechanisms functioned but also consider how the nuts and bolts of the systems physically worked, how and when they came together, and, finally, how they flew apart at the very end.

Acknowledgments

Since 2003 the historical and archaeological sequence of the ancient city has been reconstructed by scholars attached to the Proyecto Arqueológico Regional El Perú–Waka'. This archaeological project represents a collection of six co-directors representing six institutions spread across two countries, cooperatively committed to archaeological research, public outreach, rainforest conservation, graduate education, and the protection of the national patrimony of the Republic of Guatemala.

10

Large-Scale Production of Basic Commodities at Salinas de los Nueve Cerros, Guatemala

Implications for Ancient Maya Political Economy

BRENT K. S. WOODFILL

Salinas de los Nueve Cerros is a Classic Maya city located at the base of the Guatemalan highlands, surrounding a salt dome and brine stream that was the only noncoastal salt source in the Maya lowlands (Figure 10.1, Dillon 1977; Dillon et al. 1988; Woodfill et al. 2015). Nueve Cerros is found in the exceptionally fertile Chixoy River valley, and its residents were able to take advantage of the thick soil deposits brought from the volcanic highlands that filled the seasonal swamps that dot the floodplain. At the time of the Spanish conquest, the region surrounding Nueve Cerros was still well known for its agricultural potential, serving as an important source of cacao, vanilla, cotton, and achiote (Caso and Aliphat 2006; Demarest et al. 2014; Van Akkeren 2012). While the city was occupied it likely served as a breadbasket for downriver cities (Dillon 1985) in addition to providing warm-weather agricultural goods that were not possible to grow in the neighboring highlands to the south.

In addition to the local resources that would have been available to the city's residents, Nueve Cerros was located at a strategic position for interregional exchange. The Chixoy River was part of the Great Western Trade Route (Demarest and Fahsen 2002; see also R.E.W. Adams 1978; Arnauld 1990; Hammond 1972; Seler 1993), a network of rivers and valleys that connected most of the western Maya world that was used for transporting a variety of other highland goods into the lowland market, particularly obsidian, jade, pyrite, and exotic feathers (Andrieu and Forné 2010; Demarest and Barrientos 2002; Hammond 1972; Woodfill and Andrieu 2012). This led to increased competition for control of

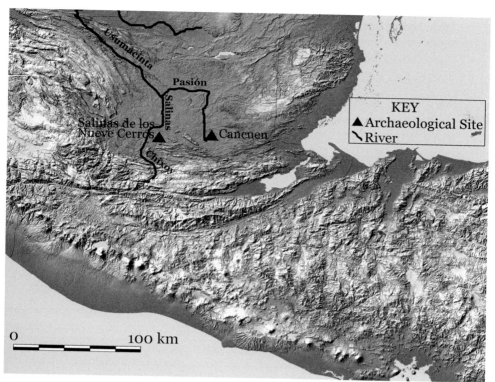

Figure 10.1. The location of Salinas de los Nueve Cerros (map produced by Marc Wolf).

these routes in the centuries before the Classic collapse (Demarest 2006, 2013; Demarest et al. 2007; Demarest and Fahsen 2002; Woodfill 2010; Woodfill and Andrieu 2012) that escalated into the destruction of Dos Pilas and the larger Petexbatún Kingdom beginning in AD 760. While the Pasión-Usumacinta route appears to have been the most heavily used through the Classic Period (Demarest 2006, 2013; Freidel et al. 2007), this branch would have been an important source for agricultural goods, salt, and other locally produced commodities as well as an alternate route connecting the highlands and lowlands.

In this chapter I briefly summarize the organization of Classic Maya salt production at Nueve Cerros before discussing the role that salt played in other parts of the local economy and the other major economic activities that occurred there. Since the project is ongoing, this is a preliminary model, albeit one that has become more refined over the past seven years of research at the site by the current archaeological project.

Salt Production

The economic and geographic center of Salinas de los Nueve Cerros was always its saltworks, which consisted of a brine stream that regularly refreshes several salt flats as it flows towards the Chixoy River. The brine spring, in turn, is born from several salt springs on the western slope of a massive salt dome covering 3 km^2 and rising nearly 200 m above the surrounding swampland. Its proximity to the river allowed for its salt to be easily exploited and commercialized. The river and the salt source have been intertwined at least as far back as the Spanish conquest, as evidenced by the changing of the name of the Chixoy to the Salinas River after the inclusion of the Nueve Cerros brine.

The earliest evidence of occupation at Nueve Cerros dates to ca. 800 BC (Woodfill et al. 2015) and is found in two distinct areas: the banks of the Chixoy River and a narrow, low ridge between the Classic saltworks and a ridge with multiple freshwater springs. By the Late Classic Period (AD 600–850), both of these areas were incorporated into a sprawling urban center (Figure 10.2) covering over 50 km^2 surrounding the salt source (Woodfill et al. 2017), with the former serving as a port and the latter as the site epicenter. In the intervening years the salt production area was heavily modified. An artificial stepped platform that contained upward of 1,200,000 m^2 of artificial fill abutted the western slope of the salt dome (Figure 10.3); it was topped by 24 structures that served as workshops and administrative buildings. During excavations undertaken there in the 1970s, Brian Dillon was able to document the salt-making process at Nueve Cerros, which appears to have remained relatively unchanged throughout the Classic Period (Dillon 1979, 1981b; Dillon et al. 1988; Woodfill et al. 2015).

The primary commodity that the brine was transformed into was a hard salt cake shaped into either a flat, round loaf or a narrow cone. Ceramic molds (classified as Cotebal Red for the loaf shape and Tzaquib Unslipped for the cone) were placed atop long, narrow ovens. As the contents boiled down, they would have been periodically topped off with fresh brine until the mold contained a solid loaf of the desired thickness, at which point the molds were broken and the finished product set aside.

There was some temporal and seasonal variation. The Maya likely scraped the salt flats and apparently brought the underlying soil onto the platform in the off season to leach the minerals out of it. By the Late Classic they had constructed dozens of specialized vessels: Atzam Red bowls that were among the

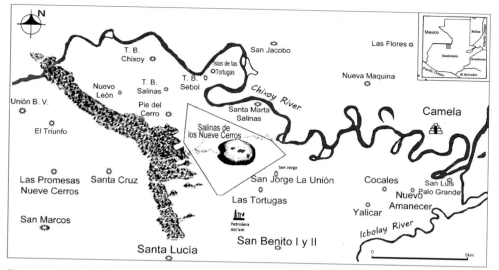

Figure 10.2. Salinas de los Nueve Cerros, showing location of the salt production zone (map produced by Carlos Efraín Tox Tiul).

Figure 10.3. Salt production zone (map produced by Marc Wolf).

largest ceramic artifacts of the New World, with thick walls and diameters approaching 2 m. These would have held the brine used to refill the molds, while allowing for some solar evaporation in order to reduce the boiling time (Dillon et al. 1988; Woodfill et al. 2015).

Evidence of Elite Control of Classic Period Salt Production

Multiple administrative structures containing well-stocked tombs of important individuals were scattered throughout the salt production zone, both on the surface and in buried earlier construction episodes. The occupant of Tomb 5, for example, was an important figure from the Early Classic who was buried with ceramic vessels and jade offerings. In order for him to continue to be active after his death, his face was removed and likely stuccoed and displayed in a visible location. During Late Classic renovations, the tomb was reopened and the face was placed back atop his skull along with multiple new offerings: 24 crude ceramic "finger bowls," 29 human finger bones, 26 obsidian prismatic blades, and a clam shell (Dillon et al. 1985; Woodfill et al. 2015)—likely the vestiges of a mass autoamputation ceremony.

The elites at Nueve Cerros tightly controlled both access to the salt source and salt production itself throughout the Classic Period if not before. The structure containing Tomb 5 was overlain by Late Classic administrative structures that were associated with salt production workshops. The salt production zone itself was adjacent to the site epicenter and other areas of monumental architecture. While there are a few convincing examples for elite goods being produced in attached workshops (Andrieu 2008, 2009b; Andrieu et al. 2014; Andrieu and Forné 2010; Aoyama 2009; Demarest et al. 2014; Emery and Aoyama 2007; Foias 2002; Inomata 2001; Inomata and Triadan 2000) at Nueve Cerros we can see that the elites were associating themselves directly with the production of a good that is definitively not elite.

This does not suggest, however, that the elites were themselves producing the salt. It is a remedial, unpleasant job: in addition to scraping the hot, blindingly white salt flats and collecting the underlying soil to leach out and accumulated minerals, workers would have spent their time doing other equally remedial and unpleasant tasks. These included tending the fire and refilling the molds as well as perpetually hauling firewood and fresh brine from the stream to feed the flames and refill the massive Atzam Red bowls found throughout the platform.

The reality of the salt-making process does not lend itself to elite participation, not only because of the level of discomfort involved in salt production but also because it required little specialized knowledge that might confer status upon its practitioners. There is ample evidence in the Classic Maya world that the elite class was more interested in symbolic control than in actual participation in management and physical labor (Andrieu et al. 2014; Aoyama 2007, 2009; Demarest 2006; Inomata 2001; Lucero 1999). It appears that Nueve Cerros is no exception. Instead, members of the Classic elite seem to have been interested in marking their presence through architecture, tombs, and likely "supervising" the actual workshop activities rather than by directly participating in the production itself.

Derivative Salt-Working Industries at Nueve Cerros

Specialized "overhang" manos and metates (Figure 10.4) were identified as part of both Prehispanic and rural contemporary salt production in Guatemala by Blanca Mijangos (2014), and 64 have been recovered in neighborhoods throughout the site to date from mound groups representing a large swath of the local socioeconomic scale. These tools, which all still contained salt residue on their tested surfaces (Mijangos 2014), were used to grind the salt cakes into small grains, which would have served a variety of functions. Along the river, for example, the residents who received the finished cakes could have produced dried, salted fish. Unfortunately, neither fish scales nor bones have been recovered through flotation of multiple soil samples, likely due to the high acidity of the soil, but there are multiple lines of evidence pointing to this being an important local industry.

1. Each of the excavated mound groups shows evidence of large-scale fishing, including large numbers of fishing weights.
2. Two of the mound groups had evidence of specialized obsidian biface production that Edgar Carpio suggested were used as fish descalers (Woodfill et al. 2015).
3. This stretch of the Chixoy contains some of the best fishing grounds in the Guatemalan interior (Dillon 1981a). During his reconnoitering on the northern banks of the river in 2015, project member Alex Rivas reported that the residents there collected an average of 10 kg of fish per person in weirs and creeks after every time the river floods. They said that if they did not collect these fish the entire valley would soon smell of dead fish.

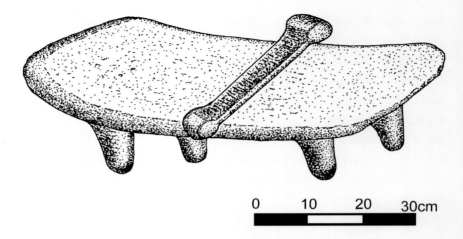

Figure 10.4. Overhang mano and metate for grinding down salt cakes (illustrated by Carlos Efraín Tox Tiul).

Neighborhoods in the rest of the site also appear to have been loci for secondary commodities involving salt due to the presence of the same grinding tools. At least one group in the southern part of the site had a dense concentration of obsidian scrapers along with the overhang manos and metates. This neighborhood was far from the river but near a vast swath of land that was archaeologically "empty" but was likely used for agriculture and arboriculture—which would have been prime grounds for hunting or animal husbandry. The presence of specialized salt-working equipment there indicates that they also depended on large quantities of finished salt made in elite workshops, which was likely used in preserving meat and/or hides. As in the case of the fish, though, it appears that there was little actual or symbolic elite involvement beyond providing the salt.

The Nonbrine Necessities of the Nueve Cerros Salt Industry

Although it is possible to examine the degree to which the salt production was embedded within the larger political system, it is difficult to reconstruct the scale of the salt production directly. There are no physical records, and the salt production zone was constantly being rebuilt and renovated and has been the focus of minimal excavations (Dillon 1979, 1990; Dillon et al. 1988). As a result, any attempts to quantify the salt output would have to take into account at least four factors that would have served as practical constraints on the Nueve Cerros salt industry: the availability of the necessary raw materials, the available labor, the market demand, and the scale and quality of ritual offerings associated with production. The last three are currently impossible to address fully, because they would necessitate both a nuanced reconstruction of shifting trade networks and detailed population estimates for the Nueve Cerros urban zone as well as much of the western Maya world. It is possible, however, to identify the raw materials required to examine the first avenue of inquiry, so that issue is addressed here.

The salt source in the Nueve Cerros site core appears to have been limitless for all intents and purposes. Dillon et al. (1988:42) estimated that about 6,000 metric tons would have been available just by scraping the salt flats throughout the dry season. Most of the brine continues to flow past the salt flats and into the Chixoy. The last formal lessee of the Nueve Cerros salt rights in the 1930s told Andrews (1983:99) that he could have produced up to 250 metric tons a year had he the necessary labor and equipment. For comparison, the entire republic of Guatemala produced about 9,000 metric tons of salt per year in the early twentieth century, which was enough to supply about 90% of the national demand (United States Department of Commerce 1917:712).

Although the brine was not a limiting factor, the salt production techniques would have necessitated other inputs that could serve as a better guide. The primary commodity created from the brine was a hard salt cake in the shape of a round, flat loaf or a narrow cone. The fundamental process for making each was fundamentally the same and would have required only firewood and ceramic molds in addition to the brine. Tovilla (2000:105) did note the addition of cornmeal into the colonial-era salt cakes at Sacapulas in highland Guatemala. If the Maya of Nueve Cerros did something similar, it could have further reduced cooking time but would not result in anything radically different. In order to make the molds, the potters would have needed two additional ingredients—clay and temper—as well as additional firewood.

Although the saltworks would have depended upon the mass production of these molds, the raw materials that went into them appear to have been as functionally limitless as the brine. Nueve Cerros is in a deep, clay-lined river valley and the Chixoy River carries large quantities of pumice and sand from farther upriver (Brian Dillon, personal communication 2011), which served as the principal temper for all the site's ceramics—including the molds. Thus, both clay and temper were readily available. This is fortunate, because it appears that the molds were single-use. The molds for the round loaves had an interior red slip, which presumably prevented the salt from sticking to the ceramic surface, but they also had an incurved lip that would have prevented the loaf from separating from the mold without breaking it. The conical molds were shoddily and quickly constructed without any internal slip and would have been too fragile to reuse, in addition to being difficult to remove without breakage. As a result, each mold represented a single salt cake: the salt workers would have needed a well-organized industry to mass produce them.

It is immediately clear that firewood is the primary input that could limit salt production on-site. As a further complication, wood is necessary for myriad activities at Nueve Cerros. The standard architecture at the site eschewed masonry vaults for perishable structures with wattle and daub walls and wooden beams, so much of the wood that could have gone into salt production was diverted to constructing and renovating structures throughout Nueve Cerros.

Firewood was necessary for making stucco, which was rare but present at the site, as well as the ubiquitous figurines and all of the other ceramic vessels throughout the site, which were often exported to other cities and regions (Woodfill et al. 2015). Possibly the largest portion of wood consumption on site, however, would have been for the daily household hearth fires. The tropical environment makes food storage problematic for obvious reasons, so it is necessary to cook fresh food daily. Based on the analysis that Lentz et al. (2014) conducted at Tikal, it appears that the residents of Nueve Cerros would have needed about 840 kg of firewood each year for each person just to feed themselves.

With regard to the salt production needs, McCracken and Smith (1998; see Woodfill et al. 2015:170) proposed a 15% efficiency for boiling brine in ceramic vessels, meaning that for every metric ton of salt it would be necessary to have 6.67 metric tons of firewood in ideal conditions. The amount of firewood needed to make each mold in the standard Maya open kiln was similarly daunting—5.2 kg of wood for each vessel. Using Cotebal Red as a guideline, a typical salt cake would have been about 0.02 m^3 and weighed 28.84 kg. This estimate assumes that the salt cake is mostly sodium chloride, which weighs 1,442 kg/m^3, meaning that each metric ton of salt would have necessitated about 35 molds, bringing the total firewood consumption to 6,852 kg per metric ton.

Proyecto Salinas de los Nueve Cerros is currently in the process of reconstructing changing patterns of land use in the site and its environs that we hope will allow us to reconstruct the quantity of available firewood and the management strategies that its residents employed. Until this investigation is finished, however, we are limited to another way to reconstruct the scale of the salt production: the quantity of molds present on site. Dillon excavated the salt production zone in addition to two elite residences near the northern slope of the salt dome in the 1970s (Dillon 1977, 1979, 1990; Dillon et al. 1988). He analyzed "slightly over 7000 sherds" from these contexts for his dissertation (Dillon 1979:25), which ranged from Late Preclassic through Terminal Classic. The two types of ceramic molds, which are were in use beginning in the Early Classic, composed nearly a third of the total assemblage (Cotebal Red 18%, Tzaquib Unslipped 13%).

Although the current archaeological project has not yet been able to return to this part of the site, the anecdotal evidence does support this ratio. Architectural fill, inevitably with multiple Cotebal and Tzaquib sherds, is visible in tractor scars and looters' pits and is eroding into the brine stream where it cuts through the platform and washes into the salt flats below. With an estimated 1,200,000 cubic meters of this fill underlying the salt production zone (Woodfill et al. 2015), there could be more than 300,000 cubic meters of mold fragments, representing over 920 million metric tons of salt, which would in turn have necessitated about 6.3 billion metric tons of firewood.

Future investigations will surely be able to replace this thought experiment with hard data, but it is nonetheless clear at present that salt was a massive industry at Nueve Cerros. While salt and derivative products were the primary commodities the city's residents traded in, within Nueve Cerros firewood likely outstripped everything else in value. In order to produce both salt and salt molds, the workshops would have been dependent not only on the immediate environs around Nueve Cerros but on a massive catchment area surrounding it.

Implications for Classic Maya Politics

Although the investigations of Classic Period Nueve Cerros are still ongoing, it is possible to isolate several major implications for our understanding of the Classic Maya economy based on what we already know. Fundamentally, the production and exchange of salt defined the site's layout, politics, and economy. Salt was produced at a massive scale and was tightly controlled by the city's elite, as evinced by the administrative and other monumental structures in and around the salt production zone.

Interestingly, the derivative industries (salted fish, leather or dried meat, etc.) that were the focus of work in the other neighborhoods throughout the site showed no such elite investment. Although elite involvement in the quotidian economy at Nueve Cerros seems to have been limited to salt production, by controlling this one commodity the elite would have inserted themselves into nearly every other economic activity that the city's residents were involved in. Salt is not only a commodity in and of itself but an ingredient in myriad others, including preserved organics and dyed textiles. Investigations in neighborhoods throughout the site have recovered evidence of large-scale production of dried fish, meat, and leather, all of which would have necessitated the use of salt. In other words, by controlling access to the salt source and doling out the final product, the site elite indirectly controlled the settlement's derivative industries without the need for actual involvement in the minutiae of these other production chains.

This investiture and involvement in the quotidian economy would explain some of the idiosyncrasies in the archaeology of Nueve Cerros—the relative dearth of hieroglyphic texts, public monuments, and fine architecture seen in its lowland contemporaries. Because of their control over the production and distribution of salt, elites did not need to invest in the more typical status-reinforcing public ritual displays for the benefit of their populace, since their citizens depended on them to obtain the salt that served as the basic economic engine of the city.

Finally, and to reiterate the main point, while salt was the primary commodity produced by residents of Nueve Cerros, this entire industry was built upon a foundation of firewood. Unlike the other "ingredients" used to produce salt (brine, clay, temper, and sun), firewood was a limited resource that required a controlled and organized management plan. The extent to which members of the elite were involved in creating and implementing this plan is unclear, but it is likely that they were involved in managing forest resource use around the settlement.

Conclusions

Nueve Cerros offers a unique perspective for understanding Classic Maya economics, as it is the only lowland urban center directly associated with a basic commodity. Salt was not only a nutritional necessity but also a desired condiment and was essential to other related material industries. By controlling the salt source, the Nueve Cerros elite not only made themselves an integral part of the Classic lowland economy but they became involved in derivative industries (that required salt) within their home city. In this respect, political power strategies at Nueve Cerros contrasted with most of its contemporaries. As at Cancuén, there was little investment in temple construction, although there is some evidence of cave ritual conducted by residents within a nearby ridge (Schwab 2013; Schwab et al. 2012) and the northern part of the site has multiple Preclassic pyramids (Woodfill et al. 2015). But most of the monumentality and public works investment at the site was focused on the salt production area and the individuals interred there.

However, the elites of Nueve Cerros, despite their specialized role in oversight of salt production and related industries, also derived power as intermediaries with the external world of exchange, as was common for Maya lowlands sites. Yet, instead of offering public ritual displays promoting the elites' role as intermediaries between the human and supernatural realm, they primarily served as intermediaries of a more secular nature, providing a mineral essential to life and the foundations of the site's economy.

III

Agriculture, Climate, Land

11

Gardens of the Maya

ANDREW R. WYATT

Many anthropologists recognize that one of the most important and fundamental elements of the economy, particularly in precapitalist societies, is the household (Netting 1993:58–60; Robin 2003:308; Wilk 1991:8; Yanagisako 1979). But how we define the household is a matter of disagreement and debate. Wilk's (1988:136) definition of a household is "an activity group in which the basic economic functions of production, consumption, inheritance, biological reproduction, and shelter are organized and carried out," and most tend to agree upon these basic functions. However, households are dynamic institutions: their structure, function, and meaning can change over time and space. Economic or political reorganization can lead to changes in household form. For example, precolonial households in much of Mesoamerica were often multifamily, multigenerational structures that were forcibly restructured as single-family units by the Spanish in the postcolonial era (Restall 1997; Wilk 1988). The household is not a static entity or "a corporate thing with the boundaries and motivation of an individual" (Wilk 1991:34). Households are embedded in economic and social networks, and changes in the political economy are often reflected in the organization of the household, although how these changes manifest varies spatially and chronologically (Arnould and Netting 1982; Robin 2003; Wilk 1991).

The basic Mesoamerican household—at least until relatively recently—generally consists of one or more residential structures with several outbuildings (e.g., kitchen, storage, ritual) situated around an open plaza (Ashmore and Wilk 1988; Schwartz 1990; Wilk 1991; Chapter 5 in this volume). Households are the primary locus of economic and subsistence activities in the Maya area, both in the past (McAnany 1993b; Wilk and Ashmore 1988) and among the historic and contemporary Maya (Farriss 1984; Redfield and Villa Rojas 1971; Restall 1997).

Household archaeology has focused on this basic cultural institution to understand different aspects of ancient Maya life, including gender (L. S. Neff 2002; Robin 2002, 2006), political economy (G. Braswell 2002; Kunen and Hughbanks 2003; Chapters 4 and 5), subsistence (H. Henderson 2003; McAnany 1992; Pyburn 1998), status (Blackmore 2011; McAnany 1993a), and ritual (Leventhal 1983; McAnany 2004; Plunket 2002). Households also are and were the primary institution for agricultural production (Kunen 2004; Murtha 2009; Ponette-González 2001; Pyburn 1998).

Many household activities take place in the houselot: residents process crops and make and repair tools, children play, and family members socialize with each other and with other households. But a great deal of the houselot is utilized for the cultivation of plants and raising animals. Killion (1992:1) terms this space "settlement agriculture," defined as "the cultivation of crops within and surrounding settlements." The agricultural systems in houselots are often arranged in concentric rings corresponding to intensity of use and maintenance as well as refuse disposal. The physical structures of a household occupy the more intensively utilized center where household activities take place. Intensively cultivated gardens are situated immediately adjacent to this area. Farther out are orchards or other forms of cultivation that require less labor (Killion 1992; McAnany 1995; see also Batún et al., Chapter 12; Fedick, Chapter 13; and Sheets, Chapter 14). Settlement agriculture is often complemented by the cultivation of large agricultural plots located at a distance from the housing compound, resulting in an infield-outfield system exhibited by many contemporary and prehispanic Mesoamerican societies (Killion 1990; Kunen 2004; Vogt 1969). These residential agricultural systems can have a high yield per land area unit, often producing sufficient food for individual households (van der Veen 2005).

Homegardens

Whereas settlement agriculture refers to a model of land use in residential settlements, here I focus on cultivated spaces. Researchers utilize a variety of names for this space; gardens, kitchen gardens, houselot gardens, homegardens, or, more academically, multistrata systems or agroforestry systems. I prefer the simpler and direct term "homegarden" to avoid confusion with horticultural garden plots located far from the residential settlement.

Homegardens are generally defined as cultivated spaces located adjacent to households or residential settlements and are utilized to grow flowers, herbs, vegetables, and fruits (Caballero 1992; Fernandes and Nair 1986; Hare et al. 2014; Killion 1990; Kumar and Nair 2004, 2006; van der Veen 2005). But rather than being clearly defined garden spaces, homegardens are often amorphous, unkept-looking spaces that take up the household's entire property and include perennial fruit and nut-bearing trees along with annual herbs and vegetables (Cleveland and Soleri 1987). In contrast to the milpa, which is sometimes located up to a day's walk or more from the household, homegardens are located immediately adjacent to the household, providing ready access for the family to plant, weed, fertilize, and harvest the garden crops (Redfield and Villa Rojas 1971). Contemporary Maya continue to maintain these garden plots in the immediate vicinity of the household (Wilk 1991). Ethnohistoric accounts by Spanish conquistadors passing through the Maya lowlands in the late 1500s document homegardens located within household clusters, filled with root crops, herbs and spices, and fruit and nut trees (Hellmuth 1977).

Homegardens are characterized not only by their proximity to the residence but by what Killion (1992:13) defines as "a polycultural mix of cultigens and useful economic species grown on small plots where the cultivator focuses on individual plants and their microhabitats by small inputs of labor on a continuous basis." Households intensify homegarden production through labor-intensive weeding, hand-watering, fertilizing, terracing, and the creation of landesque capital such as terrace walls, garden walls, raised beds (Leech 2003; Magcale-Macandog and Ocampo 2005; Netting 1968, 1974; van der Veen 2005). Fertility is maintained through the regular application of "food waste, excrement, and other debris produced by household members and dooryard animals" (Killion 1992:6). Homegardens are also the primary site of genetic innovation in terms of manipulating cultivars and experimenting with new plants (Coomes and Ban 2004; Gleason 1994).

It is generally believed that the role of homegardens in household economic strategies is to provide a "supplementary" or "secondary" source of food, such as condiments, medicines, spices; nonfood items such as dyes, construction materials, or ornamentals (Netting 1977) and a source of food in times of famine (Marcus 1982). This represents a common misconception, and rigid distinctions should not be drawn between the cultivation of primary staples, such as maize and beans, in outlying fields, and the cultivation of crops in homegardens. However, maize is a common homegarden crop (Doolittle 1992), with families in the Puuc area of the Yucatán in Mexico providing up to 25% of their maize crop from homegardens (Dunning 1996:59). And outfields often provide the supplementary crops that are common in homegardens, particularly when these outfields are lying fallow.

Homegardens provide food or materials for crafts to sell in markets, an important source of supplementary income for families (Eder 1991; Reyes-García et al. 2012; Vogl et al. 2002; Wiersum 2006), and create space for family activities, communal gatherings, and relaxation and pleasure. The economic value of homegardens is substantial, providing household income and allowing a level of economic freedom to the women who most often maintain them (Coomes and Ban 2004; McGee and González 1999; Wooten 2003).

Archaeology of Homegardens

Homegardens can be difficult to identify archaeologically, and the plants cultivated in these spaces leave little trace. Archaeologists often utilize chemical testing of soils adjacent to household structures to identify homegarden spaces (Dahlin et al. 2005; Wells et al. 2000). Food-processing activities and soil amendments may raise soil phosphate levels through time. Chemical analysis of soils has been utilized to identify potential agricultural areas near households at the sites of Sayil (Dunning 1992; Killion et al. 1989; Smyth et al. 1995), Xunantunich (J. Braswell 1998; Robin 1999), in other areas in the Belize River valley (Ball and Kelsay 1992), in the Petexbatún (Dunning et al. 1997), and in the Three Rivers area of northwestern Belize (Hughbanks 1998).

Researchers uncovered evidence of homegardens at the site of Cerén in El Salvador (Sheets 2002), a site with remarkable preservation after being buried in ash from an eruption of the Loma Caldera volcano in approximately the late sixth or early seventh century. Cerén has provided an invaluable source of paleoethnobotanical evidence regarding crops and agricultural techniques of ancient Mesoamerica (Lentz et al. 1996). Ridged fields for the cultivation of maize and several varieties of root crops were identified immediately adjacent to household structure. Excavations in suspected homegardens at the site of Seibal revealed lower sherd densities but larger sherd size, possibly indicating that residents used "chamberpots" to transport night soil (human waste) to the gardens for fertilizer (Tourtellot 1993). Charcoal was recovered from terrace beds at the site of Chan, indicating the intensive application of fertilizer in the form of household ash (Wyatt 2008b).

The distribution of households in settlement survey can also act as a proxy for the presence of homegardens. The space requirements for homegardens require room between residential settlements, particularly if they provide a more significant part of household subsistence and/or income (Killion 1990, 1992). A more dispersed settlement pattern suggests a greater focus on settlement agriculture and homegardens, a pattern that we see in much of Mesoamerica and the Maya lowlands (Reina and Hill 1980).

But how do gardening practices respond to a shifting socioeconomic landscape? The intensive labor requirements of homegardens fluctuate with available space, population density, household makeup, and market demands, suggesting that external factors significantly influence the composition and labor requirements of the homegarden (e.g., S. Barthel and Isendahl 2012). Research on Kofyar agricultural systems in Nigeria, for example, demonstrates that increasing population, reduction of available land, and the availability of markets require a set of mechanisms to schedule and balance household labor and affect the crops chosen for cultivation (G. D. Stone, Johnson-Stone, and Netting 1984; G. D. Stone, Netting, and Johnson-Stone 1990; M. P. Stone et al. 1995).

Gardens are an inseparable part of the household. The physical space of the household consists of structures devoted to habitation, cooking, and storage, and the space surrounding these structures is given over to cultivation. Like the household, garden spaces are both conservative and fluid: conservative in that they produce stable sources of subsistence, medicine, and other important household necessities, but fluid in that they are adaptable and subject to the vagaries of social, political, and economic forces.

In this chapter I examine household agricultural practices in two sites—one in the past and one contemporary—and how they responded to changes in the political economy. The Precolumbian Maya site of Chan in Belize provides us with a 2,000-year history of a farming community amid the dynamic political landscape of the Belize River Valley. The Lacandón community of Mensabak provides us with a contemporary data set during a time of rapid political, social, and economic change. Both sets of data help illuminate how changes in the political economy are reflected in homegardening practices.

Chan

Chan is a small ancient Maya agrarian community located approximately 4 km southeast of Xunantunich in the upland terrain between the Macal and Mopán drainages of the Belize River in western Belize (Figure 11.1). Occupied from the Early Preclassic Period to the Early Postclassic Period (1000 BC–AD 1200,

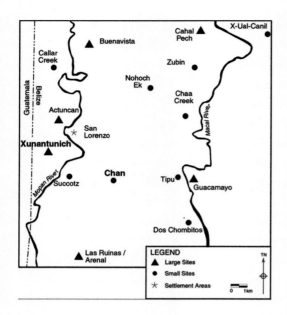

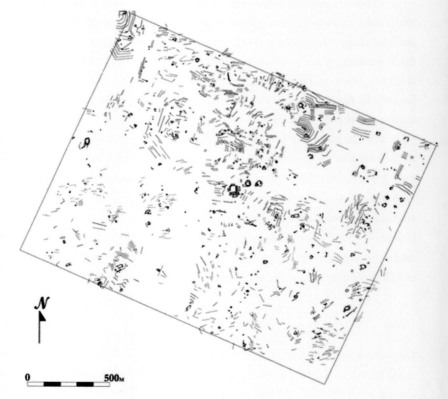

Figure 11.1. Location of Chan (*above*) and map of Chan terraces (*below*).

Chan's period of highest population and intensive land use was during the latter part of the Late Classic Period, AD 670–800/830 (Robin 1999).

While Chan is a comparatively small site, similar in size and organization to other minor centers and rural sites (Iannone and Connell 2003), the density of agricultural terraces makes it unique as a center of agricultural productivity. Sites throughout the Belize River valley and the Vaca Plateau to the south are heavily terraced (A. Chase and D. Chase 1998b; L. T. Neff 2008), but with 304 terraces per square kilometer Chan has one of the highest densities in the entire Maya area (Wyatt 2008a:112–118). Because of its central location in the Belize River Valley and the high-quality soil located in the area, Chan was likely a hub of agricultural production (Robin 2012; Robin et al. 2008).

The residents at Chan produced for their own households but also traded within the site in both lithic materials and limestone (Robin 2013), and exported agricultural production to nearby centers (Wyatt 2008a). People from a range of status levels resided at Chan, with complex ritual practices conducted within the site core, but also in more peripheral neighborhoods where early settlers at the site established long-term ties to the landscape (Blackmore 2011). Far from being a homogeneous settlement of simple farmers, research reveals that Chan was an internally differentiated population with a complex village economy.

Terrace Agriculture at Chan

Although the Maya lowlands are comparatively flat, extensive areas of undulating terrain and steep hillsides remain suitable for agricultural terracing. Thousands of hectares of hillsides in the Río Bec region (Turner 1983), the Maya Mountains (A. Chase and D. Chase 1998b), and the Petexbatún (Dunning and Beach 1994) have been transformed through the construction of terraces. Terraces serve multiple purposes, including soil conservation, ease of cultivation, and water retention (Donkin 1979; Wilken 1987). Yet, while terraces are major investments in landesque capital, they are often constructed and managed at the local level. Donkin (1979:33) indicates that terraces were "undoubtedly constructed piecemeal by single families or small groups of families, and, unlike irrigation, their maintenance involved cooperation at a level no higher than that of the village community." Although large and complex terrace systems may be organized at the suprahousehold level (Denevan 1987; Lansing 1991; Malpass 1987; Turner and Johnson 1979), terrace systems built and managed at a household or corporate group level are ultimately more common (Feinman et al. 2002; Mathewson 1984; Netting 1968, 1974; Ortiz Aguilú et al. 1993; M. Smith and Price 1994; A. Sullivan 2000).

The settlement survey of Chan mapped a landscape of households and terraces dispersed across the landscape (Figure 11.1). The map of Chan indicates that beyond the site core there is little nucleation of settlement: households are dispersed somewhat evenly over the landscape, each with a set of terraces located nearby. Some terrace sets present an extensive and organized arrangement of steps descending a hillside situated among a residential group, whereas other terrace sets consist of one or two short terraces associated with a small housemound or two. Some areas display a greater density of structures, possibly suggesting the presence of neighborhoods, although the houselots do not diminish in size. Household structures in the more densely settled areas are often larger, with larger terraces as well, in both height and length. Other areas of Chan are settled more sparsely, with smaller household structures and terraces of lesser height and length. Despite the suggestion that terraces may represent areas leveled for the construction of residential structures or ritual performance, we suggest that the terraces surrounding households and household clusters at Chan are sites of agricultural production, although the suite of crops likely changed over the 2,000-year history of the site. The settlement at Chan does not indicate a planned agricultural system constructed and managed by a central authority, as has been postulated for other sites (Beach et al. 2002; A. Chase and D. Chase 1998b). The dispersed distribution of settlement and the location of terraces adjacent to household structure indicate intensively managed infields fundamental to a system of settlement agriculture. The consistent need to maintain terraces requires that houses remain close to their fields, creating a dispersed settlement pattern (Dunning 2004:99; Netting 1993), much as we see at the Chan site.

Excavations at Chan indicate intensive labor practices in the form of water management features and soil amendment practices. In the northern part of Chan, excavations uncovered an irrigation channel running across a terrace bed (Figure 11.2). This irrigation channel likely kept crops watered during the dry season while draining excess water in the rainy season. The supply of water for irrigation on the terrace bed probably came from several small *aguadas* (rain-fed natural or artificial depressions) located adjacent to a cluster of housemounds farther up the hillside. Excavations also revealed the extensive use of natural springs and underground water sources. On one of the hillsides the residents constructed a structure to collect water from a natural spring. Water from a hillside spring passed into the structure through a small opening in the south-

Figure 11.2. Irrigation channel on terrace bed at Chan (*left*) and interior of the springhouse at Chan (*below*). The stone basin for collecting water is located in the center of the photo (*below*). The walls running through the structure were later constructions after its use as a springhouse was terminated.

eastern corner and collected in a stone-lined basin (Figure 11.2). Residents built this "springhouse" in the Late Preclassic, very early in Chan's history, although its use for the collection of springwater ended sometime in the Early Classic. There is no mention of similar structures anywhere else in the Maya area, so it is difficult to assess its purpose; however, ritual, household, and agricultural uses of the structure and the collected springwater are all likely. This evidence of varied water management strategies suggests that water control was clearly in local hands and that the farmers here had an intimate knowledge of local geological and hydrological conditions. Although individually these features did not require significant labor for construction, the constellation of different forms of water management together likely required constant labor to maintain.

Excavations on terrace beds indicate more intensive labor practices in the form of soil amendments. Archaeobotanical analysis identified the presence of very small pieces of pine charcoal on planting surfaces, which we interpreted as one element of ash from household fires (Wyatt 2008b). Although a great deal of carbon from different species was recovered from terrace beds, the presence of nonlocal pine suggested that it was placed there purposefully. Many contemporary households still collect household ash and use it as fertilizer in gardens. The presence of pine on the terrace beds at Chan indicates that the residents here were utilizing this more labor-intensive form of soil management. The highest concentrations of jute snail shell (*Pachychilus* sp.) were also recovered on terrace planting surfaces, again indicating the purposeful addition of organic material to fertilize the soil.

The two lines of evidence presented here suggest that terraces at Chan served as homegardens. First, the dispersed settlement pattern indicates that spaces surrounding household structures were purposefully maintained and that the terraces within these spaces served as agricultural production. Second, the intensive labor practices suggested by the presence of household ash and jute shell as fertilizer are characteristics of homegarden management.

So how did household agricultural production at Chan respond to the rise and fall of regional centers and the changing social and political contexts of the region over 2,000 years? Terrace construction developed throughout the occupation of the site. Farmers at Chan possibly constructed the first terraces as early as the Middle Preclassic, which were spread throughout the site by the Late Preclassic (Wyatt 2008a:296–297). These early terraces were often well built, some walls being nearly 2 m wide and constructed of large stone, despite their location in the hinterlands of the site. Residents continued to build and extend terrace walls, which covered much of Chan by the Early Classic. However, in the Late Classic residents began to construct terraces in less-than-ideal locations, such as steep drainages. The presence of more roughly cut loosely fitted stone in terrace walls indicates a focus on rapidity and functionality rather than aesthetics. This substantial expansion of terrace construction in the later years of the Late Classic corresponds to the rise of the nearby center of Xunantunich and represents a response to increasing demands for agricultural production. While households responded to the social and political changes in the region through construction and extension of terraces, evidence suggests that they were not subject to the coercive pressures of nearby centers.

At Chan we have evidence of intensive homegarden activities developing within the context of a dynamic political landscape. This is visible in the growing population at Chan, the elaboration of class structure, and the construction and expansion of agricultural terraces. But what does this mean at a smaller scale? How are these changes reflected at the microscale of the household? Blackmore (2012) addresses this through her work in the Northeast Group and the development of ritual and hierarchy in several households in this neighborhood. But are political and economic changes also reflected in homegardens? Is it possible to see how the structure and composition of gardens change, if in fact they change at all? Are homegardens subject to a dynamic political economy with labor scheduling, cultivation techniques, and the suite of cultivated plants reacting to changes? Or do they remain stable and predictable sources of food, medicine, and other plant resources despite a changing sociopolitical landscape?

Archaeological excavation can only bring us so far, as the primary components of gardens—plants—are difficult to recover in open-air contexts. The annual variations in plant composition are all but invisible, and the specifics of intensive labor practices remain opaque. We can turn to ethnographic data, however, to assist in our understanding of how changes in the political economy affect residential homegarden practices.

Mensabak

To understand the impact of a dynamic political economy on homegardening practices in a contemporary setting, the Lake Mensabak Homegarden Project conducted ethnographic research at the Lacandón Maya community of Mensabak in Chiapas, Mexico. Research took place over one month in June 2011 and two months in May and June 2013, with a short two-week field season in January 2014. We interviewed residents regarding homegardening practices, conducted inventories of plants, and created maps of houselots. As homegardens are evolving entities, we will continue to return to Mensabak to update our data and take note of changes.

Lacandón Maya

The Lacandón are a Maya-speaking people who originated from indigenous communities fleeing the Spanish in the colonial era (Palka 2005a, 2005b). Settling in the dense forests of southern Mexico and northwestern Guatemala, the Lacandón developed a distinct culture characterized by non-Christian religious practices, a language closely related to Yucatec, and more superficial characteristics, including long hair and long, plain cotton smocks called "xikuls" worn by both men and women (McGee 2001).

Until the 1970s the Lacandón Maya remained relatively isolated from the rest of Mexico, although they had contact with neighbors, including trade in products from the Lacandón forest, such as tobacco and cacao, for tools and food that they were unable to grow for themselves. Recent research has revised earlier interpretations of the Lacandón Maya as isolated and "primitive" remnants of the ancient Maya, understanding that their isolation from mainstream Mexican culture is not complete; that they participate in local economic networks; and that their traditions, while outwardly non-Christian and non-Mexican, are relatively contemporary and have been subjected to the same forces of culture change as those of other Maya groups (McGee 2001; Palka 2005a, 2005b).

Since the 1970s, with the arrival of more extensive logging and associated construction of logging roads, the expansion of cattle ranching in the area, and oil prospecting, the formerly isolated Lacandón Maya have now had more extensive contact with Mexican society, resulting in dramatic culture change (McGee 2001). The Lacandón forest has also become a popular destination to visit "untouched" nature, as the forests where the Lacandón Maya live have been designated as protected areas. Some Lacandón Maya have therefore found employment with CONANP (Comisión Nacional de Áreas Naturales Protegidas), acting as park rangers and guides. This influx of tourism has brought money to some individuals in the Lacandón Maya community, creating a significant break with the socioeconomic system of the past several centuries; whereas age and family were once an indicator of social status, access to money has now replaced this older system (McGee 2001).

Mensabak

Mensabak is a Lacandón Maya community located in central Chiapas, about 60 km to the southeast of the city of Palenque (Figure 11.3). The community is located on the shore of a series of deep lakes, Lake Mensabak and Lake Tzibana being the largest. The village is home to 14 households and approximately 110 individuals. Several stores offer minimal food and household goods, operated by individual households, that can bring in a small but reliable income.

A small group of families, several of whom are still living in the community,

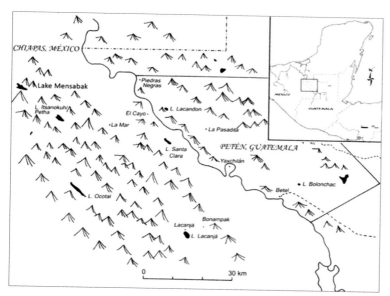

Figure 11.3. Location of Lake Mensabak (*left*) and aerial view (*below*) of surveyed and mapped gardens (*shaded*).

founded the modern village of Mensabak in the late 1960s. Archaeological evidence indicates that people have lived around the lake since the Preclassic. Several sites with rock art dating to the precolonial period are found on cliff faces around the lake. Archaeological sites and shrines surrounding the lakes indicate the area was an important pilgrimage site throughout Maya prehistory (Palka 2014).

Like many Lacandón communities, Mensabak has been relatively isolated, although the past twenty years have brought significant changes. Tourism has brought money to some, whereas others have benefited from jobs working for the park service, as the land surrounding the lake, including the community, is now a protected area. Some individuals and families now have money and are even able to hire Tzeltal workers to cultivate their fields, whereas others have very little. These economic differences are also reflected in access to political power for some (McGee 2001; McGee and González 1999). Some residents of the community have lived there in the same household for over thirty years yet do not hold any positions of economic or political importance. Much younger members work for tourist agencies or CONANP and therefore have access to money as well as political influence. Still others have small businesses manufacturing tourist items or operating small stores and have a small income.

Members of the community (primarily men) who earn their livelihood by interacting with tourists visiting the community have generally chosen to maintain the long hair and clothing of the traditional Lacandón. The others in the community who make their living elsewhere (working for the police or other Mexican agencies) have generally chose to abandon the look of the traditional Lacandón. These interacting political, economic, and cultural factors make Mensabak an ideal location for understanding rapid social and political change on the microscale.

The Lake Mensabak Homegarden Project (LMHGP)

The LMHGP conducted inventories of cultivated spaces surrounding households in the community of Mensabak (Figure 11.3). We interviewed members of seven households regarding plant use and cultivation practices and also utilized laser survey equipment to plot in all structures and each individual plant and tree of five households. This provided us with an accurate count of both the species present in the gardens and the number of individual specimens of each. At Mensabak we identified a surprising amount of variety and variability among households, reflecting the social and economic status of the households.

The data from the five households mapped by the LMHGP were chosen from different social strata, representing households with differing access to political and economic power. The following discussion includes data on the size of each garden, a description of the species present, and more anecdotal information on plant choice, management practices, and attitudes toward their homegardens. The five households discussed below are those of the families of José and Luisa, Mincho and Adela, Enrique and María, Rafa, and Pablo and Sebastiana, although we conducted interviews with most residents of the community. Although all Mensabak households have been interviewed and inventoried to a degree, these five homegardens reflect the more comprehensive interviews, mapping, and inventories conducted over several field seasons in the community by different researchers and therefore are the most reliable.

The gardens at Mensabak range from 1,904 m² to 3,599 m² and are composed of a total of 135 different species, which include food, medicinal, industrial, and ornamental plants and a mix of both indigenous and introduced plants. All houselots shared some similarities: all had a separate fenced in area for cultivating vegetables, all had chickens, and all were maintained on a regular, almost daily basis by different members of the family. In keeping with Killion's (1992) settlement agriculture model, the areas of highest use were located near the residential structures, becoming less maintained farther out toward the edges of the property. Although more traditional Lacandón houselots did not have definite boundaries, the households in Mensabak were distinctly separated from one another, often by hedges, because of the restricted space in the community. Despite these similarities, there were some significant differences. For example, only one household had pigs; pigs are illegal because this is protected area, but the village *comisario* (mayor or representative) kept several.

Although no layout of a homegarden at Mensabak is "typical," they have certain similarities. The most common plants found in Mensabak homegardens are citrus varieties (*Citrus* sp.), including *lima* (lemon, *C. limon*), *limón* (key lime, *C. aurantifolia*), *toronja* (grapefruit, *C. paradisi*), *mandarina* (mandarin orange, *C. reticulata*), and *naranja* (orange, *C. sinensis*). Many of the citrus varieties appeared to be opportunistic individuals that grew wild from discarded fruits or seeds, yet no attempt was made to thin out or otherwise maintain the trees.

The total numbers of plant species present and the variety and ubiquity of plant species varied significantly among households (Figure 11.4). Table 11.1 shows all the plant species identified at Mensabak and the total number of in-

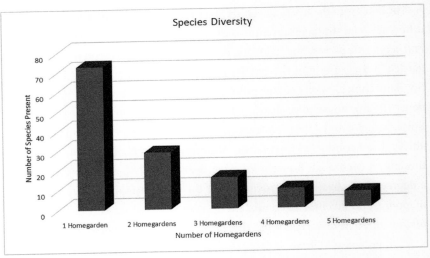

Figure 11.4. Varying diversity of plant use among Mensabak households.

dividual plants of each. Of the 135 total species present, 71 (53%) are found in only one of the household gardens, and only 8 species (.06%) are present in all 5 gardens mapped. The 8 species found in all homegardens include *annona* (*Annona reticulata*), *limón* (*Citrus aurantifolia*), *mandarina* (*C. reticulata*), *bitz* (*Inga vera*), banana (*Musa acuminata*), avocado (*Persea americana*), mango (*Mangifera indica*), and sugarcane (*Saccharum officinarum*).

Not only are a high number of plant species present in Mensabak homegardens but the diversity among different households is significant (Figure 11.4). This is consistent with research in homegardens in other parts of the world. In central Amazonia diversity among household homegardens is an indication of differences in soil texture and fertility (Junqueira et al. 2016), whereas differences in plant composition in homegardens in northern Thailand are a reflection of cultural differences between Hmong and Mien residents (Srithi et al. 2012). Socioeconomic differences are a significant factor in accounting for diversity in homegardens (Coomes and Ban 2004; Wiersum 2006). Access to land and resources—such as plant cuttings and fertilizer—impact homegarden composition, allowing wealth and status to be displayed.

Although all areas of Mensabak houselots were cultivated and utilized to different degrees, each houselot included an area set aside and fenced in for the cultivation of vegetables, herbs, and some fruits. These garden areas included

Table 11.1. List of plants identified in Lacandón homegardens

Lacandón name	Spanish/English name	Scientific name	# Plants
akunte'	subim	*Acacia collinsii*	12
k'ak'che'		*Aegiphila monstrosa*	2
ki	agave	*Agave fourcroydes*	1
mushanche	Christmasbush	*Alchornea latifolia*	1
xu'u	ajo/garlic	*Allium sativum*	5
	cebollín/chives	*Allium schoenoprasum*	55
tzo la	amaryllis	*Amaryllis sp.*	1
	piña/pineapple	*Ananas comosus*	9
	piña (ornamental)	*Ananas sp.*	1
'oopil k'aax	anona del monte/annona	*Annona montana*	1
p'opox	guanabana	*Annona muricata*	10
'oop	anona/annona	*Annona sp.*	18
	cacahuate/peanut	*Arachis hypogaea*	6
ox	castaña/breadfruit	*Artocarpus altilis*	2
	yaka	*Artocarpus heterophyllus*	1
	carambola/starfruit	*Averrhoa carambola*	1
	bambú/bamboo	*Bambusa vulgaris*	3
k'ak'che'		*Bauhinia rubeleruziana*	1
kushu	achiote/annato	*Bixa orellana*	12
	buganvila/bougainvillea	*Bougainvillea buttiana*	25
	repollo/cabbage	*Brassica oleracea*	15
cha'am	pinuelo	*Bromelia pinguin*	5
	brugmansia	*Brugmansia suaveolens*	1
chaca	gumbo limbo	*Bursera simaruba*	1
	nance	*Byrsonima crassifolia*	25
sak wowo/ te u si	calathea	*Calathea lutea*	4
se puhon	caléndula/calendula	*Calendula officinalis*	1
chankalá		*Canna edulis*	9
topshi'	platonillo	*Canna lutea*	8
ik	chile	*Capsicum annuum*	9
put	papaya	*Carica papaya*	6
	hule/rubber	*Castilla elastica*	4
ko'och	guarumo	*Cecropia peltata*	2
	cedro/cedar	*Cedrela odorata*	5
chi'ib	pacaya	*Chamaedorea tepejilote*	7
	limón/lime	*Citrus aurantifolia*	33
	naranja agrio/bitter orange	*Citrus aurantium*	1

(continued)

Table 11.1.—*continued*

Lacandón name	Spanish/English name	Scientific name	# Plants
	lima/lemon	*Citrus limon*	4
	toronja/grapefruit	*Citrus paradisi*	6
	mandarina/mandarin orange	*Citrus reticulata*	53
	naranja/orange	*Citrus sinensis*	93
	cajera	*Citrus sinensis var.*	2
itzunte		*Clerodendrum ligustrinum*	2
	chaya	*Cnidoscolus aconitifolius*	3
bachich		*Coccoloba sp.*	1
	coco/coconut	*Cocos nucifera*	4
	café/coffee	*Coffea arabica*	26
	cilantro	*Coriandrum sativum*	14
lu'uch	jícara	*Crescentia cujete*	3
chipilin	incaña	*Crotalaria longirostrata*	2
aj ku'um	escoba	*Cryosophila stauracantha*	6
	sacate limón/lemon grass	*Cymbopogon citratus*	2
mam		*Dasylirion sp.*	1
hanan	behuco	*Desmoncus ferox*	1
chiah		*Dieffenbachia sp.*	1
	batata/yam	*Dioscorea bulbifera*	1
pets'k'in		*Enterolobium cyclocarpum*	1
	perejil	*Eryngium foetidum*	20
	ficus	*Ficus benjamina*	2
kopoh	matapalo	*Ficus obtusifolia*	2
	hinojo/fennel	*Foeniculum vulgare*	1
k'ante'	madre de cacao	*Gliricidia sepium*	1
	algodón/cotton	*Gossypium hirsutum*	1
ts'ubtok		*Hampea stipitata*	1
tamaní	tulipán	*Hibiscus rosa-sinensis*	52
lemu	pitahaya	*Hylocereus undatus*	1
bitz		*Inga vera*	33
	camote/sweet potato	*Ipomoea batatas*	7
	lechuga/lettuce	*Lactuca sativa*	15
lek	calabaza/calabash	*Lagenaria siceraria*	5
tzakatz	cabeza de mico	*Licania platypus*	17
	lychee	*Litchi chinensis*	3
	tomate/tomato	*Lycopersicum esculentum*	16
	mango	*Mangifera indica*	26

Lacandón name	Spanish/English name	Scientific name	# Plants
tz'in	yuca/cassava	*Manihot esculenta*	47
ya	sapodilla	*Manilkara achras*	1
	chico zapote	*Manilkara chicle*	3
haas	zapote	*Manilkara zapota*	2
	guaya	*Melicoccus bijugatus*	2
	yerba buena/mint	*Mentha citrata*	15
ak'sak'in	four o'clock	*Mirabilis jalapa*	6
koko ak	balsamina	*Momordica balsamina*	3
bo'ox	plátano/plantain	*Musa acuminata*	38
	rambutan	*Nephelium lappaceum*	1
k'utz	tabaco/tobacco	*Nicotania tabacum*	7
sa kash	albahaca/basil	*Ocimum basilicum*	12
	nopal	*Opuntia sp.*	4
tutz	corozo	*Orbignya cohune*	4
	orchidia	Orchidaceae	15
kubuj	zapote bobo	*Pachira aquatica*	2
on	aguacate/avocado	*Persea americana*	19
	frijol/bean	*Phaseolus vulgaris*	1
	pimienta/allspice	*Pimienta dioica*	1
	anis/anise	*Pimpinella anisum*	8
	Mexican mint	*Plectranthus sp.*	5
ha'as	mamey	*Pouteria sapota*	12
pichik	guayava/guava	*Psidium guajava*	10
	rabano/radish	*Raphanus sativum*	25
k'och	castor bean	*Ricinis communis*	9
	rosa/rose	*Rosa sp.*	6
	palma royal/royal palm	*Roystonea borinquena*	6
	ruda loca	*Ruta graveolens*	1
	caña de azucar/sugarcane	*Saccharum officinarum*	57
	cana rojo	*Saccharum officinarum var.*	1
mumun che		*Saurauia yasicae*	1
	chayote	*Sechium edule*	14
	yerba mora/black nightshade	*Solanum nigrum*	5
ju'jup	jocote	*Spondias mombin*	8
ah boh	jocote jobo	*Spondias purpurea*	1
chakalte'	caoba/mahogany	*Swietenia macrophylla*	1
	maravilla/marigold	*Tagetes erecta*	5

(continued)

Table 11.1.—*continued*

Lacandón name	Spanish/English name	Scientific name	# Plants
koyok/kolok	chirillo	*Talisia floresii*	2
waya	guaya	*Talisia olivaeformis*	3
	tamarindo/tamarind	*Tamarindus indica*	1
	almendra/Indian almond	*Terminalia catappa*	1
	cacao/chocolate	*Theobroma cacao*	1
tuch	huevos de chucho	*Thevetia ahouai*	3
	san nicolás	*Tradescantia spathacea*	15
makal	macal	*Xanthosoma yucatanense*	43
	macalito	*Xanthosoma yucatanense var.*	3
	maize, corn	*Zea mays*	1
	gengibre/ginger	*Zingiber officinale*	3
buche'			1
chakotop			1
chimahun			2
chukche'			4
ch'ukche'			1
isiche'			4
k'okoche			2
popiste			2
sosa			1
suri			1
topche'			1
ts'ak k'ite			1
tupimil			1
ukuch			1

some raised beds or, if they were located on hillsides, terraces. The most common plants cultivated in the areas included *cebollín* (*Allium schoenoprasum*), cilantro (*Coriandrum sativum*), tomato (*Lycopersicum esculentum*), yerba buena (*Mentha citrata*), basil (*Osimum basilicum*), and chile (*Capsicum anuum*). The garden areas were not old, however; the gardens were a product of a nongovernmental organization (NGO) representative who spent time in Mensabak several years earlier and had persuaded different households to adopt these gardens with the idea of creating greater independence from markets.

Discussion of Mensabak Gardens

Data suggest that there is no "typical" garden at Mensabak and that a substantial degree of variability exists. Lot size ranges from 3,599 m^2 to 1,904 m^2 and the number of plant species present in each garden ranges from 77 to 35. The number of unique species in each homegarden is quite high, and their use is variable as well. Some homegardens are used primarily for subsistence, whereas others are focused more on aesthetics.

The differences in these gardens appear to reflect differences in access to political or economic power. Households with greater access to money or power have larger garden spaces and more species of plants. Perhaps the clearest example of this is the household of Mincho and Adela, wealthy residents who still hold political influence as a result of Mincho's role as former *comisario* and who also have the largest garden, the most plant species, and the most unique species. However, there are mitigating factors; Mincho's brother Enrique, the current town *comisario*, has a relatively small houselot and fewer plants. But his plot is new and under development, and he is also exchanging the advantage of more space for a central and more visible location. Enrique has also purchased more unique and "showy" plants in the nearby town of Palenque, which, combined with his more visible houselot, have created a very clear display of wealth and power.

Pablo and Sebastiana, in contrast, fall on the other end of the spectrum. While Pablo does have a job, he does not have a great deal of economic resources and has very little political power in the community. Their homegarden is comparatively small and has fewer species. Similarly, Rafa works for CONANP and thus has access to some economic power (although less than Mincho or Enrique), but he exerts little political influence. Rafa's status is reflected in his smaller garden with fewer species. Several households not discussed here were inventoried, and most of these less well-off households had significantly smaller homegardens and fewer plants. Interviews with residents also indicate that more well-off households purchase more plants and particularly medicines in town, whereas the less well-off households spend more time and energy foraging for these in the surrounding forests.

To sum up the Mensabak data, short-term changes in the political economy are reflected in the size and composition of homegardens. Over the past several decades Lacandón Maya in communities such as Mensabak have become less isolated; more incorporated into the national Mexican and global economies and social and economic systems that gave authority to community residents based on age and family have been replaced by systems privileging wealth and political authority. Enrique and Mincho represent these changes at Mensabak, as their increased wealth has provided them with more political and economic influence.

Ethnohistoric data indicate that "traditional" Lacandón gardens were fairly uniform in terms of layout and composition (Baer and Merrifield 1971; McGee 2001; Nations and Nigh 1980; Soto-Mayor 1983; Tozzer 1907). Remaining isolated from external economic and political systems, Lacandón Maya managed homegardens for subsistence and cash crops for sale and trade (such as tobacco and cacao). But as socioeconomic changes descended upon the Lacandón communities, their homegardens transformed as well.

Gardens are very visible means to display wealth (Clunas 1996; Francis 2008; Leech 2003). As status evolved into a reflection of wealth and external political power, rather than age or family, homegardens acted as sites to display this status. Homegardens could be large or small, and unique plants could be selected that exhibited access to money. With wealth, people could purchase more land, establish a larger homegarden, and purchase plants that others did not have access to. In this way, the homegarden, the cultivated space in the houselot, is a way to signify the status of the family to others, both in the community and outside it. Both Enrique's family and Mincho's family use the land that they have acquired, their ability to purchase unique plants, and the modifications to the landscape (the terraces on Enrique's land), to show to the rest of Mensabak and visitors their status.

Short-term changes in the political economy are very quickly reflected in changes in the composition and organization of the homegarden. Rather than being stable predictable spaces for mitigation against changes in the political economy, homegardens are dynamic.

Conclusions

Wilk (1991) discusses socioeconomic impacts in Q'eqchi' Maya communities in southern Belize. Similar to the Lacandón, the Q'eqchi' have been isolated, but they have interacted with the Belizean and global economy to a greater extent and adjust their crops, work schedules, and household organization to adapt to market fluctuations. Given their relatively marginal status, mitigation of risk is an important factor in their decision making. The Q'eqchi' turn to the tradition of maize agriculture when market forces prevent them from selling rice, cacao, or other market crops (Wilk 1991:140–141). The Q'eqchi' can move from a position of economic integration or retreat from this integration if necessary. The dynamic nature of their agricultural production, as well as scheduling of labor, mobility, and household structure, allows them to adapt. In fact, Wilk (1991:39) sees the household as primarily an adaptive structure. With this in mind, this chapter has focused on the homegarden as site of adaptation and asked the question whether homegardens (or settlement agriculture) represent a dynamic and adaptive structure or a place to mitigate risk and allow households to retreat in times of economic uncertainty.

This discussion of houselot spaces at the Precolumbian Maya site of Chan and at the contemporary Lacandón Maya community at Mensabak provides complementary data toward understanding the impact of the political economy on household production. At Chan we can see the evolution of household agricultural space over 2,000 years: it grew as a village and a community while nearby political centers such as Xunantunich rose and fell. Residents intensively cultivated the spaces surrounding their households, building terraces on the hilly terrain. These terraces grew to cover much of the Chan landscape and show us how the residents responded to changes in the political economy, albeit in a broad way. We can see broad changes, but shorter-term changes and differences in socioeconomic status can be invisible to us.

The Mensabak data can provide us with a model with more fine-grained data. What we see there is that the changes in the political economy, instigated by a retreat from isolation and incorporation into the regional and global economy, have created differences in wealth and access to power. These are reflected in the immediate household surrounding: the homegarden. These spaces are not simple utilitarian spaces that provide only a particular kind of subsistence but spaces that allow individuals to display their wealth and status to others.

12

Yucatec Land and Labor before and after Spanish Incursions

ADOLFO IVÁN BATÚN ALPUCHE,
PATRICIA A. MCANANY, AND MAIA DEDRICK

In a book about economic production and the circulation of things, this chapter deals with an immobile entity—land—and another that is highly mobile—human labor. Both entities are intricately linked to spheres of authority and were valued and deployed differentially and across the sea change that swept through Mesoamerica in the sixteenth century. To advance understanding of the dynamic realms of land and labor, Yucatec ethnohistorical sources are employed judiciously and found to provide invaluable relational information that can be juxtaposed with archaeological materials from both colonial and precolonial contexts. This chapter straddles a profound temporal divide and refers to both ethnohistorical and archaeological materials. In Western economic theory, land and labor represent fundamental components of economic production but as this chapter reveals, many Western concepts (such as private property) cannot be applied categorically to the manner in which authority was claimed over land in Yucatán. Significantly, a labor theory of value—dismissed by Western economists analyzing industrialized production (Stanish 2017:142)—resonates with the manner in which labor and value were entangled in the preindustrialized Maya region (see also King 2016).

This chapter builds from insights provided by influential ethnohistorian Sergio Quezada (2014), who suggests that a seismic shift in the perception of land and labor occurred between precolonial and colonial times. Quezada's framework emphasizes the *relative lack* of private property, tribute-in-kind, and market-driven production prior to Spanish colonization of Yucatán. Can such a stark and polarizing framework be sustained by additional ethnohistorical research and by archaeological evidence relevant to Postclassic and earlier times? We interrogate Quezada's model through presentation of additional evidence—both archaeological and ethnohistorical—from the eastern Yucatec town of Tahcabó and from Buena Vista, Cozumel. The goal is to generate a more complex and realistic model of these foundational aspects of Yucatec society.

Holding and Inheriting Land, Yucatec-Style

In *Maya Lords and Lordship* Quezada (2014:21) writes: "Simply put, the contact-era Maya lacked a concept of private land-ownership." Additionally, Quezada (2014:21) maintains that Yucatec Mayan has no term that conveys the notion of exclusive rights over an object. This assertion strikes a reader familiar with Classic Period hieroglyphic texts—which contain a plethora of possessive grammatical constructions—as a bit odd. In the political realm, furthermore, Quezada (2014) suggests that networks of patron-client relations were not physically constituted on the ground in a spatially delimited manner but rather selectively cultivated and maintained through personal relationships. Thus, polities resembled nodal networks of alliances rather than the territorially demarcated provinces presented by Ralph Roys (1957) in his magisterial work *The Political Geography of the Yucatan Maya*. While the territorial boundedness of nation-states is widely acknowledged to be a nineteenth-century phenomenon, completely removing the geometry of space and boundedness from considerations of premodern polities likely is pushing Postclassic polities into a realm of abstractness that defies the pragmatics of grounded expressions of authority (see also Davenport and Golden 2016).

An example of authority grounded in landscape is provided by Susan Kepecs (2003:259), who employs a resource-extraction point of view to argue that private property is a salient concept for the salt beds off the north coast of Yucatán. She cites the relevant account of encomendero Juan de Urrutia in the *Relaciones histórico-geográficas de la gobernación de Yucatán* (Garza et al. 1983:249). Urrutia likens authority over salt-producing areas to real-estate holdings. Bishop Diego de Landa (Tozzer 1941:189) likewise described salt beds as the property of individual families.

By way of wills and other documents written in Yucatec Mayan during colonial times, Matthew Restall (1995, 1997) documents inheritance of dwellings, houselots, and other private possessions within family lines. Restall (1997:206–

216) juxtaposes this very clear sense of private and inheritable property with the larger land holdings of the *cah* (community) in which all community members had a stake. But a clear-cut polarization between private and communal did not exist either. By the eighteenth century legal records of several *cahob* (plural of *cah*) examined by Restall (1997:206–211) reveal that buying, selling, and pursuing litigation over landholdings was relatively common. The 150-year legal battle over a prized cenote (sinkhole: *dzonot* in Mayan) known as Tontzimín is probably the best-known example (Alexander 2012:11; Roys 1939).

Furthermore, Alexander (2012:10) notes that lands possessing distinctive features—such as deep soils, wet or dry sinkholes, or the remains of an old town (*labcah*)—were particularly desirable because fruit trees flourished in those microenvironments. Mention of tree crops, their high value, and the desire to plant tree crops is a leitmotif of colonial sources. Tree species and orchards were associated with high status and figure into creation narratives and Classic Maya royal iconography, such as the trees shown on the sarcophagus of K'inich Janaab Pakal I of Palenque. By virtue of their longevity, tree species violate the philosophy of communally held land, use of which rotates among members of a *cah* or otherwise constituted community. Michael Emch (2003) provides a useful case study of the tension that accompanied the conversion of community-held land to cacao orchards when such cultivation was expanded in southern Belize to meet the global demand for chocolate.

The thin soil that covers most of Yucatán further accentuates the value of microenvironments on which economic tree species can be grown. Such value may be accrued by human creation of soil retention features such as terraces, windbreaks, and walls. Alternatively, enhanced-value locales can be a function of local geomorphological processes acting upon porous limestone to create solution sinkholes (locally called cenotes if water-filled or *rejolladas* if dry). Even smaller water retention features called *sartenejas* and *huayás* also are noted and highly valued. Such places continue to hold special significance and often were associated with specific families who—during colonial times—might live in a large community located many kilometers away (Alexander 2012:10; see also Farriss 1984). According to Restall (1997:Table 15.6), land containing such features often was bequeathed as property or inherited. Thus, a simple equating of private property with residence and houselot—on the one hand—and communal property with lands of the *cah* located distant from dwellings—on the other—cannot be sustained on the basis of evidence.

Restall (1997:178) also emphasizes the use of stone mounds to demarcate landholdings away from towns during precolonial times and maintains that the *cah* exerted authority over the far-flung mosaic of landholdings—even those associated with specific patronymics (Restall 1997:169). Hence private and communal cannot be construed as mutually exclusive categories but rather as places where different kinds of authority intersected and could be asserted. While an idiom of *control* over land often is used in English (with overtones of exclusivity), ethnohistorians more frequently employ the idiom of *authority*, with the connotation that land might be subject to different kinds of authority that range from inheritance patterns to historical claims and labor expenditures, to name just a few.

Granted, these examples come from the Colonial Period after Spanish imposition of *reducción* (forced nucleation into mission towns) and territorially based laws that regulated land use, sale, and inheritance. Nonetheless, during earlier times, evidence indicates that the concept of communal landholdings did not exist to the exclusion of family-based and inheritable claims to place.

A salient Postclassic example comes from Cozumel Island, where an extensive network of wall demarcations has been amply documented by Freidel and Sabloff (1984:84–90) and by Batún Alpuche (2009). Wall patterns suggest a division of space into some form of jurisdictional holdings, even at places spatially remote from clusters of dwellings. Upon close survey of lands around the Postclassic site of Buena Vista (located on the southeastern part of Cozumel Island), Batún Alpuche (2009:269) found 229 demarcated lots within 5.2 sq km. This extreme partitioning of land departs from the kinds of apportioning conducted by communities for communal-use lands. The island of Cozumel, upon superficial examination, does not seem to possess enhanced economic potential, but Batún Alpuche (2009:263) argues for an intensive production system based upon the construction of apiaries, wall networks, wells, *sacbeob* (raised causeways), and skillful use of *rejollada* (dry sinkholes) and *huayás* (shallow breaks in surface limestone). Figure 12.1 illustrates the material imprint of this landscape modification to the northeast of the center of Buena Vista. With meticulous attention to soil features, wind exposure, and moisture retention within different production zones, Postclassic farmers differentially used the land around Buena Vista for gardening, tree cropping, beekeeping, and possibly cochineal production through cactus gardens in the shallow soils of the flat *tzekel* zones (Batún Alpuche 2009:267). We return to the labor implications of this microengineered landscape below.

Even on the more expansive landscape of mainland Yucatán, lands of a *cah*

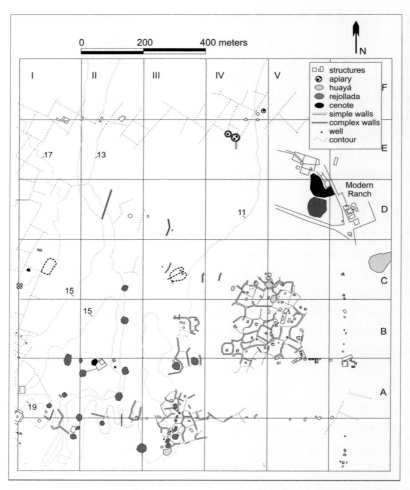

Figure 12.1. Postclassic agricultural landscape to the northeast of Buena Vista, Cozumel Island (after Batún Alpuche 2009).

within the zone of cenotes did not constitute a uniform plain as is often claimed. Around the archaeological site of Xuenkal in Yucatán, Munro-Stasiuk and colleagues (2014) have deployed remote sensing to locate sinkholes. They detect pronounced clustering of Classic Period settlement around dry sinkholes that contain deep soils, offer the possibility of growing highly valued trees and root crops, and often contain an accessible source of water. Kepecs and Boucher (1996) provide another archaeological example of a proprietary relationship between dwelling and productive landscape features from Chikinchel in northeastern Yucatán, which parallels the previous discussion of salt beds.

Adolfo Iván Batún Alpuche, Patricia A. McAnany, and Maia Dedrick

The precolonial and postcolonial town of Tahcabó, located north of Valladolid in eastern Yucatán, is located in a dense landscape of cenotes, dwellings, and *rejolladas* (Figure 12.2). In fact, the colonial grid was set to accommodate the location of six *rejolladas* and two cenotes—essential life-nourishing, natural landscape features. Today the *rejolladas* are privately held and often partitioned internally into multiple holdings that sometimes are marked by wall constructions. The density of *rejolladas* does not greatly diminish along survey transects away from the town center. Both Pre-Columbian and colonial dwellings often cluster near the edge of such features, suggesting proprietary claims to these fertile depressions. In the center of the colonial grid of Tahcabó is a large Pre-Columbian shrine situated immediately north of one of the deepest *rejolladas* at Tahcabó (labeled "A" on Figure 12.2). It is hard to ignore the spatial linkage between this old and venerable structure (likely a patron-deity shrine) and the rich fertility of a deep *rejollada*. True to Spanish colonialism's strategy of co-optation of Pre-Columbian sacred locales, a seventeenth-century ramada church was built to the north of the shrine by robbing stones from the older structure (Figures 12.2 and 12.3). These ritual structures emphasize how the cognitive experience of landscape—naming,

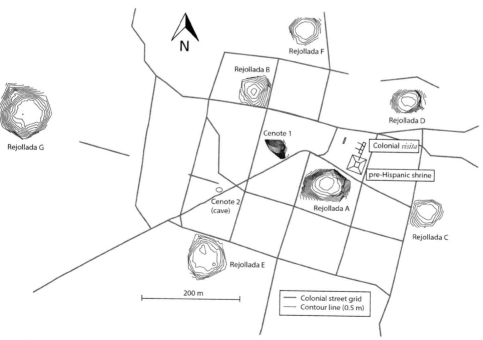

Figure 12.2. *Rejolladas* and other cultural features within the colonial grid of Tahcabo, Yucatán (map by Alf Berry and Maia Dedrick).

Figure 12.3. Back wall of seventeenth-century *visita* with the mounded topography of the precolonial shrine in the background (photo by Patricia A. McAnany).

claiming, and building close to *rejolladas*—is a prevalent pattern during both Pre-Columbian and colonial times that is intertwined with religious ideologies.

Not all land is equally productive in Yucatán, which likely amplifies and spatially complicates patterns of holding and inheriting land. The economic importance of natural features (sinkholes and fissures) to farmers seeking a livelihood from a limestone plateau creates a pattern of differential magnetism in the sense that certain parts of landscapes are highly desirable either because of natural geomorphological formations or because of the input of human labor to create high-productivity microenvironments. Regardless of proximity to settlement (although often spatially correlated), such locales were named and claimed in the past as well as in the present.

At Tahcabó and elsewhere *rejolladas* are preferred locales for Ch'a Chaak ceremonies conducted at the end of the dry season to encourage the onset of rain. Emblematic of enhanced fertility, a sinkhole—whether wet or dry—is the place at which supernatural forces that undergird rain and fertile soil can be encountered and propitiated. In this sense, these forces of nature had ultimate

Adolfo Iván Batún Alpuche, Patricia A. McAnany, and Maia Dedrick

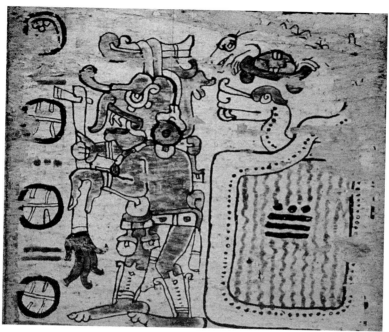

Figure 12.4. Postclassic Codex Madrid, folio 6a, showing the deity Chaak brandishing a torch and an axe (from famsi.org, accessed August 8, 2018).

authority over land and its productivity, as indicated on page 6a of the Codex Madrid, which shows Chaak standing next to a sinkhole and brandishing a torch and an axe (Figure 12.4).

Thus, archaeological evidence plus colonial documents intimate considerable complexity in land rights and include what might be called privatization (if such a term can be applied to highly partitioned landscapes such as the those found on Cozumel Island). Given the mosaic quality of natural features formed in a limestone substrate, the built and/or natural features claimed by families were not always clustered within settlements but rather could be several kilometers away. Indicative of a domesticated landscape, the naming and claiming of such features did not mean that access to places with built or natural agricultural features was open to all or necessarily closed to all but a few. Rather, overlapping spheres of authority may have exerted claims to landscape. This appears to have been the situation on both sides of the profound trauma and dislocation of Spanish colonization.

Mobilizing Networks of Labor

In reference to labor arrangements, Sergio Quezada (2014:20) is of the opinion that indigenous lords and colonial overlords demanded different kinds of obligations. According to Quezada, the former—in contrast to colonial officials—did not levy onerous demands for tribute but rather emphasized the mobilization of labor. Within a community (*cah*), a group might organize into a *mulmenyah* (work party), so that labor demands were spread across a kin group, which lessened the intrusiveness of labor drafts.

This position partially accords with archaeological evidence from precolonial times. Construction of massive architectural complexes in the northern lowlands (built from the Early Classic Period onward and even earlier in some places) suggests that labor drafts (whether voluntary or coercive) played a large role in creating the built landscape of monumental stone buildings—many with elaborate stone façades. On the western (Puuc) side of the peninsula, Tomás Gallareta Cervera (2016) has examined the large ceramic bowls and basins associated with hosting communal work parties at the Puuc site of Kiuic. But stone had to be quarried and transported; clay for pottery had to be quarried, shaped, and fired; and food and drink for large communal feasts had to be supplied. In short, labor alone would not have been sufficient without the contribution of goods and foods. Any attempt to make a sharp distinction between precolonial from colonial practices on the basis of labor tribute in the former and tribute in labor and goods in the latter is much too simplified and, as we shall see below, conflicts with ethnohistorical accounts of Postclassic tribute arrangements.

Labor is central to the idea of corvée or some kind of motivation to contribute time and energy to a production effort, whether that production is agricultural or architectural. Admittedly, archaeologists lack a specific understanding of how the impressively scaled-up built environment of northern lowland archaeological sites came about. Were these landscapes—both urban and rural—built with voluntary or compulsory labor (including captives)? In the Andean region to the south, the discovery of *huacas* (mounds) constructed with layers of packed (and sometimes marked) bags of stone construction fill called *shicra* has permitted the idea that community segments provided the construction material needed for shrine construction (Stanish 2017:202). This finding puts a more voluntary spin on monumental construction in the Andes. Internal stone bins have been documented as a construction technique for Maya pyramids and could indicate the presence of partitioned work party contributions that worked

Adolfo Iván Batún Alpuche, Patricia A. McAnany, and Maia Dedrick

in the same manner as *shicra* bags. Yet the argument that Pre-Columbian Maya peoples were conditional co-operators (per Stanish 2017) in the creation of a landscape of monumentality has not been formulated (and space precludes its formal elaboration here).

For decades archaeologists have noted the contrast between the northern and southern lowlands. Communities in the north clearly made a greater investment in monumental buildings and a lesser investment in the trappings of royalty, such as stone-carved hieroglyphic texts, tomb burials, jadeite adornments, and polychrome ceramics (with a few outstanding exceptions). Based on this material contrast, the central paradox of rulership—identified by Kurnick (2016) as the promotion of group solidarity while simultaneously promoting the royal *otherness* of the ruling family—may have been ameliorated in the northern lowlands, where social difference was understated relative to the south.

If styles of governance did underlie this contrast, then the conditions under which labor was enfranchised to build the elaborate stone buildings of the north may have been more inclusive than in the south. The repetitive motifs—handpecked into stone—that adorn the façades of Puuc buildings, for instance, indicate a large labor force of skilled masons who nevertheless need not have been literate. Decades ago Feeley-Harnik (1985) reminded us that civic pride and personal fame can be associated with contributing to the creation of a mortuary shrine for a dead ruler. Being massive does not mean that a structure was created with coerced labor.

Beyond the built environment created for supernaturals, governance, and residence lies a landscape created for the production of food, goods, and raw material extraction—the specialized production zones described by Batún Alpuche (2009) for Buena Vista, by Scarborough and Valdez (2003) for northwestern Belize, and by King (2016) and others for Colhá, Belize. In reference to Postclassic salt production around Emal, Yucatán—a specialized extraction zone—Kepecs (2003) envisions an intensified labor situation with extensive use of captives within an essentially commercialized production arrangement. From this perspective, the labor of captives could be construed as private property. As Kepecs (2005:130–135) documents, indigenous production of Yucatán's "briny diamonds" was greatly disrupted by Spanish usurpation of the saltworks, which then became focused on supplying salt to colonial Mexico City.

Many archaeologists (including Freidel and Sabloff 1984; Kepecs 2003; Masson and Freidel 2013) argue that during the Late Postclassic Period in particular considerable labor was expended for the purpose of surplus production. Produced items—whether salt, cacao, cotton, or honey, to name just a few highly desirable ones—circulated through multiscalar trading networks. Kepecs (2003), in particular, envisions a kind of strategic interdependence among production locales. In effect, labor would be funneled into producing things that emphasized (or capitalized upon) the *situatedness* of a locale. Thus, Emal, which was located on the northern coast, developed *salinas* (saltworks).

Likewise, Batún Alpuche (2009:16) argues that the dense wall networks of Buena Vista created resource-intensive zones that allowed surplus production and participation in regional and commercialized trading networks (with the input of prodigious amounts of labor). The role of Cozumel as a trading hub has long been recognized (Sabloff and Rathje 1975) but Batún Alpuche (2009:266–267) argues that Cozumel also participated as a supplier of highly desired and valuable goods—such as food items, honey, cotton, and possibly cochineal. The heavy investment in landesque capital around Buena Vista also suggests the possibility that authority over these improved parcels was held by a restricted group of one or more families who supervised a labor force engaged through a variety of mechanisms that likely included captive labor.

Tahcabó (which can be translated as the place of bee hives) is described in the *Book of Chilam Balam of Chumayel* as a place "where the Itzas stirred the honey" (Roys 1967:70). Apiaries apparently were once plentiful in the *cah* of Tahcabó. During recent excavations in a Colonial Period structure, Maia Dedrick uncovered a plug for a log beehive. This finding, along with the account of an encomendero who was given the labor and products of Tahcabó and the Island of Cozumel, indicates continuity in the labor of honey production across the many fractures of colonialism. Several pages of the Codex Madrid, which likely was produced less than 100 km from Tahcabó (Chuchiak 2004; Paxton 2004:114), address ritual practice surrounding beekeeping (Vail and Aveni 2004:5). To this day, Yucatán is known as a specialized production locale for apiaries, although log beehives are scarce and the stingless bee has been replaced largely with hybridized Old World bees.

Labor and landscape were closely entangled, especially in Postclassic Yucatán, where local production could be linked to regional trade, as has been suggested for Buena Vista. In this regard, cotton was a particularly important crop and had been since Preclassic times. Piperno and Pearsall (1998:149) consider the eastern side of the Yucatán Peninsula to have been a locale of independent cotton domestication. Growing, harvesting, cleaning, spinning, and weaving cotton requires a large number of skilled laborers. Such labor was

Adolfo Iván Batún Alpuche, Patricia A. McAnany, and Maia Dedrick

much in evidence and commented upon by sixteenth-century Spaniards who occupied Yucatán (Patch 1993:27) and carved the landscape into encomiendas (awards of indigenous labor and produce). Sixteenth-century encomendero Diego de Contreras (who was awarded the labor and produce of the people of Tahcabó and also of Cozumel Island) thought nothing of demanding woven cloth (*mantas*) in tribute. In 1579 he wrote that "we are sustained by maize given to us by the Indians of our encomiendas and also several turkeys, and every four months they [all households within a *cah*] give us cotton *mantas*, which we sell to sustain our houses, women, and family" (Garza et al. 1983:104 [our translation]).

Diego de Contreras also states that during precolonial times the *cah* sent the following tribute to Namon Cupul, lord of nearby Ek' Balam: maize, turkeys, cotton (both raw and woven), and fish from cenotes (Garza et al. 1983:186). We cannot independently verify the truth of this assertion; but if we accept his statement, then we accept the not-so-surprising idea that, contrary to Quezada's assertion, tribute goods were a mainstay of Pre-Columbian politics. Labor related to production-beyond-subsistence—whether for tribute or trade—flourished before Spaniards sailed within sight of Cozumel Island.

In short, the time before and after Christopher Columbus cannot be neatly separated into labor drafts during the former and product extraction during the latter. Rather, both times had locally specific labor arrangements that included the coerced labor of captives or colonized peoples, community projects in which labor was voluntarily provided, and labor to produce surplus production that was either traded or extracted as tribute. There is scholarly consensus that the final category of tribute-related labor was greatly amplified during colonial times, but this trend is difficult to confirm until more colonial contexts are excavated. Relatedly, Quezada (2014:5) is able to demonstrate through archival sources the progressive evisceration of the authority of local Yucatec lords (*batabob*) throughout the Colonial Period. Insofar as colonial tribute demands were negotiated through indigenous lords, the evisceration of their authority through the centuries of the Colonial Period would have exposed communities directly to tribute demands that may have been less negotiable.

Discussion and Final Thoughts

Discourse about Spanish colonialism often seeks to reduce the complexity of Pre-Columbian times and to impose models of modernity upon Post-Columbian times. One model (some would say illusion) of modernity is the territorially inscribed nation-state, which today is proving to be an ephemeral political arrangement in danger of extinction. When all is said and done, politics is composed of relational networks, which at certain times and places take on the appearance of territorial integrity. But this appearance is not a unidirectional trend of modernism.

Any study of the Spanish colonial process (which emphasized violence and disruption leading to high levels of mobility) leaves one wondering how indigenous peoples of the Yucatán Peninsula survived the atrocities and maintained a sense of cultural identity. It is extraordinary that any practice relating to land and labor from the time before Spaniards could be compared to the time following the sixteenth century. Despite the loss of indigenous sovereignty and the terror of colonial times, ways of experiencing and valuing landscape, local ecological knowledge, specific skill sets, and concepts of the heritability of land and other possessions survived, albeit in tension with Spanish legal institutions and extractive requirements.

Cain and Leventhal (2017:183) revisit the importance of land and language to contemporary people of Tihosuco who assert that the experience of landscape—particularly the *monte* (forested area)—provides a place of refuge and is integrally tied to cultural identity. Against the backdrop of a legal trend toward privatization of communally held lands (known as ejidos in México), the threat of land loss is omnipresent. In an existential sense, such loss is not calculated in hectares but instead is perceived as a chipping away of the capability to experience landscape in its diverse forms, each dimension of which provides distinctive sustenance. The pushback against land commodification within indigenous Maya communities in Mexico, Belize, and elsewhere is not a negation of the value of land but quite the reverse. It is an assertion that the relational experience of humans with land (often called labor) is valued above all else and simply is not alienable under any circumstances (Cain and Leventhal 2017:188). This philosophy likely has great time depth.

Land and labor are complex entities that do not exist in single definitional states but rather are suspended within relationships of ever-shifting authority. As the locus of authority shifts, such change reverberates and impacts particularly the places where different kinds of authority intersect and can be asserted. We suggest that this conception (or model) more closely approximates reality than older categorical models and that it is more congruent with archaeological evidence. Shifting the discussion away from "control over" and toward "authority to" recognizes the role of negotiation in the always politicized arenas of land and labor. Additionally, this construct allows inclusion of what might be called "ultimate authorities" or supernatural forces that were perceived to play a structuring role in the disposition of land and labor.

Early culture-area presentations of the Maya lowlands—particularly the northern part—emphasized a homogeneous plain of thin soil punctuated by sinkholes. The reality is quite the opposite. The Yucatec landscape contains hot spots of differential magnetism that attract humans because of enhanced qualities, such as soil accumulation or moisture retention. These valued locales were named and claimed and often removed from the common pool of land resources. Such hot spots could be created by human labor or by geomorphological processes; either way, the value of these locales was enhanced because of increased production potential. Land and labor were closely intertwined in the creation of locales of specialized productivity that fed the interdependent networks within which labor and goods circulated to create the complex economies that existed both before and after Spanish incursions.

13

Maya Cornucopia

Indigenous Food Plants of the Maya Lowlands

SCOTT L. FEDICK

Ancient Maya society was based on an agricultural economy. Plants make up the majority of foodstuffs in Maya diets, ancient and modern. Given a large number of edible plants and knowledge of their biological properties, food systems can be adapted and adjusted to take advantage of heterogeneous environments and changing political, demographic, and climatic factors. The purpose of this chapter is to provide a synthesis of the nuts-and-bolts basics of Maya subsistence: a compilation of indigenous food plants that were available to the ancient Maya. Coupled with other works in this volume on agricultural landform transformations and complex and varied cultivation practices, a full consideration of the cornucopia of food plants should dispel lingering views on limitations of the Maya lowlands environment and inherent susceptibility of the agricultural economy to failure or collapse.

Escaping the Maize Maze

The Maya diet of today is dominated by the triad of maize, beans, and squash, maize being the clearly dominant component of the diet, included in the vast majority of prepared dishes (e.g., Salazar et al. 2016). Early ethnographic studies of the Maya, and early archaeological characterizations of ancient Maya agriculture and diet, strongly emphasized the importance of maize as the subsistence base of Maya economies from ancient through modern times. The early ethnographies consistently described Maya agriculture as dependent on slash-and-burn (also shifting or swidden) cultivation, in which a plot of forest was cut, dried, then burned, followed by the planting of maize, supplemented by beans and squash (forming a milpa field). According to these early ethnographers, milpa fields were cultivated for a year or two before the plot was left unused, allowing the forest to regrow for at least ten years before being utilized in the same manner again. Early researchers presented the milpa cycle as a land extensive system believed to be the only sustainable cultivation practice possible in an environment consistently described as cursed with thin soils of low fertility and high susceptibility to erosion and weed infestation. While early ethnographic works did mention other food plants as cultivated or gathered by the Maya, maize was universally assumed to dominate the agricultural system, diet, and thoughts of Maya farmers.

The ethnographic emphasis on milpa farming, and the dominance of maize in the diet, is traced in part to social and economic conditions of the Colonial Period that followed European contact (see Fedick 2017). When the Spanish first encountered the Maya, they were exposed to food plants that were novel and difficult to accept as proper food (Schwartz 1990:54–55). Spanish agriculture and diet were based on Old World grains including wheat, barley, rye, oats, and millet and beans or peas such as chickpeas, broad beans, and lentils (G. Herrera 2006). The Spanish did come to recognize maize and beans as closest to the Old World staples that they were used to (Farriss 1984:33). Before European contact, maize was already established as a commodity used to pay tribute to Maya overlords (Patch 1993:20; Roys 1972:61). The Spanish continued this practice into the eighteenth century, collecting maize as the only food plant demanded as annual tribute (Patch 1993:28). The Spanish also demanded that the rural Maya produce a surplus of maize and beans, which was either purchased or confiscated by Spanish grain merchants and government agents, to feed the growing urban population of non-Maya (Farriss 1984:45–46; Patch 1993:98). Maize and beans also became important commodities to the Spanish, who used them as marine provisions and to feed growing colonies throughout the Spanish Caribbean (Farriss 1984:33, 369).

An emphasis on milpa cultivation and maize is also a result of postcontact warfare and Maya resistance to foreign domination. During attempts at subjugation of the Maya by Spanish conquistadors and administrators, one strategy was to break up and relocate long-established Maya communities (the policy of *reducción*), in part by destroying stable and fixed elements of their agricultural system. This meant destroying perennial crops, which tied families to specific holdings of land (see Farriss 1984:161–162; McAnany 1995:66–79). A Spanish royal ordinance issued by Tomás López Medel in 1552 specifically prohibited the Maya from having groves within their towns and ordered them to be burned if present (Ortiz Yam 2009). The Spanish chroniclers mention the destruction of orchards and the great distress that this caused the Maya (see Hellmuth 1977:423–425; Puleston 1968:64, 66). Perennial crops, particularly trees, can take years after they are planted to begin producing food but can then continue to produce for many years or decades. Annual crops, as the name implies, produce food for a single growing season. Thus, government policies that constantly move people around or deny land tenure rights promote the cultivation of annual crops, such as maize, and shifting cultivation practices that preclude or discourage fixed plot systems.

One form of Maya resistance to foreign domination was to flee control and adopt a mobile form of settlement and agriculture that was not fixed in space, allowing for relocation at a moment's notice (see Farriss 1984:72–73). For the fleeing Maya, agriculture relying on annual crops with seeds that could be stored and transported was the obvious solution.

Regional populations had dropped precipitously by the time ethnographers took to the field, and the Maya had lived under foreign domination for generations. As a result, the Maya had adapted their agricultural strategies and crop use to drastically different social and economic conditions but managed to retain their traditional ecological and botanical knowledge.

Changing Perceptions among Archaeologists about Ancient Population Levels and Agricultural Practices

Prior to the 1960s, when archaeologists made attempts to characterize ancient Maya population levels and agricultural practices, they were working under the adopted ethnographic assumption that the Maya practiced land-extensive, long-fallow slash-and-burn "shifting" cultivation and that this implied low regional populations. This was reflected in early population estimates put forth by archaeologists for the Maya lowlands, which were commonly calculated to average about 12 people per square kilometer (Culbert and Rice 1990). By the 1960s archaeological projects were beginning to expand investigations out from the temples and palaces of civic-ceremonial centers and into the surrounding forests. What the archaeologists found was very unexpected; a multitude of house foundations scattered across the landscape, suggesting population levels that could not have been supported by the long-fallow milpa farming as characterized in the ethnographic descriptions.

Archaeologists began to consider other crops and other cultivation systems that might have been used in ancient times. Bronson (1966) suggested that root crops served the ancient Maya as a dietary alternative or supplement for maize. Puleston (1968) argued that the *ramón* tree (*Brosimum alicastrum*), one of the most common species in the forests of the Maya lowlands, could have served as a maize-alternative subsistence base. Wilken (1971) suggested a wide range of cultivation technologies and crops, particularly tree crops, that were available to the Maya and would have been cultivated with stable, forest farming methods.

While various plants were being considered as alternatives or supplements to the ancient Maya diet, investigators began to discover evidence for previously unrecognized cultivation methods represented by engineering features such as raised or drained fields in wetlands and terraces on hill slopes. Following a synthesis of new data and evolving perceptions about the agricultural potential of the Maya lowlands (Harrison and Turner 1978), the "myth of the milpa" (Hammond 1978) was declared overturned, replaced by a new paradigm of intensive agriculture supported by a variety of agricultural engineering practices. This new model of ancient agriculture was more in line with the new regional population estimates that envisioned variable densities of between 100 and 250 people per square kilometer (Culbert and Rice 1990).

While the myth of the long-fallow milpa system may have been put to rest, in many, if not most, academic circles maize remained as the single staple thought to dominate the envisioned intensively cultivated plots and the diet of the ancient Maya. This continuing focus on maize, and seeming resistance to notions of crop diversity, is attributed to two factors; the lack of physical or archaeological evidence for crops other than maize and the significant impression of maize in the ethnohistoric and ethnographic records.

Archaeological Identification of Ancient Maya Plant Use

Attempts at recovering plant remains from lowland Maya archaeological sites has a short and until recently not very productive history of research. It was long assumed that plant remains, even in carbonized form, would not preserve in the humid environment of the Maya lowlands. Systematic attempts at recovery of carbonized plant remains by means of flotation methods began in the 1970s but still have not become standard practice in Maya archaeology. A few notable archaeological projects and paleoethnobotanists have doggedly pursued plant recovery and have contributed successfully to compiling lists of identified plants. Recent methodological advances in recovery and identification of pollen, phytoliths, and starch grains have also contributed to growing lists of ancient plant remains (e.g., Lentz 1999; Morell-Hart 2011; Simms 2014; K. Thompson et al. 2015).

While the efforts of paleoethnobotanists have greatly expanded the data on ancient plant use, caution must be exercised in interpreting the importance of represented plant species in the actual subsistence economy of the ancient Maya (see Vanderwarker 2006:66–78). Some plants are much more likely than others to be preserved, recovered, and identified through the archaeological record. Taphonomic or formation processes introduce biases that determine which plants enter the archaeological record and which do not (for formation process and plant remains, see Miksicek 1987; for interpretive issues with the pollen record, see Fedick 2010; Ford 2008; Ford and Nigh 2015:91–93). An example of this bias is the differential representation of maize and manioc in the archaeological record. Maize (*Zea mays*) is one of the most frequently recovered plants from archaeological sites, in large part because it is preserved through durable carbonized cob fragments as well as pollen, phytoliths, and starch grains, all of which are identifiable to the species level for this domesticated plant. In contrast, manioc or yuca (*Manihot esculenta*), suggested by some as a possible staple of the ancient Maya, introduced from South America in ancient times, has been very elusive in the archaeological record. The edible tubers of manioc consist of delicate tissue that does not readily preserve, and the plant produces few or no diagnostic seeds, pollen, or phytoliths. While a few carbonized stem and tissue fragments from manioc had been recovered, it was not until investigations at the site of Joya de Cerén in El Salvador that manioc was positively identified as an intensively cultivated crop extending back to the sixth century BC. Casts of manioc stems and tubers were recovered from cavities left in volcanic ash and the soils buried beneath the ash at Cerén, verifying manioc not only as a crop but as a staple grown in monoculture fields (Sheets et al. 2012). Recently paleoethnobotanists have managed to recover and identify manioc starch grains (e.g., Morell-Hart 2011; Simms 2014).

Maize is likely to remain the most commonly represented species in the archaeological record because of the many ways in which it can be identified to the species level from archaeological deposits and sediments. We should not, however, let this seemingly inherent bias in recovery potential shape our perceptions of ancient Maya agriculture and resource use. A comprehensive listing of indigenous food plants, as initiated here, serves as a guide to archaeologists and paleoethnobotanists, identifying what plants to look for and prompting consideration of what parts of these plants might be identifiable through carbonized fragments, pollen, phytoliths, starch grains, or even distinctive chemical residues.

Sources and Methods

The current summary and discussion focuses only on indigenous *food* plants of the Maya lowlands and is based on twenty-eight ethnographic, ethnobotanical, and botanical studies published since the 1930s that contain scientific taxonomic identifications of plants to species level, both domesticated and non-domesticated, and that are described as being used as food by Maya residing in the lowlands (below 800 m elevation) of Mexico's Yucatán Peninsula, northern Guatemala, Belize, and adjacent areas of Honduras and El Salvador (see the appendix table). The sources include ethnobotanical studies for specific Maya groups (Anderson et al. 2003; Atran 1993; Atran and Ek' 1999; Atran et al. 2004; Cook 2016; Steggerda 1943), general ethnobotanical summaries for the lowland Maya (Balick and Arvigo 2015; Barrera Marín et al. 1976; S. Coe 1994; Lundell 1938; Marcus 1982; Roys 1931; Sosa et al. 1985), botanical summaries that include ethnobotanical information (Arellano Rodríguez et al. 2003; Balick et al. 2000; Meerman 1993; Standley and Record 1936; Standley and Steyermark 1949; Vázquez-Yanes et al. 1999; Williams 1981), ethnobotanical studies of milpa fields and home gardens (DeClerck and Negreros-Castillo 2000; Herrera Castro 1994; Terán et al. 1998), and ethnobotanical studies of specific plants or families of plants (Calvo-Irabién and Soberanis 2008; Castillo Mont et al. 1994; Colunga-García Marín et al. 1993; Lira and Caballero 2002; Makkar et al. 1998). Sometimes the cited sources identified a plant as edible but did not specify which part of the plant was used as food; in these few cases, other literature on edible plants was consulted to determine the part or parts most likely eaten (qualified by a "?" in the appendix table). Dozens of other botanical, ethnographic, and ethnobotanical works on the Maya lowlands were also reviewed and considered in the background of the study but are not cited here because the species identified are redundant for those included in the works cited above. It should be noted that the food-plant list does not include nonvascular edible plants (such as mosses and bryophytes) or mushrooms and other forms of fungi. Many indigenous edible plants present in the Maya lowlands probably have not been reported as being recognized as food by the Maya; those plants are not included in the current list.

In compiling the present list of indigenous food plants (appendix table), one of the significant tasks was to identify which plants were actually indigenous to the Maya lowlands. Native distribution of each plant was verified through the Germplasm Resources Information Network (GRIN), maintained by the United States National Plant Germplasm System (https://npgsweb.ars-grin.gov/gringlobal/taxon/taxonomysearch.aspx, accessed June 2017). A second authority used for native distributions is Kew Science: Plants of the World Online (http://powo.science.kew.org, accessed June 2017). Various other sources were used to identify native distributions if a species was not included in the GRIN or Kew databases. It should also be noted that the origin of some plants is still debated among botanists.

Chronologically, the goal was to include food plants that were present in the Maya lowlands at the time of European contact, generally placed about AD 1520. Eliminating plants from the list that were introduced to the Maya area from the Old World during postcontact times was fairly straightforward. A number of plants that were reported as cultivated or gathered in the Maya lowlands, however, had apparently been introduced from other parts of the Americas, specifically from other areas of Mesoamerica, from farther south in Central America, and from South America. In researching these plants, it was found that the timing for their introduction into the Maya lowlands was almost always uncertain. Many (but not all) of these introduced American plants have now been identified archaeologically as having been present in the Maya lowlands prior to European contact. These plants are included here as "indigenous" plants of the Maya lowlands but are identified as likely introductions from elsewhere in the Americas prior to contact.

Another task involved in compiling the plant list was dealing with inconsistencies and changes in taxonomic nomenclature. Over the years plants have been renamed, previously separate species have been grouped into individual species, synonyms have been recognized, and debates continue over many taxonomic designations. The current plant list follows taxonomic nomenclature of the Angiosperm Phylogeny Group (APG), as currently maintained and updated on the Missouri Botanical Garden website (www.mobot.org/MOBOT/research/APweb/, accessed June 2017) and associated Tropicos website (www.tropicos.org, accessed June 2017). Scientific names and authorities for each species were also verified for APG nomenclature using the Taxonomic Name Resolution Service, version 4, maintained by the iPlant Collaborative (http://tnrs.iplantcollaborative.org, accessed June 2017) in collaboration with the Missouri Botanical Garden.

Diversity of Maya Food Plants

The literature review has identified 497 species of plants that are reported as being used as food by the Maya (appendix table). Of this total, 451 are known to have native distributions that include the Maya lowlands, while the other 46 species have native distributions in other areas of the Americas but were likely present in the Maya lowlands prior to European contact. It is important to note that several of the edible species included in the plant list may be toxic in their natural state and require processing before consumption.

To summarize the taxonomic diversity of Maya food plants, 38 orders, 100 families, 296 genera, and an impressive cornucopia of 497 species of food plants are represented. The growth habit by species includes 176 tree, 26 palm (tree), 2 cycad (tree), 61 shrub or tree, 52 shrub, 95 herb, 57 vine, 14 lianas (long-stemmed, woody vines), 9 succulent, and 5 grass. Edible parts of the plants consist of 263 fruits or berries; 69 leaves; 65 seeds or nuts; 30 flowers; 30 roots, rhizomes, tubers, or bulbs; 26 shoots, buds, or stems (other than palm); 24 pods; 19 inflorescences, peduncles, or spadices; 18 stems (heart of palm); 10 gums, latexes, or saps; 6 arils; 5 oils; 5 barks; 4 pads (a distinctive form of stem); and 3 grass grains. Some plants have more than one edible part; only parts specified as eaten by the Maya are enumerated here, while other parts identified as edible are included in the appendix table (with a "?" following the part eaten).

Plants of Potentially Greatest Economic Significance

The ethnobotanical evidence indicates that ancient Maya subsistence economy need not have relied on maize as a sole subsistence staple (see Fedick 2017). While other potential food plants have been suggested as major dietary components, the complete listing (appendix table) emphasizes the large number of candidates. Maize, as a grain crop, is of course recognized as both a dietary staple and a commodity that could have been stored and transported to relieve local or regional food shortage (see Staller 2010). Only three other edible grain-producing grasses were identified (*Lasiacis divaricata*, *L. ruscifolia*, and *Phragmites australis*), which are relatively unproductive as grain crops.

Seeds and nuts are the closest analogs to maize in terms of compact, storable, portable, and nutritious foods that could serve both as staples and commodities. The accompanying list includes 65 plant species with edible seeds or nuts. Beans are included by botanists as producing seeds, and the list includes the familiar vining and herbaceous beans such as the common bean (*Phaseolus vulgaris*) and lima (*P. lunatus*). Edible seeds are also produced by seven species of trees in the bean (Fabaceae) family, including the very common, productive, and nutrient-dense guanacaste (*Enterolobium cyclocarpum*). Several species and varieties of squash (*Cucurbita argyrosperma, C. lundelliana, C. moschata*, and *C. pepo*) are grown primarily for seeds. Moving beyond the maize-beans-squash triad of subsistence crops, the Amaranthaceae family includes six species of amaranth (*Amaranthus caudatus, A. dubius, A. hybridus, A. retroflexus, A. spinosus*, and *A. viridis*) that produce an abundance of seeds as well as edible leafy greens and have served as important components of other indigenous American diets and market systems (e.g., Aztec). The seeds/nuts of several trees also represent nutritious, storable, and transportable foods of potential significance, particularly the now well-known *ramón* tree (*Brosimum alicastrum*) and the lesser-known *ramón colorado* (*Brosimum costaricanum*) as well as the provision tree (*Pachira aquatica*) and the domesticated cashew (*Anacardium occidentale*). Edible seeds are also produced by a variety of other trees, shrubs, and vines, as well as sunflowers (*Helianthus annuus*), cycads (*Dioon mejiae* and *D. spinulosum*), and a nontoxic variety of physic nut (*Jatropha curcas*). Another seed of known importance in ancient Maya economy and ritual is cacao (*Theobroma cacao*).

Roots, rhizomes, and tubers are used as major crops throughout the tropics and semitropics, and many of these are stored in the ground for extended periods. For the Maya lowlands, the most likely of the 30 kinds of root/rhizome/tuber food-plants to have served as major crops or commodities are manioc or yuca (*Manihot esculenta*), malanga or makal (*Xanthosoma violaceum* and *X. yucatanense*), sweet potato (*Ipomoea batatas*), arrowroot (*Maranta arundinacea*), canna (*Canna indica* and *C. tuerckheimii*), and several species of New World yams (*Dioscorea bartlettii, D. convolvulacea, D. floribunda, D. polygonoides*, and *D. trifida*), as well as other species found in wetlands, such as cattail (*Typha domingensis*). Most, if not all, of these species are known to be ground and dried for storage and transport.

Greens, primarily in the form of leaves, are widely used by the lowland Maya as food. Edible leaves would be available for harvest through most of the year, while preservation methods of drying could enable leaves to be stored and used as commodities. Dried leaves are crumbled into powder and added to soups and stews. Of the 69 species of edible leaves found in the Maya lowlands, the most likely to be significant sources of nutrition are chaya (*Cnidoscolus aconitifolius*), amaranth (species listed above for seeds), chenopodium (*Chenopodium ambro-sioides* and *C. berlandieri*), and portulaca (*Portulaca oleracea* and *P. pilosa*).

Fruits (and berries), primarily from trees, are the most numerous form of food plant, with 262 different indigenous species being used. With such an abundance of fruits, methods of processing and preservation would certainly have been well developed by the ancient Maya. Examples of the most likely fruits that could serve as major crops or commodities include mamey (*Pouteria sapota*), chico sapote (*Manilkara zapota*), jocote or hog plum (*Spondias pur-purea*), guava (*Psidium guajava*), papaya (*Carica papaya*), and several species of annona (*Annona* sp.), as well as members of the palm (Arecaceae) family, such as the fruit of the coyol (*Acrocomia aculeata*). Several species of chilis (*Cap-sicum* sp.), readily dried for storage and transport, were also likely important market items.

Domestication and American Introductions

The domestication of local plants and the introduction of food plants from other areas of the Americas, both domesticated and wild, are significant aspects of Maya subsistence economy. The identified food plants presented here repre-sent a range from gathered wild plants to domesticated and cultivated varieties, both indigenous to the Maya lowlands, and those probably introduced during antiquity from the north or south.

Recent research has identified 18 food plants that have been studied in enough detail to indicate that they were likely domesticated *in* the Maya lowlands (Agu-irre-Dugua et al. 2013; Colunga-García Marín and Zizumbo-Villarreal 2004; Makkar et al. 1998). Some of these plants may also have been independently domesticated elsewhere. Of these 18 domesticates, 7 are fruiting trees: the hog plum (*Spondias purpurea*), papaya (*Carica papaya*), cacao (*Theobroma cacao*), black sapote (*Diospyros nigra*), mamey (*Pouteria sapota*), guava (*Psidium gua-java*), and calabash (*Crescentia cujete*; used as food, but domesticated primar-ily for use as bowls), along with the fruit of the shrub/tree nance (*Byrsonima crassifolia*) and the young inflorescence of a palm (*Chamaedorea tepejilote*). Five other indigenous Maya domesticates are herbaceous plants with edible leaves, tubers, seeds, and/or fruit: sweet potato (*Ipomoea batatas*), a chile (*Capsicum annuum*), lima bean (*Phaseolus lunatus*), and two kinds of euphorbia, chaya (*Cnidoscolus aconitifolius*) and physic nut (*Jatropha curcas*). The vining jícama (*Pachyrhizus erosus*) of the bean family (Fabaceae) produces an edible root, while vanilla (*Vanilla planifolia*), a vining orchid, was domesticated for the fragrant and flavorful fruit (pod). An herbaceous cactus, pitahaya (*Hylocereus undatus*) was domesticated by the Maya for fruit, while a succulent, henequen (*Agave fourcroydes*), was domesticated for both food and fiber. Another 8 food plants are identified as native to the Maya lowlands and possibly domesticated there (qualified with a "?" in the appendix table), although more research is needed to verify in situ domestication (Colunga-García Marín and Zizumbo-Villarreal 2004).

At least 33 species of domesticated food plants incorporated into Maya fields and gardens come from elsewhere in the Americas and are included here as "indigenous" food plants, likely used by the Maya prior to European contact (see Colunga-García Marín and Zizumbo-Villarreal 2004 for most of these plants). Of these, 19 are from South America, most notably the fruiting trees soursop (*Annona muricata*) and cherimoya (*Annona cherimola*), the peach palm (*Bactris gasipaes*), and herbaceous plants with edible leaves, fruits, or tubers, including a very productive amaranth (*Amaranthus caudatus*), blue tarro or malanga (*Xanthosoma violaceum*), and manioc (*Manihot esculenta*); sweet potato (*Ipomoea batatas*) is thought to have been domesticated in both South America and the Maya lowlands. Another 11 domesticated plants are from other parts of Mesoamerica, most notably avocado (*Persea americana*), cushaw squash (*Cucurbita argyrosperma*), pepo squash (*Cucurbita pepo*), tomato (*Lycopersicon esculentum*), tomatillo (*Physalis pubescens*), and the common bean (*Phaseolus vulgaris*). It is still uncertain whether moschata squash (*Cucurbita moschata*) was domesticated in South America or Mesoamerica. From the eastern United States comes the domesticated sunflower (*Helianthus annuus*).

Interestingly, 37 *wild* food plants ultimately originated from outside of the Maya lowlands and may well have been spread into the Maya area by human agency. Of these wild species, 19 originate in South America, 10 from elsewhere in Mesoamerica but outside of the Maya lowlands, 7 from elsewhere in Central America but outside of the Maya lowlands, and 1 from the Maya highlands. The significant number of plants introduced into the Maya lowlands from elsewhere in the Americas indicates the cosmopolitan nature of Maya agriculture and plant use.

In addition to the plants discussed above, the list includes a great variety of primarily lesser-known species ranging from cactus and succulents to epiphytes and aquatic plants, including edible parts from bark, sap, latex, and oils to flowers, inflorescences, shoots and stems to pads, pods and peduncles. Most of these plants probably served as minor foodstuffs or as flavorings and spices. Many probably functioned as "famine foods," only eaten out of necessity when more productive or nutritious foods were not available for whatever reasons.

Other Implications of the List

The food-plant list in the appendix focuses on the range of edible plants that could have been incorporated into the ancient Maya subsistence economy and many candidates for the market economy. While they are beyond the scope of this chapter, other implications of the list are worth evaluating for future research.

As discussed, the interpretation of ancient plant remains involves many problematic issues. Perhaps most serious of all is the use of pollen data to make inferences about the presence and use of food plants and about deforestation (Fedick 2010; Ford 2008; Ford and Nigh 2015:91–93). This issue has been explored by Fedick and Islebe (2012) with a preliminary list of indigenous food plants of the Maya lowlands. Pollen from different kinds of plants is not equally represented in the pollen rain that settles on land or in bodies of water, which forms the fossil pollen record that is recovered from sediments. The number of pollen grains that a flower produces, and how many pollen grains may potentially contribute to the pollen record of sediments, is strongly associated with pollination strategy. Plants that rely on pollination by wind (anemophilous plants) produce a large number of pollen grains that are generally small. These plants contribute large amounts of pollen to the pollen rain and the subsequent pollen record. Plants that rely on pollination by animals (zoophilous plants) or insects (entomophilous plants) generally produce small amounts of pollen, the grains of which are mostly larger. With rare exceptions, plants that are pollinated by animals or insects contribute only small amounts of pollen to the pollen record. It is a well-established fact that a strong bias exists in the pollen record of sediments (see Bradley 2015:410; Pearsall 1989:253). Animal/insect-pollinated taxa not only dominate the Maya forest (Ford 2008) but also dominate the food plants that were available to the ancient Maya. From a preliminary overview (Fedick and Islebe 2012), the data show that of the approximately 500 indigenous food plants known to be used by the lowland Maya less than 8% of those species are wind pollinated plants. The overwhelming majority of those food plants are pollinated by animals or insects and would be highly under-represented, if not absent, in the pollen record. It should be noted that maize is a prolific producer of pollen, producing about 25 million grains per cob (Aylor et al. 2003). Maize pollen is distributed by both wind and insects, and the domesticated form of this grass is generally considered to be easily distinguished by pollen identification from other wild grasses of the Poaceae family. Again there is a strong bias in favor of maize identification in the archaeological and sedimentary record.

Plants with a range of adaptations to drought conditions are represented in the plant list. Long-term droughts have recently received prominent discussion as a primary factor in the social and demographic disruptions of the Terminal Classic Period (for a critical review, see Iannone 2014). Different species of plants respond in specific ways to water stress, depending on the physiology of the plant. This fact has received scant attention in the agricultural-collapse scenarios that have been suggested to associate with droughts. The food plants of the list have undergone preliminary evaluation for drought resistance by Fedick and Santiago (2012). The study uses stem growth process and photosynthetic pathway (C_3, C_4 or CAM [Crassulacean Acid Metabolism]) to classify plants as drought resistant, moderately drought resistant, or drought vulnerable with low drought resistance. We found that 71 percent of the food plants are drought resistant, 3 percent are moderately drought resistant, and 16 percent are drought vulnerable. It is interesting to consider the photosynthetic pathways represented among the food plants, and how archaeologists have made inferences about ancient Maya diet using stable carbon isotope analysis of skeletal material to determine the relative amounts of diet represented by C_3, C_4 or CAM plants. With few exceptions, Maya archaeologists interpret any C_4 indicators as originating from consumption of maize, harking to the ethnographic data discussed earlier. There are, however, 15 Maya food plants, other than maize, that follow the C_4 pathway, and another 28 plants that follow the CAM pathway. These data confound a simplistic interpretation of maize consumption—again a bias in favor of maize identification.

Conclusions

The long-term stability of ancient Maya residential settlements and the generally high settlement densities demonstrated for the region over long periods suggest agricultural practices that were stable and resilient. The simple slash-and-burn techniques of the milpa, as characterized in early ethnographies as based on maize, beans, and squash, and incorporating an abandonment period of unmanaged regrowth, were certainly different in ancient times. Complex and interwoven with the mosaic landscape, agricultural fields were more likely to have been what is sometimes described in more recent research as a high performance milpa, making use of the great variety of crops and practicing managed regrowth that incorporates perennial food plants (Ford and Nigh 2015). These fields would have been supplemented by productive and diverse homegardens within settlements as well as by long-term manipulation of the surrounding forest, transforming the "wild jungle" into a managed mosaic (e.g., Fedick 1996; Ford and Nigh 2015; Lentz, Magee, et al. 2015). The cornucopia of indigenous Maya food plants provides the key to understanding the complexity and diversity of the ancient Maya subsistence economy.

Acknowledgments

I would like to thank several of my colleagues who supplied much valued comments on various drafts of this paper: Eugene Anderson, Mary Baker, Anabel Ford, Lucia Gudiel, Gerald Islebe, David Lentz, Cameron McNeil, Shanti Morell-Hart, Laura Pontow, Louis Santiago, and Andrew Wyatt.

14

Service Relationships within the Broader Economy of Cerén, a Young Maya Village

PAYSON SHEETS

Documenting service relationships among commoner households in ancient villages often proves challenging for archaeologists. Fortunately, however, the Classic Period small Maya village of Cerén, El Salvador, is preserved sufficiently well that service relationships between households and their special facilities, and the villagers who used them, can be perceived. It is a "young Maya village" because it has existed for a very short time. I define a household service relationship as a voluntary set of activities that benefit the community as a whole or at least components of the community beyond the household. The material correlates of service behavior by household members and their recipients provide clues regarding the social networks of the village.

This chapter begins with a focus on the nature of service relationships of Cerén households, within the social network of the community, and then explores economic implications and repercussions. The service relationships were embedded within household activities, but it appears that they conflicted for time and effort with routine household obligations such as agriculture and intrahousehold activities. Agriculture as well as food storage, processing, serving, structure maintenance, and other standard household activities require major efforts and are to be assumed when other obligations are considered below. I am confident that children took part in many basic household activities. At another level, time and effort conflicts may have occurred with a household's part-time specialization, where members of each household produced something in greater quantities than they needed for their own consumption (Sheets 2000). Surplus production in any year could have been in agriculture or part-time specialization or both. In any event, surplus production was necessary for exchanges in one of the many marketplaces in the Zapotitán valley (Sheets 2000). Members of every household was dependent on markets to obtain the items that they needed but could not produce themselves, including a jade celt, obsidian tools, polychrome pottery serving vessels, and pigments (hematite, limonite, and cinnabar).

Before doing research for and writing this chapter I had not done a comparative analysis of the households in terms of their very different service obligations and the differences in items that needed to be obtained by exchanges in a marketplace. Taking this approach has changed some of my understandings about how life was lived in Cerén. One important item that is found in every household is well documented in terms of distribution: copal. Every household had an incense burner; indeed every kitchen, *bodega* (storehouse), and domicile had its own *incensario* (censer). Each tested positive for copal. What is unknown is whether household members had to travel to a market to obtain the copal. The copal tree (*Protium copal*) grows well in the wet tropical lowlands but not in the highly seasonal areas such as El Salvador (David Lentz, personal communication 2017), so people probably imported the sap up into the highlands and into the Zapotitán valley. Copal apparently is the item transported the longest distance into Cerén households. Service relationships along with the economics of exchanges of surplus production helped create a social web of interdependencies within the community. In addition, at the highest level, households participated in the regional economy by exchanges made at one of the approximately one dozen marketplaces in the area.

The variety of service relationships is, of course, not the only factor that likely generated differences among Cerén households. As Cameron (2016) points out, small-scale societies have internal differentiation in a variety of statuses. To those statuses I add the principle of first occupancy, where the first families who founded Cerén would more likely be of higher status than the more recent arrivals. Because all the households considered here were in the center of town, they all were probably among the early founders and thus may not have differed much in that category. The emergence of part-time specializations per household seems to have generated a spontaneous interdependency. Ground-penetrating radar apparently detected the likely later arrivals dozens of meters south of the central area.

The evidence for service relationships includes artifacts (presence and absence), plant materials, proximities, and foot traffic. The proximity of a house-

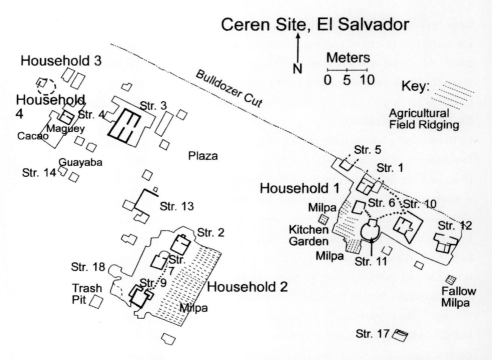

Figure 14.1. Map of Cerén. Household 1 had a service relationship with the two religious buildings east of it. Household 2 had a service relationship with the sauna to its south. Note the dotted lines showing major foot traffic. Household 4 grew specialty crops.

hold to a special facility, such as a sauna or a religious building, suggests the possibility of a service relationship. The well-trod informal paths linking household buildings to special facilities strengthen that relationship. The four dotted lines on the map (Figure 14.1) record those paths.

The Young Maya Village of Cerén

The Cerén village was stratigraphically and chronologically "sandwiched" between two volcanic eruptions (Sheets 2002). Understanding the eruptions, chronology, and preservation resulting from the second eruption is essential before exploring the service relationships. The first was the cataclysmic eruption of Ilopango volcano in the early sixth century, possibly in AD 535 (Dull et al. 2010) or more likely 539. The magnitude of that eruption eliminated all forms of floral and faunal life (including human of course) in what is now El Salvador. A few decades later sufficient weathering and plant succession occurred to permit Maya agriculturalists to colonize central and western El Salvador. As a part of that immigration a few families settled on the west bank of the Río Sucio, thus founding the town of Cerén. I estimate that the founding occurred about AD 590, plus or minus a decade or so. The achievements of this nascent community are impressive, given that only some three generations lived there before it was entombed by the second eruption. The villagers' achievements were dramatically terminated by the eruption of the Loma Caldera volcanic vent (C. Miller 2002) in the AD 660s. The magma worked its way upward and began to contact the water of the Río Sucio only 600 m north of town. The first perceptible clue of environmental instability was an earthquake of about 4 on the Richter scale. That would not have caused great concern, as earthquakes of that magnitude are quite common. The next component must have been fearsome, as steam began escaping from the vent, creating a defining shrieking noise so loud that two people yelling to each other, face-to-face, could not hear themselves.

This type of eruption (phreatomagmatic) is not uncommon in El Salvador and occurred fairly often along the fissure from the Zapotitán valley to Ilopango caldera, so I believe it is likely that Cerén residents had an oral tradition to flee immediately. Presumably they fled south, probably using the *sacbe*. We have yet to find a person in town killed by the eruption. Some of the footprints headed south that we found along the *sacbe* may well be from persons escaping.

The next stage was the eruption proper, when a massive steam explosion propelled a cloud of fine, moist volcanic ash blasting across the landscape at velocities between 50 and 200 km/hr. The cloud was 100°C because it was a steam explosion: a pasty mass coated buildings, thatch roofs, maize plants, and about everything else in and around the town. That steam explosion was so violent that it blasted away the river water for a short while, allowing for a dry phase of the eruption to deposit cinders and some volcanic bombs across the landscape. Then the river water again flowed over the vent, causing the second steam explosion and pasty layer to blast in and coat whatever was still exposed. That alternation of steam explosions and dry phases occurred fourteen times until the village was buried under 4–7 m of stratified volcanic ash within days. The first and third steam explosion layers are what helped preserve very fine details of activity areas, individual plants growing in milpas, and root crop fields and sealed all the foods stored in the household and ritual buildings. For instance, a pot holding hundreds of squash seeds in the community ritual building was perfectly preserved: the seeds had not changed in size, weight, or shape in 1,400 years in spite of the hot moist tropical climate (and I was sorely tempted to eat just one but finally decided that archaeologists should never eat their data). Burial was sufficiently deep and of such a nature that the village was isolated from the usual agents of bioturbation. No tree roots, burrowing animals, insects, or people got down to the Classic Period village and affected its preservation.

Service Relationships and Household Economics

Seasonality must have had a marked effect on service relationships, the most obvious example being the middle-of-the rainy season harvest ceremony at Structure 10, hosted by Household 1 (see below). It probably took place in August, when the maize has just matured. Fully 94% of the annual rainfall occurs in May through October. It is unknown whether Structure 10 was utilized at other times of the year. All households at Cerén invested most of their agricultural efforts of planting, microtopographic field maintenance, weeding, harvesting, and storing foodstuffs during that rainy season. Therefore, all other things being equal, households would have more time available for service relationships during the dry season.

This section examines the service relationships of two households in detail, in the contexts of their broader household economics, noting another household where the part-time economic specialization was unusual, as specialty crops were the focus.

Household 1

Of the small sample of excavated households in the village, the service activities of Household 1 evidently were the most time and effort intensive (Figure 14.2). This household apparently supported the functioning of the two religious buildings located immediately to the east of the household (Sheets 2006). Those religious buildings are at the highest elevation in the site and overlook the river that drains the valley. At Structure 10, closer to the households (Figure 14.2), a ceremony celebrating the harvest was actually underway at the time of the eruption (Brown and Gerstle 2002). The most obvious physical evidence of this household's service relationship is the food preparation for ceremonial participants provided by its members. The compaction of the ground surface from the household's buildings directly to Structure 10's entrance is clear evidence of considerable back-and-forth foot traffic (mapped as dotted lines in Figure 14.1).

Figure 14.2. Household 1, on the far right, was responsible for maintaining the two religious buildings and their functioning. Structure 12 on the far left was where the diviner practiced. Structure 10 in the middle is the village ceremonial building where the harvest ceremony was in process when the volcano erupted.

This household had an overabundance of metates and manos (Sheets 2002:47–56). One was used regularly for internal consumption and was deeply eroded from long use. It was on the floor of the kitchen. What is striking is that four others, with minimal wear, were mounted on *horquetas* (sturdy forked posts) to be used by a standing person. Three of the four were found still mounted, while one was in storage position upside-down on the ground between the two *horquetas*. When a ceremony in Structure 10 needed ground food, presumably maize, household members would mount the metates on the *horquetas*, clean them, and grind large quantities. The reason that one was unmounted is unknown. It could be because the three were supplying sufficient ground food or because a fourth food grinder was unavailable.

The supplying of food from the household to the ceremonial participants presumably had some indirect socioeconomic implications, as it generated obligations or gratitude that could be reciprocated by material exchanges from participants to the members of Household 1 (Figure 14.2). The community could count on Household 1 to supply the food that formed an essential component of the rituals giving thanks for the harvest and presumably setting up the conditions for success in the next growing season by traditional rituals. In addition to the large amounts of ground maize provided by Household 1, some maize was husked/shucked, ground, processed, and served within Structure 10, surely with considerable religious importance.

Two other aspects of the Household 1's service relationship to the religious complex involves tools (Sheets 2006). In excavating the Household 1 structures, I was surprised to find no antler *tapiscador* (corn husker). That was clarified by finding a *tapiscador* in the north corridor of Structure 10, next to a *horqueta*-mounted metate. This is the part of Structure 10 closest to Household 1, and I believe the members of the household loaned their *tapiscador* for the ceremony. Two other *tapiscadores* were stored temporarily on a high shelf near the other, also likely on loan. A *tapiscador* would not be kept permanently in a structure that was only occasionally utilized, unprotected, as it would be chewed by rodents. The same reasoning applies to the elegant deer skull headdress found on the shelf of the most sacred room inside Structure 10. If unprotected, it would have been easily destroyed by gnawing rodents, so I suspect that it was carefully curated within one of the household's actively occupied buildings when ceremonies were not being held.

Another aspect of a service relationship involves structural maintenance. No architectural smoothing tools were found in Structures 10 or 12, but the household had plenty of them. *Bajareque* (wattle-and-daub) architecture needs constant attention in filling cracks, replacing the cane and horizontal reinforcements, rethatching every decade or two, and smoothing the fine clay-tephra mix used for finishing the wall surfaces. The lowest meter of the cane reinforcements is within the zone of moistening from capillary moisture and thus will decompose sufficiently after a decade or two to require replacement. Each building was demolished down to its foundation (floor) and then entirely rebuilt. The grass thatch roof and all the wooden beams and supports were removed, and new thatch was obtained. The walls were entirely eliminated, so new vertical poles were emplaced, laced together by horizontal vines and then remudded on both sides. Every year or two both buildings would have needed a new application of a "sacrificial surfacing" of fine clay-tephra plastering to the bottom meter of all walls, to replace the erosion created when capillary moisture moves upward with dissolved salts. When the moisture dries, the salts are left behind and force particles of wall to fall off every day. The new coating must be applied before the wall becomes too undercut. Presumably, Household 1 members provided this major service for both Structures 10 and 12.

The archaeological record of Household 1 provided a clear example of re-modeling of *bajareque* architecture in Structure 6, their *bodega*. Just prior to that fateful day in August, the household members had completely removed all walls and roofing and had initiated replacing all elements. They had finished replacing all the poles that would reinforce the walls and support the roof and had completed the roofing support beams and the thatch. They had finished the mudding of the front (east) wall that included the doorway and had just begun the mudding of the other three walls. The mudding was completed only to a height of 36 cm when the eruption occurred and sealed the building and its contents as a time capsule for our edification.

Marilyn Beaudry-Corbett's ceramic functional analyses (Beaudry-Corbett et al. 2002:57) provided an insight into Household 1's support of the feasting and harvest ceremonies in Structure 10. She recognized "Household 1's greater need for long-term storage and commodity transfer containers. Structure 6, the storeroom, had more jars without handles and utilitarian bowls with handles than did other storeroom structures. The storage and commodity transfer functions, similar to maize processing, could relate to Structure 10 activities performed by Household 1 members."

Household 1 members provided labor-intensive service to the religious buildings, evidently doing maintenance to both by rethatching them at least every couple decades and replacing the internal pole reinforcements and then remudding at about the same interval of time. The wall smoothers found only in the Household 1 buildings and not in the religious buildings provide evidence of their architectural service and activity. The periodic reconstructing of the diviner's building (Structure 12) would have taken extra time due to the deliberate fragility of its wattle-and-daub walls (Figure 14.2). Those walls enclosed Ilopango Tierra Blanca Joven (TBJ) tephra, encased in earthen adobe on the outside and inside surfaces, resulting in a very weak wall that may have had great religious import. The service responsibilities were especially complex and time-consuming for Structure 10, in maintaining the structure and in grinding maize. The production of feasts is a powerful mechanism for initiating, maintaining, and reproducing social relations (Brown and Gerstle 2002). However, the time and effort commitments inevitably would conflict with other efforts such as part-time occupational specialization. The part-time occupational specialization of Household 1 was the manufacture of ground-stone tools: manos, metates, and donut stones, as evidenced by the tools used for their manufacture and the abundance of them broken in manufacture or not completed (Sheets 2000).

Such a heavy set of service relationships can have a negative economic impact on the productivity of a household in the intravillage exchanges of products resulting from part-time household specializations. Service would not only limit economic exchanges within the village but, importantly, would probably limit their surplus production for market exchanges, where they could have taken their surplus ground-stone artifacts or agricultural production. At the market they could have exchanged them for the items that were only available there: obsidian prismatic blades, polychrome vessels, and a jade axe. Those service relationships could also be a reason for the more humble construction of their domicile and their *bodega*, when compared to those of Household 2. The household members simply may not have had the time and effort to build as substantially as did their neighbors.

Household 2

Household 2 is located only 45 m southwest of Household 1 (Beaudry-Corbett et al. 2002). The service relationships of Household 2 were quite different from those of Household 1, being focused on a single building: Structure 9, the sauna (Figure 14.3). The initial construction of the sauna was a significant effort because it had a beehive-shaped firebox in the center, surrounded by an extensive bench and enclosed in massive rammed-earth walls, roofed with a *bajareque* dome, and protected by a thick thatch roof (McKee 2002). However, following construction, the time and effort that went into maintenance was considerably less than Household 1's maintenance of two religious structures. That could at least partially explain why Household 2's domicile was on a higher platform, was larger, with a niche under the bench, and was built with higher quality earthen architecture (the mixture of clay and tephra was more appropriate for durability) than the domicile of Household 1. In addition, the household's *bodega* was more substantial in size and platform height and even had an internal table and a sizable front porch (Figure 14.3).

The sauna (Structure 9) is located only 6 m south of the *bodega* (Structure 7) of Household 2. In excavating the ground surface between the two, a zone of compaction slightly over 1 m wide was discovered from the east side of the *bodega* directly to the entrance of the sauna (Figure 14.1). This is evidence of considerable foot traffic between the two. The discovery of an unusual number of ollas for water stored in the *bodega* and a considerable amount of pine sticks (Beaudry-Corbett et al. 2002) points to servicing the functioning of the sauna.

Figure 14.3. Household 2 and the sauna. The household's domicile on the left and the storehouse in the center were involved in maintaining the building and the functioning of the sauna on the right. All were buried under 5 m of volcanic ash.

The water was used for making steam by pouring it over the firebox in the center of the sauna, evidenced by the tiny erosional channel formed by excess water running out of the entrance. Water presumably was also used to rinse sauna users after exiting. The split pine sticks likely were used to start the fire in the firebox and could also have functioned as torches inside the sauna. Without the torches the interior of the sauna would have been almost pitch black, as the small doorway would have been covered. The only light, in daytime use, would come through the tiny ventilation hole in the roof. On a sunny day it would have been a strong but narrow ray only 10 cm in diameter; on a cloudy day, it would have been a diffuse and weaker small cone of light.

As with Household 1, the only architectural surfacing-smoothing tools were found in Household 2 buildings and not in or around the sauna being serviced. Presumably, Household 2 members were responsible for patching cracks in the earthen architecture, maintaining the walls, applying the sacrificial surfacing to the lower meter of the outside walls, and rethatching the thick extensive roof at least every two decades. The thatch roof was essential to preserve the earthen dome. One architectural aspect of the sauna relieved Household 2 members of a substantial amount of maintenance: the walls are solid earthen construction ("terre pise" or rammed earth) and thus did not have to be completely removed to reinsert reinforcing poles. Further, the dome was constructed of cane reinforcements that were mudded on both sides (top and underneath). Because the canes were well above the zone of capillary moisture, the dome would last indefinitely, so long as the thatch roof kept it dry from the rains.

Evidently, the amount of time and effort expended by Household 2 in service relationships to the sauna was only a small fraction of the time and effort expended by Household 1 for the two religious buildings and their functioning. As mentioned above, it is therefore likely that Household 2 members invested more effort in constructing their domicile and *bodega*, resulting in more substantial buildings than the comparable ones in Household 1. Household 2 members spent more effort in achieving a more suitable mixture of clay, volcanic ash, and other components of their earthen architecture.

Detailed artifactual analyses can elucidate the differences in service commitments between Household 1 and 2. If Household 1 had less time to produce a surplus in food or artifacts than Household 2, in part because of greater service obligations, then Household 1 should have fewer artifacts than Household 2 that came from marketplaces. Table 14.1 displays the artifactual record.

There are similarities and significant differences when comparing the two households in terms of the items obtained in one of the marketplaces in the

Table 14.1. A comparison of artifacts from Cerén Households 1 and 2

	Obsidian	Polychrome vessels	Jade	Cinnabar	Shell	Other
Household 1	4 complete prismatic blades, 5 partial blades, 2 scrapers	3 serving vessels (2 bowls, 1 dish)	1 celt	none	1 mother of pearl	1 hematite lump, 3 hematite cylinders
Household 2	4 complete prismatic blades, 10 partial blades, 3 macroblades, 1 scraper	9 serving vessels (bowls and cylinder vessels)	1 celt, 7 jade beads	graded hues of cinnabar in 5 miniature ceramic paint pots	1 *Spondylus*, 1 cowrie	1 jet and 1 incised shell bead, 2 incised shell pendants, lump of specular hematite, hematite and limonite pigment, 2 hematite cylinders

Zapotitán valley. It appears that these differences were directly related to their different service obligations. Both households had four prismatic blades that were complete and remained in storage for future use. In both cases the yet-to-be used blades were stored high in the thatch of the roof, well away from activities of old or young household members who could damage them. Child-proofing was done.

When Cerénians converted a complete stored prismatic blade to use, they broke it into segments at least 3 cm long but rarely over 5 cm long. The blade segments were held by hand, not hafted. Household 1 had five partial blades that were in use, while Household 2 had twice that number. They were similar in numbers of scrapers, but Household 2 had three macroblades and Household 1 had none. The macroblades are the only sharp tools found in their household that could cut a fresh tree gourd into two hemispheres. A single macroblade outweighed all other obsidian artifacts in each household, a significant factor given the need to transport obsidian from the source and the occupational specialization involved in its manufacture and its availability for exchange in a marketplace. Obsidian artifacts have economic value not only in their exchange ratios but also in their weight/volume and the specialist's time and effort. Cerénians did not manufacture obsidian tools within the village, but they did re-sharpen scrapers by percussion blows onto the ventral surface.

Household 2 had three times more polychrome vessels for serving food and drink than Household 1. Most polychrome vessels were made in the Copán valley in what is now Honduras, but some may also have been made in Chalchuapa. Both loci are at significant distances from Cerén, too distant for Cerénians to make the trips. Both households had a single jade celt, certainly the most expensive item that any household needed to obtain by exchanges in a market.

Beyond that, Household 2 had some very special items. One such possession was a necklace that included seven finely manufactured jade beads. The necklace also included a bead of dark gray stone or jet, a shell bead with a five-pointed star incised into it, and two incised shell pendants. Stored together with the necklace was an extraordinary graded set of cinnabar pigments in five miniature ceramic paint pots, presumably used in their part-time occupational specialization of painting hemispherical gourds. Because cinnabar is mercuric sulfide (HgS), it might be problematic to use the gourds for food serving. Fortunately, they were painted with cinnabar only on the outsides. Household 1 had one mother of pearl shell, while Household 2 had a *Spondylus* shell and a cowrie shell. Household 1 members also had a hematite nodule and three hematite cylinders. They owned a miniature metate on which the hematite cylinders were abraded to make a fine red powder, likely for body painting. They also had a domesticated duck with its leg tied to a pole in their *bodega* and some painted gourds. The duck might have been obtained at the market or obtained locally. The painted gourds could also have come from anywhere, with a good possibility that they were obtained from Household 2 nearby (Sheets 2000). It is clear from the detailed household comparisons that Household 2 members had considerably more items from a market, which could in part derive from their lesser obligations for service relationships with their sauna, therefore freeing up more time and effort to generate exchangeable surpluses.

Household 3

Excavation of a 2 × 2 m test pit encountered a small portion of a kitchen belonging to Household 3 (Sheets 2006). Its construction mirrors Household 1's kitchen in that both had thin thatch roofs and walls of pole and thatch, presumably to facilitate air circulation and to ease rebuilding in case of fire. Both had easily replaceable tephra floors and well-used metates for grinding maize daily. Most of the kitchen is still unexcavated, and the other buildings of the household are untouched and remain as intriguing anomalies in the geophysical data. The only unusual item encountered in the small area of the kitchen that was excavated was a large pottery vessel that was in elevated storage and fell on the floor and broke when the roof fire burned the two-ply cordage that had been tying it to a roofing member. It was full of a bright-red liquid paint that splashed on the floor when the pot broke. The coloring agent almost certainly was *Bixa orellana*, otherwise known as achiote. It can be used as a coloring and flavoring agent in foods, but the unusual volume in this case makes that use unlikely. Rather, it may have been stored in the kitchen as body painting for people who were taking part in the harvest ceremonies at the community feasting building (Structure 10) at the time of the eruption. Thus, this may point to a possible service relationship of this household to the community, but the evidence is rather slim.

Household 4

Household 4 is strikingly different from the others, in that the part-time occupational specialization in growing specialty crops also provided a service to the community. As Cerénians received specialty crops, the items provided in exchange had economic implications. This section begins with consideration of those specialty crops and then turns to what the household members kept in their bodega.

Household 4 is known only for one building, Structure 4 (Figure 14.4), and the extensive specialty crop garden to its south and west (Sheets 2006). Approxi-

Figure 14.4. Household 4, the storehouse, buried under 7 m of volcanic ash. In the foreground was the agave garden and the place where cacao was cultivated. A series of chili plants grew to the left of the building.

mately 70 mature *Agave americana* (maguey) plants were growing in a lunate-shaped zone. That species provides only fiber, in contrast to the highland Mexican species. The long fibers were harvested by cutting the long pulpy leaves and taking them to the pole on the east side of the building. A pair of sticks were tied to the pole such that each leaf could be pulled through them, separating the fiber from the pulp. The fibers were twisted into strands of varying thicknesses, then two strands were twisted together to make two-ply string. The stronger strings were used for tying roofing members to the poles that supported the roofs, and the thinner strings were used to suspend pottery vessels in all three kinds of household structures. Because each household needed approximately five mature agave plants to supply its needs, and the strings in both primary uses lasted well over a year, the fiber production from this household supplied well over a dozen additional households and probably closer to two dozen. This likely supplied the entire village with its fiber-for-twine needs, given its small size as presently known. The reciprocal items exchanged by villagers probably varied widely. It appears likely that there was enough fiber left over to take to a market for exchanges.

A cacao tree was growing southwest of the structure, with a flower that was just about to open. Had the eruption delayed a few weeks, the flower could have been pollinated and grown into a full pod loaded with cacao (chocolate) seeds. Cacao seeds were stored inside the building in two different forms (details below).

A dense stand of *Tithonia rotundifolia* (mirasol) was growing just northwest of the structure, and it is probable that the household planted, maintained, and harvested it. As a fast-growing annual with a strong stem, it was used to make the vertical poles that reinforced the *bajareque* walls and supported the roofs, the front walls and swinging front doors of houses, and even portable fences (Lentz and Ramírez-Sosa 2002). The plants discovered in the small test pit were many times more than Household 4 would need in a year. Because no boundary of the field was encountered it is not possible to estimate how many households could have been supplied. It is clear that the pole-reinforcing needs were met for at least a few households beyond this one.

A line of mature chile plants, perennials in a tropical climate, was discovered on the west of the building. Their production could have supplied many households beyond their own. As with the *Tithonia*, however, the boundaries of the plants is yet unknown, so an estimate of the number of households cannot be made.

As one would expect, a striking diversity of botanical resources was stored inside Structure 4 (Sheets 2006). Four pottery vessels stored cacao. One had unprocessed seeds, two had processed cacao, and one even had seeds in the bottom, a cotton gauze cloth as a separator, and chiles above, reminiscent of Mexican mole sauce. That vessel also contained a mouse on top of the chiles, presumably taking advantage of the people not being present, because they were attending the harvest ceremony.

Cotton is represented in a number of forms, ranging from the gauze mentioned above to two cotton cloths, cotton seeds, and apparent production of cotton seed oil. Two fragments of a very fine-weave cotton cloth were on top of the shelf. Cotton seeds were stored inside a ceramic vessel and were ground on the metate mounted atop the forked *horqueta* poles just north of the structure, probably to extract cottonseed oil for cooking. The cacao and the cotton products would have been excellent goods to take to a market to exchange for the items mentioned below. One intriguing item was a ball of bees' wax. It could have been obtained by household members, likely along with honey, which was probably used for sweetening the cacao. Alternatively, they may have obtained it in the marketplace.

In contrast to the botanical richness, the market-obtained goods stored in the structure were comparatively limited: seven partial and no complete prismatic blades as well as two partial macroblades. As with the other households, all sharp obsidian tools were stored up in the roofing thatch, at predictable locations, presumably to protect the sharp edges as well as to "childproof" the residences.

The building contained seven polychrome vessels, a relatively large number for a *bodega*, perhaps at least in part because the building initially was constructed to be a domicile. It was later remodeled by removing the sleeping bench in the inner room and became a *bodega*. Nevertheless, it continued to have some domicile functions. For instance, someone consumed a corn meal gruel from a polychrome bowl just before the eruption, along with a yellowish liquid from a cylinder vessel. The bowl still retains the finger marks from someone's last supper, and other vessel still retains a yellowish stain midway down its inside. It may have been a fermented maize "chicha" drink.

The only jade item was a celt. The building contained a few lumps of hematite, one of which had mica mixed in with it: a "poor person's specular hematite." A spill of hematite in a liquid, presumably water, was preserved on the floor.

Because of Household 4's proximity to Structure 3, the community building for adjudicating disputes, deciding community events scheduling and organization, and other village matters, it is possible that this household had a service relationship to rethatch its huge roof and repair cracks and apply the sacrificial surfacing. I think this is likely, but more excavations will need to be done to test the suggestion.

If we can extrapolate the market-obtained items in the *bodega* to the full Household 4 assemblage, then it would rank as intermediate between the other two households. Its service time and effort obligations in tending so many special crops and depulping the agave leaves were considerable and may have interfered with market activities more than the service obligations of Household 2 and less than those of Household 1. But that is a big "if": the need for more research is clear.

The differentiation of households' part-time occupational specializations may well have had its roots in times prior to the immigration and founding of the Cerén village. It is possible, for instance, that a Household 1 member may have been a successful diviner many generations earlier and that through time the household took on a more substantial religious role in the community. Analogous roles for the other households prior to the immigration may have existed and then developed after the village was founded. This, of course, is speculative but important to consider, given the short time the village existed.

Conclusions

This chapter focuses on the service relationships of Cerén households in the context of demanding and necessary household obligations of maintaining their buildings and their functioning, agriculture, food storage-processing-consumption, and other activities. Each household's service commitments varied greatly in their nature and their magnitude. When I tabulated each household's market-obtained goods, an inverse relationship to service became clear. That is, the greater the service obligations, the fewer market-obtained goods the household had. The sample of households is very small, but the inverse relationship can be cast as a testable hypothesis when the remainder of Household 4's structures are excavated, along with other households.

If the inverse relationship between market goods and service relationships held true in ancient times, it could be part of explaining a puzzle that has troubled me for decades. Significant architectural variation among households became clear in excavations done from 1978 through 1996. Household 1 had a more modest domicile, *bodega*, and kitchen when compared to the other households. Household 1's domicile was smaller in floor area, less elevated, and had fewer internal features than Household 2. Likewise, the *bodegas* differed significantly in size and elevation. In addition, the quality of the mixture of ingredients in the earthen architecture differed, resulting in more cracking generated by the clay component during the wet-dry oscillations. Household 1 members had service relationships to the community considerably greater than those of the other households: they had to maintain two religious buildings structurally, along with their functioning. It appears possible that their service commitments were part of time conflicts with travel to markets for exchanges to obtain specialist items and long-distance traded items. Greater service obligations may have had a negative impact on a household's abilities to participate more fully in the regional economy. The Cerén households' service obligations clearly were not of the annual cargo system, as they were connected with fixed architectural facilities or long-growing crops. Furthermore, I see no evidence of aggrandizing within the community or egregious exploitation of the proletariat by powerful elites and royals.

This chapter explores the possible conflicts in time and effort between service obligations to the community and participation in the regional economy as reflected in market-obtained goods. The apparent inverse relationship should be considered within the larger context of all the household activities of building construction, maintenance, and refurbishing, along with agricultural and other household activities. Agriculture in the rainy season involved microtopographic field preparation, planting, weeding, harvesting, and storage, followed by food processing, serving, and consumption. Families also participated in internal as well as community rituals, marriages, illnesses and curings, divinations, saunas, and myriad other activities.

IV

Political Elites, Wealthy Persons,
and Economic Administration

15

A Discrepancy between Elite Office and Economic Status in the El Palmar Dynasty

A View from the Guzmán Group of El Palmar, Mexico

KENICHIRO TSUKAMOTO

To what extent did the political achievement of members of a social group correlate with their economic status in Classic Maya society? To address this question, I examine economic aspects of a social group who held the title *lakam* (meaning "banner" in Yucatec Mayan). Epigraphic data from a hieroglyphic stairway at El Palmar suggest that a descendant of this social segment played the role of an ambassador in forming an alliance of the Copán, El Palmar, and Kaanul dynasties, representing a significant political achievement (Tsukamoto and Esparza 2015). Nevertheless, the portrayal of *lakamob* in courtly scenes painted on polychrome vessels is not consistent with such a specific duty. Polychrome vessels from the Petén region suggest that *lakamob* operated less like ambassadors and more like tribute collectors or participants in a military or ritual procession (Lacadena 2008). These epigraphic and iconographic data may indicate that the *lakam* title includes diverse roles and duties (see also Freidel et al. 2016). While the epigraphic and archaeological data from a single site are thus not fully representative of the activities associated with this office, the material remains from the Guzmán Group at El Palmar offer new perspectives on the economic activities that ambassadorial *lakamob* performed and their relative social standing within the noble class.

Politics and Economy in Classic Maya Society

Scholars have investigated the relationship between politics and economy in Classic Maya society over decades (Brumfiel and Earle, eds. 1987; Masson 2002b;

McAnany 1993a, 2010). One key question is the relationship of production activities, wealth, and political rank. The study of political economy has tended to focus on the issue of control of production and exchange by ruling elites (Brumfiel and Earle, eds. 1987; Sanders 1981). Other approaches evaluate the degree of product specialization and standardization as a correlate of centralization (Costin 1991).

More recently, this top-down perspective has been critiqued, as it obscures the complex interplay of resource management and consumption among different social segments (Masson 2002b; Murakami 2016; Sheets 2000; Shimada 2007; West 2002). For Classic Maya society, multiple lines of evidence indicate that different modes of production, exchange, and consumption coexisted and did not represent sequential stages of political development. Rather, these modes represented facets of a multidimensional Maya economic system (Houston and Inomata 2009:256). Several case studies at Classic Maya sites have demonstrated the existence of a market exchange (Dahlin and Ardren 2002; Garraty and Stark, eds. 2010; King and Shaw 2015; S. Martin 2012; L. Shaw 2012). Gift exchange and tribute obligations existed alongside market commerce, and these modes were mutually complementary (Masson and Freidel 2013). Moreover, mercantile sector success may not have earned much respect in Classic Maya society (Tokovinine and Beliaev 2013), signaling a complex relationship between political elites and merchants.

Studies of gift exchange in the Maya area have focused on the movement of elaborate polychrome pottery vessels, but possession of some of these polychrome serving vessels does not always correlate with exceptional wealth (Ball 1993; Hendon 1991; West 2002). The degree of elaboration separates the most rare and restricted vessels from those more casually made and widely distributed (Reents-Budet 1994). Ball (1993) identifies two stylistic subgroups in a polychrome ceramic group; the village-tradition polychromes versus the more elaborate serving vessels termed palace-school products. In addition to the use of polychrome paints, palace-school pottery is decorated with hieroglyphic texts and sophisticated iconographic images. Village-tradition polychromes, in contrast, have relatively simple, modest iconographic and geometric decorations. Palace-school products were likely circulated within elite spheres through gift giving and/or exchange and were used as mortuary offerings (Ball 1993; Fry 1981; Reents-Budet et al. 1994; Reents-Budet, Guenter, et al. 2012), while the village traditional polychrome vessels were broadly produced by and distributed among different households in the polity. The elaborate Late Classic polychromes could have been closely associated with feasts, likely cementing social ties and/or competing for prominence among peers in prestigious displays (R. E. W. Adams 1971; Ball 1993; C. Halperin and Foias 2010; Hendon 1991, 2003; Reents-Budet 1994; West 2002).

Who produced the most elaborate polychrome pottery that contains glyphic texts and sophisticated iconographic images? Unlike the Old World, where attached artisans without political authority seem to have produced specialized items for their rulers (Costin 1991), the study of the rapidly abandoned site of Aguateca suggests that the elites themselves were engaged in the manufacture of the most elaborate polychrome vessels (Inomata, Triadan, Ponciano, Terry, et al. 2001; Inomata, Triadan, Ponciano, Pinto, et al. 2002; see also M. Coe 1977). These elite artisans specialized in the productions of multiple classes of fine craft objects (Inomata 2007; Shimada 2007). Classic Maya elites were thus skilled persons who sometimes served as courtiers, carvers, artisans, scribes, painters, and warriors (Houston and Inomata 2009). High-level crafting was one realm in which ruling elites exercised and displayed their prerogative knowledge, consolidating and maintaining social distinctions within the noble class as well as beyond it (Inomata 2001). Epigraphic studies of polychrome vessels also support this interpretation. Producers' signatures have been deciphered, including those of royal descendants (Stuart 1989).

To what degree were elites living in outlying areas of the epicenters of Maya sites involved in the production, distribution, and consumption of finest goods such as the elaborate polychrome pottery? I address this question by analyzing materials recovered from the Guzmán Group at El Palmar.

El Palmar

El Palmar is located at the east edge of the Karstic Uplands of the central Yucatán Peninsula, which encompasses the southeastern state of Campeche in Mexico and the northern Petén region of Guatemala (Figure 15.1). Primary and secondary centers in this region include such sites as Calakmul (Snake dynasty, Kaanul), Becán, Río Bec, Tikal, Río Azul, and La Milpa, all within 90 km of El Palmar. Epigraphic evidence indicates that the two powerful dynasties of Tikal and Kaanul (its capital was Calakmul after AD 650) provoked intensive geopolitical interactions in this region during the period between AD 393 and 736 (S. Martin and Grube 2008). The El Palmar dynasty was involved in these political dynamics during the seventh and eighth centuries (at least); it was especially employed as part of Kaanul's hegemonic strategies (Tsukamoto et al. 2015; Tsukamoto and Esparza 2015). Stela 12, located at the civic core or Main Group of El

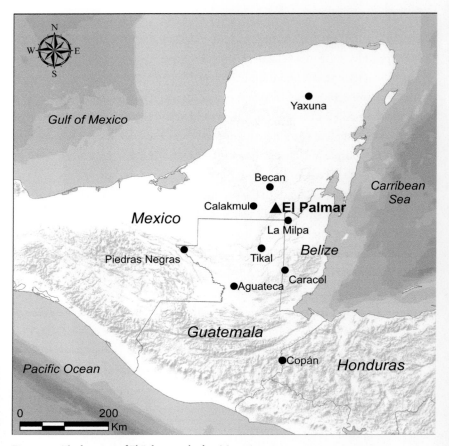

Figure 15.1. The location of El Palmar and other Maya sites.

Palmar, depicts the most powerful ruler of the Snake dynasty, Yuknoom Ch'een II (Esparza and Tsukamoto 2011).

The Main Group consists of monumental structures and numerous carved monuments that were erected on eight plazas. Octavio Esparza Olguín, the project epigrapher, has identified the royal title of El Palmar, which consists of two different glyphic blocks, *sakho'ok*(?), "white valley" and *wak piit*(?) *ajaw*, "the lord of six litters." The meaning of *sakho'ok* and the reading of *piit*(?) remain tentative, but this set of two glyphic blocks undoubtedly represents the royal title of the El Palmar kingdom.

Even though our excavations at the Main Group were limited, the identification of the El Palmar royal title enabled us to study interregional interac-

Figure 15.2. El Palmar courtly scene drawn on the polychrome vessel of El Señor de Petén, recovered by Cortés de Brasdefer (1996).

tions through textual data (Tsukamoto 2014b; Tsukamoto and Esparza 2015). With help from several epigraphers, especially Simon Martin, we have identified polychrome vessels with this same royal title, presumably produced at El Palmar. One of these is the cylinder polychrome vessel of El Señor del Petén, found by Fernando Cortés de Brasdefer at Icaiché, a medium-sized center located about 18 km east of El Palmar (Cortés de Brasdefer 1996; see also Šprajc 2008:93–94). This finely elaborate painting vessel depicts four individuals with glyphic texts, most likely illustrating a courtly scene of El Palmar (Figure 15.2). The protagonist of the scene is an El Palmar ruler Aj Sak Bohb Pat (Zender 2004:222), who carries the royal title of *sakho'ok*(?) *baahkab wak piit*(?) *ajaw*. He and two seated princes are flanked by two *ajk'uhuunob*. This evidence, together with other artifacts featuring the El Palmar royal title found at distant sites (Tsukamoto 2014b:309–315), suggests that El Palmar rulers used elaborate polychrome vessels as gifts, exchanged between polities for the purpose of establishing, maintaining, and/or strengthening political ties.

Guzmán Group

Textual evidence is not limited to the Main Group of El Palmar. Ground reconnaissance undertaken in 2007 and 2009 has so far identified eight outlying (or *plazuela*) groups surrounding the Main Group (Tsukamoto et al. 2010). One of these is the Guzmán Group, located 1.3 km north of the Main Group (Figure

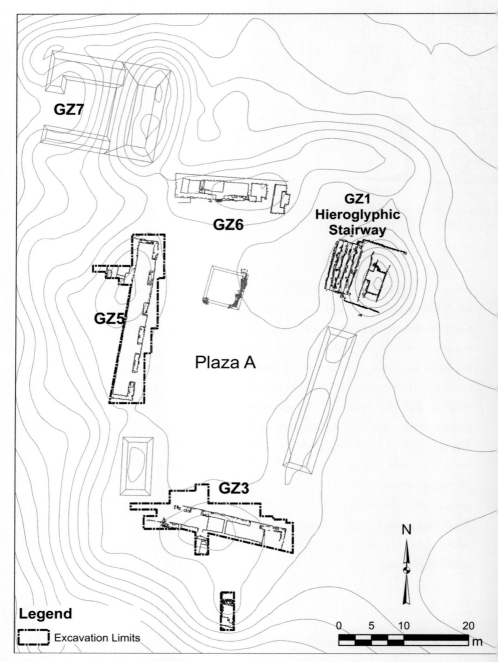

GZ7

GZ6

GZ1
Hieroglyphic
Stairway

GZ5

Plaza A

GZ3

N

Legend

⌐ ¬
└ ┘ Excavation Limits

0   5   10   20
━━━━━━━━━━━━━━━━━ m

Figure 15.3. Map of the Guzmán Group.

15.3). It constitutes a small plaza formed by seven structures (Structures GZ1–GZ6 and GZ9) and represents a typical household plaza with an eastern shrine, an arrangement commonly found in the southern Maya lowlands at sites such as Caracol (D. Chase and A. Chase 2004) and Tikal (Becker 2003b, 2004). A reservoir is located about 120 m northeast of the Guzmán plaza. Outside the plaza is an architectural compound, including Structure GZ7, the most elaborate in the group.

The Guzmán Group has been a focal point of our research since 2009, when we detected a hieroglyphic stairway attached to the eastern shrine (Structure GZ1). Structure GZ1 is a temple structure with a single upper room that was originally vaulted with finely cut cornices. The interior space of the room is furnished with two low masonry benches at its north and south ends. Two cord holders made from red jar necks would have held back a curtain on the western wall, as observed in courtly scenes depicted on elaborate polychrome vessels (e.g., Kerr 1998). A stratigraphic excavation penetrating the floor of the upper shrine detected a series of renovations with a burial (Burial 1), associated with two polychrome vessels. A platform in front of the shrine's doorway as well as the wide tread width of the stairs were very likely designed for theatrical performance (Tsukamoto 2014a).

The hieroglyphic stairway of Structure GZ1 consists of six steps; inscriptions carved on the first to the fifth steps record historical events (Tsukamoto and Esparza 2015). Epigraphic readings suggest that the protagonist of the inscriptions carved on the stairway was not a ruler but a descendant of a social group who held the title of *lakam*. The protagonist's name is Ajpach' Waal, whose family line is traced from his mother and father to probably his great-grandfather, emphasizing patrilineal succession of the *lakam* title. The text lists the patrilineal *lakam* ancestors along with the El Palmar rulers, representing their proximity to the royalty over generations.

The inscription also depicts Ajpach' Waal's political role with emphasis on his interpolity relationships. According to the inscriptions, he traveled to Copán in AD 726 in order to have an audience with Copán's ruler, Waxaklajuun Ubaah K'awiil. In the text he repeatedly states his close relationship with Copán's ruler, rather than the El Palmar ruler. The text reveals that Ajpach' Waal carved and owned the stairway, implicitly claiming that this stairway was not awarded by El Palmar's ruler. The royal title of the Kaanul dynasty appears on the stairway, but the relational glyph is eroded. Nevertheless, the spatial arrangement of the royal titles of Copán, El Palmar, and Kaanul on the stairway suggests that this diplomatic event was a part of Kaanul's political strategy to encircle Tikal, and Ajpach' Waal played the role of ambassador, mediating for the three allies (Tsukamoto 2014b). Unlike the interpretation of Lacadena (2008:23), who has suggested "a minor-level rank title" for *lakamob*, the text of the Guzmán stairway implies a higher political status, at least for Ajpach' Waal. The location of the hieroglyphic stairway, the genealogical list of *lakamob*, the protagonist's claim to the ownership of Structure GZ1, and the number of *lakamob* in courtly scenes of painted vessels all strongly suggest that the Guzmán Group was the activity space of *lakamob*, who held high political esteem.

Is the *lakamob*'s political status reflected in the spatial and material settings of the Guzmán Group? To address this question, we extensively excavated Structures GZ3, GZ5, and GZ6 around the plaza during the field seasons from 2010 to 2016. These investigations determined that people first occupied the Guzmán plaza by the Early Classic Period (AD 250–600), continuing up to the Terminal Classic Period (AD 800–950). We have found Late Preclassic sherds, but no associated structure has been detected. The excavations yielded a sizable amount of archaeological features, including termination deposits, a cache, and middens. Moreover, stratigraphic excavations penetrating the floors of the structures unearthed ten burials with offerings, all of which were interred within cists, delimited by stones that supported horizontal capstones.

Structure GZ3 is a rectangular structure that defines the south end of the plaza. It consists of a pair of east and west rooms, each with a doorway facing the plaza and a stone bench at the east end of the room. The east and west rooms are similar, although the west room appears to have been more important, with an opening to the south side of the structure that offers a view of highest pyramidal temple (Temple I) of the Main Group. Termination deposits, including a greenstone celt, were mostly found on the floor of the west room but were also present on the floor of the east room. The elaborateness of burials beneath the floor was also different between the east and west rooms. Burial 8 was located beneath the floor of the west room, in front of the access to the south part of the structure. It consisted of an adult with two vessel offerings. Beneath the bench of the west room was a *chultun* (a storage pit dug into limestone), which had been reused to deposit midden refuse and burials. Burials 9 and 10 in the *chultun* were interred without offerings. The east room of Structure GZ3 also yielded a burial (Burial 6) beneath the floor in front of the bench, but no offerings were found.

The most elaborate offering was found not at Structure GZ1, to which the hieroglyphic stairway was attached, but at Structure GZ5, which closes the west end of the plaza. The structure consists of a single rectangular room with five doorways. The function of the structure remains elusive, but its single large space was likely not designed for domestic use. The excavation exposed an elaborate stone bench covered with stucco not in the rectangular room but behind the structure. Unlike the west room of Structure GZ3, there was no access to this bench from the frontal room of Structure GZ5, suggesting a sharp division of space associated with the plaza and the areas behind the plaza. The excavations uncovered Burial 5 outside the south wall of the structure, which is probably a secondary burial judging from the incomplete condition of the skeleton. In contrast, Burial 7, the most elaborate burial at the Guzmán Group, contained an adult with five polychrome and monochrome vessels. It was located beneath the floor of the frontal room on the central axis of the structure.

Structure GZ6 is a rectangular structure that closes the north end of the plaza. The excavations uncovered three rooms that are not interconnected via interior doorways; each room has its own entrance (Tsukamoto et al. 2015). The west room constitutes a rectangular space with a throne-like bench at its center and a low lateral bench at its west end. The central room is a small quadrangular space with a single doorway to the plaza. This sort of small cubicle has been reported at the site of Nohoch Ek in the upper Belize Valley. Connell (2003:39) interprets such rooms as storage spaces for sumptuary items received as tribute or gifts. The east room is a T-shaped rectangular space. Unlike the other rooms of Structure GZ6, it has a doorway on the east side, probably indicating a focus on private activities.

Excavations detected three burials beneath the floor of Structure GZ6. Burial 2 was recovered underneath the lateral bench and consists of an individual with a brown monochrome bowl. Burial 3 was beneath the floor located at the east corner of the west room and contains an individual accompanied by a possible sacrificial victim and an elaborate red monochrome vessel. Burial 4 was located at the center of the east room and contained an individual without offerings.

In summary, the structures surrounding the plaza of the Guzmán Group were designed for both public and private activities. Some burials beneath the floors of the four structures were associated with ceramic vessels; others had no offerings. Burials 1, 7, and 8 had polychrome vessels. No lithic, shell, or other materials were included as offerings in the burials. We also found a large number of polychrome sherds from other contexts, including a midden, termination deposits, and construction fill, but the characteristics of these polychrome vessels were surprisingly different, as discussed below.

Ceramic Assemblage at the Guzmán Group

The construction of the hieroglyphic stairway suggests that writing skill was a critical practice pertaining to the political and economic status of *lakamob*. The transmission of prerogative knowledge is cross-culturally integral to differentiating a "house" from other social segments (Gillespie 2000). Writing or carving glyphic texts as an embodied action was closely tied to power and ideological dimensions in Classic Maya society (Inomata 2001). The polychrome vessels that depict El Palmar's courtly scenes attest to this important social context. People cannot maintain their writing skills without everyday practice. Because the Classic Mayan language was likely distinct from quotidian spoken languages (Houston et al. 2000), continuous writing practice in daily life must have been required to maintain skills.

Based on this reasoning, I expected to recover a significant number of ves-

Figure 15.4. Serving vessels recovered from the Guzmán Group: (*a*), (*d*), (*g*) Chantuori Black-on-Orange type, (*a*) and (*d*) bowls, (*g*) plate; (*b*) Desquite Red-on-Orange type, tripod plate; (*c*), (*h*), (*j*)–(*m*), (*o*)–(*q*) Tinaja Red type, (*c*), (*h*), (*j*)–(*m*), (*o*), and (*q*) bowls, (*p*) dish; (*e*) Saxché Orange Polychrome type, cylinder vase; (*f*) Zacatal Cream Polychrome type, tripod bowl; (*i*) Infierno Black type, plate; (*n*) Corona Red type, bowl.

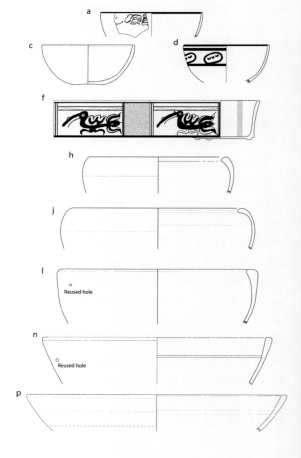

sels with glyphic texts from the excavations at the Guzmán Group. Our excavations at the Guzmán Group from 2010 through 2014 yielded 13,546 sherds (excluding eroded sherds), of which 5.13% ($n = 695$) represented polychrome vessels. We also recovered 13 complete vessels. The percentage of polychrome sherds accords well with those documented at Dos Pilas (5.58%) and Aguateca (5.29%) (Foias and Bishop 1997:278, Table 3), suggesting that the ceramic assemblage of the Guzmán Group is unaffected by biased sampling strategies, despite some differences in the contexts investigated among these sites.

In the ceramic assemblage, we have identified only three sherds with glyphic texts. Twelve complete vessels from the burials lack glyphic texts. The same is true for other artifacts, including lithics, shells, and bones recovered from the excavations. Of the three sherds, one set of glyphs was on a bichrome vessel (not a polychrome), exhibiting black text and lines drawn on an orange slip (Figure 15.4a). The other two sherds are too eroded or fragmented for the glyphs to be

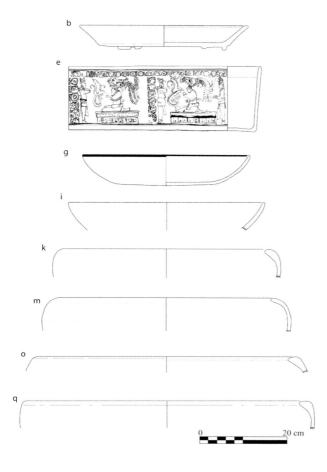

read with confidence. These three sherds were part of termination deposits laid down before the abandonment of the Guzmán Group between ca. AD 760 and 850, suggesting that the *lakamob* produced or consumed these after the building of the hieroglyphic stairway, but not before.

Mortuary offerings often provide crucial information about people's socioeconomic status. There are some ceramic vessels with iconographic images in burials, middens, and construction fill. One of the two polychrome vessels recovered from Burial 1 is a cylinder vase that depicts mythological scenes with three bands of pseudo-glyphs (Figure 15.4e). The presence of vessels with pseudo-glyphs in the burial does not necessarily indicate the illiteracy of the interred person, just as the presence of mortuary offerings embellished with glyphs cannot attest to the literacy of the interred (Houston and Stuart 1992). Indeed, several vessels buried as mortuary offerings of Jasaw Chan K'awiil at Tikal contain pseudo-glyphs (Calvin 2006). Although the mythological scenes on the vase are complex, its quality and elaboration do not match those of palace-school products exemplified by a courtly scene of the El Señor de Petén's vase. Burial 1, interred beneath the floor of Structure GZ1's room, may represent the *lakamob*'s ancestor, but we have no direct evidence of his specific identity. Another polychrome vessel is a Zacatal Cream Polychrome tripod bowl with slightly outcurved sides and three tiny supports (Figure 15.4f). On the cream slip, two water birds were drawn on the wall, probably symbolizing the watery underworld (Tsukamoto et al. 2015:216). Despite its symbolic image, I hesitate to say that this vessel is of the finest quality.

As I mentioned previously, the most elaborated mortuary offering at the Guzmán Group was not Burial 1 of Structure GZ1 but Burial 7 of Structure GZ5. Burial 7 includes two cylinder vases, a small bottle-shaped vessel, and a polychrome plate. One of the cylinder vases has polychrome decorations with a simple dot design, while another is a reddish-black monochrome. Small bottle-shaped vessels from other sites are identified as tobacco flasks, with residues containing pounded tobacco and slaked lime (M. Coe and Houston 2015:166, Figure 100). The bottle from Burial 7 indeed contained slaked lime, with residues observed spilling out of the mouth. The polychrome plate is decorated with a jaguar image, resembling a sacrificial jaguar entity identified on at least one other example (a tripod plate) found elsewhere (Reents-Budet 1994:344, Figure 68). However, the jaguar drawn on the Burial 7 plate does not hold a decapitated sacrifice, unlike the plate reported by Reents-Budet and colleagues. The Burial 7 jaguar is instead surrounded by bands, between which five pairs of red squares were painted, alluding to the initial process of drawing glyphs. I suggest that the jaguar is a spirit companion or *way*. In addition to the plate of Burial 8, Burial 4 of Structure GZ3 contained a polychrome plate decorated with simple dots and lines.

Most polychrome sherds from construction fill, middens, or termination rituals exhibit simple or modest images; only two sherds represent elaborate iconographic images. One, which depicts a priest-like person, came from the construction fill of Structure GZ1; the other, with a mythological image of a cormorant, derives from a midden or ritual dump in the *chultun* of Structure GZ3. The latter fragment represents the most elaborate iconographic image in the Guzmán Group, but no other sherds contained either sophisticated iconographic images or glyphic texts.

Reconstructing Feasts

Elsewhere I have demonstrated the devotion of *lakamob* to feasting in the plaza of the Guzmán Group, through the close examination of ceramic assemblages recovered from a termination ritual (Tsukamoto 2017). Refitting sherds resulted in 201 reconstructed vessels, of which 53 vessels were identified as plates, dishes, or bowls. Although we could not reconstruct these vessels in their entirety, the preservation of more than 10% of their rim perimeters allowed me to measure their rim diameters. A total of 53% of these vessels exceeded 30 cm in maximum diameter, including 3 plates over 35 cm in diameter (Figure 15.4b, g, and i) a 58 cm diameter dish (Figure 15.4p), and two bowls that are over 60 cm in diameter (Figure 15.4o and q). Two plates from Burial 7 and Burial 8 measure 39 cm and 30 cm in diameter, respectively. We also recovered polychrome and monochrome cylinder vases that may have used for special beverages such as *atole* and liquid chocolate.

Ethnoarchaeological and archaeological studies have demonstrated that people used large plates, dishes, or bowls over 30 cm in diameter for feasts (Crown 1994; Mills 2007; Nelson 1991; Pauketat and Emerson 1991; Spielmann 1998). While some of large vessels from our excavations are polychromes, the majority of them are red monochromes. As many of these vessels from the termination deposits have traces of wear, I suggest that *lakamob* hosted feasts repeatedly after the building of the hieroglyphic stairway.

Lithic Assemblages

The analysis of lithic materials indicates that craft production also took place at the Guzmán Group. The excavations from 2010–2012 yielded a total of 3,477 lithic materials, 98% of which were made of chert (Table 15.1). Chert artifacts include finished products such as oval bifaces ($n = 95$), end scrapers ($n = 28$), and domed smoothers ($n = 13$), as well as cores and debitage. A sizable number of cores ($n = 96$) and debitage, including decortification flakes ($n = 1,054$) and flakes without apparent use wear ($n = 1,015$) suggest that the *laka-mob* were chipped stone producers (Table 15.1). However, this activity does

Table 15.1. The distribution of lithic types recovered from the Guzmán Group during 2010–2012 field seasons

Lithic types	n	%	Weight (g)	%
Barkbeater	3	0.09	760	0.59
Chisels	3	0.09	642	0.50
Cores	96	2.76	26854	20.79
Decortication flakes	1054	30.31	19005	14.71
Doomed smoothers	13	0.37	5317	4.12
Drills	6	0.17	239	0.18
Eccentrics	1	0.03	32	0.02
End scrapers	28	0.81	2399	1.86
Flakes with useware	967	27.81	19739	15.28
Flakes without useware	1015	29.19	5362	4.15
Greenstone celts	3	0.09	148	0.11
Hammerstone	8	0.23	3655	2.83
Knives	7	0.20	235	0.18
Laurel-leaf bifaces	1	0.03	9	0.01
Manos	4	0.12	2940	2.28
Metates	2	0.06	734	0.57
Microflakes	22	0.63	3	0.00
Other polished stones	4	0.12	525	0.41
Oval bifaces	95	2.73	19527	15.12
Picks	7	0.20	756	0.59
Pounders	29	0.83	11378	8.81
Prismatic blades	45	1.29	45	0.04
Projectile points	8	0.23	264	0.20
Side scrapers	2	0.06	225	0.17
Unifacial blades	8	0.23	28	0.02
Unknown bifaces	5	0.14	859	0.67
Unidentified	41	1.18	7495	5.80
Total	3477	100.00	129175	100.00

not reflect specialized artisanal production: the workmanship of an anthropomorphic eccentric flint (Tsukamoto et al. 2015:210, Figure 9g), recovered from the termination ritual deposits of Structure GZ6 does not match the quality of eccentric flints found by Eric Thompson at the Main Group in 1936 (J.E.S. Thompson 1936). The excavations also yielded a total of three barkbeaters at the Guzmán Group. Barkbeaters are well-known implements for the manufacture of bark or *amate* paper throughout Mesoamerica. We found a barkbeater fragment under Structure GZ1-Sub 1, suggesting that the implement was used at the beginning of the Late Classic Period or before. We also found an exhausted barkbeater under the hieroglyphic stairway. These materials may indicate that some of the inhabitants at the Guzmán Group engaged in the production of bark paper, but this does not necessarily imply that the *lakamob* carried out scribal practices.

Discussion

The artifact assemblages of the Guzmán Group indicate an interesting gap between political position and economic status in Classic Maya society. In terms of their political position, the textual evidence of the hieroglyphic stairway records the significance of *lakamob*'s role in the El Palmar dynasty. The genealogical list of *lakamob*, along with El Palmar's successive rulers, emphasizes the *lakamob*'s continuous proximity to royalty over generations. The diplomatic event with Copán and Kaanul highlights their high-level political responsibilities. Even though the textual evidence of the Guzmán stairway centers on the political role of a single person, Ajpach' Waal, two polychrome vessels recovered from other sites represent two or three individuals who also held the title of *lakam* (Lacadena 2008), signaling that multiple persons could have held the same political office. The hieroglyphic stairway at the Guzmán Group exemplifies the correlation between the importance of writing skill and political power in Classic Maya society.

Nevertheless, the scarcity of glyphic texts on artifacts other than on the stairway is revealing with respect to the relative lack of scribal activities. While *lakamob* may have been literate, present data do not confirm or negate this possibility. The production and distribution of polychrome vessels with glyphic texts clearly were not activities undertaken with any regularity at the Guzmán household. The paucity of polychrome vessels with hieroglyphic texts at present leads to the inference that the activity of writing, as prerogative knowledge, was highly restricted. There remains the chance of a sampling bias, and excavation at additional contexts may further refine this perspective. The Guzmán Group data reflect the probability of competition within the intragroup hierarchy among the elite residents.

The differential access to resources thus suggests that tensions existed among the members of the Guzmán Group and that maintaining solidarity would have contended with visible internal distinctions of privilege. The slightly differing architectural design of the east and west rooms of Structure GZ3 may reflect such distinctions, as do the diversity of mortuary offerings and the limited access to vessels decorated with fine iconographic designs. Lithic materials indicate the daily practice of craft production, and the absence of chipped stone tools in the burials suggests that ceramic vessels played a more important role in expressing socioeconomic status. All the burials shared the same mortuary cist features. Pottery vessel grave goods marked and simultaneously constrained *lakamob*'s personhood. Feasting provided another context where tensions could also have been mitigated or, alternatively, fomented among *lakamob* and their noble peers. A number of worn-out large vessels recovered from different contexts most likely indicate that people organized feasts several times after the creation of the plaza space and construction of the hieroglyphic stairway. Large plates and vases with fine iconographic images could have been used to serve sumptuary foods and drinks, enhancing the significance of ritual events in the community. Theatrical performances on the stairway may also have been closely interrelated with feasting.

What kinds of economic activities were *lakamob* engaged in? One of the politico-economic roles they may have played was tribute collection (Lacadena 2008). The central room of Structure GZ6, a small cubicle like those reported at other sites (Connell 2003:39), may represent a physical space associated with tribute collection and storage. If so, *lakamob* played an important role in the economic transactions of the dynasty. The doorway of the central room at Structure GZ6 is suggestive, in that it faces the plaza, providing a view of activities in that space to persons gathered in the plaza. No cord-holders or other features were found that would have concealed activities in the room, despite their common use at the Guzmán Group, as in the case of Structures GZ1 and GZ3.

Conclusion

This chapter examines the relationship between sociopolitical status and production activities at the Guzmán Group of El Palmar. The archaeological and epigraphic data suggest that the inhabitants of the Guzmán Group, most likely *lakamob*, had differential access to resources. Not all the inhabitants shared the same resources; instead, internal diversity is evident. While the hieroglyphic stairway illuminates the political significance of written language to the public, limited members may have exercised the prerogative of the scribal arts. The available data have not fully resolved the issue of literacy; more excavations are needed. Structure GZ7, the largest architectural compound in the Guzmán Group, is a good candidate for continued investigation of this question.

Lakamob were not uniformly linked to particular economic activities. They appear to have served as ambassadors, tribute collectors, producers of stone tools and paper, carvers, theatrical performers, feast organizers, and warriors or banner men. The ambassadorial duties of *lakamob* are not fully reflected in their economic activities or prized possessions.

El Palmar was one of the major cities that participated in interregional networks of Maya dynasties. Future research may detect important features such as marketplaces, workshops, and residences of other officials such as *ajk'uhuun* (a religious specialist), providing insights into the nature of economic activities not only at El Palmar but also among Classic Period Maya cities.

Acknowledgments

The El Palmar Archaeological Project has been carried out under permits of the Instituto Nacional de Antropología e Historia, Mexico, with the valuable contributions of co-director Javier López Camacho and project staff members Luz Evelia Campaña Valenzuela, Hirokazu Kotegawa, Xanti Ceballos Pesina, Araceli Vázquez Villegas, and Octavio Esparza Olguín. The project was supported by the National Science Foundation (BCS-11640), the Japan Society for the Promotion of Science Postdoctoral Research Fellowship (15J00280), and KAKENHI (a Grants in Aid for Scientific Research Program) (21402008).

16

Bundling the Sticks

A Case for Classic Maya Tallies

ALEXANDRE TOKOVININE

A scene from a recently published cylinder vase once painted by an artist from Motul de San José (M. Coe and Houston 2015:Pl. XVIII) offers a rare glimpse of the celestial court of God D during the latest creation event. Of all the potentially significant details, our attention is drawn to the three animals apparently in charge of the accounting. The vulture (*us*) seems to be adding numbers on a sheet of paper. The opossum (*uch*) is grasping a screenfold codex. However, the third accountant, the dog (*ook*), does not seem to be holding anything at all. This image illustrates, perhaps more than anything else, the gap in our understanding of the Classic Maya accounting practices. We know that they delivered taxes (*patan*), made payments (*tojool*), engaged in various market activities, and amassed fortunes worth tens of thousands cacao beans (Stuart 2006; Tokovinine and Beliaev 2013). But how were these transactions recorded? The goal of this chapter is to present evidence of another form of record-keeping in the Maya area, which may have been the principal way of recording economic transactions. As we are going to see below, the Classic Maya term for it was "sticks." The most appropriate etic term would be "tallies," defined here as notational systems adapted to specific media such as wooden sticks.

As shown by the contributions to this volume, Maya studies are undergoing a paradigmatic shift in acknowledging the contribution of markets and market exchange to the ancient Maya economies. The shift is supported by several lines of evidence. Certain spaces within the urban cores of Maya cities have been identified as markets based on ethnohistoric analogies, artifact distribution, and soil chemistry (Cap 2011; Dahlin et al. 2010; Chapter 22). A combination of specialized production and uniform distribution of artifacts between households also points to the presence of markets (D. Chase and A. Chase 2014b; Masson and Freidel 2013). The distribution of certain artifacts such as fine polychrome pottery, however, suggests that other mechanisms were also involved (Eppich, Chapter 9; LeCount 2016; Tsukamoto, Chapter 15). It has been argued that the objects circulating through the prestige networks of Maya nobles were inalienable possessions and not commodities (Callaghan 2013; Kovacevich 2013b). Finally, investigations of the ports of trade such as the city of Cancuén (Demarest et al. 2014) attest to the scale of long-distance trade during the Classic Period, not so dissimilar from the sixteenth-century state of affairs (Piña Chan 1978).

The major role of market exchange in the ancient Maya economies has two important implications. First, the specialized producers, consumers, and traders of commodities must have relied on monies. Several potential nonperishable media of exchange, particularly shell and jade beads, have been identified in the contributions to this volume and earlier publications (Freidel et al. 2016; Freidel and Reilly 2010; Masson and Peraza 2014a:277–298), in addition to the perishable monies such as cotton mantles and cacao beans described in the ethnohistoric sources (Blom 1934; Tozzer 1941:96). The second implication is that a system of accounting must have existed to record financial transactions. Loans are of particular relevance here, as the shared terms for credit and profit in the Mayan languages demonstrate a considerable antiquity of the practices (Tokovinine and Beliaev 2013). Although Gaspar Antonio Chi, for example, explicitly stated that contracts were not written down in the native script (Tozzer 1941:231), a view also expressed in the 1593 court case cited by Blom (1934:437–438), it is hard to imagine a total lack of accounting. Contact Period sources are somewhat vague on the notion of interest, but the Yucatec terms *naj* and *p'axlil* refer to a profit made on a nonequivalent loan (Barrera Vásquez et al. 1995:550, 683–684). "Interest" is *uyar tumin* in Ch'orti' (Hull 2016:235) and *jol tak'in* in Tzotzil (Laughlin 1975:157) and Ch'ol (Aulie and Aulie 1978:67). Ch'orti' also features *paxi* "to gain an advantage over" (Hull 2016:327), which may be related to the Yucatec *p'axlil*. In a rather volatile political climate of the Classic Maya world, trading, especially long-distance trading, entailed a lot of risk-taking. Consequently, loan-givers risked as well and probably expected additional rewards for the exposure to a potential loss of their investments.

It is also reasonable to assume that similar accounting practices were applied not only to the transactions between market agents but also in the context of taxation and other economic interactions with the state. The term for price and loan repayment, *tojool*, is cited along with the more appropriate *patan* ("tax" and "labor") in references to taxation in Classic Maya inscriptions (Tokovinine and Beliaev 2013:175–176). A scene of presenting bundles of cotton mantles (*ubte'*) at the court of Motul de San José rulers (K1728; Tokovinine and Beliaev 2013:Figure 7.2b) is described in the hieroglyphic commentary as "the interest [*najal*, see above], the cotton mantles of K'eblaj Muut are presented (*nawaj*) [as] a [loan] payment [*tojool*] of/to *sajal* . . . Muut." Therefore, the scene depicts either a royal arbitration of a dispute over an interest payment (from K'eblaj Muut to a *sajal*) or taxation in the form of an interest on an earlier loan to be repaid as cotton mantles (K'eblaj Muut's mantles paid by the *sajal* to the king). A text on a stone panel from Jonuta (Tokovinine and Beliaev 2013:Figure 7.2d) mentions how the protagonist adorns himself (the text uses an intransitive verb derived from an undeciphered term for chest pectorals) "with jade [and] with shell beads" (*ta ikitz ta k'an*, the objects used as monies according to Freidel et al. 2016) as a "(loan) payment" (*tojool*).

A set of transactions of the kind hinted in the abovementioned scene on the Motul de San José vessel would have been hard to commit to memory. The latest summary on Classic Maya accounting tools (Freidel et al. 2016) shares a consensus view among Mayanists that economic transactions were facilitated by tallies/ tokens and probably recorded in the hieroglyphic books, much like the one held by a vulture in the mythical scene on a vessel described at the beginning of this chapter. Yet it is doubtful that Classic Maya analogs of Sumerian contracts on clay tablets ever existed (Van De Mieroop 2005). As noted above, we have no Contact Period confirmation of financial contracts written in the indigenous script. As for the Classic Period, epigraphic sources suggest extremely low levels of literacy (Houston 1994, 2008; Houston and Stuart 1992). Very little evidence of spontaneous production of writing such as literate graffiti has been found, as confirmed in the latest comprehensive overview of the subject (Źrałka 2014:131–139).

A somewhat more arcane argument for low literacy levels among the elites themselves addresses the issue of knowledge transfer recently pondered by Eberl (2017). For example, creating fine polychrome serving vessels required a lot specialized knowledge of raw materials and production processes, especially at the firing stage, because many pigments were potentially unstable (Houston et al. 2009:66–68). Some workshops, such as the one at Motul de San José (Halperin and Foias 2010), had access to literate artists. Yet elite makers of fine polychrome vessels at other Classic Maya sites were illiterate, whereas their literate elite neighbors were unable to make painted polychromes (see also Tsukamoto,

Chapter 15). Elite craftspeople at Aguateca were literate and produced elaborate ceramic artifacts (Inomata et al. 2014b:39–48), but their inscribed polychrome vessels were nonlocal (Houston 2014b). The presence of literate artists at Holmul/La Sufricaya is evidenced in the inscriptions on modeled stucco, carved stone, murals, and graffiti, but locally produced texts appear only on Terminal Classic modeled and carved vessels (Estrada Belli et al. 2009; Estrada Belli and Tokovinine 2016). The makers of fine polychromes at Holmul had been illiterate all along (Tokovinine 2006a). A similar divide between real texts on modeled vessels and imitations on polychrome pottery is attested at Copán (Coggins 1988; Tokovinine 2004). Perhaps the strangest case is offered by the contemporaneous early eighth century workshops of inscribed polychromes at Naranjo, which radically differed in style and even in some orthographic conventions of the texts and yet shared some uniquely local allographs, which also appeared on Naranjo carved monuments (Tokovinine 2006b).

Given the low levels of literacy and sociocultural barriers to technology transfer evidenced in these cases, it is very unlikely that most market agents, even among the elites, could record financial transactions using hieroglyphic manuscripts. Of course, one could hypothesize the existence of a small group of highly specialized palace accountants effectively monopolizing the recording process, but this scenario would contradict the apparent lack of archaeological and textual evidence of a substantial top-down involvement of the royal court in the market activities. Consequently, recording devices, if there were any, should have been accessible to people with no exposure to writing and with limited knowledge of numbers.

Tallies are one of the most cross-culturally widespread and oldest forms of record-keeping and may be traced back to Upper Paleolithic humans, who relied on notched animal bones to record lunar cycles and possibly historical events (Marshack 1991). The Western tradition of tally sticks stretches from references in Ancient Greek and Roman texts to nineteenth-century accounting practices (Baxter 1989). In the New World, the Middle Horizon Wari and later Inka *khipu* are the most well-known examples of a complex tally system that was adequate for the administrative needs of a large bureaucratic state (Conklin 1982; Urton 1998, 2003; Urton and Brezine 2005). Various indigenous cultures in North America relied on tally sticks to keep track of the lunar and solar calendars and possibly other ritual cycles (Marshack 1989; Murray 1989). Archaeological evidence such as the Presa de la Mula rock carving (Murray 1979) indicates that the tradition of tallies extends into Mesoamerica.

Students of Mesoamerican cultures have been reluctant to consider the role of tallies in the local record-keeping practices. It seems that the implicit assumption is to see tallies and writing systems as an evolutionary sequence, so that Classic Mesoamerican societies no longer needed tallies because of the invention of writing. However, tallies and written documents often coexist. European accounting practices relied on tally sticks well into the nineteenth century (Baxter 1989; Goetzmann and Williams 2005). Even with relatively widespread literacy and accessible writing implements, as in the case of the medieval Novgorod republic, tallies were instrumental in recording business transactions (Kovalev 2007). In South America, *khipu* tallies had been a viable alternative to the Spanish documents until they were banned by the colonial authorities attempting to monopolize the public records (Urton 2002). Therefore, we need to consider the traits that make tallies such an efficient accounting tool. Tallies are durable, transportable, and can cross language barriers. Simple practices like split tallies make them nearly impossible to forge (Goetzmann and Williams 2005). Tallies recording outstanding obligations such as taxes and credit effectively function as money (F. Martin 2014).

Ethnographic Evidence of Maya Tallies

There is ethnographic evidence of tallies in the Maya area. The relatively well-known Chamula wooden calendar board (Gossen 1974; Marshack 1974) was a functional tally used by the Tzotzil Maya to track the solar year-based ritual calendar, much like other indigenous tally traditions in the Americas. Yet the most significant case is a set of six tally sticks in the collections of the Peabody Museum of Archaeology and Ethnology, Harvard University (record number 06-60-20/C3944; Figure 16.1). The sticks were donated to the museum by Edward Thompson, who likely collected them himself during his stay in northern Yucatán. I have been unable to find references to these tallies in Thompson's published and unpublished writings. According to the note left with the sticks, they were "said by the Natives to record work done." The note goes on to report that "when the sticks are full or the work is finished they are kept by employer as receipts" and that "each man's name is on his sticks." It would be tempting to speculate that the sticks were used by Thompson's hacienda workers, but there is no definitive match between the names on the sticks and his records.

All six sticks have four sides, and at least one of the corners between the long sides of every stick is notched. None are "complete" in the sense of using

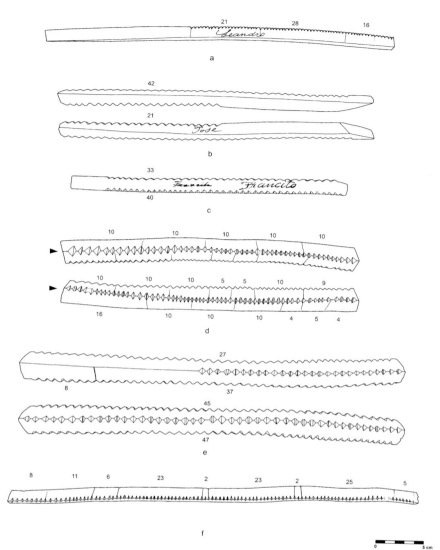

Figure 16.1. Tally sticks in the Peabody Museum collection: (*a*) stick A; (*b*) stick B; (*c*) stick C; (*d*) stick D; (*e*) stick E; (*f*) stick F (drawings by Alexandre Tokovinine).

all the corner space. Given Thompson's description, it is safe to assume that the notches represent counts of days, which may or may not be continuous. The smallest number of notches on a stick is 63; the largest is 164. The number of notches on a single corner varies from 21 to 105. In addition to the corner notches, thin incised lines segment the counts into groups. The lines always touch the notched corner that they refer to. The lines are only absent on sticks

B and C (Figure 16.1b, c). The same corner-notch count on stick D (Figure 16.1d) is provided with two sets of lines. One set segments the count into 10 + 10 + 10 + 5 + 5 + 10 + 9. The other set segments the same count into 16 + 10 + 10 + 10 + 4 + 5 + 4. The lines on stick A (Figure 16.1a) split the count into 16 + 28 + 21. The lines on stick F (Figure 16.1f) evoke a recurrent unit of 25 that is presented as 8 + 11 + 6, 23 + 2, 23 + 2, 25, plus a possibly incomplete set of 5 notches. A single line on stick E (Figure 16.1e) apparently splits the total count of 164 into 100 + 64. The positioning of that line in relation to an incomplete set of notches on the next corner of the same stick (where the count was likely interrupted) suggests that the notches were added and read in a boustrophedon pattern.

The totals of notches on individual corners and the way in which they are further segmented by the lines strongly suggests that the users relied on a decimal numeral system and not on a traditional Maya vigesimal numeral system. For example, the total on one corner count of stick D is 100 (Figure 16.1d) and is subdivided into 10 + 10 + 10 + 10 + 10. However, the reliance on a decimal system is not surprising, because by the time the sticks were collected by Thompson the indigenous numeral system had long been out of use in the Yucatán and the corresponding words had been replaced by Spanish loans.

Only sticks A, B, and C feature names (Leandro, José, and Francito) and thus conform to Thompson's description (Figure 16.1a–c). The name "Francito" on stick C is recorded twice (Figure 16.1c): the first (earlier?) iteration is in smaller letters and appears smudged or crossed-over; the second (later?) iteration is written in larger letters by a different hand. Once again, this fits a picture of Maya workers submitting the notched sticks, which are then labeled, relabeled, and stored by the employer(s). Of the labeled sticks, only stick A features additional lines segmenting the count into 16 + 28 + 21 (Figure 16.1a). The corner counts of stick B are 42 (complete) and 21 (incomplete). The counts of Stick C are 33 and 40. In contrast to many European tallies, the design of the sticks implies that they were not meant to be split into halves, so it is unclear whether the record was duplicated. The first two sets of count marks on stick A may be represented as 7×3 and 7×4. The intervals on stick B are $7 \times 3 \times 2$ and 7×3. The common multiple of 7 may reference the 7-day week. The count on stick C does not visibly follow this pattern, so that person's labor obligations may have been arranged differently.

The function of sticks D–F is unclear. They could not be used in the same way as the first three, although it is still possible that the stick owner could be identified by an attached label or by the unique shape of the stick. Stick D with its alternative segmentation of the same count is the likeliest candidate for the same group as sticks A–C. It is interesting that one of its segmentations of 16 + 10 + 10 + 10 + 4 + 5 + 4 is somewhat similar to the count of 16 + 28 + 21 on stick A. The count on Stick B may be presented as 2 × 21 + 21. Perhaps we are dealing with the records of individuals, who sometimes worked together. The intervals of 10, 15, and 20 days were common in labor arrangements for hacienda workers in Mexico and Guatemala (Katz 1974:25; Schmolz-Haberlein 1996:242).

The counts on sticks E and F are harder to interpret as labor records. Stick E (Figure 16.1e) contains a long count of days segmented as 47 + 45 + 8 + 37 + 27. If one assumes that the count of 27 is incomplete, the potential total could be close to half of the tropical year. The interval of 92 days (47 + 45) and the possible interval of at least 92 days (45 + 27 + 20 judging from the remaining space) suggest that the count refer to lunar months or to the time between solar solstices and equinoxes (e.g., Vernal Equinox—Summer Solstice—Autumnal Equinox). Stick F (Figure 16.1f) features a recurrent number of 25 days with a further subdivision into 8 + 11 + 6 or 23 + 2. The count could refer, for example, to observational lunar months with gaps around the time of the new moon. However, 25 days would also equal the amount of days it took to earn enough to buy a quintal of beans in 1934 prices in highland Guatemala (Schmolz-Haberlein 1996:241). The number of days in a month minus Sundays would also be about 25.

Maya Tallies and Tokens in the Archaeological Record

The artifacts in the Peabody Museum collection attest to the Maya tally stick accounting practices in the early twentieth century and to their apparent co-existence with the Spanish record-keeping and writing. Although it is highly unlikely that such perishable objects will ever be found in the ancient Maya archaeological record, several portable elite artifacts made from more durable materials potentially reflect the presence of tally sticks during the Classic Period.

One of the most striking collections of elite tallies comes from the burial in Urn 26 in Temple II at the archaeological site of Comalcalco, Mexico (Armijo Torres et al. 2000; Zender 2004:248–263; Zender et al. 2001). The occupant of the urn, a local priest named Aj Pakal Tahn, was interred with a bundle of 52 shell and bone "pendants," which should rather be described as tallies or tokens. The tokens were in paired sets (Figure 16.2a–b). One side of the pair was covered with an inscription, whereas the other side had grooves, so that the pair could be tied together with the inscribed sides facing each other and thus hidden from view. The perforations in the top section of either half of the set would then allow attaching the tied tokens to a master cord with the rest of the collection. The inscriptions on each pair detailed a single activity, usually an auto-sacrifice in the presence of a specific deity. Therefore, the complete set was a tangible, durable, and portable record of Aj Pakal Tahn's most significant ritual accomplishments. It is potentially significant that the inscribed sides of

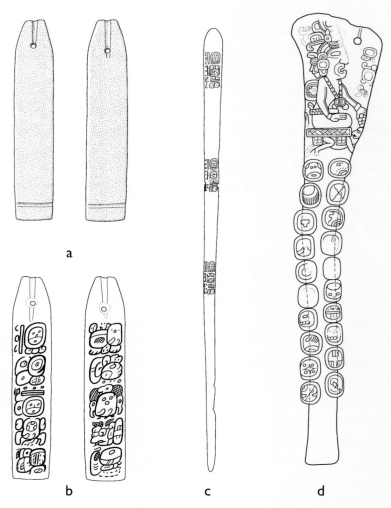

a

b   c   d

Figure 16.2. Tally-like elite artifacts: (*a*) and (*b*) shell tokens (Pendants 7A/7B), Urn 26, Comalcalco; (*c*) bone "awl" (4P-113(15)/2, MT. 26), Burial 116, Tikal; (*d*) unprovenanced "Stendahl bone" (after Barthel 1968:Figs. 1, 2).

the tokens could only be seen once each pair was untied, implying that the public display and manipulation of these objects probably did not entail reading. At least four other urn burials at Comalcalco contained similar tokens. Those in Urn 18 of Temple III were also inscribed, but their preservation was much worse (Armijo Torres et al. 2000:316–317). The implication is that the tokens in Urn 26 are indicative of a widespread practice, which is only sparsely reflected in the material record because of preservation issues.

Classic Maya bone implements have also been previously identified as potential tallies, although the problem is that various emic terms indicative of function correspond to the same awl-like shape of the artifacts and they all appear in bundles. The list includes "weaving bones" (Houston and Stuart 2001:64–65), "scratching bones" (Stuart 2005:117), "offering bones" (Stuart 2013), "perforating bones" (Lacadena García-Gallo 2003:82), and even "canoe bones" (Moholy-Nagy and Coe 2008:Figure 189–191). Consequently, potential bone tallies or tokens may be identified as such only based on the information they contain. Freidel et al. (2016:36, Figure 2) describe a bundle of awl-like bone implements discovered in Burial 39 at El Perú–Waka' and suggest that the objects could serve as tallies rather than weaving tools. A similar bundle of "hairpins" was uncovered in Burial 3 in Structure 209 at Baking Pot (Audet 2006:245–246, Figure 5.42)

A significant set of such objects comes from the Burial 116 in Temple 1, Tikal (Jones 1987; Moholy-Nagy and Coe 2008:61–62, Figures 189–207). Many of these artifacts look like awls, but only a few are labeled as "bones" (*u-baak*) of the royal occupant of the tomb without any further functional clarification. Some twenty bones feature self-contained inscriptions, sometimes in sets of two, with topics ranging from lists and historical events to calendars. The 4P-113(15)/2, MT. 26 artifact illustrated here (Figure 16.2c) references an important ritual cycle called "3×11 *pik*." Some bones in the set were plain. Just as in the case of the Comalcalco set, the significance of these artifacts lies in the choices of medium and format, which imply the existence of alternative record-keeping practices involving tallies or tokens.

Perhaps the most significant Classic Period elite tally-like object is a deer bone of unknown provenience in the Stendahl collection (T. Barthel 1967). Judging by its style, the artifact was made around AD 400. The carving shows an enthroned deity, probably God D, casting incense or divination stones above two columns with a full set of the twenty day names from the sacred 260-day calendar arranged in a boustrophedon pattern following a counterclockwise direction (Figure 16.2d). The days are listed sequentially, although the count starts with the Ajaw day instead of Imix, just as in a similar count on an Early Classic vessel from Tikal (K5618, MS1638, MNAE 11138-A, B: Reents-Budet 1994:114–149, 327, Figure 4.40). The shift to Ajaw in combination with God D's imagery could reference the Winal creation narrative (Callaway 2009). Yet the artifact may also serve as a calendar aid, much like the ethnographically documented North American stick tallies.

Some of the so-called rasps—long bones with parallel grooves—are also candidates for simple tally sticks. Of the seven such rasp bones found at Tikal (Moholy-Nagy 2003a:61, Figure 124), only four have deep grooves and could function as musical instruments (Moholy-Nagy 2003a:Figure 124a, b, e, f). A rabbit femur with horizontal marks is too small for a rasp (Moholy-Nagy 2003a:Figure 124g). The remaining two long bones have fine parallel incisions and not grooves (Moholy-Nagy 2003a:Figure 124c, d).

Textual and Visual References to Classic Maya Tallies

Given the presence of tallies in the ethnographic record and the existence of Classic Period elite artifacts indicative of similar accounting practices, it is possible to interpret several passages in Classic Maya inscriptions as references to stick tallies. An important contributing factor here is the recent reevaluation of the significance of the verb *tz'ak* in Hieroglyphic Mayan (Estrada Belli and Tokovinine 2016:158–159). The common approach among epigraphers is to treat this verb as a single root that means "to count, to accumulate, to put in order" (Boot 2009:176) or "to file, align, arrange something" (Stuart 2005:89). However, it seems that the same **TZ'AK** logogram spells two different *tz'ak* roots, one of which is a positional verb plus its derivations, whereas the other root is a CVC transitive.

Kaufman and Norman (1984:134) reconstruct *tz'äk* "complete" as a positional and a transitive verb stem for Proto-Ch'olan. The positional verb—"to take place in a certain order"—is combined with the -bu causative suffix and becomes a transitive verb *tz'akbu* "to succeed" or "to complete." This verb and its participle (*tz'akbuul*) usually refer to dynastic succession and more opaque statements when rulers "complete" the actions of their predecessors (Houston 1998; S. Martin 2003:38, Stuart 2003a, 2011:3–4; Stuart et al. 1999:32). Unfortunately, the most productive analogies for this interpretation come from Yucatec dictionaries and texts and not from the Ch'olan languages, which are much more closely related to Hieroglyphic Mayan (Houston et al. 2000). The only Ch'olan analogy is provided by Acalán Chontal Paxbolón-Maldonado papers, where -tz'ak functions as a numerical classifier in the count of rulers (Smailus 1975:27–34).

The second root—a transitive verb tz'ak—means "to add, to bring together" in Ch'orti' (Hull 2005:109). Its nominalized form—tz'ahk—signifies "bundle, collection, joint" (Wisdom 1950:734). The adjective tz'akar may be translated as "bundled, joined" (Wisdom 1950:737). Acalán Chontal uses the cognate tz'akal in the context of tribute bundles (Smailus 1975:87).

The meaning of tz'ak seems to entail assembling a totality of something. It distinguishes this verb, for example, from Ch'orti' nut', which also means "to join" but as in mending a piece of torn clothing (Wisdom 1950:548), or from tzik, which means "to count" but not specifically when summing-up (Wisdom 1950:729). The -es/-se causative suffix may be added to the tz'ak stem as in Ch'orti' tz'akse "to adjust, to modify" (Hull 2005:109) and Ch'ol ts'aktesan "to complete" (Aulie and Aulie 1978:122).

The most common form of this transitive root in the Classic Maya inscriptions is a nominalized form tz'a[h]ka' or tz'a[h]kaj that refers to the elapsed time. Its literal translation would be "something that is brought together/added (or pertains to this act)." The expression utz'ahka' usually occurs before a count of time separating different events (a so-called distance number), but occasionally no distance number is present. For example, utz'ahkaj in block H24 on Tikal Stela 31 introduces a count of days, months, and years to the next event (Jones and Satterthwaite 1982:Figure 52), but utz'ahkaj in blocks F15, H6, and H9 of the same inscription is immediately followed by clauses that begin with a date. It is clear from these contexts that the expression refers to the elapsed time that is somehow "brought together" like a bundle. It is, perhaps, a reflection of a broader Mesoamerican concept of time that can be added up into bundles like Aztec xiuhmolpilli and earlier representations of year-bundles at Teotihuacán (Fash et al. 2009:206–209). This interpretation is confirmed by two unusual expressions: winik tz'ak-tuunil-a' or winik tuun tz'ahka' ("person of one score of brought together stones [years]") on the recently discovered frieze on Holmul Building A-sub (Figure 16.3a) and huli ucha' tz'ahk uwinikhaab ti ajawlel "it came, the second bundling of his k'atun in kingship" on Hieroglyphic Stairway 1 at Dos Pilas (Houston and Mathews 1985:11, Figure 7c).

The passage of time is also one of the contexts in which the tz'ak verb–proper is used. The Calendar Round date on Toniná Fragment 35 (Houston and Mathews 1985:11, Figure 7a) was probably 6 Eb 0 Mol. Most inscriptions would refer to that day as Mol's "seating" (chum mol) or "edge of the haab Yaxk'in" (ti'

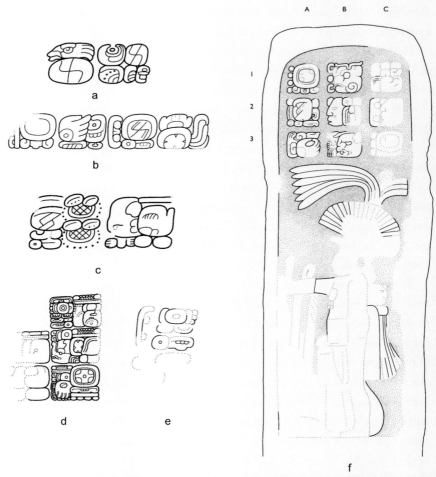

Figure 16.3. "Adding-up the sticks" expression in Classic Maya texts: (*a*) detail of the stucco frieze on Building A, Group II, Holmul; (*b*) detail of Fragment 35, Toniná; (*c*) detail of Stela 32, Naranjo; (*d*) and (*e*) details of Stela 12, Piedras Negras; (*f*) Stela 5, El Chal (drawings by Alexandre Tokovinine).

haab yaxk'in). However, the Toniná text (Figure 16.3b) uses a different expression: "since it had arrived, Yaxk'in added-up the sticks" (*huliiy utz'ak[aw] te' yaxk'in*). Therefore, it seems that Yaxk'in's tenure begins with its "arrival" and ends with an accounting act in which the "sticks" are put together. If completing a *k'atun* involves putting together "stones" (a reference to monuments?), Yaxk'in's "sticks" are probably calendar sticks used in counting days. Alternatively, the metaphor may reference a courtly accounting practice, which the personified months would also adopt.

A courtly setting is certainly in place for another context of the "adding-up the sticks" expression. The scene on Naranjo Stela 32 (I. Graham 1978:86) features an elaborate palanquin. The main inscription states that the royal protagonist visited the city of Ucanal under the auspices of a local ruler with some regional political ambitions. An additional inscription in finer incised characters that grace the steps of the palanquin details gifts from a subordinate lord named K'uk' Bahlam (Stuart 2006:133–134): "[On the day] 8 *Imix* 14 *Suutz'* K'uk' Bahlam gave two scores in/with the precious jewels (*ikaatz*) at . . . ; eleven [days] and seven months past, [on the day] 12 *Eb* 5 *K'anasiiy* K'uk' Bahlam put the sticks together, five scores; he is giving in/with the precious jewels (*ikaatz*). Then it happened, [the day] 8 *Ajaw*." It seems that collecting the "sticks" marks the second and final tribute-payment act. It is also directly linked to the statement about the size of the payment.

Haab months and taxpayers are not the only ones who "add up sticks." According to the main inscription (Figure 16.3d) and a caption to the scene (Figure 16.3e) on Piedras Negras Stela 12 (Stuart and Graham 2003:61–63), the captives *utzakaw te'* "added-up the stick(s)." We know that Classic Maya war captives were not always sacrificed. Defeated Yich'aak Bahlam of Ceibal was famously reinstated as a vassal of the victorious Dos Pilas king (S. Martin and Grube 2008 [2000]:61–63). A similar fate befell K'an Joy Chitam of Palenque after he was captured by a Toniná rival (Stuart 2003a). The narrative on the so-called Denver and Brussels "panels" describes how one of the recently captured lords was subsequently "summoned" to the court of the victorious king along with other vassals (Beliaev and Safronov 2004; Biró 2005:2–8; Houston 2014a). Therefore, it is quite possible that the inscription on Stela 12 refers to future payments of ransom and/or tribute: the captives were literally presenting tallies or token proving their worth to the captors.

It is perhaps worth mentioning here that the most common term for captives in Hieroglyphic Mayan is "bone" (*baak*). It is widely assumed that the designation refers to a practice of keeping the long bones of captives as trophies, as described by Landa (Tozzer 1941:120–123). The ample archaeological evidence of dismemberment does not include any cases of human bones with inscriptions identifying them as trophies, although tagged ancestral bones do occur (Fitzsimmons 2009:167–169). For instance, well-known depictions of a royal captive in the abovementioned set of Burial 116 at Tikal are on deer bones (Moholy-Nagy and Coe 2008:61, Figure 201a, b). In other words, that captive was connected to a set of two bones, but they were not his bones. Consequently, the captives-as-bones metaphor may carry a double significance: military trophies but also tallies or tokens.

The final case of "adding up sticks" is provided by El Chal Stela 5 (Figure 16.3f). Like the nearby Stela 4, this monument actually glorifies the exploits of the Ucanal ruler Itzamnaaj Bahlam, whose political patronage extended over El Chal and other sites in the region (Carter 2016:244). If the Calendar Round date on Stela 5 is reconstructed as 4 Lamat 1 Pax, it corresponds to AD 727 or relatively early in Itzamnaaj Bahlam's reign. It predates the much larger Stela 4 dedicated by Itzamnaaj Bahlam in AD 760 in celebration of a *k'atun* midstation. In contrast to Stela 4, the subject of the text and image on Stela 5 is not the calendar. The carved scene is very eroded, but it probably depicts a palanquin with a seated protagonist protected by a standing deity statue. The inscription states that a lady from the ruling family of the site of El Chorro (Palka 1996) "added up the sticks" before Itzamnaaj Bahlam. Given that El Chorro is located west of the Petexbatún region, it is highly unlikely that its queen or princess paid tribute to or was captured by the Ucanal lord. Yet the distance would not be unusual for a marriage alliance, and there are similar depictions of royal brides in palanquins (S. Martin 2008). Therefore, it is tempting to interpret the act of "adding up the sticks" as presentation of a dowry or some other economic transaction that accompanied the marriage arrangement.

Although Contact Period authors do not explicitly mention transactions involving stick tallies, at least one specific tribute-related gloss, (*y*)*ubte'*, attested in Classic Period inscriptions (Tokovinine and Beliaev 2013:175) and Yucatec dictionaries (Barrera Vásquez et al. 1995:980–981), is a combination of the term for a piece of cloth (*ub*) and *te'*. Together, *ub* and *te'* denote a piece of cloth of standardized size used in tribute transactions. Another Yucatec term for tribute, *ximte'*, appears to consist of a numerical classifier for cacao and *te'* (Barrera Vásquez et al. 1995:944–945). Consequently, it is the "stick" part of these *difrasismos* that seemingly qualifies an object as a tribute/tax item.

If transactions with tallies and tokens are mentioned in such a diverse range of contexts, why don't we see them depicted in the Classic Maya palace scenes? The answer to that question is that these objects are indeed present but have been consistently misclassified. The best candidates here are the so-called bundles of quills (Coe and Kerr 1998:97–101; Freidel et al. 2016). In a scene of tribute mantle presentation as "payment" on a vessel from Motul de San José (see Just 2012:148–151, Figure 86–92; Tokovinine and Zender 2012:58–59), all the participants with the exception of two torch-holding servants have identical small bundles of stick-like objects in their headdresses (Figure 16.4a). The same bundles appear in the headdresses of the protagonists of other courtly scenes painted by Motul de San José artists, including royal audiences (Figure 16.4b) and several pulque-presentation events (Figure 16.4c; see Tokovinine 2016:17–19). While it is theoretically possible to ascribe the presence of these bundles to collective expressions of artistic inclination, the quill interpretation really struggles to explain large plates with identical stick bundles before the ruler's throne in the same scenes, precisely where one expects a display of wealth like bags of cacao beans (Figure 16.4b, c). One palace scene from the set (M. Miller and Martin 2004:Pl. 7) even shows an attendant carrying a plate of stick bundles

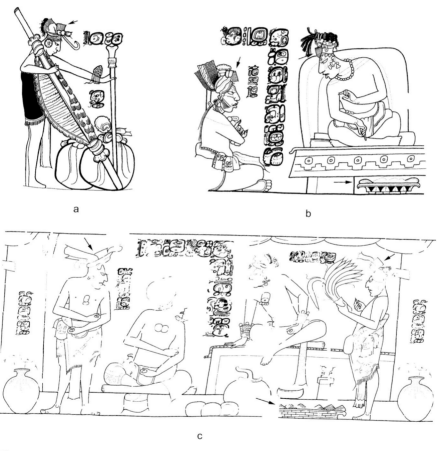

a

b

c

Figure 16.4. Possible tally stick bundles in Classic Maya palace scenes on Motul de San José pottery: (a) detail of a Late Classic vase (K1724); (b) detail of a Late Classic vase (PC.B.564/K2784); (c) detail of a Late Classic vase (TA 32A-1-3/K30177) (images courtesy of Justin Kerr).

to the ruler's throne, where another plate of stick bundles already sits next to a pile of tribute mantles and feathers. The implications are that Maya nobles carried records in the form of bundled stick tallies or tokens and that such objects were apparently standardized enough to be deposited in large numbers and displayed as statements of one's wealth. Moreover, given the ethnohistoric data that shared drinks were a way of sealing contracts among the Early Colonial Maya (Tozzer 1941:96), one is left wondering if the true meaning of the "image with pulque" scenes could involve contractual obligations or taxation.

The final context of tallies in Classic Maya texts concerns a rather enigmatic term for captives that is almost as common as "bone." It has remained poorly understood despite an extensive discussion of its known occurrences and spellings by Martin (2004) and Velásquez García (2005). The term may be spelled with a single character (T78:514), which could be preceded by ya- and followed by -he (likely a phonetic complement) (Figure 16.5a). The -AJ character can also be added (Figure 16.5b), perhaps as a spelling of the -aj "person" suffix (Houston et al. 2001:6–7). Yet the same T78:514 character may also be preceded by ye- (Figure 16.5c), so that the expression is written as ye-he-TE' (Figure 16.5d) and ye-TE' (Figure 16.5e). As pointed out by Martin (2004:110), T78:514 substitutes for the usual TE' logogram in a different lexical context once, but the unique-

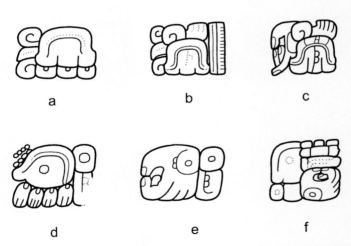

a   b   c

d   e   f

Figure 16.5. Examples of T78:514: (*a*) ya-T78: 514-he (Dzibanché Hieroglyphic Stairway, Block 5:B2); (*b*) ya-T78: 514-AJ (Dzibanché Hieroglyphic Stairway, Block 13:A3); (*c*) ye-T78: 514 (Yaxchilán Lintel 35:C1); (*d*) ye-he-TE' (Yaxchilán Hieroglyphic Stairway 5: 82); (*e*) ye-TE' (Toniná Monument 153:A3); (*f*) ye-TE' K'IN-ni-chi (Motul de San José Stela 1:C4) (drawings by Alexandre Tokovinine).

ness of the example implies that T78:514 and **TE'** usually have different readings even though -*te'* was part of the phonetic value of T78:514.

The amount of variation in the spelling of this possible term for captives is consistent with the way *difrasismos* appear in the Classic Maya script. The most relevant cases would be *saak sak ik'il*, "seed, white breath" (Kettunen 2005), and *saak mijiin*, "seed, child of father." Both are spelled with conflations, flexible reading order, and underspellings. T78:514 and its variants are characterized by the same set of patterns. If this assumption is correct, T78:514 likely stands for a conflation of **TE'** with a logogram that would most likely be **EH**, "tooth," and potentially a third glyph with a reading that begins with *a*-, as the examples prefixed by **ya**- appear to indicate. Bernal Romero (2015) recently proposed a similar interpretation of T78:514 although he did not consider the possibility of a *difrasismo*.

If the *difrasismo* hypothesis is correct, the most complete form of the expression will consist of *y-eh-te'-(aj)*, "his/her *ehte'* (person)," and *y-a . . . -te'-(aj)* "his/her *a . . . te'* (person)." Given the similarity of T78:514 to the **AT** "stinger" glyph (Lopes 2005), the second half of the kenning could be *y-at-te'-(aj)*. The term *ehte'* probably features the Ch'olan gloss *eh*, "tooth" (Kaufman and Norman 1984:119), so its literal meaning would be "tooth wood/stick/spear." Although no such term is attested in the Contact Period sources, Yucatec *julte'* "throwing spear" (Barrera Vásquez et al. 1995:244) and *nabte'* "hand spear" (Barrera Vásquez et al. 1995:546) are good analogies. The translation of *ehte'* as a kind of weapon would certainly fit the lexical contexts such as the personal name Ye[h] te' K'inich, "the tooth-spear of the Sun God" (Figure 16.5f), popular with Motul de San José rulers (Tokovinine and Zender 2012). Halberds or *macuahuitl*-like weapons with spear points and rows of triangular blades or shark teeth are frequently depicted in Classic Maya imagery. The second half of the *difrasismo* might denote a similar weapon ("stinger spear"), but it is tempting to consider the possibility that a completely different class of objects was evoked. Tzeltalan languages share a gloss *aht* "to count" (as in accounting) (Ara 1986:246; Kaufman 1972:94; Laughlin 1975:48). In Colonial Yucatec, *atal* means "to be paid" or "something paid" (Barrera Vásquez et al. 1995:18). If such interpretation of the T78:514 and related glyphs is correct, the captives were referred to as people who pertained to the weapons and the accounting devices of the captor, his "halberd (person)" and "tally (person)." The first part of the *difrasismo* evokes warfare as a means of procuring captives, while the second implies that ransom or tribute would be paid. At least two war narratives at Palenque and

Tikal conclude by placing the captives and captured items in a "house of *eh te'/aht te'*," perhaps a dedicated repository of trophies and tribute.

Conclusion

This chapter began by acknowledging the lack of studies of tallies and tokens in Mesoamerica. In contrast to implicit assumptions among scholars, tallies and writing often have complementary roles in accounting practices. There is a widespread indigenous tradition of tallies in the Americas. Tally sticks and tally boards were still in use in the Maya area in the twentieth century. A collection of sticks in the Peabody Museum was likely related to labor accounting, although the possibility of a calendrical function of at least two tallies cannot be discarded. The presence of elite tally-like bone and shell artifacts during the Classic Period suggests that tallies could have been used by the Classic Maya. Such practices would inspire the creators of special objects such as tallies and tokens in Comalcalco and Tikal burials.

Textual evidence offers the strongest case for tallies in Classic Maya accounting practices. The expression of "adding-up/putting-together the sticks" occurs in the context of time-keeping, taxation, captive tribute or ransom, and marriage arrangements. One of the terms for captives also potentially evoked tally sticks. Small bundles of tally sticks are depicted in the scenes of Classic Maya courtly life. These objects are usually tied to a headdress or placed in large plates to be displayed along with other items indicating wealth and social status.

The presence of tally sticks has several important implications for our understanding of the Classic Maya economy. First, it broadens the context in which we can identify display and use of accounting tools. It also implies that at least some accounting practices were not restricted to the members of the literate social class and/or to those versed in the prestige Hieroglyphic Mayan or Classic Ch'olti'an language. Consequently, Classic Maya elites had potentially less control of the economic records compared to a scenario when all the transactions were recorded exclusively in the codices.

One major question is the degree of standardization. The bundles of tallies appear highly standardized in the scenes on Motul de San José ("Ik' school") pottery. However, there is no comparable set of images from elsewhere. For example, no stick bundles appear in the possible market scenes on Structure Sub 14 in the North Acropolis at Calakmul. Yet the stick bundles are present in the headdresses of some secondary (*anaab*?) officials in Room 3 and dignitaries in Rooms 1 of Structure 1 at Bonampak (Miller and Brittenham 2013:184–185, 220–221). The tribute-givers in the scene on Tikal MT 67 have bundles of small shells in their headdresses, much like the characters on Calakmul murals. Such shell beads have been identified in the Classic Maya archaeological record as potential monies (Freidel et al. 2016). So it is possible that tally sticks were one of several ways of displaying and recording tribute/tax obligations.

Nevertheless, at least within the political and economic domain of Motul de San José rulers, tally records of tribute or debt may have served as equivalents of value as long as their owners were expected to get a similar amount of goods or labor—after all, the word "loan" has a substantial time depth in Mayan languages (Tokovinine and Beliaev 2013:172–173). Yet such arrangements would require a substantial amount of trust among all of the potential participants in the transactions. It is unclear if compliance could be enforced. Any systemic breakdown in trust would have been devastating, as it would instantly invalidate large holdings of potential goods and services. The breakdown in trust has already been highlighted as one of the sociopolitical factors in the so-called Classic Maya collapse (Golden and Scherer 2013). Evidence of a trust-based accounting system adds an additional dimension to that model.

Acknowledgments

This research would not be possible without the support of the Peabody Museum of Archaeology and Ethnology, Harvard University. I greatly appreciate the efforts by the museum curatorial assistant Emily Pierce Rose who provided access to the ethnographic collection of Maya tallies and its acquisition history. This manuscript has improved enormously thanks to comments and suggestions from this volume's reviewers and editors, as well as from many colleagues including Gary Urton, Anthony Aveni, Stephen Houston, Dmitri Beliaev, Nicholas Carter, Albert Davletshin, Sergey Vepretskiy, and Traci Ardren. As always, I remain solely responsible for any errors or omissions.

17

Maya Economic Organization and Power

A View from Elite Households at Aguateca

DANIELA TRIADAN AND TAKESHI INOMATA

Control over the production and distribution of goods is often interpreted as a means of power in prehistoric societies, and the degree of centralization of the economy is seen as correlated with the degree of social and political complexity (e.g., Earle 1994a). In state-level societies elites often controlled all spheres of the economy, affecting even the subsistence economy of individual households (e.g., R. M. Adams 1981; D'Altroy and Earle 1985; Paulette 2016). In contrast to Earle (1994a), we do not believe that there is a clear division between subsistence and political economy but prefer to look at three general classes of goods that may or may not represent different economic spheres in a given society: prestige goods, which are highly valued, often exotic items and/or the raw materials to produce them; utilitarian goods such as ceramics, lithics, textiles, and hides; and foodstuffs. Of course, what constitutes a prestige good depends on social and cultural definitions and often also on elite propaganda. It is possible to make something a prestige item by making it inaccessible, or prohibitively expensive, or simply by forbidding anybody but the elites to use it.

It has long been argued that the Maya had a prestige economy (e.g., Rathje 1971) in which elites controlled the access to precious and rare goods and in some cases were involved in their production. For example, Reents-Budet (1994:36–71) found that elites, and in some cases members of royal families, painted the most valuable polychrome ceramic serving vessels that were often exchanged as gifts between high-ranking nobles from different polities. Prestige goods such as jade and quetzal feathers clearly bestowed social status on Maya elites. It has been less clear to what degree elites controlled the production and distribution of utilitarian goods and foodstuffs (although many Maya scholars have worked on reconstructing the Maya economy, including Foias and Bishop 2013; Masson and Freidel 2002; Wells and Davis-Salazar 2007). This is precisely what added to debates about how complex the organization of the Maya economy was.

Our work at the Late Classic site of Aguateca in the southwestern Petén, Guatemala, revealed that the city was attacked, and the elite residences that were located along the causeway leading to the royal palace were burned and rapidly abandoned (Inomata et al. 2002; Inomata and Triadan 2003, 2010, 2014). This led to unusual in situ artifact assemblages in and around these elite houses

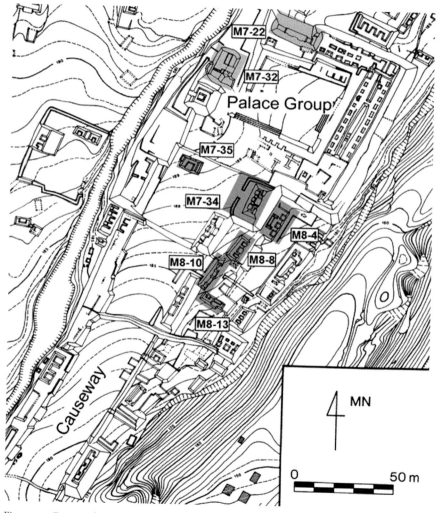

Figure 17.1. Excavated structures.

(Inomata and Triadan 2010, 2014). These artifact assemblages provide unique information on elite household organization and can be used to evaluate the households' economic activities.

We completely excavated six elite structures in the causeway area and two structures in the royal palace complex that were probably the residence of the royal household and the official audience building of the king (Figure 17.1; Inomata et al. 2001; Inomata and Triadan 2010, 2014). The latter two buildings were not rapidly abandoned, however, and we are not using them in the analysis that we are presenting here.

In the case of Aguateca we have demonstrated not only that prestige goods were important as symbols of social status but that the elites had the ultimate control over prestige goods because they actually made them in and around their own houses (Inomata 2001; Inomata et al. 2002; Inomata and Triadan 2000). We also showed that each structure was occupied by a single household, because specific activities were clearly carried out in different rooms of each structure (Inomata et al. 2002; Inomata and Triadan 2010, 2014). In this chapter we focus on utilitarian goods to assess how centralized the economy at Aguateca was. We are interested in the question of how much control the royal court had over these more mundane spheres of the economy and whether elite households were actively involved in their own subsistence economy. Specifically, we are presenting data on ceramic production and use, storage capacity, food processing, and food consumption.

Ceramic Assemblages

All six structures had a large number of whole and reconstructible vessels. They ranged from 31 in Str. M7-35 to 82 in Str. M8-10. All residences had fairly similar assemblages of storage, cooking, and serving vessels (Figures 17.2 and 17.3). Proportions of Cambio/Encanto vessels range from 10% in Str. M8-4 to 30% in Str. M7-34. Tinaja Red vessels make up 35 to 58% of the assemblages. The proportion of Saxché-Palmar Polychrome vessels is the most consistent, ranging from 19 to 28% of the assemblages, and all structures had some nonlocal ceramics. The assemblage of Str. M8-4 seems to have the most variability (Figure 17.3). The assemblage from Str. M7-13 may not be complete, because we did not completely excavate the West Room and western exterior of this structure, so more storage vessels might still be found in and around that room. Data from a Guatemalan restoration project that extended the excavation in

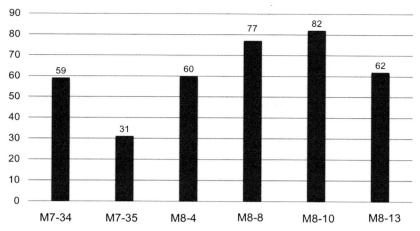

Figure 17.2. Number of reconstructible vessels per structure.

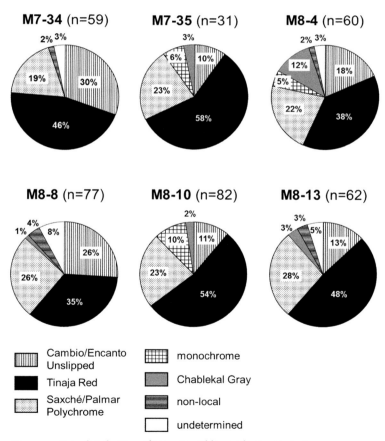

Figure 17.3. Type distributions of reconstructible vessels per structure.

this structure is not comparable to our data. Str. M7-34 may have been originally an elite residence that was later used for more public purposes such as feasting; or that may have been the building's function from the beginning (see the discussion in Inomata, Triadan, and Ponciano 2010:114–137). The ceramic assemblage, however, does look similar to those of the elite residences (Figure 17.3). The difference in the overall quantities of vessels found in the structures may reflect different household size.

Foias and Bishop (2013) have shown that most of the vessels were probably made locally by many households. They could not find any evidence for specialized production of these ceramics, except for some of the polychromes. We believe that elite households made the majority of their pottery. For instance, large-thin walled storage vessels were probably not moved very far from where they were found. They are technically extremely difficult to make and very fragile. In support of this assumption, we found one such vessel in the North Room of Str. M8-8. The vessel lacked its rim but clearly continued to be used as a storage container in that room.

In addition, we found several ceramic disks in the northern addition and the outside of the South Room of Str. M8-4, as well as outside Strs. M8-13 and M7-34 (Figure 17.4). They were the worked and reused bases of jars and bowls and in the case of Str. M8-4 many had clay residue (Inomata 2014b:Figure 14.5, 2014c:40–45, Figures 3.5–3.8). They may have been used like molds for building vessels or for mixing pastes. In the American Southwest (Puebloan) region, people were using bases of jars called "pukis" for that purpose (Fontana et al. 1962:58; Goddard 1945:4; Guthe 1925:27, 33). Reina and Hill (1978:22, 79–113) have recorded the use of broken vessel bases for forming vessels for modern Maya potters. Emery and Aoyama (2007) have shown that all elite households, including the royal court, were engaged in lithic and shell production for basic tools as well as more sophisticated ornaments. Thus, in addition to other crafting activities, we may have direct evidence for ceramic manufacture in these households.

As mentioned, all of the assemblages also contained a few imported ceramics. All but Str. M7-34 had some Chablekal Fine Gray vessels (Figure 17.5), and most had some additional imported pots (Figure 17.3). Str. M8-4 had by far the highest proportion of imports (16% of its assemblage) and also the highest proportion of Chablekal Gray (12% of its assemblage: see Figure 17.3). Chablekal Gray was produced downriver from Aguateca, most likely in an area around Palenque in the plains of the lower Usumacinta River (Foias and Bishop 2013:352–353).

Figure 17.4. Ceramic disks.

Figure 17.5. (*a*)–(*c*) Chablekal Gray vessels; (*d*) unnamed imported vessel.

These imported vessels were most likely gifts. Interestingly, they exhibited much variation in forms among the assemblages of the six structures. In some cases, they came from different areas, indicating that each household had its own individual external relations, probably with elites in other cities. Tsukamoto and Esparza (2015) have recently demonstrated a similar situation at El Palmar, where the text of a hieroglyphic stairway in an outlying group mentions a new title of a minor noble and his relationship with the royal court of Copán (see also Chapter 15). Str. M8-4 not only had had the highest proportion of Chablekal Gray but was also the only structure where we found five unusual pottery bells made of this type (Triadan 2006, 2014:11, 34–35, Figures 2.19, 2.20).

Storage and Food Processing

Storage and food-processing activities were carried out in one of the side rooms of each excavated structure and also in side additions or behind the structures (Figure 17.6), clearly indicating that the elites of Aguateca practiced what Smyth (1989:92–93) calls domestic storage (see also Vidal-Lorenza et al. 2016:274–281). Triadan (2000) previously analyzed the food storage and food-processing capacities of elite households. Here we present more complete data that were only available after we completed all of our laboratory analyses. All structures had large storage jars of the Cambio Unslipped or Encanto Striated types (Figure 17.7). Their quantities ranged from 3 jars in Str. M7-35 to 19 jars in Str. M8-8. They were probably used for dry food staples, such as shelled corn. All of the structures also had numerous smaller jars of the Tinaja Red ceramic group that probably stored water or other liquids (Figure 17.8). We base the postulated difference in stored contents on the form of the vessels. Cambio and Encanto jars are wide-mouthed, which facilitated easy access to stored goods, while Tinaja Red jars have narrow necks and omphalic bases, which facilitated carrying them on the head and minimized the spilling of liquid contents (Reina and Hill 1978:121, Figures 37a and 37b, 240, Plates 397, 251, 414). The quantities of Tinaja Red storage jars range from 10 (Str. M7-35) to 22 vessels (Str. M8-10). The total storage jars present in the different structures ranged from 13 in Str. M7-35 to 34 in Str. M8-8 (Figure 17.8). We only included jars that had a maximum diameter larger than 11 cm in this analysis. As mentioned, Str. M8-13 may have had a few more storage vessels than we recovered.

More informative in terms of the actual storage capacity for each household may be the total volume of the storage jars (Figure 17.9). Inomata calculated vessel volumes using the 3-D capacity of the Bentley Microstation V8i drawing program (Inomata, Triadan, and Estela Pinto 2010:181–192, Table 8.1). Volume estimates for Strs. M7-35 and M8-10 are derived from Tonoike's thesis (Tonoike 2001:Table 1). Following the same procedure, Tonoike used an earlier version of the program. Inomata and Tonoike calculated vessel volumes based on profile

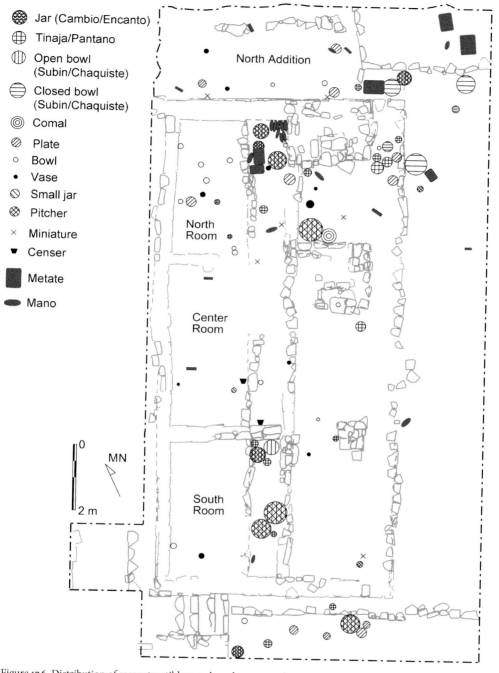

Figure 17.6. Distribution of reconstructible vessels and manos and metates in Str. M8-4.

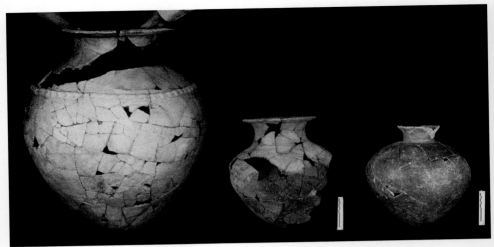

Figure 17.7. Types of storage jars (*left to right*): Cambio Unslipped, Encanto Striated, Pantano Impressed (Tinaja Red Group), all shown at the same scale.

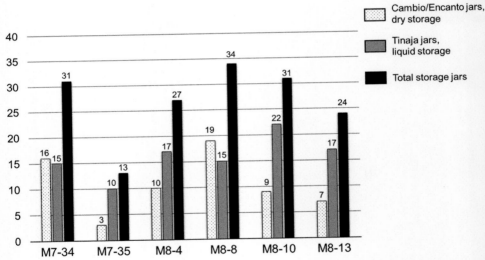

Figure 17.8. Storage jars per structure, including only jars with a maximum diameter greater than 11 cm.

drawings of the reconstructible vessels. These drawings were then scanned, and a three-dimensional image was generated. The program has a calculus function that allows to calculate the volume of the three-dimensional images. The capacities of the jar forms were calculated up to the neck or the most restricted portion of the orifice (Tonoike 2001:4). We should emphasize that all volumes

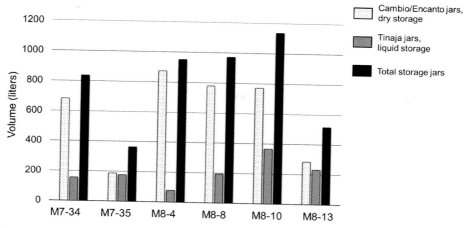

Figure 17.9. Storage jars per structure, indicating storage volume per structure in liters.

presented here are conservative estimates. Based on their maximum diameter and weight, we added an estimated capacity of 58,000 cm^3 or 58 liters for each of two Encanto Striated jars (vessel nos. 14B-3 and 14B-15). The vessels were too fragmented to calculate their volume from their profiles. This resulted in a total of 116,000 cm^3 or 116 liters that we added to the calculations for Str. M8-13 (see Inomata, Triadan, and Estela Pinto 2010:181–192, Table 8.1). Similarly we added a capacity of 6 liters for one Tinaja Red jar from Str. M8-4 (vessel no. 23A-82) and 70 liters for a Cambio Unslipped jar from Str. M7-34 (vessel no. 21A-4), based on their weight only, because they were too fragmented to allow an estimate of their maximum diameter.

The overall storage capacity ranged from 364 liters in Str. M7-35 to 1,137 liters in Str. M8-10 (Figure 17.9). Dry storage volume ranged from 169 liters in Str. M7-34 to 873 liters in Str. M8-4, which would be approximately 26.2 to 135.3 kg of dry shelled maize based on Smyth's (1991:39, Table 2.4) equations for modern Yucatec Maya, if these large vessels were indeed used for maize storage. (Following Benedict and Steggerda [1936] and Steggerda [1941] he calculates that 1 m^3 or 1,000 liters equals 155 kg of kernel maize.) This translates to a range from 1.5 to 7.5 persons that could have been sustained for 30 days (Figure 17.10), again following Smyth (1991:39, Table 2.4), who lists 0.6 kg of dry kernel maize per person as the daily consumption for Yucatec Maya. Str. M8-4 had the most dry storage capacity, but in general the volumes were similar for Strs. M8-4, M8-8, M8-10, and M7-34. If those vessels contained shelled maize, then each of these households could have sustained 6 to 7.5 persons for a month. Strs. M7-35 and M8-13 had markedly lower dry storage capacities that equaled only 1.5 to 2.5 persons that could have been sustained for a month and thus may indeed represent smaller households. The liquid storage volume capacity ranged from 78 liters in Str. M8-4 to 232 liters in Str. M8-10. Thus, even though Str. M8-4 may have had the largest dry storage capacity, it had the lowest liquid storage capacity of the six households. Figure 17.11 shows that the sizes of storage vessels varied in different households. The differences in overall storage capacity again may indicate differences in household size.

We emphasize that the storage vessels probably did not represent the total storage capacities of each households. The actual amounts of shelled maize that could have been stored in those jars were pretty low and may have only held the supply for one month for households of varying sizes. They were probably used for the daily food needs of each household. People may also have stored other foodstuffs, and the majority of the maize harvest may have been stored as ear maize on the stalk and in cribs that were made of perishable materials (Smyth 1991:20–25; see also Vidal-Lorenza et al. 2016). However, pottery jars provide containers that can be sealed and thus prevent loss from rodents and other varmints. Pithoi and amphorae, large clay storage jars, were widely used in the Mediterranean for domestic storage (e.g., Christakis 1999) as well as long-distance transport. And storage experiments at the Maya site of Cuello have shown that maize kernels stored in a *chultun* in an open container preserved better than corn on the cob (Miksicek 1991:79). Miksicek argues that sealed ceramic jars would have been suitable for long-term grain storage. Smyth (1991:25) states that properly dried shelled maize can be stored up to one year in Yucatán by modern Maya farmers. Unhusked ear maize, packed in cribs, can be stored for up to three years (Smyth 1991:25). Nevertheless, the assemblages show clearly that each elite household had its own food storage capability.

Each household was also engaged in food processing, and metates and manos were often found associated with storage and cooking vessels (Figure 17.6). Large metates, which were most likely used for grinding maize, were predominantly made from local limestone (Figure 17.2; Inomata 2014a:61, 65, Figures 5.19, 5.26). A few large metates that were made from quartzite or igneous rock were imported to the site. Although superior in grinding performance and durability, these are rare and indicate that people at Aguateca did not have regular access to these materials. The quantities of metates ranged from 1 in Str. M7-35 to 8 in Str. M8-8 (Figure 17.13). Consistent with a lower number of storage ves-

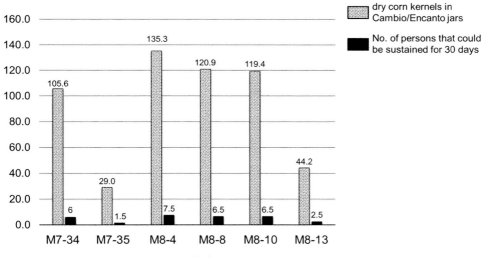

Figure 17.10. Maize storage capacity and subsistence per structure.

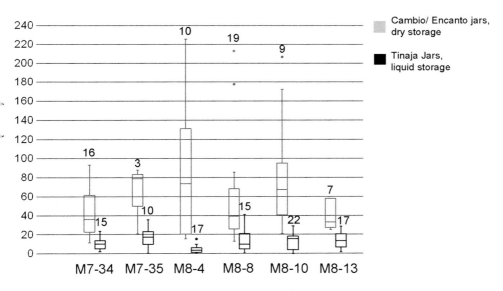

Figure 17.11. Range of storage vessel volumes per structure in liters.

sels and the lowest maize and overall storage capacity, Str. M7-35 had only 1 large metate (compare Figures 17.10 and 17.13). Areas around the structure were not as extensively excavated as the other buildings, so there could have been more grinding implements. Overall, though, Strs. M7-35 and M8-13 seemed to have housed smaller households than Strs. M8-4 and M8-8.

Figure 17.12. Large limestone metate from Str. M8-8.

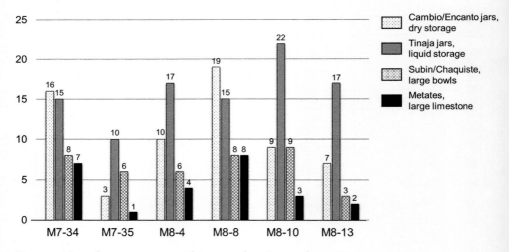

Figure 17.13. Large limestone metates and storage and serving vessels per structure.

Food Serving

All structures also had large open and closed bowls that were probably used for cooking and serving food (Figures 17.14–17.16). Str. M8-10 had the greatest number of bowls, but Str. M8-4 had the overall largest capacity for holding food in terms of volume (Figures 17.13, 17.15). This is clearly because the household had

Figure 17.14. Chaquiste Red (*left and upper right*) and Subin Red bowls of the Tinaja Red Group.

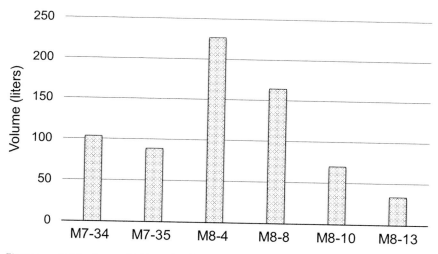

Figure 17.15. Total volume of Subin Red and Chaquiste Red bowls per structure in liters.

more very large bowls that could hold 50 liters or more than any of the other structures (Figure 17.16). In general, the bowl volume data follow the pattern seen in the storage volume, although here Str. M8-10 had the second lowest volume (compare Figures 17.9 and 17.15). Even though this context has the most bowls (n = 9, Figure 17.13), it has the smallest bowls of the six households (Figure 17.16).

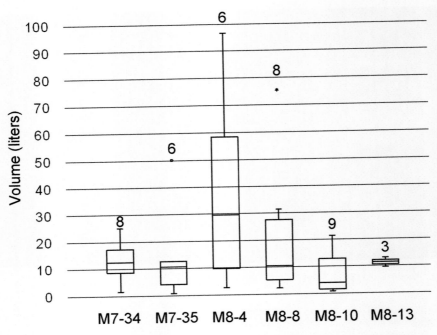

Figure 17.16. Range of Subin Red and Chaquiste Red bowl volumes per structure in liters.

The inhabitants of Str. M8-4 may have hosted more communal or feasting events than the other households. As mentioned, this household had the highest variability in ceramics, the most imports, and also the very special fine gray pottery bells. In addition, it contained the highest number of cylindrical vases (Inomata, Triadan, and Estela Pinto 2010:181–192, Table 8.1), which may have been used for serving cacao and other beverages (LeCount 2001:944–947). It also had the most figurines (Triadan 2007:273, 283, Table 1, 2014:10, 14, Table 2.1), and the most shell and bone ornaments and musical instruments (Inomata and Emery 2014:142, Table 8.2) compared to the other households, and also considerable quantities of greenstone ornaments (Inomata and Eberl 2014:89, 94, Figure 6.9). The head of the household was probably involved in making and safeguarding the royal regalia. We found parts of a royal headdress in the South Room of this structure (Inomata and Eberl 2014:92–94), together with evidence for refashioning pyrite mirrors into ornaments, possibly for special regalia (Inomata and Eberl 2014:96–110). We also found fragments of a bone

Daniela Triadan and Takeshi Inomata

carved with an inscription that mentions a royal youth of the royal family of Aguateca (Houston 2014a:264, 266, Figure 12.6b) on the bench in the Center Room. People living in this house may have been wealthier or may have had a slightly higher status than those in the other households, and they may have been more involved in administrative duties, which included hosting and feeding guests.

Food Consumption

We compared the faunal remains from each structure to assess what kinds of animal foods elites in these households may have consumed and whether the households had different consumption patterns. The analysis of all faunal remains was carried out by Kitty Emery (2010, 2014) and the data presented here are based on her tables (Emery 2010:Appendix 2B, 303–307, 2014:Table 9.5, 169–170). She also provided the minimum numbers of individuals (MNIs) that we are using here (Emery 2014:Table 9.5). We only considered the remains of vertebrate animals that may have been eaten, such as deer, turtles, dogs, armadillos, and others. Cats such as jaguars were most likely used for ritual purposes. *Pomacea flagellata*, a large river snail that has been used as a food resource by the Maya since the Preclassic (R. Harrigan 2004; Miksicek 1991:78–79) and *Pachychilus indorum*, the jute snail, consumed as early as the Preclassic Period (e.g., Healy et al. 1990), were very rare, indicating that they were not a major food source for the Late Classic elites at Aguateca. Although marine gastropod shells and river bivalves are abundant in all residences and may have been eaten, the majority were used to make ornaments and as scribal implements, such as ink pots (Emery 2014; Inomata et al. 2002). Of course, the large river clams that were used as ink pots may very well have ended up in a stew before the shells were used.

Except for Str. M8-10 the assemblage of vertebrate animals appears similar in all the households (Figure 17.17). They all had deer and dog. Most also had turtles, except for Str. M7-35. In addition, peccary, agouti, and armadillo may have been used as food. Deer was especially significant to the diet; each household had parts of two or three deer, except for Str. M8-10, which had a noticeably larger quantity: eight deer and two peccaries. We should note that many of the faunal remains found in and around the structures do not represent straightforward food garbage. In most cases, animal products were also used for other purposes, such as making personal ornaments and ritual paraphernalia, like headdresses. The remains reflect those activities (see Emery 2010, 2014).

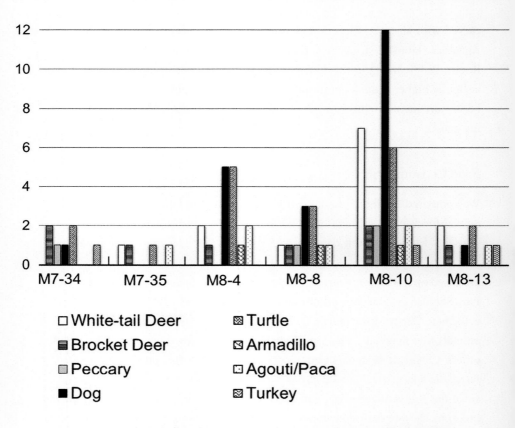

Figure 17.17. Distribution of vertebrate animals that may have been used for food by structure.

Conclusions

The assemblages of elite households at the Classic Period site of Aguateca indicate that each household was a relatively autonomous economic unit of production and consumption of staples and utilitarian goods. While individual households specialized in the production of a variety of prestige items, there is little evidence for central control of any sphere of the economy by the royal court or elites. Individual households also seem to have maintained their own long-distance relationships with other elites from different areas, which may or may not have aligned with the official foreign policy of the court. Thus, an intriguing question remains: why did Maya elites, in contrast to elites of complex societies in other parts of the world, seemingly not develop and use a centralized economy as a means of power and political control?

Daniela Triadan and Takeshi Inomata

Acknowledgments

Our work at Aguateca was funded by the National Science Foundation, the National Geographic Society, the Foundation for Advancement of Mesoamerican Studies (FAMSI), the Mitsubishi Foundation, the Sumitomo Foundation, and the H. John Heinz III Charitable Trust. Research permission was granted by the Instituto de Arqueología e Historia of Guatemala. We like to thank Marilyn Masson, David Freidel, and Arthur Demarest for inviting us to contribute to this volume, and especially Marilyn Masson for doing an incredible job in the herculean task of bringing this volume to a speedy fruition.

V

Economic Exchange Spheres

Routes, Facilities, and Symbolic Contexts

18

Economic Interactions and the Rise of Sociopolitical Complexity in the Maya Lowlands

A Perspective from the Mirador-Calakmul Basin

RICHARD D. HANSEN, EDGAR SUYUC,
STANLEY P. GUENTER, CARLOS MORALES-AGUILAR,
ENRIQUE HERNÁNDEZ, AND BEATRIZ BALCÁRCEL

The economic interactions of early social and political formations were crucial catalysts in the development of incipient polities because they established the parameters of subsistence goods and wealth pertinent to the advent of specializations and exchanges that influenced the resultant success or failures of an administrative elite (e.g., Brumfiel and Earle, eds. 1987; Clark and Blake 1994; Masson and Freidel 2002). The natures of economic and political formations and interactions in Mesoamerica have been debated for decades (e.g., Andrews 1983; Berdan 1982; Boehm de Lameiras 1991; Clark and Blake 1994; Evans 1980; Marcus 1973; Masson and Freidel 2002; Santley 1986; Santley and Richards 2007; Sheets et al. 2015; M. Smith 1979), but the real business of ancient Maya exchange can always use new scrutiny. One of the key components of such a study involves ethnohistoric and ethnographic evaluations as well as technological analyses of hard data.

Archaeological mapping, excavations, and investigations in 51 ancient cities of varying sizes in the Mirador Basin of northern Guatemala have revealed a variety of data relevant to the economic catalysts that were involved in the rise of social, political, and economic sophistication among the Preclassic Maya. New technologies recently implemented in the Mirador Basin and other areas of Mesoamerica are helping to reveal and understand the nature of sociopolitical structure and vital economies among early complex societies.

It can be emphasized, though, that the real "business" of the early Maya dealt initially with agricultural productivity and the formation of an administrative centralized organization to deal with the lack of critical resources such as water. Importantly, a powerful distribution mechanism developed in the form of a sophisticated causeway system to distribute goods and commodities and facilitate unification among a web of sites in the Mirador Basin (Figure 18.1). The initial formation and success of these kick-starting administrative formations led to a variety of other economic indicators such as the importation of exotic shells, domestic fauna, obsidian, jade, basalt, granite, coral, ceramics, and other lithic tools. These exchanges demonstrate the varying degrees of social and economic power that provided the foundations of rank, status, and functional requirements during the rise of Maya civilization. The aggregated religious, political, and social ideology provided the foundations for a relatively homogeneous society throughout the Maya lowlands by the Middle and Late Preclassic periods. The economic manifestations of these ideologies are well represented in the archaeological record. The use of a sophisticated LiDAR system to survey the Mirador Basin, combined with the archaeological data, has allowed a new perspective of the "nuts and bolts" of ancient Maya settlement distributions and, by extrapolation, associated economies in northern Guatemala. These data provide a model that is consistent with ethnohistoric and ethnographic data for Mesoamerica and confirm the models of previous scholars whose perceptions were particularly accurate and visionary. Marcus (1973), Martin and Grube (2008 [2000]), and Arnaya, Guenter, and Zender (2003) have proposed settlement and complex interaction models based on epigraphic data. Archival research by Roys (1957), Chuchiak (2003, 2017), and Okoshi Harada and Quezada (Okoshi and Quezada 2008; Quezada 2014) also provide useful comparative colonial-era models of complex sociopolitical and economic structure from ethnohistorical sources.

Based on the models initially presented by Kansky (1963), Santley (1986) proposed four economic models that have been considered for various Mesoamerican societies, particularly for Aztec political and economic systems (Figure 18.2). These systems include (a) Bounded Networks, (b) Interlocking Networks, (c) Solar Networks, and (d) Dendritic Networks. Santley came to the conclusion that Aztec regional economic organization was dendritically organized, which correlated with the causeway formations and settlement hierarchies in and out of the Basin of Mexico. We propose that the Aztec dendritic system as perceived by Santley was an imperial economic structure of great antiquity and that the

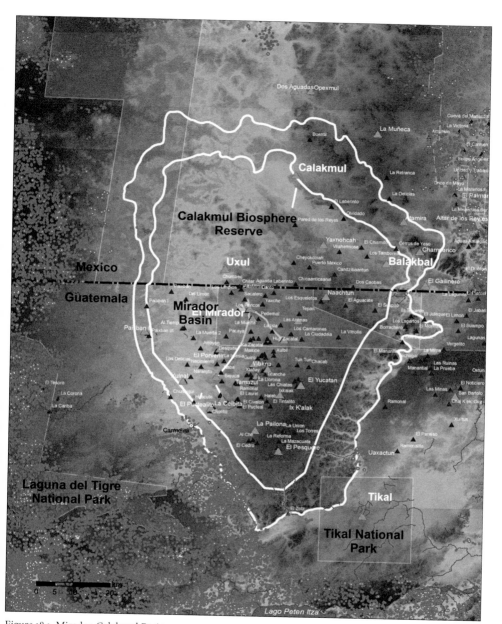

Figure 18.1. Mirador-Calakmul Basin.

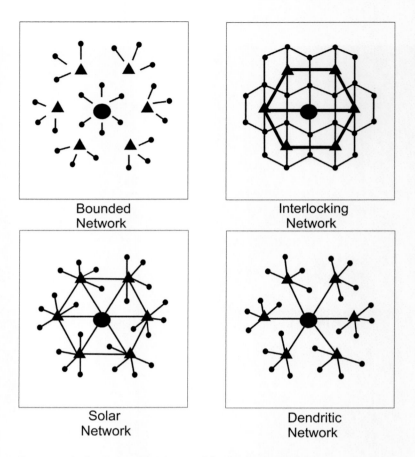

Figure 18.2. Settlement/economic systems (after Santley 1985:232).

early Maya polities of the Mirador Basin, dating to the Middle and Late Preclassic Periods, were configured in a similar sociopolitical economic structure.

The Aztec capital of Tenochtitlán was the dominant center in the Mexican highlands at the time of the conquest in 1519. Detailed mapping of the basin by Luis González (1973) located 222 sites connected by 229 roadway segments (Santley 1986:228), as shown in Figure 18.3. Tenochtitlán and Texcoco were major urban centers, 21 sites were provincial centers (previously small autonomous political units), and the remainder were agricultural villages. The roadways were elevated masonry constructions known to have crossed the lake in causeway formations. In a topological study to measure network connectivity Santley (1986) and Smith (C. Smith 1976b) noted three variables: (1) number of roads, (2) number of settlements, and (3) number of separate isolated points. Among the possible outcomes were Bounded Network systems, where specialization is underdeveloped and the primary focus is on agricultural production for internal consumption. In Interlocking Network systems each market center is linked to several higher-level centers as well as lower-level centers (C. Smith 1976b:320, cited in Santley 1986:224). As Smith (1976b:320) points out, "Goods flow to and from other systems and regions but are also exchanged within the local system at each level." These more complex systems occur where "(1) population density is high, (2) a significant

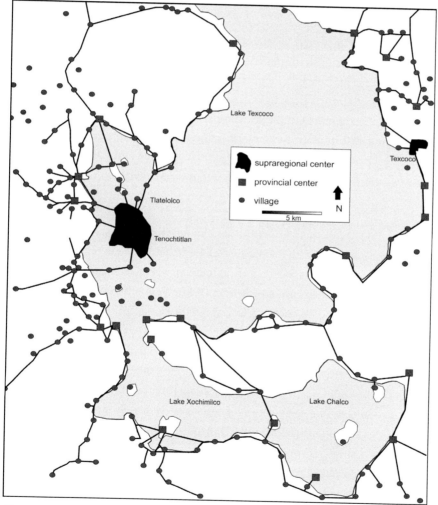

Figure 18.3. Settlement systems in the Basin of Mexico (after Santley 1986).

proportion of the population maintains highly specialized activity regimes, (3) goods are shipped in bulk from center to center, and (4) the transportation system is efficient enough to permit high volume circulation of people and goods from one point on the economic landscape to another" (Santley 1986:225).

The gulf between Bounded Networks and Interlocking Networks has several variable economic structures (Figure 18.2) that Santley termed "Solar Networks": In these structures lesser capitals are linked directly to the "Alpha" capital by transportation networks, but the lesser capitals are also linked directly to each other, allowing logistical, political, and economic support within each subpolity. Such systems allow for horizontal movements of goods and supplies, although a primary emphasis is on the connections to move up the settlement hierarchy (Santley 1986:226).

Dendritically organized systems involve minimal interaction between sites of equivalent size and status (Santley 1986:226; see also E. Johnson 1970), but the vertical linkages are the primary catalyst of the movement of goods. According to Santley (1986:226), "Bulking is a primary determinant of system structure in dendritic economies. Rural areas are serviced by one and only one higher order center that inhibits horizontal communication between centers of lower rank. All connections in such systems—both economic and political—lead to a primate center that maintains total control over its hinterland."

The Mirador-Calakmul Basin

The largest sites within the Mirador-Calakmul Basin of northern Guatemala and southern Campeche, Mexico, are situated in a geographic setting similar to that of the Aztec capital of Tenochtitlán. While Tenochtitlán was surrounded by Lake Texcoco and linked by causeways to the surrounding settlements (Figure 18.3), the sites of El Mirador, Nakbé, and Tintal were surrounded by massive *bajo* (seasonal swamp) systems and were linked by large causeways to surrounding settlements (Figure 18.4). The Mirador-Calakmul Basin, also known as the Cuenca Mirador or Reino Kan (Kaan Kingdom), has unique cultural remains dating to the earliest periods of Maya civilization, including a series of buildings and cities that are among the most monumental of the Prehispanic era (I. Graham 1967; Hansen 1984, 1990, 2001, 2005, 2012b, 2016a, 2016b, 2017; Hansen and Balcárcel 2008; Hansen, Barcárcel, et al. 2006; Hansen, Suyuc, et al. 2006; Hansen et al. 2008; Hansen et al. 2018; Matheny 1987; Matheny et al. 1980). A tropical forest surrounds the area. Due to the geographical, chemical,

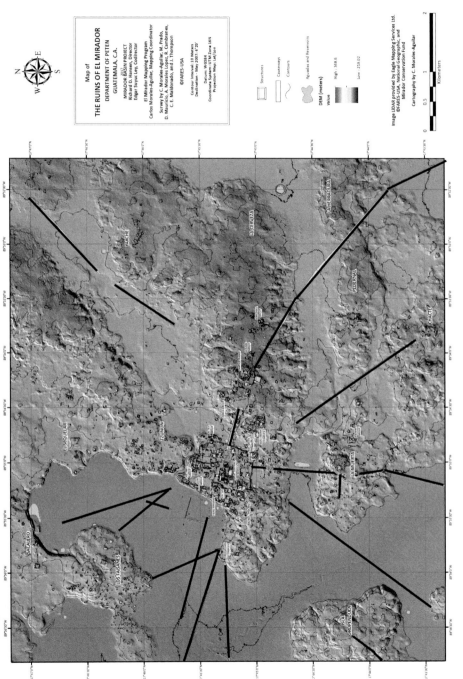

Figure 18.4. El Mirador causeways.

and mineral characteristics of the terrain, it overlaps with at least six distinct forest macrocommunities of flora, thus creating exceptional biodiversity in the area (Castañeda and Hansen 2008, 2016). These types of forests are located within a defined geographic area, which is important because it represents a much more variable biodiversity in a circumscribed area with a symbiotic interdependence. The resultant diversity may have led to varied agricultural capabilities and capacities that would have been useful in tribute and distribution systems.

Geographically, the entire system is easily identified by a variety of satellite photographs, particularly infrared images. It is surrounded by a range of low, karstic limestone hills that frame the entire basin, encompassing about 800,000 hectares. This system includes at least 10 Preclassic monumental cities and more than 70 smaller sites, although at present at least 50% of the basin is still awaiting exploration. The recent LiDAR survey of nearly 3,100 square kilometers within the core area of the basin has now located 100% of the sites within the sphere of research, demonstrating the unique quantity and density of ancient cities within its geographical confines (Figure 18.1). It is likely that the unsurveyed areas in Campeche and Guatemala contain at least five other large-scale archaeological sites with monumental architecture and dozens of smaller sites, while additional major sites are located on the Campeche side of the border. The primary archaeological sites of the Guatemalan side in the Preclassic periods are El Mirador, Tintal, Nakbé, Wakná, Xulnal, and El Pesquero, while sites like Yaxnohcah, Mucaancah, Balakbal, and Calakmul lie on the Campeche side of the basin system. These sites are located over a series of slightly elevated plateaus surrounded by extensive, tree covered seasonal swamps known as *akalches* or *bajos*. The ruins are covered by a tropical/semitropical forest with trees that range in height from 25 to 40 m (82 to 131 ft.). Nearly 40–50% of the Mirador-Calakmul Basin is dominated by *bajos*, which consist of seasonal swamps covered by broad low forests mostly of inkwood trees (*palo tinto*). Anciently, however, *bajo* forests do not seem to have been as common, based on the pollen and isotope data (see below). Instead the area seems to have contained wet, grassy marshlands, known as *civales,* which are probably what attracted the first inhabitants to the region, at least by 2600 BC (Hansen 2017:310–311).

Based on pollen, isotope, and stratigraphic data, it can be proposed that the evolution of lacustrine systems found in the basin followed a process that had lakes, savannas, and oak scrub forest by the Pleistocene. However, due to major climate change by about 7000 to 6000 BC, the area became dominated by restricted lakes and what appears to have been lush tropical forest. The lake systems matured into perennially wet marsh systems known as *civales* by about 2000 BC to about AD 200 and then converted to *bajos*, seasonal swamps with low scrubby forests dominated by inkwood trees (*tintales*).

The Beginnings of Occupation and Cultural Complexity

Pollen data and associated AMS dates from lake cores and from excavated domestic structures directly on bedrock under early Middle Preclassic platforms suggest that the basin was occupied by humans by approximately 2600 BC, with evidence of corn (*Zea*) pollen from a series of lakes along the western edge of the basin (Wahl 2005; Wahl, Byrne, et al. 2006, 2007; Wahl, Schreiner, et al. 2007; Wahl, Schreiner, and Byrne 2001; Hansen 2012b, 2016a, 2016b; Hansen et al. 2002; see below). This is consistent with the evidence for early *Zea* cultivation from other areas of the Maya lowlands (Dunning et al. 2002; M. Pohl et al. 1996; Karen Pope et al. 2001; Wyatt 2008a). Burned posts in bedrock postholes at Nakbé and the AMS dating of cores from the peripheral lakes have identified the presence of this Preceramic occupation (Beta 345809, Beta 345806, Beta 345805, CAMS 94189). It is clear that by the Middle Preclassic Period (ca. 1000–800 BC) settlements with elevated vertical-walled platforms, thin plaster floors, and wattle-and-daub houses were built and utilized (see Hansen 1998, 2005, 2012b).

The presence of such concentrated and large settlements raises the question as to why such demographic densities did not form on Late Petén Itzá or near the smaller lakes located along the western edge of the Mirador Basin. Supposedly ideal locations, such as Ceibal, which is currently being investigated by Inomata and his associates (e.g., Inomata et al. 2013) were only sparsely occupied in this early period. These locations would have provided ample water, fish, and other aquatic resources and a comfortable standard of living for early Maya settlers. These resources could have formed the initial foundations for economic growth. Pollen, isotope, and phytolith studies demonstrate that the bajos, as we know them today, were originally *civales* (Figure 18.5) or perennial wetland marshes during the periods of early Maya occupation in the Mirador Basin (Castañeda and Hansen 2016).

In this mature lacustrine system aquatic vegetation such as water "lechuga" (*Pachira*), grasses, water lilies, and small shrubs were likely responsible for filtration of water, serving as natural composters. The filtration of human waste

Figure 18.5. Cival Pesquero.

through the biomass in *civales* would have rendered an effective and manageable control of human effluents, reducing disease and contamination (Vogelmann et al. 2016; Wu et al. 2018). The *civales* would also have been effective in retaining humidity and attracting other natural resources such as animals (reptiles, amphibians, birds, fish, mollusks), water, and, particularly, organic muck. The organic muck or mud was probably the most important single resource of the *civales*, since the Maya transported it by the thousands of cubic meters from the wetlands to the numerous terraces built both within the civic centers of the cities and near major causeway systems where transport of food and plant products would have been facilitated (Hansen 2012a; Hansen et al. 2002; Hansen et al. 2018; Martínez et al. 1999). The extreme productivity of the muck, which was rich in organic nutrients, would have allowed an intensive and sustainable agriculture with corn (*Zea mays*), squash, cotton, gourds, and palms (Bozarth 2007; Bozarth and Hansen 2001; Hansen et al. 2002; Martínez et al. 1999; see below). The extensive terrace and muck systems became the economic engines that allowed the formation of administrative and economic hierarchies, indicative of an emergent social complexity in the basin (Hansen 2012a, 2016a). Similar adaptations to perennial marshes and swamp environments have been noted throughout other areas of tropical America (Hoopes 2012:246–249).

LiDAR imagery has shown extensive terrace systems that are ubiquitous throughout the Mirador Basin system, such as those near the Sacalero Causeway at El Mirador, near the community of Isla Gavilán on the Tintal-Mirador Causeway, the Palma Causeway at Nakbé, the Wakná terrace system, the Paixbancito terrace systems, and the terraces near the Mirador–Eastern Campeche causeway (Hansen et al. 2018). Such extensive agricultural systems in many ways replicate those that were identified by Arlen and Diane Chase in the area of Caracol through LiDAR images or the terrace system identified at Chan, Belize (A. Chase et al. 2011; A. Chase and D. Chase 2016a, 2016b; A.S.Z. Chase and Weishampel 2016; Wyatt 2008a).

The carbon isotope signatures in various stratigraphic levels in excavations throughout the Mirador Basin have shown the presence of grasses and probably corn (C-4 plants) during the periods of Preclassic occupation (Hansen et al. 2000, 2002; Jacob 2000). However, after the Preclassic collapse around AD 150 the isotope signature indicates a dramatic change to C-3 plants consistent with contemporary forest species (Hansen 2012a; Hansen et al. 2002; Jacob 1994, 1995). This change indicates an abrupt cessation of economic and demographic activity in the area, further exemplified by the presence of numerous Late Preclassic vessels found on the stucco floors of plazas, platforms, patios, and structures across entire sites (see below).

The ancient cities of this area had major architectural development—which implies a vast knowledge and management of natural resources—before many of the other lowland cities existed. The beginning of the sociopolitical development of the area in such early periods is due to several crucial factors, including the use of the natural environment of the marshes (wetlands) that fostered economic and administrative stability founded on a high agricultural productivity. Political, economic, and social powers were expressed in the large-scale architectural development and in the planned urban design throughout the Mirador-Calakmul system area.

In addition, developed centers were interconnected by a complex web of causeways (*sacbeob*) that made the transporting of edible goods, commodities and merchandise, raw materials, military enforcement, and administrative officials easier and quicker, creating a homogeneous society of unprecedented size and authority in the Maya lowlands. These causeways range from 30 to 50 m wide and from 2 to 6 m high on intersite connections throughout the Mirador Basin. At the ancient city of El Mirador, eight intersite causeways were detected (Figure 18.4); these connect not only to the suburban areas but also to other distant sites located in the northern Petén and southern Campeche regions (Morales-Aguilar et al. 2017).

In accordance with the dendritic models proposed by Santley and Vance, the primary site was connected politically, socially, and economically with peripheral monumental sites, which were in turn connected with smaller satellite sites. In the case of the Mirador Basin, however, this model is visible in the elaborate causeway system that formed the foundations of social, economic, and political unification of the major sites, both to the primary site and to the peripheral satellite sites (Figure 18.4). Major centers in the Mirador Basin such as El Mirador, Xulnal, Nakbé, Tintal, La Ceibita, El Pesquero, and Wakná had primary causeway systems that represented key communication systems between and among the sites, suggesting political and economic unions. Secondary causeways linked suburbs and sites to the peripheral satellite sites. A major causeway extended from the Candelaria River area to El Mirador and then continued on to other major centers to the northeast and southwest of El Mirador. Major causeways linked the primary centers to El Mirador, such as El Mirador–Tintal, El Mirador–Nakbé, El Mirador–Candelaria, and El Mirador–Eastern Campeche. Smaller causeways radiated out from the primary sites to smaller satellite centers and settlements such as Tintal–La Ceibita and Nakbé–Nakbé North, indicating an actual physical paradigm that is dendritic in nature and replicates the system identified over a thousand years later in the Aztec area, as indicated by Santley (1986). This sociopolitical complexity formed what seems to be one of the earliest political states of the Western Hemisphere (Hansen 1982, 2001, 2005, 2012b, 2016a, 2016b; Hansen et al. 2018; Hansen and Guenter 2005; Matheny 1987; see also Carneiro 1970, 1981 for definitions).

Cultural Characteristics and Features

As previously indicated, the first Maya settlements in the Mirador–Calakmul Basin system occurred by about 2600 BC, but this evidence is only visible in lake cores from three separate locations and excavations below the earliest platforms at Nakbé. The most visible sedentary occupation began by about 1000 to 800 BC, with an early development at sites such as Nakbé, El Mirador, La

Isla, Xulnal, Wakná, and El Pesquero. The greatest concentration of data for the area and material for the early Middle Preclassic Period comes from the site of Nakbé, but increased exploration and excavations are identifying additional early centers in the basin, including recent new discoveries of architecture and platforms dating to the Middle Preclassic at El Mirador, Xulnal, and El Pesquero (Hansen 2016a:347–362).

The economic manifestations of this period are expressed in the importation of exotic goods from the beginning of the Middle Preclassic Period (ca. 1000 to 600 BC). Imported items such as shell (*Strombus* shells from the Caribbean, tusk shells from the Pacific), obsidian from San Martín Jilotepeque and El Chayal sources in the highlands of Guatemala, jade from the Motagua River valley, basalt, granite, and exotic stones from the highlands of Guatemala, and coral from the Caribbean have been recovered in primary archaeological deposits. These materials reflect long-distance trade during that era that covered distances as great as 450 km (e.g., Hansen 2005, 2016b). Although the presence of *Strombus* shells has been discussed elsewhere (Hansen 2012b, 2016b), the shell repertoire of the Mirador Basin project has been analyzed by Feldman (2008). The economic importance of *Strombus* shells has been substantiated by the discovery of *Strombus* shell workshops elsewhere at Cahal Pech and Pacbitún, Belize, by Hohmann and colleagues (2018). In addition, another shell imported in the early Middle Preclassic Period is the small gastropod *Prunum apicinum* (Marginellidae), which has been found only in early ceremonial and ritual contexts. In spite of extensive excavations throughout the Mirador Basin, the use of *Strombus* shells, often with the original spines intact and frequently biconically drilled (Figure 18.6), appears only in the earliest contexts of the Mirador Basin, as do the Marginellidae. They do not appear to have been used as jewelry or decoration and have been recovered in areas of ritual/ceremonial use, but their presence is a clear indicator of the capacity of an elite hierarchy to import exotic goods as well as the establishment of merchant routes that would have allowed such interactions. Another shell that appears only in the Middle Preclassic Period in the Mirador Basin is the Pacific tusk shell, the Scaphopoda, typically a deep water shell that imbeds itself into sediments. It is likely that these shells could have been used as ornaments, due to the relative ease with which they could have been placed on strings as necklaces.

It is entirely possible that the use of some of these shells, such as *Strombus* and *Prunum apicinum*, served as some form of currency, similar to those from the Pacific south sea islanders, since they are totally absent from the subsequent

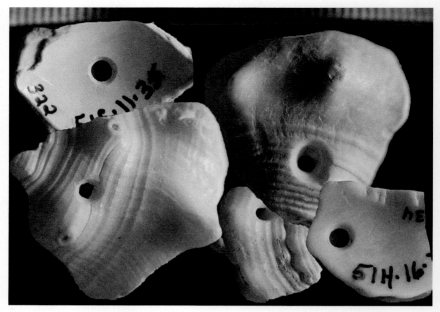

Figure 18.6. Perforated *Strombus* shells from Nakbé.

Middle Preclassic occupations and the extensive Late Preclassic deposits from the area (see also Freidel et al. 2016). Furthermore, *Spondylus* shells do not appear in the Mirador Basin until the Late Preclassic Period, and then without spines: as shaved shells with biconical apertures as expected for suspended ornaments or jewelry.

Other exotic items of economic importance include obsidian, imported into the Mirador Basin during the Middle Preclassic Period from San Martín Jilotepeque as indicated by X-ray diffraction analysis by Ray Kunselman (University of Wyoming). This obsidian was apparently transported into the sites of El Mirador and Nakbé in raw nugget form and was initially worked at the site, judging from the presence of obsidian cortex and core shatter there. This implies that the original importers of obsidian were also focused on the economic advantages of controlling not only the importation of the obsidian but the specialized process of working the stone into prismatic blades and tools. After about 300 BC the source of obsidian appears to have shifted from San Martín Jilotepeque to El Chayal (F. Nelson 1985; Nelson and Clark 1990, personal communication 2013). The obsidian assemblages of Late Preclassic sites in the Mirador Basin currently contain virtually no cortex, suggesting that the materials probably moved into the basin in prepared core form or perhaps as finished blades.

Jade was imported into the basin no later than 700 BC, as indicated by the presence of a jade offering on a sealed Middle Preclassic altar at Nakbé (Altar 4). Granite mortars and metates were also imported in the Middle and Late Preclassic Periods, indicating not only the wealth that permitted the import of such exotics but the sophistication of the transport systems that brought these bulky materials into the Mirador Basin from vast distances, including the Maya Mountains and the highlands of Guatemala. Quartz crystals have also been recovered from Late Preclassic contexts in the Mirador Basin, suggesting the ritual and ceremonial importance of such stones, particularly in association with water, reservoirs, and water collection mechanisms.

More localized materials were also incorporated into the economic systems, such as chert and alabaster. These resources were probably critical in the development of sites such as La Florida (in the southwest area of the basin), which had an arroyo surrounding the site with abundant nodules of chert littered across the floor of the arroyo. Excavations by the Mirador Basin Project in the site of La Florida, in the southwestern section of the basin, have identified dense deposits of chert debitage in numerous areas of the site (up to 1 m thick), suggesting that chert tool production may have been an important contribution to the socioeconomic development of the Mirador polities. By the Late Preclassic Period banded chert from Colhá was clearly imported into the basin, indicating another viable economic link with the eastern periphery of the Maya area.

The use of lime as an architectural agent reached its maximum utilization during the Middle and particularly the Late Preclassic Period. Experimental research by Tom Schreiner and members of the Mirador Basin Project has demonstrated the manufacturing techniques, the quantities of stone and wood, and the impact that lime production had in local economies (Schreiner 2000a, 2000b, 2001, 2002ba, 2003, 2004). The burning of limestone required vast amounts of wood, so it is likely that the lime kilns were located near the sources of wood, which would have been increasingly scarce near the major urban centers of the Mirador Basin. This strategy would have altered the economic structure of the transport required to move vast amounts of lime along the causeways to the civic centers where the larger amounts of construction were occurring (Drennan 1984; Schreiner 2001, 2002a).

During the Middle Preclassic Period from 800 to 400 BC, pyramids of up to 26 m in height as well as great platforms, residences, and stone monuments were built at Nakbé, Xulnal, El Mirador, Wakná, El Pesquero, possibly at La Ceibita, and reportedly at Yaxnohcah (Campeche). Monumental architecture is indicative of the existence of a sophisticated society, comparable to at least a complex chiefdom. Toward the end of the Middle Preclassic Period (600–400 BC), however, the first intrasite and intersite causeways were built to connect the different settlements, suggesting a centralized power marked by a higher level of political, social, and economic organization (Hansen 1994b, 1998, 2000, 2001, 2005, 2012b, 2016a, 2016b, 2017; Hansen et al. 2018; Hernández et al. 2016). It is likely that a state level of organization was developed by this time (Hansen 2001, 2005, 2012a, 2016b). The causeways are known to have connected El Mirador, La Isla, Nakbé, La Muerta, Isla Gavilán, Arroyón, Tintal, La Ceibita, and possibly the Wakná and Xulnal sites with the other major centers (Hernández et al. 2016). A major causeway that appears to date earlier than the Classic Period, judging from the extensive erosion in the middle of the Laberinto Bajo, is also visible by satellite extending to the southwest from Calakmul, suggesting a possible link to the sites farther south such as Yaxnohcah (Campeche) or the Mirador area, although the evidence for a dense Preclassic occupation at Calakmul is limited or absent.

By about 350 BC (7.0.0.0.0 in the Maya Long Count system), the beginning of the Late Preclassic Period, the principal focus of power appears to have been transferred from early sites such as Nakbé and Wakná to massive sites such as El Mirador and Tintal. These sites developed at an exceptional growth rate, with pyramids that reached monumental dimensions. During this period (ca. 350 BC to AD 150), there seems to have been an unprecedented emphasis on monumental architecture (Hansen 1990, 1998, 2001, 2005, 2012a, 2016b; Hansen et al. 2008). In El Mirador, Nakbé, Tintal, Wakná, La Ceibita, Xulnal, and several unidentified sites at the eastern edge of the basin, great pyramidal structures were built reaching heights of 30 to 72 m (98 to 236 ft.). This characteristic extends to sites such as Calakmul, Yaxnohcah, and Balakbal (in Mexico) located in the far north of the same geographical system. Platforms consisting of millions of cubic meters of construction fill were built or modified in these ancient cities, indicating a significant and unparalleled control of economic resources and labor on the part of the administrative elite.

The Late Preclassic Period was also characterized by a remarkable uniformity in ceramics, the ubiquitous Chicanel Ceramic Sphere, produced throughout the entirety of the Maya lowlands, with finishes and forms, often with waxy red, black, or cream slips or combinations of them, that even extended to vessels for domestic use (bowls and cooking pots) and incense burners. Vessels with

Preclassic forms, such as everted rims or medial flanges, were also carved from jade and alabaster. As Forsyth (2003, 2005) has repeatedly emphasized, no other period of Maya occupation had such great ceramic uniformity over such a wide area. This suggests a uniform cultural conformity throughout the Maya area that reflects an economic and political standardization that seems to have prevailed in the Maya lowlands during that era. The Chicanel Ceramic Sphere of the Late Preclassic Period (300 BC to AD 150) represents the greatest diffusion and/or assimilation of similar types, forms, tempers, pastes, and surface slips in Maya history (Figure 18.7). No period of Maya occupation had such unprecedented uniformity, suggesting that economic and utilitarian conventions were adopted throughout the Maya lowlands, probably as the result of a state impetus. Neu-

Figure 18.7. Examples of Late Preclassic ceramics.

tron Activation analyses of 572 ceramic samples from throughout the basin by Ron Bishop and Erin Sears suggest that the Middle Preclassic ceramics appear to have been locally manufactured or restricted to individual sites. By the Late Preclassic Period, ample evidence shows abundant exchanges throughout the sites of Tintal, La Florida, Nakbé, and El Mirador (Bishop 2004a, 2004b). Exotic ceramics, particularly those depicting a fine true resist decoration and fine ash-tempered paste were imported into the basin, most likely from the highlands of Guatemala and El Salvador.

Preclassic architecture consisted of specific ritual forms with patterns that came to be universal in the lowlands. Preclassic Maya settlements and buildings were organized according to specific alignments as well as strategic triangulations and orientations (see Hansen 1998, 2000; Šprajc et al. 2009). Political and ideological powers were also expressed in the architectural art that decorated all major building façades. Stelae, altars, and stone and stucco panels were erected as ideological and historic symbols (Argyle and Hansen 2016; Hansen 1990, 1992a, 1998, 2000, 2001, 2012b, 2016a, 2016b; Hansen et al. 2008; Hansen and Guenter 2005). Centers had great populations, resulting in dense urban residential areas. This population contributed to the construction of platforms, causeways, temples, palaces, reservoirs, walls, agricultural terraces, and hydraulic systems, which represent the investment of millions of man-days of labor (Hansen 2012a, 2016b; Hansen et al. 2018).

Another factor that stimulated and fostered the cultural sophistication of the early Maya was the emphasis on a uniform, consistent religious ideology. Monumental architectural art in the form of deity portraits decorated the façades of building, flanking stairways, and lined the primary staircases of buildings. Both low-relief and high-relief art appeared toward the end of the Middle Preclassic Period (ca. 600–400 BC), in which architectural sculpture emerged as an expression of authority and power through large masks and associated panels that represented deities and supernatural profiles that were part of a complex cosmology that flourished in the iconographic elements of the Middle and Late Preclassic periods (ca. 600 BC to AD 150).

Another powerful innovation that began during the Late Preclassic Period, ca. 300–200 BC, was the introduction of triadic-style architecture, which consisted of large pyramidal platforms with three distinct structures on the summit. These tripartite constructions, formed by a dominant central structure flanked by two smaller buildings facing each other, constitute the most frequent architectural form during that period (Hansen 1998, 2000, 2001, 2012b, 2016a; Hansen and

Balcárcel 2008; Morales-Aguilar et al. 2008; Velásquez-Fergusson 2013). At least 35 triadic structures have been identified at El Mirador, which suggests that the Mirador Basin could be the likely source of this architectural pattern that subsequently spread to other parts of the Maya area. The construction of such massive buildings with a uniform architectural layout is indicative of high levels of ideological homogeneity in the society; this standardized format is expressed in the largest and most ritually significant structures at the sites of the Mirador-Calakmul Basin. This particular architecture and associated architectural art may have served as an effective manipulative mechanism of organic solidarity of the society by an administrative political and ideological hierarchy by creating a standardized religious and political ideology that apparently was widely accepted and encouraged, judging by the depth and breadth of its expression (see Drennan 1976).

By the Late Preclassic Period (ca. 350 BC to AD 150) the Preclassic occupations throughout the Mirador Basin and elsewhere in the Maya area had reached their maximum demographic densities. The increased use of stone-lined agricultural terraces and transfer of rich organic mucks from the marshes to urban terraced gardens continued to provide the economic impetus for the formation and consolidation of a highly stratified society. Large-scale earthen dams were also built to control land erosion and create water containment systems. According to phytolith (microscopic silicate remains of the cellular structures of plants) studies conducted by Steven Bozarth (University of Kansas), corn, squash, cotton, gourds, palms, and a variety of fruit trees were grown in the gardens that were placed throughout the civic centers (Bozarth 2007). The agricultural wealth of the garden-terrace systems provided crucial economic resources for the increase in labor, importation of exotic products, construction of complex hydraulic systems, establishment of a military force, and the great architectural construction programs with plazas, dams, causeways, walls, moats, platforms, and temple-pyramids. The resultant organic solidarity generated by the political, economic, and ideological foundations further consolidated the prestige and economic power of rulers, as suggested by the royal Late Preclassic tombs in Tikal, Wakná, and San Bartolo (W. Coe and McGinn 1963; Hansen 1992a, 1998; Roach 2005; William Saturno, personal communication 2009).

In the Late Preclassic Period, sculpture in the form of stelae began to appear in much smaller formats compared to both previous and later periods (Figure 18.8). This interesting paradox seems contrary to the normal pattern in which rulers placed large and impressive stelae and altars to commemorate important calendrical or dynastic historical information. Monuments believed

El Chiquero Stela 1
Drawn: E. Ortega, R. Hansen

Figure 18.8. Illustration of Stela 1 from El Chiquero.

to have been erected in the late Middle Preclassic and early Late Preclassic Periods ranged from 4 to 5 m in height. Toward the latter part of the Late Preclassic Period (ca. 100 BC to AD 150), small monuments (1 m high or less) began to be placed in the sites with fine incisions and hieroglyphic texts in small panels (Hansen 1991, 1992a, 2001). It would appear that an important focus shifted toward the portraiture of rulers and the historical documentation of their activity on stone, ceramics, and stucco through texts.

A profound demographic demise is evident at most of the investigated sites in the Mirador area toward the end of the Late Preclassic Period, ca. AD 150. Residential structures of varying sizes and locational distributions as well as ritual and public buildings were abandoned, leaving behind ceramics and lithics directly on the stucco or packed-earth floors. The collapse of El Mirador, Nakbé, Tintal, Wakná, Xulnal, El Pesquero, Tamazul, and other sites at the end of this period (ca. 150 AD) coincides with what took place at other important centers, such as Uaxactún, Ceibal, Cerros, Colhá, Becán, and the central area of Yucatán, Dzibilchaltún, Komchén, the north coast of Yucatán, Isla Cancún, Edzná, Santa Rosa Xtampak, and many others (Hansen 1990:216–221). This suggests that a more global threat may have faced these societies, such as adverse climate change. But it was the massive deforestation and sedimentation of the rich *bajo* mucks *combined* with a possible drought condition that rendered the coup de grâce for the major societies in the central Maya lowlands. Yet other sites such as Naachtún seem to have experienced growth at this time, and it is possible that migrants or refugees from elsewhere in the Mirador Basin may have settled in the northeastern part of the basin and/or the coastal regions of the Caribbean (Morales-Aguilar and Hiquet 2013). Curiously, where the Preclassic presence was minimal or absent, as at Naachtún, Tikal, Uxul, and Dzibanché, the populations seem to have survived the stresses more adequately, often flourishing in the Early Classic while the larger Late Preclassic sites did not. This suggests that an anthropogenic impact may have rendered the Preclassic sites less habitable in later periods.

The multicausal factors of resource overexploitation and environmental stresses may have led to conflict issues as well as possible disease and malnutrition (investigations pending) as well as other potential stresses that may have simultaneously converged to disintegrate or degrade the centralized state system. The collapse of a superpower allowed political and economic rivals such as Tikal—possibly with Teotihuacán's help—to emerge and grow to dominance during the Early Classic Period. It is interesting that certain sites that later developed into powerful centers in the Classic Period were located within the fertile inland river valleys or close to lakes, lacustrine systems, or the coast (for example, Palenque, Lamanai, Copán, Quiriguá, Yaxhá, Piedras Negras, Yaxchilán, Dos Pilas, Tamarindito, Altun Ha, and Cobá). These sites did not have significant population levels in the Preclassic. This suggests that the proposed models for the rise of cultural complexity due to demographic pressures, social and military conflict, or prowess, trade routes, and competition for scarce resources were not the primal causal factors, because there was plenty of space for expansion toward those areas with abundant resources during the Preclassic Period (see Hansen 1984).

Conclusions

While the geographic and economic similarities between the dendritic formations of Tenochtitlán and the sites of the Mirador Basin are striking, the stark reminders of the social and political formations of Maya polities in the Yucatán Peninsula during the sixteenth century serve as a caution. Okoshi Harada and

Quezada (2008:141) propose the formation of administrative space at the time of the conquest, on the basis that lineages were a dominant factor in polity administration and that polities were "en realidad entidades sustentadas más en relaciones políticas, rituales, ceremoniales, y de parentesco que territoriales, y no necesariamente ocupaban un espacio continuo" (in reality entities sustained more by political relationships, rituals, ceremonies, and social ties than by terri-

Figure 18.9. Row of monuments, *calzada*, El Mirador.

tory, and didn't necessarily extend over continuous space). The ethnohistorical data indicate that during the sixteenth century, "los 'límites' para los Mayas de Yucatán no eran líneas físicas, sino el 'alcance de la jurisdicción'" (that is, boundaries weren't fixed in physical space but were jurisdictional concepts) according to Okoshi and Quezada (2008:142). Often, these "líneas divisorias" (boundaries) were trails or roadways, on which stones were placed (*p'iktunilob*) as markers (Okoshi and Quezada 2008:143). It is likely that similar markers, commonly found along the Preclassic causeways of the northern Petén (Figure 18.9), were clear economic and political billboards useful in commerce and other economic interactions of the area.

In the case of the Mirador Basin, the dendritic formation of the polities, as evident by the web of causeways that linked major centers, followed by shorter and lesser causeways to peripheral and adjacent sites, is consistent with what is known from later Aztec social, political, and economic structure. The similarities of Aztec economic and sociopolitical structures within the Middle and Late Preclassic in the Mirador Basin are a fascinating indicator of the continuity and influence of cumulative knowledge and economic perspectives. The use of technologies such as LiDAR will allow the geophysical manifestations of economic structure to become more evident. Such insights will provide new opportunities and challenges for scholars interested in the sociopolitical and economic formation of Maya polities. Expanded use of technology, including portable XRF (X-ray fluorescence) systems, LiDAR, and DNA will further contribute to defining and refining our knowledge of ancient economic structures.

Acknowledgments

Appreciation is extended to the University of Utah, the Foundation for Anthropological Research and Environmental Studies (FARES), FARES-Guatemala, the Association of Friends of the Naturaland Cultural Heritage of Guatemala (APANAC), the Mamel Foundation, Global Conservation and its director, Jeff Morgan, the Morgan Family Foundation, the Rosalinde and Arthur Gilbert Foundation, the Selz Foundation, the Pettit Foundation, the Jay I. Kislak Foundation, Linda Pierce, Spencer Kirk, and the U.S. Department of the Interior International Affairs Program.

19

Classic Maya Interaction Networks and the Production and Consumption of Cotton Fiber and Textiles

DORIE REENTS-BUDET AND RONALD L. BISHOP

Sixteenth-century accounts of tribute and taxation among the Yucatec Maya provide an impressive list of commodities in circulation at the time of Spanish contact while also affording a glimpse of the interlaced threads of socioeconomic relationships underlying these acts of material exchange (Tozzer 1941). These Colonial Period documents indicate that cotton fiber and finished cloth, both as bulk material and finished textiles, were among the most important commodities not only in the open market but also for tax and tribute obligations throughout Mesoamerica (see Las Casas 1875–1876; Motolinía 1971; Sahagún 1950–1982, 1989; Stark et al. 1998). The well-developed nature and importance of cloth to the economic exchange systems—in the Maya region and highland Mexico and extending into Central America—suggest a raw materials and finished goods interaction network of depth and longevity extending back at least into the Early Classic Period. The inventory of exchange materials found at Classic Maya sites substantiates this assessment, limited as it is to mostly nonperishable substances such as obsidian and marine shells. Yet most items listed in the sixteenth-century documents were perishable materials, with cloth being paramount in quantity and socioeconomic usefulness. Unfortunately, only minuscule fragments and meager indications of the presence of cloth and other woven materials have survived in the archaeological record (see Coggins and Shane 1984:147; Fash 1991:100–103; García-Moreno and Granados G. 2000; Mahler 1965:591–593; Plitnikas 2002). Therefore, all reconstructions of Classic Period Maya exchange systems are based on an incomplete picture of the economic landscape and unavoidably lack extensive consideration by scholars of the socioeconomic and political roles of such perishable materials as cotton fiber and textiles as well as their networks of production and distribution.

This chapter offers initial indications of three primary acquisition and exchange networks concerning cotton fiber and textiles among the Classic Period Maya. It compares the sixteenth-century cotton configurations in Yucatán with distributional patterns of decorated Classic Period ceramics found in southern Mexico, Guatemala, and Honduras. These modest patterns link cotton-producing regions with key archaeological sites. Their Classic Period sociopolitical positions suggest that they were important economic and political centers and thus likely prime distributors and consumers of cotton and textiles. Their pathways across the Maya realm hint at the importance of cotton to the political and economic foundations of Classic Period society. The data also support Patricia McAnany's description of Maya statecraft as the construction of networks of supply and alliance that created a political economy emphasizing exchange relationships (McAnany et al. 2002). Richard Blanton and colleagues (1996) assert that such a system frequently emphasizes prestige items—such as cotton cloth—because they offer a ready opportunity to reduce power competition locally while encouraging external competition and access.

A prestige-goods exchange system concentrates on commodities that are (1) difficult to acquire, (2) come from a long distance, (3) require labor-intensive expertise and special artistic or knowledge-based abilities, and (4) often embody qualities of intrinsic value based on ideology (Blanton et al. 1996; Clark 1997; Helms 1993; Monaghan 1990; Urban and Schortman 2012). The specific growing conditions and quantity of labor needed to produce cotton for cloth-making and the specialized skills required to produce cloth and high-quality textiles point to cotton cloth being as important to the Classic Period economic exchange system as it was for Colonial Period Yucatán (Hendon 2006; Karen Pope et al. 2001). Yet how can the exchange networks and roles of a nonsurviving commodity be discerned in the archaeological record?

This chapter examines the Classic Period pictorial ceramics to search for traces of networks of economic interaction with an eye to uncovering underlying mechanisms of producers and consumers. We use archaeological data and ceramic paste compositional analyses to proffer indications of ancient social, political, and economic networks as well as acquisition tactics by the Maya ruling elite. We propose that cotton cloth was a top-tier if not the most important commodity in the Classic Period political exchange economy. We further propose that competition for control over cotton-growing lands and ready access to cotton fiber and textiles (both plain and luxury) was a prime motivation driving network formation and polity interaction—both benign and belligerent.

Given the dearth of cotton and textile evidence in the archaeological record, we look to the ancient pictorial record to explore the importance of textiles during the Classic Period. The primary source is the polychrome pottery that often features narratives of political history, culture myths, and religious ideology (M. Coe 1973; Reents-Budet et al. 1994; Robicsek and Hales 1981). Many depict the exchange of goods taking place in elite architectural contexts (Figure 19.1), and cloth is the most prominently displayed item, whether as a diplomatic gift, ceremonial offering, or tribute or tax payment (Figure 19.2) (Houston and Stuart 2001; Reents-Budet 2007). We acknowledge that the pictorial pottery self-selects the elite strata as the social unit under study and thus privileges exchange pertaining to a prestige economy. Yet the colonial-era evidence describes a prestige economy in full flower during the early sixteenth century and specifies cloth as a seminal component thereof. These documents also chronicle the importance of cloth in the petty economy (e.g., Brumfiel and Earle, eds. 1987; Claussen and van de Velde 1991; Earle 1982; McAnany 1993a). We suggest that the same pattern characterized the Classic Period. The pictorial record constitutes a clear but pale reflection of the broader importance of cotton fiber and cloth to the economic system as an integrated horizontal and vertical structure crosscutting the social strata (Freidel 1981; McAnany 1989).

Dominating the Classic Period painted scenes is a finely arrayed male seated on a bench-throne and receiving a stack of items from subordinate visitors (Reents-Budet 2000). The limited inventory of commodities emblematizes the concept of "tribute/tax": the pile variously includes a *Spondylus* shell or greenstone body adornment (e.g., an earflare), a sheath of quetzal feathers, and bundles or baskets containing cacao or other unidentified items (Houston 1997; McAnany et al. 2002). Typically, all sit atop a stack of folded cloth. In many scenes only the folded fabric is rendered, or a finished textile is draped over a presenter's arm. Pottery made in the region bracketed by Río Azul (Guatemala) and Dzibanché (Quintana Roo) is notable for its frequent scenes of the presentation of piles of cloth taking place in elite architectural spaces (e.g., M. Coe 1973:cat.27, 33 [Kerr Photographic Archive K6059, Gardiner Museum of Ceramic Art G83.1.129]). The social context and accompanying hieroglyphic texts imply that these scenes variously represent a diplomatic gift, tax payment, or obligatory tribute recompense. These images suggest that the region may have been a notable cotton- and/or textile-producing

Figure 19.1. Diplomatic gift reception inside a palace-like structure. Note the stack of cloth and sheath of quetzal feathers behind the enthroned lord and the bundle of cacao beans in front of the bench throne. Photograph © 2020 Museum of Fine Arts, Boston. Gift of Landon T. Clay, 2004.2204.

Figure 19.2. The presentation of a war captive and tribute payment of decorated textiles. Photograph © 2020 Museum of Fine Arts, Boston. Gift of Landon T. Clay, 1988.1170.

area during the Classic Period (Piña Chan 1978; also see Masson 2002b for Postclassic production and exchange patterns in southern Quintana Roo).

Other scenes render elite feasting events during which cloth served as a principal gift item for the gathered guests (Figure 19.3; Acuña 1984; Berdan and Anawalt 1997; Brumfiel 1987, 1997; J. Pohl 1994; Sahagún 1950–1982). Classic

Figure 19.3. Detail of a gift offering or tribute payment of a stack of cloth and a basket holding greenstone and shell earflares. By permission of Justin Kerr, K1651. Photograph courtesy of Justin Kerr.

Maya feasts closely resemble those described in sixteenth-century indigenous and Spanish sources, whose goals included (1) social or political advancement through wealth acquisition—for both giver and receiver, (2) prestige building, and (3) alliance formation (Junker 2001; Monaghan 1990; M. Smith et al. 2003). The presentation of gifts, especially prestige items, was central to the event's success. The ample gifts bound together the feasting and production systems into a type of trickle-down economy embedded in a sociopolitical framework. In such a system gifting stimulated the economy through increased production, enhancement of exchange and social networks, and redistribution of wealth.

Comparable to the Classic Maya evidence, sixteenth-century highland Mexican documents describe cloth as an essential component of social and political interaction and a key economic indicator in gauging personal and state power (Berdan 1975). Cloth also served as a kind of currency in exchange for other commodities, service labor, and sociopolitical support. Its tribute importance is underscored by the gross numbers demanded by the Mexica state; for example, the *Matrícula de tríbutos* (1980) registers a tax payment of 51,600 mantles every eighty days from the Mexica subject polities, with the province of Tepequacuilco (Guerrero) alone owing 36,044 textiles a year. Most were of cotton fiber expertly woven and elaborately decorated. Thus, Mexica control over prime cotton-producing lands, such as those in Veracruz, Tabasco, and Guerrero, was crucial to securing the quantities of fiber and woven cloth needed to sustain the Aztec state and the Mexica economy.

The prominence of cloth as a tribute item was due to two sociopolitical factors. First was the use of cloth in the general market system, its exchange value holding firm throughout the Aztec Empire (Motolinía 1971:374; Sahagún 1950–1969, Bk. 9:46). Second, cloth was crucial to the politicized feasting system, a practice especially characteristic of the Mexica ruling elite but also present among lower-tier nobles and nonelites elsewhere in Mexico (cf. Brumfiel and Earle, eds. 1987; Hicks 1994; J. Pohl 1994). The multiple lines of evidence discussed above suggest that feasting held an equally dominant position in the Classic Maya economy and that cloth was the foremost prestige commodity bestowed on the attendant guests (Reents-Budet 2007).

Cloth embodies most of the characteristics of a luxury item as defined by Blanton and his colleagues (1996): (1) cotton is difficult to acquire due to the plant's agronomic requirements, (2) cotton growing and cloth production involve labor-intensive work and specialized skill and artistry, and (3) textiles display valued physical and social properties. First, successful cotton cultivation requires long-term control over environments with specific soil types and weather patterns (Berger 1969). Intensive and skilled labor is needed to tend the fastidious plant, harvest the fiber, process the raw material, spin the fibers into workable thread, and weave the final product. The best cotton-growing lands in Mesoamerica are found in the Veracruz and Tabasco coastal plains, along Guatemala's Pacific Coast, and in the lower Motagua River valley and adjacent coastal plain of northern Honduras. Although Yucatán's soils are not particularly well suited to the cotton plant, its wet-dry seasonal pattern matches the plant's distinctive agronomic cycle. Not surprisingly, then, the sixteenth-century tax tallies, such as the 13,480 mantles assessed annually against the town of Maní (Tozzer 1941:94), point to cotton being an important Yucatecan crop and textiles being vital to its political economy.

The agronomic, production, social, economic, and political characteristics of cotton and textiles as a key luxury good may shed light on the nature of Late Classic Maya economics and political history and reveal cotton/cloth exchange networks like those recorded for sixteenth-century Mexico. Furthermore, these networks may disclose elements of the strategies of Classic Maya elites to acquire and distribute this valuable commodity—either as raw fiber or finished material. Finally, the data may expose certain conditions of suppliers and producers with which to address the question of whether trade or tribute was the dominant mechanism of economic wealth and power acquisition among the Classic Maya. We look to the painted pottery to examine these topics.

The Maya Ceramics Project's combined studies of ceramic style and paste composition via instrumental neutron activation analysis (NAA: Bishop et al. 1982; Bishop and Blackman 2002) have detected three interaction networks based on the finding of pottery made in one area and traded to another (Figure 19.4). Each links a major population center with a cotton-producing zone, a pattern that we believe is not coincidental, which illuminates production and acquisition strategies relatable to Classic Period economic and sociopolitical configurations. The strongest ceramic exchange pattern links Guatemala's Pacific coast and the southern highland center of Kaminaljuyú, evidenced by highland ceramic types (e.g., Santa Rita Micaceous, Montel Alto Red, Fleshware) found at Escuintla and other centers along the coastal plain (H. Neff and Bové 1999; H. Neff et al. 1989; Robinson et al. 1998). Two-way interaction is denoted by Pacific coast–produced pottery excavated at a number of southern highland sites as well as Kaminaljuyú, where coastal vessels were excavated from elite architectural contexts in the site core and the Miraflores administrative compound (Arroyo et al. 2002; Reents-Budet et al. 2019).

Teotihuacán played an important Early Classic role in this interaction zone, as demonstrated by Puebla-produced Thin Orange pottery, green obsidian, and other Teotihuacán luxury goods discovered at Kaminaljuyú and the same Pacific coast sites where Kaminaljuyú-produced ceramics have been found (Bové 1990; G. Braswell 2003a). In particular, excavation data reported by Bové and Medrano (2003) at the Early Classic Pacific coast centers of Balberta and Montana indicate an allied interaction initially based on trade with Teotihuacán and later outright colonization by the central Mexican behemoth. At this time during the later decades of the Early Classic Period, a drop in Kaminaljuyú-produced pottery is noted in the Pacific coast ceramic assemblages, signaling a temporary shift in relations between the coastal and adjacent highland centers when Teotihuacán influence was most prevalent.

Evidence at Kaminaljuyú also indicates some level of Early Classic relations with Tikal, which prompted the suggestion that Kaminaljuyú was a corridor for Teotihuacán influence from the Pacific coast into the Petén lowlands (Bové 1990; Sanders and Michels 1977). The epigraphic record clearly records the AD 378 arrival at Tikal of Teotihuacán agent Siyaj K'ahk' and the forced replacement of Tikal's long-standing ruling dynasty (Stuart 2000). However, the hieroglyphic texts indicate a route not through Kaminaluyú but rather via El Perú–

Figure 19.4. A seated nobleman presents an offering of a large bundle, a stack of decorated cloth, *Spondylus* shell, and a sheath of long feathers. By permission of Justin Kerr, K4339. Photograph courtesy of Justin Kerr.

Waka' in the northwestern Petén, far from the southern highlands–Pacific coast zone (Guenter 2014a:151). This northern Petén route is of particular importance in light of Teotihuacán's vigorous trade and sociopolitical relations with Veracruz (Gómez Chávez 2017:106–107; Rattray 2004). The combined data intimate a route from Teotihuacán to southern Veracruz's and Tabasco's cotton-growing regions and likely continuing up the Usumacinta River. It is worth noting that a similar linkage between the Valley of Mexico and the cotton-growing regions of the Gulf Coast plains was well established during Aztec hegemony nearly

1,000 years later. It is possible that this Late Postclassic network was simply the continuation of a long-standing economic system focused on cotton and cloth.

The demise of Teotihuacán in the seventh century led not only to a reestablishment of Tikal-centric rule at the site but also the reemergence of person-centric rulership at Pacific coast sites, which is affirmed by monumental architecture and sculpture at such centers as Bilbao and El Baúl (Chinchilla 1996). At this time, too, the ceramic record reveals a resurgence of relations among the Pacific coast, the southern Maya highlands, and the Motagua River valley (Valdés and Wright 2004:351–355). This tripartite network links three regions along established economic interaction corridors that control cotton, cacao, obsidian, and jade and greenstone—four primary commodities of prestige value.

The second network indicated by Classic Period ceramic exchange patterns connects Tikal and Copán. As primary centers overseeing production and interaction networks in their respective regions, their relationship linked the central Petén to the Motagua River valley and adjacent coastal Honduran plain, both being cotton-growing regions that increasingly came under the control of Copán during the Early Classic Period (Sharer 2004:299–311). Fragmentation of the political landscape in the Comayagua and Sula valleys to the east at that time may have accelerated Copán's fortunes and the growth of the Tikal-Copán relationship (Schortman and Urban 2004). Ceramic evidence signals direct ties between Copán and the Tikal area as well as highland Guatemala, the latter being a reflex of the highland-lowland trade in obsidian and jade (Reents-Budet et al. 2004). Teotihuacán played a small but fleeting role at Copán, buttressing its Tikal and seemingly also southern highlands–Kaminaljuyú links.

Sites in Belize likely were ancillary players in this network, as implied by the epigraphic records from Pusilhá and Nim Li Punit in southern Belize (G. Braswell et al. 2008; S. Martin and Grube 2008:201). Connections to northern Belize are indicated by the relatively large quantities of Motagua jade found at Altun Ha (Pendergast 1982, 1990) and Altun Ha–produced pottery excavated from elite contexts at Copán (e.g., Longyear 1952:64, Figure 108; Reents-Budet et al. 1994:201). Only inconclusive evidence of Teotihuacán is present at Altun Ha itself, limited to one stemmed green obsidian biface blade from a postabandonment offering in a Late to Terminal Classic structure (Pendergast 1990:13) and a postinterment offering atop Tomb F-8/1, located in a peripheral Early Classic temple dated to ca. AD 250 (Pendergast 1982:260–262). The cache, which contained 248 Pachuca green obsidian objects and 23 Teotihuacán-related pottery vessels, is the core evidence of Teotihuacán's presence at Altun Ha. Yet Pendergast (2003:247) interprets the find as suggesting no more than a fleeting moment of interaction at best. Alternatively, given the quantities of Motaguá jade at Altun Ha, perhaps the Altun Ha cache denotes interaction with Copán in its role as the primary Early Classic broker—if not controller—of the Motagua jade trade, which reached Teotihuacán. This model casts Altun Ha as the Belizean nexus in a long-distance network supervised by Copán, which funneled Motagua jade into the northern Petén lowlands and points northwest. It views the Teotihuacán artifacts at Altun Ha as having come through Copán as part of this jade-centered configuration. Regardless of the correct interpretation of the Altun Ha cache, sites in Belize likely were contributing players in the Tikal-Copán network connecting prime cotton-producing areas in southern Mesoamerica (Figure 19.5).

The third principal cotton network implied by the ceramic evidence is located in the southern Campeche to northwestern Petén corridor and extends northwest into the Tabasco coastal plain via the Usumacinta River. The wealth

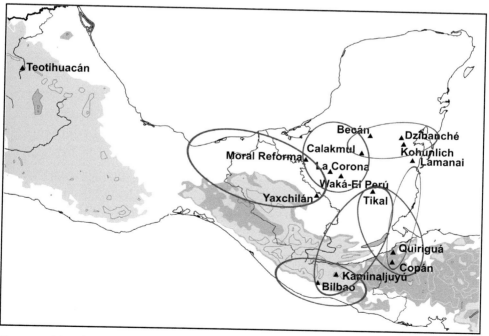

Figure 19.5. Map of southern Mesoamerica showing the three Late Classic Period interaction networks distinguished by patterns of ceramic exchange and linked to major cotton-producing regions. They commingle into two large systems overlapping the Calakmul and Tikal polities.

of Preclassic El Mirador and the subsequent rise of Calakmul as a leading Classic Period power implies long-standing control over commodity acquisition networks, including those supplying cotton and textiles. Our ceramic evidence shows an increasingly strong Middle to Late Classic relationship between Calakmul and sites in the Mirador Basin and along the San Pedro Mártir River. For example, high-status pottery made at Calakmul was exported south to La Corona and sites along the river including El Perú–Waka', La Joyanca, La Florida, and Moral-Reforma near its confluence with the Usumacinta River. No pottery from the southern Petén region or the Pacific coast has been found among the sampled ceramics at Calakmul, the San Pedro River sites, or those in the Mirador Basin. Siyaj K'ahk's route into the central Petén via El Perú–Waka' is no surprise given that the San Pedro is the only navigable river in the region and thus provides ready passage between the cotton-producing Veracruz-Tabasco zone and the northern Petén lowlands (see Guenter 2014b:151-152). Granted, from Calakmul's viewpoint, the corridor encounters the Piedras Negras and Yaxchilán polities that often were at odds with Calakmul and each other. Yet the presence of Late Classic Calakmul-produced pottery at Yaxchilán implies some level of collaborative relations that may have countered the forces of Piedras Negras and permitted trade access via the Usumacinta River to the Tabasco lowlands and the Gulf Coast networks into central Mexico.

Surprisingly, we have no compositionally based ceramic evidence from Calakmul to indicate out-flowing connections to Yucatán and Quintana Roo. This runs counter to the numerous eastern Campeche and Quintana Roo ceramic types in the Calakmul corpus, including Petkanché Orange, Azcorra Ivory, Moro Cream, and Chimbote Cream polychromes (Boucher and Dzul 2006; Domínguez Carrasco 1994a, 1994b). The Chimbote ceramic group in particular is closely associated with Becán (Ball 1977). Similarly, our ceramic analyses have not identified imports to Calakmul from any of the eastern Quintana Roo sites in spite of Early Classic records at Resbalón and Dzibanché detailing robust dynastic relationships, including the origin of Calakmul's Late Classic ruling dynasty, among these centers (Grube 2004; S. Martin 2004). Furthermore, colonial documents list large amounts of cotton textiles as tax payments nearby in southern Yucatán, and the Dzibanché region has acceptable conditions for growing cotton. It would not be surprising if southern Quintana Roo was a subsidiary cotton and textile source for Calakmul, a topic requiring further research.

In summary, the Maya Ceramic Project's compositional data indicate three main zones of interaction that link major centers with prime cotton-producing regions—the greater Calakmul polity and Tabasco lowlands, Kaminaljuyú and the Pacific coast, and Tikal and northern Honduras/Copán (secondarily connected to Belizean and Caribbean coastal routes). When considered from a pan–southern Maya political perspective, these networks form two principal zones of economic interaction that coincide with the primary Late Classic political spheres—the Calakmul and Tikal polities—whose bellicose relations and political machinations are well documented by epigraphic and archaeological data (S. Martin and Grube 1995, 2008). Our ceramic investigations imply analogous control over chief cotton-producing regions and hypothesized cotton fiber/textile networks. Such exclusionary control would promote each polity's relatively consistent access to the cotton fiber and cloth so important to a politically based, prestige-goods exchange economy. The exclusive control networks also would reduce local competition for power while encouraging external competition and access (Blanton et al. 1996).

A final consideration in the economic role of cotton and textiles is the location of production. World patterns of cotton production point to the likelihood that during the Late Classic Period at least some of the labor-intensive processing of raw cotton took place near the cultivation area. Yet archaeological evidence, such as the widespread distribution of spindle whorls and weaving batons, implies that some of the skilled-labor fabrication was done at the consumer end. Both commoners and members of the elite likely contributed such labor, as noted in sixteenth-century Spanish writings and preserved in the Classic Period archaeological record (e.g., the remains of weaving activities in an elite residential structure at Aguateca, Guatemala: Inomata and Triadan 2014).

These factors favor a tribute-based economic system that theoretically would drain resources from the cotton-producing regions, as suggested by the generally fewer Classic Period manifestations of wealth on the Pacific coast and in the Tabasco lowlands than in the Petén lowlands. Yet these two regions are not devoid of prosperity, manifested as monumental art and architecture and imported luxury goods from a variety of locales both near and far. Therefore, similar to McAnany's study of cacao (McAnany et al. 2002), the Classic Period ceramic distributional patterns, identified via neutron activation analysis, and their implied cotton/textiles networks intimate an economic system combining both trade and tribute in a multidimensional structure that fluctuated in response to the political fortunes of the competing polities and supply zones during the Classic Period.

20

The Political Geography of Long-Distance Exchange in the Elevated Interior Region of the Yucatán Peninsula

BENIAMINO VOLTA, JOEL D. GUNN, LYNDA FLOREY FOLAN, WILLIAM J. FOLAN, AND GEOFFREY E. BRASWELL

The boundaries of ancient polities were not always marked by fortifications, natural geographic features, or unoccupied buffer zones. Fortunately, in the case of the Classic Maya, economic and political systems often were coterminous because commerce was only partially commodified (G. Braswell 2010). Put another way, rulers sought to manage the exchange of certain goods within their territory, and the frontier of their economic control often coincided with the limit of their political sovereignty. The study of trade routes and networks, therefore, can help us better understand political organization.

In this chapter we reconstruct in broad strokes the patterns of exchange in the Elevated Interior Region (EIR) of the Yucatán Peninsula using data on the distribution of obsidian, ceramics, and other long-distance trade goods. Our goal is to understand to what extent these patterns paralleled changes in the political geography of the region. We suggest possible trade routes into and across the EIR based on least-cost analysis and integrate them into our analysis of the regional political economy. Finally, we discuss how these data contribute to our understanding of unresolved issues in the political and economic organization of the region.

Physical Environment and Potential Routes

The EIR is a hilly karst upland that forms the spine of the Yucatán Peninsula, extending approximately 250 km from central Campeche, Mexico, into northern Petén, Guatemala (Figure 20.1). It has been defined by Dunning and colleagues (2002) as the entire portion of the Yucatán Peninsula with appreciable topographic relief north of the La Libertad Arch, stretching from the northwestern corner of the Ticul Escarpment in the north to the Petén Lakes District in the south, and from the Edzná Valley in the west to the Hondo River in the east. We employ their terminology for the sake of consistency but reduce its extent to the area that has been previously referred to as karst plateau, Karstic Mesoplano, or Central Karstic Uplands (Folan et al. 2011; Gunn et al. 2014; Reese-Taylor 2017).

Major ancient cities of the EIR include the massive Preclassic center of El Mirador and its subsidiaries as well as the Preclassic to Classic metropolis of Calakmul. The dominant structural feature of this limestone plateau is the eastward arching north-south anticlinal fold that acts as watershed divide for the central part of the peninsula (Gates 1999). The Candelaria River drains the southwestern

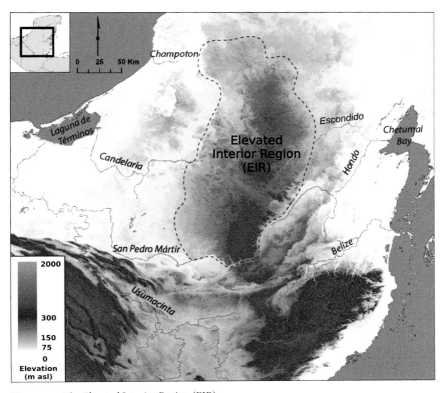

Figure 20.1. The Elevated Interior Region (EIR).

flank of the EIR toward Laguna de Términos and the Gulf of Mexico, whereas the Hondo and Escondido systems flow toward Chetumal Bay and the Caribbean to the east. The region is split in two—into the Petén karst plateau to the south and the southern Campeche karst plateau to the north—by the *bajo* El Laberinto, one of the largest of the many seasonally inundated karst solution depressions that characterize the region. Starting in the Middle Preclassic, most major settlements in the central Maya lowlands were established in upland areas at the edges of large *bajos* (R.E.W. Adams 1980; Bullard 1960:364). Reasons may have included access to water and other wetland resources, abundant chert and clay, agricultural use, and, under certain conditions, strategic advantages for transportation (Dunning et al. 2002:268; Gunn et al. 2014:107; Hansen et al. 2002).

In the absence of the physical remains of ancient roads and paths, least-cost path calculations attempt to quantify environmental conditions (e.g., ruggedness of topography) and other variables that would have influenced the choice of paths across the landscape (D. White and Surface-Evans 2012). This analysis results in the most cost-efficient routes between given origin and destination points based on these variables. Clearly, this may or may not correspond to the route a human actor would have taken. Least-cost path calculations are necessarily based on assumptions about past environmental conditions and cannot take into account the historical and cultural dimensions of routes (Conolly and Lake 2006; Herzog 2014). Nonetheless, they provide likely options that can be evaluated against archaeological evidence.

Using data on the topography and hydrography of the EIR, our least-cost path analysis suggests that there are three main east-west routes across the EIR (Figure 20.2; Volta and Gunn 2012). All three routes combine sections of river travel from the coasts with overland segments. These could have been used throughout the history of human occupation in the region, although the specific hydrological conditions of inland *bajos* at different points in time may have affected the relative efficiency of each path (Hansen and colleagues, Chapter 18). An additional suggested north-south route skirts the western edge of the plateau, approximating the path of the Camino Real used during the Spanish conquest of Petén in the late seventeenth century (Arias 2012). A slightly less cost-efficient path has been proposed for this area and may have been used instead: the "royal road" connecting the Pasión region and the western part of the EIR (Figure 20.3; Canuto and Barrientos 2013b; Demarest et al. 2014:Figure 5; Freidel et al. 2007:187). An additional consideration is that the construction of regional causeway systems across *bajos*, many of which date to the Preclas-

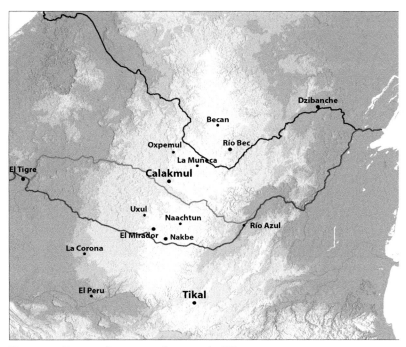

Figure 20.2. East-west least-cost paths across the EIR.

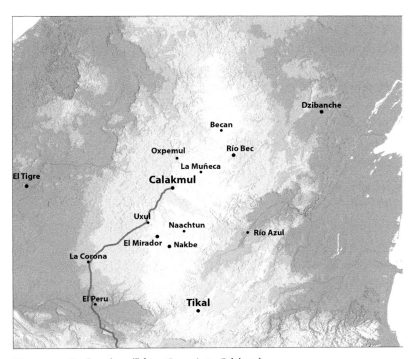

Figure 20.3. The "royal road" from Cancuén to Calakmul.

sic Period, would have lowered transportation costs and provided more direct routes between sites in the EIR (Bolles and Folan 2001; Folan et al. 1995; Hansen et al. 2002; Hansen et al., Chapter 18; Rivas 2014).

Political History

The EIR was home to some of the earliest hierarchical societies of the Maya lowlands. Starting in the latter half of the Middle Preclassic, around 600 BC, massive civic-ceremonial centers were constructed at sites like Nakbé, Wakná, and Xulnal in the southern part of the region (Hansen 2012b; Hansen et al. 2002). Hansen (2012b) and colleagues have argued that centralized rulership emerged during this period, followed by the establishment of the first lowland Maya kingdom at El Mirador at the beginning of the Late Preclassic (ca. 400 BC to AD 150). We now know that major sites farther north like Calakmul, El Zacatal, Uitzilná, Mucaancah, and Yaxnohcah also present important Middle and Late Preclassic occupations (Folan et al. 1995; Reese-Taylor 2017; Šprajc 2008, 2012).

With the abandonment of El Mirador and other centers in the Terminal Preclassic, the center of power shifted southeast and off the EIR to Tikal in the Early Classic (ca. AD 250–600). A little-understood "Bat Head" (Suutz') polity centered at Naachtún rose to power in the southern half of the EIR during this period (Grube 2005). The Suutz' rulers were involved in the event of AD 378 that epigraphers have described as a Teotihuacán *entrada* (Stuart 2000). The relationship between the Bat Head dynasty, the Early Classic rulers of Calakmul, and the Kaan (or "Snake Head") dynasty is unclear (S. Martin 2005; Nondédéo et al. 2015).

The political history of the late Early Classic and the first century of the Late Classic (ca. AD 537–695) was dominated by the conflict between the rulers of Tikal and the Kaan dynasty, which established itself at Calakmul. The degree of centralization of these rival polities has been debated since the early 1970s, with a "strong" camp describing them as hegemonic states and a "weak" camp seeing them as the central nodes of two loose networks of shifting political alliances (e.g., Marcus 1973; S. Martin and Grube 1995; Mathews 1991). The Kaan rulers of Calakmul were ascendant for 150 years but suffered a crushing reversal of fortune in AD 695 at the hands of Tikal. In the ensuing balkanization of the Terminal Classic (ca. AD 750–900), many centers in the EIR that had been affiliated with the Kaan polity were rapidly abandoned (e.g., Uxul) or erected monuments that reasserted their newfound independence (e.g., Naachtún, Oxpemul, La Muñeca).

Patterns of Exchange

The Preclassic

At about 1000 BC the earliest pottery-using villages of the Maya lowlands obtained obsidian from El Chayal, Guatemala. Between 900 and 700 BC El Chayal was supplemented by minor amounts of material from San Martín Jilotepeque and Ixtepeque (Aoyama 2017:Table 2; Ebert et al. 2015:Table 4). During the later Middle Preclassic, beginning around 700 BC, most obsidian consumed in the lowlands came from the San Martín Jilotepeque (SMJ) source in the Kaqchikel highlands (e.g., F. Nelson 1985:Table 8). El Chayal again gradually emerged as the dominant source during the Late Preclassic period at many lowland sites, including El Mirador (Fowler et al. 1989; F. Nelson and Howard 1986:Table 2), but SMJ maintained importance, accounting for about one-quarter of the obsidian consumed at many sites (see also Hansen et al., Chapter 18). Ceibal is a notable exception to this pattern of resurgence of the importance of El Chayal. There roughly 90% of the obsidian consumed in the Late Preclassic continued to come from SMJ (Aoyama 2017:Table 2; Nelson et al. 1978, see also Golitko and Feinman 2015:218–221). These distinct patterns may be associated with two separate trade routes from the Guatemalan highlands to the lowlands during the Late Preclassic Period: the overland route through Alta Verapaz to the Chixoy-Pasión-Usumacinta fluvial network and the riverine route linking the Motagua Valley to the Caribbean coast (Arnauld 1990).

In addition to obsidian from the Guatemalan highlands, Middle Preclassic contexts at Nakbé contain *Strombus gigas* (conch) shell from the Caribbean and jade from the Motagua region (Hansen 2012a:152; Hansen et al., Chapter 18). This indicates that long-distance trade connections between the EIR and both the highlands to the south and the eastern coast of the peninsula were already well established at an early date (Lohse 2010:326). During the Middle and Late Preclassic Periods, all sites in the EIR shared the extremely similar ceramics of the Mamom and Chicanel spheres, with very little imports except for Usulután wares indicating indirect contact with El Salvador at the end of the latter period (Culbert 2003; Demarest and Sharer 1982). Overall, there is little evidence for differences in procurement patterns of trade goods within the EIR during the Preclassic Period.

We do not yet know if some Preclassic lowland centers of the EIR had preferential access to obsidian or if it was evenly distributed based on population size and necessity. Put another way, we do not know if Preclassic exchange was dyadic or polyadic in nature or if it was somehow market-based (see Hirth 1998). If an early state did develop at El Mirador during the Late Preclassic Period, an administered market economy could have emerged at that time (Hansen et al., Chapter 18).

The favored routes from the Caribbean into the EIR in the Preclassic likely approximated the two southernmost least-cost paths (light and medium gray in Figure 20.2). The shared portion of these routes connects Chetumal Bay—where important trading ports such as Cerros and Nohmul were established—with the EIR via the Hondo River. The routes split near the site of Río Azul, which also has an important Late Preclassic occupation (R.E.W. Adams 1990:34). The southern branch continues southward along the Azul/Tikal waterway before veering west toward Nakbé and El Mirador, whereas the northern branch crosses the watershed divide in the vicinity of Yaxnohcah and follows the Tomatillal River in the *bajo* El Laberinto toward Calakmul (see Gunn et al. 2014:107). Shell from the Caribbean, as well as jade and obsidian traded down the Motagua, would have been carried along these routes.

After reaching the center of the EIR, both routes continue west toward the Caribe and Las Golondrinas, two tributaries of the Candelaria River, and the site of El Tigre/Itzamkanak, another large Preclassic center with ties to the EIR (Vargas 2010). Vargas and Ochoa (1982:101) have hinted at the importance of the Candelaria as a transport route from the Laguna de Términos into the EIR, but its connection to the *bajo* El Laberinto through its tributaries has generally been overlooked (Gunn and Folan 2000:Figure 9.1; but see Hansen et al., Chapter 18). Reese-Taylor and Walker (2002:90) have suggested that many Late Preclassic centers were established in strategic locations along riverine and overland portage routes. Considering evidence that at least some inland *bajos* were perennial lakes or wetlands until the end of the Late Preclassic (Dunning et al. 2002), it is tempting to link the founding of major centers like El Mirador, Yaxnohcah, and Calakmul with favorable locations along or between major waterways (e.g., Reese-Taylor et al. 2016:315). With the environmental changes that occurred at the end of the Late Preclassic, some of us have suggested that Calakmul resorted to hydrological engineering to maintain the strategic advantage of its location overlooking the *bajo* El Laberinto, whereas Yaxnohcah and El Mirador would have become cut off from major routes crossing the EIR (Gunn et al. 2002, 2014).

The Early Classic

Throughout the Early and Late Classic Periods, El Chayal obsidian was the dominant source at virtually all lowland Maya sites except those in the southeastern Maya periphery (e.g., Aoyama 1999; G. Braswell 2003b; G. Braswell and Glascock 1998, 2007; F. Nelson 1985). Despite this, uneven patterns of exchange began to appear in the archaeological record of the EIR in the Early Classic. Although El Chayal obsidian is prevalent throughout most of the lowlands in the Classic Period, some sites had more access to it than others. Among the sites in the EIR that relied largely on El Chayal obsidian are Calakmul and its neighbor Uxul (Andrieu 2009b; G. Braswell 2013; G. Braswell and Glascock 2011). Very little obsidian has been excavated at Calakmul, especially compared to Tikal (G. Braswell 2010; G. Braswell and Glascock 2011). Moreover, green obsidian from Pachuca, Mexico, has been found in large quantities in Early Classic Tikal but not at Calakmul. This suggests that Early Classic Calakmul did not have strong connections—either direct or indirect—with Teotihuacán. In contrast, it is particularly striking to note much more significant use of green obsidian at Uxul (G. Braswell 2013:Table 1) and Naachtún (Nondédéo et al. 2015:117) during this period. These two cities would later become secondary centers of Calakmul; in the Early Classic, however, they participated in a bounded elite interaction sphere that was focused around Tikal and likely based on polyadic exchange.

Starting around AD 350, a little-understood polity associated with an emblem glyph in the form of a bat head (Suutz') rose to power on the southern part of the EIR (Grube 2005; Marcus 2012). The Suutz' polity was based at Naachtún in the fourth and fifth centuries AD (Nondédéo et al. 2015). The relationship between the Suutz' dynasty and the Early Classic rulers of Calakmul is unclear, especially because only two monuments dating from before AD 600 have been recovered at the latter site (Martin 2005:Figure 2). As G. Braswell (2013:169) has noted, the distribution of green obsidian from the Central Mexican source of Pachuca in this period suggests that certain EIR sites had indirect ties with Teotihuacán, likely mediated by Tikal. Pachuca obsidian was in no way commodified in the Maya region during the Early Classic and would have been exchanged only along political alliance channels (G. Braswell 2013:169; Spence 1996). Thus, this Early Classic elite interaction sphere—which included Uxul and Naachtún but not Calakmul—would have coincided at least in part with the political network of the Suutz' polity. Centers taking part in the "Tikal connection" (Rathje 1977) such as Río Azul, El Perú–Waka', and Naachtún also shared cylinder tripod vessels associated with real or presumed interaction with Teotihuacán and more in general with participation in Early Classic elite exchange networks (Patiño 2016:51–54; L. Sullivan 2002:204–211; Varela and Braswell 2003:253). With the exception of one possible example—a Balanza Black vessel from a tomb in Structure II (Carrasco et al. 1999:52; Mumary 2016:112)—this ceramic form has not been found at Calakmul (Domínguez 1994a).

Data from the regional center of Uxul demonstrate the existence of multiple overlapping exchange spheres in this period. During the entire Classic Period, the ceramics of Uxul bear strong similarities to those of Calakmul. The materials making up the Tzakol Period Aak complex of Uxul closely mirror those of the Kaynikté complex of Calakmul, including both Petén-centric wares and groups and types originating in the Río Bec region such as Triunfo and Maxcanú (Domínguez 1994a; Dominguez and Folan 2015:16–17; Dzul 2013:446). It is reasonable to suppose that exchange with Calakmul played a significant role in the economy of Uxul throughout its history, and these ties clearly were well established by the Early Classic. Despite this, the relative abundance of green obsidian at Uxul also indicates participation in a Tikal-focused elite network (or at least a Naachtún-focused subnetwork) that excluded Calakmul during this period.

Calakmul did have access to large amounts of jade in the Early Classic, including the elaborate masks found in Tomb 1 of the Lundell Palace (Folan et al. 1995). Given the great quantities of jade found at Calakmul compared to Tikal, it is likely that the elites of the two cities participated in different jade procurement networks. Moreover, as Woodfill and Andrieu (2012:201–204) have pointed out, the presence of large amounts of Early Classic jade debitage at Tikal indicates that jade was imported to that city as raw material. This is unlike Calakmul, where jade appears in finished form. In fact, Tikal so far is a unique case as an importer of raw jade in the Early Classic Maya lowlands.

Two separate Early Classic exchange systems can thus be identified in the central region. Woodfill and Andrieu (2012) have discussed the domination by Tikal of the "Great Western Trade Route" descending from the highlands through the Chixoy-Pasión-Usumacinta network (see also Demarest et al. 2014). Freidel et al. (2007:196) argue that, thanks to their alliances with Yaxhá and Río Azul, the Early Classic rulers of Tikal also controlled the eastward trade routes on the Belize and Hondo river drainages (Figure 20.1). Nonetheless, it is necessary to clarify what such control really entailed. Did Tikal elites actively block obsidian trade to Calakmul, so notably poor in the material, or did the city just consume so much of it that very little made it into the EIR? Likewise,

B. Volta, J. D. Gunn, L. Florey Folan, W. J. Folan, and G. E. Braswell

was jade bound for Calakmul carried down the same corridors as jade destined for Tikal, or did it follow alternate routes?

If they were needed, alternate routes for obsidian and jade to reach Calakmul would have been from the Caribbean coast by means of the more northerly Escondido drainage, or from the Gulf Coast through the Candelaria River (Figure 20.2). The western route would have provided Calakmul with indirect access to goods traded down the Usumacinta corridor through El Tigre/Itzamkanak, which would have controlled trade on the upper Candelaria system as it did in the Conquest Period (Scholes and Roys 1968). The eastern route would have passed through Dzibanché—the city where the kings of the Kaan dynasty apparently resided before moving to Calakmul (Nalda 2004; Velásquez 2005)—and reached La Muñeca, located strategically at one of the shortest overland crossings between drainages on either side of the EIR. La Muñeca would become a secondary center of the Late Classic Kaan regional state, likely mediating interactions with the Río Bec region (Grube 2005; Marcus 1973). As previously noted, trade between Calakmul and this region was already important during the Early Classic and may already have been mediated by La Muñeca (Domínguez and Folan 2015:16–17).

The Late Classic

Political struggles for control of trade routes characterized the Late Classic, with distinct geopolitical conditions occurring before and after the collapse of the Kaan dynasty. Starting in the early seventh century AD, Kaan rulers either conquered or forged alliances with kingdoms throughout the lowlands (Martin and Grube 2008). Demarest and colleagues have argued that the political network built by the three Yuknoom kings effectively encircled the sphere of influence of Tikal, enabling Calakmul to access important trade routes to the southern highlands, the Caribbean, and the Gulf Coast (Demarest et al. 2014; Demarest and Fahsen 2003). Evidence from La Corona (Canuto and Barrientos 2013b) indicates that the overland trail on the western flank of the EIR was used in combination with the Pasión River route, especially in the second half of the seventh century when the Kaan lords had control of the trading centers of Cancuén—which they founded in AD 656—and Dos Pilas (Demarest et al. 2014).

Status goods such as jade and feathers seem to have been the principal materials that moved through this Kaan-controlled trade corridor. As iconographic evidence from Calakmul suggests, however, commodities such as salt were probably also traded (Carrasco et al. 2009). Andrieu and colleagues' (2014) reanalysis of jade from the trading port of Cancuén indicates that preforms were produced in workshops under elite control and then distributed to "consumer" sites such as Calakmul. As Kovacevich (2013a:270) has pointed out, down-the-line models for market exchange do not apply to the Pasión-Usumacinta route. Not all centers along this route had equal access to jade, suggesting that political alliances dictated, or at least influenced, access to the material. Kovacevich argues that trade in prestige goods such as jade took the form of emissary trade, with elite individuals or their representatives accompanying the goods.

Despite the position of Calakmul at the center of a vast political network, most of its economic sphere remained heavily focused on its immediate hinterland. The great city continued to receive very little obsidian during the Late Classic; as at most sites throughout the lowlands, these materials came predominantly from El Chayal and increasingly from Ixtepeque by the end of the Late Classic. Comprehensive data from other centers in the EIR is lacking, but it appears that sites located farther south, such as Uxul and Naachtún, enjoyed greater access to obsidian (G. Braswell 2013:163; Nondédéo et al. 2013:131). Large quantities of this material are also reported from Early and Late Classic contexts at La Corona (Andrieu and Roche 2015:341). Uxul and Naachtún both formed part of the territorial core of the Kaan polity during the seventh century, and La Corona was either a key ally or a trade entrepôt under direct control of Calakmul (Canuto and Barrientos 2013b; Grube et al. 2012; Marcus 1973). The relative abundance of obsidian at these sites compared to the political capital parallels the situation during the Early Classic. Nonetheless, whereas the restricted distribution of green obsidian can be tied to gift-giving among Early Classic elite networks, obsidian from El Chayal and Ixtepeque in the Late Classic was consumed by elite and commoner households alike (G. Braswell and Glascock 2011:128). Therefore, as in the Early Classic, its continued paucity at Calakmul suggests the existence of a bounded redistributive or administered distribution system centered around Tikal (G. Braswell 2010:135; but see Hutson, Chapter 4; Masson and Freidel 2012, 2013).

The ceramics of Calakmul and surrounding sites in the EIR indicate the existence of a tightly knit regional economy clearly focused on the Kaan capital. Diagnostic groups and types of the Late Classic Ku ceramic complex of Calakmul, such as Tinaja, Infierno, Cambio, and Encanto, are found in large quantities in the Baak complex of Uxul (Dzul 2013:448–450), the early facet of the Maax complex of Naachtún (Patiño 2015:21–27), at Oxpemul (Domínguez et al. 2011:55), and in the El Mirador region (Forsyth 2003). Materials originating in the Río

Bec and Chenes regions also are present at Uxul and sites located farther north, indicating the continuation of the exchange ties established in the Early Classic (Domínguez and Folan 2015:17).

In the eighth century the power vacuum left after the military defeat of Calakmul by Tikal created both challenges and opportunities for small, strategically located entrepôts such as La Corona and Cancuén (Canuto and Barrientos 2013b; Demarest et al. 2014). The gradual decline of the former and the explosive florescence of the latter demonstrate the uncertainty of outcomes accompanying increased elite involvement in long-distance trade toward the end of the Classic (McAnany 2013:243). Despite political turmoil, most sites throughout the Maya lowlands continued to receive obsidian from El Chayal and increasingly from Ixtepeque by the end of the Late Classic. As Golitko and colleagues (2012:513) have shown, the decay pattern for Ixtepeque obsidian in relation to distance from the Caribbean, which began during the Late Classic, became more clearly defined in the Terminal Classic. This pattern reveals the growing importance of coastal routes after the collapse of Kaan control and the subsequent political instability in the southern lowland region.

The Terminal Classic

As the rulers of newly independent kingdoms competed to display their status in the vacuum left by the dissolving Kaan polity, they sought access to highly valued goods from throughout the Maya world. At the same time, the exchange of more basic commodities such as obsidian became more diversified as the lowland economy was linked to broader Mesoamerican trade spheres (P. Rice 1987a).

Braswell and Glascock (2011:Figure 10.4) have assigned obsidian from the Terminal Classic occupation at Calakmul to Guatemalan (El Chayal, Ixtepeque, and San Martín Jilotepeque) and central Mexican (Pachuca, Ucareo, and Zaragoza) sources. El Chayal obsidian is found at Naachtún together with materials from the central Mexican sources of Otumba, Ucareo, and Zacualtipán. Other long-distance trade goods found at the site in this period include alabaster, pyrite, jade, serpentine, and schist from the Guatemalan highlands, pink granite from the Maya Mountains of Belize, and *Spondylus* from the Pacific coast (Nondédéo et al. 2012:221). If the economic sphere of Calakmul and its secondary centers gives the impression of having been closed in the Late Classic, it clearly was not bounded in any appreciable sense during the Terminal Classic.

Patterns of ceramic exchange also diversify in the Terminal Classic. Domínguez (1994b) and Boucher and Dzul (2006) have identified imports at Calakmul from the lower Usumacinta (Fine Grays and Fine Oranges) and the northern lowlands (Cehpech Slate wares) accounting for approximately 4% of the total (see also Rice, Chapter 25). Although the population of Uxul seems to have declined rapidly at the beginning of the Terminal Classic, similar types of imports have been identified (Dzul 2013:450–451). The ceramics of Naachtún indicate even broader contacts: they include Holmul-style vessels from the Belize Valley to the east, Fine Grays and Fine Oranges from the lower Usumacinta region to the west, and slate wares from the north (Nondédéo et al. 2013; Patiño 2015:14).

Braswell and colleagues (2004:185) have suggested that Chichén Itzá was the primary importer of Ucareo and Pachuca obsidian in the lowlands. For sites in the EIR, contact with the Terminal Classic economic network established by Chichén Itzá in the northern lowlands was likely mediated through the Chenes and Río Bec regions (Boucher and Dzul 1998). At the same time that established Terminal Classic Period routes were abandoned due to political turmoil in the southern lowlands and trade moved toward the coast, it appears that the north-south overland route also became an important corridor into the EIR. The site of Edzná may have also functioned as an intermediary for the trade in fine-paste ceramics from the Usumacinta and other items from the Gulf Coast (Boucher and Dzul 1998).

Discussion

Our brief overview of changes in exchange patterns in the EIR through time highlights the complexity of lowland Maya trade. The relative importance of trade routes was variable and in all periods was linked both to accidents of political geography and to broad economic patterns. We have used least-cost analysis to suggest a few paths across the EIR (Volta and Gunn 2012). Although the east-west routes that we discuss have received much less attention than the riverine corridors farther to the south, we argue that they played a key role in relation to social developments in the EIR. Beginning with the emergence of social hierarchies in the Middle Preclassic, the procurement, display, and redistribution of prestige goods were key to the creation and maintenance of social difference between emerging elites and commoners (e.g., Clark and Blake 1994).

There are clear associations between the positions occupied by many large early centers on the EIR and least-cost routes across the region. Calakmul and Yaxnohcah both sit on the edges of the *bajo* El Laberinto, the main corridor across the EIR. Similarly, El Mirador and Nakbé are both within short distances of the least-cost route across the southern half of the EIR (Figure 20.2). Furthermore, these routes can account for the importance of Chetumal Bay communities as entry points for goods from Honduras and highland Guatemala, as indicated by Golitko and colleagues' (2012) network analysis. In later times the association of the more northerly Escondido route with Calakmul and of the Hondo system with Tikal would also justify the existence of an Early Classic "buffer zone" between the two as proposed by Adams (1991:195).

A focus on routes and the actual mechanisms of trade raises the issue of political control over different forms of exchange. Although the exchange of prestige items such as jade could not have taken place without substantial elite involvement, it bears emphasizing that a certain degree of political control may have been involved in all Classic Maya trade. The key features of polyadic exchange can be recognized in the closed network in which Tikal, Naachtún, and their allies participated in the Early Classic (G. Braswell 2010:130). As we have noted, in the case of the distribution of green Pachuca obsidian and Teotihuacán-related ceramics, the limits of exchange appear to have coincided with the boundaries of the political alliances of the Suutz' polity. It should be noted that the Suutz' emblem glyph appears on Early Classic Stela 114 and Late Classic Stelae 59 and 62 from Calakmul (Martin 2005:10), indicating that Calakmul may have had some sort of political relationship with the Suutz' dynasty in the Early Classic. Nonetheless, the exclusion of Calakmul from this network, despite exchange in other goods that occurred with some of its members, speaks to the boundedness of the system. Put another way, the differential distribution of green central Mexican obsidian and cylindrical tripod vessels at sites in the EIR during the Early Classic suggests a type of exclusive or exclusionary relationship based on political allegiance and elite gift-giving focused on claiming ties with Teotihuacán.

As the Kaan dynasty rose to power in the early Late Classic, the EIR sites fell under its influence and were absorbed into its economic system. The Calakmul interaction sphere was held together by two very different political strategies. The first and perhaps better known is the establishment of alliances or patronage relationships between the Yuknoom kings and distant centers through military action, elite intermarriage (mostly hypogamy), and the gifting of prestige goods (Martin and Grube 1995). The second is the more direct control over centers in the core region of the Kaan polity. As Grube (2005) has argued, the use of toponymic titles instead of full emblem glyphs at sites in the EIR during the seventh and early eight centuries indicates a relationship of subordination between the local ruler and the Kaan overlord. We suggest that this core area constituted a regionally bounded interaction sphere into which limited amounts of materials from other regions were traded (G. Braswell et al. 2004:168). Although diplomatic visits and supervision of rituals by Kaan kings did occur, lavish gift-giving was not necessary to secure the allegiance of local rulers in this area.

Secondary centers such as Uxul, Oxpemul, and Naachtún likely had tribute obligations toward the Kaan rulers. Tribute may have included dietary staples to support the growing population of Calakmul as well as textiles and other craft products. Exchange of other goods within the region may have been accomplished within markets, as suggested by Andrieu (2013) for chert, although the degree of control exerted by elites is still unclear. In the case of obsidian, Andrieu and Roche (2015:340–341) have recently observed that scarcity seems to have been the norm in the northern portion of the EIR. At sites in the Río Bec region obsidian makes up an even smaller fraction of the lithic assemblage than at Calakmul. Although this pattern is suggestive, more data are needed to determine the actual distribution of obsidian in the region.

The contrast between Calakmul's political control of trade routes in the Late Classic and the paucity of obsidian in the city suggests that the lower perceived value of this material relative to prestige goods such as jade and feathers did not warrant the same level of elite involvement in its procurement and distribution. For example, whereas jade preforms were traded directly from Cancuén to Calakmul, Demarest and colleagues' (2014:203) discovery of a cache of more than 800 exhausted or partially exhausted obsidian cores at Cancuén suggests that this material was traded within the site's immediate region rather than with Calakmul. What is clear, however, is that the massive levels of obsidian consumption at Tikal are related to the scarcity of this material at Calakmul. As Braswell and Glascock (2011:128) observe, very little obsidian was allowed to leave the boundaries of the Tikal polity. In this sense, Tikal would have acted as an obsidian "sink" preventing more substantial amounts of it from reaching the EIR (see also Masson and Freidel 2013:218).

Conclusion

The general patterns of exchange that we have discussed for the EIR illustrate the close relationship between trade and the political geography of the region. Beginning with the establishment of the Preclassic centers of Nakbé and El

Mirador and ending with the depopulation of the region during the Terminal Classic, exchange was an integral part of the political developments that occurred on the EIR for almost two millennia. Leaders sought to control and administer the flow of goods into the region, at the same time seeking out objects to serve as material symbols of their power. The distribution of green obsidian in the Early Classic traces the outlines of the political alliances built by the local Suutz' dynasty (and probably by Tikal) on the basis of real or claimed ties with Teotihuacán. In the Late Classic the Kaan rulers went to great lengths to procure jade and other exotic goods with which to adorn their royal courts and to send off as lavish gifts for allies and subordinate kings. At the same time as it provides suggestions of the paths through which these goods were carried to the royal court, the analysis of exchange goods also sheds light upon the local relationships upon which the Calakmul polity was ultimately built. And once the Kaan dynasty began to lose its grip on power, the rapid increase in long-distance trade signals both the lifting of previously undetectable controls and the rise of new rulers who were eager to assert their power in the changing political landscape.

21

An Intracoastal Waterway and Trading Port System in Prehispanic Northwest Yucatán, Mexico

FERNANDO ROBLES CASTELLANOS,
ANTHONY P. ANDREWS, AND RUBÉN CHUC AGUILAR

In 1999 the senior authors of this chapter embarked on an archaeological survey of the northwest corner of the Yucatán Peninsula, which included the coastline from the port of Celestún to the port of Progreso. At the onset of the project we had a number of research objectives, which included a settlement pattern study from 800 BC to the present, an investigation of coast-inland dynamics through time, and the role that this region played in larger events in the northern lowlands and beyond. Owing to an unusual series of events, the main one being the urbanization of a large part of northwest Yucatán, in 2003 the project transitioned from being a pure research effort into an extensive series of salvage or Cultural Resource Management (CRM) projects under the supervision of Robles. So the research continues to this day. In this chapter we include the coastline to the east of the research area as well, between Progreso and the Bocas de Dzilám, as our focus is on the intracoastal waterway that runs between Celestún and Dzilám de Bravo (Figure 21.1).

Geography and Ecology

The northwest corner of the peninsula of Yucatán is, and most likely always was, the most arid region of the entire Maya lowlands. This region has four major distinct physiographic zones. (1) The coast is a narrow barrier beach with low dunes and dune vegetation that runs from the Celestún peninsula to Progreso and beyond to Dzilám Puerto. Hurricanes and storms have cut open and closed many passes along this beach, allowing for the flow of seawater into the estuar-

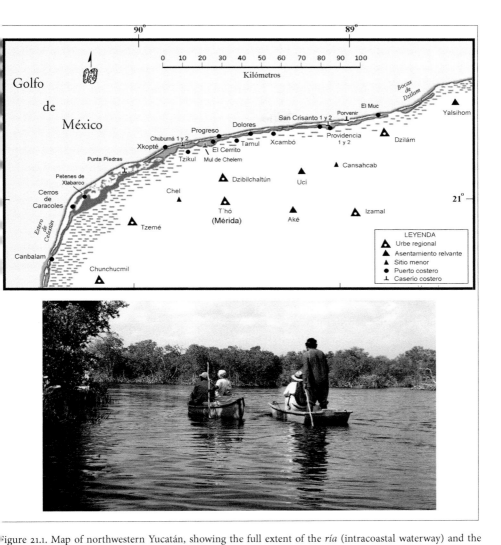

Figure 21.1. Map of northwestern Yucatán, showing the full extent of the *ría* (intracoastal waterway) and the location of Prehispanic coastal trading ports along its length as well as major nearby settlements in the interior (*top*). People traveling in shallow canoes along the interior of the *ría* near Xlabarco, much as Prehispanic travelers would have done (*bottom*).

ies behind the coast. (2) The mangrove zone is the estuary or *ciénaga* (marshy swamp) that runs parallel to the coast, populated mostly by extensive stands of mangroves interspersed with occasional bodies of open water. This zone is often referred to by locals as the *ría* (estuarine river), and separates the coastal zone from the mainland. (3) The *tzekel or sabana* (savanna-like zone) is the edge of the mainland on the inland side of the mangrove swamps. Solid limestone bedrock underlies this zone, which has a sparse scrub vegetation, consisting mostly of grasses and xerophitic bushes (often spiny) and cacti. During the dry season this area is bone dry, while in rainy season large areas become wetlands. Scattered sporadically throughout the wetlands of the mangrove and *tzekel* zones are hammocks or islands of high jungle, known as *petenes*. They are generally round or long and can vary in length or diameter from a few hundred meters up to two or three kilometers. These have dense concentrations of mangroves, palm trees, hardwoods, and logwood (*Haematoxylum campechianum*). In some instances the *petenes* have soil deposits in their centers and sometimes freshwater cenotes or springs (*ojos de agua*). The *petenes* are almost always surrounded by grassy wetlands. (4) The interior or inland zone, an extensive limestone plain covered with a low thorny scrub forest, is also defined as a subtropical dry forest, with very shallow soils; in many places the surface is raw bedrock. The mean annual temperature is 25°C, and the mean annual rainfall is 650 to 700 mm. Fresh water is easily available in most places: many cavities in the limestone enable easy access to the water table, which is generally less than 4 m from the surface.

Running between the coastal dunes and the *tzekel*, through the mangroves, is a continuous estuarine zone that connects an endless series of interior lagoons of varying sizes. These lagoons contain brackish water of variable salinity, as they are fed by fresh rainwater seeping from the interior water table and infusions of sea water from openings in the barrier beach. As noted above, these passes are constantly opening and closing owing to storms. As a result, the physiography and vegetation of the entire estuarine zone are in constant flux. Channels connecting lagoons open and close. The flow of water has also been altered throughout history by human projects such as port facilities, causeways, saltworks, and shrimp farms.

Even though it is shallow in most places, the *ría* forms a fluvial corridor 215 km long running along the entire coast from the open estuary of Celestún to the Bocas of Dzilám. Even today, and specially in the rainy season, large sections of it are navigable in shallow craft (Figure 21.1). In Prehispanic and historic times evidence indicates that the water level was higher; it is quite likely that the *ría* was navigable in its entire length. The strongest evidence in support of such a notion is the location of many Prehispanic sites at varying intervals along the entire waterway (see the section below on previous research and farther below for discussions of sites along the *ría*). Most of these sites, which often have port facilities (docks, piers, and so forth), are located on the inland side of the *ría* or on islands in the *ria*. Only three sites are located on the coastal barrier beach, which are set on the south side of the dunes, facing the *ría*: Xcopté, Progreso, and Providencia 2. Another site, on the open coast, Chuburná 1, lies today on an island in the middle of a pass connecting the open sea and the *ría*. The remains of a fifth site, Cauich, on the open coast just north of Punta Palmar, were recovered in 2000 but have since disappeared. Owing to changes in coastal morphology, we do not know whether the original location of these last two sites was facing the open coast or facing the *ría*. For documentation of these sites, see the reports by Robles et al. (2000, 2001, 2003). In short, if the *ría* were navigable, travelers would have no reason to follow along the open coast—it was much safer to travel along the inland waterway.

Water levels may have been higher in historic times as well. Maps of the nineteenth and early twentieth century show a continuous river following along the entire north coast of Yucatán. Examples are shown in the 1848 map of Nigra de San Martín, the Hubbe and Andrés Aznar Pérez map of 1878, the 1901 Estado Mayor map, the 1910 Antonio Espinosa map, the maps in Albino Lope's 1928 *Geografía de Yucatán,* and the maps in Vega's 1967 *Geografía novísima de Yucatán,* among many others. For a while we thought this was an illusion of the mapmakers, who surely did not have aerial photographs or firsthand knowledge of the *ría*. However, twenty-five years ago, a ninety-year-old fisherman in Celestún told Andrews that before the coastal highway was built in the 1920s they would follow the *ría* all the way to the port of Sisal, more than 54 km away . . . under sail! Two other elderly informants confirmed this information. Additional evidence of the navigability of the river dates back to the eighteenth century, as the cartographer Juan de Dios González noted: "From the above-mentioned *salinas* [of Celestún] there is a waterway that extends to Sisal" ("De las citadas salinas [de Celestún] hay una especie de brazo de agua que se dilata hasta Sisal": González 1766). In fact, over the years, several elderly informants along the coast have noted that the water levels were higher during the first half of the twentieth century and the waterway was much more navigable than now. During the middle of the twentieth century the water levels of the *ría* were much lower, owing to the construction of causeways from the mainland to the barrier beach without bridges or culverts. This drying up of the *ciénaga* was first noted by Arturo Schafer (1893), who attributed it to the construction of three causeways at Progreso across the *ciénaga* for a highway and two train lines to the interior, built without bridges or culverts. Also, passes between the sea and the *ría* between the 1920s and 1980s were quickly closed, to enable the use of the coastal road. As a result, large parts of the *ría* had little or no water flow and were very dry, especially during the dry season. Today a major restoration process is underway: the causeways have bridges and culverts, and bridges are built over passes opened by storms. (For a more-in depth discussion of the drying-up process and current restoration projects, see Battlori et al. 1999.)

In contrast to the agricultural communities of the interior, the Prehispanic coastal settlements were clearly involved with a different way of life, primarily focused on the exploitation of marine resources (fishing, shellfish, marine mammals, salt, and dyewoods), and serving as commercial hubs in the extensive trade networks that girded the peninsula. Most coastal settlements were points of entry not only for marine products but also for long-distance goods that came from many other regions of Mesoamerica and Central America.

Archaeological research at coastal sites in northwestern Yucatán has revealed extensive trade ties with distant localities in the Gulf of Mexico—as far as the coasts of Campeche, Tabasco, and Veracruz. It is now clear that the ports of northwestern Yucatán were heavily involved in long-distance trade with the west, from Late Preclassic times onward, throughout the Classic Period (250 BC to AD 1050). Ceramic evidence tentatively suggests that while the early coastal communities were settled and inhabited by local northern Maya peoples throughout the Late Preclassic and Early Classic periods, around 700 AD the trading ports of northwest Yucatán came under the control of foreign traders linked to the western Chontal and/or Zoquean peoples of the Tabasco-Southern Campeche coast. Following that, sometime after 900 AD, these trading ports became part of the trading sphere of Chichén Itzá, which stretched from central Mexico to lower Central America.

After around AD 1050 the coastal settlements of northwestern Yucatán were abandoned, probably as part of the societal and cultural collapse of the Maya area that unfolded during the eighth to eleventh centuries AD. Interestingly, there is no significant evidence of a Postclassic reoccupation anywhere along this coast or along the river (Robles et al. 2003). However, small amounts of Postclassic ceramics have been recovered from Cerros de Caracoles, in the *ría* north of Celestún, and at Xcambó, near Telchac Puerto, evidently ephemeral occupations. At Xcambó there are two small Postclassic shrines, indicating its continued status as a pilgrimage shrine after the abandonment of the site in Terminal Classic times. It continued to be used as a religious shrine in historic times, until the present (Quintal Avilés 2000; Sierra Sosa 1999, 2004a, 2004b).

Archaeological research during the last half century has provided us with a

Fernando Robles Castellanos, Anthony P. Andrews, and Rubén Chuc Aguilar reasonably good inventory of sites on the northwest coast. The river comes to an end near the modern port of Dzilám de Bravo, where travelers going further east would have had to continue along the open coast, for approximately 10 km, where they entered a canal leading to the Bocas de Dzilám. After navigating the calm waters of the Bocas, navigators had to return to the open sea to continue eastward, until they encountered the mouth of the Río Lagartos, some 40 km. This section of open coast without an inland waterway is the longest open water passage on the north coast of the peninsula and represents a cultural frontier between western and eastern Yucatán. The idea of an east-west divide in northern Yucatán has been discussed by several archaeologists working on the coast, including Robles and Andrews (1986:94–95), Kepecs and Gallareta (1995:288), and Burgos et al. (2008:49). The ceramics recovered from coastal sites east of the Bocas of Dzilám are very different from those of the northwestern sites and exhibit close ties to the Caribbean coast of Quintana Roo. Also, in contrast to the northwestern coast, the shorelines of northeastern Yucatán, the north coast of Quintana Roo, and the east coast were all densely settled in Postclassic times.

Previous Research

Our current vision of the Prehispanic and historic past of the northwest coast unfolded gradually over a century and a half. The first reports of Prehispanic mounds and artifacts on the northwest coast of Yucatán date to the nineteenth century. These remains were found in the course of the construction of the port of Progreso and the highway to Mérida, beginning in the 1850s. The stones from the mounds were utilized in the construction of the road across the estuary adjoining the coast (Andrews and Robles 2016; Frías and Frías 1957:20, 66). In the process of dismantling the mounds numerous artifacts turned up (Frías and Frías 1957:45). A small collection of these was reported by Father Crescensio Carrillo y Ancona (1886:275), a noted historian and later bishop of Yucatán. This collection was recovered from a single excavation made in 1883 and included a zoomorphic vase of a coatimundi (*pizote*), made of Plumbate pottery, which came from an unspecified location near Progreso. (For a discussion of the artifacts, see Andrews and Robles 2016.) The collection also included a cranium (Boas 1890). Some of the mounds were still standing at the end of the century. Holmes (1895–1897) and Edward Thompson (1932) visited Progreso in 1895, leaving brief accounts of the archaeological remains. During their visit they also made a collection of artifacts, which are currently located in the Field

Museum of Natural History in Chicago (see Andrews and Robles 2016 for a discussion of these artifacts). On the basis of these preliminary explorations, Progreso is recorded as a Prehispanic settlement in the *Atlas arqueológico de la República Mexicana* (Instituto Panamericano de Geografía e Historia 1939), and in the Tulane Map of 1940 (Kramer and Lowe 1940).

For more than seventy years no further archaeological explorations were conducted on the northwest coast. The first archaeological survey was conducted by Jack Eaton (1978) in 1968, as part of his reconnaissance of the western and northern coasts of the peninsula, which he conducted under the auspices of the Middle American Research Institute of Tulane University. He located and reported several Prehispanic sites along the northwest coast between the Celestún peninsula and Dzilám de Bravo. Most of these were small midden sites, the remains of fishing and/or salt-making camps and hamlets. Some had the remains of substantial mounds and were likely trading ports and/or salt-making centers. These include Cerros de Caracoles, Xcopté, San Crisanto 1 and 2, and Providencia (Eaton 1978; see also Ball 1978).

The next archaeological survey of the northwest coast was conducted by Andrews, as part of the *Atlas arqueológico del Estado de Yucatán*, a project of the Instituto Nacional de Antropología e Historia of Mexico, between 1976 and 1980. Andrews was also reconnoitering salt-making sites as part of his dissertation research on Prehispanic Maya salt production and trade. In this survey Andrews and several colleagues accurately relocated all of the previously reported sites on the northwest coast and added several more. Among the more prominent new sites were Petenes de Xlabarco, Tzikul, Xcambó, Chumhabín, and three sites in the Bocas de Dzilám region. All these sites were reported in the *Atlas arqueológico del Estado de Yucatán* (Garza and Kurjack 1980), and several were noted in the dissertation and book on salt by Andrews (1980, 1983). Canbalám, another site, south of Celestún, was likely the port for the city of Chunchucmil (Dahlin et al. 1998; Shook and Proskouriakoff 1951). The sites in the Bocas de Dzilám are El Cerrito, Punta Cerrito, El Remate, and Paso Holuntún (Garza and Kurjack 1980).

The first large-scale excavation of a Prehispanic settlement on the north coast of Yucatán took place at Xcambó, between 1996 and 1999, under the direction of Thelma Sierra Sosa (Sierra 1999, 2004a, 2004b) of the Instituto Nacional de Antropología e Historia. Xcambó lies on a large *petén* (hammock island) on the south side of the estuary that stretches behind the north coast. This project involved a detailed mapping and settlement pattern study of the site, excavations and restoration of most of the monumental architecture, and some limited excavations in domestic structures. The occupation of the site began in the Middle Preclassic Period (ca. 800–300 BC), when the settlement was likely a small salt-making and fishing village. The major period of occupation and construction of the majority of the masonry structures took place during the Early and Late Classic Periods, ca. AD 300–700. Evidence of subsequent occupation is scarce. A couple of shrines date to the Postclassic Period.

Xcambó lies in the middle of an extensive complex of salt pans and was a major salt-producing port from Preclassic times onward. It was also an important riverine trading port complex for goods moving along the estuary and could ship its salt a considerable distance to the east or west. The north edge of the settlement was lined with stone wharfs that could handle a large number of canoes and goods. The remains of an extensive array of salt pans lie to the west of the site. To the north of the site on the northern edge of the estuary adjoining the barrier beach is another set of salt pans known as Xtampú; these are still exploited today by the inhabitants of Dzemul, a town 12.5 km in the interior. There are two *sacbe*s from Xcambó into the interior, one headed in the direction of Dzemul (which could only be followed a short distance). Another *sacbe*, which leads to the interior site of Misnay, is 1,280 m long. The settlement of Xcambó has more than a dozen monumental structures around its plaza, including two temple pyramids, a steam bath, and the remains of several civic and/or elite domestic structures. Stretching to the east and west of the plaza are the remains of many domestic structures, which likely housed the bulk of the population. An internal *sacbe* connects the plaza to an elite domestic structure at the east end of the site.

Xcambo's strategic location allowed it to participate in long-distance exchange with faraway places. Ceramics recovered from the excavations include wares from the west and southern coasts of Campeche, the Guatemalan Petén, Tabasco, and Veracruz. Obsidian, turquoise, greenstone, and basalt artifacts and a couple of stone sculptures from the Guatemalan Petén suggest trade links that extended far beyond the Gulf Coast. While Xcambó's main trade with the interior would have been salt and marine products, it is also likely that its long-distance luxury goods were also traded to the interior, to major markets such as Izamal. Sierra's research included a survey, mapping, and test-pitting at the site of La Providencia, 28 km east of Xcambó, another Classic Period estuarine port complex that included a main site on a hammock, a complex of salt pans, two *sacbe*s leading to sites in the interior, and a coastal fishing and salt-making hamlet on the barrier beach to the north.

Sierra believes Xcambó was abandoned sometime after AD 700 but continued as a pilgrimage destination, as reflected in the presence of Postclassic shrines. In the early Colonial Period, the people of Dzemul continued to exploit the saltworks of Xtampú, which is referred as the "port of Dzemul." It is likely that Xcambó continued to be a shrine in historic times. In 1882 it was reported that an idol was venerated there, and sometime in the first half of the twentieth century the people of Dzemul built a ramada chapel at the site and made annual peregrinations to the site that were accompanied by the Virgin of Dzemul, which continue to this day (Sierra 1999, 2004a, 2004b; see also Quintal Avilés 2000).

In 1999 a new archaeological project was developed, under the direction of the authors of this chapter. It involved an intensive survey of the northwest corner of the peninsula of Yucatán, which included the coastline from the Celestún peninsula to Progreso. After 2003 the research efforts morphed into a series of *salvamentos* (salvage projects), as large parts of the area west and north of the city of Mérida were in the process of urbanization. These investigations are ongoing under the direction of Robles and have been conducted by several teams of archaeologists, including Ángel Góngora, Nancy Peniche, Carlos Cortés, Rubén Chuc, Ana María Padilla, Susana Echeverría, Teresa Ceballos, Socorro Jiménez, Mónica Rodríguez, Edgar Medina, David Anderson, Crorey Lawton, Erin Westfall, and Angélica Torres. These salvage efforts are similar to CRM projects in North America. The developments include the construction of new roads and highways and residential areas covering thousands of hectares. While this new research did not result in the discovery of many new coastal sites, we did develop new perspectives on the ecological and cultural relationships of the coast, the long estuary that runs behind the coast, and nearby inland areas.

The field surveys recorded all human settlements, from the Middle Preclassic Period to the twenty-first century, including historic towns, villages, ports, haciendas, and ranchos. When possible, many of the historic sites were mapped with various degrees of accuracy, and surface materials were collected. Among the coastal sites that we recorded were "portlets" linked to large henequen haciendas in the interior. These include Real de Salinas and Venezia on the Celestún River and Xtul, San Benito, Miramar, and Mina de Oro on the north coast (Andrews et al. 2006, 2012; Millet et al. 2014). We also mapped and excavated two nineteenth-century logwood-cutter settlements in the far northwest of our research area, adjoining the coastal swamps. One of these, Kaxek, was more of a camp than a permanent settlement. The other, San Francisco de Paula, was a permanently occupied village of Africans and their descendants (Andrews et al. 2015).

In 2002 Ángel Góngora located a new site on an island in the *ría* between Mina de Oro and Dzilám de Bravo, known as El Muc, which was later surveyed by Rafael Burgos and Miguel Covarrubias (Burgos et al. 2008; Góngora 2002c). In 2004 Burgos and Covarrubias began a series of salvage projects in the Prehispanic province of Ah Kin Chel, the capital of which was Izamal. These projects—a mix of surveys and excavations—registered a large number of sites in the periphery of Izamal, between Izamal and the coast, and revisited a number of previously reported sites along the coast, adding important new data on each. A new site, El Remate, was registered in the Bocas de Dzilám; this was likely the locale of the port facilities of Paso Holuntún. Among the more important results of these projects was the tracing of trade routes between Izamal and the coast and the identification of El Muc as a probable port of Dzilám González. El Muc has several small stone platforms, some of which may have served as wharves, and several elevated stone circles in the surrounding *ciénaga*, which were likely salt-storage platforms. The site was in the midst of a salt-producing area (Burgos et al. 2008; Covarrubias et al. 2012; Covarrubias and Burgos 2016).

One of the major coastal discoveries of recent times was the identification of a Prehispanic port complex near the modern port of Chicxulub by Rubén Chuc. This consisted of an inland site (Tamul 1) closely linked to a nearby site in the estuary (Tamul 2), which had saltworks and served as a trading port, much as Xcambó and Providencia had (Chuc 2007, 2012).

In the course of the last twenty years, the authors also reexamined the evidence for a Prehispanic port complex at Progreso and nearby El Cerrito as well as at three other estuarine ports, Petenes de Xlabarco, Xcopté, and Tzikul (Andrews and Robles 2016; Robles et al. 2000, 2001, 2003). Taken together, these estuarine ports appear to represent a Prehispanic trading network pattern, which is the subject of this chapter.

Development of Settlements along the Northwestern Coast of Yucatán

The ceramic column of northwest Yucatán reveals a continuous occupation of the region from the latter half of the Middle Preclassic Period to the present. The periods of heaviest population and activity are the latter half of the Middle Preclassic (800–400 BC) and the Late and Terminal Classic (AD 600–1050). Somewhat surprisingly, we have not found any substantive evidence of settlement along the coast until Late Preclassic times (300 BC to AD 250). We find this disconcerting, as evidence at sites in the interior indicates Middle Preclassic trade with Veracruz in the form of Olmec-style greenstone ornaments and green-gray basalt hand axes from the Tuxtla Mountains. And trade was going both ways: Nabanché pottery, a prominent group of Middle Preclassic ceramics from northern Yucatán, has been recovered at the Olmec site of La Venta (Andrews V 1986; Von Nagy 2003). It may just be a matter of time before we identify a Middle Preclassic port on the northwest coast. A likely port may have been located at Canbalám, south of Celestún. This was the port for the nearby city of Chunchucmil, which was occupied in Middle Preclassic times (Andrews 1990; see also papers in Hutson 2017).

During the Late Preclassic and the subsequent Early Classic Period, we begin to see a trend towards denser settlements across northern Yucatán, which may have been part of a process of rural to urban migration (Robles et al. 2003:108). In this period the number of rural sites areas appears to decline, and in the northwest we see the emergence of towns, such as Chunchucmil, Tzemé, Oxkintok, Chel, Komchén, Aké, Izamal, and Ichcanzihó or T'hó (Mérida). This latter site developed into a full-blown urban center in the Early Classic Period, covering an area of 9 km^2 (Ligorred 2004; see also Fernández del Valle 1992; Peña Castillo 2002; Vargas de la Peña and Sierra 1991). By that time Chunchucmil, Tzeme, Chel, Uci, Cansahcab, and Dzilám González may have also been in the early stages of urbanization (Robles et al. 2003:108; see also Hutson 2017).

During the Late Preclassic Period, a number of small settlements appear along the northwest coast, often in the vicinity of salt pans (Figure 21.2). The growth of towns in the interior probably created a demand for salt and marine products at this time. By the Early Classic Period some of these settlements evolved into prominent ports, notably Cerros de Caracoles, Tzikul, Tamul, Xcambó, San Crisanto, and La Providencia (Andrews 1980, 1983; Ceballos 2003; Chuc 2007, 2012; Eaton 1978; Robles et al. 2000, 2001, 2003; Sierra 2004a, 2004b). During this period, Xcambó and San Crisanto developed into major salt producers, probably exporting salt to distant regions in the Gulf of Mexico and possibly even to the Guatemalan Petén via the Campeche coast (Andrews 1983:31; Sierra 2004b). An interesting pattern that develops during the Late Preclassic and Early Classic Period is the location of almost all of the sites on the *ría*—not on the open coast. This suggests that the *ría* was the main avenue of transportation and commerce from the very beginning of human activity on the coast.

Tzikul is probably the largest of the Early Classic ports along the *ría* (Figure 21.2). It is situated on the south side of the estuary in the *tzekel* zone, south of

Fernando Robles Castellanos, Anthony P. Andrews, and Rubén Chuc Aguilar

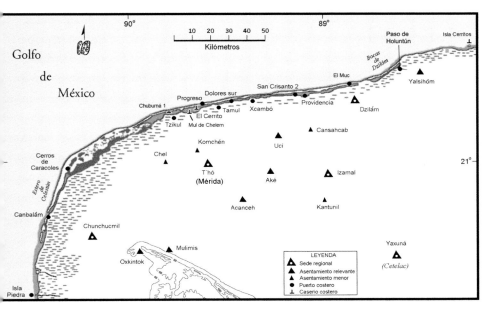

Figure 21.2. Map showing the location of ports along the *ría* of northwestern Yucatán during the Late Preclassic and Early Classic Periods (ca. 250 BC–AD 600) and major nearby contemporary settlements in the interior (*top*). Map of the Early Classic coastal settlement of Tzikul, on the south edge of the *ría* of Chuburná, part of the intracoastal waterway (*bottom*).

the modern port of Chuburná, and covers an area of at least 1.5 km². The monumental core of the site has a central plaza measuring 100 m on each side, and the north and south sides are flanked by 5 m high mounds. The core also includes a small ball court and a steam bath (*temaxcal*). Most of the ceramics recovered from the surface and looters' pits date to the Late Preclassic/Early Classic, with a handful of Middle Preclassic sherds.

It is most likely that sites like Canbalám, Tzikul, Xcambó, and La Providencia were part of a string of ports through which trade goods from the Gulf of Mexico and the Guatemalan Petén entered northwestern Yucatán. We have small amounts of green obsidian at a few sites along the coast and larger amounts appear at sites in the interior, indicating trade with the city of Teotihuacán in the central Mexican highlands. Ceramics from northwestern Yucatán have been recovered in the Merchant's Barrio of Teotihuacán, dating to the Xolalpan phase (AD 350–550), corroborating the existence of regular commerce between northern Yucatán and central Mexico (Ceballos 2003; Ceballos and Jiménez 2006; Rattray 1984).

During Late and Terminal Classic times (AD 550–1100), the number and size of sites across northwest Yucatán increased, with several hundred sites recorded to date. In fact, during this period this region reached its highest population and saw the formation of three polities, with their capitals at Chunchucmil, Tzeme, and Dzibilchaltún. These three polities have distinct ceramic traditions.

The coastal sites, however, belong to a different ceramic tradition, which is closely linked to ceramics of central and southern Campeche. This suggests that they were part of a separate entity independent of the cities of the interior. This coastal "entity" stretched from Sabancuy on the southern Campeche coast to the Bocas de Dzilám on the central north coast (Ball 1978; Jiménez 2002, 2009, 2012; Jiménez et al. 2006).

While most of the Early Classic sites on the northwest coast continued to grow during the Late Classic Period (Figure 21.3), three sites on the *ría* were abandoned around AD 500–600—Cerros de Caracoles, Tzikul, and Tamul (Figure 21.2). With the abandonment of Tzikul, Xcambó continued to grow and prosper (Figure 21.4), and eventually became the most prominent port complex on the north coast. Much of its trade goods from the Gulf Coast likely came via other prominent ports along the *ría*, such as Canbalám, Progreso (and the adjoining island of El Cerrito in the *ría*), and Petenes de Xlabarco, all of which were occupied during Late Classic times (Figure 21.3). Petenes de Xlabarco likely replaced Cerros de Caracoles, which was abandoned during the Early Classic

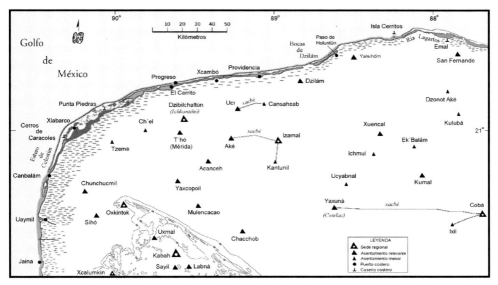

Figure 21.3. Map showing the location of ports along the *ría* of northwestern Yucatán during the Late Classic Period (ca. AD 600–800) and major nearby contemporary settlements in the interior.

Period. Farther to the east of Xcambó were several additional ports along the *ría*, notably La Providencia and El Muc.

Sometime around AD 800 Xcambó was abandoned (Jiménez 2002), and many of the coastal sites of the Late Classic Period went into decline. During the following Terminal Classic Period (ca. AD 800–1100), the bulk of trading activities on the northwest coast appear to be channeled through four main ports on the *ría*: Canbalám, Petenes de Xlabarco, Xcopté, and Progreso (and the adjoining island of El Cerrito), as indicated in Figure 21.5.

In all of these ports we see a continuation of the "Campeche" ceramics of the previous period, but there is a strong presence of Sotuta complex ceramics associated with Chichén Itzá. At Xcopté, in addition to large amounts of Sotuta complex ceramics, we recovered several fragments of green obsidian from Pachuca, Hidalgo, and one turquoise bead. As noted above, Father Carrillo recovered one of the finest Plumbate vessels of the northern lowlands at Progreso. Plumbate is also found at Canbalám, along with several types of Sotuta ceramics and a few blades of green obsidian and fragments of greenstone artifacts. Another site with a noteworthy collection of Sotuta complex ceramics is Yapak, which is located in the *ría* between Sisal and Xkopté. Taken together, the data appear to indicate that, following the Late Classic collapse, the surviving ports

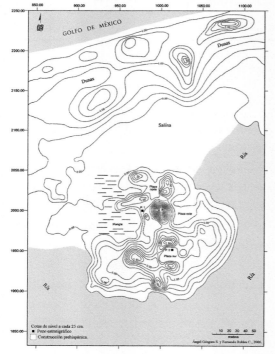

Figure 21.4. Aerial view of the monumental port of Xcambó (*top*). During the Late Classic Period Xcambó became the dominant coastal settlement of the *ría* of northwestern Yucatán. Map of the port of Xkopté, on the outer sandbar of the *ría* (*bottom*). Established by the Itza in the beginnings of the Terminal Classic, in the ninth century, Xkopté monitored and possibly controlled the trade along the *ría*. It may have controlled the traffic between the Campeche-Tabasco coast and northwestern Yucatán.

of the northwest coast of Yucatán were incorporated into the long-distance trading networks that Chichén Itzá established between the north coast, the Gulf of Mexico, and beyond (Andrews 1978; Ball 1978; Robles and Andrews 1986). The keystone of these networks was Isla Cerritos, located some 40 km east of the Bocas of Dzilám. Isla Cerritos was most likely the main trading port

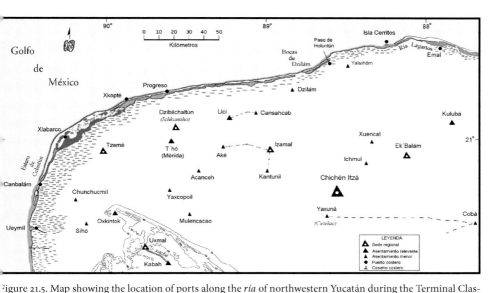

Figure 21.5. Map showing the location of ports along the *ría* of northwestern Yucatán during the Terminal Classic Period (ca. AD 800–1050) and major nearby contemporary settlements in the interior.

of Chichén Itzá, and much of its trade probably originated there (Andrews and Gallareta 1986; Andrews et al. 1988; Gallareta et al. 1989).

Around AD 1000–1100, with the collapse of Chichén Itzá and its trading networks, the entire northwest corner of Yucatán saw a precipitous decline in population (Robles et al. 2003). Only at a handful of sites have we recovered small amounts of Postclassic ceramics—mostly of the types Mama (Mayapán) Red, and Yacman Striated (AD 1100–1542). For the most part these are surface materials and are not associated with any masonry structures, with the exception of the shrines at Xcambó. This may have been due in large part to a combination of three factors: (1) the dramatic population growth of the Late and Terminal Classic Period, which likely exceeded the carrying capacity of the region; (2) climate change, in the form of extended droughts, which would have severely depressed agricultural production (Dahlin et al. 1998; Hodell et al. 2001; Leyden et al. 1996), and (3) sea level rise, another effect of climate change, which probably led to saltwater intrusion into the freshwater table all along the low-lying near-coastal plain (Dahlin et al. 1998:11–12). It is also highly probable that the droughts that affected the northern lowlands in the Terminal Classic Period would have diminished the flow of fresh water from inland areas to the coasts, which would have exacerbated the extent of saltwater intrusions in the interior. This may have been a major factor in the collapse of Chunchucmil (Dahlin et al. 1998:11–12). As a consequence of these factors, we see the collapse of the major regional capitals in the northwest, such as Chunchucmil, Tzeme, and Dzibilchaltún, and a severe disruption of the coastal trade networks.

When the Spaniards arrived in northwestern Yucatán, extensive areas of the region were uninhabited. All the surviving villages and towns were far from the coast, and their inhabitants primarily focused on inland agricultural pursuits (Okoshi Harada 1993; Roys 1957). Historic sources hint at the existence of Pre-hispanic hamlets at Sisal and Chuburná, but we do not have any archaeological evidence of these. The presence of small fishing and salt-producing hamlets during the Colonial Period is well documented at Sisal, Chuburná, Xtampú, Chavihau (Acú), and Santa Clara. Sisal was the only port of northern Yucatán during the Colonial Period.

During the nineteenth century, following independence and the growth of commerce, the coastal areas became active again. Small ranchos along the coast began supplying the interior with salt, fish, and coconuts. In the first half of the century coastal products, such as salt and logwood, and products from the interior, such as leather hides, sugar, and cotton, became major exports (Andrews et al. 2006; Millet 1984, 1985, 1990; Millet et al. 2014). After 1870 the henequen industry took off. Yucatán became a major supplier of this fiber to the United States and Europe, where it was used in the manufacture of bailer twine, cordage, and ropes. The vast majority of the henequen was grown in northwestern Yucatán and exported from Progreso. In the early twentieth century several prominent henequen families built special ports along the northwest coast of Yucatán, to ship henequen to Progreso (Andrews et al. 2012). But the henequen industry collapsed during the first half of the twentieth century. The main economic activities of the coast today are fishing, salt and coconut production, and summer tourism. Almost the entire coastline, from Sisal to Telchac, is populated by summer homes.

Conclusions

When we began our research on the northwest coast many years ago, we had no idea that the swamps behind the coast were once a navigable waterway. And we gave no credence to the maps of the nineteenth and early twentieth centuries that showed the *ría* as a continuous body of water. Our views were further influenced by the largely static estuary landscape of the mid- to late twentieth century. Large areas of the *ciénaga* had no flowing water and often were bone dry during the dry season. We did not understand that this desiccated landscape was humanmade during the first half of the twentieth century (Batllori et al. 1999).

One of the first things we came to realize was that the Yucatecan coastal landscape was much more dynamic than we had ever imagined. Even in our lifetime we have seen many new passes open. Owing to more informed environmental engineering, today the *ría* has more water, more flow, and a much richer flora and fauna than fifty years ago. We believe this was the case in Prehispanic and historic times.

In the course of our surveys we were surprised by the near absence of Prehispanic settlements on the open coast. We assumed that people chose to settle on the inland sides of the *ría* as a precaution against hurricanes. The few sites on the outer barrier beach are located on its south side, protected by sand dunes, at the edge of the *ría*. It is obvious that they are located in a position to use it. Most of the sites are located on *petenes* along the *ría* or on solid ground on its south shore. This settlement pattern eventually made it clear that the *ría* was an intracoastal waterway, the main avenue of transport and trading activities in Prehispanic times. And the sites along the *ría* form an elaborate trading port system that underwent changes through time. Why else would they settle along a swampy estuary? The archaeological evidence clearly documents the use of the *ría* as a major thoroughfare from Late Preclassic through Terminal Classic times. The decline of these activities during the Postclassic Period is still not well understood but may be due in part to changes in climate and sea level.

Acknowledgments

We would like to thank several people and institutions for their support. Eduardo Battlori originally located the 1893 Schafer article, and Rafael Burgos managed to retrieve copies of it. Battlori also provided the logistics for our trip to the Petenes de Xlabarco. Landy Pinto Bojórquez and Blanca González Rodríguez, then curator and director, respectively, of the Museo Regional de Antropología "Palacio Cantón" in Mérida, kindly assisted us in many ways in our examination and recording of the ceramic vessels from the museum, as did Christopher Phillipp and Gary Feinman with the materials from the Field Museum of Natural History in Chicago. Thelma Sierra kindly reviewed our section on

Xcambó and offered several useful comments. Over the years we have benefited tremendously from the assistance of many students and young archaeologists, from Yucatán, Louisiana, and Florida, who have carried out most of the fieldwork. Joann and Will Andrews have always helped us in a variety of ways. We also have a huge debt of gratitude to the people of the coast, many of whom worked with us and guided us, others who allowed us to interview them, and many others who offered us hospitality everywhere we went. The Instituto Nacional de Antropologia e Historia provided permits and support for several of our projects, and the National Geographic Society supported our work with several grants.

22

The Difference a Marketplace Makes

A View of Maya Market Exchange from the Late Classic Buenavista del Cayo Marketplace

BERNADETTE CAP

Scholars have long suggested that marketplace exchange was a practice of the Classic Maya (e.g., Bullard 1960; Freidel 1981; Fry 1979; Rands and Bishop 1980), but the application of Hirth's (1998) empirically based distributional approach to identify ancient marketplace exchange has contributed to the current resurgence of studies of Maya economic organizations and growing evidence for Classic Maya marketplace exchange. Hirth's (1998) basic premises have been well described in prior chapters of this volume, and his model has been refined in numerous works (e.g., Minc 2006; Watts and Ossa 2016). The perspective of household production practices has been especially significant (Feinman and Nicholas 2010; Stark and Garraty 2010). Household assemblage studies conducted at multiple Classic era Maya sites reveal that a variety of goods were exchanged through marketplaces, such as local and nonlocal ceramics, obsidian blades, ritual paraphernalia, and marine shell, among others (e.g., D. Chase and A. Chase 2014a; Eppich and Freidel 2015; García 2008; Halperin et al. 2009; Hutson et al. 2016; Masson and Freidel 2012, 2013; Moholy-Nagy et al. 2013; Sheets 2000; Shults 2012). These goods vary in significance at different sites, but widespread distribution of nonlocal items points toward marketplace exchange as a primary means of provisioning households, often (but not always) cross-cutting sociopolitical boundaries (Hutson, Chapter 4; Hansen and colleagues, Chapter 18, Volta and colleagues, Chapter 20). Marketplace exchange practices have been identified successfully at both major and minor centers, which indicates the pervasiveness and embedded nature of the practice within Classic Maya society.

At the foundation of investigations into Pre-Columbian marketplace exchange is the inference that marketplace facilities existed within many settlements, but these have been examined at only a handful of Classic Period Maya sites (e.g., Bair and Terry 2012; Cap 2015a; A. Chase et al. 2015; Dahlin et al. 2010; Jones 1996, 2015; Keller 2006; L. Shaw and King 2015; Wurtzburg 1991). Sometimes such efforts have been met with skepticism (Feinman and Garraty 2010; L. Shaw 2012). But the identification of marketplace spaces is essential to gain a fuller understanding of the complexity of marketplace exchange and the context for distributional studies.

Excavating marketplaces directly reveals the types of goods exchanged at the locality. This becomes especially important for the study of goods that may not be easily discernible as trade goods through household distributional studies (e.g., ubiquitous goods made of abundant local raw materials). Lack of preservation or rarity of an exchanged good may prevent us from identifying all of the different types of items exchanged in a marketplace. But by comparing findings from the marketplace with household consumption and production practices, we can create a more robust view of marketplace exchange practices. Thus, the identification of a marketplace provides a check against household economy studies and vice versa. The diversity of the goods identified in a marketplace venue provides information on the needs/desires of marketplace participants and has broader implications on the production practices and exchange relationships within and between settlements.

Marketplaces are centralized locales where multiple people meet and interact. Given the dispersed settlements in which the Classic Maya lived, attending a marketplace might provide an opportunity to engage with more people than one would on a daily basis. If we assume that marketplaces were open to all members of society, then it is likely that people from varied identities could have come into contact with each other. Nearly all of the posited marketplaces among the Classic Maya are located within the architectural center of sites, which has implications for interpretations regarding the role of the site center and the elite living there in the organization of marketplace exchange networks.

As important as the identification of marketplaces is, they have been challenging to identify archaeologically. Primary texts or pictorial representations provide the strongest evidence for marketplace exchange in the ancient world, but among the Classic Maya there are no unambiguous direct references to marketplaces (although see Carrasco Vargas et al. 2009 and S. Martin 2012 for a possible exception). This has caused archaeologists to anticipate the configuration of Maya marketplaces from ethnohistorical documents and ethnographic studies (e.g., Cap 2015a; Cortés 1929:87; Dahlin et al. 2007; Hirth 2009b; Landa 1941:94-96; Malinowski and de la Fuente 1982; McBryde 1945; Oviedo y Valdes 1851:401; Ximénez 1666–1772:94).

Marketplaces were often located within plazas. Only a few examples are known of Classic Maya marketplaces built of stone (e.g, Folan et al. 2001; Jones 1996, 2015; Laporte and Chocón 2008). Plazas most conducive to marketplaces are those with open access to the public, with supporting features, such as roadways or administrative buildings. As public events, plazas that are delimited by public structures, rather than private residences, are more likely to be chosen for marketplaces (Dahlin et al. 2010:198). Based on these expectations, scholars have suggested that marketplaces existed at many Maya sites, including Caracol (A. Chase et al. 2015), El Ceibal (Tourtellot 1988), Cobá (Folan 1983:51–52), Quiriguá (Jones et al. 1983; Schortman 1993), Tikal (Jones 1996, 2015), and Yaxhá (Bullard 1960:360), among others (Masson and Freidel 2013:Figure 8.6).

Directly Investigating Marketplaces

Recognizing that plazas are the likely locales of Classic Maya marketplaces is only the first step in the process of identifying a marketplace venue, however. Empirical investigation of a posited marketplace is essential in order to document evidence for associated activities and features built to accommodate them, which can vary. Marketplaces where organic goods were prevalent will have less visible remnants of exchange due to the poor preservation of organics in the tropical lowlands, for example. Sweeping or reuse of the space for different activities can also obscure the archaeological record. Because of these issues, I and others have worked to refine the suite of archaeological correlates and methods used to identify marketplaces among the Classic Maya (Becker 2015; Cap 2015a; Dahlin et al. 2010; Hirth 2009b; Keller 2006; L. Shaw 2012).

The primary activities conducted in a marketplace and the infrastructure built to accommodate them include (1) exchange of goods; (2) production of goods; (3) storage of finished goods and raw materials between marketplace sessions; and (4) maintenance of the marketplace. Many other activities take place in marketplaces, but these four behaviors are linked to a set of material archaeological expectations used in this study (Table 22.1). All four may not occur in all marketplaces, and some are associated with nonmarketplace plaza activities. Some correlates of marketplaces are thus stronger than others,

Table 22.1. Archaeological correlates of ancient marketplaces

Marketplace activity	Archaeological expectation
Exchange of goods	Currency, measurement tools, discrete concentration of artifacts by raw material type, stalls as indicated by prepared surfaces, postholes or daub outlining the edges and pathways clear of debris, discrete concentrations of chemical groups associated with other lines of evidence indicative of exchange.
Craft production	Macro- and micro-sized debris from the production of lightweight materials and/or a focus on end-stage production, prepared work surfaces and production features (e.g., loom posts), high concentrations and/or distinct spatial patterning of elements associated with production activities.
Storage	Storage pits that would likely be empty except for stray finished goods, raw materials, and/or tools of production.
Food preparation	Discrete concentrations of food debris and serving vessels, hearths, cooking pits, high concentrations and/or discrete spatial patterning of phosphorous, potassium, and calcium.
Maintenance	Concentrations on the edges of the plaza space representing swept debris from the main activity area, successive resurfacing on the plaza surface, overlapping postholes from repair to structure walls, high concentrations of phosphorous that pattern spatially with clusters of trash debris.
Administration	Special buildings adjacent to vending area.

so multiple lines of evidence are important. The archaeological expectations presented in Table 22.1 can be used to identify many different kinds of marketplaces but are best suited to those that met in the same location multiple times with a stable arrangement of vendor stalls; where the types of goods vendors exchanged were consistent over long periods and included some durable raw materials; where architectural features were built to house and separate vendors; and where cleaning practices were such that some trash was left within the marketplace. This focus presents a bias, but in this early stage of ancient Maya marketplace identifications these correlates provide a foundation from which to expand.

Scholars have investigated plazas for evidence of marketplaces at the Classic Period sites of Caracol (A. Chase et al. 2015): Chunchucmil (Dahlin et al. 2010), El Ceibal (Bair 2010; Tourtellot 1988), Ma'ax Na (L. Shaw and King 2015), Sayil (Wurtzburg 1991), Motul de San José (Bair and Terry 2012), and Xunantunich

(Keller 2006). These studies have generally provided inconclusive evidence of marketplaces due to limited collection strategies or limitations of empirical evidence that could be interpreted in multiple ways.

I developed an extensive research strategy to investigate a posited marketplace at the site of Buenavista del Cayo, Belize. Results derive from multiple lines of evidence that meet expectations of a marketplace, specifically, where chert and limestone bifaces, obsidian blades, and organics were exchanged by vendors operating from wattle-and-daub stalls during the Late Classic. This case study confirms the existence of Classic Maya marketplaces and provides a basis to reexamine the data and interpretations of the few previously investigated posited marketplaces at other sites. The Buenavista del Cayo marketplace also demonstrates the unique qualities of a specific marketplace.

The Buenavista del Cayo Late Classic Marketplace

Buenavista del Cayo (hereafter referred to as Buenavista) is situated along the Mopán River in west-central Belize (Figure 22.1). It was one of several major centers in the river valley that saw political power shifts from the Preclassic to Terminal Classic (900 BC–AD 890). Buenavista emerged as a leading political center by the Early Classic Period, as indicated by a marked increase in population density (Ball and Taschek 2004; Peuramaki-Brown 2012) and evidence for divine rulership (Yaeger et al. 2015). A shell gorget worn by an Early Classic king interred in the site's Central Plaza was incised with a text that names him as Naah Uti' K'ab, the king of Komkom, which Yaeger et al. (2015) infer could be the ancient name of Buenavista. During the Late Classic, the site of Komkom is documented in stela texts to have experienced at least two episodes of conflict with the larger center of Naranjo, located 14 km to the west (Grube and Martin 2004:II.44, II.58; Helmke and Kettunen 2011:42, 63). These texts reveal that leadership at Buenavista vacillated between periods of independence and subjugation. Buenavista reached its peak in political power prior to the end of the Late Classic (AD 670–780), when there was a decline in settlement density (Ball and Taschek 2004; Peuramaki-Brown 2012) and a concomitant rise in political power and settlement density at the site of Xunantunich, located 5 km south along the Mopán River. Occupation of Buenavista extended into the Terminal Classic (AD 780–890) and continued to be the home of a ruling family (Helmke et al. 2008). A Terminal Classic termination deposit associated with one of the site's large temple pyramids (Cap 2015b) speaks to a decline at the site in this

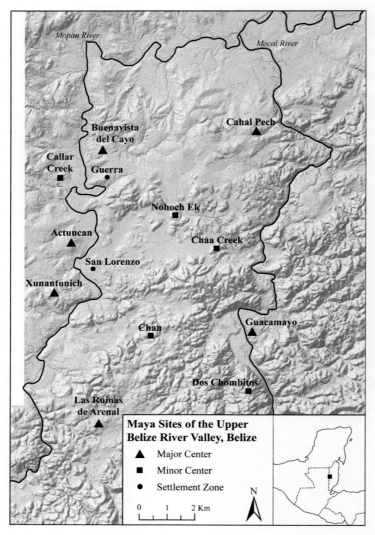

Figure 22.1. Location of Buenavista del Cayo within the Mopán River valley, Belize.

period, however, and foreshadows its abandonment in the Postclassic (Ball and Taschek 2004).

Based on this brief history, several different factors could have fostered the development of a marketplace exchange network at Buenavista. They include the increase in settlement density over time, which could impact resource availability; clear evidence for sociopolitical stratification that could have supported a variety of roles, such as economic administrators and merchants; and communication networks within the site and interregionally that could facilitate the safe movement of people and goods across boundaries. Differentially distributed natural resources in the river valley, such as chert, slate, and agriculturally rich soils (Cap 2015a), as well as the site's location along a major water route, could have contributed to the organization of exchange networks.

There are no mounded features within the Buenavista site core that meet expectations of a built marketplace facility. The East Plaza best fits expectations of a marketplace (Figure 22.2), in part because it has the widest entryways and largest areal footprint, with the ability to hold anywhere from 3,000 to 24,000 people, should occasions have arisen for the entire plaza space to be filled (Cap 2015a:Table 4.1). Causeways located to the north and south of the plaza would have facilitated entry of people and goods into the space. The structures that delimit the East Plaza include a temple pyramid (Str. 3) and a T-shaped structure (Str. 16) that possibly formed a Preclassic E-Group (Yaeger et al. 2016), and two rectangular structures of unknown function (Strs. 15 and 17). The form and function of these four structures neither specifically inform on nor hinder a marketplace interpretation of the East Plaza.

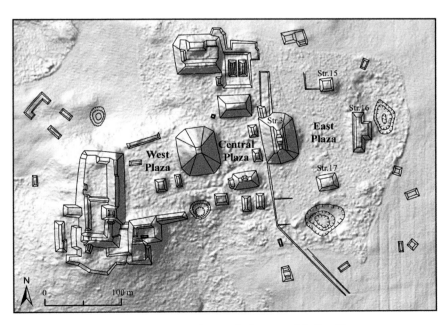

Figure 22.2. Buenavista del Cayo site core showing the location of the East Plaza.

Previous research in the East Plaza conducted by the Mopan-Macal Triangle Project, directed by Joseph Ball and Jennifer Taschek, recorded and tested a dense chert lithic deposit adjacent to Str. 15 that consisted primarily of end-stage chert biface debitage (Kelsay 1985). The discovery of such a large deposit in a plaza and the singular focus on end-stage production preliminarily met expectations of a marketplace and warranted further research.

My investigations of the East Plaza focused on the recovery of multiple lines of evidence that provided a view of activities and features at the macro- and microscale (Cap 2015a). The methods I used included a remote sensing survey, conducted by Bryan Haley, over a 11,600 m^2 area that consisted of ground-penetrating radar and electromagnetic induction; a systematic shovel test survey ($n = 188$); and horizontal excavations over a combined total area of 217 m^2 (Figure 22.3). The study area included adjacent off-plaza space to provide a comparative dataset and the opportunity to locate middens. During excavations, my team and I collected all macroartifacts (greater than ¼ inch in diameter), a 2- to 4-L soil sample that was put through flotation to recover microartifacts (less than ¼ inch in diameter) and botanical materials, and a 4 oz. soil sample that was later analyzed using a weak acid extraction and inductively coupled plasma atomic and optical emission spectrography for multielemental chemical concentrations.

Ceramics collected from vertical excavations indicate that the East Plaza was an activity area as early as the Middle Preclassic (900–300 BC). During the Late Classic occupation, the East Plaza was a multifunctional venue. Multiple lines of evidence indicative of marketplace activities and facilities are concentrated in the plaza's northern sector (Figure 22.4). Differences in the spatial distribution of macro- and microartifacts across the plaza indicate that cleaning did occur, but not at a level that obscured distinct activity areas.

The north sector of the East Plaza stands out from the rest of the study area, as the highest densities of macroartifacts are located there. Statistical analysis of macroartifact densities (using Moran's I formula and Ord-Getis Gi*) reveals significant segregation of artifacts by raw material type (Figure 22.4). The densest cluster of ceramic sherds and organics (as indicated by levels of phosphorous in soils) was found in the same location in the southern half of the north sector. Lithics were concentrated in the northern half of this sector. Obsidian artifacts were clustered in one area, while chert and limestone debitage clustered together in two distinct areas, designated as the east and west lithic production zones. The spatial segregation of objects according to raw material category meets expectations of a marketplace where goods are sold in adjacent stalls.

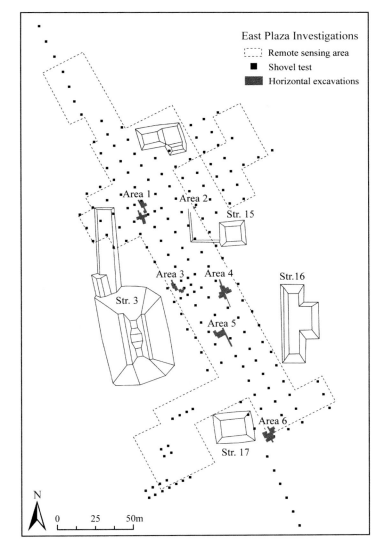

Figure 22.3. Excavations conducted in the Buenavista del Cayo East Plaza.

Chert debitage made up the largest portion of the inorganic debris recovered from the East Plaza. The eastern chert production zone extended over a 20 × 40 m area and consisted of a lens of debitage that was between 15 and 20 cm and had a maximum density of 211,437 macroflakes/m^3 of soil (Heindel et al. 2012). The presence of chert microdebitage in this zone suggests that the macrodebitage was found in situ. Directly below the chert debitage was a limestone cobble

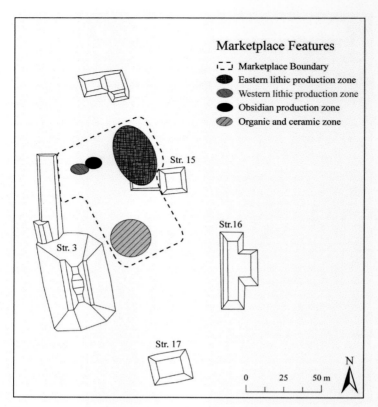

Figure 22.4. Artifact concentrations and activity areas in the north sector of the Buenavista del Cayo East Plaza.

ballast that would have supported a prepared surface for knapping. The lens of debitage was bisected by a second limestone coble ballast in which two post-molds were found, indicating resurfacing of the activity floor and the presence of a wooden superstructure. These architectural features, along with ceramics found within the deposit, revealed that accumulation of the debitage occurred throughout the duration of the Late Classic and possibly into the Terminal Classic. In contrast, the western chert production zone covered only a 10 × 10 m area that had a diffuse lens of debitage with a maximum density of 5,146 macro-flakes/m^3 of soil recovered from on and above the final Late Classic occupation surface. Microchert debitage was also present. I suggest that the volumetric differences and the distinct spatial separation between the production zones reflect two different knappers/knapping groups.

In both the eastern and western chert production zones, 80–90 percent of the chert debitage was 4 cm or smaller in length, had no cortex, and had the physical traits of biface thinning flakes that are created in the final stages of biface production. A few resharpening flakes were also present in each production zone. We recovered only six biface fragments from the entirety of both production zones.

The density of chert debitage recovered is higher than what is typically found in households at Buenavista and other settlements in the Mopán River valley (Connell 2000; Peuramaki-Brown 2012; Robin 1999; Yaeger 2000) but is lower than densities found at intensive chert workshops (e.g., Hearth 2012; Vandenbosch 1999; Whittaker et al. 2009). The emphasis on the last stage of production, however, is unique compared to other production zones and meets expectations of marketplace production practices. In a marketplace we should expect to find few finished goods because they would be removed for use elsewhere, as is the case here.

The location of limestone knapping overlapped with both chert production zones. In the eastern zone, limestone debitage occurred at a density of 58,062 flakes/m^3 of soil and all of the flakes were biface thinning flakes. The density of limestone debitage in the west production zone was only 644 flakes/m^3 of soil, of which 87% were biface thinning flakes. A small assemblage of microlimestone shatter in the western zone indicates that the debitage was recovered from a primary context. Limestone bifaces were absent.

I interpret the attributes of the limestone assemblage in both production zones as evidence for the finishing of limestone bifaces in the East Plaza in a similar way and for the same purposes that chert bifaces were also finished in the plaza. In addition to the spatial overlap, the same general kinds of tools were produced, which leads me to suggest that the same knappers worked both materials.

The concentration of obsidian artifacts in the north sector consisted of 360 fragments that were mostly blade fragments, but nearly a third of the assemblage was core reduction debitage. This high percentage of debitage, coupled with the presence of micro-obsidian fragments, indicates that obsidian blade production took place within this portion of the East Plaza. The majority of the blade fragments were medial sections, which are typically the most usable part of the blade. The average length of medial fragments, however, was only 1 cm, which likely would have limited their usability for many tasks. Therefore, I suggest that all of the obsidian artifacts collected from this zone are production waste. The lack of cortex on any of the obsidian debitage and dominance of final series blades suggests that cores were preformed prior to their entry into the East Plaza and the final stages of blade production took place there, as is expected in a marketplace.

Portable X-ray Florescence (pXRF) analysis completed at the Field Museum Elemental Analysis Facility on a portion of the assemblage (n = 341) revealed that the overwhelming majority (92%) of the fragments were El Chayal obsidian, which was the most commonly exploited obsidian source during the Late Classic among the lowland Maya (Dreiss and Brown 1989; Golitko et al. 2012; Meierhoff et al. 2012; Hutson, Chapter 4; Hansen and colleagues, Chapter 18; Volta and colleagues, Chapter 20). The remainder of the tested samples came from the Ixtepeque and San Martín Jilotopeque obsidian sources.

Finally, in addition to the presence of a superstructure in the eastern chert production zone, macro- and microdaub recovered in three areas of the north sector are interpreted as evidence for wattle-and-daub structures. The best evidence for a wattle-and-daub structure is in the excavation area designated as Area 4 (Figure 22.3), where an alignment of two postholes and a concentration of macrodaub rest directly on top of the last occupation surface. The highest densities of microdaub were present along this alignment. Linear distributions of the highest densities of microdaub indicate the presence of a daub-covered wall between the obsidian production zone and western chert and limestone production zone. A similar linear pattern of microdaub was also present in the ceramic and organic rich zone. I was not able to expose an entire wall or wattle-and-daub structure, but the strong patterning and spatial association of the microdaub to other lines of evidence suggest to me that daub-covered walls were erected to create a space for and divide activities in the plaza. Given the other strong lines of evidence for a marketplace in the north sector, I interpret these findings as evidence for marketplace stalls.

Marketplace Exchange at Buenavista

Multiple lines of evidence recovered from the East Plaza north sector converge to provide strong empirical support that a marketplace existed there during the Late Classic. I suggest that the goods exchanged in this marketplace included chert and limestone bifaces, obsidian blades, organics, and possibly ceramics. I cannot exclude the possibility that other types of goods were exchanged in the marketplace due to poor preservation of organics and the potential for items sold in small quantities to be rare finds. Scholars who applied the household-based distributional studies have inferred that chert tools, obsidian blades, organics, and ceramics were exchanged through marketplaces (e.g., D. Chase and A. Chase 2014a; Hutson et al. 2016; Masson and Freidel 2012, 2013). The findings in the Buenavista East Plaza not only provide direct confirmatory evidence for these inferences but contribute additional information that allows for more complex understandings of Classic Maya marketplace exchange.

The evidence for obsidian blade production in the Buenavista marketplace demonstrates that cores were transported across the landscape and blades were produced as needed. I cannot discern from this study the exact ways in which obsidian reached the site, but an open network of exchange that was not tightly restricted by social or political boundaries is implied by the presence of obsidian from three different obsidian sources. Ruling elites likely would have been important in forging and sustaining relationships that brought obsidian into the site and allowed safe passage between polities. The dominance of El Chayal among the tested fragments is evidence that Buenavista was linked into the major obsidian trading networks for the Late Classic, while the presence of San Martín Jilotopeque and Ixtepeque obsidian could indicate multiple trading connections of either the obsidian knapper or those who facilitated obsidian exchange networks.

Obsidian production debris typically makes up less than 5% of household assemblages in the Mopán River valley (Connell 2000; Peuramaki-Brown 2012; Robin 1999; Tritt 1997; Yaeger 2000), indicating that households obtained most of the blades that they consumed through trade. The only other known locations of obsidian blade production in the wider region are located at a posited marketplace at Xunantunich (Cap 2019; Keller 2006) and at a household workshop in the hinterlands of the El Pilar settlement, located 13 km north. With so few production locales within the valley, the East Plaza north sector was likely an important and primary venue for the acquisition of obsidian blades.

Chert and limestone are naturally abundant in the Mopán River valley and are ubiquitous in household artifact assemblages or architecture. At the valley-wide scale, multiple household studies have shown that not all households produced their own chert and limestone bifaces, including those studied at Buenavista (Connell 2000; Hearth 2012; Peuramaki-Brown 2012; Robin 1999; Yaeger 2000). Given the heavy focus on the last stage of biface production in the Buenavista marketplace, there are likely households or workshops where earlier stages of production occurred. We have yet to identify such locales within the Buenavista settlement, but specialized household workshops where chert bifaces were produced have been located in hinterland households of other centers in the valley (Hearth 2012; Vandenbosch 1999; Whittaker et al. 2009).

Exchange for bifaces could have occurred at household workshops, but a marketplace would have been an efficient method to engage with a with a larger group of people.

The Buenavista marketplace is the first case study to offer evidence that limestone bifaces were part of Classic Maya marketplace exchange practices. Limestone is often soft and breaks in an irregular manner that would make it a poor-quality material for knapping tools. A hard crystalline limestone occurs naturally in the Mopán River valley that does fracture predictably, however. Limestone bifaces were produced in the Buenavista marketplace at a lower rate than chert bifaces, suggesting that they were consumed in lower quantities. Chert is more brittle than limestone, which could result in higher breakage rates and consequently more production of chert tools than limestone tools. Alternatively, the lower rate of limestone production could be related to the use of the limestone bifaces versus chert tools. Lithicist Rachel Horowitz examined limestone bifaces recovered from households across the Buenavista settlement and found that breakage patterns and usewear on tool edges were indicative of use against hard materials (Horowitz et al. 2019). As a more durable stone, limestone tools could have been used for a special or limited set of activities that were not suitable for chert bifaces. The option to acquire both chert and limestone tools in the Buenavista marketplace highlights the complexity of the lithic economy and choices available to Maya consumers.

The evidence for multiple lithic tool production activities in the Buenavista marketplace offers an additional new insight: some vendors were also the producers of the goods that they exchanged. Production in the marketplace would allow producer-vendors to make goods to custom order and offer repair services. Conducting part of the production process in the marketplace could have been a strategic act on the part of vendors, because it would have provided an opportunity for customers to evaluate the value of an object directly in relation to the skill and labor involved.

Ethnohistorical texts provide accounts of a variety of merchants in the early colonial Maya highlands and lowlands, including long-distance and local traders, itinerant or professional merchants, and go-betweens (Feldman 1985; Tokovinine and Beliaev 2013). It would be a very special case if direct empirical evidence for these traders were to be recovered archaeologically, however. Recognition of the producer-vendors in the Buenavista marketplace consequently provides a unique perspective on the way vendors and consumers interacted in marketplace exchange systems.

The discovery that organic goods were exchanged in the Buenavista marketplace may not be surprising given that many items within ethnohistorically documented Mesoamerican marketplaces were organic. The soil chemical analysis conducted does not identify the specific kinds of organics present, but the empirical documentation of organics in a marketplace does raise questions about the availability and access to organic goods, such as food. The hinterland settlement around Buenavista is dispersed across the landscape, but soils within a 3 km radius of the site center vary in their productive qualities. Could access to good-quality soils and raw materials have contributed to the development of marketplace exchange?

The goods that I propose were exchanged in the Buenavista marketplace are all staple household items, indicating that the marketplace served in part as a source for household provisioning. There is not yet a large enough database to conduct a household-based distributional study in the Buenavista settlement to discuss the full impact of the marketplace on Buenavista household economies and vice versa. The diversity of goods available, however, would have made the marketplace an efficient method of exchange for both the vendors and consumers in terms of the time and effort it would take to forge exchange relationships and to travel to the site center. The efficiency of a marketplace increases as it becomes regularized and predictable, which could result in a more stable and reliable exchange network. The presence of wattle-and-daub structures and evidence for floor resurfacing are indications of an enduring presence of the marketplace. As a result, it would have served as a mechanism to integrate the settlement economically. Given that marketplaces are also social events, the Buenavista marketplace may also have impacted social organization within the settlement.

The archaeological record of the Buenavista marketplace does not provide direct evidence for the administration of the marketplace, but I infer from its location within the site center and its enduring presence throughout the Late Classic that it was administered. The elites living in the site center were integral to the sociopolitical and religious events that would have taken place in the site center and were likely candidates to also play a role in the marketplace. The degree to which they were entangled with the marketplace is open to debate, however. One of the potential low-cost, high-yielding ways elites could have gained power and wealth through the marketplace was to control access to the marketplace venue by charging fees to participate (Freidel 1981; Hirth 2010; Masson and Freidel 2013; C. Smith 1976b). They also could have taken direct control over trade routes, production, or the pricing system, which would create a higher degree of control and possibly add political motivations to the organization of the exchange network (Polanyi 1957; C. Smith 1976b). Alternatively, the marketplace could have been administered by a merchant class with ruling elites playing an indirect role as consumers or benevolent sponsors of marketplace activities.

Conclusion

The Buenavista marketplace case study demonstrates the successful archaeological identification of a Classic Maya marketplace. Some of the findings of this study mirror broad patterns of Classic Maya marketplace exchange practices observed in household-based distributional studies, which highlights the complementarity of the two approaches. In other cases, the view from the Buenavista marketplace is unique and adds a level of complexity to our understanding of Classic Maya marketplace exchange. The study presented here illustrates that marketplace identifications are essential to provide a more comprehensive view of Classic Maya marketplace exchange (see also Hutson et al. 2016). There also is still much to learn about the diversity of marketplaces over time and space. A growing number of scholars have argued through contextual and household-based distributional studies that marketplaces existed at several other sites in the Maya lowlands, which would suggest that more marketplaces have yet to be investigated empirically, which could provide a comparative dataset.

Acknowledgments

This research was conducted in conjunction with the Mopan Valley Archaeological Project with permission from the Belize Institute of Archaeology. Funding was provided by a National Science Dissertation Improvement Grant (BCS-0810984); the Samuel J. and Connie M. Frankino Charitable Foundation; the Geological Society of America; and the University of Wisconsin–Madison Latin American, Caribbean, and Iberian Studies Program, with additional support for LiDAR imagery from the Alphawood Foundation (awarded to the Western Belize LiDAR Consortium and collected by NCALM, the National Center for Airborne Laser Mapping).

23

Decentralizing the Economies of the Maya West

CHARLES GOLDEN, ANDREW SCHERER,
WHITTAKER SCHRODER, CLIVE VELLA,
AND ALEJANDRA ROCHE RECINOS

The editors of this volume have asked the chapter authors to focus on the "nuts and bolts" of Maya economies, the "specific evidence for agents, facilities, transport mechanisms, webs of debt, constraints and freedoms, strategies for and challenges to stability, and commodities that were made and exchanged according to gradations of value." Here we address some of these issues for the Classic Period (AD 250–810) kingdom of Piedras Negras, using a healthy mixture of archaeological data with a bit of ethnographic insight and more than a dash of speculation. First we briefly outline what we see as a fundamentally important role of the market in the operation of the kingdom: trust. Then we move quickly through the archaeological evidence for production and exchange of food, lithics, bone tools, and ceramics, in the Piedras Negras kingdom and adjacent regions, all of which, we argue, support the growing body of evidence for market trade as a driver of the Classic Period economy (Figures 23.1–23.3).

Marketing Trust in Classic Period Maya Kingdoms

While the particulars of trade, value, and profit as well as the integration of market and polity undoubtedly differed in many details from better-known Postclassic and historical examples in Mesoamerica, the body of archaeological evidence supports the presence of marketplaces and some form of market economy in the Classic Maya lowlands. This does not negate the presence or importance of other forms of trade and exchange; "down-the-line" trade, indi-

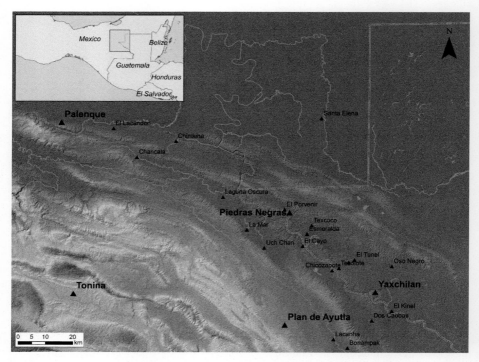

Figure 23.1. Regional map encompassing Piedras Negras and its neighbors (map by Whittaker Schroder).

vidual barter and exchange, courtly tribute, and gifting and redistribution all played a part in Precolumbian economies. But these nonmarket modes of exchange are inefficient and would not have provided the sort of economic "gravity" to move significant quantities or qualities of long-distance trade goods to major political capitals and small hinterland sites across the landscape. Our ongoing research has only begun to focus archaeological excavations on an area that we believe constitutes a marketplace at Piedras Negras. While we discuss some preliminary findings from that ongoing research here, we also focus our discussion more broadly on patterns of production and consumption evident in archaeological data at Piedras Negras and hinterland sites that strongly suggest marketing.

We also want to emphasize that market trade was not simply a faceless utilitarian exchange of goods. Rather, many if not most participants in Maya markets, like markets throughout the ancient world, were minimally acquainted with histories of interaction that enmeshed market participants in relational webs with others. The effect is that markets can build trust in participant communities. We do not have space in this chapter to offer a full discussion of the role that trust among group and individual actors plays in state cohesion (see Golden and Scherer 2013 for a more complete discussion). In brief, however, the coherence of a well-functioning state depends in no small part on the cultivation of trust among its participants. People need not have expectations of immediate or direct reciprocity, à la Mauss's *The Gift* (1925). Instead, individuals and collectives are engaged with and morally committed to society and the state with the expectation of more generalized reciprocity in the form of social, economic, and infrastructural goods that participation in the state can provide (Uslaner 2000–2001:573–579; see also Houston et al. 2003; Houston and Inomata 2009:28–42).

To build generalized trust requires the regular associations of people outside the immediate family, above the level of the household, and outside the groups with whom one interacts regularly. The work of political scientists and psychologists suggests that the weaker the preexisting social ties between the participants, the more diverse the relationships between members, and the riskier the engagement itself, the higher the levels of generalized trust as an outcome of successful associations (Stolle 1998:504). Conversely, the more one participates in associations only with preexisting strong in-group trust, the more the scope of generalized trust in the polity as a whole decreases over time (Stolle 1998:521).

Marketing brings together people from disparate households who do not see one another on a daily basis and involves potentially significant danger in getting to market and in the market exchange itself. States from Babylon to the Triple Alliance to the USA typically protect buyers and sellers to some degree by regulating currency values and offering consumer protection laws, among other practices. Nevertheless, even where such protections exist in the ideal, the real practice of the marketplace involves risk. A fair trade or an unscrupulous deal is a potential outcome of any exchange (even in a currency-based economy), highlighting the potential peril of these engagements.

In our own experiences, the fastest way to build trust in the communities where we work is to patronize local shops and eateries. Everyone in town has an opinion about which proprietor is trustworthy and which is devious. Anyone can make atoles, but some vendors make the "best" atoles, and other vendors make atoles that are "best avoided." Participating in local marketing is an opportunity, as marked outsiders, to demonstrate faith in the local community

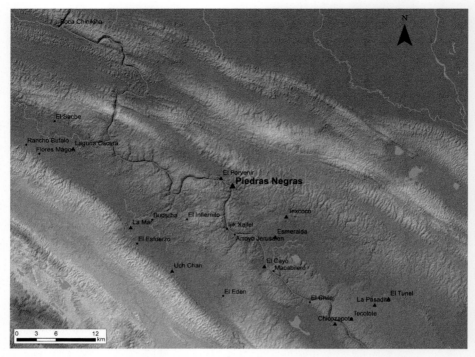

Figure 23.2. Map showing Piedras Negras and outlying settlements mentioned in text (map by Whittaker Schroder).

and the products it produces and for the vendors to get to know us. The Chiik Nahb murals at Calakmul (Carrasco et al. 2009; S. Martin 2012) present graphic representations of these experiences during the Classic Period: men, women, and children involved in the public exchange of raw materials and prepared goods. Patrons try the food, pinch the dough, and inhale potent snuff. As in modern markets the buyers assess the quality of food, pottery, and weaving needles; they also assess the trustworthiness of the vendor—and the vendor assesses the seller.

During the Early Classic Period, most of the Piedras Negras kingdom's population lived in the near vicinity of Piedras Negras. Markets there helped to create a sense of community that fostered the state. As populations spread across the landscape, as new market centers arose around noble courts, and as movement across the landscape was increasingly regulated over the course of the Late Classic Period, people participated more frequently in local markets and less commonly with those at the polity capital (Figure 23.2).

Food Production

What, then, is the archaeological evidence for marketing? We begin with food. Although markets were just one of a variety of avenues of exchange and acquisition for the provisioning of household supplies of venison and other game, dried fish, and various fruits and vegetables, here we focus on the bulk storable foodstuff: maize. Soil chemistry around Piedras Negras and its hinterlands indicates that maize was grown virtually anywhere with good earth and drainage (Fernández et al. 2005; K. Johnson et al. 2007). We have identified terraces in abundance on pedestrian survey and in LiDAR data throughout the region (Golden et al. 2016). There are also channeled and dammed fields in the surroundings of hinterland sites such as Budsilhá and Rancho Búfalo. Indeed, even lacking these intensive systems, modern interlocutors in the region around Piedras Negras report that as many as three crops per year can be harvested in some areas. One harvest, Golden and Scherer have been told, feeds the family: food produced beyond that goes to market (Figure 23.3). All of these data support the inference that maize was produced during the Classic Period well beyond the needs of regular household consumption.

To date, we have not identified any special-purpose food storage structures. Modern practice is often to store dried maize in the field, covered by a palm roof, and ideally at an elevated point where wind can pass through to reduce moisture. There, owls and hawks can reduce pests like rodents that might eat maize stored in the closed confines of the house or outbuildings. Grain stored in such conditions can last more than another growing season but must be used or sold soon lest it rot or be consumed by vermin. We infer, therefore, that surplus crops during the Classic Period could be stored for a limited time and then were ultimately exchanged for other goods at regional markets, providing access to maize for those who experienced bad harvests or otherwise needed to supplement what their households could produce. Some markets were located at polity capitals, but other markets appeared at smaller centers as populations expanded over the countryside. There is no evidence that the dynastic court had any significant direct role in food production during the Classic Period (Murtha 2015; Webster 1985), but by sponsoring central markets they surely encouraged production and were able to reap some of the rewards via taxation.

Some maize was likely traded in bulk. However, maize was also processed to create value-added goods sold at a markup: nixtamal, tamales, pozol, and atoles among other items. Indeed, what is a market without its food vendors?

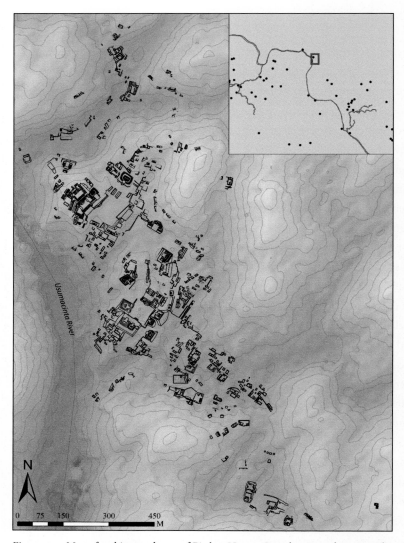

Figure 23.3. Map of architectural core of Piedras Negras. Boxed area on the map indicates the S-sector, a cluster of structures and patios proposed as the marketplace of the city (map by O. Alcover-Firpi, after maps by Tatiana Proskouriakoff, Fred Parris, and Zachary Nelson).

People across Mesoamerica today enjoy the opportunity to dine in the market on atoles, roasted corn, tamales, and other foodstuff, and we expect that people in the past were little different in this regard. Indeed, we can turn again to the murals of Calakmul for images of people enjoying precisely these market treats.

Human bone chemistry demonstrates that the residents of the Piedras Negras kingdom had among the highest isotopic signatures for maize consumption in the Maya area. At least during the eighth and early ninth centuries AD everyone enjoyed comparable access to maize regardless of status (Scherer et al. 2007). Similarly, the bone isotopes indicate that people of all classes had access to similar quantities of meat and fish throughout much of the seventh and early eighth centuries AD. Things shifted, though, in the years before or immediately after political collapse. Some individuals demonstrate noticeably lower levels of maize consumption, and the isotopic signatures of meat consumption diversify among individuals, indicating uneven access to terrestrial and riverine protein sources. Such changes in the ability of different households and individuals to access maize and protein sources resulted in part, we argue, from the unraveling of market exchange systems as the dynasty foundered.

Lithic Production

We turn next to obsidian. More than 95% of all the obsidian in the Late Classic Period Piedras Negras kingdom comes from the El Chayal source in Guatemala, the remainder coming largely from San Martín Jilotepeque and a scant minority from other sources in Mexico and Guatemala. At Piedras Negras itself the evidence for the production of obsidian blades from prismatic cores is scant. Hruby (2006) has noted that the obsidian assemblage at the kingdom's capital includes few small obsidian prismatic cores, likely because the cores arrived at Piedras Negras already heavily depleted or workable obsidian arrived in such small quantities that available cores were used to the point of exhaustion.

In marked contrast, some 10 km to the west in Chiapas, our preliminary excavations at the small palace and residential complex of Budsilhá revealed a remarkable obsidian workshop (Figure 23.4). Excavations of part of a single excavation unit in a single day, in the final occupational episode of a structure at Budsilhá, recovered far more obsidian than has been excavated at Piedras Negras in more than ten field seasons. This sample includes nearly all stages of blade production (Scherer et al. 2013). Analysis by Clive Vella demonstrates that high-quality prepared core preforms were imported to Budsilhá. Expert blade makers produced tools with nearly uniform blade dimensions averaging 1.9 by 0.9 cm during all stages of reduction. While these craftspeople may not have been the sole producers of obsidian blades in the region, they were probably among the major producers.

Clark (1986) estimates that a skilled producer could extract 100 prismatic

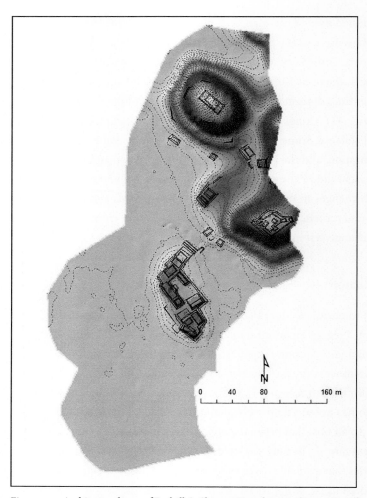

Figure 23.4. Architectural core of Budsilhá, Chiapas. Boxed area indicates area of obsidian workshop (map by Bryce Davenport, Jeffrey Dobereiner, and Charles Golden).

blades per core, suggesting at the upper limit that 2,300 prismatic blades could have been manufactured from the 23 whole but much-reduced cores found in the excavations. We suspect, however, that the polyhedral cores brought into Budsilhá were smaller than those to which Clark's estimates apply. Nonetheless, as a small sample of the probable total of cores to be found at Budsilhá, such estimates do help us to conceptualize the high levels of production. Indeed, we recovered even more fragments of polyhedral cores, suggesting that the number of blades produced was significantly greater.

C. Golden, A. Scherer, W. Schroder, C. Vella, and A. Roche Recinos

If a skilled part-time craft specialist could have produced 62.5 blades in one hour (Clark 1986:39; see also Aoyama 1999:115), the upper estimate number of 2,300 blades for 13 cores could have been produced in a mere 41.6 person-hours of work. While our obsidian sample from Budsilhá includes more than 3,000 pieces of obsidian debitage and more than 400 unifacial and bifacial tools, in addition to the cores, the entirety of the sample might be the product of a single episode of production occupying less than a week's work for a few producers. However, the distribution of tools and debitage, which tended to be packed against the base of the staircase or against wall bases and out of the main patio and walkway spaces, suggests that the materials recovered at Budsilhá repre-sented extended and multiple episodes of production. We infer that occupants swept the patio, interior building spaces, and walkways clear of potentially dangerous production debris, resulting in the high concentrations of obsidian recovered. We do not know precisely how long the small patio was the site of obsidian production. However, we feel confident that it functioned as such for well over a century during the Late Classic Period, based on the construction stratigraphy and evidence for blade production associated with earlier phases of construction.

The sheer number of obsidian blade fragments found in the same excava-tions seems to indicate that lithic producers at Budsilhá were major produc-ers of obsidian implements in the region but were unlikely to have been the sole consumers of these objects (Aoyama 1999:115). Indeed, all other regional settlements, including Piedras Negras itself, have yielded data suggesting that residents were primarily consumers, not producers, of finished blades. Clark (1986:36) argues that a family of 5 persons would consume an estimate of 10 complete blades per year. The estimate of 2,600 blades produced from 23 cores at Budsilhá would have fulfilled the obsidian needs of 260 families, or at least 1,300 people, for a year.

However, Budsilhá was likely not the only producer sending blades to mar-ket at Piedras Negras. Visual analysis of blades suggests that the majority of obsidian from Budsilhá was coming from El Chayal, with only a few fragments likely to come from Mexican sources. Indeed, pXRF analysis of the cores from Budsilhá carried out by Jeffrey Dobereiner (personal communication, 2015) indicates that all cores came from El Chayal, suggesting to us that producers of blades at Budsilhá used only cores from El Chayal. The blades at Piedras Negras have a wider variety of sources, including the Mexican sources of Zara-goza, Ucareo, and Pachuca, which likely entered into exchange in the city from multiple sources. Blades are widely distributed across all households at Piedras Negras and in all hinterland sites in varying quantities, further supporting the notion that blades from Budsilhá and elsewhere were disseminated through markets, perhaps at Piedras Negras or just as likely in markets at Budsilhá, La Mar, or other nearby lordly centers. The Budsilhá workshop sits beneath the view of a noble palatial residence, which supports the suggestion of elite oversight of import and production of the obsidian.

In contrast to the obsidian data, small-scale production of monofacial and bifacial chert tools was widespread, with a wide range of producer skill evident in the assemblage. This may perhaps reflect the widespread availability of raw material and the ease of making a usable tool. Nonetheless, some trade in finished products or resharpening of bifacial tools may have taken place in a provisionally identified marketplace just southeast of the South Group at Piedras Negras, in the "S-sector." There Hruby (2006) identified the only possible chert workshop dump at the site, consisting of about 3,000 late-stage percussion and pressure flakes from biface reduction and resharpening. These findings echo the identification of marketplace lithic production and resharpening by artisans who demonstrated their prowess to buyers at Buena Vista del Cayo, Belize, by Cap and her colleagues (Cap 2011; Cap et al. 2015, Chapter 22).

Recent excavations carried out by Alejandra Roche Recinos and Mallory Matsumoto (Roche Recinos 2017) in the S-sector reaffirm Hruby's identification of this sector as the possible location of a marketplace. The evidence of production mainly comes from the amount of obsidian microdebitage found throughout the excavations. The absence of finished obsidian tools in this area, aside from a single blade and one biface, stands in stark contrast to domestic contexts at Piedras Negras where finished tools usually abound in the archaeological record (Hirth 2009b:95). Similar patterns are also evident in the chert sample from the S-sector, which includes large quantities of microdebitage, chunks, flakes, and chunks with cortex but few finished tools. For both, the specific technological types of debitage signal the objects manufactured, including prismatic blades for obsidian and bifaces for chert. Moreover, there is evidence from this probable marketplace for the importation and reworking of jade adornments. We recovered a jade earflare that appears to have been intentionally broken in antiquity, and among the refinished objects recovered was a small jade disk that appears to be a dental inlay in need of a tooth.

Investigations by Whittaker Schroder at El Infiernito, Chiapas, a defensively positioned hilltop site halfway between Piedras Negras and La Mar, have uncovered distinct assemblages of chert tools between the Late Classic (AD 600–810) and Terminal Classic (AD 810–900) Periods. A patio group at the northern end of the epicenter of the site seems to have been a center of chert tool production during the Terminal Classic Period based on the high quantity of chert debitage and percussion tools, including hammerstones and a fragment of a deer antler. Many of the chert flakes associated with this patio group are large (between 5 and 10 cm in length) and exhibit 10–50% cortex. This chert is coarse-grained and of local origin and is found in all excavated patio groups with Terminal Classic occupations across the site.

In Late Classic assemblages within the same structures the recovered chert is fine-grained and of a nonlocal variety. Again, this chert is evident across all excavated Late Classic patio groups across the site. However, evidence of stone tool production using the finer-grained chert is on a smaller scale, consisting of either completed projectile points or smaller late-stage debitage. These data suggest that tools made of nonlocal chert were available to the inhabitants of El Infiernito at markets during the Late Classic Period, while shifting trade networks led patio groups to rely more on local stone tool production with chert from nearby sources during the Terminal Classic Period.

Intriguingly, a final lithic category encountered in our research consists of small nodules of hematite that form naturally in local soils. These have been recovered in a variety of contexts at La Mar, Budsilhá, and Piedras Negras. We find these in various stages of production, from raw nodules to finished tesserae ready to be set in mirrors. It is possible that people produced complete mirrors in their homes and traded these products at markets or paid them as tribute and tax. Alternatively, it could be that craftspeople gathered individual tesserae at markets or palace storehouses to form completed mirrors at centralized workshops.

Bone Tool Production

In contrast to obsidian blade production in a limited number of workshops, analyses by Emery and Sharpe (Emery 2007; Sharpe 2011; Sharpe and Emery 2015) of shell and bone tools found in hinterland sites and at Piedras Negras strongly suggest that many "commoner" households were sites of production, with no obvious oversight by courtly personages. For other discussion of bone tools as products or implements, see Chapters 7 and 8. "Elite" households were primarily users of finished products. That these tools typically take the form of pins and weaving needles—together with the widespread presence of spindle whorls—strongly suggests that textile production (perhaps not surprisingly) took place in elite and nonelite households alike, though elites may have purchased their weaving implements in the markets rather than producing them. Considerable numbers of finished bone pins and needles, along with other bone ornaments and tools in various stages of production, were recovered during the 2016 excavations in the S-sector marketplace at Piedras Negras. Certainly some shell and bone implements, as exemplified by inscribed objects found in burials and other deposits at Piedras Negras, may have been produced or finished by elite artisans (Inomata 2001; Inomata and Triadan 2000). Such unusual implements with nametags or other unique features (e.g., Fitzsimmons et al. 2003), however, were likely inalienable in some sense and outside the market economy.

Ceramic Production

Golden, Scherer, and colleagues (Golden et al. 2008; Golden and Scherer 2013; similarly, see Volta and colleagues, Chapter 20) have argued elsewhere that the distribution of distinctive Classic Period ceramics was significantly delimited by the political boundaries of the Piedras Negras kingdom. Of particular note, resist-decorated pottery from the Santa Rosa group constitutes a majority of Late Classic polychrome ceramics at Piedras Negras itself and is found in significant amounts at hinterland sites, but the limits of its distribution correspond roughly with the limits of the Piedras Negras polity. Beyond those borders it is found only in very limited quantities (Arroyave et al. 2006; Arroyave and Meléndez 2005; Muñoz 2004, 2006; cf. Forné 2006:144–145). We believe that markets might offer a reasonable explanation for these patterns of distribution. Santa Rosa group ceramics are technologically distinct from positive painted Classic Period polychromes. It may be that a relatively limited number of producers made the Santa Rosa materials found in and around Piedras Negras itself, with these wares then distributed widely through markets. Anyone not participating in market exchange in the Piedras Negras vicinity may simply not have had regular access to such materials.

More circumstantial evidence for marketing and the organization of trade is presented by the distribution of two well-known and more widely distributed fine paste wares. Chablekal group ceramics, likely manufactured in Tabasco, appear shortly after AD 750 at Piedras Negras, and are evident imports from their likely area of manufacture in Tabasco (Bishop et al. 1982; Cabadas-Báez et al. 2017; Foias and Bishop 1997, 2007; Rands and Bishop 1982). While they are always a small minority of the ceramic assemblage at Piedras Negras, they are widely distributed and appear in a variety of elite and nonelite residential contexts there (Muñoz 2006:124–128), a pattern most easily explained through trade in a market system (Hirth 1984). Intriguingly, though compositional analysis by Bishop, Rands, and Holley (1982) demonstrates that only a few of the multiple loci where Chablekal ceramics were produced are represented in the Piedras Negras assemblage. One possible explanation is that particular trade ties were maintained between the communities of manufacture and the individuals or corporate groups that moved the ceramics to market in the Piedras Negras kingdom (see also Triadan and Inomata, Chapter 17; Rice, Chapter 25).

In contrast, many thousands of fragments of the slightly later fine-paste ceramics of the Tres Naciones and Altar groups have been found at Yaxchilán, near where they may have been manufactured (Cabadas-Báez et al. 2017; Forné et al. 2010; López Varela 1989; cf. Bishop et al. 1982), while only small quantities have been found in limited locations at Piedras Negras. This suggests to us that such materials were not widely accessible through markets and may instead have been imported to Piedras Negras as gifts, tribute, or taxes (Muñoz 2004, 2006). On the other hand, the presence of imitation fine orange ceramics at Piedras Negras and hinterland sites El Porvenir and El Infiernito in higher proportions than the Altar group may be due to efforts by potters to provide access to similar wares (Kingsley et al. 2012; Muñoz 2004:24–25).

The distinct limits of distribution in pottery do not reflect challenges to its transportation. After all, we find small quantities of finely made trade wares imported from Yucatán and the Pacific littoral in and around Piedras Negras well into the early Postclassic Period (Kingsley et al. 2012). Nor do they simply reflect the limits of technological know-how. Rather, we argue that they represent choices by consumers of pottery available in markets that they frequented. Sites of production and exchange, like Budsilhá with its obsidian workshop, exhibit a greater mixture of regional ceramic styles than is evident at Piedras Negras itself, presumably because its residents maintained relatively wide-ranging participation in regional markets where their obsidian products were exchanged.

In particular, La Selva, the site of an elite residence near Budsilhá, shows a relatively high proportion of quartz-tempered, thin-walled jars associated with Palenque, Chinikihá, and their environs during the Late Classic Period (Jiménez 2013; Schroder and Jiménez 2016). Additionally, examples of these same forms, but made of local carbonate pastes, have been documented at La Selva.

This distribution, along with the blending of different forms and technologies of production, can best be explained by the availability of these ceramics at markets along the frontier of the kingdoms of Piedras Negras and Palenque.

Other Materials

Our archaeological evidence for trade and marketing of more perishable materials is scant. We have to turn to epigraphy, iconography, and a bit more supposition to flesh out the picture. Cacao, a marketed luxury in later periods, thrives in the Usumacinta Basin and may have been raised in scattered plots by small growers or raised on elite plantations, as suggested for Belize (e.g., McAnany et al. 2002). Pelts, feathers, medicinal plants, and other forest products as well as many other products were likely also collected for trade. They may simply escape our ability to trace their production, movement, and use in the archaeological record.

Conclusion

In summary, we suggest that Piedras Negras and neighboring kingdoms of the Maya west had at least three major economic domains with areas of overlap that remain to be fully defined. First, while dynastic rulers received luxury goods in direct tax and tribute, and likely sponsored and taxed central markets, the royal court otherwise had very limited oversight of much of the economy. Markets at the dynastic center may have been one of the few loci for exchange in the Early Classic Period, but over the course of the Late Classic Period other markets outside the direct purview of the kings and queens appeared throughout the polity.

Second, we argue that the movement of some truly long-distance goods, like obsidian, ceramic "trade wares," and likely jade, was regulated by exchange networks outside of the royal courts centered on noble courts at places like the site of Budsilhá. As Masson and Peraza (2014) have argued for Postclassic Mayapán, we believe that Classic Period elites similarly maintained the interpersonal long-distance connections and sponsored trade expeditions that fostered the flow of goods to their households. Raw or partially processed materials were then worked into finished products by expert artisans under the watchful eye of elites and then exchanged through regional markets (Inomata 2001; Inomata and Triadan 2000; Kovacevich 2006).

Third, individuals and small-scale collectives at the household or village level produced maize in quantities typically exceeding the needs of the household, as well as other foodstuffs, bone and chert tools, honey, textiles, dried fish, meat, pelts, and perishable forest products, among other goods. They must have consumed some portion of these at the home, while some went to taxes collected by local lords or as gifts to kin and neighbors or were exchanged in simple person-to-person barter. Some portion also went to be exchanged in marketplaces.

Finally, the participation of farmers, commoners, and courtiers from a range of corporate groups in the kingdom helped to foster trust among participants in the market who might otherwise rarely come into contact with one another. During the Early Classic Period, marketing activities largely took place in the dynastic capital, which fostered the functions of the state. As populations grew over the course of the Late Classic Period, as movement across the landscape become more difficult as a result of interpolity conflict, and as local markets provided access outside the capital to many of the same goods and services that were found at Piedras Negras, trust became more fragmented, adversely impacting the coherence of the state itself. We are not arguing that more rural markets brought about the collapse of the Piedras Negras kingdom. Rather, the dynamics of market participation were yet another important component of political behavior, which we plan to explore further in upcoming excavations at Piedras Negras. It is quite evident that understanding the nuts and bolts of the marketplace will give us more than merely economic insights into the rise and fall of Classic Period kingdoms.

24

A Stone Duty?

Flake Ritual Deposits and the Missing Workshops of the Maya Lowlands

CHLOÉ ANDRIEU

The question of the organization of lithic production during the Classic Period was very controversial in the 1990s, largely because Maya workshops of all kinds appeared so scarce or difficult to find (Moholy-Nagy 1990; Potter and King 1995; P. Rice 1987a). Lithic analysis played an important role in this debate because it is particularly well adapted for determining both production and distribution patterns (Aldenderfer et al. 1989; Clark 2003; Speal 2009). In that debate, the scarcity of workshops in the Maya area in general, and their absence from Maya civic-ceremonial centers in particular, has often been emphasized and discussed (Potter and King 1995; P. Rice 1987a, 2009; but see Cap, Chapter 22). These data, in their time, supported a very important argument used to define Maya economic organizations. In fact, when there was still a decentralist vs. centralist opposition in that debate (Aoyama 2001; Potter and King 1995), the lack of Maya workshops in the epicenters was very often used as an argument in considering that Maya economies were at the very least decentralized, with a low level of specialization and low levels of exchange of daily goods (Arnauld 2005; McAnany 1993b; P. Rice 1987a; Webster 1985), as opposed to prestige items that were more clearly centralized (Potter and King 1995; P. Rice 1987a; Tourtellot and Sabloff 1972). However, recent studies have shown that Maya economies were more complex and diverse than anything that could be encompassed by the centralist/decentralist debate (A. Chase and D. Chase 2004; Demarest et al. 2014). A growing number of studies also support the idea that exchanges in the Mayan area were probably much more important during the Classic Period than previously thought (King, ed. 2015; Masson and Freidel 2013; McAnany 2010).

Today the question of the degree of elite involvement in the Classic economy is still under debate (Clark 2003; King, ed. 2015; Masson and Freidel 2013). During these last ten years, most of the work on the Maya economy has dealt with patterns of exchanges. Marketplaces in particular have become a major topic lately, while more and more works show that exchanges, even of daily goods, were probably much more important than previously thought (King, ed. 2015; Masson and Freidel 2013; McAnany 2010; L. Shaw 2012). The popular view that the Maya classic economy differed from central Mexico by lacking commercialized exchange has now been challenged (Hirth and Pillsbury, ed. 2013; King, ed. 2015). The implications of this new perspective on Maya exchange systems have fully considered the organization of production. Logically, if there were more exchanges than previously thought, then more surplus production should be recognized. Here I refer to specialization in the sense of production in higher quantities than for household consumption: in other words, production for exchange (Costin 1991, 2001, see also Masson et al. 2016). If we want to understand the structure of these exchanges, we need to have a clear idea of the way production was handled and therefore need to reconsider the old question of the lack of workshops in the Maya epicenters and their scarcity in the Maya lowlands.

In this chapter I examine the practice of depositing specific flakes in a royal or elite context and stress that this practice should also be studied for its economic impact on the organization of production. I also suggest that it could indicate a form of tribute offered as a duty by certain workshops. Such a hypothesis enables us to overcome the opposition between centralists and noncentralists, or the control versus independent hypothesis, because it would indicate that both systems coexisted in a same city.

The Misidentification of the Maya Workshops

Workshops are defined as places where craftspeople produced goods in a larger quantity than for the producer's own consumption (Clark 1986, 1997, 2003; Hester and Shafer 1992; Shafer and Hester 1983;). A "workshop" therefore implies a quantitative evaluation of production, compared to an estimation of a quantity consumed by each household (Clark 1986). However, as various authors have stressed, the scarcity of Maya workshops is probably due in part to causes that are structural to certain organizations of production: for instance, if specialization was of low intensity (or resources were scarce) in certain regions, fewer concentrations would exist or they would be harder to recognize (P. Rice 2009). The existence of systems such as itinerant craftspeople that are very difficult to observe in archaeological records could also go a long way to explain the absence of workshops, as shown in southern Campeche for the Late Classic Period, for instance (Andrieu 2013). Finally, the tendency for such workshops to be located in the periphery of the cities, in zones that have been less excavated, could also explain the lack of workshop visibility, as archaeologists still tend to study civic ceremonial centers more than peripheral settlements.

However, another reason for this apparent scarcity of known workshops in the Maya lowlands could be the complex systems of reuse and relocation of the debitage, especially in urban contexts. Lithic and ceramic waste were reused in construction fill for utilitarian reasons in the Mayan area and were also intentionally deposited in caches and burials. Moholy-Nagy (1990, 1997) is the first to have underlined the importance of certain strong concentrations of obsidian and chert production waste in ritual contexts. She stressed the fact that these concentrations of debitage in ritual elite context could be also secondary deposits taken from workshops and on this basis suggested that a distinction be made between what would be a primary and a secondary workshop, the latter representing a deposit of relocated workshop waste. This proposal was highly criticized at the time, leading to a whole debate on the relevance of distinguishing between the place where the knapper actually sat and worked and the middens where the debitage was disposed (Healan 1992; Moholy-Nagy 1992; Hester and Shafer 1992). However, Moholy-Nagy was not referring to that distinction (Clark 2003), but rather to a far more complex process than the difference between the primary knapping locus and workshop middens: the very ritual pattern of depositing great quantities, sometimes tons, of lithic debitage above or within royal burial chambers or under stelae—a behavior that Mayanists have regularly documented (Johnson 2016:329).

Interestingly, since Moholy-Nagy's work, the high concentrations of debitage in symbolic contexts within the epicenters have barely been taken into account in the study of the Maya economic organization, although the question of the relationship between power and the economy during the Classic Period is still a major issue and we mostly rely on spatial correlations to discuss such questions (Clark 2003). Lithic debitage is commonly found in caches and burials (W. Coe 1959) but also in the so-called special deposits that include concentrations of obsidian and chert production waste found among royal or elite burials or under stelae (Moholy-Nagy 1997). The term "special deposits" refers to the fact that these contexts do not correspond strictly to caches or funeral offerings. Very dense concentrations of flakes are also deposited together in strange contexts such as on top of elite burials. Such deposits differ from the normal construction fill material in that they are very dense, with compact amounts of flakes that are never mixed together with ceramic or other debris, unlike the normal construction fill material. The chert and obsidian are separated, and even sometimes stratified, as observed at Tikal (W. Coe 1990 2:336). This peculiar feature type contrasts with construction fill material and was clearly intentional. The ritual practice of depositing flakes instead of finished objects was a recurring behavior (Eberl 2005:98).

Many hypotheses have been formulated about the symbolic meaning of this practice (Baudez 2002:233–234; Calligeris 1998; M. Coe 1988:232). Coe (1988) first noted that these deposits are often layered, perhaps representing the different strata of the underworld. More recently, other authors suggest that these features could be a representation of the Earth Monster (Fitzsimmons 2009) or related to a cult to the sun god (Źrałka et al. 2017). Others insist that depositing mostly production waste meant that the value of what was deposited resided more in the symbol of the raw material than in the form of the offered objects and that the raw material functioned as metaphors of different cosmogonic entities (Baudez 2002; Calligeris 1998). It has also been suggested that such a practice was meant to warn future architects about the location of a burial nearby (Hall 1989). However, this interpretation does not explain why debitage is also very common in cache deposits. Still others have suggested that the presence of flakes and production waste in ritual deposits is an indication that certain production activities were ritualized, such as eccentric manufacture (Hruby 2006, 2007).

Economic interpretations hypotheses have also been offered. Concentrations of specific debitage in symbolic contexts implied a form of economic control over certain aspects of production (Andrieu 2009a; Andrieu et al. 2011; Moholy-Nagy 1997, 2003a) or distribution of obsidian (Aoyama 2001; Hruby 2006; Johnson 2016). But the economic impact of this practice has not been fully explored, and intersite comparisons are needed. In lithic analysis every stage of debitage can be analyzed and identified, so it is particularly well suited to analyzing steps in the production process as well as the types of products made (Clark 1986). Therefore, a logical first question regarding this practice would be to determine what production process or *chaîne opératoire* is reflected in ritually deposited flakes.

Comparisons of the Technological Attributes
of Symbolic Flake Deposits

In order to gain a better understanding of this practice in terms of organization of the production, I assembled information on 67 flake deposits from 26 Classic era Maya lowland sites for which a description of the deposited material was available (Andrieu 2009b). From these, I selected the deposits with more than 50 flakes, with the idea that this degree of concentration is more likely to yield significant information regarding production characteristics (Andrieu 2009b; Andrieu et al. 2011). The discovery of only a single flake or even 10 diagnostic flakes from a single secondary context would not be enough to indicate whether a tool was produced in situ in a ritual setting. I selected 34 burial deposits documented from over 20 sites. Table 24.1 lists the source materials for this study.

The comparative sample underscores the fact that ritual debitage deposits are clearly associated with royal or elite contexts during the Early and Late Classic Periods. It is even more interesting that these curious deposits of flakes and cores from high-elite contexts were composed of debitage from the same production process or *chaîne opératoire* (Leroi-Gourhan 1945). Trachman and Titmus (2003:108, 116) analyzed a few obsidian deposits from Dos Hombres and Lamanai, concluding that they derived from blade production. The same conclusion was reached in a study of a sample of 3,000 flakes and cores from three Late Classic deposits in Yaxchilán, pertaining to two burial deposits and one stela cache (Brokmann 2000:118). Moholy-Nagy (2003a:34) studied a sample of 2,000 pieces from Burial 200 at Tikal, the majority of which consisted of prismatic blades production debris. Aoyama (2001:352) reports an Early Classic deposit found in the Gran Corniza Platform at Copán that contained 4,835 pieces of obsidian. He estimates that this production corresponds to the debitage of 16 prismatic cores. Payson Sheets (1983:96) analyzed a sample of 1,356 pieces from a deposit at Quiriguá containing several thousand obsidian fragments in a cache in the acropolis; it was also mostly composed of waste related to blade production. Johnson (2016:325–327) performed a full and detailed analysis of obsidian debitage in burial and cache contexts at Caracol and reached the same conclusions.

Ceremonial chert deposits also consist of production debris that is similar among sites compared. Except at La Corona, where my analysis of lithic material above royal Burial 6 identified burned debitage deriving from hard percussion techniques (Andrieu and Roche 2015), every other comparative context

Table 24.1. Burials covered with lithic debitage, in addition to four caches and deposits over ten sites

Site	Preclassic	Early Classic	Late Classic	Source
Altar de Sacrificios			Tomb 128	Willey 1972:180
Altun Ha		Tomb E-1/2 Tomb 4/7		Welsh 1988:292, 293
Baking Pot			Burial 1 Burial 2	Audet 2006:176–179, 186
Bonampak			Tomb 2	Tovalín et al. 2014:46–47
Buenavista del Cayo		Burial 384-1		Yaeger et al. 2015
			Burial 88B11	Taschek and Ball 1992:492
Caracol		Burial 24 Burial SD. C87E1		A. Chase and D. Chase 1987:15, 43, 61; D. Chase and A. Chase 1996:67–68, 75
Chau Hiix			Tomb 1	Geller 2014:24
La Corona		Burial 6		Andrieu and Roche 2015
Dos Hombres		Burial, Structure B-16		Trachman and Titmus 2003:108
Dos Pilas			Burial 30	Demarest et al. 1991:20
El Perú–Waka'		Burial 8	Burial 60	Lee 2005
Lamanai		Burial N9-56		Pendergast 1981:39
La Milpa		Number of burials not specified, Early Classic		Hammond and Tourtellot 2006:97
Nakum		Burial 8		Źrałka et al. 2017
Piedras Negras		Burial 10 Burial 13		Hruby 2006:315–322
Río Azul		Burial 1 Burial 19 Burial 23		R.E.W. Adams 1986:420; Hall 1989:54, 109, 177
Tamarindito			Burial in Str. 44	Demarest 2006
Tikal		Burial 125 Burial 23 Burial 24	Burial 116 Burial 196	Moholy-Nagy 1997:293; W. Coe 1990:2:336, 540, 543, 607; Hellmuth 1967
Uaxactún	Burial A20 Burial A22			A. Smith 1950:96, 101; Valdés and Fahsen 1995:202
Yaxchilán			Burials 52, 50	Brokmann 2000:108, 112

Table 24.2. Deposits with lithic debitage

Site	Preclassic	Early Classic	Late Classic	Source
Altar de Sacrificios		Cache 6	Cache 2 under Stela 16	Willey 1972:180, 212
Lamanai			Cache N10-43	Pendergast 1981:41
Calakmul			Cache 8	Carrasco 2003:158
Holmul				Hruby et al. 2006:328
Pusilhá			Stela E	Joyce 1932:17
Tres Islas		Estela 1 Estela 2 Estela 3		Barrios 2006:62
Quiriguá			Cache in the Acropolis	Sheets 1983:96
Tikal		Cache 120 Cache 8		W. Coe 1990:214, 324, 426
Yaxhá			Under Stela 30	P. Rice 1984:192
Yaxchilán			Deposit 36, Under Stela 10	Brokmann 2000:118

contained chert debitage related to later stage bifacial production. At Holmul, for instance, an offering of thousands of chert and chert flakes from a Late Classic deposit was composed of mostly bifacial thinning flakes (Hruby et al. 2005). Hruby's analysis of flakes from Burial 10 at Piedras Negras also revealed primarily bifacial thinning flakes (Hruby 2006:319); the same is true for Burial 13 debris at Piedras Negras (Table 24.2; Hruby 2006:321). Hruby emphasized that the entire production process was not represented and that refitting the flakes together was not possible. Examples of such flake features from special deposits at Tikal were studied by Clark and Parry, who similarly reported a "predominance of biface thinning flakes" (quoted in Moholy-Nagy 1991:196). Similarly, Taschek and Ball (1992:492) report mostly soft hammer bifacial thinning flakes from a lithic deposit above Late Classic Burial 88B11 at Buenavista del Cayo.

Whenever we look at the composition of other flake deposits in elite contexts in the lowlands (where a description is available), the same production stage is almost always represented. Obsidian deposits are invariably composed of irregular blades and polyhedral cores (i.e., waste from the production of prismatic blades), while chert deposits consist of mostly bifacial thinning flakes. These features indicate a clear and specific selection of certain flakes. They are not random samples of debris; instead, they are from specific production phases and processes that are not usually found concentrated in construction fill (Andrieu 2009b, 2013). These deposits represent workshop production waste that was reused in secondary contexts. Even if there were clear symbolic reasons for this practice (M. Coe 1988), the deposits also provide us with important information about craft organization. This is all the more interesting because this specific lithic waste is almost never found in concentrations in other contexts, except for workshops.

Case Studies

When workshop mounds have been analyzed and studied, they tend to be oriented toward the production of either bifacial tools (Hester and Shafer 1984; Lewis 2003; Masson 2001b; Potter 1993; Roemer 1991; Whittaker et al. 2009) or prismatic blades (Neivens and Libbey 1976; Roemer 1991). These two categories of lithic objects were widely distributed in most lowland houses, albeit in different quantities from one region to another (Andrieu 2009b, 2013), implying that both their production and exchange were frequently and regularly undertaken. While concentrations of such production waste are related to two manufacturing processes, symbolic flake concentrations likely reflect the economic importance of stone tool economies to Maya society. In other words, it is not necessary to choose between opposing ritual or economic explanations for understanding secondary ritual debris deposits. Such links are explored in ritual economy frameworks (Wells 2006). To demonstrate such links, in the following section I compare ritual deposits from two different cases, including Early Classic Naachtún and Late Classic (Cancuén).

Naachtún: A Unique Concentration of Bifacial Thinning Flakes

A single type of flake deposit was found in Naachtún in northeastern Petén (Philippe Nondédéo and Lilian Garrido, dirs., Centre National de la Recherche Scientifique and Instituto de Arqueología e Historia) and at El Juilín, a settlement near Naachtún, located 4 km from the epicenter. Various flake deposits were found there associated with an Early Classic stela. There were four dense concentrations of chert flakes: under the stela, in the construction fill of the floor associated with the stela, in a cache in the platform on which the monument rested, and in the fill of a crypt burial that was also associated with

Table 24.3. Composition of the lithic material found in the El Juilín (Naachtún) Stela deposits

Material	Quantity	Percentage
Large hard flakes (between 8 and 10 cm)	20	0.20
Medium hard percussion flakes (between 8 and 6 cm)	38	0.50
Small hard percussion flakes (between 6 and 3 cm)	114	1.50
Large soft percussion flake (between 8 and 10 cm)	29	0.30
Medium soft percussion flakes (between 8 and 6 cm)	412	5.10
Small hard percussion flakes (between 6 and 3 cm)	7285	91.00
Thin biface preform	8	0.10
Laminar cores	11	0.10
Blade fragments	46	0.60
Very small flakes, soft percussion flakes and fragments (less than 3 cm)	22	0.30
Total	7985	100

the monument (Andrieu 2015). All these various features dated to the Early Classic Period. My analysis of the material from these deposits showed that the large majority of the 7,985 fragments of chert collected in these contexts represent bifacial production waste (Table 24.3). No significant difference was found in the composition in any of the different deposit contexts excavated (Andrieu 2016).

Despite the presence of a small percentage of blade production waste (0.6%) that was evenly distributed over the four contexts of flake deposit, the majority of the material collected corresponds to bifacial production waste. However, when compared with experimental data on the production of thin bifaces (Chauchat and Pelegrin 2004), or even thick bifaces (Andrieu 2013), it clearly appears that the first stages are very underrepresented, while small bifacial thinning flakes of later stages are the most common (91%). This could indicate that these flakes correspond to the reduction of preforms, a hypothesis supported by the presence of eight thin biface preforms in these same contexts as well as by the lack of cortical flakes ($n = 28$). The absence of finished objects is also striking, showing yet again the importance of depositing waste and not objects in certain rituals. Therefore these deposits, like all the other chert flake deposits referred to in this chapter, are related to bifacial production. Regarding the economic impact of such a practice, the interesting data lie in the comparison with the rest of the lithic collection from Naachtún. In fact, bifacial thinning flakes are extremely scarce across the rest of site, whether in residential structures, burial contexts, or civic ceremonial buildings. In the Naachtún project's seven years of excavations, only 786 bifacial thinning flakes were collected over the entire site, representing less than 0.1% of the Naachtún lithic production. No concentration of more than 7 flakes was found in any residential excavation unit (Andrieu 2016). This finding suggests that bifaces were not produced by each household; instead they were acquired from specialist producers (Andrieu 2013). Therefore the ritual flake deposits represent unique concentrations of such production waste for the entire site as a whole, where no workshop has yet been found.

Cancuén

Another interesting case study was carried out in Cancuén (Arthur Demarest and Paola Torres, dirs., Vanderbilt University, IDAEH), in the Pasión region at the frontier between the Maya highlands and lowlands. There two major flake deposits were found dating to the Late Classic Period.

Kaan Maax

The first feature was found inside the burial of Kaan Maax, the last king of the site, dating to the end of the Late Classic Period, around 800 AD (Fahsen and Barrientos 2006). Here many flakes of obsidian (n = 695) and cores (n = 57) were found at the king's feet, while 1,049 fragments of chert were found around his head (Barrientos et al. 2005). The analysis of the lithic deposit shows that every flake in this grave is related to very specific productions. All the obsidian flakes come from a prismatic blade production process. Most of the materials found are irregular blades (n = 213), with some core rejuvenation flakes (n = 199), prismatic cores fragments (n = 53), and, interestingly, a number of destruction flakes (n = 92). Destruction flakes had no technical purpose other than destroying the core. Their presence implies that core destruction was part of the ritual. Because of this ultimate stage, the assemblage is a bit anomalous compared to others discussed. However, the debris found represents the same production process. The only missing element is the finished object: the prismatic blades themselves.

Table 24.4. Description of the chert material found in Kaan Maax's (Cancuén) burial

Material	Quantity	Percentage
Large hard percussion flakes (between 8 and 10 cm)	1	0.1
Medium hard percussion flakes (between 8 and 6 cm)	1	0.1
Small hard percussion flakes (between 6 and 3 cm)	43	4.1
Large soft percussion flake (between 8 and 10 cm)	0	0.0
Medium soft percussion flakes (between 8 and 6 cm)	6	0.6
Small soft percussion flakes (between 6 and 3 cm)	701	66.8
Very small flakes, soft percussion flakes and fragments (less than 3 cm)	293	28.0
Thin biface preform	4	0.5
Total	1049	100.0

The same coherence is apparent when looking at the chert assemblage. I distinguished three different kinds of cherts, all very fine and homogeneous. All debris reflect the same production process. The majority of the 1,045 chert flakes found in this grave are small bifacial thinning flakes from the production of arrow points or laurel leaf bifaces (Table 24.4). Once again, we note the presence of 4 thin biface preforms.

As for the Naachtún deposits, the primary stages are clearly underrepresented, as we did not find any other kind of percussion flakes or even large bifacial thinning flakes; curiously, no refitting was possible either. However, once again the flakes came from the same bifacial production process. Here too these flakes deposited in Kaan Maax's burial were not a random assortment of flakes but instead represented a specific aspect of production and lacked finished tools.

El Achiote

Another impressive example from Cancuén was beneath a stela at El Achiote, a peripheral settlement 4 km from Cancuén where 8 eccentrics, 4,050 chert bifacial thinning flakes, as well as 682 complete obsidian prismatic cores were found. The obsidian cores are all prismatic cores, related to prismatic blade production. If we apply the ratio of 100 blades per core that is sometimes used (Aoyama 2001), these cores would have produced 68,200 blades. However, their measurements vary from 1.5 to 4 cm in diameter, meaning that they are not all totally

Table 24.5. Description of the chert material found in El Achiote's (Cancuén) stela deposit

Type of flakes	Quantity	Percentage
Large hard percussion flakes (between 8 and 10 cm)	7	0.2
Medium hard percussion cortical flakes (between 8 and 6 cm)	72	1.8
Large soft percussion flake (between 8 and 10 cm)	10	0.2
Medium soft percussion cortical flakes (between 8 and 6 cm)	17	0.4
Medium soft percussion flakes (between 8 and 6 cm)	30	0.7
Small hard percussion cortical flakes (between 6 and 3 cm)	93	2.3
Small hard percussion flakes (between 6 and 3 cm)	212	5.2
Small soft percussion cortical flakes (between 6 and 3 cm)	375	9.3
Small soft percussion flakes (between 6 and 3 cm)	1942	48.0
Very small flakes, soft percussion flakes and fragments (less than 3 cm)	1287	31.8
Thin biface preform	5	100
Total	4050	

exhausted. Even if we apply very conservative estimates of 25 blades per core, the cores from this deposit would still have produced around 17,050 blades, many more than the 8,302 obsidian prismatic blades collected in the entire site.

The analysis of the chert flakes showed once again that they are related to bifacial production (Table 24.5). The composition of this deposit is a little different because cortical flakes were included, which were absent in the other deposits. But the same pattern is observed: a few thin biface preforms are present, and the last stages of biface production are overrepresented. If we compare the material from these deposits with the bifacial thinning flakes and the cores found in the rest of the site, the concentration of the ritual deposit is distinctive. Across the rest of Cancuén, only 10% of the prismatic cores were found in general contexts. Most showed signs of reworking for the removal of secondary flake debitage. Bifacial thinning flakes are more evenly distributed at this site. They were utilized and modified into small drills in workshop settings at Cancuén. For this reason, their presence within the epicenter does not reflect thin bifacial production but an industry geared toward the fabrication of drills (Andrieu et al. 2011). Even so, no concentration of more than 600 flakes was found in nondeposit (general or nonritual) contexts, which makes the El Achiote the densest concentration of production waste in the entire site.

Flake Deposits and Workshops

At both Naachtún and Cancuén these ritual deposits were composed of the same flakes, coming from the same production process (bifacial and prismatic blade production) as other flake deposits described in the published literature. In both cases, concentrated debris representing specific production stages or trajectories was not concentrated elsewhere at the same sites. In all cases, certain stages of production were overrepresented, while others are underrepresented. These inconsistencies indicate that the deposits do not correspond to in situ production but rather that they were probably taken from workshop contexts. Therefore, without necessarily contradicting previous symbolic interpretations, these flake concentrations also reflect ties to practices of production and exchange. Representing secondary contexts, these deposits do not tell us anything about the original location in which the tools were made. The lithic waste was probably gathered and transported in order to be deposited in a royal burial or under stelae. But these deposits imply a relationship between elites and a certain types of production activity. One possible explanation would be that this indicates a form of control that elites had over production (Andrieu 2009a, 2013; Clark and Parry 1990; Costin 1991; Moholy-Nagy 2008b). However, the word "control" encompasses such a wide variety of economic situations (Clark 2003; Costin 2001; Demarest et al. 2014) that it is probably not a very useful term.

Concentrations of debitage from chert bifacial production and obsidian prismatic blade production are found in localities other than in symbolic contexts, in what appear to be independent workshops at the periphery of major cities. The contrast between these two types of contexts is striking. They were probably linked to different social status settings, although the two context types sometimes coexist in the same cities. El Pedernal, for instance, less than 1 km from the city of Río Azul, is a small site, considered to be a satellite, where a number of biface workshops have been found (R.E.W. Adams 1990:30; Lewis 2003; Potter 1993:286). Río Azul exhibits various flake deposits containing debitage from the same production trajectories (R.E.W. Adams 1986:420) as those documented at El Pedernal. This pattern could indicate that at least two coexisting systems of production and distribution of the same tools and debris were present in the same city at the same time: one providing the palace, for example, and the other for the rest of the population. The major question to be resolved is the relationship between the known workshops found in the periphery of the cities and these special flake deposits in royal or elite contexts.

Discussion: A Lithic Duty? The Tribute Hypothesis

It has been suggested many times that some crafting activities were ritual actions in themselves (Hruby 2007; Reents-Budet 1998). Even flakes were often treasured, confirming this ritualization of the action of producing. As a matter of fact, in the case of these flake deposits, the action seems to have had greater value than the product itself, which frequently is not found in ritual contexts. However, not all crafting actions were ritualized. If we look at the little-known lithic workshops corresponding to the very same production activities, no hint of any ritual whatsoever is associated with those deposits. In these known workshops this same lithic waste was left in domestic trash pits with no special treatment associated with it (Lewis 2003; Neivens and Libbey 1976:145–147; Potter 1993). This clearly shows that not all crafting actions were ritualized, but only a certain portion of them: probably crafting actions in a special social context, which leads us to suppose that not all these productions were performed in the same social context. It is also clear that the focus of the ritual lay more on the action itself: the production appears to have had greater value than the finished objects, which are always absent from these special deposits. Interestingly, these two very different contexts of discovery of the same lithic waste are sometimes found in the same sites for the same periods (such as in the case of Río Azul or Buenavista del Cayo), implying that the two social contexts of production could exist together and do not correspond to different aspects of economic organization. Taken together, they could be explained by a form of ritualized production of certain tools that would have been made for a specific event. That would be a ritualized assigned production (Hirth 1996) or in other words a tribute in action or a lithic duty. This enables me to suggest a model whereby some knapping actions were made as a tribute, with trash ritually stored in special deposits.

A strong argument in favor of a duty system is the etymology of the word used to designate the tribute: *patan*, which comes from *pat*, meaning "to do, to fabricate, to create" (Stuart 1995). We know that tribute was very important in Classic Maya economies and is one of the most represented scenes on classic Maya polychrome vases. However, we have never really studied the way this system of vertical exchanges functioned with the rest of the economy (McAnany 2013). We should probably explore further the possibility that there was a system of tribute not only between cities but among the members of a same political entity (that would be taxes in fact, as emphasized by M. Smith 2014). That would help us to understand the relationships unifying the various units of a sociopolitical entity. Although the Mexica system of taxes was probably different, we should take into account that each *calpul* was paying a tax. Certain *calpulli* of artisans in particular had to pay their tribute in working time for their *atlepetl*. The known Maya area workshops are often found at a distance of less than 5 km from an epicenter, which could indicate that the same workshops were producing lithic tools and giving a part of their labor or working time to the epicenter. An important consequence of this model (if confirmed) would be that it could help us to overcome the long-standing opposition between the "centralist" and "noncentralist" hypotheses, which would no longer make sense, given that both systems would have coexisted. For further research, we would need to quantify the proportion of this assigned production relative to the rest of the production and understand what it implies in terms of redistribution. A few calculations are already possible: if compared with experimental data (see Andrieu 2013; Chauchat and Pelegrin 2004) in Cancuén, the chert debitage found in Kaan Maax's royal burial corresponds quantitatively to the production of about 10 and 29 knives. Such a quantity could easily have been made in a ritual as a form of tribute. The chert debitage found under the stela would represent a little more, between 39 to 115 knives, which does not represent a high proportion of the knives in the site and still could have been made in a ritual as a tribute. Barely 20% of the total number of knives from the site would have been produced in that social context. However, the obsidian collection in these contexts is more problematic. Taken together, Kaan Maax and the cache in Cancuén represent a concentration of more than 90% of the obsidian cores found in the site and gathered in an elite ritual context. This would then have a much stronger economic impact in terms of production centralization, which has yet to be understood. However, such differences enable us to show the diversity of Maya economic systems in a concrete and calculable way, which we now need to study and quantify systematically.

Conclusion

Very little attention has been paid lately to the study of production, partly because of the lack of known workshops (with a few notable exceptions, such as Lewis 2003; Masson 2001b; Masson et al. 2016; Roemer 1991; Shafer and Hester 1983; Whittaker et al. 2009). The recent focus on distribution patterns has opened up new perspectives on Maya economies. The next step, in my opinion, is to return to the study of production. More work should be carried out on the variable contexts and contents of flake deposits, from both workshops and ritual features, which can reveal valuable economic information and key links between ordinary production and symbolism in the ritual economy. It is as important to study these special flake deposits as it is to investigate workshops; together they contribute to a better understanding of the organization of production during the Classic Period. My initial assessment in this chapter suggests that tribute, and a possible duty system of tribute, was probably a significant element of Classic era Maya city economies, but this mechanism and its impacts on the broader system of the mobilization of resources should be more systematically investigated, quantified, and understood. The technological and quantitative study of special flake deposits and workshops contributes significantly toward better models of the economic relationships of peripheries and epicenters.

25

Terminal Classic Interactions between the Western Petén Lakes Chain and the Western Lowlands

PRUDENCE M. RICE

Of the myriad inputs and outputs of Maya economies, I discuss only one here: a rather scarce type of pottery in the Petén lakes area called Jato Black-on-Gray. What can this small "nut" among the "nuts and bolts" of the business of Terminal Classic economic exchange in central Petén tell us that we don't already know? The answer to this question demands a wide-angle lens. Throughout Mesoamerica, the Late and Terminal Classic or Epiclassic Periods (ca. 700–950 BC) were characterized by social, political, and economic transformations, bookended by the collapses of Teotihuacán and the southern lowland Mayas and the northern florescence in the Maya lowlands. All these transformations had complex causes and consequences, including migrations, new patterns of "international" commerce, development of new urban power centers, and the spread of the Quetzalcoatl "cult." Unsurprisingly, new and different interaction spheres emerged. The central lakes region of the Department of Petén, northern Guatemala, was hardly isolated from these changes in the surrounding regions. Here I discuss Jato Black-on-Gray pottery in the Terminal Classic in the western lakes district as evidence of poorly known interactions with the western lowlands.

Background: The Central Petén Lakes and the Western Lowlands in the Terminal Classic

The lakes district comprises a string of eight bodies of water of varying sizes extending about 80 km east-west through the Petén lowland forests. The region's inhabitants experienced the demographic upheavals of the southern lowland Terminal Classic, although generally to a much lesser degree than in other areas

(D. Rice and P. Rice 1990). In particular, the large basin of Lake Petén Itzá witnessed more and greater demographic continuities than the eastern lakes. The basin appears to have experienced in-migration of groups from the Petexbatun/Pasión area (D. Rice 1986), marked by the introduction of C-shaped structures, defensive settlement patterns, and new weaponry (bows and arrows). At the eastern end of Lake Petén, the port site of Ixlú became an important nexus of interior overland trade and responded to the challenge of intersecting with circumpeninsular coastal commerce by constructing or expanding its facilities (P. Rice and D. Rice 2016).

The Late Classic Río Chixoy-Usumacinta riverine trade route was the core of a major Late Classic economic network joining the highlands, the lowlands, and the Gulf Coast (Demarest et al. 2014). The Middle Usumacinta drainage was dominated by centers such as Yaxchilán and Piedras Negras, plus other sites outside the river basin proper, such as Palenque and Toniná. Yaxchilán in particular was tied to the western Lake Petén Itzá center of Ik'a'/Motul de San José: Yaxchilán's ruler had two wives from Ika'a' (S. Martin and Grube 2008:128). During the Terminal Classic Period, coastal and internal commerce was reorganized from the Chontalpa/Acalán region of the lower Río Usumacinta/Laguna de Términos area. People from the Middle Usumacinta area might have emigrated eastward, including toward Chichén Itzá, as seen by the introduction of carved lintels and fine-paste pottery.

Some groups from the western lowlands, including the Acalán/Chontalpa area, also might have migrated into central Petén. Nonlocal "influences" are long known in Late and Terminal Classic material culture, including monuments with text, multiple registers, pointed tops, decorated borders, squared glyph cartouches, sequential day glyphs, seated gesturing figures, and figures with non-Maya traits (P. Rice 2004:223–226). Some of these innovations may accompany the introduction of a highland (Mexican) Venus-based calendar (Lacadena 2010:384–387) and also complex associations with the emerging Quetzalcoatl "cult." They might have been introduced through the Gulf Coast/Usumacinta trade network.

These interregional economic and political interactions had long-term impacts on language and language change in the Maya lowlands. Numerous loanwords entered Mayan languages, especially Mixe-Zoquean words from the multilingual Gulf Coast/Tabasco/Acalán region (Justeson et al. 1985:69). In Yucatán, east-west dialectal differences in the late books of the *Chilam Balam* likely began in the Terminal Classic (Hofling 2009:77). Contacts between the western lowlands and the lakes region may have contributed Chontal vocabulary to Itzaj (Hofling 2018).

Pottery production and exchange experienced both continuities and changes during these turbulent centuries. The distinct eastern and western ceramic spheres of the Late Classic Period (Forsyth 2005) continue to be evident in the Terminal Classic and especially later in the Postclassic in the lakes region. Arlen Chase's (1983:1215–1216) archaeological study of the Tayasal-Paxcaman region of western Lake Petén Itzá suggested early "co-existence of two ethnic groups" associated with new imported pottery types, including slate ware (some with trickle decoration), Plumbate, and fine paste wares. The occasional presence of Plumbate and Fine Gray paste ware—absent in the eastern lake basins—suggested that the residents of the (western) Lake Petén basin participated in a different trade network (A. Chase 1983:1217). This is evident in the little-known Jato Black-on-Gray type, which drew inspiration from local and imported black and gray wares.

Terminal Classic/Epiclassic Black- and Gray-Ware Ceramics

Among the multiple spheres of political and economic interaction in the Terminal Classic Period, two are evidenced by the distribution of fine paste ceramics: one associated with Fine Gray wares and traditions and another associated with Fine Orange. Widely traded and copied, Fine Orange was manufactured in the Gulf Coast/lower Usumacinta region (e.g., Sabloff 1982) and may be associated with commercial interactions dominated by Acalan. Various groups, types, forms, and decorative schemes in this ware continued through the Postclassic Period. Fine Gray wares present a contrast, with fairly restricted distributions. One reason for the gray wares' restriction might be their origins in the upper/middle regions of the Late Classic Usumacinta trade route. When those polities fell, along with their trading nodes and partners in the southern lowlands, fine gray wares also ceased to be produced.

Fine Gray Ware: Chablekal and Tres Naciones Groups

Gray pottery became prominent in the late Late Classic and Terminal Classic Periods in parts of the Maya lowlands, along with new fine monochromes, slipped and unslipped, along the Gulf Coast. These ceramics, which have markedly different temporal and regional distributions, include Epiclassic slate wares in the northern lowlands and two Fine Gray paste wares.

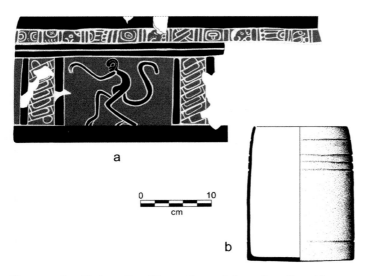

Figure 25.1. Jato Black-on-Gray (Campo Composite) vase from Tayasal Structure T30a. Ht. 18.2 cm; diam. 13.5 cm.

The Chablekal group of Fine Gray paste ware began to be produced in the Gulf Coast region, possibly Tabasco (Golden et al., Chapter 23) in the early eighth century. Forms include tripod plates and small bowls with composite shapes and three or four small round or nubbin supports (Figure 25.1). These occur as monochromes or decorated types with incising, modeling, black or red paint, and fluting, often in combination. Chablekal was rarely found beyond the western parts of both the northern and southern Maya lowlands. At Cancuén in far southern Petén, Chablekal was uncommon in elite structures but composed 15–35% of fine wares in lower-status structures and middens (Callaghan et al. 2004; Forné et al. 2010). It was not a typical part of elite mortuary furniture, although at least one vessel was from a burial. Chablekal has not been identified in central Petén.

Chablekal disappeared and was followed by Tres Naciones Fine Gray ware, a marker for the Terminal Classic Period. Possibly manufactured near Yaxchilán (Golden et al., Chapter 23), Tres Naciones had a fairly restricted distribution, being rare in the northern lowlands, eastern Petén, and Belize but common in southwestern Petén at Ceibal and Altar de Sacrificios, especially as incised *molcajetes* (pottery grater bowls). Tres Naciones has been identified in central Petén only at Nixtún-Ch'ich', in the western Lake Petén Itzá basin. Forms include a hard-fired, narrow-necked jar with a flaring rim and a tan-gray color. A barrel-shaped vase has a "bead rim": its eroded exterior was either fireclouded or had a thin black wash or slip. Two pyriform vase bases and five fragments of an unnamed molded-carved type were also recovered.

In general, in the central Petén lakes region, gray-ware pottery, whether imported (Fine Gray paste wares, slate wares) or local, is always rare. About two dozen unidentified gray-ware sherds have been noted at lakes area sites other than Nixtún-Ch'ich'. At most of these sites, as at Uaxactún and Tikal, Fine Orange paste ware was present, but not Fine Gray.

Black-Slipped Infierno and Achote Ceramic Groups

Two black-slipped ceramic groups are known in Petén in the Late and Terminal Classic Periods. The Carmelita Incised type, of the Late Classic (700–830 AD) Infierno group, is known from Uaxactún, Ceibal, and the Mirador Basin but was not identified at Tikal. Pottery of the Terminal Classic Achote group is present at Tikal, Uaxactún, and Ceibal and was recovered in burials at the first two sites. The paste is fine- to medium-textured, compact, calcite-tempered, and pink to tan in color. Decoration may be incised and gouged-incised; forms include tripod plates, dishes with nubbin feet, pyriform vases with pedestal bases, miniatures, and flasks. Neither the Infierno nor the Achote group was abundant in the central Petén lakes area.

Jato Black-on-Gray Type

Jato Black-on-Gray (hereafter JBG) is a rare—hence largely ignored—Terminal Classic (ca. 830–950 AD) type in central Petén, including Tikal and Uaxactún. In the lakes area, fragments are scarce, although whole pots are frequently found in burials. Forms include cylindrical vases, tripod plates, and straight- and round-sided dishes. These feature black painting, minimally as circumferential rim and/or basal bands, on a medium to dark gray background that may be the matte clay body or a slip. The paste is fine-textured (usually tempered with volcanic ash) and often has a pinkish core.

An unusual Jato Black-on-Gray cylindrical vase was recovered near Structure T30a at Tayasal, on the western end of the Tayasal Peninsula in Lake Petén Itzá (Pugh et al. 2012:14). This vase (Figure 25.2) has broad, black-painted lip, medial, and basal bands. The body is divided into two panels, separated by

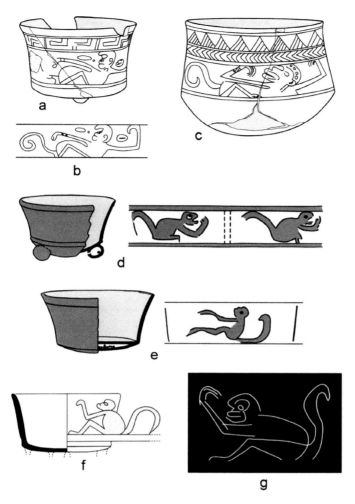

Figure 25.2. Common bowl forms and monkey decoration: (*a*)–(*c*), postslip fine incising on small, red-orange-slipped Terminal Classic bowls from Burial 22, Structure M14-15, El Perú–Waka' (redrawn from Eppich 2007:Figure 9c, d); (*d*) and (*e*) small, fine-incised bowls of Late Classic Chablekal Fine Gray, with roulette-stamping (*d*) and punctations (*e*); note rattle ball in base and support (redrawn from Rands 1973:Figure 21d, e); (*f*) Unnamed Incised Red-on-Brown Dichrome tetrapodal bowl from Ceibal, Tepejilote Phase (redrawn from Sabloff 1975:Figure 285); (*g*), monkey on Late Classic Carmelita Incised bowl (redrawn from Skousen 2009:Figure 23i).

groove-incised guilloches or mat-like motifs. Each panel has a groove-incised, black-painted, dancing spider monkey (*Ateles geoffroyi*), facing left with an upraised left forelimb. Above the panels is a band of gouge-incised pseudo-glyphs with faint traces of cinnabar, also noted in the monkey's foot.

JBG can be considered a syncretistic or hybrid type that shares characteristics of both gray-slipped (Chablekal) and black-slipped (Infierno and Achote) ceramic groups. Shared traits include not only colors but also decorative modes, motifs (monkeys), forms (vases, tripod plates), and uses as suggested by recovery in burial contexts and caches.

Monkey Motifs

Spider monkey images are frequently depicted on these Epiclassic gray and black wares. They are a distinctive feature of Chablekal decoration, incised or sometimes painted with groove-incised outlining, typically (but not exclusively) seated or reclining and facing left. One forelimb or arm is stretched forward; the paw or "hand" may be in several positions (see Figures 25.1, 25.2). The other arm, if shown, is behind the body, usually curled behind the head but sometimes scratching the back.

At Piedras Negras, local painted and incised gray-ware types dating 740–850 AD often featured monkeys, likely emulating Chablekal bowls (Muñoz 2002:9). The loose posture may indicate dancing (Eppich 2007). These primates appear in decorative fields with punctated dots or rocker-stamping filler and are topped by bands with angular chevrons or step-frets.

Carmelita Incised (Infierno group) bowls with monkey motifs are present in the Mirador Basin (Skousen 2009) and at Ceibal. In both areas the slip may grade to gray or brown. At Ceibal three varieties of Carmelita Incised were recognized and feature chevrons, steps, punctations, and postslip incised or groove-incised simians (Sabloff 1975). Some examples are similar to JBG cylinders from Uaxactún. In addition, a bowl of an unnamed dichrome type in an unidentified brown ware was decorated with three seated incised and red-painted monkeys (Figure 25.1f). All these Ceibal vessels were recovered in middens.

At Flores a partially reconstructible Cubeta Incised straight-sided bowl featured a postslip incised seated spider monkey (Figure 25.3c). The creature faced right and had an unusual head, perhaps showing only the large, mask-like area of unpigmented skin around the eyes. Originally there may have been two monkeys, separated by an angular, vertical mat motif as on the Tayasal T30a monkey vase.

Besides monkeys, another motif on some of the black- and gray-ware pottery, although much rarer, is a T-shaped tau or *ik'* sign. *Ik'*-shaped vents were placed on an Achote tripod plate in a burial at Tikal and on Tres Naciones dishes in Tabasco. In the lakes area *ik'*/tau vents appeared on the supports of a JBG tripod

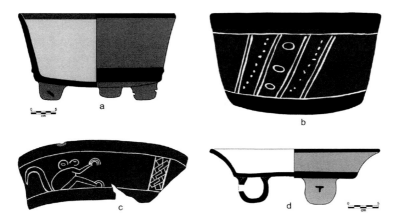

Figure 25.3. Jato Black-on-Gray group and related vessels from the Petén lakes area: (*a*) Jato dish from the Zacpetén mass grave (Operation 1000) at the northwest corner of the Group A temple assemblage: note the basal ridge and diagonal vents in supports; (*b*) and (*c*) vessels from Flores public works excavations (drawn from personal photographs; no scale): (*b*) Trece Gatos Fine-Incised straight-sided dish (see also Gámez 2007:Fig. 7): usewear is evident on the lip; (*c*) partially reconstructible Cubeta Incised (Achote group) straight-sided dish with a postslip monkey and crude vertical braid divider; (*d*), Jato tripod from a burial in Str. Q19 on the eastern of the Quexil Islands (Schwarz 2004:243–246): the interior is slipped black; note *ik'* shaped vents in the supports.

from a burial of a young female at Quexil (Figure 25.3d). A fine-incised JBG sherd from Nixtún-Ch'ich' and another from Ixlú featured an *ajaw* sign.

Classificatory Issues: A JBG Ceramic Group

JBG was originally identified as a type in the Danta ceramic group in the Terminal Classic Tepeu 3 complex of Petén Gloss ware at Uaxactún (R. Smith and Gifford 1966:158, 173). This can now be regarded as a misclassification based on few sherds and few available comparators at the time. With the recovery of more whole vessels and fragments, it is evident that JBG decoration includes not only black painting but also multiple plastic modes—fluting, punctation, prefire and postfire fine incising, groove incising, and gouge incising—alone or in combination.

Comparisons with late black- and gray-slipped or paste-ware ceramic groups and types from northern, western, and southwestern Petén reveal that JBG has a classificatory structure parallel to the black-slipped Achote and Infierno groups and the Chablekal group of Fine Gray. Thus, it is now clear that JBG is best iden-

Table 25.1. Parallel decorated types in the Chablekal, Infierno, Achote, and Jato ceramic groups of the Late and Terminal Classic system

	CERAMIC GROUP					
	Gray Chablekal	Black Infierno		Black Achote	Black-on-Gray Jato	
Dec. Mode	Type	Type	Var.	Type	Type	Variety
Monochrome	X	X		X	Jato Black-on-Gray	Jato
Incised	X	X		X	Trece Gatos Fine-Incised	Prefire
						Postfire
			X		Maranta Groove-Outlined	Maranta
Composite	X		X		Campo Composite (includes black paint plus 2 other modes)	Unspecified
Fluted	X		X			
Gouged-incised				X		
Punctated				X		
Red-painted	X					
Plano-relief		X				
Impressed				X		

tified not as a type but as a distinct, albeit small, ceramic group, with decorative mode providing the basis for type discrimination (Table 25.1).

In decorative modes, the JBG group is closely related to the Late Classic Chablekal ceramic group in Fine Gray ware. Like Chablekal, the JBG group features black painting (especially circumferential bands) frequently combined with plastic decoration: fine incising may be used to create motifs, groove incising may be used to outline black-painted motifs, and gouge incising appears in glyph bands. Monkeys, seen on the Tayasal vase now classified as Campo Composite, are particularly common in Chablekal (Figure 25.1d, e). The decorative layout of this vase follows that of several Terminal Classic decorated types (e.g., in Fine Orange paste ware), with the body of the vase divided into two nearly identical main panels flanked by narrow columns. On the Tayasal vase these vertical frames separating the monkey panels have angular, groove-incised guilloches or mat motifs also seen on the Cubeta Incised (Achote group) monkey dish from Flores (Figure 25.3c). Both are analogs to Telchac Composite in the Chablekal group.

Morphologically, JBG forms—vases, tripod plates, small bowls—follow traditional Petén forms and lack the small, relatively deep, composite-silhouette bowls with out-flaring sides, slightly bulging, rounded base, and three or four supports characteristic of Chablekal. JBG group forms are closest to those in rare Tres Naciones Fine Gray ware, although lacking the common grater bowl or *molcajete* of Tres Naciones at Ceibal and Altar de Sacrificios.

Monkeys and Mortuary Contexts

JBG group pottery is notable for its recovery in mortuary contexts in the Petén lakes region. A Campo Composite vase was found with a burial on the shore of Lake Macanché (Figure 25.4); two Jato tripod dishes were recovered with skeletal remains at Zacpetén (Figure 25.3a); and a Jato tripod was inverted over the head of a female burial on the eastern Quexil Island (Figure 25.3d). At Tayasal a Jato tripod was recovered with an interment of a young female (A. Chase 1983:544) and the Campo Composite monkey vase (Figure 25.2) was likely from a disturbed interment. The Trece Gatos Fine-Incised dish at Flores (Figure 25.3b) probably came from a burial.

Monkey pots of various types were also found in interments elsewhere. At El Peru–Waka', Chablekal vessels with incised monkeys were recovered in burials (Eppich 2007). In the Mirador Basin 18 out of 23 monkey pots, primarily Carmelita Incised (Infierno group) and Telchac Composite (Chablekal group) types, were associated with mortuary remains or looters' trenches into burials (Skousen 2009).

Black and gray ceramics of the Infierno, Achote, Chablekal, and Tres Naciones groups lacking simian images occurred more widely as mortuary furniture. Poite Incised (Tres Naciones) tripod grater bowls or *molcajetes* were recovered at Ceibal in four burials (one a female) and a cache (Sabloff 1975:211). Achote Black pots appear in Terminal Classic interments at Uaxactún, Ceibal, and Tikal, which had at least three tripod dishes in burials. One, with heavy use wear (Culbert 1993:Figure 98b, c2), came from Bur. 201, a young female ("girl") intruded into anciently looted Burial 200 in Room 1 at the front of Group 5D-22-1st in the north-central (rear) portion of the North Acropolis (W. Coe 1990, 3:870). Another, a tripod plate from P.D. 133 with mend holes (Culbert 1993:Figure145b), had *ik'*/tau signs cut into the supports.

Ik' is translated as wind, breath, scent (especially of flowers) and animating or vitalizing energy, essence, or soul. The occasional presence of this sign on JBG

Figure 25.4. A Campo Composite vase found in a Terminal Classic burial on the mainland at Lake Macanché (see P. Rice 1986:263). Ht. 14.5 cm.

and other black- or gray-ware pottery may be explained by this glyph occurring in several Classic textual death expressions, equating the loss of breath with the loss of life and soul (Houston et al. 2006:143, 228). It also may be significant that the ceramics of interest were black and/or gray: in Maya directional color associations black is associated with west—perhaps the darkness that follows the setting of the sun and its entry into the dark, watery Underworld. Moreover, the word for black in various Maya languages is *ek'* or *ik'*.

Similar associations among monkeys, death symbolism, and mortuary contexts were noted in recent study of Maya primate imagery on Late Classic polychromes (Rice and South 2015). For example, at Tikal two Late Classic Saxché Orange Polychrome barrel-shaped vases with bands of crawling monkeys were recovered in a tomb in Structure 5D-22-1st in the Central Acropolis (Culbert 1993:Figure 146c–d). A stylistically Late Classic or Terminal Classic polychrome bowl with a monkey image from Topoxté Island held a child's remains (Hermes 2000, Figure 151-1). Three painted vessels with monkey images came from burials at Caracol, one Early Classic and two Late–Terminal Classic (www.caracol.org, accessed August 18, 2019). Unprovenienced cylinder K7007 bears two incised monkey images in odd poses: semiprone with limbs outstretched as if swimming, vaguely reminiscent of the *danzante* figures in early Oaxaca. Their eyes, not clearly shown, may be closed, suggesting that they are dead.

Monkeys and monkey images are associated with death in other ways in the Classic Period. A spider monkey skeleton was found at Tikal with the Early Classic burial of a woman—perhaps "Woman of Tikal"—and child directly south of the Temple of the Inscriptions (Hattula Moholy-Nagy, personal communication 2014). Two incised bones from ruler Jasaw Chan K'awiil's Burial 116 in Tikal's Temple 2 showed a monkey with the Maize God and several other creatures in a canoe sinking to the Underworld, and a codex-style vase (K3433) depicts two monkeys in a canoe. In north coastal Belize fragments of large Palmar Orange Polychrome plates featuring bands of stylized primates were scattered over monumental structures as part of their ritual termination ("death") and abandonment (Mock 1997:179).

The association between monkeys and death/mortuary practice can be partially interpreted in light of the *Popol Vuh* origin myth (see Christenson 2003; Tedlock 1996). The Hero Twins Hunapuh and Xbalanque—who magically turned their abusive older stepbrothers into monkeys—were summoned by the angry Underworld lords One Death and Seven Death to play their noisy ballgame in Xib'alb'a. During their stay the Hero Twins employed trickery to survive many trials, finally sacrificing then resurrecting a dog, a human, and Hunapuh himself. After this astounding feat the Xibalban lords requested that the same be done to them. The Twins sacrificed the lords but did not bring them back to life, thus metaphorically defeating the powers of death itself. It may have been this death-and-resurrection theme that led to the Late Classic Period placement of pottery with monkey imagery as burial furniture (or scattered over terminated buildings). As with the images of simians in canoes, monkeys may have been thought to assist with the journey of the dead to their final resting place.

Discussion

What do these associations of black- and gray-slipped pottery, monkey imagery, and mortuary contexts mean? None of the burials are elaborate in terms of other goods or construction, and there is little to suggest elite statuses other than the distinctiveness of the types themselves. Perhaps black wares and gray wares substituted for polychromes as mortuary furniture for some nonelites who may have had certain ritual roles in life. Or maybe gray wares accompanied individuals who died of specific causes thought to have been visited by the Lords of Death. Or perhaps particular beliefs or myths concerning monkeys and death gained currency in the Late–Terminal Classic western lowlands and/or among Western Chontal speakers but were not shared more broadly. Might it be significant that several of these vessels were interred with young females?

Were the JBG and other black and gray vessels intended as burial furniture or were they food service pieces first? Usewear on the Carmelita monkey pots from the Mirador Basin suggests the latter (Skousen 2009), as it does on the Trece Gatos Fine-Incised dish from Flores, but the specificity of the motif may suggest otherwise. The recovery of Poite Incised grater bowls in burials at Ceibal seems anomalous: were these used in preparation of ingredients for mortuary rituals rather than ordinary domestic kitchen activities? Perhaps the vessels with monkeys were key components of an assemblage made and used specifically and repeatedly for serving foods at funeral rites and then buried with the deceased.

A Ceramic System and Production

The most appropriate summation of the observations collated here is that the new Jato Black-on-Gray ceramic group, together with Chablekal, Infierno, and Achote, and their shared styles, modes, and motifs, constitute a ceramic "system" in the western part of the southern lowlands during the Late and Terminal Classic Periods. The concept of a ceramic system was initially developed in connection with pottery analysis in the southwestern United States in the 1950s (e.g., Wheat et al. 1958) and has been haltingly adopted into Maya archaeology (see Aimers 2013; see also Aimers 2014). A ceramic system is a higher-order integrative unit consisting of "homologous types that are related in terms of aspects of decoration: design elements, element execution, design field layout, and the like" (J. Henderson and Agurcia 1987:432). It incorporates "roughly contemporaneous pottery types that range over a wide area . . . almost inevitably crosscuts several wares . . . [and] is extensive in distributional range" (Gifford 1976:12).

What do a ceramic system and the decorative sharing mean economically, in terms of potters' and consumers' interactions, choices, and behavior? The few applications of the system concept in the Maya area have shed little light on this issue. Some applications have noted how the concept aids the procedure of classification itself, but without also illustrating enhanced interpretations of the "meaning" of the material. Identification of a ceramic system highlights shared stylistic and technological conventions through long-distance interactions—but what kinds of conventions, why are they shared, and through what kinds of interactions? That is, we know the structural parts and properties of a system (types, slips, motifs) but we don't yet know the agential *processes* (human behavior and decision-making) underlying the sharing and transmission of those parts. There is no reason, of course, to expect that a single process or set of processes will underlie all ceramic systems.

Perhaps we can develop a broader understanding of ceramic systems through attention to "systems" as they are conceived in cybernetics, informatics, and systems theory. Most simply put, a "system" is an organized and interconnected set of components forming a complex whole. A material or artifact system (see https://en.wikipedia.org/wiki/System, accessed August 18, 2019) can be considered to be a designed (not nature-based), open (accepting external influences; not closed), dynamic (not static), physical whole. With respect to pottery economics, the interacting components of a ceramic system include inputs (clay, temper, pigment, tools, fuel); outputs (fired objects of various wares, types, forms, decorations); a "processor" (one or more potters); a "control" (the behavior, decisions, and knowledge of potters, in response to input supply and output demand); feedback (consumers' acquisition: again, supply and demand); a boundary (social, political, economic, geographic); an interface (with another ceramic system or collection of like goods); and the environment (natural and cultural). A ceramic system is part of an overarching sociocultural and economic (super)system—lowland Maya, in this case. In addition, a ceramic system comprises multiple subsystems created in large part through the interactions of these components.

The proposed western lowland Epiclassic black-slipped and gray-surfaced/slipped ceramic system is a designed, open, dynamic, material system. Its openness and dynamism are evidenced by the presence of highly varied decoration—red paint, black paint, punctations, impressions, plano-relief carving, and multiple kinds of incising—contributing to definition of types in the various constituent groups. We do not know the intended functions of the several vessel forms and decorative modes in the system's participating groups, but they clearly were used in diverse contexts.

Discussion and Conclusions: Interactions, Emulations, and Hybrids

What does the study of the Terminal Classic central Petén Jato Black-on-Gray ceramic group contribute to the theme of this volume, the "business" of Maya exchange? JBG is only a small "nut" among the "nuts and bolts" of this business, but it does shed light on some of the goings-on during the turbulent late Late and Terminal Classic or Epiclassic Periods in the southern lowlands.

The western area of the central Petén lakes zone saw considerable in-migration and introductions of new architecture and iconographic elements and programs in sculpture and ceramics during the late Late and Terminal Classic Periods. With respect to pottery, some of these appear to have come from the northern (Mirador) and western parts of Petén, where the variable incising (rather than polychrome painting) of monkey motifs passed from imported Late Classic Chablekal Fine Gray paste ware farther to the west. It appears that Terminal Classic potters in the western lakes district also emulated certain gray- and black-slipped and decorated wares of the western and southwestern lowlands. JBG is one such emulation, but the pottery appears to represent more complex reworkings of borrowed technology and iconography beyond simple imitations. JBG combines typical central Petén forms (tripod plates, vases) and mortuary use with distinctive nonlocal aspects of color (gray and black, and probably associated firing techniques), and decoration found among more widely exchanged earlier and contemporaneous wares and groups such as Fine Gray, Achote, and Infierno. These latter were present in the lakes area in only small quantities, probably as rare imports.

It is impossible from the small sample of JBG pottery to propose organizational or locational arrangements of production or circulation. We have not carried out compositional analyses to assess where the vessels were made: are they local to the lake-basin communities—and, if so, where—or imports from farther afield? My gut reaction is that they are local, a proposition that obviously needs testing. Irrespective of geochemical provenance, however, if I am right, the presence of this unusual hybrid in burials in the lakes area suggests that (1) the lakes' residents gained familiarity with these wares in other areas and copied them at home; or (2) potters in these western and southwestern regions moved into the lakes district and produced their familiar forms and decoration with local resources; or (3) some combination of both.

The Epiclassic black- and gray-ware ceramic system is one of two systems I have proposed, the other more narrowly circumscribed by Postclassic decorative structures in the Petén lakes district (Rice 2013). Both appeared during times of societal conflict and stresses. The Epiclassic in the broader region of interest—the northern, central, western, and southwestern lowlands of Yucatán, Petén, and adjacent Chiapas—was a time of population movements and "collapse" of dynastic rule and order. Social, political, economic, and demographic transformations involved migrations or intermarriage, warfare, new patterns of trade, and the spread of new belief systems, cults, or ideologies. Ceramic systems, at least in these two cases, may be an outcome of efforts to adjust to and accommodate different needs, beliefs, and practices in areas experiencing the stresses of in-migration and related interactions.

The components in the system that are most difficult to address with respect to ceramics—at least at this stage in its application to Maya products—are "control," "boundary," and "interface." We know relatively little about the organization of Late and Terminal Classic pottery production and exchange and how it intersects with other economic activities, such as marketing. The fluid circumstances of the Terminal Classic in the southern lowlands likely meant that potters' traditional "operating conditions"—access to the usual resources, regular customers, and known pottery functions—may have fallen apart. This might be accompanied by potters' sense of loss of control and awareness of newly influential (or suddenly collapsed) social and other boundaries, although it is noteworthy that both proposed systems, Epiclassic and Postclassic, transcended political boundaries. On the one hand, the transformations may have limited potters' creativity and economic success; on the other hand, they might have stimulated innovation through new interfaces (e.g., with the west). Potters apparently did not feel obligated to adhere to strict decorative canons and sensed few if any constraints in these circumstances: they could accept, reject, combine, and innovate at will.

Innovation—the sine qua non of the business world today—refers to the processes of introducing new ideas, workflows, methods, services, or products into a business, typically leading to increased value/profit. Pottery of the JBG group, including vases and dishes with distinctive monkeys and *ik'* motifs, reveals that the western lakes area was part of a larger western lowland Epiclassic ceramic system, but it was also a transitional area of overlap of old ideas and forms. If JBG was produced locally, as I suspect, this suggests that innovation was alive and well among potters in the lakes region and that the new product was valued as mortuary furniture. Regardless of where it was produced, innovation, through processes of adoption and adaptation, engaged potters in the production and exchange "business" in Terminal Classic central Petén. In other words, rather than being a "dead zone" of depopulation and decline, Lake Petén Itzá and the western lakes region in general seem to have been a relatively thriving area of cultural and intellectual interchange and "business" in the Terminal Classic. The existence of this integrative black- and gray-ware ceramic system in western Petén provides a point of contrast with the portrayal of Terminal Classic lowland politico-economic fragmentation and balkanization.

Acknowledgments

The pottery reported here was recovered in fieldwork beginning in the 1970s, funded by NSF grants BNS-7813736 to Don S. Rice and myself; DBS-9222373 and SBR-9515443 to Don S. Rice, myself, and G. D. Jones; NEH grant RZ-50520-06 to myself, Don S. Rice, and Rómulo Sánchez Polo; and the Heinz Latin American Archaeology Program. Fieldwork at Tayasal was carried out by NSF grants BCS 1219646 and BCS 0917918 to Timothy Pugh. Thanks are due to the Guatemalan Instituto de Antropología e Historia for fieldwork permits and to Don Rice for the final figures.

26

Maya Economics

Through a Glass, Sideways (One More Time)

NORMAN YOFFEE

At the Society for American Archaeology (SAA) meeting in 2015 I drifted into a session on Maya trade. I heard a number of excellent papers and was frankly astonished to learn about the new work on trade and markets in Maya-land (see below). I wrote to David Freidel, who gave one of the papers, to ask about what I thought I was hearing about markets and marketplaces, accounting, and merchants. A few weeks later I received a request from David and Arthur Demarest and Marilyn Masson to contribute to a volume on the "nuts and bolts" of Maya business. I was flattered by the request and accepted. I have been working in the last years on trade in Mesopotamia and elsewhere and thought that these chapters would bring me up to date on Maya research. Is there really a kind of revolution in how Maya archaeologists (and others) now understand ancient economies?

This book of essays does not conceal the sense of excitement about what Mayanists are discovering about Maya economy, especially about markets and trade, but also about household production and distribution. Norman Hammond's *Ancient Maya Civilization* (1982) discusses ethnohistoric information about Indian "canoes" (that is, large boats) bearing staples as well as luxury goods, citing J.E.S. Thompson's (1962:14) comparison of Chontal Maya as the "Phoenicians of Middle America." He also quotes Jeremy Sabloff (Hammond 1982:238): "long-distance trade was principally in exotic or elite goods. . . . [Such] trade was controlled by the theocracy and was used to support its position as the ruling class. Merchants did not exist as a separable sociopolitical entity." (This view of the role of merchants in ancient societies was not limited to the Maya;

see Earle 1994a.) In Hammond's words (1982:239): "Merchants may have existed as a class of craftsmen in the Preclassic and Early Classic periods, but not as a distinct stratum in society." He cautioned, presciently: "Whether these . . . interpretations will survive the impact of further research is uncertain."

Arthur Demarest (2004:173) writes: "There is no doubt . . . that Maya rulers and their courts controlled long-distance and regional exchange of many luxury goods." He also notes a "reciprocal exchange" among elites in the form of dowries and gifts (2004:173). Stephen Houston and Takeshi Inomata (2009:287) were undecided: "Traders must have existed, but little is known of them for the reason that, in most places, they might have operated at the margins of dynastic societies." Furthermore: "Did the Classic Maya even have marketplaces?" (Houston and Inomata 2009:250).

Alexandre Tokovinine and Dmitri Beliaev, Marilyn Masson and David Freidel, and Patricia McAnany in a revolutionary new volume (Hirth and Pillsbury, eds. 2013) no longer doubted the presence and importance of traders and markets (see Hutson 2017; King, ed. 2015).

Older explanations about trade and markets, based on venerable theories of ancient economies (see below), have now been discarded, for good reasons, as the essays in this volume show. If new explanations, based on new research, do not dispute the existence of markets, there is disagreement about the nature of markets, how royal courts interact with markets (that is, control them or not) (Chapters 2, 3, 8, 17, 20, and 22, among others), whether there are various kinds of markets (local, regional, interregional), and whether these markets are a "system," and whether long-distance trade and local production are normal and long-standing aspects of Maya city-states. Indeed, Doyle (2016) argues that the first markets formed in E-groups in Preclassic cities, ritual places in which worshippers from near and far exchanged goods.

As it happens, many of these questions (about the identity and status of merchants and their relation to the city-state government) are also being studied by Mesopotamianists, especially those researching the Old Assyrian trading system (Larsen 2015 is the go-to book). There are some good reasons for comparing Maya and Mesopotamian states. For example, both regions produced only ephemeral instances of territorial states. For most of the Preclassic and Classic Periods in Maya-land and for most of the time in Mesopotamia from the appearance of the earliest cities in the late fourth millennium BC until the first millennium BC, each region consisted in a congeries of city-states (for the Maya, see Grube 2000; for Mesopotamia, see Van De Mieroop 2016; but see

Hansen et al., Chapter 18, for a notable exception). These city-states (in each region) fought against one another, creating ephemeral hegemonies, which soon dissolved into the constituent city-states. Also, both regions had an overarching "civilizational" umbrella of belief-systems and cultural norms that made the Maya Maya and, *mutatis mutandis*, Mesopotamians Mesopotamians. Furthermore, these political and cultural systems conditioned and affected the economies of the two regions, if not in the ways that previous economic researchers have thought.

In this chapter I consider aspects of ancient trade and economics, as I have gleaned from the essays in this book, in a "controlled comparison." I also indicate how a such a comparative study can advance the inquiry into questions of theoretical interest in both regions (and beyond). I also want to consider aspects of economic theory used in some of the essays in this volume and to speculate whether some recent studies about Mesopotamian economics and politics may allow new questions to emerge in the study of Maya economics and society. One area in which Maya studies on the economy is more highly developed than those on Mesopotamia is household production and distribution (Chapters 4, 5, 6, 10, and 11 and others in this volume). Although these chapters can stimulate new thoughts about Mesopotamian economics on the household level (e.g., Chapter 14), I do not address these matters in this chapter.

The Maya and Me

In 1972 I was hired by the Department of Anthropology, University of Arizona, and thus became a colleague of two Maya archaeologists, Pat Culbert and Bill Rathje (until 1993, when I decamped for Michigan and worked with a number of students who studied the Maya). Every year Pat and I taught (for about a dozen years) an "early civilizations seminar." We selected a theme for each seminar, such as cities, kingship, or warfare. We began the seminar with each us lecturing on our favorite areas. Then we read and discussed with the seminarians books and articles from around the world that were pertinent to our theme. This was essentially my introduction to Maya archaeology. Also, in our archaeological core course for grad students we faculty members attended each other's lectures and occasionally commented on issues from our own perspectives. Bill Rathje discussed Maya trade, and we argued about possible Mesopotamian comparisons.[1]

In 1986 Pat Culbert invited me to a School for American Research seminar on Maya political history. The participants included archaeologists and epigraphers, and the aim was to employ both material culture and newly deciphered textual data to reconstruct "political history" (Culbert 1991), which is what I try to do in my Mesopotamian research. My outsider role in the conference was occasionally to serve as a check on the enthusiasms of Linda Schele and Peter Mathews, who were the main informants on Maya inscriptions. My refrain was: "in Mesopotamia we have been able to read, for more than a century, the proclamations of kings and the list of their accomplishments. We have learned that much of what kings say is propaganda, which is valuable for many reasons, but often do not 'correctly' depict historical events or the cause and effect of political change. Mesopotamianists have other texts, economic and legal texts, which can be used (alongside the propaganda and ideology in royal inscriptions) to write history, and we can rely on archaeological analysis to consider the claims made in the royal inscriptions." It is obvious that Mayanists are now writing history using both inscriptions and material culture.[2] The ability of (most) Maya archaeologists cheerfully to discard once cherished views as new research shows their fallacies is abundantly displayed in this volume and admirable.

The Study of the Ancient Economy, Then and Now

Maya archaeologists have long traced the movements of goods, but there has been the question of how bulk goods such as obsidian cores and salt and agricultural products were transported in the absence of draft animals and wheeled vehicles. Chapters 3, 10, 20, and 21 discuss extensive sea and river transport by means of boats and so solve many of the questions about how goods were moved. Also, labor was cheap and humans could carry goods for relatively long distances. There is now also evidence of accounting practices and the use of "money": equivalencies measured by cacao beans and shells, among other things, that facilitated the exchange of goods. But who were the traders of the goods? In particular, what was their connection to the royal courts? Does Alexander Tokovinine's reference (Chapter 16) to a rich accountant who had a lot of cacao bean, refer to profit from trade and specialized traders? What do authors mean when they say that "the Maya" or "they" traded?

In the 1970s and 1980s trade was not a major subject in archaeological theory. Many archaeologists marched under the banner of "New Archaeology," which emphasized that cultures were (extrasomatic) adaptations to environmental conditions (Oka and Kusimba 2008). Culture change occurred when environmental conditions changed, and new "adaptations" were responses to these new conditions. Also, "systems theory" proponents described essentially closed systems in which local conditions and social units could be viewed in a flow-diagram in which external contacts were of little interest (see Brumfiel 1992 for a critique of this thinking). In these "systems" people were placed in boxes, with little regard for situations in which some people might be in more than one box: for example, in a kin-group box and in a merchant-group box. This kind of "systems-thinking" is fatal to the understanding of the role of (Mesopotamian or Maya) traders (as I discuss below, but see Rice, Chapter 25, for a refreshingly dynamic application).

Now, such lack of engagement with trade studies in archaeology and the role of trade in social development was not without challenges in the 1970s. In Maya studies, Bill Rathje (1971) argued that the need to trade for distant resources like ground-stone and salt was the "prime mover" that led to the development of lowland cities and states.[3] Philip Kohl (1978) argued that production in Mesopotamian cities was critical to the understanding of social stratification in the third millennium BC. In Europe people wondered how early social stratification developed from societies without much stratification. The answer, it was speculated, was trade (see Sherratt 1997). That is, trade provided mechanisms for the creation of status and wealth beyond ascribed kinship roles. Long-distance traders were required to establish social and cultural ties with nonkin in order to disembed goods from local contexts and bring them to the home of the traders. Mary Helms's oft-cited study (1993) showed with ethnographic examples the force of distant goods in denoting and demonstrating the power of nascent leaders. Such leaders claimed special ties to the gods through the control of new symbols obtained from distant places. Archaeologists, of course, recovered nonlocal goods in rich burials and highly charged places. But if distant goods in a society could be documented, who brought those goods from the far-away places? What role did these "traders" have within their society? Many archaeologists were content simply to point to the foreignness of objects.

Also, in the 1960s, 1970s, and 1980s, the prevailing economic theory in anthropology and archaeology was derived from the works of Karl Polanyi—and also those of Max Weber and M. I. Finley. To be brief, Weber famously thought that ancient cities (in the Old World) were "consumer cities" in which commerce in towns came from rural rents and that commodity production was unimportant (Weber 1958). Finley followed Weber in declaring that "imports alone motivated trade, never exports" (Finley 1954:63, see also 1973). He also held that Asian cities had no assemblies or associations that held important power to make decisions and to serve as "democratic" governments. Polanyi explained why this was the case by arguing that pre-Classical economies (in the Old World) were largely redistributive: rural goods flowed into the palace (or temple) estate and were then allocated to retainers of the palace. Polanyi's article (1957) on Old Assyrian trade considered that traders were state employees, there were no markets, and there was no profit and loss. It is remarkable that some economic historians and archaeologists still cite Polanyi in the face of about fifty years of studies that have refuted him on every point (e.g., Renfrew and Bahn 2008). Mayanists, as in this book, and Mesopotamianists, beginning with Kohl (1978), are at pains to characterize production in cities that was expressly destined for export and what the effects of such production means for the social and economic structure of ancient cities.

I shall not belabor Polanyi's distinction between "substantivist" economics (in which the flow of goods in a society was determined by social relations) as against "formalist" economics (King, Chapter 2), in which laws of supply and demand govern economic relations in all societies. (Polanyi's influence in trade studies in archaeology is explored at length in Oka and Kusimba 2008.) Most onlookers agree that one must understand both social relations and principles of economic behavior (in anthropology ever since the convincing analysis in Pryor 1977). What remains to be evaluated, however, is Polanyi's (and many others') fundamental distinction between "public" and "private" spheres of economic relations: that is, governmental and nongovernmental action and actors. Is a trader only a private person and thus unconnected to governmental institutions, *or* is a trader under the control of a ruler and royal court? I turn to a brief characterization of Old Assyrian trade in Mesopotamia to problematize the public-private distinction.

Old Assyrian Trade (in Brief)

An exceptionally distinguished group of scholars has studied the history and archaeology of the Old Assyrian trading system (for recent publications, see Atici et al. 2014; Barjamovic 2011, 2018; Hertel 2013; Larsen 2015; Michel 2011; Veenhof 1997, 2008).[4] The Old Assyrian commercial system is doubtless the best-documented example of a long-distance trade network in the ancient world. We know it from some 23,000 merchant records written on clay tablets from the private archives of about 500 Assyrian traders living at the site of ancient Kanesh (modern Kültepe) in central Turkey. The site has been and is being excavated by a series of Turkish archaeologists and their colleagues (Atici et al. 2014). The site consists of two major mounds, the acropolis with its palace and temples and the lower town in which lived merchants, Anatolians, Assyrians, and others (outlying habitations and activities areas are also known). Altogether it is estimated that the site covers 150 hectares, with a population over 25,000. Kanesh was the hub of an Assyrian trading system that included three dozen other settlements in Anatolia (Asiatic Turkey).

At least 100 multistory houses have been excavated over the years in the lower town. The private archives of merchants were found there. Although the site's duration is from around 1950 BC to 1750 BC, a massive conflagration occurred around 1840 BC. The fire sealed the houses and preserved the tablets (and other materials). In Mesopotamia the sacking and burning of a site resulted in the preservation of archives of all sorts. We owe our knowledge of such excavated archives as at Ebla and Mari to the successful conquests by their enemies.

The tablets dating to the years from around 1895 to 1865 BC contain most of the information on the Assyrians' activities at Kanesh, from which some quantitative calculations about the goods moved in the trade can be derived. During this period of thirty years, Assyrian traders moved about 100 tons of tin and more than 10,000 textiles. The transport was by means of donkey caravans from Assur to Kanesh, a distance of about 1,000 km. The fabrics were high-quality woolen textiles, some from southern Mesopotamia, Babylonia, weighing on average about 3 kilos each. One fabric could buy a house.

This trade was organized and carried out by merchants, private entrepreneurs who maintained their own organization, the *kārum*. This word means "harbor, dock, quai" according to the Akkadian dictionaries, but at Kanesh it refers to a social institution, the community of traders. These Assyrian traders lived in the lower town of Kanesh (Kültepe) alongside non-Assyrian residents of the city. The traders acquired the large quantities of tin from the south and the east of Mesopotamia, regions that were long known to Mesopotamians. However, we know very little about this southern and eastern trade network other than that Assyrians bought tin in Assur. The Kanesh texts are almost exclusively concerned with the trade from Assur to Kanesh.

Assyrian merchants traded tin and textiles (and some other things) in

Anatolian markets for gold and silver, which were relatively (in comparison to northern Mesopotamia) plentiful. Textiles that cost about 7 shekels of silver in Assur could be sold in Anatolia for 14 shekels. Tin was at least twice as expensive in Anatolia as in Assur. Even with the costs of transport, including payments for bridges, roads, accommodation at inns en route, and payoffs to local warlords, the Assyrian merchants made great profits (and texts also report losses). Assyrian merchants made money not because they controlled any source of goods. They knew how to get goods from where they were plentiful and how to move them to where they were scarce. Merchants also shared investments in partnerships, accumulating "bags" of capital to finance their businesses. Disputes in Kanesh were settled in the assembly of merchants (Michel 2000). From these Assyrian texts we draw a picture of private initiative, risk-based and profit-seeking behavior, free-floating capital, and similar modern features within a world that had been characterized (in previous generations) by centralized ownership of land and water, fixed prices, and state merchants (Yoffee and Barjamovic 2018). Some Mesopotamianists have argued that the Old Assyrian trading system, which hardly mentions the palace in Assur at all, was an anomaly in Mesopotamian history.

However, this analysis simply underscores the nature of the sample that we have recovered. There was undoubtedly a palace (and temples) in Assur in the Old Assyrian Period. We have little knowledge of these institutions, beyond a few royal inscriptions mentioning actions of kings. Our sample comes from the remarkable excavations of merchant houses (mainly) at Kanesh. Most of the archives from the third millennium BC, by contrast, come from temples and palaces, and these focus on internal activities of these "Great Estates." Now scholars read from these tablets about transactions on behalf of palaces and temples in which traders who were specialized in the acquisition and transport of distant goods (Steinkeller 2013). Lapis lazuli, which was transported from Afghanistan as early at 3500 BC, also was moved by traders in the Old Assyrian Period. A common opinion today is that the Old Assyrian trading system was not anomalous in Mesopotamian history, although the detailed records from Kanesh are quite singular.

Trade and the State in Comparative Perspective

It is not necessary to describe the Old Assyrian trading system further in order to bring it into comparative perspective with Maya trade and to consider the possible implications for economies in the ancient world more generally. In any case I am not arguing that something like the Old Assyrian trading system and the administration of the traders in Kanesh in a self-governing body is necessarily the same as the system in a Maya city. What may be comparable is this: first, the Assyrian trading system depended on the fragmented nature of regional politics, similar to the Maya system of competing city-states. Whereas the Old Assyrian trading system did not require the royal organization of trade, it involved a complex of legal and political institutions of collective government in which the traders themselves were also part of the machinery of the state. The association of traders in Kanesh facilitated transport through hostile territories and arranged a system of treaties with local rulers of kingdoms en route and in Anatolia. However, in one of the rare Old Assyrian royal inscriptions, the ruler of Assur himself campaigns in the south in order to guarantee the access of merchants to Babylonian goods and trade routes. The palace in Assur could thus collect taxes on the activities of the traders.

The home-city of traders, Assur, was the home of the ruler; his title is not king but "viceroy" of the patron deity of the city of Assur (the divine Assur). The ruler of Assur, the city, shared governance with "The City," an assembly of great men and lesser men. This assembly is known from the Kanesh documents as a judicial body, making decisions about the leaders of trading houses and sending these decisions to the *kārum* in Kanesh, the judicial authority of the lower town traders. The city assembly thus monitored fundamental aspects of the traders in distant Anatolia. Officers of the state in Assur witnessed investment agreements and supervised tax-collection in Assur.

The point of the foregoing is that *there is no clear distinction* between the community of traders and the institutional arenas of rulers in the Old Assyrian Period. This kind of political system is also known from the great trading cities of late medieval Italy and the Hanseatic cities of northern Europe (De Roover 1963; Spufford 2002). In the Old Assyrian case this conclusion is derived from the study of the private documents of the merchants, the sort of data that are not clearly present in the corpus of Maya inscriptions. It should come as no surprise that markets and traders are barely visible in royal inscriptions (either in Mesopotamia or in Maya inscriptions), because traders and markets played no role in the sacred and formal political ideology of kings or in the propaganda about royal warfare and alliances, which are the dominant subjects in royal inscriptions.

Public and Private in the Economy of Early Cities and States

The contributors in Sabloff and Lamberg-Karlovsky (1975), which might have been a harbinger of trade studies to come, had little to say about the nature of long-distance trade and the state. Several authors were still debating Polanyi's positions on "aboriginal economies" and their putative lack of markets. Dalton (1975, 1982:112) seems to have thought comparison between Trobriand islanders and the Maya was apt, though he wondered whether "foreign trade" required at least some aspects of market behavior (1982:89). Sabloff and Freidel (1975:373) and Rathje (1975: 436) tentatively considered, respectively, ideas about "controlling centers . . . of long-distance trade" and "population participation in . . . commerce."

As economic anthropology has been liberated from Polanyi's (and Weber's and Finley's) strictures, the present volume now joins *Merchants, Markets, and Exchange in the Precolumbian World* (Hirth and Pillsbury, eds. 2013); *Archaeological Approaches to Market Exchange in Ancient Societies* (Garraty and Stark, eds. 2010); *Interweaving Worlds: Systemic Interactions in Eurasia, 7th to 1st Millennia BC* (Wilkinson et al., eds. 2011); *Tying the Threads of Eurasia: Trans-Regional Routes and Material Flows in Transcaucasia, Eastern Anatolia and Western Central Asia, c. 3000–1500 BC* (Wilkinson, ed. 2014); and *Trade and Civilization in the Pre-Modern World* (Kristiansen et al., eds. 2018).

The new research in several of the chapters in this volume that identifies physical markets in Maya-land is of great interest. In Mesopotamia the most common word for market is simply "street," and this is where local markets flourished and where perishables and other commodities were exchanged. The word "harbor" (*kārum*) denotes a place where long-distance traders and family-firms were located, as at Kanesh, and also the social institutions of the "harbor." The *kārum* at Kanesh was, I emphasize, not the exclusive enclave of Assyrians. Polanyi and his followers had asked the question: is trade a "public" (governmental) institution, controlled by the state and traders are public employees of the state, or is trade a private entrepreneurial affair, with profit and loss, choice, rationality guiding the flow of goods? If Polanyi was wrong about the "embeddedness" of the economy and trade within social and political institutions, we can now discuss the "entanglements" of economic and political spheres. Charles Golden and his colleagues (Chapter 23) have reminded us that modern governments support trade in various ways and that modern traders seek to influence governmental policy and can also be officials of the state or work with governments, as well as being social and economic elites.

Mesopotamia had various forms of elites, including elites who had ties, including contractual ties, with the royal court, and urban leaders who were "mayors" and judges and formed councils of elders (ethnic/kin-group nobility), especially in the countryside, but who necessarily had contact with the royal court. They could also lead opposition to ruling dynasties and their courtiers. "Eliteness" cannot be essentialized, as the sources of their status could vary so greatly. Similarly, "elite" is not a category or "class" of people. In Maya studies I wonder whether the term "elite" covers over different kinds of elites and the various relations of various elites with the royal court.

At something like the other end of the social spectrum from eliteness, I offer a footnote to Batún, McAnany, and Dedrick (Chapter 12). In the very centralized state of the "Third Dynasty of Ur," ca. 2100–2000 BC, outlying villages subject to the Ur III state were responsible for delivering reeds (Steinkeller 1987) and pots (Steinkeller 1996) to the capital. After this work was done, which took about half a year, the villagers could and did work for themselves. In the subsequent Old Babylonian Period, there are contracts in which shepherds managed palace and temple herds in outlying pastures, keeping for themselves newborn lambs over and above the quotas for which they were responsible (Finkelstein 1968; Postgate 1975).

I advocate further that terms like "integrated," used by some to describe the evolution and nature of Maya cities and states (and complex societies in other areas too), should be reconsidered. "Integration" tends to make people think that religion and/or politics brought together various groups of people in a cooperative and beneficent arrangement. Such attempts at societal "integration," however, may well have made states more fragile and decomposable (as Scott 1998 tells us). Maya cities, like Mesopotamian ones, were aggregations of various people: villagers who moved into urban places, people of various statuses and social orientations, ethnic groups. These groups of people formed the urban population but could also become organized cells of resistance to the goals of leaders in times of stress. The Late Classic boom in the construction of temples and monuments may well have constituted such a stress on the majority of the population in cities and in the countryside. Once flourishing cities were progressively abandoned (McAnany et al. 2015; Grube 2016), as even Mesopotamianists are aware.

If traders were part of the order of Maya urban government, as I have speculated may have been the case, the "collapse" of the Maya cities need not (in theory) and did not (in practice) mean the end of trade in the Maya region.

Trade and traders did not simply survive the Maya urban dislocations: they seem to have prospered as a result of them (e.g., Chapters 5, 8, 25, and 16). As in the Old Assyrian case, the lack of centralized political regimes provided relatively unhindered access to goods and transportation routes.

Finally, if my emphasis in this comment is to break down economic and political institutions and to suggest possible entanglements of trading and courtly spheres, Mayanists need no urging in seeing the differences among Maya cities/states (Chapter 16). Mayanists are careful to note that there are various kinds of city-states in different regions and in different times and with a variety of relations with near neighbors—and so there are a variety of mechanisms of trade and exchange. Nonetheless, throughout the Maya region, communication for exchange among Maya cities required new technologies of numeracy and equivalencies that were the standards by which goods were valued. These were transmitted to and shared by Maya cities (Freidel et al. 2016). Markets were social constructions and had to be sustained by agreements between governments and traders, who—as I have tentatively suggested—were neither (necessarily) independent of the royal courts nor organized by the courts. Masson (2002b:8) stresses the complementary institutions of exchange, transfers of goods, tribute (see Chapter 19), gifting, feasting, and the marketplace. I cannot improve on that picture; I only suggest that these institutions be further broken down to see that Maya "agents" were not limited in their participation to one or another of them. Are Maya elites differentiated into ritual, military, mercantile, ritual, and political spheres (and subspheres: see Freidel 2018)? Are the interests of these elites not only complementary but also sometimes opposing? And how do competing interests (and interest groups) garner support or/and promote resistance among non-elite citizens (in and out of cities, villagers and farmers)? These (and other) questions are stimulated by the research in this volume.

Author's Note: My chapter (Yoffee 1991) in *Classic Maya Political History* (Culbert 1991) attempted a Mesopotamianist's perspective on Maya elites, especially political elites. This essay is my second "sideways" look at the Maya, now focusing on Maya economics. I thank David Freidel, Arthur Demarest, and Marilyn Masson for the invitation to attend the SAA panel in Orlando and also the participants who sent me their papers in advance of the session. I am grateful to David Freidel and Arthur Demarest for answering many questions and for sending me PowerPoints and other illustrations.

Notes

1. Whatever small value there may be in this chapter is due to the engagement with cross-cultural research and especially the importance (to a Mesopotamianist) of Maya archaeology that was inculcated in me at the University of Arizona, Department of Anthropology. I wish that I could show this chapter to Pat and Bill.

2. Linda and Peter and I became good friends in Santa Fe, and I regret that a paper that Linda and I had planned to write together never came to pass.

3. Guillermo Algaze (2008) makes a similar argument for the "Sumerian break-out." Both Rathje's and Algaze's views of the rise of the state are similar to Arnold Toynbee's "challenge and response" theory of state development.

4. "Old Assyrian" refers to a stage in the Assyrian dialect of the Akkadian language family and is known mainly from the trading records found at Kanesh.

27

Conclusion

The Ties That Bind

MARILYN A. MASSON

Many perspectives offered by the contributors to this book advance the frontier of studying the organization of Maya economies. David Freidel (Chapter 1) reviews the themes and issues treated in our chapters, from the perspective of sites and regions, classes of data in our interdisciplinary field, and the battery of methodological and theoretical approaches at our disposal. How has this book helped to sharpen the data and rigor with which economic dimensions of Maya society are studied? Primarily, the chapters represent case studies for how to address a range of questions, drawing on many categories of material culture and their contextual and distributional analysis, taking into consideration variable political and social strategies and constraints. These nuanced approaches derive from specific places and times, revealing that different sets of artifacts track variable practices and processes that push the field beyond a one-size-fits-all model of market commerce or other modes of exchange. The contributors do not adhere to a simple, universalistic party line. We have collectively risen to the challenges laid out by David Freidel, Eleanor King, and Arthur Demarest and colleagues in Chapters 1–3 by documenting temporal and spatial variation in intersecting aspects of local and regional economies, drawing closer to defining a more emic framework for Pre-Columbian Maya market systems and other distinctive, if related, exchange systems. In this chapter I discuss the following recurring themes: degrees of autonomy and interdependence, labor, markets and merchants, boundedness and regional economies, movements of people and things, social affiliations, the interrelatedness of the concepts of value with the model of integrated, complex economies, and the strengths and pitfalls of ethnohistorical analogy. I conclude by recognizing that the time has come for Mayanists to draw on their own empirical data, rather than receiving wisdom from comparative treatises that contrast our region to that of central Mexico.

Autonomy, Interdependence, and Labor Specialization

The question of autonomy, or its synonym, self-sufficiency, has pervaded literature on Maya economies at the household, community, and polity scales for some time (e.g., Masson and Peraza 2004). This issue relates not only to household provisioning (Horowitz et al., Chapter 7) but also to spheres of exchange, seen by some to have been separate from one another (e.g., Scarborough and Valdez 2009). These concepts are reconsidered in the chapters of this book, mostly benefiting from the approach of examining relative rather than absolute qualities of autonomy, pertaining to specific production practices, contexts, or artifact types. The influential concept of prestige exchange was once part of a favored model for the economic foundations of New World states, along with the notion of a primary (and separate) distributive tribute economy supplying goods essential to daily life.

The authors in this volume observe that households and towns direct efforts toward degrees of self-provisioning but also take advantage of specific types of opportunities for economic interdependency at the community or regional scales. Such research questions within this book reflect the data and social contexts studied. Working at elite residences often coincides with the study of the production and exchange of sumptuary goods not pertinent to market exchange, for example.

Agricultural production has been traditionally associated with peasant economies regarded as self-sufficient, and such characterizations can go too far (Masson and Peraza 2004). Clearly, residents of cities or towns that invested heavily in cultivation, such as Caracol, Chan, and El Mirador (Chapters 8, 11, 18) would have consumed much homegrown food, but they were nonetheless interdependent on producers for other essential craft goods, as Diane Chase and Arlen Chase point out; agricultural surpluses would have enabled such purchases. Cerén (Chapter 14) and Mayapán (Chapter 5) farmers were also dependent on exchange for goods deemed essential to daily life. The quest to self-provision was a cross-cultural concern for premodern cities, but annual climatic fluctuations and other factors also prompt the institutionalization of options for food trade (Freidel and Shaw 2000; Masson and Peraza 2014a:407). Even when grain shortages are supplemented by imports or exchanges, in times of famine, impoverished sectors can disproportionately suffer (e.g., M. Davis 2001; Pounds 1973:433). Immense settlements with full commitments to cultivation like Caracol may have buffered such hardships, internally and externally (Chapter 8). Batún, McAnany, and Dedrick also emphasize the importance of labor directed toward surpluses for trade (Chapter 12). This was true not only for agriculture but also in large-scale salt production at Emal (Kepecs 2003) and at Salinas de Nueve Cerros (Woodfill, Chapter 10). On a smaller scale, the home gardens of Mensabak were not simply risk reduction mechanisms to guard against economic or subsistence strife. Rather, they were dynamic features, responding to larger, changing political and economic conditions, as Andrew Wyatt argues (Chapter 11). These gardens ultimately developed into expressions of wealth in terms of diversity or quantity of plants grown, as inequality became more pronounced in the community. Increasing demands for agricultural production, presumably beyond the community of Chan itself, resulted in expansion of terrace construction (Wyatt, Chapter 11).

It is probable that most agriculturalists of the Pre-Columbian Maya area did not cultivate the full suite of 497 plant food species documented by Scott Fedick (Chapter 13); El Mirador residents were also concerned with botanical diversity (Hansen et al., Chapter 18). As Fedick observes, some specialized plants, including many drought-resistant species, would have been desirable commodities in marketplace exchange. In a complex, interdependent economic system at the settlement, regional, and sometimes interregional scales, variation in geographical and ecological resources presents opportunities for local specialization and exchange between environmental zones. Is there a maize bias in dietary reconstructions due to factors of preservation and biased colonial and ethnographic analogies as Fedick suggests? Probably. Piña Chan (1978) compared tribute items from colonial polities in the peninsula, which were diverse and variable (Masson and Peraza 2014a:Figure 6.1). While Demarest and colleagues (Chapter 3) point out that heterogeneity in the tropical lowlands was not comparable to the hailed diversity of parts of central Mexico, what matters most is whether diversity and variation in natural resources were great enough to trigger occupational specialization, exchange, and interdependencies (e.g., Feinman and Nicholas 2004). The Colhá project (Hester and Shafer 1994; Shafer and Hester 1991; Potter and King 1995). Rathje (1971) revealed that the Maya area was sufficiently diverse to foster significant exchange dependencies. Chapters by Chase and Chase (Chapter 8), Hansen and colleagues (Chapter 18),

Fedick (Chapter 13), and Batún and colleagues (Chapter 12) reiterate this point. As early as the Middle Preclassic (Hansen et al. Chapter 18, Volta et al. Chapter 20), the desire for nonlocal items stoked interregional relationships that set the stages for commercial development, even if they may have originally been part of different kinds of exchanges, as Hansen and colleagues suggest (e.g., bride-wealth, gifting). Reents-Budet and Bishop (Chapter 19) advance this argument further, identifying strategic ties of Calakmul and Tikal networks that linked them to prime cotton-producing regions. A striking parallel for cacao, rather than cotton, was reported by Grant Jones for the Petén Itzá at Contact, as observed by Hernán Cortés; Lord Can Ek was connected to coastal subject towns, "who served him by cultivating certain cacao plantations for which the land was very suitable" (G. Jones 1989:103).

The prerogatives of autonomy or ownership would have been critical factors in complex economic relationships between humans and the environment. As Batún and colleagues eloquently state, labor is often definable as the relationship between humans and land (and its natural resources). Landesque capital in the form of orchards grown over years or decades and other coveted natural resources such as cenotes and other moisture traps was negotiated and defined by the labor investments of family groups. The Spanish colonial contention that land was communally held glosses over the proprietary rights of family groups and their cultivated features, even if elites would occasionally insert themselves into the politics of use (Freidel and Sabloff 1984:183; McAnany 1995). The archaeological record of the Postclassic Period, in which houselots and attached fields at Mayapán are delineated by boulder walls, and earlier at Chunchucmil and Cobá (Dahlin and Ardren 2002; Folan 1983), and the stone-lined field plots at Cozumel provide strong support for stakeholder ownership of gardens, fields, and orchards (Chapter 12 and Freidel and Sabloff 1984:181). It is important to remember that farmers were sometimes specialists, too, cultivating surplus (year-round or part-time) for exchange for craft goods as argued for rural Mayapán through time (Chapter 5). Salt-workers, fishers, and those working in other subsistence industries, including slaves, also constitute individuals who engaged in specialized labor, at least intermittently (Batún et al., Chapter 12; Restall 2001:359).

Alexandre Tokovinine's discussion (Chapter 16) of labor tallies from the early twentieth century and their potential time depth in the Maya area underscores the importance of labor, not only in terms of household production and exchange but as a commodity in its own right (see also Kepecs 2003). Human service (labor), as Sheets (Chapter 14) illustrates, was an essential mechanism for the operation of integrated economic institutions across hierarchical and horizontal systems. His chapter also emphasizes the voluntary, cooperative nature of some labor contributed at the community level (as do Batún et al., Chapter 12). Service roles and farming likely took place in concert with the seasonality of the agricultural cycle, as Sheets reminds us.

Controlled labor was an asset in its own right, for purposes unrelated to market exchange, as proposed by Ringle, Gallareta, and Bey (Chapter 6) in their consideration of the finely built stone houses of the Late Classic Puuc region. Creating fine masonry was (and still is) a revered occupation in northwest Yucatán. Did Puuc lords allocate masons' efforts in nonroyal house construction as part of the deployment of political and social capital? Such gifting, compellingly argued by these authors, adds the dimension of labor (service) to a realm of dispensation of goods formerly considered primarily from the perspective of portable artifacts. The inalienable permanence of fine houses, as they emphasize, would have represented a powerful and enduring symbol of affiliation and patronage. In smaller settlements, the construction and maintenance of public facilities may be been delegated as service obligations to individual families (Sheets, Chapter 14). The limited use of hieroglyphics, aside from the stairway, at the Guzmán Group of El Palmar may similarly reflect restricted allotments to subroyal elites by lords controlling scribal arts, in that ruling elites exercised "prerogative knowledge" (Tsukamoto, Chapter 15). Paper was made at this group, as recovered barkbeaters indicate. Is it possible that writing was confined to this medium at the group, or were these *lakamob* making bark paper destined for use by limited members of El Palmar society? Unfortunately, such questions are unanswerable due to paper's status as a perishable good.

Sergio Quezada's (2014:13, 21) negation of the Pre-Columbian existence of family-owned landholdings, based on patterns observed for the Colonial Period, is implausible. He also considers production activities only in the context of patronage and collectives, without mentioning producers' options in the marketplace. The fragile state of life on the peninsula after a century of warfare, disease, famine, and conquest spanning the late Pre-Contact and early Contact periods in the peninsula (Masson and Peraza, eds. 2014) was not equivalent to the height of prosperity of the Mayapán regime (Masson and Peraza 2014b). Quezada's (2014:14) diminutive view of the Mayapán confederacy echoes old downtrodden characterizations of the Postclassic Period (e.g., H. Pollock 1962), which have now been challenged. Batún and colleagues effectively argue that more complex economic institutions regarding land tenure endured into the colonial era.

The realm of service occupations, however part-time, as presented by Sheets (Chapter 14), is an important topic that has been understudied in our field, except for crafters or artisans in the service of elites. We have wrangled with this issue at Mayapán (Masson and Peraza 2014a:288, 294, 376, 421). Where did corvée laborers, including soldiers, drafted from beyond the city's boundaries reside while on temporary duty? To what degree might "ordinary" (noncrafting, commoner, not particularly wealthy) houses reflect families engaged in seasonal service industries, or do they mostly represent agriculturalist specialists living in the city who farmed plots within and beyond the urban zone? Market vendors provided services for communities, even making objects on demand in marketplaces as Cap reports (Chapter 22).

Artifact and botanical concentrations at Cerén attest to labor specialization. Individual dwellings in proximity to such features as a sauna and a ritual structure also suggest service affiliations. Household 4, with its array of specialized plants, provides a strong indication of a need for such items not duplicated in the gardens of every dwelling. Surely this was also true at other sites, and it is for villages today (Wyatt, Chapter 11; Russell and Farstad 2016). Monumental buildings at Mayapán are regularly flanked by small "custodial" houses (Peraza and Masson 2014b:72–74, Delgado et al. 2020). In fact, these are the only dwellings within monumental spaces; palaces are located beyond the main plazas (Hare et al. 2014). Duties such as guarding ritual architecture (and deity effigies installed within them) as well as cleaning and maintaining the edifices are implied. This site's custodians were often (but not always) engaged in a range of activities, including fine crafting of figurines, censers, or metal objects; they were presumably retained by elite patrons (Paris 2008; Peraza et al. 2015). Service industries can also be indicated by concentrations of specific artifacts, such as manos, for places that prepared food and residential groups with high densities of serving wares that suggest responsibilities of hosting feasts (Sheets, Chapter 14; Triadan and Inomata, Chapter 17; Tsukamoto, Chapter 15). How interesting it is to note that ritual and royal (respectively) headdresses were housed within dwellings at Cerén and Aguateca (Chapter 14, Chapter 17)! Here we see such responsibilities replicated at the village and political center scales.

A high degree of production self-sufficiency is inferred for elite residences at Aguateca analyzed by Triadan and Inomata (Chapter 17), in terms of food preparation and the manufacture of ordinary pottery as well as high-value artisanal crafts (Inomata 2001). These results are important, as the issue of production self-sufficiency has been underexamined with regard to high-status contexts, compared to commoners (e.g., Lohse and Valdez 2004; Masson and Peraza 2014b; Robin 2013; Masson et al. Chapter 5; D. Chase and A. Chase, Chapter 8; Horowitz et al., Chapter 7). Households like those of Aguateca certainly possessed the skills to manufacture ordinary storage and cooking vessels, given that they were already engaged in making finer pots (Inomata 2001). It is also true that some secondary elite households (for example, House Z-39) at Mayapán engaged in chert, shell, and obsidian crafting on a scale similar to commoner contexts (Masson et al. 2016). But production for household use would not have meant that each household was an island unto itself, given responsibilities to the community, perhaps including feasting and the manufacture and storage of important regalia. Similarly, the *lakam* household of El Palmar engaged in fine crafting, hosted feasts, and participated in an ambassadorial manner in political matters, as Tsukamoto reports (Chapter 15).

But would elites (beyond Aguateca) generally have made their own ordinary pottery—and if so, why? At Mayapán and Laguna de On (Masson 2000:Figure 4.6; Masson et al. 2016) we have employed Stark's (1985) criteria for identifying pottery production areas in the absence of kilns or wasters. Foremost is an incredibly dense overall quantity of sherds, at Mayapán in outlier proportions, especially in places where other activities such as feasting events (and preparations for them) are unlikely to have occurred. Such contexts, of which there are few, at these two Postclassic sites correlate with other markers such as potting hearths, molds (potters also made figurines), or caches of pigments unlike those found at nonpotting contexts (Delgado et al. 2020). Triadan and Inomata (Chapter 17) convincingly point out that exceptionally large storage vessels (made by elites) would have been fragile and difficult to transport, a good reason for their onsite manufacture. The production of low numbers of anomalous vessels would not generate the quantity of debris diagnostic of a workshop making ordinary pots in large numbers. At Mayapán, too, such large storage vessels are also present (Peraza and Masson 2014a:Figure 3.17). They are rare, and no evidence suggests their manufacture at workshops.

The fact that storage and food processing occurred within Aguateca elite households reflects scant reliance on service outside of the household for these quotidian functions. Elites' license to exercise a degree of self-determination and agency is also reflected by distinctive practices or material culture. Such findings represent an important line of inquiry as idiosyncratic details representing maker choices likely reflect aspects of social identity (Tsukamoto, Chapter 15; Peraza and Masson 2014a). As at Aguateca, a lack of spatial segregation of food storage and preparation activities is also noted at Mayapán's public buildings and also at Xochicalco's central edifices. Preparations for feasting and other ceremonial occasions were conducted onsite in these public realms. Metates and vessels used for storage (food and water) and food preparation formed important proportions of assemblages at Mayapán's halls and temples (Masson and Peraza, eds. 2014:123, 125); similar results were found at Xochicalco by Cyphers and Hirth (2000). Faunal analysis at Mayapán reveals that entire carcasses of deer were butchered at public buildings (Masson and Peraza 2013). Some crafting also occurred at Mayapán's public buildings (spinning, weaving, figurine and effigy censer making), perhaps reflecting the onsite manufacture of items needed for building-specific events (Peraza et al. 2015). Activities leading up to the events seem to have been symbolically important (e.g., McAnany 2010; Wells and McAnany 2008). Alternatively (or complementarily), onsite preparations were a matter of *costumbre* or convenience. Greater spatial activity segregation is reported by Sheets at Cerén (Chapter 14), with surplus food preparation falling under the responsibilities of a particular household.

Markets and Merchants

This volume was an outgrowth of prolonged (and sometimes heated) arguments of the co-editors on the matter of the significance of Maya market institutions prior to the Postclassic Period, following Masson and Freidel's papers (2012, 2013) in this regard. David Freidel and I rallied analogies and comparisons of archaeological correlates of Classic and Postclassic era Maya market-oriented production and exchange and the critical relationship of these activities to daily life, political economy (its permeation at all social scales), and the general stability of Classic era city states.

Our arguments contributed to an emerging set of literature in Maya archaeology that also reconsidered the market question, such as recent works by Tokovinine and Beliaev (2013), Masson and Freidel (2012, 2013), McAnany (2013), King and Shaw (2015), L. Shaw (2012), Dahlin et al. (2010), and many others referenced in this volume. Despite some doubts (Chapter 3), marketplace facilities do matter (Chapter 1), representing key infrastructural evidence best considered in combination with other categories of data (A. Chase 1998; Hirth 1998; King, Chapter 2; D. Chase and A. Chase, Chapter 8; Cap, Chapter 22).

Recent work represents a second wave of scholarly attention directed toward the issue of Maya area market systems. Fine-grained studies of the circulation of different types of polychrome pottery within Tikal by Fry (2003) and Culbert (2003), for example, reflect a long tradition of consideration of market exchange for this site (Jones 1996). Fry and Culbert observe that a minority of polychrome types at Tikal were restricted, perhaps gifted or redistributed via nonmarket mechanisms. They report that most polychrome vessels and well-made nonlocal types were broadly distributed, likely obtained at Tikal's markets (Culbert 2003:65–68; Fry 2003: 150, 162–166). These authors also suggest that certain pots were obtained within neighborhoods, perhaps from producer-vendors. Even for the Aztec realm, considered to represent the height of commercial development for the Pre-Columbian New World, and despite Spaniards' eyewitness accounts, scholars were late in recognizing the importance of pre-Contact market systems to other key processes of socioeconomic development (Blanton 1996:80; Kowalewski 1990:54). In my opinion, studies of the Classic Maya are now undergoing a similar process, without the benefit of as many near-contemporary ethnohistorical sources.

Most colleagues arguing for the importance of markets do not negate the probability that goods were exchanged in other ways as well, through gifting or redistribution. Tsukamoto, Triadan and Inomata, and Reents-Budet and Bishop (Chapters 15, 17, 19) report production specifically geared toward items destined for restricted gifting or other exclusive forms of consumption. Some elites at Aguateca also seem to have received gifts from distant realms (Chapter 17), and this type of reciprocity is well chronicled in the literature, as discussed in detail in Chapters 17 and 19 (and elsewhere: e.g., Ball 1993; Foias and Bishop 2007; Inomata 2001; Reents-Budet et al. 1994, 2012). To what degree did multiple economic spheres operate independently of one another, sometimes framed as "dual economies," "prestige economies," or "domestic" versus "political" economies (e.g., D'Altroy and Hastorf 2001:4; Scarborough and Valdez 2009)? My colleagues and I have argued that the circulation of various goods of different value (and social context of production) formed components of a greater, more integrated, complex economic system (Freidel et al. 2016; Masson and Freidel 2012), as has Michael Smith (2004:77). There is no denying the existence of sumptuary restricted goods kept out of the marketplace and reserved for internoble gifting, or what Freidel and Reilly (2010) refer to as "treasure," which elites manipulate in all complex societies (M. Smith 2004:89).

Yet the process by which goods of middling worth, with more general distributions, achieve their value pivots from the reference point of treasures, as Lesure (1999) has argued for greenstone axes. The serpentine celt is a referent to a jade one, the notched and perforated olive shell tinkler is a referent to objects carved as death heads, and presumably, this relationship existed between more common and more rare polychrome vessels. Such objects were regarded along a continuum of value, precisely because elites promoted their worth in costume, display, and by assigning them symbolic properties (Freidel et al. 2016; Freidel and Reilly 2010). This continuum bridges the realms of restricted circulation and marketplace acquisition. Even chert artifacts and raw materials were considered according to a hierarchy of value linked to desirable properties (Horowitz et al., Chapter 7; Andrieu, Chapter 24). A perspective that considers integrated spheres of economic circulation and the relationships between objects circulated via different exchange modes of exchange does not negate the benefits of studying patterns specific to a single mode. Diane Chase and Arlen Chase (Chapter 8) use this approach in a classification of institutions crafted specifically to examine aspects of Caracol's economy. Michael Smith (2004:77) argues compellingly that household economies were integral components of political economies: the latter do not exist in a detached manner unrelated to the productive and distributive processes in which the majority of society toiled.

Maya archaeologists are likely to welcome evidence for functional differentiation among places within the Maya realm. Demarest and colleagues (Chapter 3) provide a clear example in Cancuén. M. Smith and F. Berdan (2003) ably demonstrated the existence of trading ports, affluent, well-connected peripheries, and core commercial nodes across the Mesoamerican Postclassic world as well as in more isolated peripheral zones. Caracol, while seemingly located in an out-of-the-way place, was strategically located in a corridor of diverse resources that contributed to its prosperity (Chapter 8). Kowalewski (1990) emphasizes the probability of functional differentiation among settlements within a region. Markets were functionally diversified among Aztec towns, as Blanton's (1996) treatise details. Competition for large and diverse market facilities resulted in variation, with politically unimportant places like Acapetlayocán delegated as a "turkey" market; political defeats sometimes resulted in the specialization of such markets that paled in comparison to city state capitals that attracted coveted and esteemed artisans and merchants (Blanton 1996:79). Mesoamerican archaeology has moved past the simple expectation that peripheries were uniformly impoverished and underdeveloped; sites located in boundary or frontier zones and other unusual, seemingly out of the way locations can exhibit great wealth (Chapter 3, Chapter 8). Sometimes, however, distant towns in supply zones were relatively impoverished, like San Martín Jilotepeque (G. Braswell 2002:303).

What proportion of exchanges was market-based, and what proportion was not? The essential issue of the relative importance of each exchange mode to the economic activities affecting the majority of members of ancient societies must be resolved across spatial and temporal analytical units. It does not suffice to adopt a tolerant general view that markets may have played a part, unquantified or compared, along with every other mode of exchange studied by anthropology. Elite-sponsored artisan crafts and gifting among nobles has been well studied for parts of the Maya area, but what proportion of exchanges do these represent for society as a whole? As Michael Smith (2004:89) points out, most societies, even those with well-developed market institutions, had sumptuary goods restricted in circulation (see also Freidel and Reilly 2010; Stuart 2006).

If key central places had large, diverse, and influential markets, enabled and encouraged by the governing class, the idea that this institution had no impact on subject towns and villages seems unlikely (Masson and Freidel 2012). How far would the reach of a given central market center have been? At El Perú–Waka' ceramics mostly represented local goods, as Eppich reports (Chapter 9); overlapping but relatively local spheres of pottery exchange were present at Piedras Negras as well (Golden and colleagues, Chapter 23). In general, compared to stone tools (chert and obsidian) and marine shell, ceramics are heavier and present greater but not insurmountable transport considerations. Exchange models relying primarily on ceramics, especially majority types in common use, will generally track more bounded exchange spheres within cities or polities (Masson 2001a:183; West 2002). Given this consideration, ceramics are not a perfect proxy for the exchange of other goods, as Eppich suggests, but ceramic economies undoubtedly formed an essential component of integrated exchange systems for Maya cities and political networks. Eppich's fine-grained chronological comparisons answer Demarest et al.'s (Chapter 3) call for tighter chronological control. Late Classic polychromes were not distributed in markets until the Terminal Classic at El Perú–Waka', in his analysis, but the Late Classic patterns are complicated. Polychromes are present in all households, with higher frequencies in elite contexts. As Fry (2003) and Culbert (2003) note at Tikal, polychromes do not represent a uniform artifact class: specific types circulated differently. Monochromes at El Perú–Waka' were probably distributed in markets in Eppich's estimation, unlike for the elite houses at Aguateca

(Chapter 17). Clearly, the intricacies and variable traditions of ceramic economies merit continued examination.

Arthur Demarest and colleagues (Chapter 3) take issue with chronological intervals represented by nonceramic artifact distributions from Classic Period Tikal, used by Masson and Freidel (2012, 2013) to argue for Classic and Postclassic distributional parity. Another run at the Tikal data by Hutson (Chapter 4) provides complementary results with respect to commoner access to high quantities of obsidian (more than elites) at this site. His findings raise new questions. It is true that Tikal was one of the Classic Period's most important political capitals (aside from its hiatus), and dwellings at smaller sites may be expected to exhibit fewer and less diverse goods. Not surprisingly, David Freidel and I stand by our findings, especially given that the 2012 article takes care to utilize the Late Classic Period (rather than the Classic Period as a whole) data, drawing on William Haviland's carefully reported chronological results. The Late Classic Period approximates the same interval length as Mayapán, 200–250 years. While the Cancuén analysis benefits from exceptional microchronology, the result of relative paucity of obsidian in commoner contexts would not be any different if all intervals of the Late Classic at this site were lumped together. That is, there was never a time when this site followed expectations of Hirth's distributional model. This point provides hope that archaeologists working with grosser temporal scales (Early Classic, Late Classic, Terminal Classic, and so forth) will generate valid results.

The relative poverty of nonelites at Cancuén is striking and provides an important wake-up call that guards against simplistic universal models for Maya city economies through space and time. It is this kind of variation that has been anticipated by archaeologists exploring the *relative* importance of Maya market institutions (Dahlin 2009; Hutson 2017; Hutson et al. 2010; Hutson and Dahlin 2017; King 2015; Masson and Freidel 2012, 2013). Ironically, however, Cancuén's distinctive characteristics are attributed to the rise in mercantile power. So in this case we have a city intricately connected to a far-reaching commercial system that defies Hirth's distributional model. Excellent! Recent investigations of the roles of merchants in Classic era Maya society emphasize their exclusion and demeaning portrayal by royals controlling the mediums of art and writing (McAnany 2010, 2013; Tokovinine and Beliaev 2013:188). Eisenstad's (1988) comparative social histories reveal a perpetual struggle between political and mercantile sectors (and religious officials), given the prospects for merchant wealth and influence. Toward the end of the Classic Period, merchants at Cancuén appear to have seized control, with poor results for lower-status sectors. This point also challenges prevailing models indicating that the amplification of market commerce, as a rule, coincides with greater commoner affluence (e.g., Hirth 1998; Masson 2000; Sabloff and Rathje 1975), as does the relative impoverishment of some, but not all, noncrafting households at Mayapán (Chapter 5; Masson and Peraza 2014a:419, Masson and Freidel 2013). Eppich (Chapter 9) importantly points out that the "rise" (and fall) of the merchant sectors began prior to the Postclassic Period (Sabloff and Rathje 1975). He proposes that at El Perú–Waka' the decline of a mercantile system is observed through time within the Classic era. The Terminal Classic marked the period of the erosion of Caracol's centralized market institutions (Chapter 8). These authors meet the challenges laid out in Chapter 3 for diachronically qualified economic analyses.

Another point of irony is that the rise of Cancuén's merchants did not result in any apparent marketplace in the city (Chapter 3). The Cancuén case fits nicely in Kowalewski's (1990) expectations of functional differentiation of centers across a regional landscape. The irony continues with Hutson's (Chapter 4) evaluation of Chunchucmil, a city more focused on commerce than politics. In this nucleus of market system exchange, replete with a marketplace, the distributional model is not a good fit. Why? Is this a case semiparallel to Cancuén, where amplified mercantile sector power suppresses access of some ordinary residents to nonlocal goods?

Even in well-developed market systems, leveling mechanisms in terms of access to nonlocal or fancy goods are expected to be incomplete (Hirth 1998; Smith 2004:89). Elites, by definition, are expected to be wealthier and are likely to possess more than commoners as a whole. That they do not possess more obsidian at Tikal according to Hutson's analysis may have more to do with the uses and relatively low value of obsidian at that site, as he argues. Our study of Mayapán's rural houses (Chapter 5) for the Terminal and Postclassic periods illustrates the point that some commoners, within and beyond the city wall, were poorer than others. As for elite versus commoner patterns, economic standing within the nonelite sector should also be expected to vary at urban places and their peripheries. The rural houses that we investigated were not uniformly impoverished, varying according to activity diversification (including crafting) as well as wealth, as is also observed in the urban zone. Surplus crafting correlates with commoner wealth in this city (Masson and Peraza, eds. 2014:419).

To what degree were markets and merchants relatively autonomous from political control? Demarest and colleagues (Chapter 3) challenge recent critiques of enduring views that premodern market systems were autonomous and self-regulating. The apolitical characterization of markets traces its roots to the writings of Adam Smith or even Classical sources before him (Graeber 2011:24–25). However, this view has been challenged. The embeddedness of market institutions and agents in social and political relationships, once thought to be a primitive trait, is now recognized as a factor shared by many systems, premodern to contemporary (King, Chapter 2; Blanton 1996; Cribb 2005:420; Feinman and Garraty 2010; Maurer 2006:17; Freidel et al. 2013). In Chapter 3 Demarest and colleagues have a point in arguing that the relative degree of market system autonomy must be investigated rather than assumed, and few would disagree with the need for models derived from empirical data. In some cases, infrastructural evidence reveals significant institutional control (Chapter 8); in others, market facilities housed in epicenters seem to have folded commercial activities into monumental settings where a suite of other centralized activities took place (e.g., Cap, Chapter 22; Dahlin et al. 2007; Jones 1996; Wurtzburg 1991). Production activities of nonroyal elites may have been relatively independent, according to Triadan and Inomata (Chapter 17). Presumably this lack of interest in quotidian supervision extended to the commoner production as well, given the efficiency of controlling mechanisms of distribution rather than production (e.g., Freidel 1981), as well as the real possibility of heterarchical exchanges between communities (Scarborough et al. 2003). Consumers and traders at Chunchucmil seem to have exercised considerable autonomy, reflected in variable domestic assemblages (Hutson, Chapter 4).

Archaeologists studying Maya economies must also look more deeply into what is meant by concepts of control or supervision of institutions such as markets (King, Chapter 2). This issue is separate from patronage or sponsorship of fine or sumptuary goods. Given the exclusion of market business and merchants from much of Maya hieroglyphic text and writing (also true in central Mexican pictorial manuscripts), analogies to the Contact Period represent useful resources from which to build models and expectations of the data. Freidel and I have discussed the issue of a nuanced degree of elite control of markets in depth elsewhere (Masson and Freidel 2012, 2013).

To summarize, ideal types such as those proposed by Carol Smith (1976b), by her own estimation, may only partially correspond to historical cases. During the Contact Period, major successful Maya area market facilities and events described by Spanish sources included the following oversight elements: security, laws governing where and when trade occurred, dispute resolution and deliberations of weights and measures (by market judges), and bureaucratic edifices for housing judges and places where purchasing agents for elites could engage in special transactions (Masson and Freidel 2013:203, Table 8.1). Blanton (1996) reveals that elites vied for the richest and most diverse markets precisely because they benefited from them, not only by taxing merchants, but due to the opportunities provided for exchanging one form of surplus for another as well as the prestige that they brought to city state capitals. Hosting, organizing, and policing major central marketplaces does not imply complete control in the sense of Smith's full elite monopoly outlined in the solar central-place model. As Freidel (1981) observed, dispersed Maya producers were beyond the reach of full elite control of production, with central place (major market event) distribution representing a more efficient option for elites. Looser local markets probably operated within neighborhoods and at smaller towns and villages in the countryside. Vendors also no doubt traded their wares from home as noted at Contact (Feldman 1978a), whether elites sanctioned this or not. The question of control benefits from consideration of sources specific to the Maya area (King, Chapter 2; Tokovinine and Beliav 2013).

Boundedness and Regional Economies

The question of the regional reach of major market nodes aligns with the struggle in the archaeology of state societies to define the term "region" (e.g., Feinman 2000; Feinman and Nicholas 2010; Kowalewski 1990). Appropriate scales of regional analysis could include estimated polity boundaries for centers and their subjects (Volta et al., Chapter 20; Horowitz et al., Chapter 7) or larger cultural and natural geographic units within vast regions like the Maya area that interacted intensively in a way that results in shared architectural, ceramic, or other artifactual styles (e.g., Masson 2001a).

It has long been clear that northwest Yucatán Maya society was distinctive compared to the southern lowlands. For all of the contributions that the Chunchucmil project made toward recognizing a commercial Early Classic center, Dahlin considered this site to be "ahead of its time" (Dahlin 2009, see also Dahlin and Chase 2014). It is anomalous compared to its contemporaries in terms of the quantity of nonlocal goods (Hutson et al. 2010; Hutson 2017). Ringle and colleagues (Chapter 6) also point out that the Puuc region reveals little evidence for the importance of market exchange to daily life. Few nonlocal goods are generally found. My colleagues and I find similar results in a rural Terminal

Classic setting near Mayapán (Chapter 5). Do these data imply weak or nonexisting market exchange? Certainly that is one viable interpretation. Were Late and Terminal Classic Maya households in Yucatán especially poor, compared, for example, to commoners at Tikal (Masson and Freidel 2012)? Possibly.

However, the Terminal Classic residents in the Mayapán area did not make their own pottery, as years of survey by my colleagues and I have determined. Yet the one abundant and diverse category of artifact at these contexts is ceramics. We infer that ceramic exchange, tied to regional markets, supplied these residents. My ongoing collaborative research with Carlos Peraza analyzing similar dwelling assemblages of this period at sites other than Mayapán reveals that this pattern is not unique to our study area. Perhaps market structures were organized more regionally and with different emphases in northwest Yucatán: ceramic trade may have been prioritized, along with other goods deriving from this region such as ground stone (reasonably abundant and diverse at Terminal Classic dwellings), foodstuffs, and other perishables. If this is true, such a system would have been bounded within a smaller region (the Puuc area, the northwestern plains, or both), with less emphasis on distant trade. The abundance of ceramics provides one line of evidence for dependency on regional exchange.

A greater boundedness seems apparent for the northwest Yucatán Puuc region (and affiliated parts of the northern plains) in terms of exchange, in striking contrast to data from Chichén Itzá, a commercial hub with diverse imports that exceeded those of any other Maya center (e.g., G. Braswell 2010; Coggins and Shane 1984; Gallareta et al. 1989). Ringle and colleagues (Chapter 6) present a strong case for the importance of a regional economy in stone working and masonry. Pottery was also especially important for the social and economic needs of this region. In the Mayapán study area we note a pervasive, significant investment in residential platforms, in contrast to modest superstructural remains (see also Carmean 1991:160). In this part of the north, economic investments seem to be following a different trajectory, emphasizing architecture, platforms, and pottery over other classes of things. Despite the boundedness of the El Mirador dendritic network proposed by Hansen and colleagues (Chapter 18), in which surrounding centers and towns may have formalized and directed their exchange activities into and out of the behemoth center, they also consider the expansive boundaries of ceramic stylistic similarities for this period (Chapter 18; Masson 2001a). There is no denying the effects of policies of political elites in influencing and directing the prospects for market success in central

Mexico, where dendritic principles were at play (except where elite actors intervened) and where the Late Aztec system was somewhat "top-heavy" (Blanton 1996:80).

Boundedness for economies centered on specific political capitals would have varied through time according to the well-documented process of shifting political landscapes. At Late Classic Calakmul, economic exchanges were more tightly focused around this major capital and its hinterland and expanded more regionally in the Terminal Classic (Volta et al., Chapter 20). These results echo those reported by Eppich for El Perú/Waka'. Of critical importance to a regional perspective is the influence of macropolitics on boundedness and economic exchange spheres. Despite Volta and colleagues' perspective on the boundedness of Late Classic Calakmul's economy, Reents-Budet and Bishop (Chapter 19) suggest that this capital was the nucleus of one of two principal zones of interaction for this period; the other was centered at Tikal. Zones of interaction involving ceramic emulation and supply zones, as Reents-Budet and Bishop document, differed from tighter economic orbits tracked by other measures at Calakmul as well as at El Mirador.

The Tikal-Calakmul enmity may have suppressed the flow of obsidian to Calakmul (Masson and Freidel 2012:478; Volta et al., Chapter 20), although, curiously, not jades. The intriguing suggestion by Beniamino Volta and colleagues that dyadic, external trade contacts were of magnified importance for Calakmul's elites, precisely because certain flows of market goods were partially suppressed, bears serious consideration. Nonetheless this capital, like Tikal, may have also exerted extensive influence in zones of strategic interest such as prime cotton-producing regions, as Reents-Budet and Bishop reveal (Chapter 19). Similar to this strategy regarding cotton-producing areas, Mayapán proactively oversaw its interests in cacao cultivation zones from afar (Roys 1962:50, 55–60; Masson and Peraza 2014a:278–280). While small quantities of essential goods like cotton or cacao could be grown in special environments in areas like relatively arid northwest Yucatán, local production did not satisfy the appetites of these regional economies. Other parts of the lowlands with more rainfall and deeper soils were more suitable for production of surplus for export.

Movements of Goods and Social Affiliations

Ceramicists have long recognized that Classic-era ceramics reflect affiliated political zones within the Maya region. Majority types with widespread distributions hint at the geographic extent of political and economic interaction. Reents-Budet and Bishop (Chapter 19) approach this problem using NAA data. Rarer, nonlocal pottery reflects external relationships of a different sort, as chapters in this volume consider.

Political dyadic relationships were significant for supplies of coveted valuables (including nonlocal vessels) not available in market settings (Volta et al., Chapter 20; Demarest et al., Chapter 3). What other factors, besides political rivalries, might have affected the geographic extent of pottery affliations? Stark (1997) proposed that population size and concentration were important factors; as these variables increase, an increase can be observed in the relative nucleation of pottery traditions. When larger numbers of producers and consumers are concentrated, they provide critical mass for robust exchange economies over more compact geographical zones, as for intervals of the Classic Maya era (Masson 2001a). Conversely, lower or more dispersed populations may correlate with broader geographical style zones, as for the Late Preclassic and Postclassic Periods (Masson 2001a). While such correlations may not apply to all historical cases, they are worth considering. It is true that the Late Preclassic and Postclassic Maya political landscapes differed in many important ways, including population sizes for urban centers as well as the number and size of contemporary political centers. Were ceramic emulation spheres broader when the peninsula was dominated by fewer dominant political capitals? The Late and Terminal Classic situation in northern Yucatán, divided by the Cehpech and Sotuta phenomenon, may represent another case of a pair of broader regional spheres of exchange and social identity emanating from the nuclei of Uxmal and Chichén Itzá (Robles and Andrews 1986).

Rarer pottery types were likely acquired via personal household ties (Triadan and Inomata, Chapter 17), which may also have brought obsidian into Chunchucmil households (Hutson, Chapter 4). At Aguateca elites exercised relative autonomy to pursue and maintain socioeconomic relationships beyond the polity. Chunchucmil, an acephalous, anomalous city, had multiple, similarly ranked elite groups that seem to have operated independently in long-distance trading ventures. The radial organization of this city also reflects the formalization of social divisions (Hutson 2016). Merchants represented social actors, as previously noted. Cross-culturally, they tend to isolate themselves (King, Chapter 2), forming insular or exclusive social groups in their own right.

Migration was an essential process for the demographic stability of cities in the preindustrial world (Kowalewski 1990; Paine and Storey 2006). Most archaeologists in the Maya area face challenges in identifying ethnic groups, due to the lack of distinctive material cultures marking migrants or rapid assimilation processes glossing difference (Masson and Peraza 2010). But peoples of the Petén Lakes region often did express themselves distinctively in architectural and ceramic forms (P. Rice and D. Rice 2009). Prudence Rice (Chapter 25) notes that transformations, migrations, and intermarriage were important processes in Terminal Classic, contributing to the introduction and distribution of a distinctive pottery type. Black-and-gray ware distributions, in her assessment, attest to integrative patterns in the western Petén that contradict a more widely held balkanization model advanced for the Terminal Classic Period. This pottery tradition represents a ceramic "system," more broadly, across the western part southern lowlands. Not yet identified are the kinds of interactions responsible for the incorporation of these vessels into local inventories. Deeper social changes beyond more conventional forms of trade are likely responsible (Rice, Chapter 25). Her chapter adopts an agent-centered approach, like many others in this volume.

Routes Connecting the Ties That Bind

Movements of people and goods, whether through migration or for travel, would ideally have followed prescribed routes through consenting territories. Passages through territories were not haphazard and were potentially dangerous, as attested to by travel accounts of colonial friars (G. Jones 1989). Fernando Robles and colleagues (Chapter 21) identify the existence of a former estuarine *ría* along which trading sites were located through the Terminal Classic Period. The Maya area literature has often considered the importance of canoe-borne traffic along coastal routes. The existence of a quieter, safer passageway represents an important contribution to the assessment of trade pathways in the north (McKillop 2002). Chapter 21 complements findings from Chunchucmil, near the western coast of the northern peninsula, with its economy that capitalized on salt and trade; the *ría* extended to the coast near this site and its port, Canbalám (Figure 21.1). Central sites along the *ría* shifted in importance and location with each period from the Late Preclassic through the Terminal Classic, sometimes spaced with strategic regularity (Chapter 21). Similarly, the Chikinchel polity to the east specialized in salt trade, especially in the Terminal and Postclassic Periods (Kepecs 2003). Anthony Andrews (1980; Andrews and Mock 2002) has long recognized the major impacts of the salt industry on

Maya commerce. Chapter 21 represents a fine blend of environmental reconstruction, use of ethnohistorical documents, and the archaeological record. It is interesting that fine sumptuary goods were also present along *ría* sites, such as turquoise and sculpture from the Petén, in addition to a wide array of less scarce valuables.

Volta and colleagues (Chapter 20) map out four least-cost routes linking important Classic Period centers. A north-south route complements the proposed royal road that connected Cancuén to Calakmul. Three others extend from the Chetumal Bay westward into the interior, two of which pass through Río Azul by way of the Río Hondo. The northern path passes by Calakmul; the southern path passes Nakbé and El Mirador. Both connect to the important Campeche center of El Tigre on the Candelaria River. The third east-west route, utilizing the Río Escondido, passes close to Calakmul but is closer to its affiliated sites of La Muñeca, Oxpemul, and Río Bec. Importantly, this route then turns northward to a different destination on the western Campeche coast. Such routes were partly aquatic and partly overland. Volta and colleagues suggest that another route may exist that generally follows the path taken for the colonial era north-south Camino Real. Roys (1972:52) mentions an additional route that connected the north (Maní province, Xiu territory) to the Río Hondo; it has yet to be investigated. Notably, there is overlap between some of the interaction zones identified by Reents-Budet and Bishop (Chapter 19) and the routes proposed by Volta et al., especially for the area bridging Calakmul and Chetumal Bay as well as the area encompassing Becán, Calakmul, La Corona, and El Perú–Waka' (sites connected by the royal road). Reents-Budet and Bishop identify additional zones that would have had their own aquatic and terrestrial routes, yet to be reconstructed, in the western, central, southern and southeastern parts of the Maya area.

Lingering Questions

While this book has taken the pulse of current research on the workings of Maya economies, much work remains to be done in the coming years. There is no broad consensus regarding the complexity of Maya systems in any given period or even farther beyond the borders of this region in greater Mesoamerica. Most controversial, and erroneous, in my view, is the insistence in certain corners on clinging to notions of the primitive when it comes to Maya monetary units, trade, and market systems. Pre-Columbian Maya society, when characterized as a whole, with little regard for temporal or spatial variation, has generally served as a straw dog for *big* theory contrasting it to the west or to Aztec central Mexico. This extensive topic, addressed by King in Chapter 2, merits its own book and can only be briefly touched upon here. The time has come for theory-builders to read and heed the evidence for Maya economic complexity, rather than continuing to draw on old assumptions that trace their roots to the "Law of Environmental Limitation" in Meggers (1954), which claimed that the tropics are no place for advanced civilization to develop or be sustained.

Comparison of Western and non-Western preindustrial states in terms of markets was long stifled due to influential models contrasting the West and the rest (King, Chapter 2; Mayer 2013). The concept of money has been at the center of this problem. General-purpose money, used to purchase any kind of other good or service available for sale, is still not considered to be a valid part of Pre-Columbian Maya economies by authors such as Speal (2014). As shell money is used as a special purpose (noncommercial) unit in well-known, nonstate ethnographic cases in anthropology, it has not inspired detailed study as a commercial currency in the Maya area despite Contact Period testimonies. David Freidel, Michelle Rich, and I (Freidel et al. 2016) recently confronted monetary questions and rallied evidence for Classic era monies and tokens (see also Baron 2018b; Freidel and Reilly 2010; Stuart 2006). While sacks of cacao beans and textile monies are perishable, specific (monetary) shell beads and pendants are not. Their properties of scarcity, standardization, distribution, and valuation provide data relevant to the identification and study of currencies.

Literate and numerate officials in Maya society, like many "bean counters" in premodern states, seem to have kept account of transactions with tallies and tokens. The consideration of tokens suggests that evidence for account-keeping does exist in plain sight, representing the best explanation for seemingly odd burial inclusions such as spindle whorls standing in for the ever-important commodity of cotton in royal graves, bone sticks alluding to tallies, and wax pallets observed in art and perhaps as grave goods (Freidel et al. 2016). McAnany (2010) argues for the representation of economic commodities (tribute goods) adorning persons attending royal courts as seen in Maya art (e.g., "walking tribute bundles"). Alexandre Tokovinine (Chapter 16) carries the tally argument forward for bone and stick tallies, a phenomenon known elsewhere in premodern courts and commerce. Tallies of goods represent a natural extension of practices of accounting and arithmetic. The status of unmarked counting sticks (or bones) as tallies is strengthened by cases where carved examples are found in association with uncarved versions; archaeologists will have to reconsider the importance of these enigmatic artifacts. Loans, credit, and profit, also previously considered to be institutions of no relevance to non-Western economies like those of the Maya area, now merit a deeper look (Chapter 16; Tokovinine and Beliaev 2013). Old World scholars have also had to overcome similar obstacles in recognizing ancient currencies in a less primitivizing framework (von Reden 2010).

An argument concerning barter markets is now underway in our field, provoked by Graeber's (2011) chapter "The Myth of Barter," in which he states, point blank, that barter markets never existed as a precursor to commercial markets that relied on debt accounts or money. That is, barter markets are nowhere documented as a means for regular daily provisioning of the needs of households within a community. This does not mean that individuals did not barter on occasion, with members of outside groups, but Graeber removes "barter markets" from the unilineal evolutionary scheme. What some refer to as barter exchanges within communities sounds more like cases of reciprocity (including delayed reciprocity) outlined by Graeber (see also King, Chapter 2) or credit advanced during market transactions. Baron (2018a:109, 111), for example, suggests that a barter-based market system preceded full monetization and market commerce at the end of the Classic Period but also considers the existence of credit account transactions in markets. Eppich (Chapter 9) advocates for the importance of barter between persons in a community but does not distinguish this from reciprocity. Graeber's position (2011:29) clarifies the matter: "Now, all this hardly means that barter does not exist—or even that it's never practiced by the sort of people that Smith would refer to as 'savages.' It just means that it's almost never employed, as Smith imagined, between fellow villagers." Graeber's point is that barter markets did not serve as an evolutionary precursor to market exchange as a means of regular, ongoing daily provisions for the goods essential to daily life. This does not mean, as Eppich states, that neighbors did not sometimes exchange things or favors (services) with each other, but that is reciprocity, not a precommerce barter market stage of development.

Barry Isaac is a renowned scholar on the topic of New World economies, with a deep well of knowledge, particularly of the Aztec realm. His views on Mesoamerican and Maya economies are cited by Demarest and colleagues (Chapter 3). Isaac (2013) is a go-to place to find a dismissive view of commercial complexity for southern Mesoamerica and even the central highlands. But to what extent is Isaac familiar with the emerging data from the Maya area? Like

Hirth and Pillsbury (2013), Isaac (2013:435) uses the term "periodic" to describe poorly developed Maya commercial institutions, in claiming that market events were scheduled on a nonregular basis and were peripheral to the mainstream economy. In fact, periodic market events, as originally proposed by Freidel (1981), were invoked to argue for regularly scheduled systematic events that could coincide with other state affairs, drawing large crowds of people. Since then arguments have expanded to suggest that marketplaces were frequently open for business at major regional centers (Masson and Freidel 2012, 2013). Support for this is found in Contact Period accounts, for example, the existence of daily markets in towns of highland Guatemala (Berdan et al. 2003:101; Feldman 1978b:12).

Blanton et al. (1993:221–222) favor a prestige goods economy for the Maya area in their model, claiming that "there is little evidence for the formation of regular interregional dependencies for goods in common use." The literature from the Maya region now has much evidence to the contrary. Such promoters of big, overarching theories and societal type characterizations ignore the subtleties of the data over space and type, as are offered in the chapters of this volume. Even in central Mexico the debate rages on. In the important 2013 volume *Merchants, Markets, and Exchange in the Pre-Columbian World*, editors Hirth and Pillsbury (2013:15), state: "The Mexican Highlands had a thriving commercial economy centered on the marketplace. What remains unclear is the degree of household participation in the marketplace, especially in rural areas at variable distances from large urban centers." This characterization contrasts with research in the Aztec countryside that has resoundingly demonstrated high levels of market integration and interdependence (e.g., Brumfiel 2005; M. Smith 2010; M. Smith and Heath-Smith 1994). Regarding Classic Maya society, Hirth and Pillsbury (eds., 2013:16) offer that "the palace was the center of elite power and governance as well as the heart of its institutional economy" . . . "Goods certainly moved across the Maya region, but by whom and in what quantity remains unclear." They write: "Salt, for example, was not widely traded within Yucatan, but individuals traveled from towns to the coast to process what they needed." This view is what McKillop refers to as the "family salt picnic" idea (personal communication, 2018), which denies the importance of salt trade in the Maya area despite years of research rallying substantial ethnohistorical and archaeological evidence (A. Andrews 1983; Andrews and Mock 2002; Kepecs 2003, 2007; McKillop 2002). Even in the Contact Period, despite a century of hardship and political dissolution, the polity of Sotuta relied on exchange of "game and fruit" for "salt and fish" with the coastal polity of Chikinchel (Landa 1941:40). Like Baron (2018b), Hirth and Pillsbury contend that "trade" became "acceptable" during the Terminal Classic Period in the Maya area, as does Blanton (Blanton 2013:32). Blanton, speaking of Maya economies, allows for "restricted" "border" markets in "weak" marginal areas, a model that flies in the face of evidence for large central places associated with centrally featured market infrastructure and activity (for recent summaries, see King, ed. 2015; Masson and Freidel 2012).

Blanton's purpose is to draw contrasts to the relative sophistication of central Mexican commerce. Similarly, by comparison to the Maya, Isaac (2013:436) notes: "In contrast, . . . the Spanish conquerors were agape . . . at the thousands of producer-vendors . . . as well as the numerous regional merchants in the Aztec Empire," although he still argues that direct barter was also the most usual mode of exchange in Central Mexican marketplaces. Exchange currencies, in Isaac's estimations, applied only to a restricted range of transactions. Most exchanges in the Aztec economy, Isaac (2013:436–437) argues, were "non-commercial and nonmonetary," and the "great majority of the Aztec Empire's inhabitants were rural peasants whose main production aim was household provisioning." Although space does not allow a prolonged refutation here, Isaac's positions seem ill informed by archaeological data that have emerged over the past twenty years. Nor does he seem to draw on the full corpus of Maya area Contact Period historical sources, including instances in which Spaniards were similarly "agape" at Maya marketplace splendor. My point here is not to equate any Maya area marketplace with Tlatelolco, but Maya Contact Period markets were not marginal or unimportant. For example, the town of Ecab was referred to as "El Gran Cairo" due to its lively commerce observed by Bernal Díaz del Castillo (Tozzer 1941:9, n. 43). A more extensive review of Contact Period Maya sources can be found in recent articles (Masson and Freidel 2012, 2013).

In conclusion, then, we are not finished. Debates generate interest and force us to build the empirical foundations of arguments ever stronger. Comparisons and contrasts to other places, other times, are what anthropologists do. The chapters of this book deliver data and inferences that attest to complex and often articulating components of Maya economies. Economic anthropology within the field of Maya archaeology is back with a vengeance.

Appendix

Indigenous Food Plants of the Maya Lowlands

SCOTT L. FEDICK

Key

Edible part: ar = aril, bk = bark, fl = flower, fr = fruit/berry, gr = grain, gs = gum/latex/sap, in = inflorescence/peduncle/spadix, lf = leaf, ol = oil, pa = pad, pd = pod, rt = root/rhizome/tuber/bulb, se = seed/nut, sh = shoot/bud/stem (other than palm), st = stem (heart of palm). ? = edible part from sources other than reported for Maya.

Ethnobotanical source: 1 = Anderson et al. 2003, 2 = Arellano Rodríguez et al. 2003, 3 = Atran 1993, 4 = Atran et al. 2004, 5 = Atran and Ek' 1999, 6 = Balick and Arvigo 2015, 7 = Balick et al. 2000, 8 = Barrera Marín et al. 1976, 9 = Calvo-Irabién and Soberanis 2008, 10 = Castillo Mont et al. 1994, 11 = S. Coe 1994, 12 = Colunga-GarcíaMarín et al. 1993, 13 = Cook 2016, 14 = DeClerck and Negreros-Castillo 2000, 15 = Herrera Castro 1994, 16 = Lira and Caballero 2002, 17 = Lundell 1938, 18 = Makkar et al. 1998, 19 = Marcus 1982, 20 = Meerman 1993, 21 = Roys 1931, 22 = Sosa et al. 1985, 23 = Standley and Record 1936, 24 = Standley and Steyermark 1949, 25 = Steggerda 1943, 26 = Terán et al. 1998, 27 = Vázquez-Yanes et al. 1999, 28 = Williams 1981. * = listed in source as a synonym.

Native distribution/domestication: CA = Central America (outside Maya Lowlands), CB = Caribbean/West Indies, MA = Mesoamerica (outside Maya lowlands), MH = Maya lighlands, ML = Maya lowlands, PT = pan-tropical for millennia, SA = South America, SE = Southeastern United

States, (G) = Germplasm Resources Information Network (GRIN), https://npgsweb.ars-grin.gov/gringlobal/taxon/taxonomysearch.aspx (accessed June 2017), (K) = Kew Science: Plants of the World Online, http://powo.science.kew.org/ (accessed June 2017), D = Domesticated.

Source for domestication: 1 = Aguirre-Dugua at al. 2013, 2 = Bai and Lindhout 2007, 3 = Castillo Mont et al. 1994, 4 = Colunga-GarcíaMarín and Zizumbo-Villarreal 2004, 5 = Makkar et al. 1998, 6 = Peters 2000, 7 = Roullier et al. 2013, 8 = Wills and Burke 2006.

Indigenous Food Plants of the Maya Lowlands

Family	Genus, species, and author	Spanish/English common name	Growth habit	Edible portion	Ethnobotanical reference	Native distribution/ domestication
Actinidiaceae	*Saurauia kegeliana* Schltdl.	capulin	tree	fr	23*, 28	ML (K)
Actinidiaceae	*Saurauia yasicae* Loes.	aguacatillo/wild orange	tree	fr	6	ML (K)
Adoxaceae	*Sambucus canadensis* L.	sauco/elderberry	tree	fr, fl	28*	ML (K)
Alstroemeriaceae	*Bomarea acutifolia* (Link & Otto) Herb.	papa de venado	vine	rt	28	ML (K)
Alstroemeriaceae	*Bomarea edulis* (Tussac) Herb.	yatzi	vine	rt	7, 28	ML (G)
Amaranthaceae	*Amaranthus caudatus* L.	pison calaloo/love-lies-bleeding	herb	lf, se	7, 28	SA (G)/D-A
Amaranthaceae	*Amaranthus dubius* Mart. Ex Thell.	calaloo/amaranth	herb	lf, se	4–7, 28	ML (G)
Amaranthaceae	*Amaranthus hybridus* L.	slim amaranth	herb	lf, sh, se	7, 28	ML (G)
Amaranthaceae	*Amaranthus retroflexus* L.	redroot amaranth	herb	lf, sh, se	28	ML (G)
Amaranthaceae	*Amaranthus spinosus* L.	spiny amaranth	herb	lf, sh, se	4, 5, 7, 28	ML (G)
Amaranthaceae	*Amaranthus viridis* L.	calalu/slender amaranth	herb	lf, se	7	ML (K)
Amaranthaceae	*Chamissoa altissima* (Jacq.) Kunth	false chaff flower	herb	lf, se?	7	ML (G)
Amaranthaceae	*Chenopodium berlandieri* Moq.	epazote/pitseed goosefoot	herb	lf, sh	2, 4, 28	ML (K)
Amaranthaceae	*Dysphania ambrosioides* (L.) Mosyakin & Clemants	epazote/Mexican tea	herb	lf, sh	1, 2, 4–7, 11, 13, 28	ML (G)
Amaryllidaceae	*Allium glandulosum* Link & Otto	gland onion	herb	fl, lf, rt	11*, 13	ML (G)
Anacardiaceae	*Anacardium excelsum* (Bertero & Balb. ex Kunth) Skeels	espavel/wild cashew	tree	se	28	ML (G)
Anacardiaceae	*Anacardium occidentale* L.	marañón/cashew	tree	fr, se	1, 2, 4, 6, 7, 17, 23, 28	SA (G)/D-SA
Anacardiaceae	*Spondias mombin* L.	ciruela cochino/wild hog plum	tree	fr	1, 2, 4, 6–8, 23, 28	ML (G)

Anacardiaceae	Spondias purpurea L.	jocote/hog plum	tree	fr	1, 2, 4, 6–8, 11, 17, 23, 25, 28	ML (G)/D-ML (4)
Anacardiaceae	Spondias radlkoferi Donn. Sm.	jocote/wild plum	tree	fr	6, 7	ML (G)
Anacardiaceae	Tapirira mexicana Marchand	caobilla	tree	fr?	7	ML (K)
Annonaceae	Annona cherimola Mill.	cherimoya/custard apple	tree	fr	1, 8, 21, 23, 25, 28	SA (G)/D-SA
Annonaceae	Annona diversifolia Saff.		tree	fr	2, 17, 28	ML (G)/D?
Annonaceae	Annona glabra L.	anona de rio/pond apple	tree	fr, gs	7, 21*, 23, 28	ML (G)
Annonaceae	Annona muricata L.	guanabana/soursop	tree	fr	1, 2, 4, 6–8, 13, 17, 28	ML (K)/D-SA
Annonaceae	Annona primigenia Standl. & Steyerm.	anona del monte/wild custard apple	tree	fr	2, 4–7, 28	ML (K)
Annonaceae	Annona purpurea Moc. & Sessé ex Dunal	soncoya/cowsap	tree	fr	1, 2, 4, 7, 8, 17, 23, 28	ML (K)/D-SA
Annonaceae	Annona reticulata L.	anona colorada/bullock's heart	tree	fr	1, 2, 4, 6–8, 17, 21, 23	ML (K)/D-SA, ML?
Annonaceae	Annona scleroderma Saff.	anona del monte/pochte	tree	fr	3, 7, 28	ML (G)
Annonaceae	Annona squamosa L.	saramuya/sweetsop	tree	fr	2, 4, 5, 7, 8, 17, 28	ML (K)/D-MA (4)
Annonaceae	Cymbopetalum penduliflorum (Dunal) Baill.	orejuela	tree	fl	17, 28	ML (G)
Annonaceae	Mosannona depressa (Baill.) Chatrou	elemuy/wild soursop	tree	fr	6*, 7*, 8*, 28*	ML (G)
Annonaceae	Rollinia jimenezii Saff.	anonillo	tree	fr	28	ML (G)
Annonaceae	Rollinia rensoniana Standl.	churumuyo	tree	fr	28	ML
Annonaceae	Sapranthus microcarpus (Donn. Sm.) R.E. Fr.	palanco	tree	fr	28	ML (G)
Apiaceae	Eryngium foetidum L.	culantro/Mexican coriander	herb	lf	4–7, 11, 13, 23, 28	ML (G)

Family	Genus, species, and author	Spanish/English common name	Growth habit	Edible portion	Ethnobotanical reference	Native distribution/ domestication
Apocynaceae	Couma macrocarpa Barb. Rodr.	leche huayo/cow tree	tree	fr, gs	6, 17*, 23*, 28	ML (G)
Apocynaceae	Dictyanthus ceratopetalus Donn. Sm.	chanchitos	vine	fr	28*	ML (K)
Apocynaceae	Echites umbellatus Jacq.	devil's potato	vine	fr	1	ML (K)
Apocynaceae	Fernaldia pandurata (A. DC.) Woodson	loroco	tree	fl, sh	2*, 28*	ML (G)
Apocynaceae	Gonolobus barbatus Kunth	Cuajayote	vine	fr	2	ML (G)
Apocynaceae	Gonolobus cteniophorus (S.F. Blake) Woodson	Orijón	vine	fr	2	ML (G)
Apocynaceae	Gonolobus edulis Hemsl.	cuayote	vine	fr	28	CA (G) (K)
Apocynaceae	Gonolobus lanugiflorus Woodson		vine	fr	2	ML (G)
Apocynaceae	Gonolobus salvinii Hemsl.	cuchamper	vine	fr	7, 28	ML (G)
Apocynaceae	Gonolobus stenanthus (Standl.) Woodson	angelpod	vine	fr	2*, 7, 28	ML (K)
Apocynaceae	Lacmellea panamensis (Woodson) Markgr.	cerillo	tree	gs, fr?	28	CA (G) (K)
Apocynaceae	Lacmellea standleyi (Woodson) Monach.	palo de vaca/milk tree	tree	fr, gs	6, 7, 23*, 28	ML (G)
Apocynaceae	Matelea gentlei (Lundell & Standl.) Woodson	orijón	vine	fr	2*	ML (G)
Apocynaceae	Plumeria rubra L.	flor de mayo/mayflower	tree	fl	4	ML (G)
Apocynaceae	Rauvolfia ligustrina Willd. ex Roem. & Schult.	amatillo	shrub	fr?	7	ML (G)
Apocynaceae	Thevetia ahouai (L.) A. DC.	cochetón/dog balls	shrub/tree	fr	4, 6, 7, 13	ML (G)
Araceae	Anthurium crassinervium (Jacq.) Schott	bird's nest anthurium	herb	se	2	SA (G)
Araceae	Anthurium scandens (Aubl.) Engl. subsp. scandens	bejuco real/pearl laceleaf	herb	fr	7, 28	ML (G)
Araceae	Anthurium schlechtendalii Kunth	cola de faisán/pheasant's tail	herb	fr	2*, 7	ML (G)

Family	Species	Common name	Growth form	Part	References	Distribution
Araceae	Lemna gibba L.	duckweed	herb	lf?	1	MA, SA (G) (K)
Araceae	Lemna minor L.	duckweed	herb	lf?	1	MA (K)
Araceae	Monstera adansonii var. laniata (Schott) Madison	hoja de sereno/Swiss cheese plant	herb	in	28*	ML (K)
Araceae	Monstera deliciosa Liebm.	pina anona/Mexican breadfruit	herb	in	8, 28	ML (G)
Araceae	Philodendron sagittifolium Liebm.		vine	in	13	ML (G)
Araceae	Philodendron warszewiczii K. Koch & C.D. Bouché	guacamayo	herb	fr	28	ML (K)
Araceae	Pistia stratiotes L.	lechuga de agua/water lettuce	herb	lf?	7	ML (G)
Araceae	Spathiphyllum blandum Schott	platanillo/wild plantain	herb	fl? in?	7	ML (G)
Araceae	Spathiphyllum phryniifolium Schott	gusnay	herb	fl, in	7, 13, 28	ML (G)
Araceae	Syngonium podophyllum Schott	pico de guara/arrowhead vine	vine	in	6, 7, 28	ML (G)
Araceae	Syngonium salvadorense Schott	conde	vine	in	28	ML (K)
Araceae	Xanthosoma violaceum Schott	malanga/blue tarro	herb	rt	6, 13, 17, 28	SA (G)/D-SA
Araceae	Xanthosoma yucatanense Engl.	malanga	herb	rt, sh	1, 2, 4, 8, 11, 26	ML (K)/D-ML?
Araliaceae	Dendropanax arboreus (L.) Decne. & Planch.	mano de león/potatowood	tree	fr?	7	ML (G)
Arecaceae	Acoelorraphe wrightii (Griseb. & H. Wendl.) H. Wendl. Ex Becc.	tasiste/palmetto	tree (palm)	se, st	6, 7	ML (G)
Arecaceae	Acrocomia aculeata (Jacq.) Lodd. ex Mart.	coyol/Mexican wine palm	tree (palm)	fr, gs, ol, st	1*, 2*, 4*, 7, 8*, 13, 14*, 17*, 21*, 23*, 25*, 28*	ML (G)/D-ML?
Arecaceae	Astrocarvum mexicanum Liebm. ex Mart.	guiscoyol/warree cohune	tree (palm)	fl, in, se, st	4*, 5*, 6, 7, 13*	ML (G)
Arecaceae	Attalea butyracea (Mutis ex L.f.) Wess. Boer	coyol real/royal palm	tree (palm)	st	13	ML (G)

Family	Genus, species, and author	Spanish/English common name	Growth habit	Edible portion	Ethnobotanical reference	Native distribution/domestication
Arecaceae	Attalea cohune Mart.	corozo/cohune	tree (palm)	fl, fr, ol, st	1*, 2*, 4*, 5*, 6, 7, 14*, 17*, 21*, 23*, 28*	ML (G)
Arecaceae	Bactris gasipaes Kunth	pejibaye/peach palm	tree (palm)	fr, st	28	CA (G)/D-SA
Arecaceae	Bactris major Jacq.	biscoyol/pork and doughboy	tree (palm)	fr	4*, 5*, 6	ML (G)
Arecaceae	Bactris mexicana Mart.	palma de espina/warrie cohune	tree (palm)	fr, st?	6, 7	ML (K)
Arecaceae	Brahea dulcis (Kunth) Mart.	soyate/rock palm	tree (palm)	fr, se	7	ML (G)
Arecaceae	Chamaedorea cataractarum Mart.	cat palm	tree (palm)	fl	13	ML (K)
Arecaceae	Chamaedorea ernesti-augusti H. Wendl.	uaya de abajo/Ernest August's palm	tree (palm)	fr? in?	7	ML (G)
Arecaceae	Chamaedorea graminifolia H. Wendl.	pacaya	tree (palm)	in	8, 21, 28	ML (G)
Arecaceae	Chamaedorea pinnatifrons (Jacq.) Oerst.	chem chem/monkey tail palm	tree (palm)	in	6, 7, 28*	ML (G)
Arecaceae	Chamaedorea tepejilote Liebm.	pacaya	tree (palm)	in, st	4, 5, 7, 10, 13, 28	ML (G)/D-ML (3)
Arecaceae	Chamaedorea woodsoniana L.H. Bailey		tree (palm)	fl, st?	13	ML (K)
Arecaceae	Cryosophila stauracantha (Heynh.) R. Evans	escoba/give-and-take palm	tree (palm)	st	6	ML (K)
Arecaceae	Desmoncus chinantlensis Liebm. ex Mart.		tree (palm)	st	4*, 5*, 7*, 13*	ML (G)
Arecaceae	Euterpe precatoria Mart. var. longevaginata (Mart.) A.J. Hend.	mountain cabbage palm	tree (palm)	st, fr?	6, 7	ML (K)
Arecaceae	Gaussia maya (O.F. Cook) H.J. Quero	palmasito/Maya palm	tree (palm)	st	4, 5	ML (G)
Arecaceae	Geonoma interrupta (Ruiz & Pav.) Mart.	pacaya/monkey tail palm	tree (palm)	in, st	6, 7, 13, 28	ML (G)
Arecaceae	Roystonea dunlapiana P.H. Allen	palma real/royal palm	tree (palm)	st	4, 5	ML (K)
Arecaceae	Sabal mauritiiformis (H. Karst.) Griseb. & H. Wendl.	botan/bay palmetto	tree (palm)	st	4	ML (G)

Arecaceae	*Sabal mexicana* Mart.	guano	tree (palm)	fr, st	1, 4, 26	ML (G)
Arecaceae	*Sabal yapa* C. Wright ex Becc.	huano/pay leaf palm	tree (palm)	fr, st	2, 6, 7	ML (K)
Arecaceae	*Scheelea lundellii* Bartlett	corozo	tree (palm)	fr, st	4, 5, 13*, 17, 28	ML (G)
Arecaceae	*Thrinax radiata* Lodd. ex Schult. & Schult. f.	Florida thatch palm	tree (palm)	fr, se, st	6, 8, 9	ML (G)
Aristolochiaceae	*Aristolochia maxima* Jacq.	guaco/duck flower	liana	pd	7, 28	ML (K)
Asparagaceae	*Agave angustifolia* Haw.	Caribbean agave	succulent	in	12	ML (G)
Asparagaceae	*Agave fourcroydes* Lem.	henequén	succulent	in	12	ML (G)/D-ML (4)
Asparagaceae	*Yucca guatemalensis* Baker	izote/spineless yucca	shrub/tree	fl, rt	2*, 4*, 5*, 6, 7, 8*, 17*, 23*, 28*	ML (G)
Asteraceae	*Acmella pilosa* R.K. Jansen	oro soos amarillo/hairy spotflower	herb	lf	7	ML
Asteraceae	*Bidens pilosa* L.	picao preto/hairy beggarticks	herb	lf	7	ML (G)
Asteraceae	*Helianthus annuus* L.	girasol/sunflower	herb	se	2	SE (G)/D-SE (8)
Asteraceae	*Pectis linifolia* L.	romero macho/narrowleaf lemonweed	herb	lf?	11	ML (G)
Asteraceae	*Porophyllum punctatum* (Mill.) S.F. Blake	piojillo/squirrel's tail	herb	lf	2, 7	ML
Asteraceae	*Porophyllum ruderale* var. *macrocephalum* (DC.) Cronquist	pápaloquelite/poreleaf	herb	lf	2	ML (G)
Asteraceae	*Tagetes lucida* Cav.	Santa María/Mexican tarragon	herb	lf	11	ML (G)
Asteraceae	*Tithonia rotundifolia* (Mill.) S. F. Blake	Mexican sunflower	herb	se?	7	ML (G)
Asteraceae	*Viguiera dentata* (Cav.) Spreng.	tajonal/toothleaf goldeneye	herb	se?	7	ML (G)
Bataceae	*Batis maritima* L.	beachwort	herb	lf, rt	7	ML (G)
Bignoniaceae	*Amphilophium paniculatum* (L.) H.B.K. var. *paniculatum*	liana de cuello	liana	fl?	6, 7	ML (G)

Family	Genus, species, and author	Spanish/English common name	Growth habit	Edible portion	Ethnobotanical reference	Native distribution/domestication
Bignoniaceae	*Bignonia aequinoctialis* L.	ajos sacha/garlic vine	vine	fl, lf	11*, 13*	ML (G)
Bignoniaceae	*Crescentia alata* Kunth	jícara/calabash tree	tree	fr, ol, se	28	ML (G)
Bignoniaceae	*Crescentia cujete* L.	jícara/calabash tree	tree	fr, lf, se, sh	7, 6, 28	ML (G)/D-ML (1)
Bignoniaceae	*Parmentiera aculeata* (Kunth) Seem.	guajilote/cow okra	tree	fr	1–6, 8, 11, 17, 19, 21*, 28	ML (G)
Bignoniaceae	*Parmentiera millspaughiana* L.O. Williams	guajalote	tree	fr	1	ML (G)
Bignoniaceae	*Stizophyllum riparium* (Kunth) Sandwith		vine	?	14	ML (G)
Bixaceae	*Bixa orellana* L.	annato/lipstick tree	shrub	se	1, 2, 4, 6–8, 11, 13, 21, 23, 25, 28	ML (G)/D-SA
Bixaceae	*Cochlospermum vitifolium* (Willd.) Spreng.	cotton flower	shrub/tree	fl	6, 7	ML (G)
Boraginaceae	*Bourreria mollis* Standl.	lima del monte/wild craboo	tree	fr?	7*	ML (K)
Boraginaceae	*Cordia alliodora* (Ruiz & Pav.) Oken	laurel blanco/salmwood	tree	fr	7, 28	ML (G)
Boraginaceae	*Cordia dentata* Poir.	flore de ángel/white manjack	tree	fr	23*, 28	ML (G)
Boraginaceae	*Cordia dodecandra* DC.	ciricote	tree	fr	1, 2, 4, 6–8, 17, 28	ML (G)
Boraginaceae	*Cordia sebestena* L.	ciricote/geiger tree	shrub/tree	fr	1, 2, 7, 8, 17, 21, 28	ML (G)
Boraginaceae	*Ehretia tinifolia* L.	roble/bastard cherry	tree	fr	6, 7, 19, 23, 28	ML (K)
Boraginaceae	*Heliotropium curassavicum* L.	salt heliotrope	herb	lf?	7, 28	ML (G)
Boraginaceae	*Tournefortia hirsutissima* L.	robo de mico/chiggery grapes	shrub	fr	6, 7	ML (G)
Boraginaceae	*Varronia globosa* Jacq.	butterfly sage	herb	lf	25*	ML (G)
Brassicaceae	*Lepidium virginicum* L.	altanisa/pepperweed	herb	lf, se, pd	2, 4, 5, 7, 28	ML (G)
Bromeliaceae	*Aechmea bracteata* (Sw.) Griseb.	piñuela	herb	fr	1, 7, 28	ML (G)
Bromeliaceae	*Aechmea magdalenae* (André) André ex Baker	pita/silk grass	herb	fr	7, 23, 28	ML (G)

Family	Scientific name	Common name	Habit	Part	References	CA (G) (K)
Bromeliaceae	Aechmea mariae-reginae H.Wendl.	espírito santo/Queen Mary bromeliad	herb	fr	28	SA (G)/D-SA
Bromeliaceae	Ananas comosus (L.) Merr.	piña/pineapple	herb	fr	1, 6, 11, 13, 14, 17, 23	ML
Bromeliaceae	Bromelia hemispherica Lam.		herb	fr	28*	ML (G)
Bromeliaceae	Bromelia karatas L.	piñuela/wild pineapple	herb	fr, in, lf, sh	1–4, 17, 25, 28	ML (G)
Bromeliaceae	Bromelia pinguin L.	piñuela/wild pineapple	herb	fr, in, lf, sh	1–4, 6, 7, 8, 13, 28	ML (G)
Burseraceae	Bursera simaruba (L.) Sarg.	gumbo limbo/tourist tree	tree	lf	6	ML (G)
Burseraceae	Protium copal (Schltdl. & Cham.) Engl.	copal/incense tree	tree	fr	4, 5	ML (G)
Cactaceae	Acanthocereus tetragonus (L.) Hummelinck	pitayita/triangle cactus	succulent	fr	2, 8, 21*, 23*	ML (G)
Cactaceae	Epiphyllum crenatum (Lindl.) G. Don	pitaya/crenate orchid cactus	vine	fr	3, 7	ML (G)
Cactaceae	Epiphyllum phyllanthus (L.) Haw.	pitaya/climbing cactus	herb	fr	3, 4*, 7, 28*	ML (K)
Cactaceae	Hylocereus undatus (Haw.) Britton & Rose	pitaya/dragon fruit	herb	fr, fl	1, 2*, 4, 5, 11, 14, 21*, 25*, 28	ML (G)/D-ML (4)
Cactaceae	Nopalea cochenillifera (L.) Salm-Dyck	nopal/prickly pear	succulent	pa	1*, 6*	ML (G)
Cactaceae	Opuntia dillenii (Ker Gawl.) Haw.	nopal/prickly pear	succulent	pa	2*	ML (G)
Cactaceae	Opuntia ficus-indica (L.) Mill.	nopal/prickly pear	succulent	pa	1, 11, 28	MA (K)
Cactaceae	Opuntia guatemalensis Britton & Rose	nopal/prickly pear	succulent	pa	4	ML (K)
Cactaceae	Pterocereus gaumeri (Britton & Rose) Th. MacDoug. & Miranda	columnar cactus	succulent	fr	8*	ML (K)
Cactaceae	Selenicereus grandiflorus (L.) Britton & Rose	tuna trepadora/night-blooming cereus	herb	fr	2*	ML (K)
Cactaceae	Selenicereus testudo (Karw. Ex Zucc.) Buxb.	pitaya/devil's gut	herb	fr	4, 5	ML (K)

Family	Genus, species, and author	Spanish/English common name	Growth habit	Edible portion	Ethnobotanical reference	Native distribution/domestication
Cactaceae	Stenocereus griseus (Haw.) Buxb.	pitayo de mayo/Mexican organ pipe	succulent	fr?	8*	SA (G)
Calophyllaceae	Mammea americana L.	mamey/mamee apple	tree	fr	2, 4, 5, 17, 21, 23, 28	ML (K)/D-SA, ML?
Cannabaceae	Celtis iguanaea (Jacq.) Sarg.	uña de gato/iguana hackberry	shrub/tree	fr	6-8, 25	ML (G)
Cannabaceae	Trema micrantha (L.) Blume	capulin/bay cedar	shrub/tree	fr?	7	ML (G)
Cannaceae	Canna indica L.	achira/canna	herb	rt	1, 6-8, 28	ML (G)/D-SA
Cannaceae	Canna tuerckheimii Kraenzl.	giant canna	herb	rt?	7	ML (G)
Capparaceae	Crateva tapia L.	tapia/garlic pear	tree	fr	7	ML (G)
Capparaceae	Cynophalla flexuosa (L.) J. Presl	limber caper	shrub/tree	pd, se, rt?	7*	ML (G)
Caricaceae	Carica papaya L.	papaya/pawpaw	tree	fr, rt	1, 4, 6-8, 11, 13, 14, 17, 21, 23, 26, 28	ML (G)/D-ML (4)
Caricaceae	Jacaratia dolichaula (Donn. Sm.) Woodson	papaya cimarrona/wild pawpaw	tree	fr	2, 6, 7	ML (G)
Caricaceae	Jacaratia mexicana A. DC.	cuaguayote/dead rat tree	tree	fr	1, 2, 4, 5, 8, 11, 21, 28	ML (G)
Caricaceae	Vasconcellea cauliflora (Jacq.) A. DC.	papaya de montaña/mountain pawpaw	tree	fr	2*	ML (G)
Chloranthaceae	Hedyosmum mexicanum C. Cordem.	palo de agua	tree	fr, lf	7, 28	ML
Chrysobalanaceae	Chrysobalanus icaco L.	icaco/coco plum	shrub/tree	fr	2, 6, 7, 17, 23, 28	ML (G)
Chrysobalanaceae	Couepia polyandra (Kunth) Rose	baboon cap	tree	fr	1, 2, 4-6, 7, 8, 17*, 21*, 23*, 28	ML (G)
Chrysobalanaceae	Hirtella americana L.	aceituna peluda/pigeon plum	tree	fr	4, 5, 17	ML (G)
Chrysobalanaceae	Hirtella racemosa Lam.	aceituna colorado/blossom cherry	shrub/tree	fr	7, 17	ML (K)

Family	Species	Common name	Habit	Parts	References	Region
Chrysobalanaceae	*Licania platypus* (Hemsl.) Fritsch	sansapote/monkey apple	tree	fr	4–7, 13, 17, 23, 28	ML (G)
Clusiaceae	*Garcinia intermedia* (Pittier) Hammel	caimito/waika plum	tree	fr	6, 17*, 23*, 28*	ML (K)
Clusiaceae	*Symphonia globulifera* L. f.	leche amarillo macho/waika chewstick'	tree	fr	7, 28	ML (G)
Combretaceae	*Combretum farinosum* Kunth	papa miel/chew stick	tree	sh	17	ML (G)
Convolvulaceae	*Ipomoea batatas* (L.) Lam.	camote/sweet potato	vine	rt, sh	1, 2, 4, 7, 8, 11, 13, 14, 17, 21, 25, 26	ML (K)/D-ML (7), SA
Convolvulaceae	*Turbina corymbosa* (L.) Raf.	aguinaldo blanco/christmas vine	vine	fl?	15	ML (G)
Costaceae	*Costus pulverulentus* C. Presl	caña de Cristo/spiral ginger	herb	fl, gs, rt	6, 7	ML (G)
Cucurbitaceae	*Cucurbita argyrosperma* K. Koch	pepito gruesa/cushaw squash or pumpkin	vine	fr, se	1, 2, 4, 26	ML (G)/D-MA
Cucurbitaceae	*Cucurbita lundelliana* L.H. Bailey	calabacilla de monte/bitter pumpkin	vine	fr	2	ML (G)/D-ML?
Cucurbitaceae	*Cucurbita moschata* Duchesne	calabaza/moschata or winter squash	vine	fr, se	1, 2, 4, 8, 13, 17, 21, 26	ML (K)/D-MA
Cucurbitaceae	*Cucurbita pepo* L.	calabaza/pepo squash	vine	fr, se	1, 2, 4, 26, 28	MA (G)/D-MA
Cucurbitaceae	*Cyclanthera pedata* (L.) Schrad.	caiba/wild cucumber	vine	fr, sh	28	ML (K), SA (G)
Cucurbitaceae	*Echinopepon wrightii* (A. Gray) S. Watson	wild balsam apple	herb	?	7*	ML (G)
Cucurbitaceae	*Lagenaria siceraria* (Molina) Standl.	guaje/bottle gourd	vine	fr, lf, sh, se, ol	2, 7, 28	PT (G)/D-MA
Cucurbitaceae	*Melothria pendula* L.	meloncito/creeping cucumber	vine	fr, lf, sh	2, 7, 16, 21	ML (G)
Cucurbitaceae	*Psiguria warscewiczii* (Hook. F.) Wunderlin	fire vine	vine	?	7	ML (G)
Cucurbitaceae	*Rytidostylis gracilis* Hook. & Arn.	chayotillo	vine	fr, lf, sh	7, 16, 28	ML (K)
Cucurbitaceae	*Sechium edule* (Jacq.) Sw.	chayote/cho-cho	vine	fr, fl, rt, se, sh	1, 4, 6, 7, 8, 11, 13, 14, 17, 23, 28	MA (G)/D-MA

Family	Genus, species, and author	Spanish/English common name	Growth habit	Edible portion	Ethnobotanical reference	Native distribution/ domestication
Cucurbitaceae	*Sicana odorifera* (Vell.) Naudin	melocotón/cassabanana	vine	fr	4, 5, 14, 28	SA (G)/D-SA
Cyclanthaceae	*Carludovica palmata* Ruiz & Pav.	palma de jipijapa/panama hat palm	tree	in	6	ML (G)
Cyclanthaceae	*Evodianthus funifer* (Poit.) Lindm.	chidra	shrub	in	28*	CA (K)
Cyperaceae	*Cyperus esculentus* L.	cebollán/yellow nutsedge	herb	rt	28	ML (G)
Cyperaceae	*Eleocharis geniculata* (L.) Roem. & Schult.	tule/spike rush	herb	rt	28*	ML (K)
Dilleniaceae	*Curatella americana* L.	chaparro/sandpaper tree	tree	se	6	ML (K)
Dilleniaceae	*Tetracera volubilis* L.	bejuco colorado	vine	gs	23	ML (K)
Dioscoreaceae	*Dioscorea bartlettii* C.V. Morton	cocolmeca blanca/wild yam	vine	rt	7	ML (G)
Dioscoreaceae	*Dioscorea convolvulacea* Schltdl. & Cham.	madre de maiz/wild yam	vine	rt	1, 7, 28	ML (G)
Dioscoreaceae	*Dioscorea floribunda* M. Martens & Galeotti	arbasco amarillo/wild yam	vine	rt	2	ML (G)
Dioscoreaceae	*Dioscorea polygonoides* Humb. & Bonpl. ex Willd.	mata gallina	vine	rt	2	ML (G)
Dioscoreaceae	*Dioscorea trifida* L. f.	mapuey/indian yam	vine	rt	28	ML (G) (K)/D-SA
Ebenaceae	*Diospyros albens* C. Presl.		tree	fr	2	MA (K)
Ebenaceae	*Diospyros anisandra* S.F. Blake		liana	fr	2	ML (G)
Ebenaceae	*Diospyros nigra* (J.F. Gmel.) Perr.	zapote negro/black sapote	tree	fr	1, 2, 6–8, 13, 28	ML (G)/D-ML (4)
Ebenaceae	*Diospyros tetrasperma* Sw.	sibil	tree	fr	2*, 8*	ML (K)
Ericaceae	*Macleania insignis* M. Martens & Galeotti		shrub	fr	7	ML (K)
Ericaceae	*Satyria warszewiczii* Klotzsch	colmillo	shrub/tree	fr	7, 28	ML (K)
Euphorbiaceae	*Acalypha polystachya* Jacq.	equilite	herb	lf, sh?	7	ML (K)

Family	Species	Common name	Habit	Parts	References	Region
Euphorbiaceae	Cnidoscolus aconitifolius (Mill.) I.M. Johnst.	chaya/tree spinach	shrub	lf	1, 6, 7, 11, 14, 17, 21*, 25, 26, 28	ML (G)/D-ML (4)
Euphorbiaceae	Cnidoscolus tubulosus (Müll. Arg.) I.M. Johnst.	mala mujer	shrub	lf	23*	ML (G)
Euphorbiaceae	Jatropha curcas L.	pinoncillo/physic nut	shrub	lf, se	1, 8, 18, 19, 23	ML (G)/D-ML (5)
Euphorbiaceae	Manihot esculenta Crantz	yuca/manioc	shrub	rt	2, 4, 6, 7, 8, 11, 13, 14, 17, 21*, 23, 26, 28	SA (G)/D-SA
Euphorbiaceae	Omphalea oleifera Hemsl.	aguacate de danta	tree	fr, se	28	ML (G)
Fabaceae	Acacia collinsii Saff.	subín blanco	tree	pd	28*	ML (G)
Fabaceae	Acacia cornigera (L.) Willd.	subín/bullhorn acacia	shrub/tree	pd, se	6, 7, 28*	ML (G)
Fabaceae	Acacia gentlei Standl.	subín/red cockspur	tree	pd	6, 7	ML (K)
Fabaceae	Acacia hindsii Benth.	carretadera/ant acacia	tree	pd	2	ML (K)
Fabaceae	Acacia mayana Lundell	piñuela/bullhorn acacia	tree	pd, se	13	ML (K)
Fabaceae	Caesalpinia pulcherrima (L.) Sw.	guacamayo/paradise-flower	shrub/tree	se	6, 7	ML (K)
Fabaceae	Calopogonium caeruleum (Benth.) C. Wright	jícama cimarrona	vine	rt	11, 19	ML (G)
Fabaceae	Canavalia ensiformis (L.) DC.	canavalia/jack bean	vine	pd, se	28	ML (G)
Fabaceae	Cassia grandis L. f.	carqué/stinking toe	tree	pd	4–6, 7	ML (G)
Fabaceae	Crotalaria cajanifolia Kunth	frijolillo	shrub	lf	7, 28	ML (G)
Fabaceae	Crotalaria longirostrata Hook. & Arn.	chipilón/castanet-plant	shrub	fl, lf, sh	2, 4, 5, 11, 28	ML (G)
Fabaceae	Crotalaria maypurensis Kunth	chipilin	shrub	lf	17	ML (G)
Fabaceae	Dalbergia glabra (Mill.) Standl.		liana	fr	1	ML (G)
Fabaceae	Dialium guianense (Aubl.) Sandwith	guapacque/logwood brush	tree	fr	3, 6, 17	ML (G)

Family	Genus, species, and author	Spanish/English common name	Growth habit	Edible portion	Ethnobotanical reference	Native distribution/ domestication
Fabaceae	*Enterolobium cyclocarpum* (Jacq.) Griseb.	guanacaste/devil's-ear	tree	pd, se	1, 2, 7	ML (G)
Fabaceae	*Erythrina berteroana* Urb.	pito/coral bean tree	tree	fl, in, lf, sh	28	ML (G)
Fabaceae	*Erythrina folkersii* Krukoff & Moldenke	colorin/coral tree	tree	fl	7	ML (K)
Fabaceae	*Erythrina fusca* Lour.	gallito/coastal coral tree	tree	fl	7, 28	ML (G)
Fabaceae	*Erythrina standleyana* Krukoff	pito rojo/coral bean tree	tree	fl	5, 6	ML (G)
Fabaceae	*Gliricidia sepium* (Jacq.) Kunth ex Walp.	madre de cacao/pea tree	tree	fl	4–7, 28	ML (G)
Fabaceae	*Haematoxylum campechianum* L.	palo de tinto/logwood	tree	se	8	ML (G)
Fabaceae	*Hymenaea courbaril* L.	guapinol/kerosene tree	tree	pd	2, 3, 5–7, 17, 28	ML (G)
Fabaceae	*Inga davidsei* M. Sousa	cola de mico	tree	pd	7	ML (K)
Fabaceae	*Inga inicuil* Schltdl. & Cham. ex G. Don	guama	tree	pd, se	2*, 17*, 28*	ML (G)
Fabaceae	*Inga pavoniana* G. Don	guama/mountian bribri	tree	pd, se	6, 7	ML (G)
Fabaceae	*Inga punctata* Willd.	paterno	tree	pd	28*	ML (G)
Fabaceae	*Inga thibaudiana* DC.	guamo de mico/broken ridge	tree	pd, se	6, 7, 27	ML (G)
Fabaceae	*Inga vera* Willd.	guama/ice-cream bean	tree	pd	2*, 6, 17*, 28*	SA (G)/D-SA
Fabaceae	*Leucaena leucocephala* (Lam.) de Wit	tepeguaje dormilón/wild tamarind	tree	se	1, 7	ML (G)
Fabaceae	*Lonchocarpus castilloi* Standl.	manchiche/cabbage bark	tree	bk	4, 5	ML (K)
Fabaceae	*Lonchocarpus guatemalensis* Benth.	frijolillo/turtle bone	tree	bk	7, 28	ML (K)
Fabaceae	*Lonchocarpus longistylus* Pittier	pitarrilla/cabbage bark	tree	bk	2, 11, 17, 25	ML (K)
Fabaceae	*Mucuna argyrophylla* Standl.	haba negra/ojo de venado	liana	se	4, 5	ML (K)
Fabaceae	*Mucuna sloanei* Fawc. & Rendle	ojo de buey/horse eye	vine	se	7	ML (G)

Family	Species	Common name		Part		ML
Fabaceae	Muellera frutescens (Aubl.) Standl.	madre de cacao/swamp dogwood	tree	fl	6	ML
Fabaceae	Pachyrhizus erosus (L.) Urb.	jicama/yam bean	vine	rt	1*, 2, 4, 6–8, 11, 14, 17, 21*, 23, 26	ML (G)/D-ML (4)
Fabaceae	Parkinsonia aculeata L.	palo verde/horse bean	tree	pd	22	ML (K)
Fabaceae	Phaseolus lunatus L.	frijol ancho/lima bean	herb	se	1, 2, 4, 8, 11, 13, 14, 25, 26, 28	ML (G)/D-ML (4)
Fabaceae	Phaseolus vulgaris L.	frijol/common bean	vine	se	1, 2, 4, 8, 17, 25, 26, 28	ML (K)/D-MA
Fabaceae	Pithecellobium dulce (Roxb.) Benth.	guamúchil/manila tamarind	shrub/tree	ar, se	2, 7, 8, 28	ML (G)
Fabaceae	Pithecellobium keyense Britton	blackbead	shrub/tree	ar, se	6, 7	ML (K)
Fabaceae	Pithecellobium lanceolatum (Humb. & Bonpl. ex Willd.) Benth.	guachimol/red fowl	shrub/tree	ar, se	7, 28	ML (G)
Fabaceae	Pithecellobium unguis-cati (L.) Benth.	guamuchillo/bread'n cheese	tree	pd	22	ML (G)
Fabaceae	Prosopis juliflora (Sw.) DC.	mezquite/mesquite	tree	pd	8, 28	ML (K)
Fabaceae	Rhynchosia minima (L.) DC.	frijolillo/least snout-bean	vine	pd	2	ML (G)
Fabaceae	Senna occidentalis (L.) Link	frijolillo/coffee senna	herb	fl, lf, pd, se	7, 17	ML (G)
Fabaceae	Senna peralteana (Kunth) H.S. Irwin & Barneby	zorrillo	shrub	se	6, 7	ML (K)
Fabaceae	Senna undulata (Benth.) H.S. Irwin & Barneby	cuilite de caballo/john crow bead	shrub	pd?	7	ML (G)
Fabaceae	Sphinga platyloba (Bertero ex DC.) Barneby & J.W. Grimes	sphinga tree	tree	pd? se?	2*	ML (G)
Fabaceae	Vigna spectabilis (Standl.) A. Delgado		vine	fl	7	ML (G)
Fagaceae	Quercus oleoides Schltdl. & Cham.	encino/oak	tree	fr	6	ML (G)

Family	Genus, species, and author	Spanish/English common name	Growth habit	Edible portion	Ethnobotanical reference	Native distribution/ domestication
Goodeniaceae	Scaevola plumieri (L.) Vahl	inkberry	shrub	fr	2	ML (K)
Heliconiaceae	Heliconia librata Griggs	plantillo	herb	sh	13	ML (K)
Heliconiaceae	Heliconia mariae Hook. f.	platanillo/wild plantain	herb	lf	6, 7	ML (G)
Icacinaceae	Calatola costaricensis Standl.	palo azul	tree	se	7, 28	ML (G)
Icacinaceae	Calatola laevigata Standl.	palo de papa	tree	fr, se?	7, 23	ML (K)
Iridaceae	Cipura paludosa Aubl.	chautillo	herb	rt	1	ML (G)
Iridaceae	Tigridia pavonia (L. f.) DC.	cebollin/tiger flower	herb	rt	28	ML (G)
Lamiaceae	Callicarpa acuminata Kunth	granadilla/Mexican beautyberry	shrub	lf	1	ML (G)
Lamiaceae	Clerodendrum ligustrinum (Jacq.) R. Br.	árbol sagrado	shrub	lf	7, 11, 21*	ML (G)
Lamiaceae	Mesosphaerum suaveolens (L.) Kuntze	canutillo/pignut	herb	lf, se	2*, 7*, 28*	ML (K)
Lamiaceae	Ocimum campechianum Mill.	albahaca de monte/wild basil	herb	lf	1*, 7, 28*	ML (G)
Lauraceae	Beilschmiedia anay (S.F. Blake) Kosterm.	anay	tree	fr	28	ML (K)
Lauraceae	Cassytha filiformis L.	hierba de fideos/jaundice tie tie	vine	fr	6	ML (G)
Lauraceae	Litsea glaucescens Kunth	laurelillo/Mexican bay leaf	tree	lf	11, 28	ML (G)
Lauraceae	Persea americana Mill.	aguacate/avocado	tree	fr	1, 2, 4, 6–8, 11, 13, 17, 21, 23, 25, 28	ML (G)/D-MA, ML?
Lauraceae	Persea schiedeana Nees	coyó/wild avocado	tree	fr	2, 4–7, 13, 17, 23, 28	ML (G)
Lecythidaceae	Grias cauliflora L.	anchovy pear	tree	fr	7	ML (G)
Loganiaceae	Strychnos brachistantha Standl.	chicoloro	shrub	fr	7	ML (K)
Loganiaceae	Strychnos panamensis Seem. var. panamensis	chicoloro	liana	fr	7, 20	ML (K)

Family	Species	Common name	Habit	Part	References	Region
Malpighiaceae	*Byrsonima bucidifolia* Standl.	nance blanco/craboo	shrub/tree	fr	1, 2, 4–8, 17, 23, 25, 28	ML (K)
Malpighiaceae	*Byrsonima crassifolia* (L.) Kunth	nance/craboo	shrub/tree	fr	1, 2, 4–8, 13, 17, 23, 28	ML (G)/D-ML (4)
Malpighiaceae	*Heteropterys lindeniana* A. Juss.		shrub/tree	lf?	7	ML (G)
Malpighiaceae	*Malpighia emarginata* DC.	acerola	shrub/tree	fr	7	ML (G)
Malpighiaceae	*Malpighia glabra* L.	acerola/Barbados cherry	shrub/tree	fr	1*, 2, 4–8, 17, 21, 23, 28	ML (G)
Malpighiaceae	*Malpighia mexicana* A. Juss.	acerola	shrub/tree	fr	28*	ML (G)
Malpighiaceae	*Malpighia souzae* Miranda		shrub/tree	fr	2, 8	ML
Malvaceae	*Abutilon permolle* (Willd.) Sweet	arepa/coastal indian mallow	shrub	fr	6	ML (K)
Malvaceae	*Bernoullia flammea* Oliv.	ampola/mapola flower	tree	se	6, 7, 28	ML (K)
Malvaceae	*Ceiba aesculifolia* (Kunth) Britten & Baker f.	ceiba/pochote	tree	bk, pd, se, sh	4–8, 17, 25, 28	ML (G)
Malvaceae	*Ceiba pentandra* (L.) Gaertn.	ceiba/cotton tree	tree	fl, fr, lf, ol, se	7, 27 17, 28	ML (G)
Malvaceae	*Ceiba schottii* Britten & Baker f.	ceiba	tree	fr?, lf?, se?	2	ML (G)
Malvaceae	*Corchorus siliquosus* L.	malvavisco/slippery burr	shrub	lf?	7	ML (G)
Malvaceae	*Guazuma ulmifolia* Lam.	guácima/bay cedar	tree	fr	4–8	ML (G)
Malvaceae	*Malvaviscus arboreus* Cav.	tulipán/white moho	shrub	fr	2, 6–8	ML (G)
Malvaceae	*Pachira aquatica* Aubl.	zapote de agua/provision tree	tree	bk, fl, se, lf	6–8, 13, 23, 28	ML (G)
Malvaceae	*Quararibea funebris* (La Llave) Vischer	rosita de cacao/swivel stick tree	tree	fl	7, 8, 11, 13, 21*, 28	ML (G)
Malvaceae	*Sterculia apetala* (Jacq.) H. Karst.	bellota/Panama tree	tree	se	28	ML (G)

Family	Genus, species, and author	Spanish/English common name	Growth habit	Edible portion	Ethnobotanical reference	Native distribution/ domestication
Malvaceae	Talipariti tiliaceum var. pernambucense (Arruda) Fryxell	sea hibiscus	shrub/tree	bk? fl? lf? rt?	7*	ML
Malvaceae	Theobroma angustifolium DC.	cacao de montaña/emerald cacao	tree	fr, se	28	CA (G)
Malvaceae	Theobroma bicolor Bonpl.	pataste/mocambo tree	tree	se	7, 8, 11, 28	ML (G)
Malvaceae	Theobroma cacao L.	cacao/cocoa	tree	fr, se	1, 2, 4, 6–8, 11, 17, 23	SA (K)/D-ML (4), SA
Malvaceae	Triumfetta semitriloba Jacq.	cadillo/burweed	shrub	?	7	ML (G)
Marantaceae	Calathea crotalifera S. Watson	hoja de berijao/waha leaf	herb	sh?	7	ML (G)
Marantaceae	Calathea lutea (Aubl.) Schult.	hoja del sal/waha leaf	herb	lf? fl?	7	ML (G)
Marantaceae	Goeppertia allouia (Aubl.) Borchs. & S. Suárez	lerén/guinea arrowroot	herb	fl, rt	4*, 5*, 28*	SA (G)
Marantaceae	Maranta arundinacea L.	camotillo/arrowroot	herb	rt	1, 3, 5, 7, 8, 14, 23, 26, 28	ML (G) (K)/D-SA
Marantaceae	Thalia geniculata L.	popal/alligator flag	herb	lf?, rt?	7	ML (G)
Melastomataceae	Arthrostemma ciliatum Pav. ex D. Don	acedillo/pinkfringe	herb	lf, sh, fl?	6, 7	ML (G)
Melastomataceae	Arthrostemma parvifolium Cogn.		herb	fr	6, 7	ML
Melastomataceae	Bellucia grossularioides (L.) Triana	duraznillo/black moir	tree	fr	6, 7	ML (G)
Melastomataceae	Bellucia pentamera Naudin	coronillo/mountain apple	tree	fr	7, 28	ML (G)
Melastomataceae	Clidemia novemnervia (DC.) Triana		shrub	fr	7	SA, ML?
Melastomataceae	Clidemia octona (Bonpl.) L.O. Williams	hojalatillo	tree	fr	7	SA, ML?
Melastomataceae	Clidemia setosa (Triana) Gleason	Santa María	tree	fr	28	ML

Family	Species	Common name	Habit	Part	References	Region
Melastomataceae	Conostegia xalapensis (Bonpl.) D. Don ex DC.	pasita/chigger nits	shrub/tree	fr	6, 7, 17, 23, 28	ML (G)
Melastomataceae	Miconia affinis DC.	sirin/chigger nits	shrub/tree	fr	6, 7, 28	SA, ML?
Melastomataceae	Miconia albicans (Sw.) Steud.	flor azul/pine ridge sirin	shrub	fr	7, 28	ML (G)
Melastomataceae	Miconia ciliata (Rich.) DC.	concha del tortuga/Maya seed	shrub	fr, se	6, 7, 28	ML (G)
Melastomataceae	Miconia lacera (Bonpl.) Naudin	sirin/chigger nits	shrub	fr	6, 7, 28	ML
Melastomataceae	Miconia neomicrantha Judd & Skean	mountain Spanish elder	shrub/tree	fr?	7*	ML
Melastomataceae	Miconia tomentosa (Rich.) D. Don ex DC.	big chigger nits	shrub/tree	fr	7, 28	SA, ML?
Menispermaceae	Disciphania calocarpa Standl.	chivitos/fringed redmaids	liana	fr	13	ML (K)
Montiaceae	Calandrinia micrantha Schltdl.		herb	lf	28	ML
Moraceae	Brosimum alicastrum Sw.	ramón/breadnut	tree	fr, gs, se	1, 2, 4, 11, 6–8, 13, 17, 21, 23, 28	ML (G)/D-ML (6)
Moraceae	Brosimum costaricanum Liebm.	ramón colorado	tree	fr, in, se	28	CA (K), ML?
Moraceae	Brosimum utile (Kunth) Oken	palo de vaca/cow tree	tree	gs	28	CA (G) (K)
Moraceae	Castilla elastica Sessé	hule/Mexican rubber tree	tree	fr?	8	ML (G)
Moraceae	Ficus americana Aubl.	matapalo/West Indian laurel fig	tree	fr	6, 7	ML (G)
Moraceae	Ficus aurea Nutt.	higuerón/strangler fig	tree	fr?	7	ML (G)
Moraceae	Ficus cotinifolia Kunth	higo/fig	tree	fr	17	ML (K)
Moraceae	Ficus crassinervia Desf. ex Willd.	higo/fig	tree	fr	6*	ML (G)
Moraceae	Ficus insipida Willd.	higo de venado/deer fig	tree	fr	6, 23*, 28	ML (G)
Moraceae	Ficus lapathifolia (Liebm.) Miq.	higo/fig	tree	fr	17	ML (K)
Moraceae	Ficus obtusifolia Kunth	huiguerilla/fig	tree	fr	2	ML (G)
Moraceae	Maclura tinctoria (L.) D. Don ex Steud.	mora/fustic mulberry	tree	fr	4, 5	ML (G)

Family	Genus, species, and author	Spanish/English common name	Growth habit	Edible portion	Ethnobotanical reference	Native distribution/ domestication
Moraceae	Morus celtidifolia Kunth	mora/Texas mulberry	tree	fr	28	ML (G)
Moraceae	Poulsenia armata (Miq.) Standl.	amate blanco	tree	fr	6, 7, 28	ML (G)
Moraceae	Pseudolmedia glabrata (Liebm.) C.C. Berg	manzanilla/cherry	tree	fr	4*, 5*, 7, 17*, 28*	ML (G)
Moraceae	Pseudolmedia spuria (Sw.) Griseb.	asta María/wild cherry	tree	fr	5–7, 17, 23	ML (G)
Moraceae	Trophis mexicana (Liebm.) Bureau	palo morillo	tree	fr	28*	ML (G)
Moraceae	Trophis racemosa (L.) Urb.	ramón colorado/red ramon	tree	fr	6, 7, 23, 28	ML (G)
Muntingiaceae	Muntingia calabura L.	capulín/jamaican cherry	tree	fr	2, 4–7, 13, 17, 23, 28	ML (G)
Myristicaceae	Virola guatemalensis (Hemsl.) Warb.	cacao volador	shrub/tree	ar, se	28	ML (G)
Myrtaceae	Calyptranthes calderonii Standl.	blossom berry	shrub/tree	fr? lf?	7	ML (K)
Myrtaceae	Calyptranthes lindeniana O. Berg	blossom berry	shrub/tree	fr	6, 7	ML (K)
Myrtaceae	Eugenia axillaris (Sw.) Willd.	escobillo/white stopper	tree	fr?	7	ML (G)
Myrtaceae	Eugenia capuli (Schltdl. & Cham.) Hook. & Arn.	cacho de venado/blossom berry	shrub/tree	fr	6, 7	ML (G)
Myrtaceae	Eugenia trikii Lundell		shrub	fr	6, 7	ML (G)
Myrtaceae	Myrcia splendens (Sw.) DC.	capulincillo/pigeon plum	shrub/tree	fr, lf?	6, 7, 23*	ML (K)
Myrtaceae	Pimenta dioica (L.) Merr.	pimienta/allspice	tree	fr, lf	2, 4*, 5–7, 11*, 13, 17*, 23*, 28*	ML (G)
Myrtaceae	Psidium friedrichsthalianum (O. Berg) Nied.	guayaba agria/Costa Rican guava	tree	fr	28	ML (G)
Myrtaceae	Psidium guajava L.	guayaba/guava	shrub/tree	fr	1, 4–8, 13, 17, 23, 25, 28	ML (G)/D-ML (4)
Myrtaceae	Psidium guineense Sw.	guísaro/Brazilian guava	shrub/tree	fr	7, 28	ML (G)
Myrtaceae	Psidium sartorianum (O. Berg) Nied.	guayabillo/wild guava	tree	fr	1, 6, 7, 23, 28	ML (G)

Family	Species	Common name	Growth form	Part	Numbers	Region
Nyctaginaceae	*Boerhavia erecta* L.	hierba blanca/erect spiderling	herb	lf?	7	ML (G)
Nyctaginaceae	*Neea psychotrioides* Donn.Sm.	hoja de salat/pigeon plum	tree	fr	6	ML (K)
Orchidaceae	*Vanilla planifolia* Andrews	vainilla/vanilla	vine	fr	1, 2*, 6, 7, 8*, 17*, 28*	ML (G)/D-ML (4)
Orchidaceae	*Vanilla pompona* Schiede	vainilla	vine	fr	28	ML (G)
Oxalidaceae	*Oxalis tetraphylla* Cav.	fourleaf pink sorrel	herb	lf, rt	28*	MA, ML?
Oxalidaceae	*Oxalis frutescens* L.	hierba cancerina/shrubby woodsorrel	herb	lf?	7, 28*	MA (K)
Passifloraceae	*Passiflora ambigua* Hemsl.	granadilla de monte/passion flower	liana	fr	7, 28	ML (G)
Passifloraceae	*Passiflora bicornis* Houst. ex Mill.	ojo de luna/wing-leaf passionfruit	vine	fr	2*	ML (K)
Passifloraceae	*Passiflora ciliata* Aiton	maracuyá/fringed passion flower	vine	fr	2	ML (K)
Passifloraceae	*Passiflora coriacea* Juss.	ala de murciélago/bat-leaf passion flower	vine	fr	2	ML (G)
Passifloraceae	*Passiflora foetida* L.	maracuyá silvestre/fetid passion flower	vine	fr	6, 7, 28	ML (G)
Passifloraceae	*Passiflora hahnii* (E. Fourn.) Mast.	passion flower	vine	fr	13*	ML (K)
Passifloraceae	*Passiflora ligularis* Juss.	granadilla/sweet granadilla	vine	fr	23, 28	ML (G)
Passifloraceae	*Passiflora mayarum* J.M. MacDougal	grandillo/wild passion flower	vine	fr	6, 7	ML (G)
Passifloraceae	*Passiflora serratifolia* L.	amapola/broken ridge granadillo	vine	fr	7, 13, 28	ML (G)
Passifloraceae	*Passiflora yucatanensis* Killip	Yucatán passion flower	vine	fr	2	ML (G)
Passifloraceae	*Turnera diffusa* Willd.	damiana/swamp bush	shrub	lf	7	ML (G)
Phyllanthaceae	*Phyllanthus acidus* (L.) Skeels.	ciruela costeña/gooseberry tree	tree	fr	23	SA (G)

Family	Genus, species, and author	Spanish/English common name	Growth habit	Edible portion	Ethnobotanical reference	Native distribution/domestication
Phytolaccaceae	*Phytolacca icosandra* L.	mazorquilla/button pokeweed	shrub	lf	7, 8, 28	ML (G)
Phytolaccaceae	*Phytolacca rivinoides* Kunth & C.D. Bouché	jaboncillo/pigeon berry	shrub	lf, sh	6, 7, 23, 28	ML (G)
Picramniaceae	*Picramnia antidesma* Sw. subsp. *antidesma*	pasa embra/wild raisin	shrub/tree	fr	6, 7	ML (K)
Piperaceae	*Piper aduncum* L.	cordoncillo/spiked pepper	shrub	lf?	7	ML (G)
Piperaceae	*Piper auritum* Kunth	hierba santa/Mexican pepperleaf	shrub	lf	1, 2, 4, 6–8, 13, 14, 17, 28	ML (G)
Piperaceae	*Piper peltatum* L.	Santa Maria/cowfoot	shrub	lf	6, 7	ML (G)
Piperaceae	*Piper umbellatum* L.	acuya	shrub	lf	7, 13	ML (G)
Plantaginaceae	*Russelia sarmentosa* Jacq.	flor de mirto rojo silvestre/red rocket	shrub	lf	6, 7	ML (G)
Poaceae	*Gynerium sagittatum* (Aubl.) P. Beauv.	caña brava/wild cane	grass	gr?	7	ML (G)
Poaceae	*Lasiacis divaricata* (L.) Hitchc.	carricillo/small cane	grass	gr	1	ML (G)
Poaceae	*Lasiacis ruscifolia* (Kunth) Hitchc.	carricillo/climbing tribisee	grass	gr	1	ML (K)
Poaceae	*Phragmites australis* (Cav.) Trin. ex Steud.	carrizo/common reed-grass	grass	gr? gs? lf? rt? sh?	7	ML (G)
Poaceae	*Zea mays* L.	maíz/corn	grass	gr	1, 4, 8, 11, 14, 17, 21, 25	MA (G)/D-MA
Polygonaceae	*Antigonon leptopus* Hook. & Arn.	flor de San Diego/coral vine	vine	rt	21*, 28	ML (G)
Polygonaceae	*Coccoloba {x} lundellii* Standl.	uva	shrub/tree	fr?	17	ML
Polygonaceae	*Coccoloba barbadensis* Jacq.	roble de la costa/wild grape	tree	fr	6	ML (K)
Polygonaceae	*Coccoloba belizensis* Standl.	uva silvestre/berry tree	tree	fr	6, 7	ML (K)
Polygonaceae	*Coccoloba diversifolia* Jacq.	uvero/pigeon plum	tree	fr	7	ML (G)

Family	Scientific name	Common name	Habit	Part	References	Region
Polygonaceae	Coccoloba spicata Lundell	uvero/wild grape	tree	fr?	7	ML (K)
Polygonaceae	Coccoloba uvifera (L.) L.	uva de playa/sea grape	shrub/tree	fr	2, 6–8, 17, 21*, 28	ML (G)
Polypodiaceae	Microgramma lycopodioides (L.) Copel.	helecho/clubmoss snakefern	herb	sh?	2	ML (G)
Portulacaceae	Portulaca oleracea L.	verdolaga/purslane	herb	lf, sh	1, 2, 4–8, 11, 13, 23, 28	ML
Portulacaceae	Portulaca pilosa L.	chisme/pink purslane	herb	lf	8	ML (G)
Primulaceae	Ardisia bracteosa A. DC.	caraso berries	shrub/tree	fr	7*	ML (K)
Primulaceae	Ardisia compressa Kunth	zacil de montaña/bill bird potter	shrub/tree	fr	6, 7, 13, 23, 28	ML (G)
Primulaceae	Ardisia escallonioides Schltdl. & Cham.	pimienta de monte/marlberry	shrub/tree	fr	7, 28	ML (G)
Primulaceae	Ardisia paschalis Donn. Sm.	cereto/bastard carboo	shrub/tree	fr	7, 28	ML (G)
Primulaceae	Ardisia revoluta Kunth	fruta de pava	shrub/tree	fr	7, 28	ML (K)
Primulaceae	Parathesis cubana (A. DC.) Molinet & M. Gómez	residán/pidgeon grape	shrub/tree	fr	6, 7	ML
Primulaceae	Parathesis sessilifolia Donn. Sm.		shrub/tree	fr	6, 7	ML (K)
Primulaceae	Stylogyne turbacensis (Kunth) Mez	pigeon berry	shrub/tree	fr	7*, 28*	ML (K)
Pteridaceae	Acrostichum aureum L.	helecho de playa/tiger bush	herb	sh	7	ML (G)
Putranjivaceae	Drypetes brownii Standl.	coquito/wild monkey aple	tree	se	6, 7	ML (K)
Rhamnaceae	Colubrina greggii S. Watson	manzanita	shrub/tree	fr?	1	MA (K)
Rhamnaceae	Sageretia elegans (Kunth) Brongn.	ciruelillo/cherry	shrub	fr	6, 7	ML
Rhizophoraceae	Rhizophora mangle L.	mangle colorado/red mangrove	tree	fr?	7	ML (G)
Rosaceae	Prunus serotina subsp. capuli (Cav.) McVaugh	capulin/wild cherry	tree	fr	28*	ML (G)
Rubiaceae	Alibertia edulis (Rich.) A. Rich. ex DC.	guayaba de monte/gibnut fruit	shrub/tree	fr	6, 7, 23, 28	ML (G)

Family	Genus, species, and author	Spanish/English common name	Growth habit	Edible portion	Ethnobotanical reference	Native distribution/ domestication
Rubiaceae	Chomelia spinosa Jacq.	cedrón prieto	tree	fr	28	ML (K)
Rubiaceae	Ernodea littoralis Sw.	yellow jugs	shrub	fr	6, 7	ML (G)
Rubiaceae	Genipa americana L.	guali/genip	tree	fr	7, 28	ML (G)
Rubiaceae	Guettarda macrosperma Donn. Sm.	pimentilla/wild grape	shrub/tree	fr	6, 7	ML (G)
Rubiaceae	Hamelia patens Jacq. var. patens	coloradillo/redhead	shrub/tree	fr	6, 7, 8, 23, 25, 28	ML (G)
Rubiaceae	Posoqueria latifolia (Rudge) Schult.	guayaba del mono/mountain guava	tree	fr	7	ML (G)
Rubiaceae	Randia aculeata L. var. aculeata	crucecita/wild lime	shrub	fr	7	ML (G)
Rubiaceae	Randia armata (Sw.) DC.	cruceta/wild lime	shrub	fr	7, 23, 28	ML (G)
Rubiaceae	Randia longiloba Hemsl.		tree	fr	2	ML (K)
Rubiaceae	Randia monantha Benth.	papache peludo/wild lime	shrub/tree	fr	6*, 7*	ML (G)
Rubiaceae	Sabicea villosa Schult.	woolly woodvine	vine	fr	7	ML (K)
Rutaceae	Casimiroa edulis La Llave & Lex.	zapote blanco/white sapote	tree	fr	8, 19, 28	ML (G) (K)/D-MA, ML?
Rutaceae	Casimiroa tetrameria Millsp.	mata abejas/woolly-leaf white sapote	tree	fr	6–8, 23, 25, 28	ML (G)
Salicaceae	Casearia corymbosa Kunth	café de montaña/billy hop	shrub/tree	fr	6, 7	ML (G)
Salicaceae	Casearia obovata Schltdl.	hueso de tortuga	shrub/tree	fr	4, 5	ML
Salicaceae	Laetia procera (Poepp.) Eichler	drunken bayman wood	tree	fr?	7	SA (K)
Salicaceae	Zuelania guidonia (Sw.) Britton & Millsp.	volador/drunken bayman wood	shrub/tree	fr	6, 7, 25	ML (G)
Sapindaceae	Allophylus cominia (L.) Sw.	palo de caja/bastard cherry	shrub/tree	fr	4–7, 23	ML (K)
Sapindaceae	Blomia prisca (Standl.) Lundell		tree	fr	4, 5	ML (K)
Sapindaceae	Cupania belizensis Standl.	palo carbon/granny betty	shrub/tree	?	7	ML (K)

Sapindaceae	*Melicoccus bijugatus* Jacq.	mamoncillo/genip	tree	fr	2	SA (G)/D-SA
Sapindaceae	*Paullinia clavigera* Schltdl.	bejuco coralero/cross vine	liana	fr	6, 7	ML (G)
Sapindaceae	*Paullinia fuscescens* Kunth	chilillo/moldy bread and cheese	liana	ar	7, 28	ML (G)
Sapindaceae	*Paullinia pinnata* L.	barbasco	liana	ar	7, 24	ML (G)
Sapindaceae	*Talisia floresii* Standl.		tree	fr	2, 4, 5, 8, 28	ML
Sapindaceae	*Talisia oliviformis* (Kunth) Radlk.	guaya/yellow genip	tree	fr, se?	1, 2, 4, 5, 8, 17, 21*, 23, 28	ML (G)
Sapotaceae	*Chrysophyllum cainito* L.	caimito/star apple	tree	fr	1, 2, 4–7, 17, 23, 28	CA (G), CB (K)/D-CA or CB
Sapotaceae	*Chrysophyllum mexicanum* Brandegee ex Standl.	cayumito silvestre/wild coco plum	tree	fr	2, 4–8, 28	ML (G)
Sapotaceae	*Chrysophyllum venezuelanense* (Pierre) T.D. Penn.	palo de sobo/wild zapote	tree	fr	7	ML (G)
Sapotaceae	*Manilkara chicle* (Pittier) Gilly	chicle macho	tree	fr	4, 7, 28	ML (G)
Sapotaceae	*Manilkara zapota* (L.) P. Royen	chico sapote/chicle	tree	fr	2, 4, 5, 7, 8, 28	ML (G)
Sapotaceae	*Micropholis melinoniana* Pierre	silión blanco	tree	fr	7	ML (G)
Sapotaceae	*Pouteria campechiana* (Kunth) Baehni	sapotillo/egg fruit	tree	fr	1, 2, 4–8, 11, 13, 17, 21*, 23*, 25, 28	ML (G)
Sapotaceae	*Pouteria durlandii* (Standl.) Baehni	mamey cederia/wild mammee	tree	fr	7	ML (G)
Sapotaceae	*Pouteria hypoglauca* (Standl.) Baehni	mamey de Santo Domingo/cinnamon apple	tree	fr	1, 2, 8, 17, 21*, 25	ML (G)
Sapotaceae	*Pouteria reticulata* (Engl.) Eyma	zapotillo negro/wild cherry	tree	fr	7	ML (G)
Sapotaceae	*Pouteria sapota* (Jacq.) H.E. Moore & Stearn	mamey/mamey apple	tree	fr, se	1, 2*, 4*, 5*, 6, 7, 11*, 13, 17*, 21*, 23*, 25*,28*	ML (G)/D-ML (4)

Family	Genus, species, and author	Spanish/English common name	Growth habit	Edible portion	Ethnobotanical reference	Native distribution/ domestication
Sapotaceae	Pouteria viridis (Pittier) Cronquist	injerto/green zapote	tree	fr	23*, 28	ML (G)
Sapotaceae	Sideroxylon americanum (Mill.) T.D. Penn.	caimitillo/milk berry	shrub/tree	fr	2, 6–8	ML (K)
Sapotaceae	Sideroxylon celastrinum (Kunth) T.D. Penn.	coma/saffron plum	tree	fr	8*	ML (G)
Sapotaceae	Sideroxylon foetidissimum Jacq.	caracolillo/false mastic	tree	fr	7, 17*, 23*, 28*	ML (G)
Sapotaceae	Sideroxylon obtusifolium (Humb. ex Roem. & Schult.) T.D. Penn.	zapotillo/jungle plum	shrub/tree	fr	7	ML (G)
Sapotaceae	Sideroxylon persimile (Hemsl.) T.D. Penn.	espino blanco/bastard cherry	tree	fr	7	ML (G)
Sapotaceae	Sideroxylon salicifolium (L.) Lam.	silión/willow bustic	tree	fr	6,7	ML (G)
Schoepfiaceae	Schoepfia schreberi J.F. Gmel.	limoncillo/gulf graytwig	tree	fr	2	ML (G)
Scrophulariaceae	Buddleja americana L.	salvia castilla/butterfly bush	shrub/tree	lf?	7	ML (G)
Simaroubaceae	Quassia amara L.	hombre grande/bitter wood	shrub/tree	bk?	7	ML (K)
Simaroubaceae	Simarouba amara Aubl.	aceituno/paradise tree	tree	fr	2*, 4*, 5*, 6*, 7*, 17*, 28*	ML (G)
Siparunaceae	Siparuna andina (Tul.) A. DC.	lemoncillo	shrub/tree	fr	28*	ML
Smilacaceae	Smilax mollis Humb. & Bonpl. ex Willd.	sarsaparillo/wild sarsa	liana	fr	6	ML
Solanaceae	Acnistus arborescens (L.) Schltdl.	gallinero/hollowheart	shrub/tree	fr	28	MH (G) (K)
Solanaceae	Capsicum annuum L.	chile/chile pepper	herb	fr	2, 4, 6–8, 14, 17, 21*, 26, 28	ML (G)/D-ML (4), SA
Solanaceae	Capsicum rhomboideum (Dunal) Kuntze	chile silvestre/wild pepper	herb	fr	2*	ML (G)
Solanaceae	Lycopersicon esculentum Mill.	jitomate/tomato	herb	fr	1, 2, 4, 6, 8, 11, 13, 14, 17, 21, 28	SA/D-SA, MA (2)
Solanaceae	Physalis angulata L.	miltomate/cutleaf groundcherry	herb	fr	7, 28	ML (G)
Solanaceae	Physalis campechiana L.	tomatillo	shrub	fr	2*	MA (K), ML?

Family	Scientific name	Common name	Growth form	Part	Refs	Region
Solanaceae	*Physalis cinerascens* (Dunal) Hitchc.	tomatillo/smallflower groundcherry	herb	fr	2	ML (G)
Solanaceae	*Physalis cordata* Mill.	miltomate/heartleaf groundcherry	herb	fr	28	ML (K)
Solanaceae	*Physalis gracilis* Miers	huevo de gato/cat's balls	herb	fr, se	6, 7	ML (G)
Solanaceae	*Physalis philadelphica* Lam.	tomatillo/green tomato	herb	fr	28	ML (G)/D-MA
Solanaceae	*Physalis pubescens* L.	tomatillo/husk tomato	herb	fr	6, 7, 11, 17, 28	ML (G)
Solanaceae	*Solanum americanum* Mill.	chilillo/American black nightshade	shrub	lf, fr	4–8, 13, 28	ML (G)
Solanaceae	*Solanum candidum* Lindl.	fuzzyfruit nightshade	herb	fr?	7	ML (G)
Solanaceae	*Solanum hirtum* Vahl	paperas/cat's balls	shrub	fr?	7	ML (G)
Solanaceae	*Solanum lanceolatum* Cav.	sosa/lanceleaf nightshade	herb	fr	6	ML (G)
Solanaceae	*Solanum torvum* Sw.	susamba/turkey berry	shrub	fr, fl? lf? sh?	6, 7	ML (G)
Talinaceae	*Talinum fruticosum* (L.) Juss.	espinaca/waterleaf	herb	lf	28*	ML (G)
Typhaceae	*Typha domingensis* Pers.	tula/southern cattail	herb	rt, sh	6, 7	ML (K)
Urticaceae	*Cecropia obtusifolia* Bertol.	guaramo/trumpet tree	tree	fr, fl	7, 27	ML (G)
Urticaceae	*Cecropia peltata* L.	guaramo/trumpet tree	tree	sh? fl? fr? lf?	7	ML (G)
Urticaceae	*Pourouma bicolor* Mart.	guaramo de montaña	tree	fr	28*	ML (G)
Urticaceae	*Urera baccifera* (L.) Gaudich. ex Wedd.	ortiga/scratchbush	shrub	fr	21	ML (G)
Verbenaceae	*Duranta erecta* L.	coralillo/pigeon berry	shrub	lf	1*	ML (G)
Verbenaceae	*Lantana camara* L.	palabra de cabellero/wild sage	shrub	fr, lf	2, 7, 8, 17	ML (G)
Verbenaceae	*Lantana citrosa* (Small) Moldenke	orégano	shrub	fr	2	ML

Family	Genus, species, and author	Spanish/English common name	Growth habit	Edible portion	Ethnobotanical reference	Native distribution/domestication
Verbenaceae	*Lantana involucrata* L.	orégano de monte/buttonsage	shrub	fr, lf	2, 7, 6	ML (G)
Verbenaceae	*Lantana trifolia* L.	cariaquito/threeleaf shrubverbena	shrub	fr	7, 13	ML (G)
Verbenaceae	*Lippia alba* (Mill.) N.E. Br. ex Britton & P. Wilson	salvia sija/bushy lippia	shrub	lf	1, 2	ML (G)
Verbenaceae	*Lippia graveolens* Kunth	orégano de monte/Mexican oregano	herb	lf	2, 6, 8, 28	ML (G)
Verbenaceae	*Lippia mexicana* Grieve	sweet leaf	herb	lf	2, 11, 28	MA (K)
Verbenaceae	*Phyla dulcis* (Trevir.) Moldenke	orases/Aztec sweet herb	herb	lf	2*, 6*, 11*, 28*	ML (G)
Verbenaceae	*Phyla stoechadifolia* (L.) Small	té de limón/southern fogfruit	shrub	lf	1*	ML (G)
Vitaceae	*Vitis bourgaeana* Planch.	bejuco de agua/wild grape	liana	fr	1	ML (G)
Vitaceae	*Vitis tiliifolia* Humb. & Bonpl. ex Schult.	uvas de monte/wild grape	liana	fr, gs, lf	1, 6, 7, 17, 23, 28	ML (G)
Ximeniaceae	*Ximenia americana* L.	chabalaca/tallow plum	tree	fr	3, 4–8, 17, 21, 23, 28	ML (G)
Zamiaceae	*Dioon mejiae* Standl. & L.O. Williams	palma teosinte/cycad	tree (cycad)	se	28	ML (G)
Zamiaceae	*Dioon spinulosum* Dyer	coyolito del cerro/giant dioon	tree (cycad)	se	8	MA (G), (K)
Zamiaceae	*Zamia polymorpha* D.W. Stev., A. Moretti & Vázq. Torres	mata ratón	shrub	rt	6	ML (G)
Zingiberaceae	*Renealmia aromatica* (Aubl.) Griseb.	wild ginger	herb	fr	7, 28	ML (K)

Bibliography

Abrams, Elliot M. 1994. *How the Maya Built Their World: Energetics and Ancient Architecture*. University of Texas Press, Austin.

———. 1995. A Model of Fluctuating Labor Value and the Establishment of State Power: An Application of the Prehispanic Maya. *Latin American Antiquity* 6:196–213.

Acuña, René. 1984. *Relaciones geográficas del siglo XVI: Antequera*. Vol. 2. Universidad Autónoma de México, Mexico City.

Adams, Richard E. W. 1971. *The Ceramics of Altar de Sacrificios*. Papers of the Peabody of Archaeology and Ethnology, No. 62, Harvard University, 63. Cambridge, MA.

———. 1978. Routes of Communication in Mesoamerica: The Northern Guatemalan Highlands and the Petén. In *Mesoamerican Communication Routes and Cultural Contacts*, ed. Thomas Lee and Carlos Navarrette, 27–36. Papers of the New World Archaeological Foundation No. 40. Brigham Young University Press, Provo, UT.

———. 1980. Swamps, Canals, and the Locations of Ancient Maya Cities. *Antiquity* 54(212):206–214.

———. 1986. *Rio Azul Reports, No. 2: The 1984 Season*. Center for Archaeological Research, University of Texas, San Antonio.

———. 1990. Archaeological Research at the Lowland Maya City of Río Azul. *Latin American Antiquity* 1:23–41.

———. 1991. *Prehistoric Mesoamerica*. Revised ed. University of Oklahoma Press, Norman.

Adams, Richard E. W., and W. D. Smith. 1981. Feudal Models for Maya Civilization. In *Lowland Maya Settlement Patterns*, ed. Wendy Ashmore, 335–349. School of American Research/University of New Mexico Press, Albuquerque.

Adams, Robert McCormick. 1981. *Heartland of Cities*. University of Chicago Press, Chicago.

Aguirre-Dugua, Xitlali, Edgar Pérez-Negrón, and Alejandro Casas. 2013. Phenotypic Differentiation between Wild and Domesticated Varieties of *Crescentia cujete* L. and Culturally Relevant Uses of Their Fruits as Bowls in the Yucatan Peninsula, Mexico. *Journal of Ethnobiology and Ethnomedicine* 9:76 (November 4, 2013, http://ethnobiomed.com/content/9/1/76).

Ahuja, Gautam. 2000. Collaboration Networks, Structural Holes, and Innovation: A Longitudinal Study. *Administrative Science Quarterly* 45:425–455.

Aimers, James J. 2014. Follow the Leader: Fine Orange Pottery Systems in the Maya Lowlands. In *The Maya and Their Central American Neighbors: Settlement Patterns, Architecture, Hieroglyphic Texts, and Ceramics*, ed. George E. Braswell, 308–332. Routledge, New York.

———, editor. 2013. *Ancient Maya Pottery: Classification, Analysis, and Interpretation*. University Press of Florida, Gainesville.

Aldenderfer, Marc S., L. R. Kimball, and April Sievert. 1989. Microwear Analysis in the Maya Lowlands: The Use of Functional Data in a Complex Society Setting. *Journal of Field Archaeology* 16:47–58.

Alexander, Rani T. 2012. Prohibido Tocar Este Cenote: The Archaeological Basis for the Titles of Ebtun. *International Journal of Historical Archaeology* 16:1–24.

Alexander, Rani T., and Susan M. Kepecs. 2005. The Postclassic to Spanish-Era Transition in Mesoamerica: An Introduction. In *The Postclassic to Spanish-Era Transition in Mesoamerica*, ed. Susan M. Kepecs and Rani T. Alexander, 1–12. University of New Mexico Press, Albuquerque.

Algaze, Guillermo. 2008. *Ancient Mesopotamia at the Dawn of Civilization*. University of Chicago Press, Chicago.

Alonzo, Juan A. 1995. La unidad habitacional Compleja C de Ixtontón, Dolores. En *Reporte 9: Atlas arqueológica de Guatemala*, 100–126. Instituto de Antropología e Historia, Guatemala City.

Anderson, E. N., José Cauich Canul, Aurora Dzib, Salvador Flores Guido, Gerald Islebe, Feliz Medina Tzuc, Odilón Sánchez Sánchez, and Pastor Valdez Chale. 2003. *Those Who Bring the Flowers: Maya Ethnobotany in Quintana Roo, Mexico*. El Colegio de la Frontera Sur, San Cristóbal de las Casas, Chiapas, Mexico.

Andrews, Anthony P. 1978. Puertos costeros del Postclásico Temprano en el norte de Yucatán. *Estudios de Cultura Maya* 11:75–93.

———. 1980. *Salt-Making, Merchants and Markets: The Role of a Critical Resource in the Development of Maya Civilization*. Ph.D. diss., University of Arizona, Tucson. ProQuest Dissertations Publishing (8025224), Ann Arbor, MI.

———. 1983. *Maya Salt Production and Trade*. University of Arizona Press, Tucson.

———. 1990. The Role of Ports in Maya Civilization. In *Vision and Revision in Maya Studies*, ed. Flora S. Clancy and Peter D. Harrison, 159–167. University of New Mexico Press, Albuquerque.

Andrews, Anthony P., Rafael Burgos Villanueva, and Luis Millet Cámara. 2006. The Historic Port of El Real de Salinas in Campeche, and the Role of Coastal Resources in the Emergence of Capitalism in Yucatán, México. *International Journal of Historical Archaeology* 10(2):179–205.

———. 2012. The Henequen Ports of Yucatan's Gilded Age. *International Journal of Historical Archaeology* 16(1)(March):25–46.

Andrews, Anthony P., Carlos Cortés Avilés, and Fernando Robles Castellanos. 2015. Proyecto San Francisco de Paula y Kaxek [Grant No. 9335-13]. Final Report to the Committee for Research & Exploration, National Geographic Society, Washington, DC.

Andrews, Anthony P., and Tomás Gallareta Negrón. 1986. The Isla Cerritos Archaeological Project, Yucatán, Mexico. *Mexicon* 8:3:44–48.

Andrews, Anthony P., Tomás Gallareta Negrón, Fernando Robles Castellanos, Rafael Cobos Palma, and Pura Cervera Rivero. 1988. Isla Cerritos: An Itzá Trading Port on the North Coast of Yucatán, Mexico. *National Geographic Research* 4(2):196–207.

Andrews, Anthony P., and Shirley B. Mock. 2002. New Perspectives on the Prehispanic Maya Salt Trade. In *Ancient Maya Political Economies*, ed. Marilyn A. Masson and David A. Freidel, 307–334. AltaMira Press, New York.

Andrews, Anthony P., and Fernando Robles Castellanos. 2016. El complejo portuario prehispánico de Progreso, Yucatán. In *Los mayas del norte de Yucatán,* ed. Ángel Góngora, 27–39. Centro INAH Yucatán, Mérida.

Andrews, E. Wyllys, V. 1986. Olmec Jades from Chacsinkin, Yucatan, and Maya Ceramics from La Venta, Tabasco. In *Research and Reflections in Archaeology and History: Essays in Honor of Doris Stone*, ed. E. Wyllys Andrews V, 11–49. Middle American Research Institute, Publication 57. Tulane University, New Orleans.

Andrieu, Chloé. 2008. Reassessment of the Lithic Assemblages of Cancuen: Preliminary Report and Research Design. Proyecto Arqueológico Cancuen, Guatemala.

———. 2009a. Irreplaceable? Or Just Not Indispensable . . . Subsistence and Complications in Lithic Raw Material Management in the Maya Lowlands. In *Non-Flint Raw Material Use in Prehistory: Old Prejudices and New Directions,* ed. Fanna Sternke, Lotte Eigeland, and Laurent-Jacques Costa, 241–248. BAR International Series 1939. Archaeopress, Oxford.

———. 2009b. Outils mayas: Distribution et production du silex et de l'obsidienne dans les Basses Terres mayas. Unpublished Ph.D. dissertation, Department of Prehistory and Technology, Université Paris Ouest, Nanterre.

———. 2013. Late Classic Maya Lithic Production and Exchange at Río Bec and Calakmul, Mexico. *Journal of Field Archaeology* 38(1):21–37.

———. 2015. Excavación en El Juilín. In Proyecto Petén-Norte Naachtun 2010–2014: Informe final de la quinta temporada de campo, ed. Philippe Nondédéo, 75–82, CNRS/Université de Paris 1/CEMCA. Report delivered to the Instituto de Antropología e Historia, Guatemala City.

———. 2016. La lítica del Juilín. In Proyecto Petén-Norte Naachtun 2010–2014: Informe final de la sexta temporada de campo, ed. Philippe Nondédéo, 230–238. CNRS/Université de Paris 1/CEMCA. Report delivered to the Instituto de Antropología e Historia, Guatemala.

Andrieu, Chloé, and Mélanie Forné. 2010. Producción y distribución del jade en el mundo maya: Talleres, fuentes y rutas del intercambio en su contexto interregional: Vista desde Cancuén. In *XXIV Simposio de Investigaciones Arqueológicas en Guatemala, 2009,* ed. Bárbara Arroyo, Adriana Linares Palma, and Lorena Paiz Aragón, 947–956. Museo Nacional de Arqueologia e Historia, Guatemala City.

Andrieu, Chloé, Olaf Jaime-Riveron, María Dolores Tenorio, Thomas Calligaro, Juan Carlos Cruz Ocampo, Melania Jiménez, and Mikhail Ostrooumov. 2011. Últimos datos sobre la producción de artefactos de jade en Cancuén. In *XXIV Simposio Internacional de Arqueología, 2010,* ed. Bárbara Arroyo, Lorena Paiz Aragón, and Adriana Linares Palma, 1017–1026. Museo Nacional de Arqueología y Etnología, Guatemala City.

Andrieu, Chloé, and Alejandra Roche. 2015. Análisis del material lítico de La Corona y La Cariba. In *Proyecto arqueológico La Corona: Informe final temporada 2014*, ed. Tomás Barrientos Q., Marcello A. Canuto, and Eduardo Bustamante, 335–346. Middle American Research Institute, Tulane University, New Orleans.

Andrieu, Chloé, Edna Rodas, and Luis F. Luín. 2014. The Values of Maya Jades: A Reanalysis Analysis of Cancuén's Jade Workshop. *Ancient Mesoamerica* 25(1):141–164.

Aoyama, Kazuo. 1996. Exchange, Craft Specialization, and Ancient Maya State Formation: A Study of Chipped Stone Artifacts from the Southern Maya Lowlands. Unpublished Ph.D. dissertation, University of Pittsburgh.

———. 1999. *Ancient Maya State, Urbanism, Exchange, and Craft Specialization: Chipped Stone Evidence from Copán Valley and the La Estrada Region, Honduras.* Memoirs in Latin American Archaeology No. 12. University of Pittsburgh.

———. 2001. Classic Maya State, Urbanism, and Exchange: Chipped Stone Evidence from the Copán Valley and Its Hinterland. *American Anthropologist* 103:346–360.

———. 2007. Elite Artists and Craft Producers in Classic Maya Society: Lithic Evidence from Aguateca, Guatemala. *Latin American Antiquity* 18(1):3–26.

———. 2009. *Elite Craft Producers, Artists, and Warriors at Aguateca: Lithic Analysis.* University of Utah Press, Salt Lake City.

———. 2011. Socioeconomic and Political Implications of Regional Studies of Maya Lithic Artifacts: Two Case Studies of the Copan Region, Honduras, and the Aguateca Region, Guatemala. In *The Technology of Maya Civilization: Political Economy and beyond in Lithic Studies* ed. Zachary X. Hruby, Geoffrey E. Braswell, and Oswaldo Chinchilla Mazariegos, 37–54. Equinox, Sheffield, UK.

———. 2017. Preclassic and Classic Maya Interregional and Long-Distance Exchange: A Diachronic Analysis of Obsidian Artifacts from Ceibal, Guatemala. *Latin American Antiquity* 28(2):213–231.

Appadurai, Arjun. 1988. Putting Hierarchy in Its Place. *Current Anthropology* 3:16–20.

———. 1996. *Modernity at Large: Cultural Dimensions of Globalization*. University of Minnesota Press, Minneapolis.

———, editor. 1986. *The Social Life of Things: Commodities in Cultural Perspective*. Cambridge University Press, Cambridge.

———, editor. 2001. *Globalization*. Duke University Press, Durham, NC.

Ara, Domingo de. 1986. *Vocabulario de lengua tzeldal según el orden de Copanabastla*. 1st ed. Universidad Nacional Autónoma de México, Mexico City.

Arellano Rodríguez, J. Alberto, José Salvador Flores Guido, Juan Tun Garrido, and María Mercedes Cruz Bojórquez. 2003. *Nomenclatura, forma de vida, uso, manejo y distribución de las especies vegetales de la península de Yucatán*. Etnoflora Yucatanense Fascículo 20. Universidad Autónoma de Yucatán, Facultad de Medicina Veterinaria y Zootecnia, Mérida, Mexico.

Arias Ortiz, Teri Erandeni. 2012. Imagen, función, uso y significado de los caminos coloniales durante la conquista de El Petén (1695–1704). Unpublished Ph.D. dissertation, Rheinische Friedrich-Wilhelms-Universität, Bonn.

Armijo Torres, Ricardo, Miriam Judith Gallegos Gómora, and Marc Zender. 2000. Urnas funerarias, textos historicós y ofrendas en Comalcalco. *Los Investigadores de la Cultura Maya* 8(2):312–323.

Arnauld, Marie Charlotte. 1990. El comercio clásico de obsidiana: Rutas entre Tierras Altas y Tierras Bajas en el área Maya. *Latin American Antiquity* 1(4):347–367.

———. 2005. Les mayas classiques: Lettrés artisans de haut rang? *Technique et Culture* 46–47:217–229.

Arnaya Hernández, Armando, Stanley P. Guenter, and Marc U. Zender. 2003. Sak Tz'i, a Classic Maya Center: A Locational Model Based on GIS and Epigrpahy. *Latin American Antiquity* 14(2):179–191.

Arnold, Jeanne, and Anabel Ford. 1980. A Statistical Examination of Settlement Patterns at Tikal, Guatemala. *American Antiquity* 45(4):713–726.

Arnould, Eric J., and Robert McC. Netting. 1982. Households: Changing Form and Function. *Current Anthropology* 23(5):571–575.

Arrow, Kenneth J. 1975. Vertical Integration and Communication. *Bell Journal of Economics* 6:173–183.

Arroyave, Ana Lucía, and Juan Carlos Meléndez. 2005. Análisis preliminar de cerámica 2005. In *Proyecto Regional Arqueológico Sierra del Lacandón, Informe preliminar no. 3*, ed. Rosaura Vásquez, Andrew K. Scherer, and Charles W. Golden, 57–62. Dirección General del Patrimonio Cultural y Natural de Guatemala, Guatemala City.

Arroyave, Ana Lucía, Fabiola María Quiroa Flores, and Juan Carlos Meléndez. 2006. Investigaciones preliminares en el sitio Zancudero. In *Proyecto Regional Arqueológico Sierra del Lacandón: Informe preliminar no. 4*, ed. Charles Golden, Andrew K. Scherer, and Rosaura Vásquez, 67–74. Dirección General del Patrimonio Cultural y Natural de Guatemala, Guatemala City.

Arroyo, Bárbara. 1995. El Preclásico Temprano en la costa central de Guatemala: Interpretaciones finales y perspectivas. In *Simposio de Investigaciones Arqueológicas en Guatemala (1994)*, ed. Bárbara Arroyo, Juan Pedro LaPorte, and Juan Antonio Valdés, 3–77. Vol. 1. Museo Nacional de Antropología y Etnología, Guatemala City.

Arroyo, Bárbara, and Gloria Ajú. 2019. Interaction and Exchange at Kaminaljuyu: Trade and Ritual. Paper presented at the 84th Annual Meeting of the Society for American Archaeology, Albuquerque, NM, 2019 (https://core.tdar.org/document/451210/interaction-and-exchange-at-kaminaljuyu-trade-and-ritual, accessed August 18, 2019).

Arroyo, Bárbara, Hector Neff, and James Feathers. 2002. Early Formative Sequence of Pacific Coastal Guatemala. In *Incidents of Archaeology in Central America and Yucatán*, ed. Michael Love, Marion Popenoe de Hatch, and Hector L. Escobedo, 35–50. University Press of America. Lanham, MD.

Ashmore, Wendy. 1994. Settlement Archaeology at Xunantunich, Belize, Central America. In Xunantunich Archaeological Project: 1994 Field Season, ed. R. M. Leventhal and Wendy. Ashmore, 10–25. Report submitted to the Institute of Archaeology, Belmopan, Belize.

———. 2010. Antecedents, Allies, Antagonists: Xunantunich and Its Neighbors. In *Classic Maya Provincial Polities: Xunantunich and Its Hinterlands*, ed. Lisa J. LeCount and Jason Yaeger, 46–65. University of Arizona Press, Tucson.

———, editor. 1981. *Lowland Maya Settlement Patterns*. School of American Research, University of New Mexico, Albuquerque.

Ashmore, Wendy, Samuel V. Connell, Jennifer J. Ehret, C. H. Gifford, L. T. Neff, and J. C. Vandenbosch. 1994. The Xunantunich Settlement Survey. In Xunantunich Archaeological Project: 1994 Field Season, ed. R. M. Leventhal and Wendy Ashmore, 248–290. Report submitted to the Institute of Archaeology, Belmopan, Belize.

Ashmore, Wendy, and Richard R. Wilk. 1988. Household and Community in the Mesoamerican Past. In *Household and Community in the Mesoamerican Past*, ed. Richard R. Wilk and Wendy Ashmore, 1–27. University of New Mexico Press, Albuquerque.

Atici, Levent, Fikri Kulakoğlu, Gojko Barjamovic, and Andrew Fairbairn, editors. 2014. *Current Research in Kültepe/Kanesh: An Interdisciplinary and Integrative Approach to Trade Networks, Internationalism, and Identity during the Middle Bronze Age*. Journal of Cuneiform Studies Supplementary Series 4. American Schools of Oriental Research, Bristol, CT.

Atran, Scott. 1993. Itza Maya Tropical Agro-Forestry. *Current Anthropology* 34:633–700.

Atran, Scott, and Edilberto Ucan Ek'. 1999. Classification of Useful Plants by the Northern Petén Maya (Itzaj). In *Reconstructing Ancient Maya Diet*, ed. Christine D. White, 19–59. University of Utah Press, Salt Lake City.

Atran, Scott, Ximena Lois, and Ediberto Ucan Ek'. 2004. *Plants of the Petén Itza' Maya/Plantas de los Maya Itza' del Petén*. Memoirs No. 38. Ann Arbor: Museum of Anthropology, University of Michigan, Ann Arbor.

Aubet, María Eugenia. 2001. *The Phoenicians and the West: Politics, Colonies, and Trade*. 2nd ed. Cambridge University Press, Cambridge.

Audet, Carolyn Marie. 2006. The Political Organization of the Belize Valley: New Evidence from Baking Pot, Xunantunich, and Cahal Pech. Unpublished Ph.D. dissertation, Department of Anthropology, Vanderbilt University, Nashville, TN.

Aulie, H. Wilbur, and Evelyn W. de Aulie. 1978. *Diccionario Ch'ol: Ch'ol-Español, Español–Ch'ol*. 1st ed. Instituto Lingüístico de Verano en coordinación con la Secretaría de Educación Pública a través de la Dirección General de Servicios Educativos en el Medio Indígena, Mexico City.

Aveni, Anthony F. 2001. *Skywatchers of Ancient Mexico*. University of Texas Press, Austin.

Aylor, Donald E., Neil P. Schultes, and Elson J. Shields. 2003. An Aerobiological Framework for Assessing Cross-Pollination in Maize. *Agricultural and Forest Meteorology* 119:111–119.

Baer, Philip, and William R. Merrifield. 1971. *Two Studies on the Lacandones of Mexico*. Summer Institute of Linguistics, Norman, OK.

Bai, Yuling, and Pim Lindhout. 2007. Domestication and Breeding of Tomatoes: What Have We Gained and What Can We Gain in the Future? *Annals of Botany* 100:1085–1094.

Bair, Daniel A. 2010. The Dirt on the Ancient Maya: Soil Chemical Investigations of Ancient

Maya Marketplaces. Unpublished MA thesis, Department of Plant and Wildlife Sciences, Brigham Young University, Provo.

Bair, Daniel A., and Richard E. Terry. 2012. In Search of Markets and Fields: Soil Chemical Investigations at Motul de San José. In *Motul de San José: Politics, History, and Economy in a Classic Maya Polity*, ed. Antonia E. Foias and Kitty F. Emery, 357–385. University Press of Florida, Gainesville.

Balick, Michael J., and Rosita Arvigo. 2015. *Messages from the Gods: A Guide to the Useful Plants of Belize*. Oxford University Press, New York.

Balick, Michael J., Michael H. Nee, and Daniel E. Atha. 2000. *Checklist of the Vascular Plants of Belize with Common Names & Uses*. Memoirs of the New York Botanical Garden, Vol. 85. New York Botanical Garden Press, Bronx.

Ball, Joseph W. 1977. *The Archaeological Ceramics of Becan, Campeche, Mexico*. Middle American Research Institute, Tulane University, New Orleans.

———. 1978. Archaeological Pottery of the Yucatan-Campeche Coast. *Middle American Research Institute*, Publication 46:69–146. Tulane University, New Orleans.

———. 1993. Pottery, Potter, Palaces, and Polities: Some Socioeconomic and Political Implications of Late Classic Maya Ceramic Industries. In *Lowland Maya Civilization in the Eighth Century A.D.: A Symposium at Dumbarton Oaks 7th and 8th October 1989*, ed. Jeremy A. Sabloff and J. S. Henderson, 243–272. Dumbarton Oaks Research Library and Collection, Washington, DC.

Ball, Joseph W., and Richard G. Kelsay. 1992. Prehistoric Intrasettlement Land Use and Residual Soil Phosphate Levels in the Upper Belize Valley, Central America. In *Gardens of Prehistory: The Archaeology of Settlement Agriculture in Greater Mesoamerica*, ed. Thomas W. Killion, 234–262. University of Alabama Press, Tuscaloosa.

Ball, Joseph W., and Jennifer T. Taschek. 1991. Late Classic Lowland Maya Political Organization and Central-Place Analysis: New Insights from the Upper Belize Valley. *Ancient Mesoamerica* 2(2):149–165.

———. 1992. Economics and Economies in the Late Classic Maya Lowlands: A Trial Examination of Some Apparent Patterns and Implications. Presented at the Wenner-Gren Foundation Symposium "The Segmentary State and the Classic Lowland Maya: A 'New' Model for Ancient Political Organization." Cleveland State University, Cleveland, OH.

———. 2004. Buenavista del Cayo: A Short Outline of Occupational and Cultural History at an Upper Belize Valley Regal-Ritual Center. In *The Ancient Maya of the Belize Valley: Half a Century of Archaeological Research*, ed. James F. Garber, 149–167. University Press of Florida, Gainesville.

Bardenstein, Carol B. 1999. Trees, Forests, and the Shaping of Palestinian and Israeli Collective Memory. In *Acts of Memory: Cultural Recall in the Present*, ed. Mieke Bal, Jonathan V. Crewe, and Leo Spitzer, 148–170. University Press of New England, Hanover, NH.

Barjamovic, Gojko. 2011. *A Historical Geography of Anatolia in the Old Assyrian Colony Period*. Museum Tusculanum Press, Copenhagen.

———. 2018. Interlocking Commercial Networks and the Infrastructure of Trade in Western Asia during the Bronze Age. In *Trade and Civilisation. Economic Networks and Cultural Ties, from Prehistory to the Early Modern Area*, ed. Kristian Kristiansen, Thomas Lindkvist, and Janken Myrdal, 113–142. Cambridge University Press, Cambridge.

Baron, Joanne. 2013. Patrons of La Corona: Deities and Power in a Classic Maya Community. Unpublished Ph.D. dissertation, University of Pennsylvania, Philadelphia, PA.

———. 2016. *Patron Gods and Patron Lords: The Semiotics of Classic Maya Community Cults*. University Press of Colorado, Boulder.

———. 2018a. Ancient Monetization: The Case of Classic Maya Textiles. *Journal of Anthropological Archaeology* 49:100–113.

———. 2018b. Making Money in Mesoamerica: Currency Production and Procurement in the Classic Maya Financial System. *Economic Anthropology* 5(2):210–223.

Barrera Marín, Alfredo, Alfredo Barrera Vázquez, and Rosa María López Franco. 1976. *Nomenclatura etnobotánica maya: Una interpretación taxonómica*. Colección Científica Etnología 36. Instituto Nacional de Antropología e Historia, Mexico City.

Barrera Vásquez, Alfredo, Juan Ramón Bastarrachea Manzano, William Brito Sansores, Refugio Vermont Salas, David Dzul Góngora, and Domingo Dzul Poot. 1995. *Diccionario Maya: Maya-Español, Español-Maya*. 3rd ed. Editorial Porrúa, Mexico City.

Barrientos, Tomás. 2014. The Royal Palace of Cancuén: The Structure of Lowland Maya Architecture and Politics at the End of the Late Classic Period. Unpublished Ph.D. dissertation, Department of Anthropology, Vanderbilt University, Nashville.

Barrientos, Tomás, Moisés Arriaza, Adriana Linares, Blanca Mijangos, Silvia Alvarado, and Claudia Quintanilla. 2005. Excavación en la Estructura L7–27 de Cancuén. In *Proyecto Cancuén, Informe preliminar no. 7, séptima temporada*, ed. Arthur Demarest, Tomás Barrientos, and L. A. Luín, 259–314. Instituto de Antropología e Historia, Guatemala City.

Barrientos, Tomás, and Arthur Demarest. 2012. Geografía sagrada y poder político en las ciudades Mayas del Río La Pasión. In *Ciudades mesoamericanas*, ed. Horacio Cabezas Carcache, 185–204. Publicaciones Mesoamericanas, Guatemala City.

Barrientos, Tomás, Brigitte Kovacevich, Michael Callaghan, and Lucía Morán. 2001. Investigaciones en el área residencial sur y sureste de Cancuen. In *Proyecto Arqueológico Cancuén: Informe temporada 2002*, 99–160. Ministerio de Cultura y Deportes, Guatemala City.

Barrios Villar, Edy Alejandro. 2006. Tres Islas: Un pueso de control comercial en el Río La Pasión. Técnico en Arqueología, Universidad de San Carlos de Guatemala. Unpublished MA thesis, Centro Universitario de Petén, Santa Elena, Flores.

Barthel, Stephan, and Christian Isendahl. 2012. Urban Gardens, Agriculture, and Water Management: Sources of Resilience for Long-term Food Security in Cities. *Ecological Economics* 86:224–234.

Barthel, Thomas. 1967. Notes on the Inscription on a Carved Bone from Yucatan. *Estudios de Cultura Maya* 6:223–241.

———. 1968. El complejo emblema. *Estudios de Cultura Maya* 7:159–193.

Bar-Yosef, Ofer. 2002. The Upper Paleolithic Revolution. *Annual Review of Anthropology* 31:363–393.

Batllori Sampedro, Eduardo, José L. Febles Patrón, and Julio Días Sosa. 1999. Landscape Change in Yucatan's Northwest Coastal Wetlands (1948–1991). *Human Ecology Review* 6(1):8–20.

Batún Alpuche, Adolfo Iván. 2009. Agrarian Production and Intensification at a Postclassic Maya Community, Buena Vista, Cozumel, Mexico. Unpublished Ph.D. dissertation, Department of Anthropology, University of Florida, Gainesville.

Baudez, Claude François. 2002. *Une histoire de la religion maya*. PUF, Paris.

Baxter, William T. 1989. Early Accounting: The Tally and Checkerboard. *Accounting Historians Journal* 16 (2):43–83.

Bayman, James M. 1995. Rethinking "Redistribution" in the Archaeological Record: Obsidian Exchange at the Marana Platform Mound. *Journal of Anthropological Research* 51(1):37–63.

Beach, Timothy, Sheryl Luzzadder-Beach, Nicholas Dunning, Jon Hageman, and Jon Lohse. 2002. Upland Agriculture in the Maya Lowlands: Ancient Maya Soil Conservation in Northwestern Belize. *Geographical Review* 92(3):372–398.

Beaudry-Corbett, Marilyn, Scott Simmons, and David Tucker. 2002. Ancient Home and Garden: The View from Household 1 at Cerén. In *Before the Volcano Erupted: The Ancient Cerén Village in Central America*, ed. Payson Sheets, 45–57. University of Texas Press, Austin.

Becker, Marshall J. 1979. Priests, Peasants, and Ceremonial Centers: The Intellectual History of a Model. In *Maya Archaeology and Ethnohistory*, ed. Norman Hammond and Gordon R. Willey, 3–20. University of Texas Press, Austin.

———. 2003a. Houselots at Tikal Guatemala: It's What's Out Back That Counts. In *Reconstruyendo la Ciudad Maya: El urbanismo en las sociedades antiguas*, ed. Andrés Ciudad Ruiz, M. J. Iglesias Ponce de León, and M. C. Martínez Martínez, 427–460. Publicaciones de la SEEM No. 6. Sociedad Española de Estudios Mayas, Madrid.

———. 2003b. Plaza Plans at Tikal: A Research Strategy for Inferring Social Organization and Processes of Cultural Change at Lowland Maya Sites. In *Tikal: Dynasties, Foreigners, and Affairs of State*, ed. Jeremy A. Sabloff, 253–280. School of American Research Press, Santa Fe, N. Mex.

———. 2004. Maya Heterarchy as Inferred from Classic-Period Plaza Plans. *Ancient Mesoamerica* 15:127–138.

———. 2015. Ancient Maya Markets: Architectural Grammar and Market Identifications. In *The Ancient Maya Marketplace: The Archaeology of Transient Space*, ed. Eleanor M. King, 90–110. University of Arizona Press, Tucson.

Beliaev, Dmitri D., and Alexandr Safronov. 2004. Ak'e i Shukal'nakh: Istoriia i politicheskaia geografiia gosudarstv maiia verkhnei Usumasinty. In *Drevnii vostok i antichnyi mir: Trudy Kafedry Istorii Drevnego Mira Istoricheskogo Fakulteta MGU*, 119–142. Vol. 6. Lomonosov Moscow State University, Moscow.

Bell, Betty. 1956. An Appraisal of Maya Civilization. In *The Ancient Maya* by S. G. Morley and G. W. Brainerd, 424–441. 3rd ed. Stanford University Press, Stanford.

Bell, Ellen, Marcello Canuto, and Robert Sharer. 2004. *Understanding Early Classic Copan*. University of Pennsylvania Museum of Archaeology and Anthropology, Philadelphia.

Benavides C., Antonio, Sara Novelo O., Nikolai Grube, and Carlos Pallán G. 2009. Nuevos hallazgos en la región Puuc: Sabana Piletas y su escalinata jeroglífica. *Arqueología Mexicana* 17:77–83.

Benedict, Francis G., and Morris Steggerda. 1936. *The Food of the Present-Day Maya Indians of Yucatan*. Publication 456, Contribution 18. Carnegie Institution, Washington, DC.

Bentley, G. Carter. 1986. Indigenous States of Southeast Asia. *Annual Review of Anthropology* 15(1):275–305.

Bentley, Jerry H. 1993. *Old World Encounters: Cross-Cultural Contacts and Exchanges in Pre-Modern Times*. 1st ed. Oxford University Press, Oxford.

Berdan, Frances F. 1975. Trade, Tribute and Market in the Aztec Empire. Unpublished Ph.D. dissertation. University of Texas at Austin.

———. 1982. *The Aztecs of Central Mexico*. Holt, Rinehart, and Winston, New York.

Berdan, Frances F., and Patricia R. Anawalt. 1997. *The Essential Codex Mendoza*. University of California Press, Berkeley.

Berdan, Frances F., Marilyn A. Masson, Janine Gasco, and Michael E. Smith. 2003. An International Economy. In *The Postclassic Mesoamerican World*, ed. M. E. Smith and F. F. Berdan, 96–108. University of Utah Press, Salt Lake City.

Berger, Josef. 1969. *The World's Major Fibre Crops: Their Cultivation and Manuring*. Centre d'Étude de L'Azote. Conzett and Huber, Zurich.

Bernal Romero, Guillermo. 2015. Glifos enigmáticos de la escritura maya: El logograma T514, yej, "filo." *Arqueología Mexicana* 23(135):78–85.

Bernhofen, Daniel M., and John C. Brown. 2005. An Empirical Assessment of the Comparative Advantage Gains from Trade: Evidence from Japan. *American Economic Review* 95(1):208–225.

Bey, George J., III, and Rossana May Ciau. 2014. The Role and Realities of Popol Nahs in Northern Maya Archaeology. In *The Maya and Their Central American Neighbors: Settlement Pat-*

terns, Architecture, Hieroglyphic Texts, and Ceramics, ed. Geoffrey E. Braswell, 335–355. Routledge/Taylor and Francis Group, London.

Bibeau, Gilles. 2008. La dépolitisation de la notion de "capital social": Pourquoi pas un retour à Karl Polanyi? *Anthropologica* 50(2):416–419.

Biró, Péter. 2005. Sak Tz'i' in the Classic Period Hieroglyphic Inscriptions (2005). Mesoweb: www.mesoweb.com/articles/biro/SakTzi.pdf (accessed August 18, 2019).

Bishop, Ronald. 2004a. Análisis por activación neutrónica de cerámicas arqueológicas del Proyecto PRIANPEG, Constancia 054-2002. Manuscript delivered to the Department of Prehispanic and Colonial Monuments, Instituto de Antropología e Historia, Guatemala City, FARES Foundation, Rupert, ID.

———. 2004b. Report on Ceramic Samples Exported for Chemical Analysis Authorized by Permit Registro Numero 26359. Manuscript on file, Foundation for Anthropological Research & Environmental Studies (FARES), Rupert, ID.

Bishop, Ronald L., and J. Blackman. 2002. Neutron Activation Analysis of Archaeological Ceramics: Scale and Interpretation. *Journal of Accounts of Chemical Research* 35(8):603–610.

Bishop, Ronald L., Robert L. Rands, and George R. Holley. 1982. Ceramic Compositional Analysis in Archaeological Perspective. In *Advances in Archaeological Method and Theory, Vol. 3*, ed. M. B. Schiffer, 275–331. Academic Press, New York.

Bishop, Ronald L., Erin L. Sears, and M. James Blackman. 2005. A través del Río Cambio. *Estudios de Cultura Maya* 26:7–40.

Black, Stephen L. 1987. Settlement Pattern Survey and Testing, 1985. In *Rio Azul Reports Number 3, the 1985 Season*, ed. Richard E. W. Adams, 183–221. University of Texas at San Antonio, San Antonio.

Blackmore, Chelsea. 2011. Ritual among the Masses: Deconstructing Identity and Class in an Ancient Maya Neighborhood. *Latin American Antiquity* 22(2):159–177.

———. 2012. Recognizing Difference in Small-Scale Settings: An Examination of Social Identity Formation at the Northeast Group, Chan. In *Chan: An Ancient Maya Farming Community*, ed. Cynthia Robin, 173–191. University Press of Florida, Gainesville.

Blanton, Richard E. 1994. *Houses and Households: A Comparative Study*. Plenum, New York.

———. 1996. The Basin of Mexico Market System and the Growth of Empire. In *Aztec Imperial Strategies*, by Frances F. Berdan, Richard E. Blanton, Elizabeth H. Boone, Mary G. Hodge, Michael E. Smith, and Emily Umberger, 47–84. Dumbarton Oaks, Washington, DC.

———. 2013. Cooperation and the Moral Economy of the Marketplace. In *Merchants, Markets, and Exchange in the Pre-Columbian World*, ed. Kenneth Hirth and Joanne Pillsbury, 23–48. Dumbarton Oaks Research Library and Collection, Washington, DC.

Blanton, Richard E., and Lane Fargher. 2008. *Collective Action in the Formation of Pre-Modern States*. Springer, New York.

Blanton, Richard E., Gary M. Feinman, Stephen A. Kowalewski, and Peter N. Peregrine. 1996. A Dual-Processual Theory for the Evolution of Mesoamerican Civilization. *Current Anthropology* 37(1):1–86.

Blanton, Richard E., Stephen A. Kowalewski, Gary M. Feinman, and Laura M. Finsten. 1993. *Ancient Mesoamerica: A Comparison of Change in Three Regions*. 2nd ed. Cambridge University Press, Cambridge.

Blom, Frans. 1932. Commerce, Trade, and Monetary Units of the Maya. *Middle American Research Series* No. 4:531–556. Tulane University, New Orleans.

———. 1934. Commerce, Trade, and Monetary Units of the Maya. *Annual Report of the Board of Regents of the Smithsonian Institution*:423–440.e Smithsonian Institution, Washington, DC.

Boas, Franz. 1890. Cranium from Progreso, Yucatan. *Proceedings of the American Antiquarian Society* (Worcester, MA), n.s. 6 (1889–1890):350–57 [preprint B, April 30, 1890].

Boehm de Lameiras, Brigitte. 1991. El estado en Mesoamerica: Estudio sobre su origen y evolución. *Revista Española de Antropología Americana* (Madrid) 21:11-51.

Bolles, David, and William J. Folan. 2001. An Analysis of Roads Listed in Colonial Dictionaries and Their Relevance to Pre-Hispanic Linear Features in the Yucatan Peninsula. *Ancient Mesoamerica* 12(02):299-314.

Boot, Erik. 2009. *The Updated Preliminary Classic Maya–English, English–Classic Maya Vocabulary of Hieroglyphic Readings.* Mesoweb Resources, http://www.mesoweb.com/resources/vocabulary/Vocabulary-2009.01.pdf (accessed August 12, 2019).

Boucher, Sylviane, and Sara Dzul G. 1997. La seriación tipológica de la cerámica del Proyecto Arqueológico Calakmul (Temporadas 1993–1997). In *Proyecto Arqueológico Calakmul: Temporada 1996–1997*, ed. Ramón Carrasco Vargas. Centro Regional de Yucatán, INAH, Mérida, Mexico.

———. 1998. La secuencia tipológica preliminar de la cerámica de Calakmul. In *Proyecto Arqueológico Calakmul: Informe de los trabajos arqueológicos, temporada 1997–1998*, ed. Ramón Carrasco Vargas, 123–146. INAH, Campeche, Mexico.

———. 2006. La secuencia tipológica preliminar de la cerámica del Proyecto Arqueológico Calakmul, Campeche (Temporadas 1993–2000). In *Los mayas de ayer y hoy: Memorias del Primer Congreso Internacional de Cultura Maya* 584–616. Vol. 1. Gobierno del Estado de Yucatán, CONACYT, INAH, UADY, Mérida, Mexico.

Bové, Frederick J. 1990. The Teotihuacan-Kaminaljuyú-Tikal Connection: A View from the South Coast of Guatemala. In *The Sixth Palenque Round Table 1986*, ed. Merle G. Robinson and Virginia Fields, 135–142. University of Oklahoma Press, Norman.

Bové, Frederick J., and Sonia Medrano Busto. 2003. Teotihuacan, Militarism, and Pacific Guatemala. In *The Maya and Teotihuacan: Reinterpreting Early Classic Interaction*, ed. Geoffrey E. Braswell, 45–80. University of Texas Press, Austin.

Bozarth, Steven R. 2007. Phytolith Analyses of the Mirador Basin. Paper presented at the 72nd Annual Meeting of the Society for American Archaeology, SAA, Austin, TX.

Bozarth, Steven, and Richard D. Hansen. 2001. Estudios paleo-botánicos de Nakbe: Evidencias preliminares de ambiente y cultivos en el Preclásico. In *XIV Simposio de Investigaciones Arqueológicas en Guatemala*, ed. Juan Pedro Laporte, Ana Clauda de Suasnavar, and Bárbara Arroyo, 419–436. Museo Nacional de Arqueología y Etnología, Ministerio de Cultura y Deportes, Instituto de Antropología e Historia, Asociación Tikal, Guatemala City.

Bradley, Raymond S. 2015. *Paleoclimatology: Reconstructing Climates of the Quaternary.* 3rd ed. Academic Press, San Diego, CA.

Braswell, Geoffrey E. 1996. *A Maya Obsidian Source: The Geoarchaeology, Settlement History, and Ancient Economy of San Martin Jilotepeque, Guatemala.* PhD dissertation, Tulane University. University Microfilms, Ann Arbor, MI.

———. 2002. Praise the Gods and Pass the Obsidian? The Organization of Ancient Economy in San Martín Jilotepeque, Guatemala. In *Ancient Maya Political Economies*, ed. Marilyn A. Masson and David A. Freidel, 285–306. AltaMira Press, Walnut Creek, CA.

———. 2003a. *The Maya and Teotihuacan: Reinterpreting Early Classic Interaction.* University of Texas Press, Austin.

———. 2003b. Obsidian Exchange Spheres. In *The Postclassic Mesoamerican World*, ed. Michael E. Smith and Frances F. Berdan, 131–158. University of Utah Press, Salt Lake City.

———. 2010. The Rise and Fall of Market Exchange: A Dynamic Approach to Ancient Maya Economy. In *Archaeological Approaches to Market Exchange in Ancient Societies*, ed. Christopher P. Garraty and Barbara L. Stark, 127–140. Boulder: University Press of Colorado.

———. 2013. Ancient Obsidian Procurement and Production in the Peten Campechano: Uxul and Calakmul during the Early Classic to Terminal Classic Periods. *Indiana* 30:149–171.

Braswell, Geoffrey, Cassandra Bill, and Christian Prager. 2008. Exchange, Political Relations, and Regional Interaction: The Ancient City of Pusilhá in the Late Classic Maya World. *Research Reports on Belizean Archaeology*, 5:51–62. Institute of Archaeology, National Institute of Culture and History, Belmopan, Belize.

Braswell, Geoffrey E., and Michael D. Glascock. 1998. Interpreting Intrasource Variation in the Composition of Obsidian: The Geoarchaeology of San Martín Jilotepeque, Guatemala. *Latin American Antiquity* 9(4):353–369.

———. 2003. The Emergence of Market Economies in the Ancient Maya World: Obsidian Exchange in Terminal Classic Yucatán, Mexico. In *Geochemical Evidence for Long-Distance Exchange*, ed. Michael D. Glascock, 33–52. Bergin and Garvey, Westport, CT.

———. 2007. El intercambio de la obsidiana y el desarrollo de las economías de tipo mercado en la región maya. In *XX Simposio de Investigaciones Arqueológicas en Guatemala, 2006*, ed. Juan Pedro Laporte, Bárbara Arroyo, and Héctor Mejía, 15–28. Museo Nacional de Arqueología y Etnología, Guatemala City.

———. 2011. Procurement and Production of Obsidian Artifacts at Calakmul. In *The Technology of Maya Civilization: Political Economy and Beyond*, ed. Zachary X. Hruby, Geoffrey E. Braswell, and Oswaldo Chinchilla Mazariegos, 119–129. Equinox, Sheffield, UK.

Braswell, Geoffrey E., Joel D. Gunn, María del Rosario Domínguez Carrasco, William J. Folan, Laraine A. Fletcher, Abel Morales López, and Michael D. Glascock. 2004. Defining the Terminal Classic at Calakmul, Campeche. In *The Terminal Classic in the Maya Lowlands: Collapse, Transition and Transformation*, ed. Arthur A. Demarest, Prudence M. Rice, and Don S. Rice, 162–194. University of Colorado Press, Boulder.

Braswell, Jennifer B. 1998. Archaeological Investigations at Group D, Xunantunich, Belize. Unpublished Ph.D. dissertation, Department of Anthropology, Tulane University, New Orleans.

Bray, Tamara L., editor. 2003. *The Archaeology and Politics of Food and Feasting in Early States and Empires*. Kluwer Academic/Plenum Publishers, New York.

Breschi, Stefano, and Franco Malerba, editors. 2007. *Clusters, Network, and Innovation*. Oxford University Press, Oxford.

Brew, J. O. 1946. *The Archaeology of Alkali Ridge, Southern Utah*. Peabody Museum Papers 21. Peabody Museum, Cambridge, MA.

Brokmann, Carlos. 2000. *Tipología y análisis de la obsidiana de Yaxchilán, Chiapas*. Collección Científica, Serie Arqueología. INAH, Mexico City.

Bronson, Bennet. 1966. Roots and Subsistence of the Ancient Maya. *Southwestern Journal of Anthropology* 22:251–279.

Brookfield, Harold C. 2001. Intensification, and Alternative Approaches to Agricultural Change. *Asia Pacific Viewpoint* 42(2):181.

Brown, Clifford T., Carlos Peraza Lope, Walter R. T. Witschey, and Rhianna Rogers. 2006. Results of Survey in Central Yucatán, México. Presented at the Society for American Archaeology, San Juan, Puerto Rico.

Brown, Linda, and Andrea Gerstle. 2002. Structure 10: Feasting and Village Festivals. In *Before the Volcano Erupted: The Ancient Cerén Village in Central America*, ed. Payson Sheets, 97–103. University of Texas Press, Austin.

Brumfiel, Elizabeth. 1987. Elite and Utilitarian Crafts in the Aztec State. In *Specialization, Exchange and Complex Societies*, ed. Elizabeth M. Brumfiel and Timothy K. Earle, 102–118. Cambridge University Press, Cambridge.

———. 1992. Breaking and Entering the Ecosystem: Gender, Class, and Faction Steal the Show. *American Anthropologist* 94:551–567.

————. 1997. Tribute Cloth Production and Compliance in Aztec and Colonial Mexico. *Museum Anthropology* 21(2):55–71.

————. 2005. Introduction: Production and Power at Postclassic Xaltocan. In *La producción local y el poder en el Xaltocan posclásico/Production and Power at Postclassic Xaltocan*, ed. Elizabeth Brumfiel, 27–42. Instituto Nacional de Antropología e Historica, Mexico City, and University of Pittsburgh, Pittsburgh, PA.

Brumfiel, Elizabeth M., and Timothy K. Earle. 1987. Specialization, Exchange, and Complex Societies: An Introduction. In *Specialization, Exchange, and Complex Societies*, ed. Elizabeth M. Brumfiel and Timothy K. Earle, 1–9. Cambridge University Press, Cambridge.

Brumfiel, Elizabeth M., and Timothy K. Earle, editors. 1987. *Specialization, Exchange, and Complex Societies*. Cambridge University Press, Cambridge.

Bullard, William R., Jr. 1960. The Maya Settlement Pattern in Northwestern Peten, Guatemala. *American Antiquity* 25:355–372.

Burgos Villanueva, Rafael, Miguel Covarrubias Reyna, Sara Dzul Góngora, and Yoli Palomo Carillo. 2008. Investigaciones arqueológicas en la región costera y al interior de la provincia histórica de Ah Kin Chel, Yucatán. *Los Investigadores de la Cultura Maya 2008* 16(2):49–61. Universidad Autónoma de Campeche, Campeche, Mexico.

Bustamante, Eduardo. 2011. Operación CR41: Excavaciones en el Grupo Habitacional 13S-2. In *Proyecto Regional Arqueológico La Corona No. 3: Temporada 2010*, ed. Tomás Barrientos Q., Marcello A. Canuto, and M. J. Acuña, 347–360. Tulane University and Universidad del Valle, Guatemala, New Orleans and Guatemala City.

Cabadas-Báez, Héctor Víctor, Berenice Solís-Castillo, Elizabeth Solleiro-Rebolledo, Sergey Sedov, Daniel Leonard, Keiko Teranishi-Castillo, Rodrigo Liendo-Stuardo, and Oleg Korneychik. 2017. Reworked Volcaniclastic Deposits from the Usumacinta River, Mexico: A Serendipitous Source of Volcanic Glass in Maya Ceramics. *Geoarchaeology*. https:///doi.org/10.1002/gea.21610 (accessed March 30, 2017).

Caballero, Javier. 1992. Maya Homegardens: Past, Present and Future. *Ethnoecológica* 1:35–54.

Cagnato, Clarissa. 2013. Excavaciones en el Grupo 13S-1. In *Proyecto Regional Arqueológico La Corona No. 5: Temporada 2012*, ed. Tomás Barrientos Q., Marcello A. Canuto, and Jocelyne Ponce, 279–288. Tulane University and Universidad del Valle, Guatemala, New Orleans and Guatemala City.

Cain, Tiffany C., and Richard M. Leventhal. 2017. Questioning the Status of Land as Commodity in Maya Quintana Roo and Belize. In *The Value of Things: Prehistoric to Contemporary Commodities in the Maya Region*, ed. Jennifer P. Mathews and Thomas H. Guderjan, 173–192. University of Arizona Press, Tucson.

Callaghan, Michael G. 2013. Maya Polychrome Vessels as Inalienable Possessions. In *The Inalienable in the Archaeology of Mesoamerica*, ed. Michael G. Callaghan and Brigitte Kovacevich, 112–127. Archaeological Papers of the American Anthropological Association, Paper 23. American Anthropological Association, Hoboken, NJ.

Callaghan, Michael G., Cassandra R. Hill, Jeanette Castellanos, and Ronald L. Bishop. 2004. Gris Fino Chablekal: Distribución y análisis socioeconómico preliminar en Cancuén. En *XVII Simposio de Investigaciones Arqueológicas en Guatemala, 2003*, ed. Juan Pedro P. Laporte, Bárbara Arroyo, Héctor L. Escobedo, and Héctor E. Mejía, 323–339. Museo Nacional de Arqueología y Etnología, Guatemala City.

Callaghan, Michael G., and Nina Neivens de Estrada. 2016. *The Ceramic Sequence of the Holmul Region, Guatemala*. No. 77. University of Arizona Press, Tucson.

Callaway, Carl D. 2009. The Birth of the Number Twenty in the Dresden Codex. In *The Maya and Their Sacred Narratives: Text and Context in Maya Mythologies, Proceedings of the 12th European Maya Conference, Geneva, December 7–8, 2007*, ed. Geneviève Le Fort, Raphaël

Gardiol, Sebastian Matteo, and Christophe Helmke, 75–87. Acta Mesoamericana. Verlag Anton Saurwein, Markt Schwaben, Germany.

Calligeris, Catherine. 1998. Fonction et signification des dépôts de fondation mayas, dans les Basses Terres, à la période classique. Unpublished Ph.D. dissertation. University Paris I-Panthéon-Sorbonne, Department of Archaeology, Paris.

Calnek, Edward E. 1974. The Sahagún Texts as a Source of Sociological Information. In *Sixteenth-Century Mexico: The Work of Sahagún*, ed. M. S. Edmonson, 189–204. School of American Research and University of New Mexico Press, Albuquerque.

Calvin, Inga E. 2006. Between Text and Image: An Analysis of Pseudo-Glyphs on Late Classic Maya Pottery from Guatemala. Unpublished Ph.D. dissertation, Department of Anthropology, University of Colorado–Boulder, Boulder.

Calvo-Irabién, Luz Maria, and Alejandro Soberanis. 2008. Indigenous Management Practices of Chit (*Thrinax radiata*) in Quintana Roo, Mexico. *Palms* 52(1):46–50.

Cameron, Catherine. 2016. The Variability of the Human Experience: Marginal People and the Creation of Power. In *Archaeology of the Human Experience*, ed. Michelle Hegmon, 40–53. Archaeological Papers 27. American Anthropological Association, Arlington, VA.

Canuto, Marcello A., and Tomás Barrientos Quezada. 2011. La Corona: Un acercamiento a las políticas del Reino Kaan desde un centro secundario del noroeste de Petén. *Estudios de Cultura Maya* 38:14–43.

———. 2013a. Cinco años de investigaciones en La Corona: Una adivinanza envuelta en un misterio dentro de un enigma. In *XXVI Simposio de Investigaciones Arqueológicas en Guatemala, 2012*, ed. Bárbara Arroyo and L. M. Salinas, 993–997. Ministerio de Cultura y Deportes, Instituto de Antropología e Historia, Asociación Tikal, Guatemala City.

———. 2013b. The Importance of La Corona. *La Corona Notes* 1(1). Mesoweb: www.mesoweb.com/LaCorona/LaCoronaNotes01.pdf (accessed August 10, 2017).

———. 2018. La Corona: Una parada aislada en el camino al poder: Análisis de interacciones sociopolíticas regionales en el noroeste de Petén. In *XXXI Simposio de Investigaciones Arqueológicas en Guatemala, 2017*, ed. Bárbara Arroyo, Luis A. Méndez Salinas, and Gloria Ajú Álvarez, 303–314. Ministerio de Cultura y Deportes, Instituto de Antropología e Historia, Asociación Tikal, Guatemala City.

Cap, Bernadette. 2011. Investigating an Ancient Maya Marketplace at Buenavista del Cayo, Belize. *Research Reports in Belizean Archaeology* 8:241–253.

———. 2015a. Classic Maya Economies: Identification of a Marketplace at Buenavista del Cayo, Belize. Unpublished Ph.D. dissertation, Dept. of Anthropology, University of Wisconsin-Madison.

———. 2015b. Initial Investigations of the Buenavista del Cayo Site Center Structure 3. Report submitted to the Belize Institute of Archaeology, Belmopan, Belize.

———. 2019. A Classic Maya Marketplace at Xunantunich, Belize. *Research Reports in Belizean Archaeology* 16:111-122.

Cap, Bernadette, Meaghan Peruamaki-Brown, and Jason Yaeger. 2015. Shopping for Household Goods at Buenavista del Cayo Marketplace. *Research Reports in Belizean Archaeology* 12:25–36.

Carmean, Kelli. 1991. Architectural Labor Investment and Social Stratification at Sayil, Yucatan. *Latin American Antiquity* 2:151–165.

Carmean, Kelli, Patricia A. McAnany, and Jeremy A. Sabloff. 2011. People Who Lived in Stone Houses: Local Knowledge and Social Difference in the Classic Maya Puuc Region of Yucatan, Mexico. *Latin American Antiquity* 22:143–158.

Carneiro, Robert. 1970. A Theory of the Origin of the State. *Science* 169(1970):733–738.

———. 1981. The Chiefdom: Precursor of the State. In *Transition to Statehood in the New World*, ed. Grant D. Jones and Robert R. Kautz, 37–79. Cambridge University Press, New York.

Carr, Robert F., and James E. Hazard. 1961. *Map of the Ruins of Tikal, El Petén, Guatemala.* Tikal Reports No. 11, Museum Monographs, University Museum, University of Pennsylvania, Philadelphia.

Carrasco Vargas, Ramón. 2003. Actividad ritual y objetos de poder en la Estructura IV de Calakmul, Campeche, Calakmul. In *Calakmul: Una antología*, ed. Carlos Angles and Marylin Domínguez, 149–166. Instituto Nacional de Antropología e Historia y Universidad Autónoma de Campeche, Campeche, México.

Carrasco Vargas, Ramón, Sylviane Boucher, Paula Álvarez González, Vera Tiesler Blos, Valeria García Vierna, Renata García Moreno, and Javier Vázquez Negrete. 1999. A Dynastic Tomb from Campeche, Mexico: New Evidence on Jaguar Paw, a Ruler of Calakmul. *Latin American Antiquity* 10(1):47–58.

Carrasco Vargas, Ramón, Verónica Vázquez López, and Simon Martin. 2009. Daily Life of the Ancient Maya Recorded on Murals at Calakmul, Mexico. *Proceedings of the National Academy of Science* 106(46):19245-19249.

Carrillo y Ancona, Crescencio. 1886. Las Cabezas–Chatas. *Anales del Museo Nacional de México* 1:3:272–78.

Carter, Nicholas P. 2016. These Are Our Mountains Now: Statecraft and the Foundation of a Late Classic Maya Royal Court. *Ancient Mesoamerica* 27(2):233–253.

Caso Barrera, Laura, and Mario Aliphat Fernández. 2006. Cacao, Vanilla and Annatto: Three Production and Exchange Systems in the Southern Maya Lowlands, XVI–XVII Centuries. *Journal of Latin American Geography* 5(2):29–52.

Castañeda Salguero, César. 1995. *Sistemas lacustres de Guatemala: Recursos que mueren.* Editorial Universitaria, Universidad de San Carlos, Guatemala City.

Castañeda Salguero, Cesar, and Richard D. Hansen. 2007. Estudios botánicos en la Cuenca Mirador: Desarrollo de vegetación y su significado cultural. In *XX Simposio de Investigaciones Arqueológicas en Guatemala*, ed. Juan Pedro Laporte, Bárbara Arroyo, and Héctor E. Mejía, 111–120. Museo Nacional de Arqueología y Etnología, Ministerio de Cultura y Deportes, Instituto de Antropología e Historia, Asociación Tikal, Fundación Arqueológica del Nuevo Mundo, Guatemala City.

———. 2008. Relación entre cambio cultural y vegetación en la Cuenca Mirador, norte de Guatemala. *Revista de la Universidad del Valle de Guatemala* 18 (2008):90–100.

———. 2016. Cultural Development and Change of Vegetation in the Mirador System. In *Mirador: Research and Conservation in the Ancient Kaan Kingdom*, ed. Richard D. Hansen and Edgar O. Suyuc L., 37–62. Foundation for Anthropological Research and Environmental Studies (FARES), Corporación Litográfica, Guatemala City.

Castillo Mont, Juan José, Negli Rene Gallardo, and Dennis V. Johnson. 1994. The Pacaya Palm (*Chamaedorea tepejilote*; Arecaceae) and Its Food Use in Guatemala. *Economic Botany* 48(1):68–75.

Ceballos Gallareta, Teresa Noemí de Jesús. 2003. La cronología cerámica de Puerto Maya de Xcambó, Costa Norte de Yucatán: Complejo Xtampú. Unpublished tesis de Licenciatura en Ciencias Antropológicas en la Especialidad de Arqueología. Facultad de Ciencias Antropológicas, Universidad Autónoma de Yucatán, Mérida, Mexico.

Ceballos Gallareta, Teresa, and Socorro Jiménez Álvarez. 2006. Las esferas cerámicas del horizonte Cochuah del Clásico Temprano (ca. 250–600 d.C) en el norte de la península de Yucatán. Parte 1: Las esferas del oeste y del centro. In *La producción alfarera en el México antiguo II*, ed. Beatriz Leonor Merino Carrión and Ángel García Cook, 561–580. Instituto Nacional de Antropología e Historia, Mexico City.

Chase, Adrian S. Z. 2016a. Beyond Elite Control: Residential Reservoirs at Caracol, Belize. *WIREs Water* 3:885–897.

———. 2016b. Districting and Urban Services at Characol, Belize: Intrasite Boundaries in an Evolving Maya Cityscape. *Research Reports in Belizean Archaeology* 13:15–18.

———. 2017. Residential Inequality among the Ancient Maya: Operationalizing Household Architectural Volume at Caracol, Belize. *Research Reports in Belizean Archaeology* 14:31–39.

Chase, Adrian S. Z., and Aubrey M. Z. Chase. 2015. Ceramic Standardization and the Domestic Economy of the Ancient Maya: Belize Red Tripod Plates at Caracol, Belize. *Research Reports in Belizean Archaeology* 12:65–76.

Chase, Adrian S. Z., and John F. Weishampel. 2016. Using LiDAR and GIS to Investigate Water and Soil Management in the Agricultural Terracing at Caracol, Belize. *Advances in Archaeological Practice* 4:357–370.

Chase, Arlen F. 1983. *A Contextual Consideration of the Tayasal-Paxcaman Zone, El Peten, Guatemala*. Ph.D. dissertation, University of Pennsylvania. University Microfilms, Ann Arbor, MI.

———. 1998. Planeación cívica e integración de sitio en Caracol, Belice: Definiendo una economía administrada del Período Clássico maya. *Los Investigadores de la Cultura Maya* (Universidad Autónoma de Campeche, Campeche) 6:26–44.

Chase, Arlen F., and Diane Z. Chase. 1987. *Investigations at the Classic Maya City of Caracol, Belize: 1985–1987*. Monograph No. 3. Pre-Columbian Art Research Institute, San Francisco.

———. 1992. Mesoamerican Elites: Assumptions, Definitions, and Models. In *Mesoamerican Elites: An Archaeological Assessment*, ed. Diane Z. Chase and Arlen F. Chase, 3–17. University of Oklahoma Press, Norman.

———. 1994. Details in the Archaeology of Caracol, Belize: An Introduction. *In Studies in the Archaeology of Caracol, Belize*, ed. Diane Z. Chase and Arlen F. Chase, 1–11. Monograph 7. Pre-Columbian Art Research Institute, San Francisco.

———. 1996. More Than Kin and King: Centralized Political Organization among the Ancient Maya. *Current Anthropology* 37(5):803–810.

———. 1998a. Late Classic Maya Political Structure, Polity Size, and Warfare Arenas. *In Anatomía de una civilización: Aproximaciones interdisciplinarias a la cultura maya*, ed. Andrés Ciudad Ruiz, M. Y. Fernández Marquínez, J. M. García Campillo, M. J. Iglesias Ponce de León, Alfonso Lacadena García-Gallo, and L. T. Sanz Castro, 11–29. Sociedad Española de Estudios Mayas, Madrid.

———. 1998b. Scale and Intensity in Classic Period Maya Agriculture: Terracing and Settlement at the "Garden City" of Caracol, Belize. *Culture and Agriculture* 20(2/3):60–77.

———. 2001. Ancient Maya Causeways and Site Organization at Caracol, Belize. *Ancient Mesoamerica* 12(2):273–281.

———. 2004. Exploring Ancient Economic Relationships at Caracol, Belize. *Research Reports in Belizean Archaeology* 1:115–127.

———. 2005. The Early Classic Period at Caracol, Belize: Transitions, Complexity, and Methodological Issues in Maya Archaeology. *Research Reports in Belizean Archaeology* 2:17–38.

———. 2007. "This Is the End": Archaeological Transitions and the Terminal Classic Period at Caracol, Belize. *Research Reports in Belizean Archaeology* 4:13–27.

———. 2008. Methodological Issues in the Archaeological Identification of the Terminal Classic and Postclassic Transition in the Maya Area. *Research Reports in Belizean Archaeology* 5:23–36.

———. 2009. Symbolic Egalitarianism and Homogenized Distributions in the Archaeological Record at Caracol, Belize: Method, Theory, and Complexity. *Research Reports in Belizean Archaeology* 6:15-24.

———. 2012. Belize Red Ceramics and Their Implications for Trade and Exchange in the Eastern Maya Lowlands. *Research Reports in Belizean Archaeology* 9:3–14.

———. 2014. Houses, Households, and Residential Groups at Caracol, Belize. *Research Reports in Belizean Archaeology* 11:3–17.

———. 2015. The Domestic Economy of Caracol, Belize: Articulating with the Institutional Economy in an Ancient Maya Urban Setting. *Research Reports in Belizean Archaeology* 12:15–23.

———. 2016a. The Ancient Maya City: Anthropogenic Landscapes, Settlement Archaeology, and Caracol Belize. *Research Reports in Belizean Archaeology* 13:3–14.

———. 2016b. Urbanism and Anthropogenic Landscapes. *Annual Review of Anthropology* 45: 361–376.

———. 2020. The Materialization of Classic Period Maya Warfare: Caracol Stranger-Kings at Tikal. In *A Forest of History: The Maya after the Emergence of Divine Kingship*, ed. T. W. Stanton and M. K. Brown. University Press of Colorado, Boulder (in press).

———. 2021. The Transformation of Maya Rulership at Caracol, Belize. In *Maya Kingship: Rupture and Transformation from Classic to Postclassic Times*, ed. Tsubasa Okoshi, Arlen F. Chase, Philippe Nondédéo, and M. Charlotte Arnauld. University Press of Florida, Gainesville.

Chase, Arlen F., Diane Z. Chase, Christopher T. Fischer, Stephen L. Leisz, and John F. Weishampel. 2012. Geospatial Revolution and Remote Sensing LiDAR in Mesoamerican Archaeology. *Proceedings of the National Academy of Science* 190(32):12916-12921.

Chase, Arlen F., Diane Z. Chase, John F. Weishampel, Jason B. Drake, Ramesh L. Shrestha, K. Clint Slatton, Jaime J. Awe, and William E. Carter. 2011. Airborne LiDAR, Archaeology, and the Ancient Landscape at Caracol, Belize. *Journal of Archaeological Science* 38:387–398.

Chase, Arlen F., Diane Z. Chase, Elayne Zorn, and Wendy G. Teeter. 2008. Textiles and the Maya Archaeological Record: Gender, Power, and Status in Classic Period Caracol, Belize. *Ancient Mesoamerica* 19(1):127–142.

Chase, Arlen F., and James F. Garber. 2004. The Archaeology of the Belize Valley in Historical Perspectives. In *Ancient Maya of the Belize Valley: Half a Century of Archaeological Research*, ed. James F. Garber, 1–14. University Press of Florida, Gainesville.

Chase, Diane Z., and Arlen F. Chase. 1996. Maya Multiples: Individuals, Entries and Tombs in Structure A34 of Caracol, Belize. *Latin American Antiquity* 7(1):61–79.

———. 2004. Archaeological Perspectives on Classic Maya Social Organization from Caracol, Belize. *Ancient Mesoamerica* 15:139–147.

———. 2014a. Ancient Maya Markets and the Economic Integration of Caracol, Belize *Ancient Mesoamerica* 25:239–250.

———. 2014b. Path Dependency in the Rise and Denouement of a Classic Maya City: The Case of Caracol, Belize. In *The Resilience and Vulnerability of Ancient Landscapes: Transforming Maya Archaeology through IHOPE*, ed. Arlen F. Chase and Vernon L. Scarborough, 142–154. AP3A Paper 24(1). American Anthropological Association, Arlington, VA.

———. 2017. Caracol, Belize and Changing Perceptions of Ancient Maya Society. *Journal of Archaeological Research* 25(3):185–249.

Chase, Diane Z., and Arlen F. Chase, editors. 1994. *Studies in the Archaeology of Caracol Belize*. PreColumbian Art Research Institute, San Francisco.

Chase, Diane Z., Arlen F. Chase, and William A. Haviland. 1990. The Classic Maya City: Reconsidering the Mesoamerican Urban Tradition. *American Anthropologist* 92(2):499–506.

Chauchat, Claude, and Jacques Pelegrin. 2004. *Projectile Point Technology and Economy: A Case Study from Paiján, North Coastal Peru*. Center for the Study of First Americans. A&M University Press, College Station, TX.

Chinchilla, Oswaldo. 1996. *Settlement Patterns and Monumental Art at a Major Pre-Columbian Polity: Cotzumalguapa, Guatemala*. Ph.D. dissertation, Department of Anthropology, Vanderbilt University. University Microfilms, Ann Arbor.

Christakis, K. S. 1999. Pithoi and Food Storage in Neopalatial Crete: A Domestic Perspective. *World Archaeology* 31(1):1–20.

Christenson, Allen J. 2003. *Popol Vuh: The Sacred Book of the Maya*. O Books, New York.

Chuc Aguilar, Rubén J. 2007. Los asentamientos arqueológicos de la región costera de Chicxulub Puerto, Yucatán: Tipología de asentamiento y producción salinera. Tesis de licenciatura en Arqueología. Facultad de Ciencias Antropológicas, Universidad Autónoma de Yucatán, Mérida.

———. 2012. Un nuevo complejo portuario maya en la costa norte de Yucatán. *Mexicon* 34(4):87–91.

Chuchiak, John F. 2004. Papal Bulls, Extirpators, and the Madrid Codex: The Content and Probable Provenience of the M. 56 Patch. In *The Madrid Codex: New Approaches to Understanding an Ancient Maya Manuscript*, ed. Gabriela Vail and Anthony F. Aveni, 57–88. University Press of Colorado, Boulder.

Ciudad Ruiz, Andrés. 1994. Exploraciones en grupos habitacionales del valle de Dolores: Ixtontón 58 e Ixtontón 45. In *Reporte 8: Atlas Arqueológico de Guatemala*, 200–219. Instituto de Antropología e Historia, Guatemala City.

Ciudad Ruiz, Andrés, María Josefa Iglesias Ponce de León, Jesús Adánez Pavón, Alfonso Lacadena, and Jorge E. Chocón. 2003. In Proyecto: La entidad política de Machaquilá (Guatemala) en el Clásico Tardío y Terminal: Informe de la temporada 2003. Ministerio de Ciencia y Tecnología, Madrid.

Claessen, Henri J. M., and Pieter van de Velde. 1991. *Early State Economics*. Transaction Publishers, New Brunswick, NJ.

Clark, John E. 1986. From Mountains to Molehills: A Critical Review of Teotihuacan's Obsidian Industry. In *Economic Aspects of Prehispanic Highland Mexico*, ed. Barry Isaac, 23–74. JAI Press, Greenwich, CT.

———. 1987. Politics, Prismatic Blades, and Mesoamerican Civilization. In *The Organization of Core Technology*, ed. Jay K. Johnson, 259-284. Boulder, CO: Westview Press.

———. 1991. The Beginnings of Mesoamerica: Apologia for the Soconusco Early Formative. In *The Formation of Complex Society in Southeastern Mesoamerica*, ed. William Fowler, 13–26. CRC Press, Boca Raton, FL.

———. 1997. Prismatic Blademaking, Craftsmanship, and Production: An Analysis of Obsidian Refuse from Ojo de Agua, Chiapas, Mexico. *Ancient Mesoamerica* 8:137–159.

———. 2003. A Review of Twentieth-Century Mesoamerican Obsidian Lithic Technology. In *Mesoamerican Lithic Technology, Experimentation and Interpretation*, ed. Kenneth G. Hirth, 15–54. University of Utah, Salt Lake City.

———. 2007. Mesoamerica's First State. In *The Political Economy of Ancient Mesoamerica: Transformations during the Formative and Classic Periods*, ed. Vernon L. Scarborough and John E. Clark, 11–46. University of New Mexico Press, Albuquerque.

Clark, John E., and Michael Blake. 1994. The Power of Prestige: Competitive Generosity and the Emergence of Rank Societies in Lowland Mesoamerica. In *Factional Competition and Political Development in the New World*, ed. Elizabeth M. Brumfiel and John W. Fox, 17–30. Cambridge University Press, Cambridge.

Clark, John E., and William J. Parry. 1990. Craft Specialization and Cultural Complexity. *Research in Economic Anthropology* 12:289–346.

Cleveland, David A., and Daniela Soleri. 1987. Household Gardens as a Development Strategy. *Human Organization* 46(3):259–270.

Clunas, Craig. 1996. *Fruitful Sites: Garden Culture in Ming Dynasty China*. Reaktion Books, London.

Cobos, Rafael. 1994. Preliminary Report on the Archaeological Mollusca and Shell Ornaments of Caracol, Belize. In *Studies In the Archaeology of Caracol, Belize*, ed. Diane Z. Chase and Arlen F. Chase, 139–147. Monograph 7. Pre-Columbian Art Research Institute, San Francisco, CA.

Coe, Michael D. 1973. *The Maya Scribe and His World*. Grolier Club, New York.

———. 1977. Supernatural Patrons of Maya Scribes and Artisans. In *Social Process in Maya Prehistory: Essay in Honor of Sir Eric Thompson*, ed. Norman Hammond, 327–347. Academic Press, London.

———. 1988. Ideology of the Maya Tomb. In *Maya Iconography*, ed. Elizabeth P. Benson and Gillett G. Griffin, 222–235. Princeton University Press, Princeton, NJ.

Coe, Michael D., and Stephen D. Houston. 2015. *The Maya*. 9th ed. Thames and Hudson, New York.

Coe, Michael D., and Justin Kerr. 1998. *The Art of the Maya Scribe*. Harry N. Abrams, New York.

Coe, Sophie D. 1994. *America's First Cuisines*. Austin: University of Texas Press.

Coe, William R. 1959. *Piedras Negras Archaeology: Artifacts, Caches, and Burials*, Museum Monograph, University Museum, University of Pennsylvania, Philadelphia.

———. 1965. Current Research (Tikal). *American Antiquity* 30:379–383.

———. 1990. *Excavations in the Great Plaza, North Terrace, and North Acropolis of Tikal*. 7 vols. Tikal Report 14. University of Pennsylvania Museum, Philadelphia.

Coe, William R., and John J. McGinn. 1963. Tikal: The North Acropolis and an Early Tomb. *Expedition* 5(2):24–32.

Coggins, Clemency Chase. 1988. On the Historical Significance of Decorated Ceramics at Copan and Quirigua and Related Classic Maya Sites. In *The Southeast Classic Maya Zone: A Symposium at Dumbarton Oaks, 6th and 7th October 1984*, ed. E. H. Boone and G. R. Willey, 95–124. Dumbarton Oaks Research Library and Collection, Washington, DC.

Coggins, Clemency, and Orrin C. Shane III, editors. 1984. *Cenote of Sacrifice: Maya Treasures from the Sacred Well at Chichen Itza*. University of Texas Press, Austin.

Colunga-GarcíaMarín, Patricia, Julian Coello-Coello, Lida Espejo-Peniche, and Lilia Fuente-Moreno. 1993. *Agave* Studies in Yucatan, Mexico II. Nutritional Value of the Inflorescence Peduncle and Incipient Domestication. *Economic Botany* 47:328–334.

Colunga-GarcíaMarín, Patricia, and Daniel Zizumbo-Villarreal. 2004. Domestication of Plants in the Maya Lowlands. *Economic Botany* 58 (Supplement):S101–S110.

Common, Michael, and Sigrid Stagl. 2005. *Ecological Economics: An Introduction*. Cambridge University Press, Cambridge.

CONAP (Consejo Nacional de Áreas Protegidas). 1999. *Plan Maestro 1999–2003 del Parque Nacional Laguna del Tigre*. Consejo Nacional de Áreas Protegidas, Conservación Internacional-ProPetén, Asociación Canan K'aax, Guatemala City.

Conklin, William J. 1982. The Information System of Middle Horizon Quipus. In *Ethnoastronomy and Archaeoastronomy in the American Tropics*, ed. Anthony F. Aveni and Gary Urton, 262–281. New York Academy of Sciences, New York.

Connell, Samuel V. 2000. Were They Well Connected? An Exploration of Ancient Maya Regional Integration from the Middle-Level Perspective of Chaa Creek, Belize. Unpublished Ph.D. dissertation, Department of Anthropology, University of California.

———. 2003. Making Sense of Variability among Minor Centers: The Ancient Maya of Chaa Creek, Belize. In *Perspectives on Ancient Maya Rural Complexity*, ed. Gyles Iannone and Samuel V. Connell, 27–41. Cotsen Institute of Archaeology, University of California, Los Angeles.

Conolly, James, and Mark Lake. 2006. *Geographical Information Systems in Archaeology*. Cambridge University Press, Cambridge.

Cook, Suzanne. 2016. *The Forest of the Lacandon Maya: An Ethnobotanical Guide*. Springer, New York.

Coomes, Oliver T., and Natalie Ban. 2004. Cultivated Plant Species Diversity in Home Gardens of an Amazonian Peasant Village in Northeastern Peru. *Economic Botany* 58(3):420–434.

Cortés, Hernando. 1929. *Five Letters of Cortés to the Emperor* (1521–1525). Translated by J. B. Morris. Norton, New York.

Cortés de Brasdefer, Fernando. 1996. A Maya Vase from "El Señor de Petén." *Mexicon* 18(1):6.

Costin, Cathy L. 1991. Craft Specialization: Issues in Defining, Documenting, and Explaining the Organization of Production. In *Archaeological Methods and Theory*, ed. M. B. Schiffer, 1–56. Vol. 3. University of Arizona Press, Tucson.

———. 2001. Craft Production Systems. In *Archaeology at the Millennium: A Sourcebook*, ed. Gary M. Feinman and T. Douglas Price, 273–328. Kluwer Academic/Plenum Publishers, New York.

Covarrubias Reyna, Miguel, and Rafael Burgos Villanueva. 2016. El paisaje arqueológico de la costa centro-norte de Yucatán. *Estudios de Cultura Maya* 47:55–92. Centro de Estudios Mayas. Universidad Nacional Autónoma de México, Mexico City.

Covarrubias Reyna, Miguel, Rafael Burgos Villanueva, and Yoli Palomo Carillo. 2012. Desarrollo costero estratégico en la región de Ah Kin Chel. *Los Investigadores de la Cultura Maya* (Campeche: Universidad Autónoma de Campeche) 20(1):165–174.

Cowan, Robin, and Nicolas Jonard. 2004. Network Structure and the Diffusion of Knowledge. *Journal of Economic Dynamics and Control* 28(8):1557–1575.

Cowgill, George. 1988. Onward and Upward with Collapse. In *The Collapse of Ancient States and Civilizations*, ed. Norman Yoffee and George Cowgill, 244–276. University of Arizona Press, Tucson.

Cribb, Joe. 2005. Money as Metaphor 1, Money Is Justice: The Origins of Money and Coinage. *Numismatic Chronicle* (2005):417–438.

Crown, Patricia L. 1994. *Ceramics and Ideology: Salado Polychrome Pottery*. University of New Mexico Press, Albuquerque.

Cucina, Andrea. 2015. Population Dynamics during the Classic and Postclassic Period in the Northern Maya Lowlands: The Analysis of Dental Morphological Traits. In *Archaeology and Bioarchaeology of Population Movement among the Prehispanic Maya*, ed. Andrea Cucina, 71–84. Springer International Publishing, New York.

Culbert, T. Patrick. 1993. *The Ceramics of Tikal: Vessels from the Burials, Caches, and Problematical Deposits*. Tikal Report No. 25, Part A. University Museum, University of Pennsylvania, Philadelphia.

———. 2003. The Ceramics of Tikal. In *Tikal: Dynasties, Foreigners, & Affairs of State: Advancing Maya Archaeology*, ed. Jeremy A. Sabloff, 47–82. School of American Research Press, Santa Fe, NM.

Culbert, T. Patrick, editor. 1991. *Classic Maya Political History. Hieroglyphic and Archaeological Evidence*. School of American Research Advanced Seminar Series. Cambridge University Press, Cambridge.

Culbert, T. Patrick, Laura J. Kosakowsky, Robert E. Fry, and William A. Haviland. 1990. The Population of Tikal, Guatemala. In *Precolumbian Population History in the Maya Lowlands*, ed. T. Patrick Culbert and Don S. Rice, 103–122. University of New Mexico Press, Albuquerque.

Culbert, T. Patrick, and Don S. Rice, editors. 1990. *Precolumbian Population History in the Maya Lowlands*. University of New Mexico Press, Albuquerque.

Cunningham-Smith, Petra, Arlen F. Chase, and Diane Z. Chase. 2014. Fish from Afar: Marine Use at Caracol, Belize. *Research Reports in Belizean Archaeology* 11:43–53.

Cyphers, Ann, and Kenneth G. Hirth. 2000. Ceramics of Western Morelos, the Cañada through Gobernador Phases at Xochicalco. In *Ancient Urbanism at Xochicalco: The Evolution and Organization of a Pre-Hispanic Society*, ed. Kenneth G. Hirth, 102–135. Vol. 2. University of Utah Press, Salt Lake City.

Dahlin, Bruce H. 2009. Ahead of Its Time? The Remarkable Early Classic Maya Economy of Chunchucmil. *Journal of Social Archaeology* 9(3):341–367.

Dahlin, Bruce H., Anthony P. Andrews, Timothy Beach, Clara Bezanilla, Patrice Farrell, Sheryl Luzzader-Beach, and Valerie. McCormick. 1998. Punta Canbalám in Context: A Peripatetic Coastal Site in Northwest Campeche, Mexico. *Ancient Mesoamerica* 9(1):1–15.

Dahlin, Bruce H., and Traci Ardren. 2002. Modes of Exchange and Regional Patterns: Chunchucmil, Yucatan. In *Ancient Maya Political Economies*, ed. Marilyn A. Masson and David A. Freidel, 249–284. AltaMira Press, Walnut Creek, CA.

Dahlin, Bruce H., Daniel A. Bair, Timothy Beach, Matthew Moriarty, and Richard Terry. 2010. The Dirt on Food: Ancient Feasts and Markets among the Lowland Maya. In *Pre-Columbian Foodways: Interdisciplinary Approaches to Food, Culture, and Markets in Ancient Mesoamerica*, ed. John E. Staller and Michael Carrasco, 191–232. Springer, New York.

Dahlin, Bruce H., Marjukka Bastamow, Timothy Beach, Zachary X. Hruby, Scott R. Hutson, and Daniel Mazeau. 2011. Phantom Lithics at Chunchucmil, Yucatan, Mexico. In *The Technology of Maya Civilization: Political Economy and Beyond in Lithic Studies*, ed. Zachary X. Hruby, Geoffrey E. Braswell, and Oswaldo Chinchilla Mazariegos, 76–87. Equinox, Oakville, CT.

Dahlin, Bruce H., Timothy Beach, Sheryl Luzzadder-Beach, David Hixson, Scott R. Hudson, Aline Magnoni, Eugenia B. Mansell, and Daniel E. Mazeau. 2005. Reconstructing Agricultural Self-Sufficiency at Chunchucmil, Yucatan, Mexico. *Ancient Mesoamerica* 16:229–247.

Dahlin, Bruce H., and Arlen F. Chase. 2014. A Tale of Three Cities: Effects of the A.D. 536 Event in the Lowland Maya Heartland. In *The Great Maya Droughts in Cultural Context: Case Studies in Resilience and Vulnerability*, ed. Gyles Iannone, 127–155. University Press of Colorado, Boulder.

Dahlin, Bruce H., Christopher T. Jensen, Richard E. Terry, David R. Wright, and Timothy Beach. 2007. In Search of an Ancient Maya Market. *Latin American Antiquity* 18(4):363–384.

Dalton, George. 1975. Karl Polanyi's Analysis of Long-Distance Trade and His Wider Paradigm. In *Ancient Civilization and Trade*, ed. Jeremy Sabloff and C. C. Lamberg-Karlovski, 63–132. University of New Mexico Press, Albuquerque.

———. 1982. Barter. *Journal of Economy Issues* 16(1):181–190.

———. 1990. Writings That Clarify Theoretical Disputes over Karl Polanyi's Work. *Journal of Economic Issues* 24(1):249–261.

D'Altroy, Terence N., and Timothy K. Earle. 1985. Staple Finance, Wealth Finance, and Storage in the Inka Political Economy. *Current Anthropology* 26(2):187–206.

D'Altroy, Terence N., and Christine A. Hastorf. 2001. The Domestic Economy, Households, and Imperial Transformation. In *Empire and Domestic Economy,* ed. Terence N. D'Altroy and Christine A. Hastorf, 3–26. Kluwer Academic Publishers, New York.

Das, T. K., and Bing-Sheng Teng. 1998. Between Trust and Control: Developing Confidence in Partner Cooperation in Alliances. *Academy of Management Review* 23:491–512.

———. 2001. Trust, Control, and Risk in Strategic Alliances: An Integrative Framework. *Organizational Studies* 22(2):251–283.

Davenport, Bryce, and Charles W. Golden. 2016. Landscapes, Lordships, and Sovereignty in

Mesoamerica. In *Political Strategies in Pre-Columbian Mesoamerica*, ed. Sarah Kurnick and Joanne P. Baron, 181–215. University Press of Colorado, Boulder.

Davies, John K. 2005. Linear and Nonlinear Flow Models for Ancient Economies. In *The Ancient Economy: Evidence and Models*, ed. J. G. Manning and Ian Morris, 127–156. Stanford University Press, Palo Alto.

Davis, Jason P. 2016. The Group Dynamics of Interorganizational Relationships: Collaborating with Multiple Partners in Innovation Ecosystems. *Administrative Science Quarterly* 61(4):621–661.

Davis, Mike. 2001. *Late Victorian Holocausts: El Niño Famines and the Making of the Third World*. Verso Books, London.

Deal, Michael. 1998. *Pottery Ethnoarchaeology in the Central Maya Highlands*. University of Utah Press, Salt Lake City.

———. 2007. An Ethnoarchaeological Perspective on Local Ceramic Production and Distribution in the Maya Highlands. In *Pottery Economics in Mesoamerica*, ed. Christopher A. Pool and George Bey, 39–58. University of Arizona Press, Tucson.

DeClerck, F.A.J., and Patricia Negreros-Castillo. 2000. Plant Species of Traditional Maya Homegardens of Mexico as Analogs for Multistrata Agroforests. *Agroforestry Systems* 48:303–317.

Dedrick, Maia. 2019. The Archaeology of Colonial Maya Livelihoods at Tahcabo, Yucatan, Mexico. Unpublished Ph.D. dissertation, Department of Anthropology, University of North Carolina at Chapel Hill.

Delgado Kú, Pedro C., Bárbara del C. Escamilla Ojeda, Marilyn A. Masson, Carlos Peraza Lope, and Douglas J. Kennett. 2020. Household Archaeology within and outside of Mayapán's Monumental Center. In *Settlement, Economy, and Society at Mayapán, Yucatán, Mexico*, ed. Marilyn A. Masson, Timothy S. Hare, Carlos Peraza Lope, and Bradley W. Russell. Center for Comparative Archaeology, University of Pittsburgh, Pittsburg, PA (in press).

Demarest, Arthur A. 1984. Proyecto El Mirador de la Harvard University. *Mesoamerica* 7:1–13.

———. 2002. Product and Exchange at Cancuen: Reconstructing the Classic Maya Political Economy. Proposal to the National Science Foundation. No. 0137639. National Science Foundation, Alexandria, Virginia.

———. 2004. *Ancient Maya: The Rise and Fall of a Rainforest Civilization*. Cambridge: Cambridge University Press.

———. 2006. *The Petexbatun Regional Archaeological Project: A Multidisciplinary Study of the Maya Collapse*. Vanderbilt Institute of Mesoamerican Archaeology, Vol. 1. Vanderbilt University Press, Nashville, TN.

———. 2012a. El cambio económico y político en Cancuén: Evidencia y controversia sobre producción, control y poder en el siglo octavo. In *XXV Simposio de Investigaciones Arqueológicas en Guatemala, 2011*, ed. Bárbara Arroyo, Lorena Paiz, and Héctor Mejia, 361–378. Museo Nacional de Arqueología y Etnología, Guatemala City.

———. 2012b. Production and Exchange at Cancuen. Final Report No. 0137639. National Science Foundation, Alexandria Virginia.

———. 2013. Ideological Pathways to Economic Exchange: Religion, Economy, and Legitimation at the Classic Maya Royal Capital of Cancuen. *Latin American Antiquity* 24(4):371–402.

Demarest, Arthur A., Chloé Andrieu, Paola Torres, Mélanie Forné, Tomás Barrientos, and Marc Wolf. 2014. Economy, Exchange, and Power: New Evidence from the Late Classic Maya Port City of Cancuen. *Ancient Mesoamerica* 25(1):187–219.

Demarest, Arthur A., Chloé Andrieu, Bart Victor, and Paola Torres. 2017. Cambio en la economía de las Tierras Bajas del sur y el seguimiento de un sistema económico nuevo en las vísperas del colapso. In *XXXI Simposio de Investigaciones Arqueológicas en Guatemala,*

2017, ed. Bárbara Arroyo, Luis Méndez Salinas, and Gloria Aju Álvarez, 55–68. Ministerio de Cultura y Deportes and Asociación Tikal, Guatemala City.

———. 2020. Monumental Landscapes as Instruments of Radical Economic Change: The Rise and Fall of a Maya Economic Network. In *Monumental Landscapes: How the Maya Shaped Their World*, ed. Brett Houk, Bárbara Arroyo, and Terry G. Powis. University Press of Florida, Gainesville.

———. 2021. The Collapse of the Southern Lowland Classic Maya Kingdoms: Recent Economic Evidence and Models for the 760–810 Disaster (or "Collapse"). In *Maya Kingship: Rupture and Transformation from Classic to Postclassic Times*, ed. Tsubasa Okoshi, Arlen F. Chase, Philippe Nondédéo, and M. Charlotte Arnauld. University Press of Florida, Gainesville.

Demarest, Arthur, Chloé Andrieu, Bart Victor, Paola Torres, and Mélanie Forné. 2017. La producción e intercambio de mercancías en el siglo octavo en las Tierras Bajas Mayas: Nuevos datos, conceptos e interpretaciones. In *XXX Simposio de Investigaciones Arqueológicas en Guatemala 2016*, ed. Bárbara Arroyo, Luis M. Salinas, and Gloria Ajú Álvarez, 937–948. Ministerio de Cultura y Deportes de Guatemala, Guatemala City.

Demarest, Arthur A., and Tomás Barrientos. 2002. Proyecto Arqueológico Cancuén, Temporada 2001: Antecedentes y resumen de actividades. In *Proyecto Arqueológico Cancuén Informe: Temporada 2001*, 1–18. Department of Anthropology, Vanderbilt University, Nashville, TN.

Demarest, Arthur A., Hector Escobedo, Juan Antonio Valdes, Stephen Houston, Lori Wright, and Katherine Emery. 1991. Arqueología, epigrafía y el descubrimiento de una tumba real en el centro ceremonial de Dos Pilas, Petén, Guatemala. *Utz'ib* 1(1):14–28.

Demarest, Arthur, and Federico Fahsen. 2002. Nuevos datos e interpretaciones de los reinos occidentales del Clásico Tardío: Hacia una visión sintética de la historia Pasión-Usumacinta. Paper presented at the XVI Simposio de Investigaciones Arqueológicas en Guatemala, Guatemala City.

———. 2003. Nuevos datos e interpretaciones de los reinos occidentales del Clásico Tardío: Hacia una visión sintética de la historia Pasión/Usumacinta. In *XVI Simposio de Investigaciones Arqueológicas en Guatemala, 2002*, ed. Juan Pedro Laporte, Bárbara Arroyo, Héctor Escobedo, and Héctor Mejía, 160–176. Museo Nacional de Arqueología y Etnología, Guatemala City.

Demarest, Arthur A., and Robert J. Sharer. 1982. The Origins and Evolution of Usulutan Ceramics. *American Antiquity* 47(4):810–822.

Demarest, Arthur, and Bart Victor. 2018. It Was the Best of Times, It Was the End of Times: Theory from Ancient Experience to the Modern Risk of Doomsday. *Academy of Management Perspectives* (under review).

Demarest, Arthur A., Bart Victor, Chloé Andrieu, and Paola Torres. 2020. Monumental Landscapes as Instruments of Radical Economic Change: Innovation, Apogee, and Collapse. In *Approaches to Monumental Landscapes of the Ancient Maya*, ed. Brett Houk, Bárbara Arroyo, and Terry G. Powis. University Press of Florida, Gainesville.

Demarest, Arthur A., Bart Victor, and Paola Torres. 2020. Changing Classic Maya Economic Regimes, Networks, and Strategies on the Eve of Collapse: A Comparative Perspective. In *Regimes of the Classic Maya*, ed. Marcello A. Canuto and Maxime Lamoureux St.-Hilaire. Cambridge University Press, Cambridge.

Demarest, Arthur, Brent Woodfill, Tomás Barrientos, Federico Fahsen, and Mirza Monterroso. 2007. La ruta Altiplano–Tierras Bajas del Occidente, y el surgimiento y caída de la civilización Clásica Maya. In *XX Simposio de Investigaciones Arqueológicas en Guatemala*, ed. Juan Pedro Laporte, Bárbara Arroyo, and Héctor Mejía, 27–44. Ministerio de Cultura y Deportes, Guatemala City.

Denevan, William M. 1987. Terrace Abandonment in the Colca Valley, Peru. In *Pre-Hispanic*

Agricultural Fields in the Andean Region, Part I, ed. William M. Denevan, Kent Mathewson, and Gregory Knapp, 1–43. Proceedings of the 45th International Congress of Americanists, BAR International Series 359(i), BAR, Oxford.

De Roover, Raymond. 1963. The Organization of Trade. In *The Cambridge Economic History of Europe*, ed. M. M. Postan, E. E. Rich, and Edward Miller, vol. 3, *Economic Organization and Policies in the Middle Ages*, 42–118. Cambridge University Press, Cambridge.

Dickson, Peter R., and J. L. Ginter. 1987. Market Segmentation, Product Differentiation and Marketing Strategy. *Journal of Marketing* 51:1–10.

Dietler, Michael, and Brian Hayden, editors. 2001. *Feasting: Archaeological and Ethnographic Perspectives on Food, Politics, and Power.* Smithsonian Institution Press, Washington, DC.

Dillon, Brian D. 1977. *Salinas de los Nueve Cerros, Guatemala.* Studies in Mesoamerican Art, Archaeology, and Ethnohistory No. 2. Ballena, Socorro, NM.

———. 1979. The Archaeological Ceramics of Salinas de los Nueve Cerros, Alta Verapaz, Guatemala. Ph.D. dissertation, Department of Anthropology, University of California, Berkeley.

———. 1981a. Camelá Lagoon: Preliminary Investigations at a Lowland Maya Site in El Quiché, Guatemala. *Journal of New World Archaeology* 4(3):55–81.

———. 1981b. Estudio sobre la fabricación de la sal por los Mayas, Salinas de los Nueve Cerros, Guatemala. *Antropología e Historia de Guatemala* series 2(3):25–30.

———. 1985. Preface to the English Edition. *The Verapaz in the Sixteenth and Seventeenth Centuries: A Contribution to the Historical Geography and Ethnology of Northeastern Guatemala*, by Karl Sapper, translated by Theodore E. Gutman, i–vii. Occasional Paper 13, Institute of Archaeology, University of California, Los Angeles.

———. 1990. Proyecto de rescate de los vasijones de salinas de los Nueve Cerros, Alta Verapaz. Final report submitted to the Instituto de Antropología e Historia de Guatemala, Guatemala City.

Dillon, Brian D., Lynda Brunker, and Kevin O, Pope. 1985. Ancient Maya Autoamputation? A Possible Case from Salinas de los Nueve Cerros, Guatemala. *Journal of New World Archaeology* 5(4):24–38.

Dillon, Brian D., Kevin O. Pope, and Michael Love. 1988. An Ancient Extractive Industry: Maya Saltmaking at Salinas de los Nueve Cerros, Guatemala. *Journal of New World Archaeology* 7(2/3):37–58.

Dockall, John E., and Harry J. Shafer. 1993. Testing the Producer-Consumer Model for Santa Rita Corozal, Belize. *Latin American Antiquity* 4(2):158–179.

Docster, Elise, Santiago Juárez, Andrew Wyatt, Ethan Kalosky and Cynthia Robin. 2008. A Changing Cultural Landscape: Settlement Survey and GIS at Chan. Paper presented at the 73rd Annual Meeting of the Society for American Archaeology, Vancouver.

Domínguez Carrasco, María del Rosario. 1994a. *Calakmul, Campeche: Un análisis de la cerámica.* Collección Arqueológica 4. Centro de Investigaciones Históricas y Sociales, Universidad Autónoma de Campeche, Campeche, México.

———. 1994b. Tipología cerámica de Calakmul, Campeche, México. *Mexicon* 16(3):51–53.

Domínguez Carrasco, María del Rosario, Leydi del Carmen Puc Tejero, and William J. Folan. 2011. Oxpemul, Campeche: Un acercamiento a la temporalidad de su asentamiento. *Estudios de Cultura Maya* 37:45–63.

Domínguez Carrasco, María del Rosario, and William J. Folan. 2015. Ceramic Traditions in the Calakmul Region: An Indicator of the Movement of Ideas or Populations? In *Archaeology and Bioarchaeology of Population Movement among the Prehispanic Maya*, ed. Andrea Cucina, 13–24. Springer, New York.

Donkin, R. A. 1979. *Agricultural Terracing in the Aboriginal New World.* Viking Fund Publications in Anthropology 56. University of Arizona Press, Tucson.

Doolittle, William E. 1992. House-Lot Gardens in the Gran Chichimeca. In *Gardens of Prehistory: The Archaeology of Settlement Agriculture in Greater Mesoamerica*, ed. T. W. Killion, 69–91. University of Alabama Press, Tuscaloosa.

Douglas, Mary, and Baron Isherwood. 1996. *The World of Goods: Towards An Anthropology of Consumption*. 2nd ed. Routledge Press, London.

Doyle, James A. 2012. Regroup on "E-Groups": Monumentality and Early Centers in the Middle Preclassic Maya Lowlands. *Latin American Antiquity* 23(4):355–379.

———. 2016. E-Groups and the Origins of Maya Exchange. Presented at the 83rd Meeting of the Society for American Archaeology, Orlando, Florida.

Doz, Yves L. 1996. The Evolution of Cooperation in Strategic Alliances: Initial Conditions or Learning Processes. *Strategic Management Journal* 17:55–83.

Dreiss, Meridith L., and David O. Brown. 1989. Obsidian Exchange Patterns in Belize. In *Prehistoric Maya Economies of Belize*, ed. Patricia A. McAnany and B. K. Isaac, 57–90. Research in Economic Anthropology, Supplement 4. JAI Press, Greenwich.

Drennan, Robert D. 1976. Religion and Social Evolution in Formative Mesoamerica. In *The Early Mesoamerican Village*, ed. Kent V. Flannery, 345–368. Academic Press, New York.

———. 1984. Long-Distance Transport Costs in Prehispanic Mesoamerica. *American Anthropologist* 86:105–112.

Dull, Robert, John Southon, Stefan Kutterolf, Armin Freundt, David Wahl, and Payson Sheets. 2010. Did the TBJ Ilopango Eruption Cause the AD 536 Event? American Geophysical Union Fall Meeting, San Francisco, Abstract V13C-2370.

Dunning, Nicholas. 1992. Ancient Maya Anthrosols: Soil Phosphate Testing and Land Use. In *Proceedings of the First International Conference on Pedo-Archaeology*, ed. J. E. Foss, M. E. Timpson, and M. W. Morris, 203–210. University of Tennessee Special Publication 93-03. University of Tennessee, Knoxville.

———. 1996. A Reexamination of Regional Variability in the Prehistoric Agricultural Landscape. In *The Managed Mosaic: Ancient Maya Agriculture and Resource Use*, ed. Scott L. Fedick, 53–68. University of Utah Press, Salt Lake City.

———. 2004. Down on the Farm: Classic Maya "Homesteads" as "Farmsteads." In *Ancient Maya Commoners*, ed. Jon C. Lohse and Fred J. Valdez Jr., 97–116. University of Texas Press, Austin.

Dunning, Nicholas P., and Timothy Beach. 1994. Soil Erosion, Slope Management, and Ancient Terracing in the Maya Lowlands. *Latin American Antiquity* 5(1):51–69.

Dunning, Nicholas, Timothy Beach, and David Rue. 1997. The Paleoecology and Ancient Settlement of the Petexbatun Region, Guatemala. *Ancient Mesoamerica* 8(2):255–266.

Dunning, Nicholas P., John G. Jones, Timothy Beach, and Sheryl Luzadder-Beach. 2003. Physiography, Habitats, and Landscapes of the Three Rivers Region. In *Heterarchy, Political Economy, and the Ancient Maya: The Three Rivers Region of the East-Central Yucatán Peninsula*, ed. Vernon L. Scarborough, Fred Valdez Jr., and Nicholas P. Dunning, 14–24. University of Arizona Press, Tempe.

Dunning, Nicholas P., Sheryl Luzzadder-Beach, Timothy Beach, John G. Jones, Vernon Scarborough, and T. Patrick Culbert. 2002. Arising from the *Bajos*: The Evolution of a Neotropical Landscape and the Rise of Maya Civilization. *Annals of the Association of American Geographers* 92:2 (2002):267–283.

Dutton, Jane E., and Joel A. C. Baum. 1996. *The Embeddedness of Strategy*. JAI Press, Greenwich, CT.

Dzul Góngora, Sara. 2013. La clasificación de la cerámica de Uxul: Temporada 2013. In *Informe técnico: Temporada 2013 del Proyecto Arqueológico Uxul*, ed. Nikolai Grube, Kai Delvendahl, and Antonio Benavides Castillo, 443–453. Report submitted to Consejo de Arqueología, Instituto Nacional de Antropología e Historia, Mexico City.

Earle, Timothy. 1982. The Ecology and Politics of Primitive Valuables. In *Cultural Ecology: Eclec-*

tic Perspectives, ed. John G. Kennedy and Robert B. Edgerton, 65–83. American Anthropological Association, Washington, DC.

———. 1994a. Positioning Exchange in the Evolution of Human Society. In *Prehistoric Exchange Systems in North America*, ed. Timothy G. Baugh and Jonathon E. Ericson, 419–437. Plenum Press, New York.

———. 1994b. Wealth Finance in the Inka Empire: Evidence from the Calchaqui Valley, Argentina. *American Antiquity* 59(3):443–460.

———. 2002. *Bronze Age Economics: The Beginnings of Political Economies*. Westview Press, Cambridge, MA.

Eaton, Jack D. 1978. Archaeological Survey of the Yucatán-Campeche Coast. *Middle American Research Institute Publication* 46:1–67.

Eberl, Markus. 2005. *Muerte, entierro y ascensión: Ritos funerarios entre los antiguos mayas*. Ediciones de la Universidad Autónoma de Yucatán, Mérida, Mexico.

———. 2017. *War Owl Falling: Innovation, Creativity, and Culture Change in Ancient Maya Society*. University Press of Florida, Gainesville.

Ebert, Claire, Mark Dennison, Kenneth G. Hirth, Sarah B. McClure, and Douglas J. Kennett. 2015. Formative Period Obsidian Exchange along the Pacific Coast of Mesoamerica. *Archaeometry* 57(S1):54–73.

Eder, James F. 1991. Agricultural Intensification and Labor Productivity in a Philippine Vegetable Gardening Community: A Longitudinal Study. *Human Organization* 50(3):245–255.

Edmonson, Munro S., translator and annotator. 1986. *Heaven Born Merida and Its Destiny: The Book of Chilam Balam of Chumayel*. University of Texas Press, Austin.

Eggers, Jamie P. 2012. Falling Flat: Failed Technologies and Investment under Uncertainty. *Administrative Science Quarterly* 57:47–80.

Eisenstad, Shmuel. 1988. Beyond Collapse. In *The Collapse of Ancient States and Civilizations*, ed. Norman Yoffee and George L. Cowgill, 236–243. University of Arizona Press, Tucson.

Emch, Michael E. 2003. The Human Ecology of Mayan Cacao Farming in the Toledo District, Belize. *Human Ecology* 31(1):111–131.

Emery, Kitty F. 2007. Aprovechamiento de la fauna en Piedras Negras: Dieta, ritual y artesanía del Periodo Clásico Maya. *Mayab* 19:51–69.

———. 2010. *Dietary, Environmental, and Social Implications of Ancient Maya Animal Use in the Petexbatun: A Zooarchaeological Perspective on the Collapse*. Archaeology Series, Vol. 5. Vanderbilt Institute of Mesoamerica, Vanderbilt University, Nashville, TN.

———. 2014. Aguateca Animal Remains. In *Life and Politics at the Royal Court of Aguateca: Artifacts, Analytical Data, and Synthesis*, ed. Takeshi Inomata and Daniela Triadan, 158–200. Monographs of the Aguateca Archaeological Project First Phase, Vol. 3. University of Utah Press, Salt Lake City.

Emery, Kitty, and Kazuo Aoyama. 2007. Bone Tool Manufacturing in Elite Maya Households at Aguateca, Guatemala. *Ancient Mesoamerica* 18(2):69–89.

Emery, Kitty F., and Antonia E. Foias. 2012. Landscape, Economies, and the Politics of Power in the Motul de San José Polity. In *Motul de San José: Politics, History, and Economy in a Classic Maya Polity*, eds. Antonia E. Foias and Kitty F. Emery, 401–418. University Press of Florida, Gainesville.

Eppich, Keith. 2007. Death and Veneration at El Perú–Waka': Structure M14-15 as Ancestor Shrine. *PARI Journal* 8(1):1–16.

———. 2011. Lineage and State at El Perú–Waka': Ceramic and Architectural Perspective on the Classic Maya Social Dynamic. Unpublished Ph.D. dissertation, Southern Methodist University, Dallas.

———. 2015. The Decline and Fall of the Classic Maya City. In *Archaeology for the People*, ed.

John Cherry and Felipe Rojas Silva, 81–94. Joukowsky Institute Publication Series. Oxbow Books, Oxford.

Eppich, Keith, and Haley Austin. 2016. WK-19: Excavaciones en los grupos de patio en el distrito del margen sureste. In *Proyecto Arqueológico El Perú–Waka': Informe No. 13, temporada 2015*, ed. Juan Carlos Pérez and Griselda Pérez, 55–130. Informe Entragado a la Dirección General del Patrimonio Cultural y Natural de Guatemala, Guatemala City.

Eppich, Keith, Haley Austin, Sarah Van Oss, Kristi Gift, Emily Haney, and Zac Cooper. 2017. Análisis cerámico, 2016: 1,300 años de tradición cerámica de El Perú–Waka'. In *Proyecto Arqueológico El Perú-Waka': Informe No. 14, temporada 2016*, ed. Juan Carlos Pérez and Griselda Pérez, 347–462. Informe Entragado a la Dirección General del Patrimonio Cultural y Natural de Guatemala, Guatemala City.

Eppich, Keith, and David Freidel. 2015. Markets and Marketing in the Classic Maya Lowlands: A Case Study from El Perú Waka'. In *The Ancient Maya Marketplace: The Archaeology of Transient Space*, ed. Eleanor M. King, 195–225. University of Arizona Press, Tucson.

Erasmus, Charles J. 1965. Monument Building: Some Field Experiments. *Southwestern Journal of Anthropology* 21(4):277–301.

Escamilla Ojeda, Bárbara. 2004. Los artefactos de obsidiana de Mayapán, Yucatán. Tesis profesional, Universidad Autónoma de Yucatán, Facultad de Ciencias Antropológica, Mérida, Mexico.

Esparza Olguín, Octavio Q., and Kenichiro Tsukamoto. 2011. Espacios de la escenografía ritual. In *Los Mayas: Voces de piedra*, ed. Alejandra Martínez de Velasco and María Elena Vega, 393–399. Ámbar Diseño, México City.

Espinoza, Antonio. 1910. *Mapa de la Península de Yucatán (México) comprendiendo los Estados de Yucatán y Campeche y el Territorio de Quintana Roo*. Amended with new topographical and astronomical date by Antonio Espinosa. Ingeniero. Scale 1:500,000. J. Solier, engraver. Barcelona: Lit. Labielle, Barcelona.

Estado Mayor, Mexico. 1901. *Croquis del Estado de Yucatán*. Memoria de la Secretaría de Guerra y Marina. Bernardo Reyes, Mexico City.

Estrada Belli, Francisco, and Alexandre Tokovinine. 2016. A King's Apotheosis: Iconography, Text, and Politics from a Classic Maya Temple at Holmul. *Latin American Antiquity* 27(2):149–169.

Estrada Belli, Francisco, Alexandre Tokovinine, Jennifer Foley, Heather Hurst, Gene A. Ware, David Stuart, and Nikolai Grube. 2009. A Maya Palace at Holmul, Peten, Guatemala and the Teotihuacan "Entrada": Evidence from Murals 7 and 9. *Latin American Antiquity* 20(1):228–529.

Evans, Susan Toby 1980. *A Settlement System Analysis of the Teotihuacán Region, Mexico, AD 1350-1520*. Ph.D. dissertation, Pennsylvania State University. University Park, PA. University Microfilms, Ann Arbor, MI.

Fahsen, Federico. 1988. *A New Early Classic Text from Tikal*. Research Reports on Ancient Maya Writing, No. 17. Center for Maya Research, Washington, DC.

Fahsen, Federico, and Tomás Barrientos. 2006. Los monumentos de Taj Chan Ahk y Kaan Maax. In Proyecto Arqueológico Cancuén: Informe de temporada 2004–2005, ed. Tomás Barrientos, Arthur Demarest, Claudia Quintanilla, and Luis Luín, 35–56, MS. Instituto de Antropologia e Historia, Guatemala City.

Farriss, Nancy M. 1984. *Maya Society under Colonial Rule: The Collective Enterprise of Survival*. Princeton University Press, Princeton, NJ.

Fash, William. 1991. *Scribes, Warriors, and Kings: The City of Copan and the Ancient Maya*. Thames and Hudson, London.

Fash, William L., Alexandre Tokovinine, and Barbara Fash. 2009. The House of New Fire at Teotihuacan and Its Legacy in Mesoamerica. In *Art of Urbanism: How Mesoamerican King-*

doms Represented Themselves in Architecture and Imagery, ed. William L. Fash and Leonardo López Luján, 201–229. Dumbarton Oaks Research Library and Collection, Washington, DC.

Fedick, Scott L. 2010. The Maya Forest: Destroyed or Cultivated by the Ancient Maya? *Proceedings of the National Academy of Sciences (PNAS)* 107:953–954.

———. 2017. Plant-Food Commodities of the Maya Lowlands. In *The Value of Things: Prehistoric to Contemporary Commodities in the Maya Region*, ed. Jennifer P. Mathews and Thomas H. Guderjan, 163–172. University of Arizona Press, Tucson.

Fedick, Scott L., editor. 1996. *The Managed Mosaic: Ancient Maya Agriculture and Resource Use.* University of Utah Press, Salt Lake City.

Fedick, Scott L., and Gerald A. Islebe. 2012. The Secret Garden: Assessing the Archaeological Visibility of Ancient Maya Plant Cultivation according to Pollination Syndrome. Paper presented at the 8th European Conference on Ecological Restoration, Ceské Budejovice, Czech Republic.

Fedick, Scott L., and Louis Santiago. 2012. Drought Resistance and Ancient Maya Agriculture. Paper presented at the 77th Annual Meeting of the Society for American Archaeology, Memphis, Tennessee.

Feeley-Harnik, Gillian. 1985. Issues in Divine Kingship. *Annual Review of Anthropology* 14:273–313.

Feinman, Gary M. 2000. High Intensity Household-Scale Production in Ancient Mesoamerica: A Perspective from Ejutla, Oaxaca. In *Cultural Evolution: Contemporary Viewpoints*, ed. Gary M. Feinman and Linda M. Nicholas, 167–188. University of Utah Press, Salt Lake City.

———. 2013. Crafts, Specialists, and Markets in Mycenaean Greece, Re-envisioning Ancient Economies: Beyond Typological Concepts. *American Journal of Archaeology* 117:453–459.

Feinman, Gary M., and Christopher P. Garraty. 2010. Preindustrial Markets and Marketing: Archaeological Perspectives. *Annual Review of Anthropology* 39:167–191.

Feinman, Gary M., and Joyce Marcus, editors. 1998. *Archaic States.* School of American Research Press, Santa Fe, NM.

Feinman, Gary M., and Linda M. Nicholas. 2000. High-Intensity Household-Scale Production in Ancient Mesoamerica: A Perspective from Ejutla, Oaxaca. In *Cultural Evolution: Contemporary Viewpoints*, ed. Gary M. Feinman and Linda Manzanilla, 119–144. Kluwer Academic/Plenum Publishers, New York.

———. 2004. Unraveling the Prehispanic Highland Mesoamerican Economy: Production, Exchange, and Consumption in the Classic Period Valley of Oaxaca. In *Archaeological Perspectives on Political Economies*, ed. Gary M. Feinman and Linda M. Nicholas, 167–188. University of Utah Press, Salt Lake City.

———. 2010. A Multiscalar Perspective on Market Exchange in the Classic-Period Valley of Oaxaca. In *Archaeological Approaches to Market Exchange In Ancient Societies*, ed. Christopher P. Garraty and Barbara Stark, 85–98. University Press of Colorado, Boulder.

———. 2012. The Late Prehispanic Economy of the Valley of Oaxaca, Mexico: Weaving Threads from Data, Theory, and Subsequent History. In *Political Economy, Neoliberalism, and the Prehistoric Economies of Latin America*, ed. Ty Matejowsky and Donald C. Wood, 225–258. Research in Economic Anthropology 32. Emerald Group Publishing, Bingley, UK.

Feinman, Gary M., Linda M. Nicholas, and Helen R. Haines. 2002. Houses on a Hill: Classic Period Life at El Palmillo, Oaxaca, Mexico. *Latin American Antiquity* 13(3):251–277.

Feldman, Lawrence H. 1978a. Inside a Mexica Market. In *Mesoamerican Communication Routes and Cultural Contacts*, ed. Thomas A. Lee and Carlos Navarrete, 219–222. New World Archaeological Foundation, Vol. 40. Brigham Young University, Provo, UT.

———. 1978b. Moving Merchandise in Protohistoric Central Quauhtemallan. In *Mesoamerican*

Communication Routes and Cultural Contacts, ed. Thomas A. Lee and Carlos Navarette, 7–17. Papers of the New World Archaeological Foundation, Provo, Utah.

———. 1985. *A Tumpline Economy: Production and Distribution Systems in Sixteenth-Century Eastern Guatemala*. Labyrinthos, Culver City, CA.

———. 2008. Archaeological Shells in the Peten: Report on Nakbe, Flores, Mirador, and La Florida. Report on file in the archives of the FARES Foundation, Rupert, ID.

Fernandes, E.C.M., and P.K.R. Nair. 1986. An Evaluation of the Structure and Function of Tropical Homegardens. *Agricultural Systems* 21(4):279–310.

Fernández, Fabián G., Kristofer D. Johnson, Richard E. Terry, Sheldon D. Nelson, and David L. Webster. 2005. Soil Resources of the Ancient Maya at Piedras Negras, Guatemala. *Soil Science Society of America Journal* 69:2020–2032.

Fernández del Valle, Patricia. 1992. Salvamento arqueológico en la ciudad de Mérida, El Vergel II. Tesis profesional. Facultad de Ciencias Antropológicas de la Universidad Autónoma de Yucatán, Mérida, Mexico.

Finkelstein, J. J. 1968. An Old Babylonian Herding Contract and Genesis 31:38. *Journal of the American Oriental Society* 88:30–36.

Finley, M. I. 1954. *The World of Odysseus*. Viking Press, New York.

———. 1973. *The Ancient Economy*. Chatto and Windus, London.

Firth, Raymond. 1967. Themes in Economic Anthropology: A General Comment. In *Themes in Economic Anthropology*, ed. Raymond Firth, 1–28. Association of Social Anthropologists Monograph 6. Tavistock Publications, London.

Fischer, Edward F. 2014. *The Good Life: Aspiration, Dignity, and the Anthropology of Wellbeing*. Stanford University Press, Redwood City, CA.

Fischer, Edward F., editor. 2014. *Cash on the Table: Markets, Values, and Moral Economies*. SAR Press, Santa Fe, NM.

Fischer, Edward F., and Bart Victor. 2014. High-End Coffee and Smallholding Growers in Guatemala. *Latin American Research Review* 49(1):155–77.

Fitzsimmons, James L. 2009. *Death and the Classic Maya Kings*. University of Texas Press, Austin.

Fitzsimmons, James L., Andrew K. Scherer, Stephen D. Houston, and Héctor L. Escobedo. 2003. Guardian of the Acropolis: The Sacred Space of a Royal Burial at Piedras Negras, Guatemala. *Latin American Antiquity* 14(4):449–468.

Flores, Rosa María. 1994. Exploraciones en Suk Che' Central. In *Reporte 8: Atlas arqueológico de Guatemala*, 295–309. Instituto de Antropología e Historia, Guatemala City.

Foias, Antonia. 2002. At the Crossroads: The Economic Basis of Political Power in the Petexbatun Region. In *Ancient Maya Political Economies*, ed. Marilyn Masson and David Freidel, 223–248. AltaMira Press, Walnut Creek, CA.

———. 2013. *Ancient Maya Political Dynamics*. University Press of Florida, Gainesville.

Foias, Antonia E., and Ronald L. Bishop. 1997. Changing Ceramic Production and Exchange in the Petexbatun Region, Guatemala: Reconsidering the Classic Maya Collapse. *Ancient Mesoamerica* 8(2):275–291.

———. 2007. Pots, Sherds, and Glyphs: Pottery Production and Exchange in the Petexbatun Polity, Peten, Guatemala. In *Pottery Economics in Mesoamerica*, ed. Christopher A. Pool and George J. Bey III, 212–236. University of Arizona Press, Tucson.

———. 2013. *Ceramics, Production, and Exchange in the Petexbatun Region: The Economic Parameters of the Classic Maya Collapse*. Archaeology Series, Vol. 7. Vanderbilt Institute of Mesoamerica. Vanderbilt University, Nashville, TN.

Foias, Antonia E., and Kitty F. Emery. 2012. Politics and Economics: Theoretical Perspectives of the Motul de San José Project. In *Motul de San José: Politics, History, and Economy in* a *Classic Maya Polity*, ed. Antonia E. Foias and Kitty F. Emery, 1–29. University Press of Florida, Gainesville.

Foias, Antonia, Christina T. Halperin, Ellen Spensley Moriarty, and Jeanette Castellanos. 2012. Architecture, Volumetrics, and Social Stratification at Motul de San José during the Late and Terminal Classic. In *Motul de San José: Politics, History, and Economy in a Classic Maya Polity*, ed. Antonia E. Foias and Kitty F. Emery, 94–138. University Press of Florida, Gainesville.

Folan, William J. 1983. Urban Organization and Social Structure of Cobá. In *Cobá: A Classic Maya Metropolis*, ed. William J. Folan, Ellen R. Kintz, and Lorraine A. Fletcher, 49–63. Academic Press, New York.

Folan, William J., Gary Gates, Beniamino Volta, María del Rosario Domínguez Carrasco, Raymundo González Heredia, Joel D. Gunn, and Abel Morales-López. 2011. Las ruinas de Calakmul, Campeche, México: Sus ciudades tributarias y su altiplanicie kárstica del Petén campechano y el norte de Guatemala. Paper presented at the XXI Encuentro Internacional "Los Investigadores de la Cultura Maya," Campeche, Mexico.

Folan, William J., Joel D. Gunn, and María R. Domínguez Carrasco. 2001. Triadic Temples, Central Plazas, and Dynastic Palaces: A Diachronic Analysis of the Royal Court Complex, Calakmul, Campeche, Mexico. In *Royal Courts of the Maya, Vol. II*, ed. Takeshi Inomata and Stephen D. Houston, 223–265. Westview Press, Boulder.

Folan, William J., Joyce Marcus, Sophia Pincemin, María del Rosario Domínguez Carrasco, Laraine Fletcher, and Abel Morales López. 1995. Calakmul: New Data from an Ancient Maya Capital in Campeche, Mexico. *Latin American Antiquity* 6(4):310–334.

Fontana, Bernard L., William J. Robinson, Charles W. Cormack, and Ernest E. Leavitt Jr. 1962. *Papago Indian Pottery*. University of Washington Press, Seattle.

Ford, Anabel. 2008. Dominant Plants of the Maya Forest and Gardens of El Pilar: Implications for Paleoenvironmental Reconstructions. *Journal of Ethnobiology* 28:179–199.

Ford, Anabel, and Ronald Nigh. 2015. *The Maya Forest Garden: Eight Millennia of Sustainable Cultivation of the Tropical Woodlands*. Left Coast Press, Walnut Creek, CA.

Formica, Piero. 2017. Why Innovators Should Study the Rise and Fall of Venetian Empire. *Harvard Business Review*, http://hbr.org/2017/01, https://hbr.org/2017/01/why-innovators-should-study-the-rise-and-fall-of-the-venetian-empire (accessed February 3, 2017).

Forné, Mélanie. 2006. *La cronología cerámica de La Joyanca, noroeste del Petén, Guatemala*. BAR International Series 1572. Archaeopress, Oxford.

Forné, Mélanie, Ronald L. Bishop, Arthur A. Demarest, M. James Blackman, and Erin L. Sears. 2010. Gris Fino, Naranjo Fino: Presencia temprana y fuentes de producción, el caso de Cancuén. In *XXIII Simposio de Investigaciones Arqueológicas en Guatemala, 2009*, ed. Bárbara Arroyo, Adriana Linares, and Lorena Paiz, 1150–1169. Guatemala City: Museo Nacional de Arqueología y Etnología.

Forsyth, Donald W. 2003. La cerámica del Clásico tardío de la Cuenca Mirador. In *XVI Simposio de Investigaciones Arqueológicas en Guatemala, 2002*, ed. Juan Pedro Laporte, Bárbara Arroyo, Héctor Escobedo, and Héctor Mejía, 657–671. Museo Nacional de Arqueología y Etnología, Guatemala City.

———. 2005. A Study of Terminal Classic Ceramic Complexes and Their Socioeconomic Implications. In *Geographies of Power: Understanding the Nature of Terminal Classic Pottery in the Maya Lowlands*, eds. Sandra L. López Varela and Antonia E. Foias, 7–22. British Archaeological Reports. Archaeopress, Oxford.

Fowler, William R., Jr., Arthur A. Demarest, Helen V. Michel, Frank Asaro, and Fred Stross. 1989. Sources of Obsidian from El Mirador, Guatemala: New Evidence on Preclassic Maya Interaction. *American Anthropologist* 91:158–168.

Francis, Jill. 2008. Order and Disorder in the Early Modern Garden, 1558–C. 1630. *Garden History* 36(1):22–35.

Freeman, John H., Glen R. Carroll, and Michael T. Hannan. 1983. The Liability of Newness: Age Dependence in Organizational Death Rates. *American Sociological Association* 48(5):692–710.

Freidel, David A. 1981. The Political Economics of Residential Dispersion among the Lowland Maya. In *Lowland Maya Settlement Patterns*, ed. Wendy Ashmore, 371–382. University of New Mexico Press, Albuquerque.

———. 2018. Maya and the Idea of Empire. In *Pathways to Complexity*, ed. M. Kathryn Brown ad George J. Bey III, 363–386. University Press of Florida, Gainesville.

Freidel, David A., Héctor Escobedo, and Stanley F. Guenter. 2007. A Crossroads of Conquerors: Waka and Gordon Willey's "Rehearsal for the Collapse" Hypothesis. In *Gordon R. Willey and American Archaeology: Contemporary Perspectives*, ed. Jeremy A. Sabloff and William L. Fash, 187–208. University of Oklahoma Press, Norman.

Freidel, David A., Héctor Escobedo, and Juan Carlos Meléndez. 2013. Mountain of Memories: Structure M12-32 at El Perú. In *Millenary Maya Societies: Past Crises and Resilience*, ed. M.-Charlotte Arnauld and Alain Breton, 235–248. Mesoweb, www.mesoweb.com/publications/MMS/15_Freidel_etal.pdf (accessed August 18, 2019).

Freidel, David A., Marilyn A. Masson, and Michelle Rich. 2016. Imagining a Complex Maya Political Economy: Counting Tokens and Currencies in Image, Text, and the Archaeological Record. *Cambridge Archaeological Journal* 27:29–54.

Freidel, David A., Kathryn Reese-Taylor, and David Mora-Marín. 2002. The Origins of Maya Civilization: The Old Shell Game, Commodity, Treasure, and Kinship. In *Ancient Maya Political Economies*, ed. Marilyn Masson and David A. Freidel, 41–86. AltaMira Press, New York.

Freidel, David A., and F. Kent Reilly III. 2010. The Flesh of the Gods: Cosmology, Food, and the Origins of Political Power in Ancient Southeastern Mesoamerica. In *Pre-Columbian Foodways: Interdisciplinary Approaches to Food, Culture, and Markets in Mesoamerica*, ed. John Edward Staller and Michael Carrasco, 635–680. Springer, New York.

Freidel, David A., and Jeremy A. Sabloff. 1984. *Cozumel: Late Maya Settlement Patterns*. Academic Press, New York.

Freidel, David A., and Justine Shaw. 2000. The Lowland Maya Civilization: Historical Consciousness and Environment. In *The Way the Wind Blows: Climate, History, and Human Action*, ed. Roderick J. McIntosh, Joseph A. Tainter, and Susan Keech McIntosh, 271–300. Columbia University Press, New York.

Freiwald, Carolyn. 2011. Maya Migration Networks: Reconstructing Population Movement in the Belize River Valley during the Late and Terminal Classic. Unpublished Ph.D. dissertation, Department of Anthropology, University of Wisconsin, Madison.

Fremont, H. 1861. *Plano del Estado de Campeche*. Agencia del Ministerio de Fomento, Campeche, Mexico.

Frías Bobadilla, Romero, and Rubén Frías Bobadilla. 1957. *Progreso y su evolución, 1840 a 1900*. Talleres Díaz Massa, Mérida, Mexico.

Friedland, Roger, and Robert R. Alford. 1991. Bringing Society Back In: Symbols, Practices and Institutional Contradictions. In *The New Institutionalism in Organizational Analysis*, ed. Walter W. Powell and Paul J. DiMaggio, 232–263. University of Chicago Press, Chicago.

Fry, Robert E. 1979. The Economics of Pottery at Tikal, Guatemala: Models of Exchange for Serving Vessels. *American Antiquity* 44:494–512.

———. 1981. Pottery Production-Distribution Systems in the Southern Maya Lowlands. In *Production and Distribution: A Ceramic Viewpoint*, ed. Hilary Howard and Elaine L. Morris, 145–168. BAR International Series 120. BAR, Oxford.

———. 2003. The Peripheries of Tikal. In *Tikal: Dynasties, Foreigners, and Affairs of State*, ed. Jeremy A. Sabloff, 143–170. School of American Research Press, Santa Fe, NM.

Gallareta Cervera, Tomás. 2016. The Archaeology of Monumentality and the Social Construction of Authority at the Northern Maya Puuc Site of Kiuic. Unpublished Ph.D. dissertation, Department of Anthropology, University of North Carolina, Chapel Hill.

Gallareta Negrón, Tomás, Anthony P. Andrews, Fernando Robles Castellanos, Rafael Cobos Palma, and Pura Cervera Rivero. 1989. Isla Cerritos: Un puerto maya prehispánico en la costa norte de Yucatán. *Memorias del II Coloquio Internacional de Mayistas* (Campeche, 1987) 1:311–32. Centro de Estudios Mayas. Universidad Nacional Autónoma de México, Mexico City.

Gallareta Negrón, Tomás, George J. Bey III, and William Ringle. 2014. Investigaciones arqueológicas en las ruinas de Kiuic y la zona Labná-Kiuic, Distrito de Bolonchén, Yucatán, México. Informe técnico al Consejo de Arqueología de INAH, Temporada 2013. On file with the Instituto Nacional de Antropología e Historia, Mexico City.

Gámez, Laura. 2007. Salvamento arqueológico en el área central de Petén: Nuevos resultados sobre la conformación y evolución del asentamiento prehispánico en la isla de Flores. *In XX Simposio de Investigaciones Arqueológicas en Guatemala, 2006,* ed. Juan Pedro Laporte, Bárbara Arroyo, and H. Mejía, 258–273. Museo Nacional de Arqueología e Etnología, Guatemala City.

García, Krista L. 2008. Maya Pottery Specialization and Standardization: Using Late and Terminal Classic Ceramics from the Upper Belize River Valley to Evaluate Market Exchange. MA thesis, Department of Anthropology, University of Alabama, Tuscaloosa.

García-Moreno, Renata, and Josefina Granados G. 2000. Tumbas reales de Calakmul. *Arqueología Mexicana* 7(42):28–33.

Garraty, Christopher P. 2009. Evaluating the Distributional Approach to Inferring Marketplace Exchange: A Test Case from the Mexican Gulf Lowlands. *Latin American Antiquity* 20(1):157–174.

———. 2010. Investigating Market Exchange in Ancient Societies. In *Archaeological Approaches to Market Exchange in Ancient Societies*, ed. Christopher P. Garraty and Barbara L. Stark, 3–32. University Press of Colorado, Boulder.

Garraty, Christopher P., and Barbara Stark. 2010. Detecting Marketplace Exchange in Archaeology: A Methodological Review. In *Archaeological Approaches to Market Exchange In Ancient Societies*, ed. Christopher P. Garraty and Barbara Stark, 33–60. University Press of Colorado, Boulder.

Garraty, Christopher P., and Barbara Stark, editors. 2010. *Archaeological Approaches to Market Exchange in Ancient Societies*. University Press of Colorado, Boulder.

Garza, Mercedes de la, Ana Luisa Izquierdo, María del Carmen León, and Tolita Figueroa, editors. 1983. *Relaciones histórico-geográficas de la gobernación de Yucatán (1579–1581)*. Vol. 2. Universidad Nacional Autónoma de México, Mexico City.

Garza Tarazona de González, Silvia, and Edward B. Kurjack Bacso. 1980. *Atlas arqueológico del Estado de Yucatán*. Instituto Nacional de Antropología e Historia, Centro Regional del Sureste, Mexico City.

Gates, Gary. 1999. Fisiografía, geología e hidrología. In *Naturaleza y cultura en Calakmul, Campeche*, ed. William J. Folan Higgins, Maria Consuelo Sánchez González, and José Manuel Garcia Ortega, 31–39. Universidad Autónoma de Campeche, Centro de Investigaciones Históricas y Sociales, Campeche, Mexico.

Geller, Pamela L. 2014. Sedimenting Social Identity: The Practice of Pre-Columbian Maya Body Partibility. In *The Bioarchaeology of Space and Place: Ideology, Power, and Meaning in Maya Mortuary Contexts*, ed. Gabriel D. Wrobel, 15–38. Springer, New York.

Gerstle, Andrea, and Payson Sheets. 2002. Structure 4: A Storehouse-Workshop for Household 4. In *Before the Volcano Erupted: The Ancient Cerén Village In Central America*, ed. Payson Sheets, 74–80. University of Texas Press, Austin.

Gifford, James C. 1976. *Prehistoric Pottery Analysis and the Ceramics of Barton Ramie in the Belize Valley*. Memoirs, Vol. 18. Peabody Museum of Archaeology and Ethnology, Harvard University, Cambridge, MA.

Gillespie, Susan D. 2000. Rethinking Ancient Maya Social Organization: Replacing "Lineage" with "House." *American Anthropologist* 102(3):467–484.

Gleason, Kathryn L. 1994. To Bound and to Cultivate: An Introduction to the Archaeology of Gardens and Fields. In *The Archaeology of Garden and Field*, ed. N. F. Miller and K. L. Gleason, 1–24. University of Pennsylvania Press, Philadelphia.

Gluckman, Max. 1960. The Rise of a Zulu Empire *Scientific American* 202(4):157–168.

Goddard, Plyni Earl. 1945. *Pottery of the Southwestern Indians*. Science Guide No. 73. American Museum of Natural History, New York.

Goetzmann, William N., and Laura Williams. 2005. From Tallies and Chirographs to Franklin's Printing Press at Passy. In *The Origins of Value: The Financial Innovations That Created Modern Capital Markets*, ed. W. N. Goetzmann and K. G. Rouwenhorst, 105–121. Oxford University Press, Oxford.

Golden, Charles, Timothy Murtha, Bruce Cook, Derek S. Shaffer, Whittaker Schroder, Elijah Hermitt, Omar Alcover Firpi, and Andrew K. Scherer. 2016. Reanalyzing Environmental LiDAR Data for Archaeology: Mesoamerican Applications and Implications. *Journal of Archaeological Science* 9:293–308.

Golden, Charles, and Andrew K. Scherer. 2013. Territory, Trust, Growth, and Collapse in Classic Period Maya Kingdoms. *Current Anthropology* 54(4):397–435.

Golden, Charles, Andrew K. Scherer, A. René Muñoz, and Rosaura Vásquez. 2008. Piedras Negras and Yaxchilan: Divergent Political Trajectories in Adjacent Maya Polities. *Latin American Antiquity* 19(3):249–274.

Golitko, Mark, and Gary M. Feinman. 2015. Procurement and Distribution of Pre-Hispanic Mesoamerican Obsidian 900 BC–AD 1520: A Social Network Analysis. *Journal of Archaeological Method and Theory* 22(1):206–247.

Golitko, Mark, James Meierhoff, Gary M. Feinman, and Patrick R. Williams. 2012. Complexities of Collapse: The Evidence of Maya Obsidian as Revealed by Social Network Graphical Analysis. *Antiquity* 86:507–523.

Gómez Chávez, Sergio. 2017. Foreigners' Barrios at Teotihuacan: Reasons for and Consequences of Migration. In *Teotihuacan: City of Water, City of Fire*, ed. Matthew H. Robb, 102–107. Fine Arts Museum of San Francisco. University of California Press, Los Angeles.

Góngora Salas, Ángel. 2002a. El sitio arqueológico del Puerto de Xkopté. MS. Centro INAH Yucatán. Instituto Nacional de Antropología e Historia, Mérida, Mexico.

———. 2002b. El sitio arqueológico de Tzikul. MS. Centro INAH Yucatán. Instituto Nacional de Antropología e Historia, Mérida, Mexico.

———. 2002c. El Sitio Dzilám 2. MS. Archivo de la Sección de Arqueología, Centro INAH Yucatán. Instituto Nacional de Antropología e Historia, Mérida, Mexico.

———. 2002d. Pozos de exploración y levantamiento topográfico en el sitio arqueológico El Cerrito, Laguna de Progreso. MS. Instituto Nacional de Antropología e Historia, Centro INAH Yucatán, Mérida, Mexico.

González, Juan de Dios. 1766. Reconocimiento y estado de la Provincia de Yucatán, por el ingeniero Juan de Dios González, en Campeche a 18 de febrero de 1766. Archivo General de Indias, México 3157, Sevilla. In *Fortificaciones en Nueva España* (1984), by José Antonio

Calderón Quijano, 392–405. Gobierno del Estado de Veracruz, Consejo Superior de Investigaciones Científicas, Escuela de Estudios Hispanoamericanos, Madrid.

González Aparicio, Luis. 1973. *Plano reconstructivo de la región de Tenochtitlán*. Instituto Nacional de Antropología e Historia, Mexico City.

Goodenough, Oliver, and Monika Gruter Cheney. 2007. Is Free Enterprise Values in Action?: A Project Précis. In *Moral Markets: The Critical Role of Values in the Economy*, ed. Paul J. Zak. Values in Action Conference Series, 2005–2006. Princeton University Press, Princeton, NJ. SSRN (October 26, 2007): https://ssrn.com/abstract=940432.

Gossen, Gary H. 1974. A Chamula Solar Calendar Board from Chiapas, Mexico. In *Mesoamerican Archaeology: New Approaches*, ed. Norman Hammond, 217–253. University of Texas Press, Austin.

Graeber, David. 2011. *Debt: The First 5,000 Years*. 2nd ed. Melville House, New York.

Graham, Elizabeth. 2002. Perspectives on Economy and Theory. In *Ancient Maya Political Economies*, ed. Marilyn A. Masson and David A. Freidel, 398–416. AltaMira Press, Walnut Creek, CA.

Graham, Ian. 1967. *Archaeological Explorations in El Peten, Guatemala*. Middle American Research Institute Publication 33. Tulane University, New Orleans.

———. 1978. *Corpus of Maya Hieroglyphic Inscriptions*. Vol. 2(2): Naranjo, Chunhuitz, Xunantunich. Harvard University, Peabody Museum of Archaeology and Ethnology, Cambridge, MA.

Granovetter, Mark. 1985. Economic Action and Social Structure: The Problem of Embeddedness. *American Journal of Sociology* 91:481–510.

Grube, Nikolai. 2000. The City-States of the Maya. In *A Comparative Study of Thirty City-State Cultures*, ed. Mogens Herman Hansen, 547–565. C. A. Reitzels, Copenhagen.

———. 2004. El origen de la dinastía Kaan. In *Los Cautivos de Dzibanché*, ed. Enrique Nalda, 117–132. Instituto Nacional de Antropología e Historia, Mexico City.

———. 2005. Toponyms, Emblem Glyphs, and the Political Geography of Southern Campeche. *Anthropological Notebooks* 11(1):87–100.

———. 2016. Die Apokalypse der Maya-Könige: Der Zusammenbruch der klassischen Maya-Städte. In *Maya: Das Rätsel der Königestädte*, ed. Nikolai Grube, 269–275. Historisches Museum der Pfalz Speyer. Hirmer Verlag, Munich.

Grube, Nikolai, Kai Delvendahl, Nicolaus Seefeld, and Beniamino Volta. 2012. Under the Rule of The Snake Kings: Uxul in the 7th and 8th Centuries. *Estudios de Cultura Maya* 40:11–49.

Grube, Nikolai, and Simon Martin. 2004. Patronage, Betrayal, and Revenge: Diplomacy and Politics in the Eastern Maya Lowlands. In *Notebook for the XXVIIIth Maya Hieroglyphic Forum at Texas*, ed. Nikolai Grube, II-1–II-95. University of Texas Press, Austin.

Guderjan, Thomas, Jeffrey Baker, and Robert Lichtenstein. 2003. Environmental and Cultural Diversity at Blue Creek. In *Heterarchy, Political Economy, and the Ancient Maya*, ed. Vernon L. Scarborough, Fred Valdez Jr., and Nicholas Dunning, 77–91. University of New Mexico Press, Albuquerque.

Guderjan, Thomas, Sheryl Luzzadder-Beach, Timothy Beach, Stephan Bozarth, and Samantha Krause. 2017. The Production of Ancient Wetland Commercial Economies in the Maya Lowlands. In *The Value of Things: Prehistoric to Contemporary Commodities in the Maya Region*, ed. Jennifer Mathews and Thomas Guderjan, 30–48. University of Arizona Press, Tucson.

Guenter, Stanley Paul. 2007. On the Emblem Glyph of El Peru. *PARI Journal* 8(2): 20–23.

———. 2014a. The Classic Maya Collapse: Chronology and Causation. Unpublished Ph.D. dissertation, Dept. of Anthropology, Southern Methodist University, Dallas, TX.

———. 2014b. The Epigraphy of El Perú–Waká. In *Archaeology at El Perú–Waká: Ancient Maya Performances of Ritual, Memory, and Power*, ed. Olivia C. Navarro-Farr and Michelle Rich, 147–166. University of Arizona Press, Tucson.

Gunn, Joel D., and William J. Folan. 2000. Three Rivers: Subregional Variations in Earth System Impacts in the Southwestern Maya Lowlands (Candelaria, Usumacinta, and Champotón Watersheds). In *The Way the Wind Blows: Climate, History, and Human Action*, ed. Roderick Mcintosh, Joseph A. Tainter, and Susan Keech Mcintosh, 263–270. Columbia University Press, New York.

Gunn, Joel D., William J. Folan, Christian Isendahl, María del Rosario Domínguez Carrasco, Betty B. Faust, and Beniamino Volta. 2014. Calakmul: Agent Risk and Sustainability in the Western Maya Lowlands. *Archeological Papers of the American Anthropological Association* 24:101–123.

Gunn, Joel D., John E. Foss, William J. Folan, María del Rosario Domínguez Carrasco, and Betty B. Faust. 2002. Bajo Sediments and the Hydraulic System of Calakmul, Campeche, Mexico. *Ancient Mesoamerica* 13(2):297–315.

Gunn, Joel D., Vernon L. Scarborough, William J. Folan, Christian Isendahl, Arlen F. Chase, Jeremy A. Sabloff, and Beniamino. Volta. 2016. A Distribution Analysis of the Central Maya Lowlands Ecoinformation Network: Its Rises, Falls, and Changes. *Ecology and Society* 22(1):20. https://doi.org/10.5751/ES-08931-220120 (accessed August 12, 2019).

Guthe, Carl E. 1925. *Pueblo Pottery Making: A Study at the Village of San Ildefonso*. Papers of the Phillips Academy Southwestern Expedition, No. 2. New Haven, CT.

Guzmán Piedrasanta, Melvin Rodrigo. 2012. Operación CR51: Excavaciones en el Grupo 13P-5 (posible Juego de Pelota). In *Proyecto Regional Arqueológico La Corona No. 4, temporada 2011*, ed. Tomás Barrientos Quezada, Marcello A. Canuto, and Josefa Iglesias Ponce de León, 347–356. Tulane University and Universidad del Valle, Guatemala, New Orleans and Guatemala City.

Hall, G. 1989. *Realms of Death: Royal Mortuary Customs and Polity Interaction in the Classic Maya Lowlands*. Unpublished Ph.D. dissertation, Harvard University, Cambridge, MA.

Halperin, Christina T. 2014. Circulation as Placemaking: Late Classic Maya Polities and Portable Objects. *American Anthropologist* 116(1):110–129.

Halperin, Christina T., Ronald L. Bishop, Ellen Spensley, and M. James Blackman. 2009. Late Classic (AD 600–900) Maya Market Exchange: Analysis of Figurines from the Motul de San José Region, Guatemala. *Journal of Field Archaeology* 34(457–480).

Halperin, Christina T., and Antonia E. Foias. 2010. Pottery Politics: Late Classic Maya Palace Production at Motul de San José. *Journal of Anthropological Archaeology* 29:392–411.

———. 2012. Motul de San José Palace Pottery Production: Reconstructions from Wasters and Debris. In *Motul de San José: Politics, History, and Economy in a Classic Maya Polity*, ed. Antonia E. Foias and Kitty F. Emery, 167–193. University Press of Florida, Gainesville.

Halperin, Rhoda H. 1984. Polanyi, Marx, and the Institutional Paradigm in Economic Anthropology. *Research in Economic Anthropology* 6:245–272.

Hamman, Sherrie, and Keith Provan. 2000. Legitimacy Building in the Evolution of Small-Firm Networks: A Comparative Study of Success and Demise. *Administrative Science Quarterly* 45:327–65.

Hammond, Norman. 1972. Obsidian Trade in the Mayan Area. *Science* 178:1092–1093.

———. 1978. The Myth of the Milpa: Agricultural Expansion in the Maya Lowlands. In *Pre-Hispanic Maya Agriculture*, ed. Peter D. Harrison and B. L. Turner II, 23–34. University of New Mexico Press, Albuquerque.

———. 1982. *Ancient Maya Civilization*. New Brunswick: Rutgers University Press.

Hammond, Norman, and Gair Tourtellot. 2006. Una segunda oportunidad: Fundación y refundación en la ciudad maya de la época Clásica de la Milpa, Belice. In *Nuevas ciudades, nuevas patrias: Fundación y relocalización de ciudades en Mesoamérica y el mediterráneo antiguo*, ed. Josefa Iglesia Ponce de León, Rogelio Valencia Rivera, Andrés Ciudad Ruiz, 93–104. Sociedad Española de Estudios Maya, Madrid.

Hannerz, Ulf. 1980. *Exploring the City: Inquiries toward an Urban Anthropology*. Columbia University Press, New York.

Hansen, Richard D. 1982. Excavations in the Tigre Pyramid Area, El Mirador, Guatemala: A New Evaluation of Social Process in the Preclassic Maya Lowlands. In *Abstracts of the 44th International Congress of Americanists,* University of Manchester, England, 1982. Summarized in *Past and Present in the Americas: A Compendium of Recent Studies*, ed. John Lynch, 133–134. Manchester University Press, 1984, Manchester, UK.

———. 1984. Excavations on Structure 34 and the Tigre Area, El Mirador, Petén, Guatemala: A New Look at the Preclassic Lowland Maya. Unpublished MS thesis, Brigham Young University, Provo, Utah.

———. 1990. *Excavations in the Tigre Complex, El Mirador, Petén, Guatemala*. Papers of the New World Archaeological Foundation, No. 62. Brigham Young University, Provo, UT.

———. 1991. An Early Maya Text from El Mirador, Guatemala. *Research Reports on Ancient Maya Writing*. 37: 19–32. Center for Maya Research, Washington, DC.

———. 1992a. The Archaeology of Ideology: A Study of Maya Preclassic Architectural Sculpture at Nakbe, Peten, Guatemala. Unpublished Ph.D. dissertation, Department of Archaeology, University of California, Los Angeles.

———. 1992b. El proceso cultural de Nakbe y el área del Petén nor-central: Las épocas tempranas. In *V Simposio de Investigaciones Arqueológicas en Guatemala*, ed. Juan Pedro Laporte, Hector L. Escobedo, and Sandra V. de Brady, 81–96. Museo Nacional de Arqueología y Etnología, Ministerio de Cultura y Deportes, Instituto de Antropología e Historia de Guatemala, Asociación Tikal, Guatemala City.

———. 1992c. Proyecto Regional de Investigaciones Arqueológicas del Norte de Petén, Guatemala: Temporada 1990. In *IV Simposio de Arqueología Guatemalteca, julio 1990*, ed. Juan Pedro Laporte, Héctor L. Escobedo, and Sandra V. de Brady, 1–36. Museo Nacional de Arqueología y Etnología, Ministerio de Cultura y Deportes, Instituto de Antropología e Historia, Asociación Tikal, Guatemala City.

———. 1994a. Investigaciones arqueológicas en el norte del Petén, Guatemala: Una mirada diacrónica de los orígines mayas. In *Campeche Maya Colonial*, ed. William J. Folan, 14–54. Universidad Autónoma del Sureste, Campeche, Mexico.

———. 1994b. Las dinámicas culturales y ambientales de los orígines mayas: Estudios recientes del sitio arqueológico Nakbe. In *VII Simposio Arqueológico de Guatemala*, ed. Juan Pedro Laporte and Héctor L. Escobedo, 369–387. Ministerio de Cultura y Deportes, Instituto de Antropología e Historia, Asociación Tikal, Museo Nacional de Arqueología y Etnología, Guatemala City.

———. 1998. Continuity and Disjunction: Preclassic Antecedents of Classic Maya Architecture. In *Function and Meaning in Classic Maya Architecture*, ed. Stephen D. Houston, 49–122. Dumbarton Oaks, Washington, DC.

———. 2000. Ideología y arquitectura: Poder y dinámicas culturales de los mayas del período Preclásico en las Tierras Bajas. In *Arquitectura e ideología de los antiguos mayas: Memoria de la Segunda Mesa Redonda de Palenque*, ed. Silvia Trejo, 71–108. Instituto Nacional de Antropología e Historia, Consejo Nacional Para la Cultura y las Artes; CONACULTA-INAH, Mexico City.

———. 2001. The First Cities: The Beginnings of Urbanization and State Formation in the Maya Lowlands. In *Maya: Divine Kings of the Rain Forest*, ed. Nikolai Grube, 50–65. Könemann Verlag, Cologne.

———. 2002. The Preclassic Collapse in the Social, Political, and Ideological Transformation from the Preclassic to Classic Periods of Maya Civilization. In *Abstracts of the 101st Annual Meeting, American Anthropological Association*, 235. AAA Session 3-083, Becoming Classic: Social, Political, and Ideological Transformations in the Southern Maya Lowlands, November 23, 2002, New Orleans.

——. 2005. Perspectives on Olmec-Maya Interaction in the Middle Formative Period. In *New Perspectives on Formative Mesoamerican Cultures*, ed. Terry G. Powis, 51–72. BAR International Series 1377. BAR, Oxford.

——. 2006. The Beginning of the End: Conspicuous Consumption and Environmental Impact of the Preclassic Lowland Maya. Paper presented at the 71st Annual Meeting of the Society for American Archaeology. San Juan, Puerto Rico.

——. 2012a. The Beginning of the End: Conspicuous Consumption and Environmental Impact of the Preclassic Lowland Maya. In *An Archaeological Legacy: Essays in Honor of Ray T. Matheny*, ed. Deanne G. Matheny, Joel C. Janetski, and Glenna Nielson, 243–291. Occasional Paper No. 18, Museum of Peoples and Cultures. Brigham Young University, Provo, Utah.

——. 2012b. Kingship in the Cradle of Maya Civilization. In *Fanning the Sacred Flame: Mesoamerican Studies in Honor of H. B. Nicholson*, ed. Matthew A. Boxt and Brian Dervin Dillon, 139–171. University Press of Colorado, Boulder.

——. 2013. The Mirador Cultural and Natural System. In *Mayab Yik'elil Kan: Los insectos tropicales del antiguo reino Kan de Mesoamérica/The Tropical Insects of the Ancient Kan Kingdom of Mesoamerica,* by José Monzón S. and Jack C. Schuster, ed. Richard D. Hansen and Edgar Suyuc Ley, 6–13. Corporación Litografica, S.A., Guatemala City. Foundation for Anthropological Research and Environmental Studies (FARES), Salt Lake City, ID.

——. 2016a. Cultural and Environmental Components of the First Maya States: A Perspective from the Central and Southern Maya Lowlands. In *The Origins of Maya States*, ed. Loa P. Traxler and Robert J. Sharer, 329–416. University of Pennsylvania Museum of Archaeology and Anthropology, Philadelphia.

——. 2016b. The Mirador-Calakmul Cultural and Natural System: A Priceless Treasure in Guatemala and Mexico/El sistema cultural y natural Mirador-Calakmul: Un tesoro invaluable en Guatemala y México. In *Mirador: Research and Conservation in the Ancient Kaan Kingdom,* ed. Richard D. Hansen and Edgar Suyuc, 9-36. Foundation for Anthropological Research and Environmental Studies (FARES), Corporación Litográfica, Guatemala City.

——. 2017. The Feast before Famine and Fighting: The Origins and Consequences of Social Complexity in the Mirador Basin, Guatemala. In *Feast, Famine or Fighting? Multiple Pathways to Social Complexity*, ed. R. J. Chacón and R. Mendoza, 305-335. Springer Press, New York.

Hansen, Richard D., and Beatriz Balcárcel. 2008. El Complejo Tigre y la Acrópolis Central de El Mirador durante el Prelásico Medio y Tardio. In *XXI Simposio de Investigaciones Arqueológicas en Guatemala, 2007*, ed. Juan Pedro Laporte, Bárbara Arroyo, and Hector E. Mejía, 339–348. Museo Nacional de Arqueología y Etnología, Ministerio de Cultura y Deportes, Instituto de Antropología e Historia, Asociación Tikal, Fundación Arqueológica del Nuevo Mundo, Guatemala City.

Hansen, Richard D., Beatríz Balcárcel, Edgar Suyuc Ley, Héctor E. Mejía, Enrique Hérnandez, Gendry Valle, Stanley P. Guenter, and Shannon Novak. 2006. Investigaciones arqueológicas en el sitio Tintal, Petén. In *XIX Simposio de Investigaciones Arqueológicas en Guatemala 2005*, ed. Juan Pedro Laporte, Bárbara Arroyo, and Héctor E. Mejía, 739–751. Museo Nacional de Arqueología y Etnología, Guatemala City.

Hansen, Richard D., Steven Bozarth, John Jacob, David Wahl, and Thomas Schreiner. 2002. Climatic and Environmental Variability in the Rise of Maya Civilization: A Preliminary Perspective from Northern Petén. *Ancient Mesoamerica* 13(2):273–295.

Hansen, Richard D., Donald W. Forsyth, James C. Woods, Eric F. Hansen, Thomas Schreiner, and Gene Titmus. 2018. Developmental Dynamics, Energetics, and Complex Economic Interactions of the Early Maya of the Mirador Basin, Guatemala. In *Pathways to Complexity: A View from the Maya Lowlands*, ed. M. Kathryn Brown and George J. Bey III, 147-194. University Press of Florida, Gainesville.

Hansen, Richard D., and Stanley P. Guenter. 2005. Early Social Complexity and Kingship in the Mirador Basin. In *Lords of Creation: The Origins of Sacred Maya Kingship*, ed. Virginia M. Fields and Dorie Reents-Budet, 60–61. Los Angeles County Museum of Art, Scala Publishers, Los Angeles.

Hansen, Richard D., Wayne K. Howell, and Stanley P. Guenter. 2008. Forgotten Structures, Haunted Houses, and Occupied Hearts: Ancient Perspectives and Contemporary Interpretations of Abandoned Sites and Buildings in the Mirador Basin, Guatemala. In *Ruins of the Past: The Use and Perception of Abandoned Structures in the Maya Lowlands*, ed. Travis W. Stanton and Aline Magnoni, 25–64. University Press of Colorado, Boulder.

Hansen, Richard D., Gustavo Martínez, John Jacob, and Wayne K. Howell. 2000. Cultivos intensivos: Sistemas agrícolas de Nakbe. In *Investigaciones arqueológicas y ecológicas en la Cuenca Mirador, 1998: Informe de la temporada de campo*, ed. Richard D. Hansen and Judith Valle, 687–700. Proyecto Regional de Investigaciones Arqueológicas del Norte del Petén, Guatemala (PRIANPEG), Guatemala City/UCLA RAINPEG, FARES Foundation, Rupert, Idaho.

Hansen, Richard D., Edgar Suyuc Ley, Adriana Linares, Carlos Morales Aguilar, Beatriz Balcárcel, Francisco López, Antonieta Cajas, Abel Morales López, Enrique Monterroso Tun, Enrique Monterroso Rosado, Carolina Castellanos, Lilián de Zea, Adelzo Pozuelos, David Wahl, and Thomas Schreiner. 2006. Investigaciones en la zona cultural Mirador Petén. *In XIX Simposio de Investigaciones Arqueológicas en Guatemala*, ed, Juan Pedro Laporte, Bárbara Arroyo, and Héctor E. Mejía, 867-876. Ministerio de Cultura y Deportes, Instituto de Antropología e Historia, Asociación Tikal, Fundación Arqueológica del Nuevo Mundo, Guatemala City.

Hanson, Craig A. 2008. *The Late Mesoamerican Village*. Ph.D. dissertation, Department of Anthropology, Tulane University. University Microfilms, Ann Arbor, MI.

Hardin, Russell. 2000. Communities and Development: Autarkic Social Groups and the Economy. In *A Not-so-Dismal Science: A Broader View of Economies and Societies*, ed. Mancur Olson and Satu Kähköhnen, 206–227. Vistaar Publication, New Delhi.

Hare, Timothy S., Marilyn A. Masson, and Carlos Peraza Lope. 2014. The Urban Cityscape. In *Kukulcan's Realm: Urban Life at Postclassic Mayapan*, by Marilyn A. Masson and Carlos Peraza Lope, 149–192. University Press of Colorado, Boulder.

Hare, Timothy S., Marilyn A. Masson, and Bradley W. Russell. 2014. High-Density LiDAR Mapping of the Ancient City of Mayapán. *Remote Sensing* 2014(6):9064–9085.

Harrigan, Kathryn Rudie. 1985. Vertical Integration and Corporate Strategy. *Academy of Management Journal* 28:397–425.

Harrigan, Ryan. 2004. Mollusca of K'axob. In *K'axob: Ritual, Work, and Family in an Ancient Maya Village*, ed. Patricia A. McAnany, 399–414. Cotsen Institute of Archaeology, University of California, Los Angeles.

Harrison, Peter D., and B. L. Turner II. 1978. *Prehispanic Maya Agriculture*. University of New Mexico Press, Albuquerque.

Hartnett, Alexandra, and Shannon Lee Dawdy. 2013. The Archaeology of Illegal and Illicit Economies. *Annual Review of Anthropology* 42:37–51.

Haviland, William A. 1970. Tikal, Guatemala, and Mesoamerican Urbanism. *World Archaeology* 2:186–198.

———. 1972. Family Size, Prehistoric Population Estimates, and the Ancient Maya. *American Antiquity* 37:135–139.

————. 1982. Where the Rich Folks Lived: Deranging Factors in the Statistical Analysis of Tikal Settlement. *American Antiquity* 47(2):427–429.

————. 1985. *Excavations in Small Residential Groups of Tikal: Groups 4F-1 and 4F-2.* Tikal Report No. 19. University of Pennsylvania Museum of Archaeology and Anthropology, Philadelphia.

————. 1992a. From Double-Bird to Ah Cacao: Dynastic Troubles and the Cycle of the Katuns at Tikal, Guatemala. *In New Theories on the Ancient Maya*, ed. Ellen C. Danien and Robert J. Sharer, 71–80. University Museum, University of Pennsylvania, Philadelphia.

————. 1992b. Status and Power in Classic Maya Society: The View from Tikal. *American Anthropologist* 94(4):937–940.

————. 2003. Settlement, Society, and Demography at Tikal. In *Tikal: Dynasties, Foreigners and Affairs of State Advancing Maya Archaeology*, ed. Jeremy A. Sabloff, 111–142. SAR Press, Santa Fe, NM.

————. 2014a. *Excavations in Residential Areas of Tikal: Non-elite Groups without Shrines: Analysis and Conclusions.* Tikal Report No. 20B. University of Pennsylvania Museum of Archaeology and Anthropology, Philadelphia.

————. 2014b. *Excavations in Residential Areas of Tikal: Non-elite Groups without Shrines: The Excavations.* Tikal Report No. 20A. University of Pennsylvania Museum of Archaeology and Anthropology, Philadelphia.

————. 2015. *Excavations in Residential Areas of Tikal: Group 7F-1.* Tikal Report No. 22. University of Pennsylvania Museum of Archaeology and Anthropology, Philadelphia.

Hayden, Brian D., and Aubrey Cannon. 1983. Where the Garbage Goes: Refuse Disposal in the Maya Highlands. *Journal of Anthropological Archaeology* 2:117–163.

Hayden, Brian, and Suzanne Villeneuve. 2011. A Century of Feasting Studies. *Annual Review of Anthropology* 40:433–449.

Healan, Dan M. 1992. A Comment on Moholy-Nagy's "The Misidentification of Lithic Workshops." *Latin American Antiquity* 3:240–242.

————. 2002. Producer versus Consumer: Prismatic Core-Blade Technology at Epiclassic/Early Postclassic Tula and Ucareo. In *Pathways to Prismatic Blades: A Study in Mesoamerican Obsidian Core-Blade Technology*, ed. Kenneth G. Hirth and Bradford Andrews, 27–35. Cotsen Institute of Archaeology, UCLA, Los Angeles.

Healy, Paul F., Kitty Emery, and Lori E. Wright. 1990. Ancient and Modern Maya Exploitation of the Jute Snail (*Pachychilus*). *Latin American Antiquity* 1(2):170–183.

Healy, Paul, Heather McKillop, and Bernetta Walsh. 1984. Analysis of Obsidian from Moho Cay, Belize. *Science* 225:414–417.

Hearth, Nicholas F. 2012. Organization of Chert Tool Economy during the Late and Terminal Classic Periods at Chan: Preliminary Thoughts Based upon Debitage Analyses. In *Chan: An Ancient Maya Farming Community*, ed. Cynthia Robin, 192–206. University Press of Florida, Gainesville.

Hearth, Nicholas F., and Scott L. Fedick. 2011. Defining the Chert Paucity Problem in the Northern Maya Lowlands: A First Approximation. In *The Technology of Maya Civilization: Political Economy and Beyond in Lithic Studies*, ed. Zachary X. Hruby, Geoffrey E. Braswell, and Oswaldo Chinchilla Mazariegos, 69–75. Equinox, Sheffield, UK.

Heindel, Theresa A., Bernadette Cap, and Jason Yaeger. 2012. Knapping in the Marketplace: Lithic Production and Marketplace Exchange at Buenavista del Cayo, Belize. *Research Reports in Belizean Archaeology* 9:29–38.

Hellmuth, Nicholas M. 1967. *Structure 5D-73, Burial 196, Tikal, Peten, Guatemala, a Preliminary Report.* Unpublished Report, Foundation for Latin American Anthropological Research, Harvard College.

———. 1977. Cholti-Lacondon (Chiapas) and Peten-Ytza Agriculture, Settlement Pattern and Population. In *Social Process in Maya Prehistory: Studies in Honour of Sir Eric Thompson*, ed. Norman Hammond, 421–448. Academic Press, New York.

Helmke, Christophe, Joseph W. Ball, Patricia T. Mitchell, and Jennifer T. Taschek. 2008. Burial BVC88-1/2 at Buenavista del Cayo, Belize: Resting Place of the Last King of Puluul? *Mexicon* 30(2): 39–43.

Helmke, Christophe, and Harri Kettunen. 2011. *Where Atole Abounds: Naranjo during the Reign of K'ahk' Tiliw Chan Chahk.* 1st Kracow Maya Conference: Archaeology and Epigraphy of the Eastern Central Maya Lowlands. Jagiellonian University, Kracow, Poland.

Helms, Mary. 1993. *Craft and the Kingly Ideal: Art, Trade, and Power.* University of Texas Press, Austin.

Henderson, Hope. 2003. The Organization of Staple Crop Production at K'axob, Belize. *Latin American Antiquity* 14(4):469–496.

Henderson, John S., and Ricardo F. Agurcia. 1987. Ceramic Systems: Facilitating Comparison in Type-Variety Analysis. In *Maya Ceramics: Papers from the 1985 Maya Ceramic Conference*, ed. Prudence M. Rice and Robert J. Sharer, 431–438. BAR International Series 345(ii). British Archaeological Reports, Oxford.

Hendon, Julia A. 1991. Status and Power in Classic Maya Society: An Archaeological Study. *American Anthropologist* 93(4):894–918.

———. 2003. Feasting at Home: Community and House Solidarity among the Maya of Southeastern Mesoamerica. In *The Archaeology and Politics of Food and Feasting in Early States and Empires*, ed. Tamara L. Bray, 203–234. Kluwer, New York.

———. 2006. Textile Production as Craft in Mesoamerica: Time, Labor and Knowledge. *Journal of Social Archaeology* 6:354–378.

Hermes, Bernard. 2000. Industria cerámica. In *El sitio maya de Topoxté: Investigaciones en una isla del lago Yaxhá, Petén, Guatemala*, ed. W. W. Wurster, 164–202. Verlag Philipp von Zabern, Mainz am Rhein, Germany.

Hernández, Enrique, Thomas Schreiner, Richard D. Hansen, Carlos Morales A., Edgar Ortega G, and Douglas Mauricio. 2016. Las calzadas y sacbeob de la Cuenca Mirador/The Causeways and Sacbeob of the Mirador Basin. In *Mirador: Research and Conservation in the Ancient Kaan Kingdom,* ed. Richard D. Hansen and Edgar Suyuc, 219–254. Foundation for Anthropological Research and Environmental Studies (FARES), Corporación Litográfica, Guatemala City.

Hernández Cruz, Rosa E., Eduardo Bello Baltazar, Guillermo Montoya Gómez and Erin I. J. Estrada Lugo. 2005. Social Adaptation Ecotourism in the Lacandon Forest. *Annals of Tourism Research* 32(3):610–627.

Herrera, Antonio de. 1945. *Historia general de los hechos de los castellanos en, las Islas, y Tierra Firme de el Mar Oceano, vol. 4 [sic]*. Editorial Guarania, Buenos Aires.

Herrera, Gabriel Alonso de. 2006 [1539]. *Ancient Agriculture: Roots and Application of Sustainable Farming*. Compiled by Juan Estevan Arellano. Ancient City Press, Salt Lake City.

Herrera Castro, Natividad Delfina. 1994. *Los huertos familiares mayas en el oriente de Yucatán.* Etnoflora Yucatanense No. 9. Universidad Autónoma de Yucatán, Mérida, Mexico.

Hertel, Thomas. 2013. *Old Assyrian Legal Practices.* Akademisk Forlag, Copenhagen.

Herzog, Irmela. 2014. Least-Cost Paths: Some Methodological Issues. *Internet Archaeology* 36. https://doi.org/10.11141/ia.36.5 (accessed August 2019).

Hester, Thomas R. 1985. The Maya Lithic Sequence in Northern Belize. In *Stone Tool Analysis: Essays in Honor of Don E. Crabtree*, ed. M. G. Plew, J. C. Woods, and M. G. Pavesic, 187–210. University of New Mexico Press, Albuquerque.

Hester, Thomas R., and Harry J. Shafer. 1984. Exploitation of Chert Resources by the Ancient Maya of Northern Belize, Central America. *World Archaeology* 16(2):157–173.

———. 1992. Lithic Workshop Revisited: Comments on Moholy-Nagy. *Latin American Antiquity* 3(3):243–248.

———. 1994. The Ancient Maya Craft Community at Colha, Belize, and Its External Relationships. In *Archaeological Views from the Countryside: Village Communities in Early Complex Societies*, ed. Glenn M. Schwartz and Stephen E. Falconer, 48–63. Smithsonian Institution Press, Washington, DC.

Hicks, Frederic. 1987. First Steps towards a Market-Integrated Economy in Aztec Mexico. In *Early State Dynamics*, ed. Henri J. M. Claessen and Pieter van de Velde, 91–107. Brill, Leiden, the Netherlands.

———. 1994. Cloth in the Political Economy of the Aztec State. In *Economies and Polities in the Aztec Realm*, ed. Mary G. Hodge and Michael E. Smith, 89–111. Studies on Culture and Society, Vol. 6. Institute for Mesoamerican Studies, State University of New York, Albany.

Hirth, Kenneth G. 1984. The Analysis of Prehistoric Economic Systems: A Look to the Future. In *Trade and Exchange in Early Mesoamerica*, ed. Kenneth G. Hirth, 281–302. University of New Mexico Press, Albuquerque.

———. 1996. Political Economy and Archaeology: Perspectives on Exchange and Production. *Journal of Archaeological Research* 4: 203–239.

———. 1998. The Distributional Approach: A New Way to Identify Marketplace Exchange in the Archaeological Record. *Current Anthropology* 39(4):451–476.

———. 2000. *Ancient Urbanism at Xochicalco: The Evolution and Organization of a Pre-Hispanic Society*. 2 vols. University of Utah Press, Salt Lake City.

———. 2008. The Economy of Supply: Modeling Obsidian Procurement and Craft Provisioning at a Central Mexican Urban Center. *Latin American Antiquity* 19(4):435–458.

———. 2009a. Craft Production, Household Diversification, and Domestic Economy in Prehispanic Mesoamerica. In *Housework: Craft Production and Domestic Economy in Ancient Mesoamerica*, ed. Kenneth G. Hirth, 13–32. Archeological Papers of the American Anthropological Association No. 19. American Anthropological Association, Alexandria, VA.

———. 2009b. Craft Production in a Central Mexican Marketplace. *Ancient Mesoamerica* 20:89–102.

———. 2010. Finding the Mark in the Marketplace: The Organization, Development, and Archaeological Identification of Market Systems. In *Archaeological Approaches to Market Exchange in Ancient Societies*, ed. Christopher P. Garraty and Barbara Stark, 227–247. University Press of Colorado, Boulder.

———. 2013. The Merchant's World: Commercial Diversity and the Economics of Interregional Exchange in Highland Mesoamerica. In *Merchants, Markets, and Exchange in the Pre-Columbian World*, ed. Kenneth G. Hirth and Joanne Pillsbury, 85–112. Dumbarton Oaks Research Library and Collections, Trustees for Harvard University, Washington, DC.

———. 2016. *The Aztec Economic World: Merchants and Markets in Ancient Mesoamerica*. Cambridge University Press, Cambridge.

Hirth, Kenneth G., Ann Cyphers, Robert Cobean, Jason De Leon and Michael D. Glascock. 2013. Early Olmec Obsidian Trade and Economic Organization at San Lorenzo. *Journal of Archaeological Science* 40:2784–2798.

Hirth, Kenneth G., and Joanne Pillsbury. 2013. Merchants, Markets, and Exchange in the Pre-Columbian World. In *Merchants, Markets, and Exchange in the Pre-Columbian World*, ed. Kenneth G. Hirth and Joanne Pillsbury, 1–22. Dumbarton Oaks Research Library and Collections, Trustees for Harvard University, Washington, DC.

Hirth, Kenneth G., and Joanne Pillsbury, editors. 2013. *Merchants, Markets, and Exchange in the Pre-Columbian World.* Dumbarton Oaks Research Library and Collections, Trustees for Harvard University, Washington, DC.

Hodell, David A., Mark Brenner, J. H. Curtis, and Thomas Guilderson. 2001. Solar Forcing of Drought Frequency in the Maya Lowlands. *Science* 292:1367–1370.

Hodges, Richard. 1982. *Dark Age Economics: The Origins of Towns and Trade A.D. 600–1000.* Gerald Duckworth, London.

Hofling, Charles Andrew. 2009. The Linguistic Context of the Kowoj. In *The Kowoj: Identity, Migration, and Geopolitics in Late Postclassic Petén, Guatemala*, ed. Prudence M. Rice and Don S. Rice, 70–79. University Press of Colorado, Boulder.

———. 2018. Itzaj Maya from a Historical Perspective. In *Historical and Archaeological Perspectives on the Itzas of Petén, Guatemala*, ed. Prudence M. Rice and Don S. Rice, 28–39. University Press of Colorado, Boulder.

Hohmann, Bobbi, Terry G. Powis, and Paul F. Healy. 2018. Middle Preclassic Maya Shell Ornament Production. In *Pathways to Complexity: A View from the Maya Lowlands*, ed. M Kathryn Brown and George J. Bey III, 117–146. University Press of Florida, Gainesville.

Holley, George. 1983. Ceramic Changes at Piedras Negras, Guatemala. Unpublished Ph.D. dissertation, Southern Illinois University, Carbondale.

Holmes, William H. 1895–1897. Archaeological Studies among the Ancient Cities of Mexico. Part I: Monuments of Yucatan (1895). Part II: Monuments of Chiapas, Oaxaca and the Valley of Mexico (1897). *Field Museum of Natural History, Anthropological Series* (New York) 1:1–338.

Hoopes, John. 2012. Imagining Human Alteration of Ancient Landscapes in Central and South America. In *The Ethics of Anthropology and Amerindian Research: Reporting on Environmental Degradation and Warfare*, ed. Richard Chacon and Rubén Mendoza, 235–267. Springer, New York.

Horowitz, Rachel A. 2017. Understanding Ancient Maya Economic Variability: Lithic Technological Organization in the Mopan Valley, Belize. Unpublished Ph.D. dissertation, Tulane University, New Orleans.

Horowitz, Rachel A., Bernadette Cap, Jason Yaeger, Meaghan Peuramaki-Brown, and Mark Eli. 2019. Raw Material Selection and Stone Tool Production: Limestone Bifaces in the Mopan Valley. *Latin American Antiquity* 30:198–204.

Houck, Charles W., Jr. 2004. *A Rural Survey of Ek Balam, Yucatan, Mexico.* Ph.D. dissertation, Department of Anthropology, Tulane University, ProQuest/UMI, Ann Arbor, MI.

Houk, Brett A. 2015. *Ancient Maya Cities of the Eastern Lowlands.* University Press of Florida, Gainesville.

Houston, Stephen D. 1994. Literacy among the Pre-Columbian Maya: A Comparative Perspective. In *Writing without Words: Alternative Literacies in Mesoamerica and the Andes*, ed. Walter D. Mignolo and Elizabeth Hill Boone, 27–49. Duke University Press, Durham, NC.

———. 1997. A King Worth a Hill of Beans. *Archaeology* 50(3):40.

———. 1998. Classic Maya Depictions of the Built Environment. In *Function and Meaning in Classic Maya Architecture*, ed. Stephen D. Houston, 333–372. Dumbarton Oaks Research Library and Collection, Washington, DC.

———. 2008. The Small Deaths of Maya Writing. In *The Disappearance of Writing Systems: Perspectives on Literacy and Communication*, ed. John Baines, John Bennet, and Stephen D. Houston, 231–252. Equinox Publishing, London.

———. 2014a. Miscellaneous Texts. In *Life and Politics at the Royal Court of Aguateca: Artifacts, Analytical Data, and Synthesis*, ed. Takeshi Inomata and Daniela Triadan, 256–267. Monographs of the Aguateca Archaeological Project First Phase, Vol. 3. University of Utah Press, Salt Lake City.

———. 2014b. Monuments. In *Life and Politics at the Royal Court of Aguateca: Artifacts, Analyti-*

cal Data, and Synthesis, ed. Takeshi Inomata and Daniela Triadan, 233–255. Monographs of the Aguateca Archaeological Project First Phase, Vol. 3. University of Utah Press, Salt Lake City.

———. 2014c. Pehk and "Parliaments." Maya Decipherment (October 7, 2014): https://decipherment.wordpress.com/2014/10/07/pehk-and-parliaments/.

———. 2016. Crafting Credit: Authorship among Classic Maya Painters and Sculptors. In *Making Value, Making Meaning: Techné in the Pre-Columbian World*, ed. Cathy Lynne Costin, 391–431. Dumbarton Oaks Research Library, Washington, DC.

———. 2017. Tributary Texts. Maya Decipherment (July 7, 2017): https://mayadecipherment.com/2017/01/07/tributary-texts/.

Houston, Stephen D., Claudia Brittenham, Cassandra Mesick, Alexandre Tokovinine, and Christina Warinner. 2009. *Veiled Brightness: A History of Classic Maya Color*. University of Texas Press, Austin.

Houston, Stephen D., Héctor Escobedo, Mark Child, Charles Golden, and René Muñoz. 2003. The Moral Community: Maya Settlement Transformation at Piedras Negras, Guatemala. In *The Social Construction of Ancient Cities*, ed. Monica L. Smith, 212–253. Smithsonian Institution Press, Washington, DC.

Houston, Stephen D., and Takeshi Inomata. 2009. *The Classic Maya*. Cambridge World Archaeology. Cambridge University Press, Cambridge.

Houston, Stephen D., and Peter Mathews. 1985. *The Dynastic Sequence of Dos Pilas, Guatemala*. Pre-Columbian Art Research Institute, San Francisco.

Houston, Stephen D., John Robertson, and David Stuart. 2000. The Language of Classic Maya Inscriptions. *Current Anthropology* 41(3):321–356.

———. 2001. Quality and Quantity in Glyphic Nouns and Adjectives. *Research Reports on Ancient Maya Writing* 47.

Houston, Stephen D., and David Stuart. 1992. On Maya Hieroglyphic Literacy. *Current Anthropology* 33(5):589–593.

———. 2001. Peopling the Classic Maya Court. In *Royal Courts of the Ancient Maya, Volume One: Theory, Comparison, and Synthesis*, ed. Takeshi Inomata and Stephen D. Houston, 54–83. Westview Press, Boulder, CO.

Houston, Stephen, David Stuart, and Karl Taube. 2006. *The Memory of Bones: Body, Being, and Experience among the Classic Maya*. University of Texas Press, Austin.

Hruby, Zachary X. 2006. The Organization of Chipped-Stone Economies at Piedras Negras, Guatemala. Unpublished Ph.D. dissertation, Department of Anthropology, University of California at Riverside, Riverside.

———. 2007. Ritualized Chipped-Stone Production at Piedras Negras, Guatemala. In *Rethinking Craft Specialization in Complex Societies: Archaeological Analysis of the Social Meaning of Production*, ed. Zachary X. Hruby and Rowan Flad. *Archaeological Papers of the American Anthropological Association* 17(1):68–87.

Hruby, Zachary X., Helios J. Hernández, and Brian Clark. 2006. Análisis preliminar de los artefactos líticos de Holmul, Cival y La Sufricaya, Guatemala. In *Investigaciones en la región de Holmul, Petén, Guatemala: Informe preliminar de la temporada 2005*, ed. Francisco Estrada Belli, 322–339. http://www.bu.edu/holmul/reports/holmul05_informe_2.pdf (accessed August 12, 2019).

Hubbe, Joaquín, and Andrés Aznar Pérez. 1878. *Mapa de la Península de Yucatán, comprendiendo los Estados de Yucatán y Campeche*. Compiled by Joaquín Hubbe and Andrés Aznar Pérez. Revised by C. Herman Berendt. Regnier, Paris.

Hudson, Michael. 2010. Entrepreneurs: From Near Eastern Takeoff to the Roman Collapse. In *The Invention of Enterprise: Entrepreneurship from Ancient Mesopotamia to Modern Times*, ed. David Larsen, Joel Mokyr, and William J. Baumol, 8–39. Princeton University Press, Princeton, NJ.

Hughbanks, Paul J. 1998. Settlement and Land Use at Guijarral, Northwest Belize. *Culture & Agriculture* 20(2/3):107–120.

Hull, Kerry. 2005. *An Abbreviated Dictionary of Ch'orti' Maya.* FAMSI report: http://www.famsi. org/reports/03031/index.html (accessed August 18, 2019).

———. 2016. *A Dictionary of Ch'orti' Mayan-Spanish-English.* University of Utah Press, Salt Lake City.

Humphrey, Caroline, and Stephen Hugh-Jones, editors. 1992. *Barter, Exchange, and Value: An Anthropological Approach.* Cambridge University Press, Cambridge.

Hutson, Scott R. 2010. *Dwelling, Identity and the Maya: Relational Archaeology at Chunchucmil.* AltaMira, Lanham, MD.

———. 2016. *Ancient Urban Maya.* University Press of Florida, Gainesville.

Hutson, Scott R., editor. 2017. *Ancient Maya Commerce. Multidisciplinary Research at Chunchucmil.* University of Colorado Press, Boulder.

Hutson, Scott R., and Bruce H. Dahlin. 2017. Introduction: The Long Road to Maya Markets. In *Ancient Maya Commerce: Multidisciplinary Research at Chunchucmil*, ed. Scott R. Hutson, 3–25. University Press of Colorado, Boulder.

Hutson, Scott R., Bruce H. Dahlin, and Daniel Mazeau. 2010. Commerce and Cooperation among the Classic Maya: The Chunchucmil Case. In *Cooperation in Social and Economic Life*, ed. Robert C. Marshall, 81–103. AltaMira Press, Lanham, MD.

Hutson, Scott R., David Hixson, Aline Magnoni, Daniel E. Mazeau, and Bruce H. Dahlin. 2008. Site and Community at Chunchucmil and Ancient Maya Urban Centers. *Journal of Field Archaeology* 33(1):19–40.

Hutson, Scott R., Aline Magnoni, Traci Ardren, and Chelsea Blackmore. 2017. Chunchucmil's Urban Population. In *Ancient Maya Commerce: Multidisciplinary Research at Chunchucmil*, ed. Scott R. Hutson, 107–138. University Press of Colorado, Boulder.

Hutson, Scott R., Aline Magnoni, and Bruce H. Dahlin. 2017. Architectural Group Typology and Excavation Sampling within Chunchucmil. In *Ancient Maya Commerce: Multidisciplinary Research at Chunchucmil*, ed. Scott R. Hutson, 51–72. University Press of Colorado, Boulder.

Hutson, Scott R., Travis W. Stanton, Aline Magnoni, Richard E. Terry, and Jason Craner. 2007. Beyond the Buildings: Formation Processes of Ancient Maya Houselots and Methods for the Study of Non-architectural Space. *Journal of Anthropological Archaeology* 26:442–473.

Hutson, Scott, Richard E. Terry, and Bruce H. Dahlin. 2016. Marketing within Chunchucmil. In *Ancient Maya Commerce: Multidisciplinary Research at Chunchucmil*, ed. Scott R. Hutson, 241–272. University Press of Colorado, Boulder.

———. 2017. Marketing within Chunchucmil. In *Ancient Maya Commerce: Multidisciplinary Research at Chunchucmil*, ed. Scott R. Hutson, 241–272. University Press of Colorado, Boulder.

Iannone, Gyles, editor. 2014. *The Great Maya Droughts in Cultural Context: Case Studies in Resilience and Vulnerability.* University of Colorado Press, Boulder.

Iannone, Gyles, and Samuel V. Connell, editors. 2003. *Perspectives on Ancient Maya Rural Complexity.* Monograph 49. Cotsen Institute of Archaeology University of California, Los Angeles.

Iannone, Gyles, Brett Houk, and Sonja Schwake, editors. 2016. *Ritual, Violence and the Fall of the Classic Maya Kings.* University of Florida Press, Gainesville.

Inomata, Takeshi. 2001. Power and Ideology of Artistic Creation: Elite Craft Specialists in Classic Maya Society. *Current Anthropology* 42(3):321–349.

———. 2007. Classic Maya Elite Competition, Collaboration, and Performance in Multicraft Production. In *Craft Production in Complex Societies*, ed. Izumi Shimada, 120–133. University of Utah Press, Salt Lake City.

———. 2014a. Grinding Stones and Related Artifacts. In *Life and Politics at the Royal Court of Aguateca: Artifacts, Analytical Data, and Synthesis*, ed. Takeshi Inomata and Daniela Triadan, 54–83. Monographs of the Aguateca Archaeological Project First Phase, Vol. 3. University of Utah Press, Salt Lake City.

———. 2014b. Synthesis of Data from the Rapidly Abandoned Buildings. In *Life and Politics at the Royal Court of Aguateca: Artifacts, Analytical Data, and Synthesis*, ed. Takeshi Inomata and Daniela Triadan, 271–319. Monographs of the Aguateca Archaeological Project First Phase, Vol. 3. University of Utah Press, Salt Lake City.

———. 2014c. Worked Sherds and Other Ceramic Artifacts. In *Life and Politics at the Royal Court of Aguateca: Artifacts, Analytical Data, and Synthesis*, ed. Takeshi Inomata and Daniela Triadan, 39–53. Monographs of the Aguateca Archaeological Project First Phase, Vol. 3. University of Utah Press, Salt Lake City.

Inomata, Takeshi, and Markus Eberl. 2014. Other Stone Ornaments and Other Stone Artifacts. In *Life and Politics at the Royal Court of Aguateca: Artifacts, Analytical Data, and Synthesis*, ed. Takeshi Inomata and Daniela Triadan, 84–117. Monographs of the Aguateca Archaeological Project First Phase, Vol. 3. University of Utah Press, Salt Lake City.

Inomata, Takeshi, and Kitty Emery. 2014. Bone and Shell Artifacts. In *Life and Politics at the Royal Court of Aguateca: Artifacts, Analytical Data, and Synthesis*, ed. Takeshi Inomata and Daniela Triadan, 127–157. Monographs of the Aguateca Archaeological Project First Phase, Vol. 3. University of Utah Press, Salt Lake City.

Inomata, Takeshi, and Daniela Triadan. 2000. Craft Production by Classic Maya Elites in Domestic Settings: Data from Rapidly Abandoned Structures at Aguateca, Guatemala. *Mayab* 13:57–66.

———. 2003. Where Did Elites Live? Analysis of Possible Elite Residences at Aguateca, Guatemala. In *Maya Palaces and Elite Residences: An Interdisciplinary Approach*, ed. Jessica J. Christie, 154–183. University of Texas Press, Austin.

Inomata, Takeshi, and Daniela Triadan, editors. 2010. *Burned Palaces and Elite Residences of Aguateca: Excavations and Ceramics*. University of Utah Press, Salt Lake City.

———. 2014. *Life and Politics at the Royal Court of Aguateca: Artifacts, Analytical Data, and Synthesis*. Aguateca Archaeological Project First Phase Monograph Series, Vol. 3. University of Utah Press, Salt Lake City.

Inomata, Takeshi, Daniela Triadan, Kazuo Aoyama, Victor Castillo, and Hitoshi Yonenobu. 2013. Early Ceremonial Constructions at Ceibal, Guatemala, and the Origins of Lowland Maya Civilization. *Science* 340(6131):467–471.

Inomata, Takeshi, Daniela Triadan, and Estela Pinto. 2010. Complete, Reconstructible, and Partial Vessels. In *Burned Palaces and Elite Residences of Aguateca: Excavations and Ceramics*, ed. Takeshi Inomata and Daniela Triadan, 180–361. University of Utah Press, Salt Lake City.

———. 2014a. Grinding Stones and Related Artifacts. In *Life and Politics at the Royal Court of Aguateca: Artifacts, Analytical Data, and Synthesis*, ed. Takeshi Inomata and Daniela Triadan, 54–83. Monographs of the Aguateca Archaeological Project First Phase, Vol. 3. University of Utah Press, Salt Lake City.

———. 2014b. Worked Sherds and Other Ceramic Artifacts. In *Life and Politics at the Royal Court of Aguateca: Artifacts, Analytical Data, and Synthesis*, ed. Takeshi Inomata and Daniela Triadan, 39–53. Monographs of the Aguateca Archaeological Project First Phase, Vol. 3. University of Utah Press, Salt Lake City.

Inomata, Takeshi, Daniela Triadan, and Erick Ponciano. 2010. The Elite Residential Area. In *Burned Palaces and Elite Residences of Aguateca: Excavations and Ceramics*, ed. Takeshi Inomata and Daniela Triadan, 53–137. Monographs of the Aguateca Archaeological Project First Phase, Vol. 1. University of Utah Press, Salt Lake City.

Inomata, Takeshi, Daniela Triadan, Erick Ponciano, Estela Pinto, Richard E. Terry, and Markus Eberl. 2002. Domestic and Political Lives of Classic Maya Elites: The Excavation of Rapidly Abandoned Structures at Aguateca, Guatemala. *Latin American Antiquity* 13(3):305–330.

Inomata, Takeshi, Daniela Triadan, Erick Ponciano, Richard Terry, and Harriet F. Beaubien. 2001. In the Palace of the Fallen King: The Royal Residential Complex at Aguateca, Guatemala. *Journal of Field Archaeology* 28(3/4):287–306.

Instituto Panamericano de Geografía e Historia. 1939. *Atlas arqueológico de la República Mexicana*. Publication 41. Instituto Nacional de Antropología e Historia, Mexico City.

Isaac, Barry L. 1993. Retrospective on Formalist-Substantivist Debate. *Research in Economic Anthropology* 14:213–233.

———. 2013. Discussion. In *Merchants, Markets, and Exchange in the Pre-Columbian World*, ed. Kenneth G. Hirth and Joanne Pillsbury, 435–448. Dumbarton Oaks Research Library and Collections, Trustees for Harvard University, Washington, DC.

Jackson, Thomas, and Heather McKillop. 1989. Defining Coastal Maya Trading Ports and Transportation Routes. In *Coastal Maya Trade*, ed. Heather McKillop, 91–110. Occasional Papers in Anthropology. Trent University, Petersborough, Ontario.

Jacob, John. 1994. Evidencias para cambio ambiental en Nakbe, Guatemala. In *VII Simposio Arqueológico de Guatemala*, ed. Juan Pedro Laporte, Héctor L. Escobedo, Sandra V. de Brady, 275–280. Ministerio de Cultura y Deportes, Instituto de Antropología e Historia, Asociación Tikal, Museo Nacional de Arqueología y Etnología, Guatemala City.

———. 1995. Archaeological Pedology in the Maya Lowlands. In Soil Science Society of America, Special Publication 44: *Pedological Perspectives in Archaeological Research*, ed. Mary E. Collins, 51–82, Madison, WI.

———. 2000. Informe de las Operaciones 801 C, 801 B, 801 A, Nakbe: Temporada 1998. In *Investigaciones arqueológicas y ecológicas en la Cuenca Mirador, 1998: Informe de la temporada de campo*, ed. Richard D. Hansen and Judith Valle, 515–519. Proyecto Regional de Investigaciones Arqueológicas del Norte del Petén, Guatemala (PRIANPEG), Guatemala City, UCLA RAINPEG, FARES Foundation, Rupert, ID.

Jiménez Álvarez, Socorro. 2002. La cronología cerámica del puerto maya de Xcambó, costa norte de Yucatán: Complejo cerámico Xcambó y complejo cerámico Cayalac. 2 vols. Tesis profesional de Licenciatura, Facultad de Ciencias Antropológicas, Universidad Autónoma de Yucatán, Mérida.

———. 2009. La esfera cerámica Canbalám. In *V Coloquio Pedro Bosch Gimpera: Cronología y periodización en Mesoamérica y el norte de México*, ed. Annick Daneels, 365–88. Instituto de Investigaciones Antropológicas, Universidad Nacional Autónoma de México, Mexico City.

———. 2012. Las esferas de interacción cerámica durante el Clásico en la costa de Campeche. In *Arqueología de la costa de Campeche: La época prehispánica*, ed. Rafael Cobos, 161–86. Universidad Autónoma de Yucatán, Mérida, Mexico.

———. 2013. Producción, consumo y distribución del período Clásico Tardío, Chinikiha, Chiapas, Mexico. Unpublished Ph.D. dissertation, Facultad de Filosofía y Letras de la Universidad Nacional Autónoma de México, Mexico City.

Jiménez Álvarez, Socorro, Teresa Ceballos Gallareta, and Thelma Sierra Sosa. 2006. Las insólitas cerámicas del litoral noroeste de la península de Yucatán en el Clásico Tardío: La esfera cerámica Canbalám. In *La producción alfarera en el México antiguo III*, ed. Beatriz Leonor Merino Carrión and Ángel García Cook, 345–70. Instituto Nacional de Antropología e Historia, Mexico City.

Jiménez Álvarez, Socorro, Aline Magnoni, Eugenia Mansell, and Tara Bond-Freeman. 2017. Chunchucmil Chronology and Site Dynamics. In *Ancient Maya Commerce: Multidisciplinary Research at Chunchucmil*, ed. Scott Hudson, 73–106. University Press of Colorado, Boulder.

Johnson, Edgar August Jerome. 1970. *The Organization of Space in Developing Countries*. Harvard University Press, Cambridge, MA.

Johnson, James Gregory. 2000. *The Chichen Itza–Ek Balam Transect Project: An Intersite Perspective on the Political Organization of the Ancient Maya*. Ph.D. dissertation, Dept. of Anthropology, University of Pittsburgh. University Microfilms, Ann Arbor, MI.

Johnson, Kristofer D., Richard E. Terry, Mark W. Jackson, and Charles Golden. 2007. Ancient Soil Resources of the Usumacinta River Region, Guatemala. *Journal of Archaeological Science* 34:1117–1129.

Johnson, Lucas M. 2016. Moving, Crafting, and Consuming Stone: An Investigation of Obsidian from Caracol, Belize, Unpublished Ph.D. dissertation, University of Florida, Gainesville.

Johnston, Robert. 2005. A Social Archaeology of Garden Plots in the Bronze Age of Northern and Western Britain. *World Archaeology* 37(2):211–223.

Jones, Christopher. 1987. The Life and Time of Ah Cacau, Ruler of Tikal. In *Primer Simposio Mundial sobre Epigrafía Maya*, 107–120. Asociación Tikal, Guatemala.

———. 1996. *Excavations in the East Plaza of Tikal*. Tikal Report Number 16. University Museum, University of Pennsylvania, Philadelphia.

———. 2015. The Marketplace at Tikal. In *Ancient Maya Marketplaces: The Archaeology of Transient Space*, ed. Eleanor M. King and Leslie C. Shaw, 67–89. University of Arizona Press, Tucson.

Jones, Christopher, Wendy Ashmore, and Robert Sharer. 1983. The Quirigua Project: 1977 Season. In *Quirigua Reports, Volume II*, ed. Robert Sharer, 1–38. University Museum Monograph 49. University Museum, University of Pennsylvania, Philadelphia.

Jones, Christopher, and Linton Satterthwaite. 1982. *The Monuments and Inscriptions of Tikal: The Carved Monuments*. University Museum University of Pennsylvania, Philadelphia.

Jones, Grant D. 1989. *Maya Resistance to Spanish Rule: Time and History on a Colonial Frontier*. University of New Mexico Press, Albuquerque.

Joyce, Thomas A. 1932. The Eccentric Flints of Central America. *Journal of the Royal Anthropological Institute of Great Britain and Ireland* 62:17–26.

Junker, Laura Lee. 2001. The Evolution of Ritual Feasting Systems in Prehispanic Philippine Chiefdoms. In *Feasts: Archaeological and Ethnographic Perspectives on Food, Politics, and Power*, ed. Michael Dietler and Brian Hayden, 267–310. Smithsonian Institution Press, Washington, DC.

Junqueira, André Braga, Nathalia Bezerra Souza, Tjeerd-Jan Stomph, Conny J. M. Almekinders, Charles R. Clement, and Paul C. Struik. 2016. Soil Fertility Gradients Shape the Agrobiodiversity of Amazonian Homegardens. *Agriculture, Ecosystems & Environment* 221:270–281.

Just, Bryan R. 2012. *Dancing into Dreams: Maya Vase Painting of the Ik' Kingdom*. Princeton University Art Museum/Yale University Press, Princeton, NJ/New Haven, CT.

Justeson, John S., William M. Norman, Lyle Campbell, and Terrence Kaufman. 1985. *The Foreign Impact on Lowland Mayan Language and Script*. Middle American Research Institute Publication 53. Tulane University, New Orleans.

Kansky, K. J. 1963. *Structure of Transportation Networks: Relationships between Network Geometry and Regional Characteristics*. Department of Geography Research Paper No. 84, University of Chicago, Chicago.

Katz, Friedrich. 1974. Labor Conditions on Haciendas in Porfirian Mexico: Some Trends and Tendencies. *Hispanic American Historical Review* 54(1):1–47.

Kaufman, Terrence S. 1972. *El Proto-Tzeltal-Tzotzil: Fonología comparada y diccionario construido, versión española e índice español*. 1st ed. UNAM, Coordinación de Humanidades, Mexico City.

Kaufman, Terrence S., and William M. Norman. 1984. An Outline of Proto-Cholan Phonology,

Morphology, and Vocabulary. In *Phoneticism in Mayan Hieroglyphic Writing*, ed. John S. Justeson and Lyle Campbell, 77–166. State University of New York at Albany Publication 9. Institute for Mesoamerican Studies, Albany, NY.

Keller, Angela H. 2006. Roads to the Center: The Design, Use, and Meaning of the Roads of Xunantunich, Belize. Unpublished Ph.D. dissertation, Department of Anthropology, University of Pennsylvania, Philadelphia.

Kelsay, Richaline. 1985. A Late Classic Lithic Finishing Station at Buenavista, Belize. Paper presented at the 50th Annual Meeting of the Society for American Archaeology, Denver, CO.

Kent, Susan M. 1990. A Cross Cultural Study of Segmentation, Architecture, and the Use of Space. In *Domestic Architecture and the Use of Space: An Interdisciplinary Cross-cultural Study*, ed. Susan Kent, 127–152. Cambridge University Press, Cambridge.

Kepecs, Susan M. 2003. Chikinchel. In *The Postclassic Mesoamerican World*, ed. Michael E. Smith and Frances F. Berdan, 259–268. University of Utah Press, Salt Lake City.

———. 2005. Mayas, Spaniards, and Salt: World Systems Shifts in Sixteenth-Century Yucatán. In *The Postclassic to Spanish-Era Transition in Mesoamerica: Archaeological Perspectives*, ed. Susan Kepecs and Rani T. Alexander, 117–137. University of New Mexico, Albuquerque.

———. 2007. Chichén Itzá, Tula, and the Epiclassic/Early Postclassic Mesoamerican World System. In *Twin Tollans: Chichén Itzá, Tula, and the Epiclassic to Early Postclassic Mesoamerican World*, ed. Jeff Karl Kowalski and Cynthia Kristan-Graham, 129–150. Dumbarton Oaks, Washington, DC.

Kepecs, Susan M., and Sylviane Boucher. 1996. The Pre-Hispanic Cultivation of *Rejolladas* and Stone-Lands: New Evidence from Northeast Yucatán. In *The Managed Mosaic: Ancient Maya Agriculture and Resource Use*, ed. Scott L. Fedick, 69–91. University of Utah Press, Salt Lake City.

Kepecs, Susan M., and Tomás Gallareta Negrón. 1995. Una visión diacrónica de Chikinchel y Cupul, noreste de Yucatán, Mexico. In *Memorias del Segundo Congreso Internacional de Mayistas*, 275–293. Universidad Nacional Autónoma de México, Mexico City.

Kerr, Justin. 1998. *The Maya Vase Book: A Corpus of Rollout Photograph of Maya Vase*. Electronic ed. Vol. 1. Associates, New York.

Kettunen, Harri. 2005. An Old Euphemism in New Clothes: Observations on a Possible Death Difrasismo in Maya Hieroglyphic Writing. *Wayeb Notes* 16: http://www.wayeb.org/notes/wayeb_notes0016.pdf (accessed August 12, 2019).

Keynes, John Maynard. 1936. *The General Theory of Employment, Interest and Money*. Macmillan and Co., London.

Kidder, Alfred, J. Jennings, and Edwin M. Shook. 1946. *Excavations at Kaminaljuyu*. Carnegie Institution of Washington Publication 561. Washington, DC.

Killion, Thomas W. 1990. Cultivation Intensity and Residential Site Structure: An Ethnoarchaeological Examination of Peasant Agriculture in the Sierra de los Tuxtlas, Veracruz, Mexico. *Latin American Antiquity* 1(3):191–215.

———. 1992. The Archaeology of Settlement Agriculture. In *Gardens of Prehistory: The Archaeology of Settlement Agriculture in Greater Mesoamerica*, ed. Thomas W. Killion, 1–13. University of Alabama Press, Tuscaloosa.

Killion, Thomas W., Jeremy A. Sabloff, Gair Tourtellot, and Nicholas P. Dunning. 1989. Intensive Surface Collection of Residential Clusters at Terminal Classic Sayil, Yucatan, Mexico. *Journal of Field Archaeology* 16(3):273–294.

King, Eleanor M. 2000. The Organization of Late Classic Lithic Production at the Prehistoric Maya Site of Colha, Belize: A Study in Complexity and Heterarchy. Unpublished Ph.D. dissertation, Department of Anthropology, University of Pennsylvania.

———. 2012. The Social Dimensions of Production and Consumption within Late Classic Colha, Belize. *Lithic Technology* 37(2):77–94.

———. 2015. The Ethnohistoric Evidence for Maya Markets and Its Implications. In *The Ancient Maya Marketplace: The Archaeology of Transient Space*, ed. Eleanor M. King, 33–66. University of Arizona Press, Tucson.

———. 2016. Rethinking the Role of Early Economies in the Rise of Maya States: A View from the Lowlands. In *The Origins of Maya States*, ed. Loa P. Traxler and Robert J. Sharer, 417–460. University of Pennsylvania Museum of Archaeology and Anthropology, Philadelphia.

———. 2018. Markets and the Maya: From Muddle to Metamorphosis in Our Models. *Codex* 26(1/2):14–29.

King, Eleanor M., editor. 2015. *The Ancient Maya Marketplace: The Archaeology of Transient Space*. University of Arizona Press, Tucson.

King, Eleanor M., and Leslie C. Shaw. 2015. Research on Maya Markets. In *The Ancient Maya Marketplace: The Archaeology of Transient Space*, ed. Eleanor M. King, 3–32. University of Arizona Press, Tucson.

Kingsley, Melanie, Charles Golden, Andrew K. Scherer, and Luz Midilia Marroquín Franco. 2012. Parallelism in Occupation: Tracking the Pre- and Post-Dynastic Evolution of Piedras Negras, Guatemala through Its Secondary Site, El Porvenir. *Mexicon* 34(5):109–117.

Kohl, Phillip. 1978. The Balance of Trade in Southwestern Asia in the Mid-Third Millennium BC. *Current Anthropology* 19:463–492.

Kohler, Timothy A., Michael E. Smith, Amy Bogaard, Gary M. Feinman, Christian E. Peterson, Alleen Betzenhauser, Matthew Pailes, Elizabeth C. Stone, Anna Marie Prentiss, Timothy J. Dennehy, Laura J. Ellyson, Linda M. Nicholas, Ronald K. Faulseit, Amy Styring, Jade Whitlam, Mattia Fochesato, Thomas A. Foor, and Samuel Bowles. 2017. Greater Post-Neolithic Wealth Disparities in Eurasia Than in North America and Mesoamerica. *Nature* 551:619–622.

Kopytoff, Igor. 1986. The Cultural Biography of Things: Commoditization as a Process. In *The Social Life of Things: Commodities in Cultural Perspective*, ed. Arjun Appadurai, 6–91. Cambridge University Press, London.

Kovacevich, Brigitte. 2006. Reconstructing Classic Maya Economic Systems: Production and Exchange at Cancuen. Unpublished Ph.D. dissertation, Department of Anthropology, Vanderbilt University, Nashville, TN.

———. 2011. The Organization of Jade Production at Cancuen, Guatemala. In *The Technology of Maya Civilization: Political Economy and Beyond in Lithic Studies*, ed. Zachary X. Hruby, Geoffrey E. Braswell, and Oswaldo Chinchilla Mazariegos, 151–163. Equinox, Sheffield, UK.

———. 2013a. Craft Production and Distribution in the Maya Lowlands: A Jade Case Study. In *Merchants, Markets, and Exchange in the Pre-Columbian World*, ed. Kenneth G. Hirth and Joanne Pillsbury, 255–282. Dumbarton Oaks Research Library and Collection, Washington, DC.

———. 2013b. The Inalienability of Jades in Mesoamerica. In *The Inalienable in the Archaeology of Mesoamerica*, ed. Michael G. Callaghan and Brigitte Kovacevich, 95–111. Archaeological Papers of the American Anthropological Association. American Anthropological Association, Hoboken, NJ.

Kovalev, Roman K. 2007. Accounting, Tag, and Credit Tallies. In *Wood Use in Medieval Novgorod*, ed. Mark Brisbane Jon G. Hather, 189–202. Oxbow Books, Oxford.

Kowalewski, Stephen A. 1990. The Evolution of Complexity in the Valley of Oaxaca. *Annual Review of Anthropology* 19:39–58.

Kramer, Gerhardt, and S. K. Lowe. 1940. *Archaeological Sites in the Maya Area* ("Tulane Map"). Middle American Research Institute, Tulane University, New Orleans.

Kristiansen, K., T. Lindkvist, and J. Myrdal, editors. 2018. *Trade and Civilisation: Economic*

Networks and Cultural Ties, from Prehistory to the Early Modern Area. Cambridge University Press, Cambridge.

Kuhn, Thomas. 1962. *The Structure of Scientific Revolutions.* University of Chicago Press, Chicago.

Kumar, B. M., and P.K.R. Nair. 2004. The Enigma of Tropical Homegardens. *Agroforestry Systems* 61/62:135–152.

——. 2006. *Tropical Homegardens: A Time-Tested Example of Sustainable Agroforestry.* Springer, New York.

Kunen, Julie L. 2004. *Ancient Maya Life in the Far West Bajo: Social and Environmental Change in the Wetlands of Belize.* Anthropological Papers of the University of Arizona No. 69. University of Arizona Press, Tucson.

Kunen, Julie L., and Paul J. Hughbanks. 2003. Bajo Communities as Resource Specialists: A Heterarchic Approach to Maya Socioeconomic Organization. In *Heterarchy, Political Economy, and the Ancient Maya; The Three Rivers Region of the East-Central Yucatán Peninsula,* ed. Vernon L. Scarborough, Fred J. Valdez and Nicholas P. Dunning, 92–108. University of Arizona Press, Tucson.

Kurjack, Edward B. 1974. *Prehistoric Lowland Maya Community and Social Organization: A Case Study at Dzbilchaltun, Yucatan, Mexico.* Middle American Research Institute, Publication 38. Tulane University, New Orleans.

Kurnick, Sarah. 2016. Paradoxical Politics: Negotiating the Contradictions of Political Authority. In *Political Strategies in Pre-Columbian Mesoamerica,* ed. Sarah Kurnick and Joanne P. Baron, 3–36. University Press of Colorado, Boulder.

Kwoka, Joshua J. 2014. Ideological Presentism and the Study of Ancient Technology: Preclassic Maya Lithic Production at San Bartolo, Guatemala. Unpublished Ph.D. dissertation, Department of Anthropology, University of Buffalo, NY.

Lacadena García-Gallo, Alfonso. 2003. *The Glyphic Corpus from Ek' Balam, Yucatán, México.* FAMSI Report (2004). http://www.famsi.org/reports/01057/index.html.

—— [Lacadena, Alfonso]. 2008. El título Lakam: Evidencia epigráfica sobre la organización tributaria y militar interna de los reinos mayas del Clásico. *Mayab, Sociedad Española de Estudios Mayas* 20:23–43.

——. 2010. Highland Mexican and Maya Intellectual Exchange in the Late Postclassic: Some Thoughts on the Origin of Shared Elements and Methods of Interaction. In *Astronomers, Scribes, and Priests: Intellectual Interchange between the Northern Maya Lowlands and Highland Mexico in the Late Postclassic Period,* ed. Gabrielle Vail and Christine Hernández, 383–406. Dumbarton Oaks Research Library and Collection, Trustees for Harvard University, Washington, DC.

Lakatos, Imre, and Alan Musgrave, editors. 1970. *Criticism and the Growth of Knowledge.* Cambridge University Press, Cambridge.

Landa, Diego de. 1941. *Relación de las cosas de Yucatán* (1566). Ed. and trans. Alfred M. Tozzer. Peabody Museum of American Archaeology and Ethnology, Cambridge.

Landes, David S., Joel Mokyr, and William J. Baumol, editors. 2010. *The Invention of Enterprise: Entrepreneurship from Ancient Mesopotamia to Modern Times.* Princeton University Press, Princeton, NJ.

Lange, Frederick W., and Ronald L. Bishop. 1988. Abstraction and Jade Exchange in Precolumbian Southern Mesoamerica and Lower Central America. In *Costa Rican Art and Archaeology: Essays in Honor of Frederick R. Mayer,* ed. Frederick W. Lange, 65–88. University of Colorado Press, Boulder.

Lansing, J. Stephen. 1991. *Priests and Programmers: Technologies of Power in the Engineered Landscape of Bali.* Princeton University Press, Princeton, NJ.

Laporte, Juan Pedro, and Jorge E. Chocón. 2008. ¿Sera un palacio? . . . ¡No! ¿Sera una acropolis? . . . ¡No!: Un conjunto de función desconcertante en el dentro de Pueblito, Petén. In *Simposio de Investigaciones Arqueológicas en Guatemala, 2007*, ed. Juan Pedro LaPorte, Bárbara Arroyo, and Héctor E. Mejía, 696–712. Museo Nacional de Arqueología y Etnología, Guatemala City.

Laporte, Juan Pedro, Lilian A. Corzo, Oswaldo Gómez, Carmen E. Ramos, Jaime Castellanos, Luisa Escobar, Irinna Montepeque, Heidy I. Quezada, and Mynor Silvestre y Rosaura Vásquez. 1999. Exploraciones arqueológicas en Calzada Mopán: Los grupos de la Acrópolis. En *Reporte 13: Atlas arqueológico de Guatemala*, 238–263. Instituto de Antropología e Historia, Guatemala City.

Laporte, Juan Pedro, Heidy Quezada, Jennifer Braswell, and María Elena Ruiz Aguilar. 1996. Una propuesta para el análisis de los artefactos de piedra tallada del *Atlas arqueológico de Guatemala*. En *Reporte 10: Atlas arqueológico de Guatemala*, 493–508. Instituto de Antropología e Historia, Guatemala City.

Larsen, M. T. 2015. *Ancient Kanesh: A Merchant Colony in Bronze Age Anatolia*. Cambridge University Press, Cambridge.

Larson, Andrea. 1992. Network Dyads in Entrepreneurial Settings: A Study of the Governance of Exchange Processes. *Administrative Science Quarterly*, 37:76–104.

Las Casas, Bernabé de. 1875–1876. *Historía general de las cosas de la Nueva España* (1561). 5 vols. M. Ginesta Press, Madrid.

Latour, Bruno. 1993. *We Have Never Been Modern*. Harvard University Press, London.

Laughlin, Robert M. 1975. *The Great Tzotzil Dictionary of San Lorenzo Zinacantán*. Smithsonian Institution Press, Washington, DC.

Lawton, Crorey. 2007. Excavaciones residenciales en el grupo O: Op 1010, 6A, 6B, y 6D. In *Proyecto arquelógico Motul de San José Informe 7: Temporada de Campo 2005–2006*, ed. Matthew D. Moriarty, Ellen Spensley, Jeanette E. Castellanos C., Antonia E. Foias, 177–198. Department of Anthropology and Sociology, Williams College, Williamstown, MA.

Leach, Helen M. 1997. The Terminology of Agricultural Origins and Food Production Systems: A Horticultural Perspective. *Antiquity* 71(271):135–148.

Leal Rodas, Marco Antonio, and Salvador López Aguilar. 1993. Reconocimiento arqueológico en la brecha topográfica Libertad-Xan (sector Tamariz–Río San Pedro). Basic Resources International, Guatemala City.

Leal Rodas, Marco Antonio, Salvador López Aguilar, María Teresita Chinchilla, José Héctor Paredes G., José Enríquez Benítez, and Marco E. Zetina Aldana. 1988. *Reconocimiento arqueológico en el noroccidente de Petén*. Instituto de Investigaciones Históricas, Antropológicas y Arqueológicas Vol. 1. Escuela de Historia, Universidad de San Carlos de Guatemala, Guatemala City.

LeCount, Lisa J. 1999. Polychrome Pottery and Political Strategies in Late and Terminal Classic Lowland Maya Society. *Latin American Antiquity* 10:239–258.

———. 2001. Like Water for Chocolate: Feasting and Political Ritual among the Late Classic Maya at Xunantunich, Belize. *American Anthropologist* 103:935–953.

———. 2010. Maya Palace Kitchens. In *Inside Ancient Kitchens: New Directions In the Study of Daily Meals and Feasts*, ed. Elizabeth A. Klarich, 133–160. University Press of Colorado, Boulder.

———. 2016. Classic Maya Marketplaces and Exchanges: Examining Market Competition as a Factor for Understanding Commodity Distributions. In *Alternative Pathways to Complexity: A Collection of Essays on Architecture, Economics, Power, and Cross-cultural Analysis*, ed. Lane F. Fargher and Verenice Y. Heredia Espinoza, 155–173. University Press of Colorado, Boulder.

LeCount, Lisa J., and Jason Yaeger. 2010. A Brief Description of Xunantunich. In *Classic Maya*

Provincial Polities: Xunantunich and Its Hinterlands, ed. Lisa J. LeCount and Jason Yaeger, 67–78. University of Arizona, Tucson.

LeCount, Lisa J., Jason Yaeger, Richard M. Leventhal, and Wendy Ashmore. 2002. Dating the Rise and Fall of Xunantunich, Belize: A Late and Terminal Classic Lowland Maya Regional Center. *Ancient Mesoamerica* 13(1):41–63.

Lee, David. 2005. WK-06: Excavaciones en la Estructura L11–38 en el Complejo Palaciego Noroeste. In *Proyecto Arqueológico El Perú–Waka': Informe no. 2, temporada 2004*, ed. Hector L. Escobedo and David Freidel, 111–142. SMU, Dallas.

Leech, Roger. 2003. The Garden House: Merchant Culture and Identity in the Early Modern City. In *Archaeologies of the British: Explorations of Identity in Great Britain and Its Colonies 1600–1945*, ed. Susan Lawrence, 76–86. Routledge, New York.

Lentz, David L. 1999. Plant Resources of the Ancient Maya: The Paleoethnobotanical Evidence. In *Reconstructing Ancient Maya Diet*, ed. Christine D. White, 3–18. University of Utah Press, Salt Lake City.

Lentz, David L., Marilyn P. Beaudry-Corbett, Maria Luisa Reyna de Aguilar, and Lawrence Kaplan. 1996. Foodstuffs, Forests, Fields, and Shelter: A Paleoethnobotanical Analysis of Vessel Contents from the Ceren Site, El Salvador. *Latin American Antiquity* 7(3):247–262.

Lentz, David, Nicholas P. Dunning, and Vernon L. Scarborough, editors. 2015. *Tikal: Paleoecology of an Ancient Maya City*. Cambridge University Press, New York.

Lentz, David L., Nicholas P. Dunning, Vernon L. Scarborough, Kevin S. Magee, Kim M. Thompson, Eric Weaver, Christopher Carr, Richard E. Terry, Gerald Islebe, Kenneth B. Tankersley, Liwy Grazioso Sierra, John G. Jones, Palma Buttles, Fred Valdez, and Carmen E. Ramos Hernández. 2014. Forests, Fields, and the Edge of Sustainability at the Ancient Maya City of Tikal. *Proceedings of the National Academy of Sciences of the United States of America* 111(52):18513–18518.

Lentz, David L., Kevin Magee, Eric Weaver, John G. Jones, Kenneth B. Tankersley, Angela Hood, Gerald Islebe, Carmen E. Ramos Hernández, and Nicholas P. Dunning. 2015. Agroforestry and Agricultural Practices of the Ancient Maya at Tikal. In *Tikal: Paleoecology of an Ancient Maya City*, ed. David L. Lentz, Nicholas P. Dunning, and Vernon L. Scarborough, 152–185. Cambridge University Press, New York.

Lentz, David, and Carlos Ramírez-Sosa. 2002. Cerén Plant Resources: Abundance and Diversity. In *Before the Volcano Erupted: The Ancient Cerén Village in Central America*, ed. Payson Sheets, 33–42. University of Texas Press, Austin.

Léon-Portilla, Miguel. 1962. La institución cultural del comercio prehispánico. *Estudios de Cultural Náhuatl* III:23–54.

Leroi-Gourhan, André. 1945. *Milieu et technique*. Albin Michel, Paris.

Lesure, Richard. 1999. On the Genesis of Value in Early Hierarchical Societies. In *Material Symbols: Culture and Economy in Prehistory*, ed. John E. Robb, 23–55. Center for Archaeological Investigations, Occasional Paper No. 26. Southern Illinois University, Carbondale.

Leventhal, Richard M. 1983. Household Groups and Classic Maya Religion. In *Prehistoric Settlement Systems: Essays in Honor of Gordon R. Willey*, ed. Evon Z. Vogt and Richard M. Leventhal, 55–76. University of New Mexico Press and Peabody Museum of Archaeology and Ethnology, Cambridge, MA.

Lewis, Brandon S. 2003. Environmental Heterogeneity and Occupational Specialization: An Examination of the Lithic Tool Production in the Three Rivers Region of the Northeastern Peten. In *Heterarchy, Political Economy, and the Ancient Maya: The Three Rivers Region of the East-Central Yucatan Peninsula*, ed. Vernon. L. Scarborough, Fred Valdez Jr., and Nicholas Dunning, 122–135. University of Arizona Press, Tucson.

Leyden, Barbara W., Mark Brenner, Tom Whitmore, Jason H. Curtis, Dolores R. Piperno, and

Bruce H. Dahlin. 1996. A Record of Long- and Short-Term Climatic Variation from Northwest Yucatán: Cenote San José Chulchacá. In *The Managed Mosaic: Ancient Maya Agriculture and Resource Use*, ed. Scott L. Fedick, 30–50. University of Utah Press, Salt Lake City.

Liendo Stuardo, Rodrigo, editor. 2008. *El territorio Maya: Memoria de la Quinta Mesa Redonda de Palenque*. Instituto Nacional de Antropologia e Historia, Mexico City.

Ligorred Perramón, Josep. 2004. T'ho, la Mérida Ancestral: Ordenamiento arqueoterritorial y caracterización urbana. Tesis Profesional. Facultad de Ciencias Antropológicas de la Universidad Autónoma de Yucatán, Mérida.

Lira, Rafael, and Javier Caballero. 2002. Ethnobotany of the Wild Mexican Cucurbitaceae. *Economic Botany* 56:380–398.

Lohse, Jon C. 2010. Archaic Origins of the Lowland Maya. *Latin American Antiquity* 21(3): 312–352.

Lohse, Jon C., and Fred Valdez Jr., editors. 2004. *Ancient Maya Commoners*. University of Texas Press, Austin.

Longyear, John M. 1952. *Copan Ceramics: A Study of Southeastern Maya Pottery*. Publication 597. Carnegie Institution of Washington, Washington, DC.

Lope, Albino. 1928. *Geografía del Estado de Yucatán*. Sociedad de Edición y Librería Franco Americana, Mexico City.

Lopes, Luís. 2005. A Reading for the "Stinger" Glyph. *Mesoweb*. http://www.mesoweb.com/articles/lopes/Stinger.pdf (accessed August 12, 2019).

López Varela, Sandra L. 1989. *Análisis y clasificación de la cerámica de un sitio maya del Clásico: Yaxchilán, Mexico*. BAR International Series, 535. British Archaeological Reports, Oxford.

Low, Setha M. 1999. *Theorizing the City: The New Urban Anthropology Reader*. Rutgers University Press, New Brunswick, NJ.

Lucero, Lisa J. 1999. Water Control and Maya Politics in the Southern Maya Lowlands. In *Complex Polities in the Ancient Tropical World*, ed. Elizabeth Bacus and Lisa Lucero, 35–49. Archaeological Papers 9. American Anthropological Association, Washington, DC.

Lundell, Cyrus L. 1938. Plants Probably Utilized by the Old Empire Maya of Peten and Adjacent Lowlands. *Papers of the Michigan Academy of Science Arts and Letters* 24:37–56.

Magcale-Macandog, Damasa, and Lovereal Joy M. Ocampo. 2005. Indigenous Strategies of Sustainable Farming Systems in the Highlands of Northern Philippines. *Journal of Sustainable Agriculture* 26(2):117–138.

Mahler, Joy. 1965. Garments and Textiles of the Maya Lowlands. In *Handbook of Middle American Indians: Archaeology of Southern Mesoamerica, Part Two, Vol. 3*, 581–593. University of Texas Press, Austin.

Makkar, Harinder P. S., Karin Becker, and Birgit Schmook. 1998. Edible Provenances of *Jatropha curcas* from Quintana Roo State of Mexico and Effect of Roasting on Antinutrient and Toxic Factors in Seeds. *Plant Foods for Human Nutrition* 52:31–36.

Maler, Teobert. 1997. *Península Yucatán*. ed. by Hanns J. Prem. Gebr. Mann Verlag, Berlin.

Malinowski, Bronislaw, and Julio de la Fuente. 1982. The Economics of a Mexican Market System: An Essay in Contemporary Ethnographic and Social Change in a Mexican Valley. In *Malinowski in Mexico: The Economics of a Mexican Market System*, ed. Susan Drucker-Brown, 51–191. Routledge and Kegan Paul, London.

Malpass, Michael A. 1987. Prehistoric Agricultural Terracing at Chijra in the Colca Valley, Peru: Preliminary Report II. In *Pre-Hispanic Agricultural Fields in the Andean Region Part I*, ed. William M. Denevan, Kent Mathewson, and Gregory W. Knapp, 45–66. Proceedings of the 45th International Congress of Americanists, BAR International Series 359(i), BAR, Oxford.

Marcus, Joyce. 1973. Territorial Organization of the Lowland Classic Maya. *Science* 180(4089):911–916.

———. 1982. The Plant World of the Sixteenth- and Seventeenth-Century Lowland Maya. In

Maya Subsistence: Studies in Memory of Dennis E. Puleston, ed. Kent V. Flannery, 239–273. Academic Press, New York.

———. 2012. Maya Political Cycling and the Story of the Kaan Polity. In *The Ancient Maya of Mexico: Reinterpreting the Past of the Northern Maya Lowlands*, ed. Geoffrey E. Braswell, 88–116. Equinox, Sheffield, UK.

Marcus, Joyce, and Jeremy A. Sabloff, editors. 2008. *The Ancient City: New Perspectives on Urbanism in the Old and New World*. School for Advanced Research Press, Santa Fe, NM.

Marken, Damien B. 2015. Conceptualizing the Spatial Dimensions of Classic Maya States. In *Classic Maya Polities of the Southern Maya Lowlands*, ed. Damien Marken and James Fitzsimmons, 123–166. University Press of Colorado, Boulder.

Marken, Damien, and Erika Maxson. 2017. Llenando depresiones: Mapa topográfico del Centro Urbano de El Perú–Waka'. In *Proyecto Arqueológico El Perú–Waka': Informe No. 14, temporada 2016*, ed. Juan Carlos Pérez and Griselda Pérez, 304–321. Informe Entragado a la Dirección General del Patrimonio Cultural y Natural de Guatemala, Guatemala City.

Marroquín, Alejandro. 1957. *La ciudad mercado (Tlaxiaco)*. Imprenta Universitaria, Mexico City.

Marshack, Alexander. 1974. The Chamula Calendar Board: An Internal and Comparative Analysis. In *Mesoamerican Archaeology: New Approaches*, ed. Norman Hammond, 255–270. University of Texas Press, Austin.

———. 1989. North American Indian Calendar Sticks: The Evidence for a Widely Distributed Tradition. In *World Archaeoastronomy: Selected Papers from the 2nd Oxford International Conference on Archaeoastronomy Held in Merida, Yucatan, Mexico, 13–17 January 1986*, ed. Anthony F. Aveni, 308–324. Cambridge University Press, New York.

———. 1991. *The Roots of Civilization: The Cognitive Beginnings of Man's First Art, Symbol and Notation*. Moyer Bell, Mount Kisco, NY.

Martin, Felix. 2014. *Money: The Unauthorised Biography*. Random House, New York.

Martin, Simon. 2003. In the Line of the Founder: A View of Dynastic Politics at Tikal. In *Tikal: Dynasties, Foreigners, and Affairs of State*, ed. Jeremy A. Sabloff, 3–46. School of American Research Press, Santa Fe, NM.

———. 2004. Preguntas epigráficas acerca de los escalones de Dzibanché. In *Los cautivos de Dzibanché*, ed. Enrique Nalda, 105–115. Instituto Nacional de Antropología e Historia, Mexico City.

———. 2005. Of Snakes and Bats: Shifting Identities at Calakmul. *PARI Journal* 6(2):5–13.

———. 2008. Wives and Daughters on the Dallas Altar. Mesoweb: www.mesoweb.com/articles/martin/Wives&Daughters.pdf (accessed August 21, 2009).

———. 2012. Hieroglyphs from the Painted Pyramid: The Epigraphy of Chiik Nahb Structure Sub 1-4, Calakmul, Mexico. In *Maya Archaeology 2*, ed. Charles Golden, Stephen D. Houston, and Joel Skidmore, 60–81. Precolumbia Mesoweb Press, San Francisco.

Martin, Simon, and Nikolai Grube. 1995. Maya Superstates. *Archaeology* 48(6):41–46.

———. 2008. *Chronicle of the Maya Kings and Queens: Deciphering the Dynasties of the Ancient Maya*. 2nd ed. Thames and Hudson, London.

Martin, Simon, Stephen D. Houston, and Marc Zender. 2015. Sculptors and Subjects: Notes on the Incised Text of Calakmul Stela 51. Maya Decipherment: Ideas on Ancient Maya Writing and Iconography. https://decipherment.wordpress.com/2015/01/07/sculptors-and-subjects-notes-on-the-incised-text-of-calakmul-stela-51/ (accessed April 7, 2017).

Martindale Johnson, Lucas R. 2014. Standardized Lithic Technology and Crafting at the "Gateway Group" from Caracol, Belize: Implications for Maya Household Archaeology. *Research Reports in Belizean Archaeology* 11:81–94.

———. 2016. Towards an Itinerary of Stone: Investigating the Movement, Crafting and Use of Obsidian from Caracol, Belize. Unpublished Ph.D. dissertation, University of Florida, Gainesville.

Martínez Hildalgo, Gustavo, Richard D. Hansen, John Jacob, and Wayne K. Howell. 1999. Nuevas evidencias de los sistemas de cultivo del Preclásico en la Cuenca Mirador. In *XII Simposio de Investigaciones Arqueológicas en Guatemala*, ed. Juan P. Laporte, Héctor L. Escobedo, Ana Claudia M. de Suasnavar, 327–336. Museo Nacional de Arqueología y Etnología, Ministerio de Cultura y Deportes, Instituto de Antropología e Historia, Asociación Tikal, Guatemala City.

Masson, Marilyn A. 2000. *In the Realm of Nachan Kan: Postclassic Maya Archaeology at Laguna de On, Belize*. University Press of Colorado, Boulder.

———. 2001a. Changing Patterns of Ceramic Stylistic Diversity in the Pre-Hispanic Maya Lowlands. *Acta Archaeologica* 72:159–188.

———. 2001b. The Economic Organization of Late and Terminal Classic Period Maya Stone Tool Craft Specialist Workshops at Colha, Belize. *Lithic Technology* 26:29–49.

———. 2002a. Community Economy and the Mercantile Transformation. In *Ancient Maya Political Economies*, ed. Marilyn A. Masson and David A. Freidel, 335–364. Altamira Press, Walnut Creek, CA.

———. 2002b. Introduction. In *Ancient Maya Political Economies*, ed. Marilyn A. Masson and David A. Freidel, 1–30. AltaMira Press, Walnut Creek, CA.

———. 2003. Laguna de On and Caye Coco: Postclassic Political and Economic Scales of Integration at Two Island Communities in Northern Belize. In *The Social Implications of Ancient Maya Rural Complexity*, ed. Gyles Iannone and Samuel V. Connell, 119–130. Monograph 49. Cotsen Institute of Archaeology, University of California, Los Angeles.

Masson, Marilyn A., and David A. Freidel, editors. 2002. *Ancient Maya Political Economies*, AltaMira Press, Walnut Creek, CA.

———. 2012. An Argument for Classic Era Maya Market Exchange. *Journal of Anthropological Archaeology* 31(4):455–484.

———. 2013. Wide Open Spaces: A Long View of the Important of Maya Market Exchange. In *Merchants, Markets, and Exchange in the Pre-Columbian World*, ed. Kenneth G. Hirth and Joanne Pillsbury, 201–228. Dumbarton Oaks Research Library and Collections, Trustees for Harvard University, Washington, DC.

Masson, Marilyn A., Timothy S. Hare, Carlos Peraza Lope, Bárbara C. Escamilla Ojeda, Elizabeth Paris, Betsy Kohut, Bradley W. Russell, and Wilberth Cruz Alvarado. 2016. Household Craft Production in the Prehispanic Urban Setting of Mayapán, Yucatan, Mexico. *Journal of Archaeological Research* 24:1–46.

Masson, Marilyn A., and Shirley Boteler Mock. 2004. Ceramics and Settlement Patterns at Terminal Classic–Period Lagoon Sites in Northeastern Belize. In *The Terminal Classic in the Maya Lowlands: Collapse, Transition, and Transformation*, ed. Arthur A. Demarest, Prudence M. Rice, and Don S. Rice, 367–401. University Press of Colorado, Boulder.

Masson, Marilyn A., and Carlos Peraza Lope. 2004. Commoners in Postclassic Maya Society: Social versus Economic Class Constructs. In *Ancient Maya Commoners*, ed. Jon Lohse and Fred Valdez, 197–224. University of Texas Press, Austin.

———. 2010. Evidence for Maya-Mexican Interaction in the Archaeological Record of Mayapan. In *Astronomers, Scribes, and Priests: Intellectual Interchange between the Northern Maya Lowlands and Highland Mexico in the Late Postclassic Period*, ed. Gabrielle Vail and Christine Hernández, 77–114. Dumbarton Oaks, Washington, DC.

———. 2013. The Distribution and Diversity of Faunal Exploitation at Mayapan: From Temple to Houselot. In *The Archaeology of Mesoamerican Animals*, ed. Christopher M. Götz and Kitty F. Emery, 233–280. Archaeobiology Series. Lockwood Press, Atlanta.

———. 2014a. The Economic Foundations. In *Kukulcan's Realm: Urban Life at Postclassic Mayapan*, by Marilyn A. Masson and Carlos Peraza Lope, 269–424. University Press of Colorado, Boulder.

———. 2014b. Militarism, Misery, and Collapse. In *Kukulcan's Realm: Urban Life at Ancient Mayapan*, by Marilyn A. Masson and Carlos Peraza Lope, 521–540. University Press of Colorado, Boulder.

Masson, Marilyn A., and Carlos Peraza Lope, editors. 2014. *Kukulcan's Realm: Urban Life at Ancient Mayapan*. University Press of Colorado, Boulder.

Masson, Marilyn A., Carlos Peraza Lope, and Timothy S. Hare. 2014. The Social Mosaic, In *Kukulcan's Realm: Urban Life at Postclassic Mayapan*, by Marilyn A. Masson and Carlos Peraza Lope, 193–268. University Press of Colorado, Boulder.

Matheny, Ray T. 1987. Early States in the Maya Lowlands during the Late Preclassic Period: Edzna and El Mirador. In *City-States of the Maya: Art and Architecture*, ed. Elizabeth P. Benson, 1–44. Rocky Mountain Institute for Pre-Columbian Studies, Denver, CO.

Matheny, Ray T., Richard D. Hansen, and Deanne L. Gurr. 1980. Preliminary Field Report, El Mirador, 1979 Season. In *El Mirador, Peten, Guatemala: An Interim Report*, ed. Ray T. Matheny, 1–23. Papers of the New World Archaeological Foundation, No. 45. New World Archaeological Foundation, Provo, UT.

Mathews, Peter. 1991. Classic Maya Emblem Glyphs. In *Classic Maya Political History: Hieroglyphic and Archaeological Evidence*, ed. T. Patrick Culbert, 19–29. Cambridge University Press, Cambridge, MA.

Mathewson, Kent. 1984. *Irrigation Horticulture in Highland Guatemala: The Tablón System of Panajachel*. Westview Press, Boulder, CO.

Matrícula de tributos–Códice de Motecuzoma. 1980 (1522–1530). Akademische Druck- u. Verlagsanstalt (ADEVA), Graz, Austria. World Digital Library (www.wdl.org/en/item/3248, accessed September 26, 2019).

Maurer, Bill. 2006. The Anthropology of Money. *Annual Review of Anthropology* 35:15–36.

Mauss, Marcel. 1925. *The Gift*. Routledge Press, London.

Maya Ambía, Carlos Javier. 2014. Actualidad de la crítica de Karl Polanyi a la sociedad de mercados. *Política y Cultura* 41:143–166.

May Ciau, Rossana, and Tomás Gallareta Negrón. 2003. La Calera. In *Investigaciones arqueológicas y restauración arquitectónica en Labná, Yucatán, Mexico: La temporada de campo de 2002*, ed. Tomás Gallareta Negrón, Rossana May Ciau, Ramón Carillo Sánchez, Julieta Ramos Pacheco, and Maribel Gamboa, 6.15–6.16. Centro Yucatán del INAH, Mérida, Mexico.

Mayer, Enrique. 2013. In the Realm of the Incas. In *Merchants, Markets, and Exchange in the Pre-Columbian World*, ed. Kenneth Hirth and Joanne Pillsbury, 309–318. Dumbarton Oaks, Washington, DC, and Trustees for Harvard University, Cambridge, MA.

McAnany, Patricia A. 1989. Economic Foundations of Prehistoric Maya Society: Paradigms and Concepts. In *Prehistoric Maya Economies of Belize*, ed. Patricia A. McAnany and Barry L. Isaac, 347–372. JAI Press, Greenwich, CT.

———. 1992. Agricultural Tasks and Tools: Patterns of Stone Tool Discard near Prehistoric Maya Residences Bordering Pulltrouser Swamp, Belize. In *Gardens of Prehistory: The Archaeology of Settlement Agriculture in Greater Mesoamerica*, ed. Thomas W. Killion, 184–213. University of Alabama Press, Tuscaloosa.

———. 1993a. The Economics of Social Power and Wealth among Eighth-Century Maya Households. In *Lowland Maya Civilization in the Eighth Century A.D.*, ed. Jeremy A. Sabloff and J. S. Henderson, 65–89. Dumbarton Oaks, Washington, DC.

———. 1993b. Resources, Specialization, and Exchange in the Maya Lowlands. In *The American*

Southwest and Mesoamerica: Systems of Prehistoric Exchange, ed. Jonathan E. Ericson and Timothy G. Baugh, 213–246. Plenum Press, New York.

———. 1995. *Living with the Ancestors: Kinship and Kingship in Ancient Maya Society*. University of Texas Press, Austin.

———. 2004. *K'axob: Ritual, Work, and Family in an Ancient Maya Village*. Cotsen Institute of Archaeology, University of California, Los Angeles.

———. 2010. *Ancestral Maya Economies in Archaeological Perspective*. Cambridge University Press, Cambridge.

———. 2013. Artisans, Ikatz, and Statecraft: Provisioning Classic Maya Royal Courts. In *Merchants, Markets, and Exchange in the Pre-Columbian World*, ed. Kenneth G. Hirth and Joanne Pillsbury, 229–254. Dumbarton Oaks, Washington, DC.

McAnany, Patricia A., Jeremy A. Sabloff, Maxime Lamoureux St.-Hilaire, and Giles Iannone. 2015. Leaving Classic Maya Cities: Agent-Based Modeling and the Dynamics of Diaspora. In *Social Theory in Archaeology and Ancient History: The Present and Future of Counternarratives*, ed. Geoff Emberling, 259–290. Cambridge University Press, Cambridge.

McAnany, Patricia A., Ben S. Thomas, Steve Morandi, Polly A. Peterson, and Eleanor Harrison. 2002. Praise the Ajaw and Pass the Kakaw: Xibun Maya and the Political Economy of Cacao. In *Ancient Maya Political Economies*, ed. Marilyn A. Masson and David A. Freidel, 123–139. AltaMira, Walnut Creek, CA.

McBryde, Felix W. 1945. *Cultural and Historical Geography of Southwest Guatemala*. Institute of Social Anthropology Publication No. 4. Smithsonian Institution, Washington, DC.

McClosky, Deirdre N. 1997. Polyani Was Right, and Wrong. *Eastern Economic Journal* 23(4):483–487.

McCracken, John, and Kirk Smith. 1998. Emissions and Efficiency of Improved Woodburning Cookstoves in Highland Guatemala. *Environment International* 24(7):739–747.

McCraw, Thomas K. 2007. *Prophet of Innovation: Joseph Schumpeter and Creative Destruction*. Belknap Press, Cambridge, MA.

McDaniels, Gene. 1969. Compared to What?! Musical composition on the album *Swiss Movement* by Les McCann and Eddie Harris. Atlantic Records, Los Angeles.

McGee, R. Jon. 2001. *Watching Lacandon Maya Lives*. Allyn and Bacon, Boston.

McGee, R. Jon, and Belisa González. 1999. Economics, Women, and Work in the Lacandon Jungle. *Frontiers: A Journal of Women Studies* 20(2):175–189.

McKee, Brian. 2002. Household 2 at Cerén: The Remains of an Agrarian and Craft-Oriented Corporate Group. In *Before the Volcano Erupted: The Ancient Cerén Village in Central America*, ed. Payson Sheets, 58–71. University of Texas Press, Austin.

McKillop, Heather. 1989. Coastal Maya Trade: Obsidian Densities at Wild Cane Key. In *Prehistoric Maya Economies of Belize, Research in Economic Anthropology, Supplement 4*, ed. Patricia A. McAnany and Barry Isaac, 17–56. JAI Press, Greenwich.

———. 1995. Underwater Archaeology, Salt Production, and Coastal Maya Trade at Stingray Lagoon, Belize. *Latin American Antiquity* 6(3):214–228.

———. 1996. Ancient Maya Trading Ports and the Integration of Long-Distance and Regional Economies. *Ancient Mesoamerica* 7:49–62.

———. 2002. *Salt: White Gold of the Maya*. University Press of Florida, Gainesville.

———. 2005. *In Search of Maya Sea Traders*. Texas A&M University Press, College Station.

McMillan, C. J., and J. S. Overall. 2017. Crossing the Chasm and over the Abyss: Perspectives on Organizational Failure. *Academy of Management Perspectives* 31(4):271–287.

Meerman, Jan C. 1993. Provisional Annotated Checklist of the Flora of the Shipstern Nature Reserve. *Occasional Papers of the Belize Natural History Society* 2(2):8–36.

Meggers, Betty. 1954. Environmental Limitation on the Development of Culture. *American Anthropologist* 56(5):801–854.

Meierhoff, James, Mark Golitko, and James D. Morris. 2012. Obsidian Acquisition, Trade, and Regional Interaction at Chan. In *Chan: An Ancient Maya Farming Community*, ed. Cynthia Robin, 271–288. University Press of Florida, Gainesville.

Meissner, Nathan J. 2014. *Technological Systems of Small Point Weaponry of the Postclassic Lowland Maya (A.D. 1400–1697)*. Ph.D. dissertation, Southern Illinois University at Carbondale. ProQuest Dissertations Publishing, Ann Arbor, MI.

Mejía, Héctor E. 2002. El Ronrón, un sitio arqueológico en el parte aguas Mopán-Chiquibul, Melchor de Mencos. In *Reporte 16: Atlas arqueológico de Guatemala*, 171–176. Instituto de Antropología e Historia, Guatemala City.

———. 2005. Reconocimiento en el área de sabana al sur del pueblo de San Francisco. In *Reporte 19: Atlas arqueológico de Guatemala*, 1–22. Instituto de Antropología e Historia, Guatemala City.

Mejía, Héctor E., Lilian A. Corzo, and Marco Antonio Urbina. 1999. Reconocimiento en la cuenca baja del río Chiquibul: Entidad política El Naranjal. En *Reporte 13: Atlas arqueológico de Guatemala*, 111–130. Instituto de Antropología e Historia, Guatemala City.

Menéndez, Damaris. 2017. WKES: Extensión de excavaciones en la Operación ES169 B, Grupo Payes, Estructura L11–54. In *Proyecto Arqueológico El Perú–Waka': Informe no. 14, temporada 2016*, ed. Juan Carlos Pérez and Griselda Pérez, 270–295. Informe Entragado a la Dirección General del Patrimonio Cultural y Natural de Guatemala, Guatemala City.

Menéndez, Damaris, and Savanah Dakos. 2017. WK19: Excavaciones en los Grupos T19-1 (LDT.39) y T22-1 (LDT.38) In *Proyecto Arqueológico El Perú–Waka': Informe No. 14, temporada 2016*, ed. Juan Carlos Pérez and Griselda Pérez, 99–155. Informe Entragado a la Dirección General del Patrimonio Cultural y Natural de Guatemala, Guatemala City.

Merk, Stephan. 2016. *The Long Silence: Sabana Piletas and Its Neighbors*. Books on Demand, Norderstedt, Germany.

Meyer, John W., and Rowan Brian. 1991. Institutionalized Organizations: Formal Structure as Myth and Ceremony. In *The New Institutionalism in Organizational Analysis*, ed. Walter W. Powell and Paul J. DiMaggio, 41–62. University of Chicago Press, Chicago.

Michel, Cécile. 2000. Les litiges commerciaux paléo-assyriens. In *Rendre la justice en Mésopotamia: Archives judiciaires du Proche-Orient ancient*, ed. Francis Joannès, 113–139. Presses Universitaires de Vincennes, Saint-Denis, France.

———. 2011. The Private Archives from Kaniš Belonging to Anatolians. *Altorientalische Forschungen* 38(1):94–115.

Mijangos, Blanca. 2014. *Las piedras y manos para moler del sitio Salinas de los Nueve Cerros: Implementos utilizados en el refinamiento de sal.* Unpublished licenciatura thesis, Universidad de San Carlos, Guatemala City.

Miksicek, Charles H. 1987. Formation Processes of the Archaeobotanical Record. *Advances in Archaeological Method and Theory* 10:211–247.

———. 1991. The Ecology and Economy of Cuello: The Natural and Cultural Landscape of Preclassic Cuello. In *Cuello: An Early Maya Community in Belize*, ed. Norman Hammond, 70–84. Cambridge University Press, Cambridge.

Miller, C. Dan. 2002. Volcanology, Stratigraphy, and Effects on Structures. In *Before the Volcano Erupted: The Ancient Cerén Village in Central America*, ed. Payson Sheets, 11–23. University of Texas Press, Austin.

Miller, Mary Ellen, and Claudia Brittenham. 2013. *The Spectacle of the Late Maya Court: Reflections on the Murals of Bonampak*. University of Texas Press, Austin.

Miller, Mary Ellen, and Simon Martin. 2004. *Courtly Art of the Ancient Maya*. Thames and Hudson, New York.

Millet Cámara, Luis. 1984. Logwood and Archaeology in Campeche. *Journal of Anthropological Research* 40(2):324–28.

———. 1985. Los canales de la costa de Campeche y su relación con la industria del palo del tinte. *Revista Mexicana de Estudios Antropológicos* 31:73–79.

———. 1990. Yucatán: Su entrada al mercado mundial de materias primas. In *Sociedad, estructura agraria y estado en Yucatán*, ed. Othón Baños Ramírez, 21–44. Universidad Autónoma de Yucatán, Mérida, Mexico.

Millet Cámara, Luis, Rafael Burgos Villanueva, and Anthony P. Andrews. 2014. Panorama histórico de la costa norte de Yucatán durante el siglo XIX y principios del XX. In *El pueblo maya del siglo XIX: Perspectivas arqueológicas e históricas*, ed. Susan Kepecs and Rani T. Alexander, 71–92. Cuadernos del Centro de Estudios Mayas, 40. Universidad Nacional Autónoma de México, Mexico City.

Mills, Barbara J. 2007. Performing the Feast: Visual Display and Suprahousehold Commensalism in the Puebloan Southwest. *American Antiquity* 72(2):210–239.

Minc, Leah D. 2006. Monitoring Regional Market Systems in Prehistory: Models, Methods, and Metrics. *Journal of Anthropological Archaeology* 25:82–116.

Mock, Shirley Boteler. 1997. Monkey Business at Northern River Lagoon: A Coastal-Inland Interaction Sphere in Northern Belize. *Ancient Mesoamerica* 8(2):165–183.

———, ed. 1998. *The Sowing and the Dawning: Termination, Dedication, and Transformation in the Archaeological and Ethnographic Record of Mesoamerica*. University of New Mexico Press, Albuquerque.

Moholy-Nagy, Hattula. 1989. Who Used Obsidian at Tikal? In *La obsidiana en Mesoamerica*, ed. M. Gaxiola G. and J. E. Clark, 379–390. INAH, Mexico City.

———. 1990. The Misidentification of Mesoamerican Lithic Workshops. *Latin American Antiquity* 1:268–279.

———. 1991. The Flaked Chert Industry of Tikal, Guatemala. In *Maya Stone Tools, Selected Papers from the Second Maya Lithic Conference*, ed. Thomas R. Hester and Harry J. Shafer, 189–202. Monograph in World Archaeology No. 1. Prehistory Press, Madison, WI.

———. 1992. Lithic Deposits as Waste Management: Reply to Healan and to Hester and Shafer. *Latin American Antiquity* 3:249–251.

———. 1997. Middens, Construction Fill, and Offerings: Evidence for the Organization of Classic Period Craft Production at Tikal, Guatemala. *Journal of Field Archaeology* 24(3):293–313.

———. 2003a. *The Artifacts of Tikal: Utilitarian Artifacts and Unworked Material*. Tikal Report No. 27, Part B. University of Pennsylvania Museum of Archaeology and Anthropology, Philadelphia.

———. 2003b. The Hiatus at Tikal, Guatemala. *Ancient Mesoamerica* 14:77–83.

———. 2008a. Appendices 5 and 6. In *The Artifacts of Tikal: Ornamental and Ceremonial Artifacts and Unworked Material*. Tikal Report No. 27, Part A. University of Pennsylvania Museum of Archaeology and Anthropology, Philadelphia.

———. 2008b. *The Artifacts of Tikal: Utilitarian Artifacts and Unworked Material*. Tikal Report 27, Part B. University of Pennsylvania Museum of Archaeology and Anthropology, Philadelphia.

Moholy-Nagy, Hattula, and William R. Coe. 2008. *The Artifacts of Tikal: Ornamental and Ceremonial Artifacts and Unworked Material*. Tikal Report No. 27, Part A. University of Pennsylvania Museum of Archaeology and Anthropology, Philadelphia.

Moholy-Nagy, Hattula, James Meierhoff, Mark Golitko, and Caleb Kestle. 2013. An Analysis of pXRF Obsidian Source Attributions from Tikal, Guatemala. *Latin American Antiquity* 24:72–97.

Monaghan, John. 1990. Reciprocity, Redistribution, and the Transaction of Value in the Meso-american Fiesta. *American Ethnologist* 17:758–774.

Monterroso Rosado, Carolina Castellanos, Lilián de Zea, Adelzo Pozuelos, David Wahl, and Thomas Schreiner. 2006. Investigaciones en la zona cultural Mirador, Petén. In *XIX Simposio de Investigaciones Arqueológicas en Guatemala*, ed. Juan Pedro Laporte, Bárbara Arroyo, and Héctor E. Mejía, 867–876. Ministerio de Cultura y Deportes, Instituto de Antropología e Historia, Asociación Tikal, Fundación Arqueológica del Nuevo Mundo, Guatemala City.

Montgomery, Shane. 2016. On the Back of the Crocodile: Extent, Energetics, and Productivity in Wetland Agricultural Systems, Northern Belize. Unpublished MA thesis. Department of Anthropology, University of Central Florida, Orlando.

Morales Aguilar, Carlos, Richard D. Hansen, A. Morales López, and W. Howell. 2008. Nuevas perspectivas en los modelos de asentamiento maya durante el Preclásico en las Tierras Bajas: los sitios de Nakbé y El Mirador. In *XXI Simposio de Investigaciones Arqueológicas en Guatemala*, ed. Juan Pedro Laporte, Bárbara Arroyo, and Héctor Mejía, 198–213. Ministerio de Cultura y Deportes, Instituto de Antropología e Historia, Asociación Tikal, Guatemala City.

Morales-Aguilar, Carlos, Richard D. Hansen, Edgar Suyuc Ley, Enrique Hernández, Douglas Mauricio, and Josué García. 2017. Comunidades mayas del Periodo Clásico en La Cuenca Mirador, Petén, Guatemala. In *XXX Simposio de Investigaciones Arqueológicas en Guatemala*, ed. Bárbara Arroyo, Luis Méndez Salinas, and Gloria Ajú Álvarez, 77–91. Ministerio de Cultura y Deportes, Instituto de Antropología e Historia, Asociación Tikal, Guatemala City.

Morales-Aguilar, Carlos, and Julien Hiquet. 2013. Naachtun en el contexto regional durante el Clásico Temprano. Paper presented at the IX Congreso Internacional de Mayistas, Campeche, Mexico, June 23–29, 2013.

Morales-Aguilar, Carlos, Douglas Mauricio, Richard D. Hansen, and Enrique Hernández. 2015. Los suburbios de la antigua ciudad de El Mirador, Petén, Guatemala. In *XXVIII Simposio de Investigaciones Arqueológicas en Guatemala 2014*, ed. Bárbara Arroyo, Luis Méndez Salinas, and L. Paiz, 497-509. Vol. 1. Museo Nacional de Arqueología y Etnología, Guatemala City.

Morell-Hart, Shanti. 2011. Paradigms and Syntagms of Ethnobotanical Practice in Pre-Hispanic Northwest Honduras. Unpublished Ph.D. dissertation in Anthropology, University of California, Berkeley.

Moriarty, Matthew D. 2012. History, Politics, and Ceramics: The Ceramic Sequence of Trinidad de Nosotros, El Petén, Guatemala. In *Motul de San José: Politics, History, and Economy in a Classic Maya Polity*, ed. Antonia E. Foias and Kitty F. Emery, 194–228. University Press of Florida, Gainesville.

Morley, Sylvanus G. 1947. *The Ancient Maya*. 2nd ed. Stanford University Press, Stanford, CA.

Morris, Earl H. 1931. Description of the Temple of the Warriors and Edifices Related Thereto. In *The Temple of the Warriors at Chichén Itzá, Yucatán*, by Earl H. Morris, Jean Charlot, and Ann A. Morris, 11–228. Carnegie Institution of Washington, Publication 406. Washington, DC.

Motolinía, Toribio de Benvente. 1971. *Memoriales o libro de las cosas de Nueva España y de los naturales de ella* (1858). Edited by Edmundo O'Gorman. Universidad Nacional Autónoma de México, Mexico City.

Mumary Farto, Pablo Alberto. 2016. Reinterpretando la información de los vasos dinásticos de los Kaan ajawo'ob. *Estudios de Cultura Maya* 47:93–117.

Muñoz, Arturo René. 2002. Ceramics at Piedras Negras, Guatemala. FAMSI: http://www.famsi.org/reports/00079/index.html (accessed September 26, 2019).

———. 2004. The Ceramic Sequence of Piedras Negras, Guatemala: Types and Varieties. Report submitted to the Foundation for the Advancement of Mesoamerican Research. FAMSI, http://www.famsi.org/reports/02055/index.html (accessed March 29, 2017).

———. 2006. Power, Practice, and Production: Technological Change in the Late Classic Ceramics of Piedras Negras, Guatemala. Unpublished Ph.D. dissertation, University of Arizona, Tucson.

Munro-Stasiuk, Mandy J., T. Kam Manahan, Trent Stockton, and Traci Ardren. 2014. Spatial and Physical Characteristics of *Rejolladas* in Northern Yucatán, Mexico: Implications for Ancient Maya Agriculture and Settlement Patterns. *Geoarchaeology* 29:156–172.

Murakami, Tatsuya. 2016. Materiality, Regimes of Value, and the Politics of Craft Production, Exchange, and Consumption: A Case of Lime Plaster at Teotihuacan, Mexico. *Journal of Anthropological Archaeology* 42:56–78.

Murray, William Breen. 1979. Description and Analysis of a Petroglyphic Tally Count Stone at Presa de la Mula, Nuevo León, Mexico. *Mexicon* 1(1):7–9.

———. 1989. A Re-Examination of the Winnebago Calendar Stick. In *World Archaeoastronomy: Selected Papers from the 2nd Oxford International Conference on Archaeoastronomy Held in Merida, Yucatan, Mexico, 13–17 January 1986*, ed. Anthony F. Aveni, 325–330. Cambridge University Press, New York.

Murtha, Timothy. 2009. *Land and Labor: Maya Terrraced Agriculture: An Investigation of the Settlement Economy and Intensive Agricultural Landscape of Caracol, Belize*. DM Verlag Dr. Muller, Saarbrucken, Germany.

———. 2015. Negotiated Landscapes: Comparative Settlement Ecology of Tikal and Caracol. In *Ancient Maya Polities*, ed. Damien Marken and James Fitzsimmons, 75–98. University of Colorado Press, Boulder.

Nakassis, Dimitri, William A. Parkinson, and Michel L. Galaty. 2011. Redistribution in Aegean Palatial Societies: Redistributive Economics from a Theoretical and Cross-Cultural Perspective. *American Journal of Archaeology* 115(2):177–184.

Nalda, Enrique, editor. 2004. *Los cautivos de Dzibanché*. INAH, Mexico City.

Nations, James D., and Ronald B. Nigh. 1980. The Evolutionary Potential of Lacandon Maya Sustained-Yield Tropical Forest Agriculture. *Journal of Anthropological Research* 36(1):1–30.

Neff, Hector, Ron L. Bishop, and Frederick J. Bové. 1989. Compositional Patterning in Ceramics from Pacific Coastal and Highland Guatemala. *Archaeomaterials* 3:97–109.

Neff, Hector, and Frederick Bové. 1999. Mapping Ceramic Compositional Variation and Prehistoric Interaction in Pacific Coastal Guatemala. *Journal of Archaeological Science* 26:1037–1051.

Neff, Linda Stephen. 2002. Gender Divisions of Labor and Lowland Terrace Agriculture. In *Ancient Maya Women*, ed. Traci Ardren, 31–51. AltaMira Press, Walnut Creek, CA.

Neff, L. Theodore. 2008. A Study of Agricultural Intensification: Ancient Maya Agricultural Terracing in the Xunantunich Hinterland, Belize, Central America. Unpublished Ph.D. dissertation, Dept. of Anthropology, University of Pennsylvania, Philadelphia.

Neivens, M., and D. Libbey. 1976. An Obsidian Workshop at El Pozito, Northern Belize. In *Maya Lithic Studies: Papers from the 1976 Belize Field Symposium*, ed. Thomas R. Hester and Norman Hammond, 137–150, Special Report No. 4. Center for Archaeological Research, University of Texas at San Antonio.

Nelson, Ben A. 1991. Ceramic Frequency and Use-Life. In *Ceramic Ethnoarchaeology*, ed. William A. Longacre, 162–181. University of Arizona Press, Tucson.

Nelson, Fred W., Jr. 1985. Summary of the Results of Analysis of Obsidian Artifacts from the Maya Lowlands. *Scanning Electron Microscopy* 2:631–649.

Nelson, Fred, and John E. Clark. 1990. Determination of Exchange Patterns in Prehistoric Mesoamerica. In *Nuevos enfoques en el estudio de la lítica*, ed. María de los Dolores Soto de Arechavelta, 153–176. Universidad Nacional Autónoma de Mexico, Mexico City.

Nelson, Fred W., Jr., and David S. Howard. 1986. Trace Element Analysis of Obsidian Artifacts from El Mirador, Guatemala. *Notes of the New World Archaeological Foundation* (Provo, UT) 3:1-13.

Nelson, Fred W., Jr., Raymond V. Sidrys, and Richard D. Hansen. 1978. Trace Element Analysis by X-ray Fluorescence of Obsidian Artifacts from Guatemala and Belize. In *Excavations at Seibal, Department of Petén, Guatemala: Artifacts*, ed. Gordon R. Willey, 153–161. Memoirs of the Peabody Museum of Archaeology and Ethnology 14. Harvard University, Cambridge, MA.

Netting, Robert McC. 1968. *Hill Farmers of Nigeria: Cultural Ecology of the Kofyar of the Jos Plateau*. University of Washington Press, Seattle.

——. 1974. The System Nobody Knows: Village Irrigation in the Swiss Alps. In *Irrigation's Impact on Society*, ed. Robert McC. Adams, Theodore E. Downing, and McGuire Gibson, 67–76. Anthropological Papers of the University of Arizona No. 25. University of Arizona Press, Tucson.

——. 1977. Maya Subsistence: Mythologies, Analogies, Possibilities. In *The Origins of Maya Civilization*, ed. Richard E. W. Adams, 299–334. University of New Mexico Press, Albuquerque.

——. 1993. *Smallholders, Householders: Farm Families and the Ecology of Intensive, Sustainable Agriculture*. Stanford University Press, Stanford, CA.

Nigra de San Martín, Santiago. 1848. *Plano de Yucatán*. H. Bourrelier and D. Theurat, New Orleans.

Nondédéo, Philippe, Lilián Garrido, Alejandro Patiño, Alfonso Lacadena, Ignacio Cases, Éva Lemonnier, Dominique Michelet, Julio Cotom, Louise Purdue, Divina Perla, Hemmamuthé Goudiaby, Giovanni González, Céline Gillot, Alejandra Díaz, Jackeline Quiñonez, Isaac Barrientos, Julien Sion, Lydie Dussol, and Mariana Colin. 2015. Una mirada hacia Naachtun después de cinco años de investigación (Proyecto Naachtun 2010–2014). In *XXVIII Simposio de Investigaciones Arqueológicas en Guatemala, 2014*, ed. Bárbara Arroyo, Luis Méndez Salinas, and Lorena Paiz, 115–123. Ministerio de Cultura y Deportes, Instituto de Antropología e Historia, Asociación Tikal, Guatemala City.

Nondédéo, Philippe, Carlos Morales, Alejandro Patiño, Mélanie Forné, Chloé Andrieu, Julien Sion, Dominique Michelet, Charlotte Arnauld, Céline Gillot, Mónica de León, Julio Cotom, Éva Lemonnier, Grégory Pereira, and Isaac Barrientos. 2012. Prosperidad económica en Naachtún: Resultados de las dos primeras temporadas de investigación. In *XXV Simposio de Investigaciones Arqueológicas en Guatemala, 2011*, ed. Bárbara Arroyo, Lorena Paiz, and Héctor Mejía, 217–225. Ministerio de Cultura y Deportes, Instituto de Antropología e Historia, and Asociación Tikal, Guatemala City.

Nondédéo, Philippe, Alejandro Patiño, Julien Sion, Dominique Michelet, and Carlos Morales-Aguilar. 2013. Crisis múltiples en Naachtun: Aprovechadas, superadas e irreversibles. In *Millenary Maya Societies: Past Crises and Resilience*, ed. Marie-Charlotte Arnauld and Alain Breton, 122–147. Mesoweb: www.mesoweb.com/publications/MMS/9_Nondedeo_etal.pdf.

North, Douglass. 1981. *Structure and Change in Economic History*. W. W. Norton, New York.

——. 2005. *Understanding the Process of Economic Change*. Princeton University Press, Princeton, NJ.

Oka, R., and C. Kusimba. 2008. The Archaeology of Trading Systems, Part 1: Towards a New Trade Synthesis. *Journal of Archaeological Research* 16:339–395.

Okoshi Harada, Tsubasa. 1993. Los canules: Estudio etnohistórico del Códice de Calkiní. Unpublished Ph.D. dissertation, Universidad Nacional Autónoma de México, Mexico City.

Okoshi Harada, Tsubasa, and Sergio Quezada. 2008. Vivir con fronteras: Espacios mayas peninsulares del siglo XVI. In *El territorio maya: Memoria de la Quinta Mesa Redonda de Palenque*, 137–149. Instituto Nacional de Antropología e Historia, Mexico City.

Oliver, Christine. 1996. The Institutional Embeddedness of Economic Activity. In *The Embeddedness of Strategy: Advances in Strategic Management*, ed. Jane Dutton and Joel Baum, 163–186. JAI Press, Greenwich, CT.

O'Mansky, Matt, and Nicholas P. Dunning. 2004. Settlement and Late Classic Political Disentegration in the Petexbatun Region, Guatemala. In *The Terminal Classic In the Maya Lowlands, Collapse, Transition, and Transformation*, ed. Arthur A. Demarest, Prudence M. Rice, and Don S. Rice, 83–101. University Press of Colorado, Boulder.

Ortiz Aguilú, J. J., J. Riviera Meléndez, A. Principe Jacome, M. Meléndez Maiz, and M. Lavergne Colberg. 1993. Intensive Agriculture in Pre-Columbian West Indies: The Case for Terraces. In *Proceedings of the Fourteenth International Congress for Caribbean Archaeology*, ed. Alissandra Cummins and Philippa King, 278–285. International Association for Caribbean Archaeology, Barbados.

Ortiz Ruiz, María Soledad. 2014. Caracterización de las estructuras anulares de la región del occidente de las tierras bajas mayas. Unpublished master's thesis, El Colegio de Michoacán A.C., Centro de Estudios Arqueológicos, La Piedad de Cabadas, Michoacán, Mexico.

Ortiz Yam, Inéz. 2009. Los montes yucatecos: La percepción de un espacio en las fuentes coloniales. In *Text and Context: Yucatec Maya Literature in a Diachronic Perspective*, ed. Antje Gunsenheimer, Tsubasa Okoshi Harada, and John F. Chuchiak, 185–203. Shaker Verlag, Aachen, Germany.

Oviedo y Valdez, Gonzalo Fernández de. 1851. *Historia general y natural de las Indias*. La Real Academia de la Historia, Madrid.

———. 1851–1855. *Historia general y natural de las Indias, islas, y tierre-firme del mar océano*. (1535). La Real Academia de la Historia, Madrid.

Paine, Richard R., and Glenn R. Storey. 2006. Epidemics, Age at Death, and Mortality in Ancient Rome. In *Urbanism and the Preindustrial World: Cross Cultural Approaches*, ed. Glenn R. Storey, 69–85. University of Alabama Press, Tuscaloosa.

Palka, Joel W. 1996. Sociopolitical Implications of a New Emblem Glyph and Place Name in Classic Maya Inscriptions. *Latin American Antiquity* 7(3):211–227.

———. 2005a. Postcolonial Conquest of the Southern Maya Lowlands, Cross-Cultural Interaction, and Lacandon Maya Culture Change. In *The Postclassic to Spanish-Era Transition in Mesoamerica: Archaeological Perspectives*, ed. Susan Kepecs and R. T. Alexander, 183–202. University of New Mexico Press, Albuquerque.

———. 2005b. *Unconquered Lacandon Maya: Ethnohistory and Archaeology of Indigenous Culture Change*. University Press of Florida, Gainesville.

———. 2014. *Maya Pilgrimage to Ritual Landscapes: Insights from Archaeology, History, and Ethnography*. University of New Mexico Press, Albuquerque.

Paris, Elizabeth H. 2008. Metallurgy, Mayapan, and the Postclassic World System. *Ancient Mesoamerica* 19(1):43–66.

Parry, William J., and Robert L. Kelly. 1987. Expedient Core Technology and Sedentism. In *The Organization of Core Technology*, ed. Jay K. Johnson and Carol A. Morrow, 285–304. Westview Press, Boulder, CO.

Pastrana, Alejandro. 1998. *La explotación azteca de la obsidiana en la Sierra de las Navajas*. Colección Científica. INAH, Mexico City.

Patch, Robert W. 1993. *Maya and Spaniard in Yucatán, 1648–1812*. Stanford University Press, Stanford, CA.

Patiño, Alejandro. 2015. Patrones de desarrollo en la cerámica de Naachtún, Petén, Guatemala. *Trace: Travaux et Recherches dans les Amériques du Centre* 67:11–38.

———. 2016. Explaining Tzakol: Social Interaction during the Early Classic. A View from Naachtún, Petén, Guatemala. *Estudios de Cultura Maya* 48:39–70.

Patterson, Erin, Elisandro Garza, and Leticia Miguel. 2012. Operaciones CR18 Y CR19: Excavaciones en el Patio Norte del Grupo 13R-II. In *Proyecto Regional Arqueológico La Corona no. 4, temporada 2011*, ed. Tomás Barrientos Q., Marcello A. Canuto, and J. Ponce, 319–334. Tulane University and Universidad del Valle, Guatemala, New Orleans and Guatemala City.

Pauketat, Timothy R., and Thomas E. Emerson. 1991. The Ideology of Authority and the Power of the Pot. *American Anthropologist* 93(4):919–941.

Paulette, Tate. 2016. Grain, Storage, and State Making in Mesopotamia (3200–2000 BC). In *Storage in Ancient Societies: Administration, Organization, and Control*, ed. Linda R. Manzanilla and Mitchell S. Rothman, 85–109. Routledge, New York.

Paxton, Merideth. 2004. Tayasal Origins of the Madrid Codex: Further Consideration of the Theory. In *The Madrid Codex: New Approaches to Understanding an Ancient Maya Manuscript*, ed. Gabrielle Vail and Anthony Aveni, 89–127. University Press of Colorado, Boulder.

Pearsall, Deborah M. 1989. *Paleoethnobotany: A Handbook of Procedures*. Academic Press, San Diego, CA.

Peña Castillo, Agustín. 2002. Informe técnico del salvamento arqueológico en Xoclán. Archivo del Centro INAH Yucatán, Mérida, Mexico.

Pendergast, David M. 1981. Lamanai, Belize: Summary of Excavation and Results, 1974–1980. *Journal of Field Archaeology* 8:29–53.

———. 1982. *Excavations at Altun Ha, Belize, 1964–1979, Volume 2*. Royal Ontario Museum, Toronto, Canada.

———. 1990. *Excavations at Altun Ha, Belize, 1964–1979, Volume 3*. Royal Ontario Museum, Toronto, Canada.

———. 2003. Teotihuacan at Altun Ha: Did It Make a Difference? In *The Maya and Teotihuacan: Reinterpreting Early Classic Interaction*. ed. by Geoffrey Braswell, 235–248. University of Texas Press, Austin.

Peraza Lope, Carlos, and Marilyn A. Masson. 2014a. An Outlying Temple, Hall, and Elite Residence. In *Kukulcan's Realm: Urban Life at Ancient Mayapan*, by Marilyn A. Masson and Carlos Peraza Lope, 105–148. University Press of Colorado, Boulder.

———. 2014b. Politics and Monumental Legacies. In *Kukulcan's Realm: Urban Life at Postclassic Mayapan*, by Marilyn A. Masson and Carlos Peraza Lope, 39–104. University Press of Colorado, Boulder.

Peraza Lope, Carlos, Marilyn A. Masson, and Wilberth Cruz Alvarado. 2015 Imágenes de los dioses: Artesanos e incensarios efigie del Posclásico en Mayapán. Paper presented at the "II Mesa Redonda del Mayab: La ciencia y las artes entre los mayas." Mérida, Mexico.

Perera, Victor. 1986. *The Last Lords of Palenque: The Lacandon Mayas of the Mexican Rain Forest*. University of California Press, Berkeley.

Peters, Charles M. 2000. Precolumbian Silviculture and Indigenous Management of Neotropical Forests. In *Imperfect Balance: Landscape Transformations in the Precolumbian Americas*, ed. David L. Lentz, 203–223. Columbia University Press, New York.

Peuramaki-Brown, Meaghan. 2012. The Integration and Disintegration of Ancient Maya Urban Centres: Charting Households and Community at Buenavista del Cayo, Belize. Unpublished Ph.D. dissertation, Dept. of Anthropology, University of Calgary, Canada.

Piña Chan, Román. 1978. Commerce in the Yucatan Peninsula: The Conquest and Colonial Period. In *Mesoamerican Communication Routes and Cultural Contacts: Papers*, ed. Thomas A. J. Lee and Carlos Navarrete, 37–66. Papers of the New World Archaeological Foundation. Brigham Young University, Provo, UT.

Piperno, Dolores R., and Deborah M. Pearsall. 1998. *The Origins of Agriculture in the Lowland Neotropics*. Academic Press, San Diego, CA.

Plitnikas, Jill J. 2002. Textile Fragments Associated with Flaked Stone Symbols from the Maya

Site of Altun Ha, Belize. *American Institute for Conservation Textile Specialty Group Post-prints* (American Institute for Conservation of Historic and Artistic Works, Philadelphia) 12:11–23.

Plunket, Patricia, editor. 2002. *Domestic Ritual in Ancient Mesoamerica*. Regents of the University of California, Los Angeles.

Pohl, John. 1994. Weaving and Gift Exchange in the Mixtec Codices. In *Cloth and Curing: Continuity and Change in Oaxaca*, ed. Grace Johnson and Douglas Sharon. San Diego Museum Papers No. 32. San Diego Museum of Man, San Diego, CA.

Pohl, Mary E. D., Kevin O. Pope, John G. Jones, John S. Jacob, Deborah R. Piperno, Susan D. deFrance, David L. Lentz, John A. Gifford, M. E. Danforth, and J. Katheryn Josserand. 1996. Early Agriculture in the Maya Lowlands. *Latin American Antiquity* 7:355–372.

Polanyi, Karl. 1944. *The Great Transformation: The Political and Economic Origins of Our Time*. Holt, Rinehart and Winston, New York.

———. 1957. The Economy as Instituted Process. In *Trade and Market in the Early Empires*, ed. Karl Polanyi, Conrad M. Arensberg, and Harry W. Pearson, 243–270. Free Press, Glencoe, New York.

———. 1975a. Marketless Trading in Hammurabi's Time. In *Trade and Market in the Early Empires: Economies in History and Theory*, ed. Karl Polanyi, Conrad Arensburg, and H. W. Pearson, 159–188. Free Press, Glencoe, IL.

———. 1975b. Traders and Trade. In *Ancient Civilization and Trade*, ed. Jeremy A. Sabloff and C. C. Lamberg-Karlovsky, 133–154. University of New Mexico Press, Albuquerque.

Polanyi, Karl, editor. 1957. *Trade and Market in the Early Empires*. Gateway, Henry Regnery, Chicago.

Polanyi, Karl, Conrad M. Arensberg, and H. W. Pearson, editors. 1957. *Trade and Market in Early Empires: Economies in History and Theory*. Free Press, Glencoe, IL.

Pollock, Adam. 2006. Investigating the Socio-economic and Socio-political Organization of Intensive Agricultural Production at Minanha, Belize. Unpublished master's thesis, Trent University, Peterborough, Ontario, Canada.

Pollock, Harry E. D. 1962. Introduction. In *Mayapan, Yucatan, Mexico*, by Harry E. D. Pollock, Ralph L. Roys, Tatiana Proskouriakoff, and A. L. Smith, 1–22. Publication No. 619. Carnegie Institution of Washington, Washington, DC.

Ponce Stokvis, Jocelyne Michelle. 2011. Operación CR42: Excavaciones en el Grupo Habitacional 13R-2. In *Proyecto Regional Arqueológico La Corona No. 3, temporada 2010*, ed. Tomás Barrientos Q., Marcello A. Canuto, and M. J. Acuña, 305–316. Tulane University and Universidad del Valle, Guatemala, New Orleans and Guatemala City.

———. 2013. Estructura 13R-10 de La Corona: Un área de actividad de la élite maya prehispánica durante el Clásico Tardío y Terminal. Unpublished *licenciatura* thesis, Universidad del Valle, Guatemala City.

Ponce Stokvis, Jocelyne Michelle, Andrea Sandoval, and Alejandro González. 2013. Excavaciones en la plataforma del Grupo 13R-II. In *Proyecto Regional Arqueológico La Corona No. 5, temporada 2012*, ed. Tomás Barrientos Q., Marcello A. Canuto, and Jocelyne Ponce, 251–258. Tulane University and Universidad del Valle, Guatemala, New Orleans and Guatemala City.

Ponette-González, Alexandra Gisele. 2001. A Household Analysis of Huastec Maya Agriculture and Land Use at the Height of the Coffee Crisis. *Human Ecology* 35(3):289–301.

Pontaza, Jorge. 2011. Operación CR44: Excavaciones en el Grupo Habitacional 13P-1. In *Proyecto Regional Arqueológico La Corona No. 3, temporada 2010*, ed. Tomás Barrientos Q., Marcello A. Canuto, and M. J. Acuña, 335–346. Tulane University and Universidad del Valle, Guatemala, New Orleans and Guatemala City.

———. 2012. Investigación del Grupo 14S-1 "El Caballito." In *Proyecto Regional Arqueológico La*

Corona No. 4, temporada 2011, ed. Tomás Barrientos Q., Marcello A. Canuto, and J. Ponce, 335–346. Tulane University and Universidad del Valle, Guatemala, New Orleans and Guatemala City.

Pontaza, Jorge, and Alejandro González. 2013. Excavaciones en el Grupo 14S-1 "El Caballito," temporada 2012. In *Proyecto Regional Arqueológico La Corona No. 5, temporada 2012*, ed. Tomás Barrientos Q., Marcello A. Canuto, and J. Ponce, 259–278. Tulane University and Universidad del Valle, Guatemala, New Orleans and Guatemala City.

Pope, Cynthia. 1994. Preliminary Analysis of Small Chert Tools and Related Debitage at Caracol, Belize. *In Studies in the Archaeology of Caracol, Belize*, ed. Diane Z. Chase and Arlen F. Chase, 148–156. Monograph No. 7. Pre-Columbian Art Research Institute, San Francisco.

Pope, Karen, Mary D. Pohl, John Jones, David Lentz, Christopher von Nagy, F. Bega, and Irvy Quitmyer. 2001. Origin and Environmental Setting of Ancient Agriculture in the Lowlands of Mesoamerica. *Science* 292 (May):1370–1373.

Pope, Kevin O., Mary E. D. Pohl, John G. Jones, David L. Lentz, Christopher von Nagy, Francisco J. Vega, and Irvy R. Quitmyer. 2001. Origin and Environmental Setting of Ancient Agriculture in the Lowlands of Mesoamerica. *Science* 292:1370–1373.

Porter, Michael. 1998. *Competitive Strategy: Techniques for Analyzing Industries and Competitors*. Free Press, Glencoe, NY.

Postgate, John N. 1975. Some Old Babylonian Shepherds and Their Flocks. *Journal of Semitic Studies* 20:1–21.

Potter, Daniel R. 1993. Analytical Approaches to Late Classic Maya Lithic Industries. In *Lowland Maya Civilization in the Eight Century A.D.*, ed. Jeremy A. Sabloff and John S. Henderson, 273–298. Dumbarton Oaks, Washington, DC.

Potter, Daniel R., and Eleanor M. King. 1995. A Heterarchical Approach to Lowland Maya Socioeconomies. In *Heterarchy and the Analysis of Complex Societies*, ed. Robert M. Ehrenreich, Carole L. Crumley, and Janet E. Levy, 17–32. Archaeological Papers of the American Anthropological Association No. 6. American Anthropological Association, Arlington, VA.

Pounds, Norman J. G. 1973. *An Historical Geography of Europe: 450 B.C.–A.D. 1350*. Cambridge University Press, Cambridge.

Prem, Hanns J. 2003a. Aspectos de los patrones de ssentamiento en la región Puuc central. In *Escondida en la selva*, ed. Hans J. Prem, 272–308. Bonn University/Instituto Nacional de Antropología e Historia. Bonn, Germany/Mexico City.

———. 2003b. *Xkipché: Una ciudad maya en el corazón del Puuc: Vol. 1, El Asientamiento*. Bonn University/Instituto Nacional de Antropología e Historia, Bonn, Germany/Mexico City.

Pryor, F. 1977. *The Origins of the Economy: A Comparative Study of Distribution in Primitive and Peasant Economies*. Academic Press, New York.

Puga, Diego, and Daniel Trefler. 2012. *International Trade and Institutional Change: Medieval Venice's Response to Globalization*. Working Papers, 18288. National Bureau of Economic Research, Cambridge, MA.

Pugh, Timothy W., José Rómulo Sánchez, and Yuko Shiratori. 2012. Contact and Missionization at Tayasal, Petén, Guatemala. *Journal of Field Archaeology* 37(1):3–19.

Puleston, Dennis E. 1968. *Brosimum Alicastrum as a Subsistence Alternative for the Classic Maya of the Central Southern Lowlands*. Master's thesis, University of Pennsylvania. University Microfilms, Ann Arbor, MI.

———. 1983. *The Settlement Survey of Tikal*. Tikal Reports 13. University Museum, University of Pennsylvania, Philadelphia.

Pyburn, K. Anne. 1997. The Archaeological Signature of Complexity. In *The Archaeology of City States: Cross Cultural Approaches*, ed. Deborah L. Nichols and Thomas H. Charlton, 155–168. Smithsonian Institution Press, Washington, DC.

———. 1998. Smallholders in the Maya Lowlands: Homage to a Garden Variety Ethnographer. *Human Ecology* 26(2):267–286.

———. 2008. Pomp and Circumstance before Belize: Ancient Maya Commerce and the New River Conurbation. In *The Ancient City: New Perspectives on Urbanism in the Old and New World*, ed. Joyce Marcus and Jeremy A. Sabloff, 247–272. School for American Research, Santa Fe, NM.

Pyburn, K. Anne, Boyd Dixon, Patricia Cook, and Anna McNair. 1998. The Albion Island Settlement Pattern Project: Domination and Resistance in Early Classic Northern Belize. *Journal of Field Archaeology* 25:37–62.

Quezada, Heidy. 1998. El Rosario 5 en la cuenca media del río Mopán, municipio de Dolores. En *Reporte 12: Atlas arqueológico de Guatemala*, 272–287. Dirección General del Patrimonio Cultural y Natural, Guatemala City.

Quezada, Heidy, Jorge E. Chocón, Mario Vásquez, and Juan Pedro Laporte. 1998. Nuevas exploraciones en El Chal, municipios de Dolores y Santa Ana. En *Reporte 12: Atlas arqueológico de Guatemala*, 1–53. Dirección General de Patrimonio Cultural y Natural, Guatemala City.

Quezada, Sergio. 2014. *Maya Lords and Lordship: The Formation of Colonial Society in Yucatán, 1350–1600*. Trans. T. Rugeley. University of Oklahoma, Norman.

Quintal Avilés, Ella F. 2000. Vírgenes e ídolos: La religión en manos del pueblo. *Mesoamerica* 39:287–304.

Ramos, Carmen E., Julio A. Roldán, José Samuel Suasnávar, and Juan Pedro Laporte. 1993. Análisis preliminar de los artefactos líticos de la región de Dolores. En *Reporte 7: Atlas arqueológico de Guatemala*, 373–401. Instituto de Antropología e Historia, Guatemala City.

Rands, Robert L. 1973. The Classic Maya Collapse: Usumacinta Zone and the Northwestern Periphery. In *The Classic Maya Collapse*, ed. T. Patrick Culbert, 165–206. University of New Mexico Press, Albuquerque.

Rands, Robert L., and Ronald L. Bishop. 1980. Resource Procurement Zones and Patterns of Ceramic Exchange in the Palenque Region, Mexico. In *Models and Methods in Regional Exchange*, ed. Robert E. Fry, 19–46. SAA Papers No. 1. Society for American Archaeology, Washington, DC.

———. 1982. Maya Fine Paste Ceramics: An Archaeological Perspective. In *Excavations at Seibal: Analysis of Fine Paste Ceramics*, ed. Jeremy A. Sabloff, 315–343. Memoirs of the Peabody Museum of Archaeology and Ethnology, Vol. 15(2). Harvard University, Cambridge, MA.

Rathje, William L. 1971. The Origins and Development of Lowland Classic Maya Civilization. *American Antiquity* 36:275–286.

———. 1972. Praise the Gods and Pass the Metates: A Hypothesis of the Development of Lowland Rainforest Civilizations in Mesoamerica. In *Contemporary Archaeology, A Guide to Theory and Contributions*, ed. Mark P. Leone, 365–392. Southern Illinois University Press, Carbondale.

———. 1975. The Last Tango in Mayapan: A Tentative Trajectory of Production-Distribution Systems. In *Ancient Civilization and Trade*, ed. Jeremey A. Sabloff and C. C. Lamberg-Karlovsky, 409–448. University of New Mexico Press, Albuquerque.

———. 1977. The Tikal Connection. In *The Origins of Maya Civilization*, ed. Richard E. W. Adams, 373–382. School of American Research, University of New Mexico Press, Albuquerque.

———. 2002. The Nouveau Elite Potlatch: One Scenario for the Monumental Rise of Early Civilizations. In *Ancient Maya Political Economies*, ed. Marilyn A. Masson and David A. Freidel, 31–40. AltaMira Press, New York.

Rattray, Evelyn C. 1984. El barrio de los comerciantes de Teotihuacán. In *XVII Mesa Redonda de la Sociedad Mexicana de Antropología*, 147–164. Mexico City: Sociedad Mexicana de Antropología.

————. 2004. Etnicidad en el barrio de los comerciantes, Teotihuacan, y sus relaciones con Veracruz. In *La costa del golfo en tiempos teotihuacanos: propuestas y perspectivas, memoria de la segunda mesa redonda de Teotihuacán*, ed. María Elena Ruiz Gallut and Arturo Pascual Soto, 493–512. Instituto Nacional de Antropología e Historia, Mexico City.

Redfield, Robert, and Alfonso Villa Rojas. 1971. *Chan Kom: A Maya Village*. University of Chicago Press, Chicago.

Reents-Budet, Dorie L. 1994. *Painting the Maya Universe: Royal Ceramics of the Classic Period*. Duke University Press, Durham, NC.

————. 1998. Elite Maya Pottery and Artisans as Social Indicators. In *Craft and Social Identity*, ed. Cathy Costin and Rita Wright, 71–89. Archaeological Papers of the American Anthropological Association, Vol. 8. American Anthropological Association, Washington, DC.

————. 2000. Feasting among the Classic Maya: Evidence from Pictorial Ceramics. In *The Maya Vase Book*, ed. Justin Kerr, 1022–1038. Vol. 6. Kerr Associates, New York.

————. 2007. Power Material in Ancient Mesoamerica: The Roles of Cloth among the Classic Maya. In *Wrapping Traditions in Ancient Mesoamerica: Ritual Acts of Wrapping and Binding in Mesoamerica*, ed. Julia Guernsey and F. Kent Reilly, 105–126. Center for Ancient American Studies, Washington, DC, and Ashville, NC.

————. 2008. The Art of Classic Vase Painting. In *Maya: Divine Kings of the Rain Forest*, ed. Nikolai Grube, 246–259. Könemann, Cologne.

Reents-Budet, Dorie L., Ellen Bell, Loa Traxler, and Ronald L. Bishop. 2004. Early Classic Ceramic Offerings at Copán: A Comparison of the Hunal, Margarita, and Sub-Jaguar Tombs. In *Understanding Early Classic Copan*, ed. Ellen Bell, Marcello Canuto, and Robert Sharer, 159–190. University of Pennsylvania Museum of Archaeology and Anthropology, Philadelphia.

Reents-Budet, Dorie, Ronald L. Bishop, and Barbara MacLeod. 1994. Painting Styles, Workshop Locations, and Pottery Production. In *Painting the Maya Universe: Royal Ceramics of the Classic Period*, ed. Dorie Reents-Budet, 164–233. Duke University Press, Durham, NC.

Reents-Budet, Dorie, Ronald L. Bishop, Jennifer T. Taschek, and Joseph W. Ball. 2000. Out of the Palace Dumps: Ceramic Production and Use at Buenavista del Cayo. *Ancient Mesoamerica* 11:99–121.

Reents-Budet, Dorie, Stanley Guenter, Ronald L. Bishop, and M. James Blackman. 2012. Identity and Interaction: Ceramic Styles and Social History of the Ik' Polity, Guatemala. In *Motul de San José: Politics, History, and Economy in a Classic Maya Polity*, 67–93. University Press of Florida, Gainesville.

Reents-Budet, Dorie, Juan Antonio Valdés, and Ronald L. Bishop. 2019. Comercio e Interacción en Miraflores-Kaminaljuyú In *Homenaje a Juan Antonio Valdés, ed.* Cristina Vidal and Edgar Carpio. Universidad de Valencia, Spain.

Reese-Taylor, Kathryn. 2017. Founding Landscapes in the Central Karstic Uplands. In *Maya E Groups: Calendars, Astronomy, and Urbanism in the Early Lowlands*, ed. David A. Freidel, Arlen F. Chase, Anne S. Dowd, and Jerry Murdock, 480–514. University Press of Florida, Gainesville.

Reese-Taylor, Kathryn, Armando Anaya Hernández, F. C. Atasta Flores Esquivel, Kelly Monteleone, Juan Carlos Fernández-Díaz, Alejandro Uriarte, Christopher Carr, Helga Geovannini Acuña, Meaghan Peuramaki-Brown, and Nicholas Dunning. 2016. Boots on the Ground at Yaxnohcah: Ground Truthing Lidar in a Complex Tropical Landscape. *Advances in Archaeological Practice* 4(3):314–338.

Reese-Taylor, Kathryn, and Debra S. Walker. 2002. The Passage of the Late Preclassic into the Early Classic. In *Ancient Maya Political Economies*, ed. Marilyn A. Masson and David A. Freidel, 87–122. AltaMira Press, Walnut Creek, CA.

Reina, Ruben E., and Robert M. Hill II. 1978. *The Traditional Pottery of Guatemala*. University of Texas Press, Austin.

———. 1980. Lowland Maya Subsistence: Notes from Ethnohistory and Ethnography. *American Antiquity* 45(1):74–79.

Reith, Joseph C. 2003. SDEP-1, Buenavista del Cayo, Belize: Functional Significance and Socio-economic Implications of an Unusual Deposit of Chipped-Stone Microliths from a Classic Maya Center in Central Western Belize. Unpublished Ph.D. dissertation, Department of Anthropology, San Diego State University.

Relaciones histórico-geográficas de la gobernación de Yucatán (Mérida, Valladolid y Tabasco). 1983. Prepared by Mercedes de la Garza, Ana Luisa Izquierdo, Ma. del Carmen León, and Tolita Figueroa. Instituto de Investigaciones Filológicas, Centro de Estudios Mayas, Vol. 2. Universidad Nacional Autónoma de México, México City.

Relaciones histórico-geográficas de las provincias de Yucatán (RHGY). 1900 (1579). Colección de documentos inéditos relativos al descubrimiento: Relaciones de Yucatán, Vol. 13. Real Academia de la História, Madrid.

Renfrew, Colin. 1975. Trade as Action at a Distance: Question of Integration and Communication. In *Ancient Civilization and Trade*, ed. Jeremy A. Sabloff and C. C. Lamberg-Karlovsky, 3–59. University of New Mexico Press, Albuquerque.

———. 1977. Alternative models for Exchange and Spatial Distribution. In *Exchange Systems in Prehistory*, ed. Timothy K. Earle and Jonathon Ericson, 71–90. Academic Press, Cambridge.

Renfrew, Colin, and Paul Bahn. 2008. *Archaeology: Methods, Theories and Practice*. Thames and Hudson, London.

Restall, Matthew. 1995. *Life and Death in a Maya Community: The Ixil Testaments of the 1760s*. Labyrinthos, Lancaster, CA.

———. 1997. *The Maya World: Yucatec Culture and Society, 1550–1850*. Stanford University Press, Palo Alto, CA.

———. 2001. The People of the Patio: Ethnohistoric Evidence of Yucatec Maya Royal Courts. In *Royal Courts of the Maya, Volume II*, ed. Takeshi Inomata and Stephen D. Houston, 335–390. Westview Press, Boulder, CO.

Reyes-García, Victoria, Laura Aceituno, Sara Vila, Laura Calvet-Mir, Teresa Garnatje, Alexandra Jesch, Juan José Lastra, Montserrat Parada, Montserrat Rigat, Joan Valles and Manuel Pardo-De-Santayana. 2012. Home Gardens in Three Mountain Regions of the Iberian Peninsula: Description, Motivation for Gardening, and Gross Financial Benefits. *Journal of Sustainable Agriculture* 36(1–2):249–270.

Rice, Don S. 1986. The Peten Postclassic: A Settlement Perspective. In *Late Lowland Maya Civilization: Classic to Postclassic*, ed. Jeremy A. Sabloff and E. Wyllys Andrews V, 301–344. University of New Mexico Press, Albuquerque.

———. 2006. Late Classic Maya Populations: Characteristics and Implications, In *Urbanism and the Preindustrial World: Cross Cultural Approaches*, ed. Glenn R. Storey, 252–276. University of Alabama Press, Tuscaloosa.

Rice, Don S., and Prudence M. Rice. 1990. Population Size and Population Change in the Central Peten Lakes Region, Guatemala. In *Precolumbian Population History in the Maya Lowlands*, ed. T. Patrick Culbert and Don S. Rice, 123–148. University of New Mexico Press, Albuquerque.

Rice, Prudence M. 1984. Obsidian Procurement in the Central Peten Lakes Region, Guatemala. *Journal of Field Archaeology* 11:183–194.

———. 1986. The Peten Postclassic: Perspectives from the Central Peten Lakes. In *Late Lowland Maya Civilization: Classic to Postclassic*, ed. Jeremy A. Sabloff and E. Wyllys Andrews V, 251–299. University of New Mexico Press, Albuquerque.

———. 1987a. Economic Change in the Lowland Maya Late Classic Period. In *Specialization, Exchange and Complex Societies*, ed. Elizabeth M. Brumfiel and Timothy K. Earle, 76–85. Cambridge University Press, Cambridge.

———. 1987b. *Macanche Island, El Peten, Guatemala: Excavations, Pottery, and Artifacts*. University Press of Florida, Gainesville.

———. 2004. *Maya Political Science: Time, Astronomy, and the Cosmos*. University of Texas Press, Austin.

———. 2009. On Classic Maya Political Economies. *Journal of Anthropological Archaeology* 70:70–84.

———. 2013. Type-Variety: What Works and What Doesn't. In *Ancient Maya Pottery: Classification, Analysis, and Interpretation*, ed. James John Aimers, 11–28. University Press of Florida, Gainesville.

Rice, Prudence M., and Donald Forsyth. 2004. Terminal Classic–Period Lowland Ceramics. In *The Terminal Classic in the Maya Lowlands*, ed. Arthur A. Demarest, Prudence M. Rice, and Don S. Rice, 28–59. University Press of Colorado, Boulder.

Rice, Prudence M., and Timothy W. Pugh. 2017. Water, Centering, and the Beginning of Time at Middle Preclassic Nixtun Ch'ich', Petén, Guatemala. *Journal of Anthropological Archaeology* 48:1–16.

Rice, Prudence M., and Don S. Rice. 2009. *The Kowoj: Identity, Migration, and Geopolitics in Late Postclassic Petén, Guatemala*. University Press of Colorado, Boulder.

———. 2016. *Ixlú: A Contested Maya Entrepôt in Petén, Guatemala/Ixlú: Un disputado entrepôt en Petén, Guatemala*. University of Pittsburgh Memoirs in Latin American Archaeology No. 12. University of Pittsburgh Center for Comparative Archaeology and Universidad Francisco Marroquín and Museo Popol Vuh, Guatemala City.

Rice, Prudence M., and Katherine E. South. 2015. Revisiting Monkeys on Pots: A Contextual Consideration of Primate Imagery on Classic Lowland Maya Pottery. *Ancient Mesoamerica* 26(2):275–294.

Rich, Michelle E. 2011. Ritual, Royalty and Classic Period Politics: The Archaeology of the Mirador Group at El Perú–Waka', Petén, Guatemala. Unpublished Ph.D. dissertation, Department of Anthropology, Southern Methodist University.

Ringle, William M. 2012. The Nunnery Quadrangle of Uxmal. In *The Ancient Maya of Mexico: Reinterpreting the Past of the Northern Maya Lowlands*, ed. Geoffrey Braswell, 189–226. Equinox Press, London.

———. 2014. Organización política maya del norte de Yucatán. In *Historia General de Yucatán: Vol. 1, La civilización maya yucateca*, ed. Sergio Quezada, Fernando Robles Castellanos, and Anthony P. Andrews, 137–161. Universidad Autónoma de Yucatán, Mérida, Mexico.

Rivas, Alexander. 2014. Traversing the Terrain: A Least Cost Analysis on Intersite Causeways in the Maya Region. Master's thesis, University of Central Florida, Tampa. *Electronic Theses and Dissertations*. Paper 4749. http://stars.library.ucf.edu/etd/4749/ (accessed August 10, 2018).

Roach, John. 2005. Oldest Known Maya Mural, Tomb Reveal Story of Ancient King. National Geographic News, December 13, 2005, http://news.nationalgeographic.com/news/2005/12/1213_051213_maya_mural.html (no longer available; accessed June 1, 2017).

Robicsek, Francis, and Donald Hales. 1981. *The Maya Book of the Dead: The Ceramic Codex*. University of Virginia Art Museum, Charlottesville.

Robin, Cynthia. 1996. Xunantunich Rural Settlement Project—1996. In Xunantunich Archaeological Project, 1996: Field Season, ed. Richard M. Leventhal, 151–172. Report submitted to the Institute of Archaeology, Belmopan, Belize.

———. 1999. Towards an Archaeology of Everyday Life: Maya Farmers of Chan Noòhol, Belize.

Unpublished Ph.D. dissertation, Department of Anthropology, University of Pennsylvania, Philadelphia.

———. 2002. Gender and Maya Farming: Chan Nóohol, Belize. In *Ancient Maya Women*, ed. Traci Ardren, 12–30. AltaMira Press, Walnut Creek, CA.

———. 2003. New Directions in Classic Maya Household Archaeology. *Journal of Archaeological Research* 11(4):307–356.

———. 2004. The Chan Project: 2004 Season. Report submitted to the Belize Institute of Archaelogy, Belmopan, Belize.

———. 2005. The Chan Project: 2005 Season. Report submitted to the Belize Institute of Archaeology, Belmopan, Belize.

———. 2006. Gender, Farming, and Long-Term Change: Maya Historical and Archaeological Perspectives. *Current Anthropology* 47(3):409–433.

Robin, Cynthia, editor. 2012. *Chan: An Ancient Maya Farming Community*. University Press of Florida, Gainesville.

———. 2013. *Everyday Life Matters: Maya Farmers at Chan*. University Press of Florida, Gainesville.

Robin, Cynthia, Jim Meierhoff, Caleb Kestle, Chelsea Blackmore, Laura Kosakowsky, and Ana Novotny. 2008. A 2,000-Year History of Ritual in a Farming Community. Paper presented at the 73rd Annual Meeting of the Society for American Archaeology, Vancouver.

Robin, Cynthia, William Middleton, Mary Morrison, and Santiago Juárez. 2002. *The Chan Project: 2002 Survey Season*. Report submitted to the Belize Institute of Archaeology, Belmopan, Belize.

Robinson, Eugenia J., H. A. Wholey, and Hector Neff. 1998. La tradición cerámica Flesh Ware en las tierras altas centrales y costa del Pacífico de Guatemala. In *XI Simposio de Investigaciones Arqueológicas en Guatemala, 1997*, ed. Juan Pedro Laporte and Hector Escobedo, 751–766. Museo Nacional de Arqueología y Etnología, Guatemala City.

Robles Castellanos, Fernando, and Anthony P. Andrews. 1986. A Review and Synthesis of Recent Postclassic Archaeology in Northern Yucatán. In *Late Lowland Maya Civilization: Classic to Postclassic*, ed. Jeremy A. Sabloff and E. Wyllys Andrews V, 53–98. University of New Mexico Press, Albuquerque.

Robles Castellanos, Fernando, and Anthony P. Andrews, with David Anderson, Crorey Lawton, Edgar Medina Castillo, Teresa Ceballos Gallareta, and Rafael Burgos Villanueva. 2003. Proyecto Costa Maya: Reconocimiento arqueológico en el noroeste de Yucatán. Reporte interino, temporada 2002: Reconocimiento arqueológico de la esquina noroeste de la península de Yucatán y primeras aproximaciónes a los temas de investigación. Informe para el Consejo Nacional de Arqueología de México. Centro INAH Yucatán, Mérida, Mexico.

Robles Castellanos, Fernando, and Anthony P. Andrews, with David Anderson, Crorey Lawton, Edgar Medina Castillo, Kimberly Sumrow, Teresa Ceballos Gallareta, Soccoro Jiménez Alvarez, and Rafael Burgos Villanueva. 2001. Proyecto Costa Maya: La interacción costa-interior entre los mayas de Yucatán. Reporte interino, temporada 2001: Reconocimiento arqueológico de la esquina noreste de la península de Yucatán. Informe para el Consejo Nacional de Arqueología de México y Propuesta de actividades de campo para la temporada 2002. Centro INAH Yucatán, Mérida, Mexico.

Robles Castellanos, Fernando, and Anthony P. Andrews, with Crorey Lawton, Edgar Medina Castillo, E. Westfall, A. Góngora Salas, Teresa Ceballos Gallareta, and Socorro Jiménez Álvarez. 2000. Proyecto Arqueológico: La costa maya: Interacción costa-interior entre los mayas prehispánicos de Yucatán. Reporte interino, temporada 2000: Reconocimiento arqueológico de la esquina noreste de la península de Yucatán. Informe para el Consejo Nacional de Arqueología de México y propuesta de actividades de campo para la temporada 2001. Centro INAH Yucatán, Mérida, Mexico.

Rocheleau, Dianne, and David Edmunds. 1997. Women, Men and Trees: Gender, Power and Property in Forest and Agrarian Landscapes. *World Development* 25(8):1351–1371.

Roche Recinos, Alejandra. 2015. Operación CR120: Excavaciones en la Estructura 12R-9. In *Proyecto Regional Arqueológico La Corona no. 7, temporada 2014*, ed. Tomás Barrientos Q., Marcello A. Canuto, and Eduardo Bustamante, 291–300. Tulane University and Universidad del Valle, Guatemala, New Orleans and Guatemala City.

———. 2017. Maya Lithic Economies at Piedras Negras, Guatemala: Production and Exchange in an Elite Architectural Complex. Master's thesis, Department of Anthropology, Brown University, Providence, RI.

Roemer, Erwin. 1991. A Late Classic Workshop at Colha, Belize. In *Maya Stone Tools: Selected Papers from the Second Maya Lithic Conference*, ed. Thomas R. Hester and Harry J. Shafter, 55–65. Monograph in World Archaeology No. 1 Prehistory Press, Madison, WI.

Rojas, Andrea. 2011. Operación CR43: Excavaciones en el Grupo Habitacional 12Q-1. In *Proyecto Regional Arqueológico La Corona no. 3, temporada 2010*, ed. Tomás Barrientos Q., Marcello. A. Canuto, and M. J. Acuña, 317–334. Tulane University and Universidad del Valle, Guatemala, New Orelans and Guatemala City.

Roullier, Caroline, Anne Duputié, Paul Wennekes, Laure Benoit, Víctor Manuel Fernández Bringas, Genoveva Rossel, David Tay, Doyle McKey, and Vincent Lebot. 2013. Disentangling the Origins of Cultivated Sweet Potato (*Ipomoea batatas* (L.) Lam.). PLoS ONE 8(5):e62707. doi:10.1371/journal.pone.0062707.

Roys, Ralph L. 1931. *The Ethno-Botany of the Maya*. Middle American Research Series 2. Dept. of Middle American Research, Tulane University, New Orleans.

———. 1939. *The Titles of Ebtun*. Publication No. 505. Carnegie Institution of Washington, Washington, DC.

———. 1957. *The Political Geography of the Yucatan Maya*. Publication 613. Carnegie Institution of Washington, Washington, DC.

———. 1962. Literary Sources for the History of Mayapan. In *Mayapan, Yucatan, Mexico*, ed. H.E.D. Pollock, 25–86. Carnegie Institute, Washington, DC.

———. 1967. *The Book of Chilam Balam of Chumayel* (1933). University of Oklahoma Press, Norman.

———. 1972. *Indian Background of Colonial Yucatán* (1943). University of Oklahoma Press, Norman.

Ruhl, T., Nicholas Dunning, and Christopher Carr. 2018. Lidar Reveals Possible Network of Ancient Maya Marketplaces in Southwestern Campeche, Mexico. *Mexicon* 40(3):83–91.

Russell, Bradley W. 2008. Postclassic Settlement on the Rural-Urban Fringe of Mayapán, Yucatán, Mexico. Unpublished Ph.D. dissertation, Dept. of Anthropology, University at Albany–SUNY.

Russell, Bradley, and Bruce Dahlin. 2007. Traditional Burnt-Lime Production at Mayapán, Mexico. *Journal of Field Archaeology* 32:407–423.

Russell, Bradley W., and Kendra J. Farstad. 2016. Ethnoarchaeology of a Three Generation Yucatec Maya House Compound. Paper presented at the 81st annual meeting of the Society for American Archaeology, Orlando, FL.

Sabloff, Jeremy A. 1975. *Excavations at Seibal: Ceramics*. Memoirs of the Peabody Museum of Archaeology and Ethnology Vol. 13, No. 2. Harvard University Press, Cambridge, MA.

———, editor. 1982. *Analyses of Fine Paste Ceramics. Excavations at Seibal*. Memoirs, Vol. 15, No. 2. Peabody Museum of Archaeology and Ethnology, Harvard University, Cambridge, MA.

Sabloff, Jeremy A., and David A. Freidel. 1975. A Model of a Pre-Columbian Trade Center. In *Ancient Civilization and Trade*, ed. Jeremy A. Sabloff and C. C. Lamberg-Karlovsky, 369–408. University of New Mexico Press, Albuquerque.

Sabloff, Jeremy A. and C. C. Lamberg-Karlovsky, eds. 1975. *Ancient Civilization and Trade*. A School of American Research Book. University of New Mexico Press, Albuquerque.

Sabloff, Jeremy A., and William Rathje. 1975. The Rise of a Maya Merchant Class. *Scientific American* 233:72–82.

———. 1980. Archaeological Research on the Island of Cozumel, Mexico. *National Geographic Society Research Papers* 11:595–599.

Sabloff, Jeremy A., and Gair Tourtellot. 1991. *The Ancient Maya City of Sayil: The Mapping of a Puuc Region Center*. Middle American Research Institute, Publication 60. Tulane University, New Orleans.

Sahagún, Fray Bernabé 1950–1982. *Florentine Codex: General History of the Things of New Spain* (1565). Translated and edited by Arthur Anderson and Charles Dibble. School of American Research and University of Utah Press, Santa Fe and Salt Lake City.

———. 1989. *The Conquest of New Spain, 1585 Revision*. Translated by Howard Cline. University of Utah Press, Salt Lake City.

Sahlins, Marshall. 1972. *Stone Age Economics*. Aldine Press, Aldine-Atherton, Chicago.

Salazar, Carmen, Daniel Zizumbo-Villarreal, Patricia Colunga-GarciaMarín, and Stephen Brush. 2016. Contemporary Maya Food Systems in the Lowlands of Northern Yucatan. In *Ethnobotany of Mexico: Interactions of People and Plants in Mesoamerica*, ed. Rafael Lira, Alejandro Casas, and José Blancas, 133–150. Springer, New York.

Sanders, William T. 1981. Classic Maya Settlement Patterns and Ethnographic Analogy. In *Lowland Maya Settlement Patterns*, ed. Wendy Ashmore, 351–370. School of American Research, University of New Mexico, Albuquerque.

Sanders, William T., and Joseph W. Michels. 1977. *Teotihuacan and Kaminaljuyu*. Pennsylvania State University, University Park.

Sanders, William T., and David Webster. 1988. The Mesoamerican Urban Tradition. *American Anthropologist* 90:521–546.

Santley, Robert S. 1983. Obsidian Trade and Teotihuacan Influence in Mesoamerica. In *Highland-Lowland Interaction in Mesoamerica: Interdisciplinary Approaches*, ed. Arthur G. Miller, 69–124. Dumbarton Oaks, Washington, DC.

———. 1986. Prehispanic Roadways, Transport Network Geometry, and Aztec Politico-Economic Organization in the Basin of Mexico. In *Research in Economic Anthropology: Economic Aspects of Prehispanic Highland Mexico*, ed. Barry L. Isaac, Supplement 2, 223–244. JAI Press, Greenwich, CT.

———. 1994. The Economy of Matacapan. *Ancient Mesoamerica* 5(2):243–266.

Santley, Robert S., and Heather M. Richards. 2007. Rank-Size Analysis of Classic Period Settlement in the Tuxtla Mountains, Southern Veracruz, Mexico. In *The Political Economy of Ancient Mesoamerica: Transformations during the Formative and Classic Periods*, ed. Vernon L. Scarborough and John E. Clark, 115–134. University of New Mexico Press, Albuquerque.

Scarborough, Vernon L., and Fred Valdez Jr. 2003. The Engineered Environment and Political Economy of the Three Rivers Region. In *Heterarchy, Political Economy, and the Ancient Maya: The Three Rivers Region of the East-Central Yucatán Peninsula*, ed. Vernon L. Scarborough, Fred Valdez Jr., and Nicholas Dunning, 3–13. University of Arizona Press, Tucson.

———. 2009. An Alternative Order: The Dualistic Economies of the Ancient Maya. *Latin American Antiquity* 20(1):207–227.

Scarborough, Vernon L., Fred Valdez Jr., and Nicholas Dunning, editors. 2003. *Heterarchy, Political Economy, and the Ancient Maya: The Three Rivers Region of the East-Central Yucatán Peninsula*. University of Arizona Press, Tucson.

Schafer, Arturo. 1893. La salubridad de la ciudad y puerto de Progreso I–III (3 articles). *El Horizonte*, 3rd series, year 4, 136 (February 26):2; (March 5):1; 137 (March 12):1.

Scheidel, Walter, and Sitta von Reden, editors. 2002. *The Ancient Economy*. Edinburgh University Press, Edinburgh.

Scherer, Andrew K., Charles Golden, and Jeffrey Dobereiner editors. 2013. Proyecto Arqueológico Busilja-Chocolja: Informe de la cuarta temporada de investigación. Report submitted to the Consejo de Arqueología, Instituto Nacional de Antropología e Historia, Mexico City.

Scherer, Andrew K., and Lori E. Wright. 2015. Dental Morphometric and Strontium Isotope Evidence for Population History at Tikal, Guatemala. In *Archaeology and Bioarchaeology of Population Movement among the Prehispanic Maya*, ed. Andrea Cucina, 109–118. Springer Briefs in Archaeology. Springer, New York.

Scherer, Andrew K., Lori E. Wright, and Cassady J. Yoder. 2007. Bioarchaeological Evidence for Social and Temporal Differences in Subsistence at Piedras Negras, Guatemala. *Latin American Antiquity* 18(1):85–104.

Schmolz-Haberlein, Michaela. 1996. Continuity and Change in a Guatemalan Indian Community: San Cristóbal–Verapaz, 1870–1940. *Hispanic American Historical Review* 76(2):227–248.

Scholes, France V., and Ralph L. Roys. 1968. *The Maya Chontal Indians of Acalan-Tixchel: A Contribution to the History and Ethnography of the Yucatan Peninsula*. University of Oklahoma Press, Norman.

Schortman, Edward M. 1993. Archaeological Investigations in the Lower Motagua Valley, Izabel, Guatemala: A Study in Monumental Site Function and Interaction. *Quirigua Reports, Vol. III*. University Museum, University of Pennsylvania, Philadelphia.

Schortman, Edward M., and Patricia A. Urban. 1991. Patterns of Late Preclassic Interaction and the Formation of Complex Society in the Southeast Maya Periphery. In *The Formation of Complex Society in Southeastern Mesoamerica*, ed. William R. Fowler, 121–142. CRC Press, Boca Raton, FL.

———. 2004. Marching Out of Step: Early Classic Copan and Its Honduran Neighbors. In *Understanding Early Classic Copan*, ed. Ellen Bell, Marcello Canuto, and Robert Sharer, 319–336. University of Pennsylvania Museum of Archaeology and Anthropology. Philadelphia.

———. 2011. *Networks of Power: Political Relations kin the Late Postclassic Naco Valley*. University Press of Colorado, Boulder.

———. 2012. Networks, Cores, and Peripheries: New Frontiers in Interaction Studies. In *The Oxford Handbook of Mesoamerican Archaeology*, ed. Deborah L. Nichols and Christopher Pool, 471–481. Oxford University Press, New York.

Schrank, Andrew, and Josh Whitford. 2011. The Anatomy of Network Failure. *Sociological Theory* 29(3):151–177.

Schreiner, Thomas. 2000a. Maya Use of Vegetal and Mineral Additives to Architectural Lime Products. In *Program Abstracts from Archaeometry: 32nd International Symposium*, (May 15–19, 2000), 246. Conaculta-INAH, Universidad Nacional Autónoma de México, Mexico City.

———. 2000b. Social and Environmental Impacts of Mesoamerican Lime Burning. Abstract in *GEOS, Unión Geofísica Mexicana, A.C.: Estudios del cuaternario* 20(3):170.

———. 2001. Fabricación de Cal en Mesoamerica: Implicaciones para los mayas del Preclásico en Nakbe, Peten. In *XIV Simposio de Investigaciones Arqueológicas en Guatemala*, ed. Juan Pedro Laporte, Ana C. de Suasnavar, and Bárbara Arroyo, 405–418. Museo Nacional de Arqueología y Etnología, Ministerio de Cultura y Deportes, Instituto de Antropología e Historia, Asociación Tikal, Guatemala City.

———. 2002a. Aspectos rituales de la producción de cal en Mesoamérica. In *Resúmenes del XVI Simposio de Investigaciones Arqueológicas en Guatemala, 2002*, 39. Ministerio de Cultura y Deportes, Dirección General del Patrimonio Cultural y Natural, Instituto de Antropología e Historia, Museo Nacional de Arqueología y Etnología, Asociación Tikal, Guatemala City.

———. 2002b. Traditional Maya Lime Production: Environmental and Cultural Implications of a Native American Technology. Unpublished Ph.D. dissertation, Department of Architecture University of California, Berkeley.

———. 2003. Aspectos rituales de la producción de Cal en Mesoamérica: Evidencias y pespectivas de las tierras bajas mayas. In *XVI Simposio de Investigaciones Arqueológicas en Guatemala, 2002*, ed. Juan Pedro Laporte, Bárbara Arroyo, Héctor L. Escobedo, and Héctor E. Mejía, 487–494. Museo Nacional de Arqueología y Etnología, Ministerio de Cultura y Deportes, Instituto de Antropología e Historia, Asociación Tikal, Guatemala City.

———. 2004. Mesoamerican Lime Burning Technology: A Possible Model for Incipient Lime Industries of the Early Near East. In The *Last Hunter-Gatherers in the Near East*, ed. Christophe Delage, 249–262. BAR International Series 1320. John and Erica Hedges, Oxford.

Schroder, Whittaker, and Socorro del Pilar Jiménez Álvarez. 2016. Clasificación multiple de la cerámica del Grupo Principal de La Selva. In Proyecto Arqueológico Busilja-Chocolja: Informe de la septima temporada de investigación, ed. Whittaker Schroder, Andrew K. Scherer, and Charles Golden, 157–192. Report submitted to the Consejo de Arqueología. Instituto Nacional de Antropologia e Historia, Mexico City.

Schumpeter, Joseph A. 1942. *Socialism, Capitalism and Democracy*. Harper and Brothers, New York.

Schwab, Gregory T. 2013. *Cave Art Study of the Nueve Cerros Survey*. Unpublished MS thesis, Department of Anthropology, St. Cloud State University, St. Cloud, MN.

Schwab, Gregory T., Mark Lentz, Seleste Sanchez, Brent K. S. Woodfill, Mirza Monterroso, and Judith Valle. 2012. Espeleoarqueología, etnohistoria y etnografia en la región Nueve Cerros. In *XXV Simposio de Investigaciones Arqueológicos en Guatemala*, ed. Bárbara Arroyo, Lorena Paiz, and Héctor Mejía, 581–90. Ministerio de Cultura y Deportes, Guatemala City.

Schwartz, Norman B. 1990. *Forest Society: A Social History of Peten, Guatemala*. University of Pennsylvania Press, Philadelphia.

Schwarz, Kevin R. 2004. Understanding Classic to Postclassic Household and Community Spatial Transformation: The Rural Maya of the Quexil-Petenxil Basins, Guatemala. 2 vols. Unpublished Ph.D. dissertation, Southern Illinois University Carbondale.

Scott, James. 1998. *Seeing Like a State: How Certain Schemes to Improve the Human Condition Have Failed*. Yale University Press, New Haven, CT.

Sears, Erin L. 2016. A Reflection of Maya Representation, Distribution, and Interaction: Ceramic Figurines from the Late Classic Site of Cancuen, Peten Department, Guatemala. Unpublished Ph.D. dissertation, Department of Anthropology, University of Kentucky, Lexington.

Seler, Eduard. 1993. On the Origin of Some Forms of Quiche and Cakchiquel Myths. In *Collected Works in Mesoamerican Linguistics and Archaeology, Volume IV*, ed. J. Eric S. Thompson and Francis Richardson, 323–325. Labyrinthos, Culver City, California.

Seligson, Kenneth. 2016a. Lord of the Ring Structures: Burnt Lime Production and the Ancient Puuc Economy. Paper given at the 81st Annual Meeting, Society for American Archaeology, Orlando.

———. 2016b. The Prehispanic Maya Burnt Lime Industry: Socio-economy and Environmental Resource Management in the Terminal Classic Period Northern Lowlands (650–950 AD). Unpublished Ph.D. dissertation, University of Wisconsin–Madison.

Seligson, Kenneth E., Tomás Gallareta Negrón, Rossana May Ciau, and George J. Bey. 2017. Using Multiple Lines of Evidence to Identify Prehispanic Maya Burnt-Lime Kilns in the Northern Yucatán Peninsula. *Latin American Antiquity* 28:558–576.

Service, Ellman R. 1962. *Primate Social Organization: An Evolutionary Perspective*. Random House, New York.

Sewell, William H. 1940. *The Construction and Standardization of a Scale for the Measurement of the Socio-Economic Status of Oklahoma Farm Families.* Technical Bulletin, Vol. 9. Oklahoma Agricultural and Mechanical College, Agricultural Experimental Station, Stillwater, OK.

Shafer, Harry J., and Thomas R. Hester. 1983. Ancient Maya Chert Workshops in Northern Belize, Central America. *American Antiquity* 48:519–543.

———. 1986. Maya Stone-Tool Craft Specialization and Production at Colha, Belize: Reply to Mallory. *American Antiquity* 51:158–166.

———. 1991. Lithic Craft Specialization and Product Distribution at the Maya Site of Colha, Belize. *World Archaeology* 23(1):79–97.

Sharer, Robert. 2004. External Interaction at Early Classic Copan. In *Understanding Early Classic Copan*, 297–318. University of Pennsylvania Museum of Archaeology and Anthropology, Philadelphia.

Sharpe, Ashley E. 2011. Beyond Capitals and Kings: A Comparison of Animal Resource Use among Ten Late Classic Maya Sites. Unpublished master's thesis, Department of Anthropology, University of Florida, Gainesville.

Sharpe, Ashley E., and Kitty F. Emery. 2015. Differential Animal Use within Three Late Classic Maya States: Implications for Politics and Trade. *Journal of Anthropological Archaeology* 40:280–301.

Shaw, Justine M. 2001. Maya Sacbeob: Form and Function. *Ancient Mesoamerica* 12:261–272.

Shaw, Leslie C. 2012. The Elusive Maya Marketplace: An Archaeological Consideration of the Evidence. *Journal of Archaeological Research* 20:117–166.

Shaw, Leslie C., and Eleanor M. King. 2015. The Maya Marketplace at Maax Na, Belize. In *The Ancient Maya Marketplace: The Archaeology of Transient Space*, ed. Eleanor M. King, 168–194. University of Arizona Press, Tucson.

Sheets, Payson D. 1983. Guatemalan Obsidian: A Preliminary Study of Sources and Quirigua Artefacts. In *Quirigua Reports, Vol. II, Papers 6–15*, ed. Robert J. Sharer, 87–101. University Museum, University of Pennsylvania, Philadelphia.

———. 2000. Provisioning the Cerén Household: The Vertical Economy, Village Economy, and Household Economy in the Southeastern Maya Periphery. *Ancient Mesoamerica* 11:217–230.

———. 2006. *The Cerén Site: An Ancient Village Buried by Volcanic Ash in Central America.* 2nd ed. Thomson Wadsworth, Belmont, CA.

Sheets, Payson, editor. 2002. *Before the Volcano Erupted: The Ancient Cerén Village in Central America.* University of Texas Press, Austin.

Sheets, Payson, Christine Dixon, David Lentz, Rachel Egan, Alexandria Halmbacher, Venicia Slotten, Rocio Herrera, and Celine Lamb. 2015. The Sociopolitical Economy of an Ancient Maya Village: Ceren and Its Sacbe. *Latin American Antiquity* 26(3):341–361.

Sheets, Payson, David Lentz, Dolores Piperno, John Jones, Christine Dixon, George Maloof, and Angela Hood. 2012. Ancient Manioc Agriculture South of the Ceren Village, El Salvador. *Latin American Antiquity* 23:259–281.

Sherbondy, Jeanette E. 1987. The Incaic Organization of Terraced Irrigation in Cuzco, Peru. In *Pre-Hispanic Agricultural Fields in the Andean Region Part II*, ed. W. M. Denevan, Kent Mathewson, and Gregory Knapp, 365–371. Proceedings of the 45th International Congress of Americanists, BAR International Series 359(ii), BAR, Oxford.

Sherratt, Andrew. 1997. *Economy and Society in Prehistoric Europe: Changing Perspectives.* Edinburgh University Press, Edinburgh.

Shimada, Izumi. 2007. Introduction. In *Craft Production in Complex Societies: Multicraft and Producer Perspective*, ed. Izumi Shimada, 1–21. University of Utah Press, Salt Lake City.

Shook, Edwin M., and Tatiana Proskouriakoff. 1951. Yucatan. *Carnegie Institution of Washington, Yearbook* 50:236–40.

Shults, Sara C. 2012. Uncovering Ancient Maya Exchange Networks: Using the Distributional Approach to Interpret Obsidian Exchange at Actuncan, Belize. Unpublished MA thesis, Department of Anthropology, University of Alabama, Tuscaloosa.

Sidrys, Raymond M. 1976. Classic Maya Obsidian Trade. *American Antiquity* 41:449–464.

———. 1979. Supply and Demand among the Classic Maya. *Current Anthropology* 20(3):594–597.

Sierra Sosa, Thelma Noemí. 1999. Xcambó: Codiciado enclave económico del Clásico Maya. *Arqueología Mexicana* 7(37):40–47.

———. 2004a. La arqueología de Xcambó, Yucatán, centro administrativo salinero y puerto comercial de importancia regional durante el Clásico. Unpublished Ph.D. dissertation, Estudios Mesoamericanos, Programa en Estudios Mesoamericanos, Universidad Nacional Autónoma de México, Mexico City.

———. 2004b. Relaciones culturales y mercantiles entre el puerto de Xcambó de la costa norte de Yucatán y el litoral veracruzano-tabasqueño-campechano. *Estudios Mesoamericanos* (Universidad Nacional Autónoma de México) 6:13–19.

Simms, Stephanie Renee. 2014. Prehispanic Maya Foodways: Archaeological and Microbotanical Evidence from Escalera al Cielo, Yucatán, Mexico. Unpublished Ph.D. dissertation, Department of Archaeology, Boston University.

Simms, Stephanie R., Evan Parker, George J. Bey III, and Tomás Gallareta Negrón. 2012. Evidence from Escalera al Cielo: Abandonment of a Terminal Classic Puuc Maya Hill Complex in Yucatán, Mexico. *Journal of Field Archaeology* 37:270–288.

Skousen, Benjamin Jacob. 2009. Monkey Pots: Inferring Meaning through Time and Space from Function, Decoration, and Context. Unpublished MA thesis, Brigham Young University, Provo, UT.

Smailus, Ortwin. 1975. *El Maya-Chontal de Acalán: Análisis lingüístico de un documento de los años 1610–12.* 1st ed. UNAM, Coordinación de Humanidades, Mexico City.

Smith, A. Ledyard. 1950. *Uaxactun, Guatemala: Excavations of 1931–1937.* Publication No. 588. Carnegie Institution of Washington, Washington, DC.

Smith, Carol A. 1976a. Causes and Consequences of Central-Place Types in Western Guatemala. In *Regional Analysis, vol. 1, Economic Systems,* ed. Carol A. Smith, 255–300. 2 vols. Academic Press, New York.

———. 1976b. Exchange Systems and the Spatial Distribution of Elites: The Organization of Stratification in Agrarian Societies. In *Regional Analysis: vol. 2, Social Systems,* ed. Carol A. Smith, 309–374. 2 vols. Academic Press, New York.

Smith, James Gregory. 2000. *The Chichén Itzá-Ek Balam Transect Project: An Intersite Perspective on the Political Organization of the Ancient Maya.* Ph.D. dissertation, University of Pittsburgh. University Microfilms, Ann Arbor, MI.

Smith, Michael E. 1979. The Aztec Marketing System and Settlement Pattern in the Valley of Mexico: A Central Place Analysis. *American Antiquity* 44:110-125.

———. 1987. Household Possessions and Wealth in Agrarian States: Implications for Archaeology. *Journal of Anthropological Archaeology* 6(4):297–335.

———. 1999. On Hirth's "Distributional Approach." *Current Anthropology* 40(4):528–530.

———. 2004. The Archaeology of Ancient State Economies. *Annual Review of Anthropology* 33:73–102.

———. 2010. Regional and Local Market Systems in Aztec-Period Morelos. In *Archaeological Approaches to Market Exchange in Ancient Societies,* ed. Christopher P. Garraty and Barbara L. Stark, 161–182. University Press of Colorado, Boulder.

———. 2014. The Aztecs Paid Taxes, Not Tribute. *Mexicon* 36:19–22.

———. 2015. Quality of Life and Prosperity in Ancient Households and Communities. In *The*

Oxford Handbook of Historical Ecology and Applied Archaeology, ed. Christopher Isendahl and Daryl Stump, 486–505. Oxford University Press.

Smith, Michael E., and Frances F. Berdan. 2003. Spatial Structure of the Mesoamerican World System. In *The Postclassic Mesoamerican World*, ed. Michael E. Smith and Frances F. Berdan, 21–31. University of Utah Press, Salt Lake City.

Smith, Michael E., Timothy Dennehy, April Kamp-Whittaker, Emily Colon, and Rebecca Harkness. 2014. Quantitative Measures of Wealth Inequality in Ancient Central Mexican Communities. *Advances in Archaeological Practice* 2(4):311–323.

Smith, Michael E., and Cynthia Heath-Smith. 1994. Rural Economy in Late Postclassic Morelos. In *Economies and Polities in the Aztec Realm*, ed. Mary G. Hodge and Michael E. Smith, 349–376. Institute for Mesoamerican Studies, University at Albany SUNY, Albany, NY.

Smith, Michael E., and T. Jeffrey Price. 1994. Aztec-Period Agricultural Terraces in Morelos, Mexico: Evidence for Household-Level Agricultural Intensification. *Journal of Field Archaeology* 21(2):169–179.

Smith, Michael E., Jennifer Wharton, and Jan M. Olson. 2003. Aztec Feasts, Rituals and Markets: Political Uses of Ceramic Vessels in a Commercial Economy. In *The Archaeology and Politics of Food and Feasting in Early States and Empires*, ed. Tamara Bray, 235–268. Kluwer Academic Publishers, New York.

Smith, Robert E., and James C. Gifford. 1966. *Maya Ceramic Varieties, Types, and Wares at Uaxactun: Supplement to Ceramic Sequence at Uaxactun, Guatemala*. Publication 28. Middle American Research Institute, Tulane University, New Orleans.

Smyth, Michael P. 1989. Domestic Storage Behavior in Mesoamerica: An Ethnoarchaeological Approach. In *Archaeological Method and Theory*, ed. Michael B. Schiffer, 89–138. Vol. 1. University of Arizona Press. Tucson.

———. 1991. *Modern Maya Storage Behavior: Ethnoarchaeological Case Examples from the Puuc Region of Yucatan*. University of Pittsburgh Memoirs in Latin American Archaeology No. 3. University of Pittsburgh, Pittsburgh.

Smyth, Michael P., Christopher D. Dore, and Nicholas P. Dunning. 1995. Interpreting Prehistoric Settlement Patterns: Lessons from the Maya Center of Sayil, Yucatan. *Journal of Field Archaeology* 22(3):321–347.

Sosa, Victoria, Salvador J. Flores, V. Rico-Gray, Rafael Lira, and J. J. Ortiz. 1985. *Lista florística y sinomimia maya*. Etnoflora Yucatanense, Vol. 1. Instituto Nacional de Investigaciones Sobre Recursos Bióticos, Xalapa, Veracruz, Mexico.

Soto-Mayor, Juan de Villagutierre. 1983. *History of the Conquest of the Province of the Itza*. English ed. Translated by R. D. Wood. Labyrinthos, Culver City, CA.

Speal, C. Scott. 2009. The Economic Geography of Chert Lithic Production in the Southern Maya Lowlands: A Comparative Examination of Early Stage Reduction Debris. *Latin American Antiquity* 20(1):91–119.

———. 2014. The Evolution of Ancient Maya Exchange Systems: An Etymological Study of Economic Vocabulary in the Mayan Language Family. *Ancient Mesoamerica* 25(1):69–113.

Spence, Michael W. 1981. Obsidian Production and the State of Teotihuacán. *American Antiquity* 46(4):769–788.

———. 1996. Commodity or Gift: Teotihuacan Obsidian in the Maya Region. *Latin American Antiquity* 7(1):21–39.

Spielmann, Katherine A. 1998. Ritual Influences on the Development of Rio Grande Glaze A Ceramics. In *Migration and Reorganization: The Pueblo IV Period in the American Southwest*, ed. Katherine A. Spielmann, 253–261. Anthropological Research Paper 51, Arizona State University, Tempe.

Šprajc, Ivan. 2008. *Reconocimiento arqueológico en el sureste del estado de Campeche, México:*

1996–2005. Monographs in America Archaeology 19, Paris. BAR International Series 1742, Archaeopress, Oxford.

———. 2012. El preclásico en el sureste del estado de Campeche, México. In *XXV Simposio de Investigaciones Arqueológicas en Guatemala, 2011*, ed. Bárbara Arroyo, Lorena Paiz, and Héctor Mejía, 850–65. Ministerio de Cultura y Deportes, Instituto de Antropología e Historia, Asociación Tikal, Guatemala City.

Šprajc, Ivan, Carlos Morales-Aguilar, and Richard D. Hansen. 2009. Early Maya Astronomy and Urban Planning at El Mirador, Peten, Guatemala. *Anthropological Notebooks* 15:3:79–101 (Slovene Anthropological Society, Slovenia, http://www.drustvo-antropologov.si/anthropological_notebooks_eng.html, http://www.drustvo-antropologov.si/AN/PDF/2009_3/Anthropological_Notebooks_XV_3_Sprajc.pdf, accessed September 1, 2018).

Spufford, Peter. 2002. *Power and Profit: The Merchant in Medieval Europe*. Thames and Hudson, New York.

Srithi, Kamonnate, Chusie Trisonthi, Prasit Wangpakapattanawong, Prachaya Srisanga, and Henrik Balslev. 2012. Plant Diversity in Hmong and Mien Homegardens in Northern Thailand. *Economic Botany* 66(2):192–206.

Staller, John E. 2010. *Maize Cobs and Culture: History of Zea mays L.* Springer, Berlin.

Standley, Paul Carpenter, and Samuel J. Record. 1936. *The Forests and Flora of British Honduras*. Field Museum of Natural History, Chicago.

Standley, Paul Carpenter, and Julian A. Steyermark. 1949. Flora of Guatemala. *Fieldiana: Botany* 24:6:1–440.

Stanish, Charles. 2017. *The Evolution of Human Co-operation: Ritual and Social Complexity in Stateless Societies*. Cambridge University Press, Cambridge.

Stanish, Charles, and Lawrence S. Coben. 2013. Barter Markets in the Pre-Hispanic Andes: Merchants, Markets, and Exchange in the Pre-Columbian World. In *Merchants, Markets, and Exchange in the Pre-Columbian World*, ed. Kenneth. G. Hirth and Joanne Pillsbury, 419–434. Dumbarton Oaks Research Library and Collections, Trustees for Harvard University, Washington, DC.

Stark, Barbara L. 1985. Archaeological Identifications of Pottery Production Locations: Ethnoarchaeological and Archaeological Data in Mesoamerica. In *Decoding Prehistoric Ceramics*, ed. Ben A. Nelson, 158–194. Southern Illinois Press, Carbondale.

———. 1997. Gulf Lowland Settlement in Perspective. In *Olmec to Aztec Settlement Patterns in the Ancient Gulf Lowlands*, ed. Barbara L. Stark and Philip J. Arnold III, 278–290. University of Arizona Press, Tucson.

———. 2007. Pottery Production and Distribution in the Gulf Lowlands of Mesoamerica. In *Pottery Economics in Mesoamerica*, ed. Christopher A. Pool and George J. Bey III, 147–183. University of Arizona Press, Tucson.

Stark, Barbara L., and Christopher P. Garraty. 2010. Detecting Marketplace Exchange in Archaeology: A Methodological Review. In *Archaeological Approaches to Market Exchange in Ancient Societies*, ed. Christopher P. Garraty and Barbara Stark, 33–58. University Press of Colorado, Boulder.

Stark, Barbara L., and Christopher P. Garraty, editors. 2010. *Archaeological Approaches to Market Exchange in Ancient Societies*. University Press of Colorado, Boulder.

Stark, Barbara, L. Heller, and M. Ohnersorgen. 1998. People with Cloth: Mesoamerican Economic Exchange from the Perspective of Cotton in South-Central Veracruz. *Latin American Antiquity* 9(1):7–36.

Steggerda, Morris. 1941. *Maya Indians of Yucatan*. Publication 531. Carnegie Institution, Washington, DC.

———. 1943. *Some Ethnological Data concerning One Hundred Yucatan Plants*. Bureau of American Ethnology, Bulletin 136. Anthropological Papers No. 29. Smithsonian Institution, Washington, DC.

Steinberg, Michael K. 1998. Neotropical Kitchen Gardens as a Potential Research Landscape for Conservation Biologists. *Conservation Biology* 12(5):1150–1152.

Steinkeller, Piotr. 1987. The Foresters of Umma: Toward a Definition of Ur III Labor. In *Labor in the Ancient Near East*, ed. Marvin Powell, 73–115. American Oriental Society, New Haven, CT.

———. 1996. The Organization of Crafts in Third Millennium Babylonia: The Case of Potters. *Altorientalische Forschungen* 23:232–253.

———. 2013. Trade Routes and Commercial Networks in the Persian Gulf during the Third Millennium BC. In *Collection of Papers Presented to the Third International Conference of the Persian Gulf*, ed. Scientific Board of the Conference, 413–431. University of Tehran, Tehran.

Stolle, Dietlind. 1998. Bowling Together, Bowling Alone: The Development of Generalized Trust in Voluntary Associations. *Political Psychology* 19(3):497–525.

Stone, Glenn Davis, M. Priscilla Johnson-Stone, and Robert McC Netting. 1984. Household Variability and Inequality in Kofyar Subsistence and Cash-Cropping Economies. *Journal of Anthropological Research* 40(1):90–108.

Stone, Glenn Davis, Robert McC Netting, and M. Priscilla Stone. 1990. Seasonality, Labor Scheduling, and Agricultural Intensification in the Nigerian Savanna. *American Anthropologist* 92(1):7–23.

Stone, M. Priscilla, Glenn Davis Stone, and Robert McC Netting. 1995. The Sexual Division of Labor in Kofyar Agriculture. *American Ethnologist* 22(1):165–186.

Storey, Glenn R. 2006. *Urbanism in the Preindustrial World: Cross-Cultural Approaches*. University of Arizona Press, Tucson.

Stuart, David. 1989. Hieroglyphs on Maya Vessels. In *The Maya Vase Book: A Corpus of Rollout Photographs of Maya Vases*, ed. J. Kerr, 149–160. Vol. 1. Kerr Associates, New York.

———. 1995. *A Study of Maya Inscriptions*. Ph.D. dissertation, Vanderbilt University, Nashville. University Microfilms, Ann Arbor, MI.

———. 2000. The Arrival of Strangers: Teotihuacan and Tollan in Classic Maya History. In *Mesoamerica's Classic Heritage: From Teotihuacan to the Aztecs*, ed. David Carrasco, Lindsay Jones, and Scott Sessions, 465–513. University Press of Colorado, Niwot.

———. 2003a. Longer Live the King: The Questionable Demise of K'inich K'an Joy Chitam of Palenque. *PARI Journal* 4(1):1–4.

———. 2003b. On the Paired Variants of Tz'ak. In Mesoweb: www.mesoweb.com/stuart/notes/tzak.pdf (accessed August 12, 2019).

———. 2005. *Sourceboook for the 29th Maya Hieroglyphic Forum, March 11–16, 2005*. Department of Art and Art History, University of Texas, Austin.

———. 2006. Jade and Chocolate: Bundles of Wealth in Classic Maya Economics and Ritual. In *Sacred Bundles: Ritual Acts of Wrapping and Binding in Mesoamerica*, ed. Julia Guernsey and F. Kent Reilly, 127–144. Ancient America Special Publication No. 1. Boundary End Archaeology Research Center, Barnardsville, NC.

———. 2011. Some Working Notes on the Text of Tikal Stela 31. Mesoweb: www.mesoweb.com/stuart/notes/Tikal.pdf (accessed August 12, 2019).

———. 2013. Report: Two Inscribed Bones from Yaxchilan. Maya Decipherment: https://decipherment.wordpress.com/2013/05/16/report-two-inscribed-bones-from-yaxchilan (accessed August 12, 2019).

Stuart, David, and Joanne Baron. 2013. Análisis preliminar de las inscripciones de la Escalinata Jeroglífica 2 de La Corona. In *Proyecto Regional Arqueológico La Corona No. 5: temporada 2012*, ed. Tomás Barrientos, Marcello A. Canuto, and Jocelyne Ponce, 187–220. Tulane University and Universidad del Valle, Guatemala, New Orleans and Guatemala City.

Stuart, David, and Ian Graham. 2003. *Corpus of Maya Hieroglyphic Inscriptions: Volume 9, Part 1: Piedras Negras*. Peabody Museum of Archaeology and Ethnology, Harvard University, Cambridge, MA.

Stuart, David, Stephen D. Houston, and John Robertson. 1999. Recovering the Past: Classic Maya Language and Classic Maya Gods. In *Notebook for the XXIIIrd Maya Hieroglyphic Forum at Texas, Part II*, 1–96. University of Texas Press, Austin.

Suchman, Mark C. 1995. Managing Legitimacy: Strategic and Institutional Approaches. *Academy of Management Review* 20(3):571–610.

Sullivan, Alan P. 2000. Effects of Small-Scale Prehistoric Runoff Agriculture on Soil Fertility: The Developing Picture from Upland Terraces in the American Southwest. *Geoarchaeology* 15(4):291–313.

Sullivan, Lauren A. 2002. Dynamics of Regional Integration in Northwestern Belize. In *Ancient Maya Political Economies*, ed. Marilyn A. Masson and David A. Freidel, 197–222. AltaMira Press, Walnut Creek, CA.

Suyuc Ley, Edgar. 2011. The Extraction of Obsidian at El Chayal, Guatemala. In *The Technology of Maya Civilization: Political Economy and Beyond in Lithic Studies*, ed. Zachary X. Hruby, Geoffrey E. Braswell, and Oswaldo Chinchilla Mazariegos, 130–139. Equinox, Sheffield, UK.

Sytch, Maxim, and Adam Tatarynowicz. 2014. Friends and Foes: The Dynamics of Dual Social Structures. *Academy of Management Journal* 57:585–613.

Sytch, Maxim, Adam Tatarynowicz, and Ranjay Gulati. 2012. Toward a Theory of Extended Contact: The Incentives and Opportunities for Bridging across Network Communities. *Organization Science* 23:1658–1681.

Taschek, Jennifer T., and Joseph W. Ball. 1992. Lord Smoke-Squirrel's Cacao Cup: The Archaeological Context and Socio-Historical Significance of the Buenavista's Jauncy Vase. In *The Maya Vase Book 3*, ed. Justin and Barbara Kerr, 490–498. Kerr Associates, New York.

Tatarynowicz, Adam, Maxim Sytch, and Ranjay Gulati. 2016. Environmental Demands and the Emergence of Social Structure: Technological Dynamism and Interorganizational Network Forms. *Administrative Science Quarterly* 61(1):52–86.

Tedlock, Dennis. 1996. *Popol Vuh: The Definitive Edition of the Mayan Book of the Dawn of Life and the Glories of Gods and Kings*. Rev. ed. Simon and Schuster, New York.

Teeter, Wendy G. 2001. Maya Diet in a Changing Urban Environment: Faunal Utilization at Caracol, Belize. Unpublished Ph.D. dissertation. Dept. of Anthropology, University of California, Los Angeles.

Teeter, Wendy G., and Arlen F. Chase. 2004. Adding Flesh to the Bones: Using Zooarchaeology Research to Answer the Big-Picture Questions. *Archaeofauna* 13:155–172.

Terán, Silvia, Christian H. Rasmussen, and Olivio May Cauich. 1998. *Las plantas de la milpa entre los mayas*. Fundación Tun Ben Kin, Yucatán, Mexico.

Thompson, Edward H. 1932. *People of the Serpent*. Houghton Mifflin, Boston (2nd ed. 1965).

Thompson, J. Eric S. 1936. An Eccentric Flint from Quintana Roo, Mexico. *Maya Research* 3:316–318.

———. 1962. Trade Relations between the Maya Highlands and Lowlands. *XXXV Congreso Internacional de Americanistas, Actas y Memorias* (Mexico City) 1:35(1):13–48.

Thompson, Kim M., Angela Hood, Dana Cavallaro, and David L. Lentz. 2015. Connecting Contemporary Ecology and Ethnobotany to Ancient Plant Use Practices of the Maya at Tikal. In *Tikal: Paleoecology of an Ancient Maya City*, ed. David L. Lentz, Nicholas P. Dunning, and Vernon L. Scarborough, 124–151. Cambridge University Press, Cambridge.

Tokovinine, Alexandre. 2004. Signification Domains and Expressions of Identity in Maya Writing. Paper presented at the 9th European Maya Conference "Maya Ethnicity: The Construction of Ethnic Identity from the Preclassic to Modern Times," Bonn.

———. 2006a. Reporte epigráfico de la temporada de 2005. In *Investigaciones arqueológicas en la región de Holmul, Petén, Guatemala: Informe preliminar de la temporada 2005*, ed. Francisco Estrada Belli, 347–365. http://www.bu.edu/holmul/reports/holmul05_informe_2.pdf (accessed August 12, 2019).

———. 2006b. Reporte preliminar del análisis epigráfico e iconográfico de algunas vasijas del Proyecto Atlas Arqueológico de Guatemala, Dolores, Petén. In *Reporte 20: Atlas arqueológico de Guatemala: Exploraciones arqueológicas en el sureste y centro-oeste de Petén*, ed. Juan Pedro Laporte and Héctor E. Mejía, 364–383. Dirección General del Patrimonio Cultural y Natural, Ministerio de Cultura y Deportes, Guatemala City.

———. 2007. Of Snake Kings and Cannibals: A Fresh Look at the Naranjo Hieroglyphic Stairway. *PARI Journal* 7(4):15–22.

———. 2016. "It Is His Image with Pulque": Drinks, Gifts, and Political Networking in Classic Maya Texts and Images. *Ancient Mesoamerica* 27(1):13–29.

Tokovinine, Alexandre, and Dmitri D. Beliaev. 2013. People of the Road: Traders and Travelers in Ancient Maya Words and Images. In *Merchants, Markets, and Exchange in the Pre-Columbian World*, ed. Kenneth G. Hirth and Joanne Pillsbury, 169–200. Dumbarton Oaks Research Library and Collection, Washington, DC.

Tokovinine, Alexandre, and Marc Zender. 2012. Lords of Windy Water: The Royal Court of Motul de San José in Classic Maya Inscriptions. In *Politics, History, and Economy at the Classic Maya Center of Motul de San José, Guatemala*, ed. Antonia Foias and Kitty Emery, 30–66. University Press of Florida, Gainesville.

Tonoike, Yukiko. 2001. The Volume of Vessels at Aguateca: Implications for Vessel Function and Household Composition. Unpublished MA thesis, Department of Anthropology, Yale University.

Torquebiau, Emmanuel. 1992. Are Tropical Agroforestry Home Gardens Sustainable? *Agriculture, Ecosystems & Environment* 41(2):189–207.

Torres, Carlos Rolando, and Juan Pedro Laporte. 1988. Reconocimiento en Suk Che', Dolores. In *Reporte 1: Atlas arqueológico de Guatemala*, 34–39. Instituto de Antropología e Historia, Guatemala City.

Torres, Paola, Arthur Demarest, Horacio Martínez Paiz, Francisco Saravia, Miryam Saravia, and Fidel Tuyuc. 2018. Geografía sagrada, monumentos e interacción política y económica en la red Transversal hacia El Caribe: Nuevos datos del epicentro de Sesakkar, Alta Verapaz. In *XXXI Simposio de Investigaciones Arqueológicas en Guatemala, 2017*, ed. Bárbara Arroyo, Luis Méndez Salinas, and Gloria Ajú Álvarez, 689–704. Ministerio de Cultura y Deportes de Guatemala, Guatemala City.

Torres, Paola, Arthur Demarest, Miryam Saravia, Francisco Saravia, and Carlos Fidel Tuyuc. 2017. Investigaciones de la temporada 2016 en Cancuen y la Transversal del Norte: Nuevas evidencias sobre el comercio clásico maya y el apogeo de las rutas de comercio de La Verapaz en el Clásico Tardío. In *XXIX Simposio de Investigaciones Arqueológicas en Guatemala 2016*, ed. Bárbara Arroyo, Luis Méndez Salinas, and Gloria Aju Álvarez, 959–968. Ministerio de Cultura y Deportes de Guatemala, Asociación Tikal, Guatemala City.

Torres, Paola, Melanie Forné, Carlos Fidel Tuyuc, Miryam Saravia, and Juan Francisco Saravia. 2017. Tipología cerámica de Cancuen: Evidencias de la relación con los vecinos cercanos y distantes. In XXXI *Simposio de Investigaciones Arqueológicas en Guatemala, 2016*, ed. Bárbara Arroyo, Luis Méndez Salinas. and Gloria Ajú Álvarez, 959–968. Ministerio de Cultura y Deportes de Guatemala, Guatemala City.

Tourtellot, Gair. 1988. *Excavations at Seibal: Peripheral Survey and Excavation, Settlement and Community Patterns*. Memoirs of the Peabody Museum. Harvard University, Cambridge.

———. 1993. A View of Ancient Maya Settlements in the Eighth Century. In *Lowland Maya*

Civilization in the Eighth Century A.D., ed. Jeremy A. Sabloff and J. S. Henderson, 219–241. Dumbarton Oaks, Washington, DC.

Tourtellot, Gair, and Jeremy A. Sabloff. 1972. Exchange System among the Ancient Maya. *American Antiquity* 37:126–133.

Tovalín Ahumada, Alejandro, José Adolfo Velásquez de León Collins, and Javier Montes de Paz. 2014. Tres tumbas en la Acrópolis de Bonampak, Chiapas, México. In *Prácticas funerarias y arquitectura en tiempo y espacio*, ed. Antonio Benavides Castillo and Ricardo Armijo Torres, 42–55. Universidad Autónoma de Campeche, Campeche, Mexico.

Tovilla, Alfonso. 2000. Of the Inspection I Made in My Province, and of the Differences and Climates That Were in It. In *Lost Shores, Forgotten Peoples: Spanish Explorations of the South East Maya Lowlands*, ed. and trans. Lawrence H. Feldman, 100–105. Duke University Press, Durham, NC.

Tozzer, Alfred M. 1907. *A Comparative Study of the Mayas and Lacandones.* Macmillan, London.

———, translator and annotator. 1941. *Landa's Relación de las Cosas de Yucatán.* Papers of the Peabody Museum of American Archaeology and Ethnology, Vol. 18. Harvard University, Cambridge, MA.

Trachman, Rissa M., and Gene L. Titmus. 2003. Pecked and Scored Initiations: Early Classic Core-Blade Production in the Central Maya Lowlands. In *Mesoamerican Lithic Technology, Experimentation and Interpretation*, ed. Kenneth G. Hirth, 108–119. University of Utah Press, Salt Lake City.

Traxler, Loa P., and Robert J. Sharer, editors. 2016. *The Origins of Maya States.* University of Pennsylvania Museum of Archaeology, Philadelphia.

Triadan, Daniela. 2000. Elite Household Subsistence at Aguateca, Guatemala. *Mayab* 13:46–56.

———. 2006. Five Fine Gray Pottery Bells from Aguateca, Guatemala. *Mexicon* 28(4):75–78.

———. 2007. Warriors, Nobles, Commoners and Beasts: Figurines from Elite Buildings at Aguateca, Guatemala. *Latin American Antiquity* 18:269–293.

———. 2014. Figurines. In *Life and Politics at the Royal Court of Aguateca: Artifacts, Analytical Data, and Synthesis*, ed. Takeshi Inomata and Daniela Triadan, 9–38. Monographs of the Aguateca Archaeological Project First Phase, Vol. 3, University of Utah Press, Salt Lake City.

Trinh, L. N., J. W. Watson, N. N. Hue, N. N. De, N. V. Minh, P. Chu, B. R. Sthapit, and P. B. Eyzaguirre. 2003. Agrobiodiversity Conservation and Development in Vietnamese Home Gardens. *Agriculture, Ecosystems & Environment* 97(1–3):317–344.

Tritt, Chad E. 1997. A Preliminary Study of Obsidian Production and Utilization at Two Classic Period Maya Sites in Central Western Belize, Central America. Unpublished MA thesis, Dept. of Anthropology, San Diego State University.

Tsukamoto, Kenichiro. 2014a. Multiple Identities on the Plazas: The Classic Maya Center of El Palmar, Mexico. In *Mesoamerican Plazas: Arenas of Community and Power*, ed. Kenichiro Tsukamoto and Takeshi Inomata, 50–67. University of Arizona Press, Tucson.

———. 2014b. Politics in Plazas: Classic Maya Ritual Performance at El Palmar, Campeche, Mexico. Unpublished Ph.D. dissertation, Dept. of Anthropology, University of Arizona, Tucson.

———. 2017. Reverential Abandonment: A Termination Ritual at the Ancient Maya Polity of El Palmar in Southern Mexico. *Antiquity* 91(360):1630–1646.

Tsukamoto, Kenichiro, and Octavio Esparza Olguín. 2015. Ajpach' Waal: The Hieroglyphic Stairway of the Guzmán Group of El Palmar, Campeche, Mexico. In *Maya Archaeology 3*, ed. Charles Golden, Stephen Houston, and Joel Skidmore, 30–55. Precolumbian Mesoweb Press, San Francisco.

Tsukamoto, Kenichiro, Javier López Camacho, Luz Evelia Campaña Valenzuela, Hirokazu Kotegawa, and Octavio Q. Esparza Olguín. 2015. Political Interactions among Social Actors: Spatial Organization at the Classic Maya Polity of El Palmar, Campeche, Mexico. *Latin American Antiquity* 26:200–220.

Tsukamoto, Kenichiro, Javier López Camacho, and Octavio Q. Esparza Olguín. 2010. El Palmar, Campeche. *Arqueología Mexicana* 101:72–77.

Turner, Billie Lee, II. 1983. *Once Beneath the Forest: Prehistoric Terracing in the Río Bec Region of the Maya Lowlands*. Dellplain Latin American Studies, No. 13. Westview Press, Boulder, CO.

Turner, Billie Lee, II, and William C. Johnson. 1979. A Maya Dam in the Copan Valley, Honduras. *American Antiquity* 44(2):299–305.

United States Department of Commerce. 1917. *Commerce Reports Nos. 76–152, Volume 2, April, May, and June*. Government Printing Office, Washington, DC.

Urban, Patricia, and Edward Schortman. 2004. Marching Out of Step: Early Classic Copan and Its Honduran Neighbors. In *Understanding Early Classic Copan*, 319–336. University of Pennsylvania Museum of Archaeology and Anthropology, Philadelphia.

———. 2012. *Archaeological Theory in Practice*. Left Coast Press, Walnut Creek, CA.

Urbana, Marco Antonio. 1998. Los sitios Maringa 2, La Vertiente y La Ponderosa en la margen oeste del río Chiquibul, municipio de Melchor de Mencos. En *Reporte 12: Atlas arqueológico de Guatemala*, 227–271. Dirección General de Patrimonio Cultural y Natural, Guatemala City.

Urton, Gary. 1998. From Knots to Narratives: Reconstructing the Art of Historical Record Keeping in the Andes from Spanish Transcriptions of the Inka Khipus. *Ethnohistory* 45(3):409–438.

———. 2002. An Overview of Spanish Colonial Commentary on Andean Knotted-String Records. In *Narrative Threads: Accounting and Recounting in Andean Khipu*, ed. Jeffrey Quilter and Gary Urton, 3–25. University of Texas Press, Austin.

———. 2003. *Signs of the Inka Khipu: Binary Coding in the Andean Knotted-String Records*. University of Texas Press, Austin.

Urton, Gary, and Carrie J. Brezine. 2005. Khipu Accounting in Ancient Peru. *Science* 309:1065–1067.

Uslaner, Eric M. 2000–2001. Producing and Consuming Trust. *Political Science Quarterly* 115(4):569–590.

Uzzi, Brian. 1996. The Sources and Consequences of Embeddedness for the Economic Performance of Organizations: The Networks Effect. *American Sociological Review* 61:674–98.

Vail, Gabrielle, and Anthony Aveni. 2004. Research Methodologies and New Approaches to Interpreting the Madrid Codex. In *The Madrid Codex: New Approaches to Understanding an Ancient Maya Manuscript*, ed. Gabrielle Vail and Anthony Aveni, 1–30. University Press of Colorado, Boulder.

Valdés, Juan Antonio, and Federico Fahsen. 1995. The Reigning Dynasty of Uaxactun during the Early Classic: The Rulers and the Ruled. *Ancient Mesoamerica* 6(2):197–219.

Valdés, Juan Antonio, and Lori E. Wright. 2004. The Early Classic and Its Antecedents at Kaminaljuyú: A Complex Society with Complex Problems. In *Understanding Early Classic Copan*, ed. Ellen E. Bell, Marcello A. Canuto, and Robert J. Sharer, 337–355. University of Pennsylvania Museum of Archaeology and Anthropology, Philadelphia.

Valeri, Valerio. 2014. Kingship (1980). In *Rituals and Annals: Between Anthropology and History*, ed. Rupert Stasch, 1–34. Hau Classics of Ethnographic Theory Series 2. Hau Society for Ethnographic Theory, Manchester, UK.

Van Akkeren, Ruud. 2012. *Xib'alb'a y el nacimiento del nuevo sol: Una visión posclásica del colapso maya*. Piedra Santa, Guatemala City.

Van De Mieroop, Marc. 2005. The Invention of Interest: Sumerian Loans. In *The Origins of Value: The Financial Innovations That Created Modern Capital Markets*, ed. W. N. Goetzmann and K. G. Rouwenhorst, 17–30. Oxford University Press, Oxford.

————. 2016. *A History of the Ancient Near East, ca. 3000–323 BC.* Blackwell, Malden, MA.

Vandenbosch, Jon C. 1999. Lithic Economy and Household Interdependence among the Late Classic Maya of Belize. Unpublished PhD dissertation, Dept. of Anthropology, University of Pittsburgh.

VandenBosch, Jon C., Lisa J. LeCount, and Jason Yaeger. 2010. Integration and Interdependence: The Domestic Chipped Stone Economy of the Xunantunich Polity. In *Classic Maya Provincial Polities: Xunantunich and Its Hinterlands,* ed. Lisa J. LeCount and Jason Yaeger, 272–294. University of Arizona Press, Tucson.

van der Veen, Marijke. 2005. Gardens and Fields: the Intensity and Scale of Food Production. *World Archaeology* 37(2):157–163.

VanDerwarker, Amber M. 2006. *Farming, Hunting, and Fishing in the Olmec World.* University of Texas Press, Austin.

Varela Torrecilla, Carmen, and Geoffrey E. Braswell. 2003. Teotihuacan and Oxkintok: New Perspectives from Yucatán. In *The Maya and Teotihuacan: Reinterpreting Early Classic Interaction,* ed. Geoffrey E. Braswell, 249–271. University of Texas Press, Austin.

Vargas de la Peña, Leticia, and Thelma Sierra Sosa. 1991. Informe de actividades del "rescate" arqueológico de Xoclán, Mérida. Centro INAH–Yucatán, Mérida, Mexico.

Vargas Pacheco, Ernesto. 2010. La legitimación de la realeza entre los mayas del Preclásico tardío: Los mascarones de El Tigre, Campeche. *Estudios de Cultura Maya* 36:11–35.

Vargas Pacheco, Ernesto, and Lorenzo Ochoa. 1982. Navegantes, viajeros y mercaderes: Notas para el estudio de la historia de las rutas fluviales y terrestres entre la costa de Tabasco-Campeche y tierra adentro. *Estudios de Cultura Maya* 14:59–118.

Vázquez-Yanes, C., A. I. Batis Muñoz, M. I. Alcocer Silva, M. Gual Díaz, and C. Sánchez Dirzo. 1999. *Árboles y brbustos potencialmente valiosos para la restauración ecológica y la reforestación.* Reporte técnico del proyecto J084. CONABIO—Instituto de Ecología, Universidad Nacional Autónoma de México, Mexico City.

Veenhof, K. 1997. "Modern Features" in Old Assyrian Trade. *Journal of the Economic and Social History of the Orient* 40:333–366.

————. 2008. The Old Assyrian Period. In *The Old Assyrian Period,* by K. R. Veenhof and J. Eidem. Orbis Biblicus et Orientalis 160.5. Academic Press, Vandenhoeck und Ruprecht, Göttingen.

Vega C., Juan Ramón. 1967. *Geografía novísima de Yucatán.* 12th ed. Librería Burrel, Mérida, Mexico.

Velásquez-Fergusson, María Laura. 2013. Juegos visuales o conceptuales: Las variantes de los conjuntos de patrón triádico en El Mirador. In *XXVI Simposio de Investigaciones Arqueológicas en Guatemala, 2012,* ed. Bárbara Arroyo and Luis Méndez Salinas, 951–960. Museo Nacional de Arqueología y Etnología, Ministerio de Cultura y Deportes, Instituto de Antropología e Historia, Asociación Tikal, Guatemala City.

Velásquez García, Erik. 2004. Los Escalones Jeroglíficos de Dzibanché. In *Los cautivos de Dzibanché,* ed. Enrique. Nalda, 79–103. Consejo Nacional para la Cultura y las Artes, Instituto Nacional de Antropología e Historia, Mexico City.

————. 2005. The Captives of Dzibanche. *PARI Journal* 6(2):1–4.

Victor, Bart, Meridith Blevins, Ann F. Green, Elisee Ndatimana, Lazaro González-Calvo, Edward F. Fischer, Alfredo E. Vergara, Sten H. Vermund, Omo Olupona, and Troy D. Moon. 2014. Multidimensional Poverty in Rural Mozambique: A New Metric for Evaluating Public Health Interventions. *Public Library of Science* (Florida) 9(9).

Victor, Bart, Edward F. Fischer, Bruce Cooil, Alfredo Vergara, Abraham Mukolo, and Meridith Blevins. 2013. Frustrated Freedom: The Effects of Agency and Wealth on Wellbeing in Rural Mozambique. *World Development* 47:30–41.

Victor, Bart, and Carroll Stephens. 1994. The Dark Side of New Organizational Forms: An Editorial Essay. *Organizational Science* 5(4):479–482.

Vidal-Lorenza, Cristina, Maria Luísa Vázquez-de-Ágredos-Pascual, and Gaspar Muñoz-Cosme. 2016. Storage Places in the Maya Area. In *Storage in Ancient Societies: Administration, Organization, and Control*, ed. Linda R. Manzanilla and Mitchell S. Rothman, 271–291. Routledge, New York.

Vogelmann, Eduardo Saldanha, Gabriel Oladele Awe, and Juliana Prevedello. 2016. Selection of Plant Species used in Wastewater Treatment. In *Wastewater Treatment and Reuse for Metropolitan Regions and Small Cities in Developing Countries*, 1–10. Cuvillier Verlag (December 2016): https://www.researchgate.net/publication/313874379_SELECTION_OF_PLANT_SPECIES_USED_IN_WASTEWATER_TREATMENT.

Vogl, C. R, B. Vogl-Lukasser, and J. Caballero. 2002. Homegardens of Maya Migrants in the District of Palenque (Chiapas/Mexico): Implications for Sustainable Rural Development. In *Ethnobiology and Biocultural Diversity*, ed. J. R. Stepp, F. S. Wyndham, and R. K. Zarger, 631–647. University of Georgia Press, Athens.

Vogt, Evon Z. 1969. *Zinacantan: A Maya Community in the Highlands of Chiapas*. Belknap Press of Harvard University Press, Cambridge, MA.

Volta, Beniamino, and Joel D. Gunn. 2012. Análisis de costo mínimo de posibles rutas de intercambio transpeninsulares en el Petén campechano. Paper presented at the 54th International Congress of Americanists, Vienna.

Von Nagy, Christopher. 2003. Of Meandering Rivers and Shifting Towns: Landscape Evolution and Community within the Grijalva Delta. Unpublished Ph.D. dissertation, Tulane University, New Orleans.

Von Reden, Sitta. 2010. *Money in Classical Antiquity*. Cambridge University Press, Cambridge.

Wahl, David B. 2005. Climate Change and Human Impacts In the Southern Maya Lowlands: A Paleoecological Perspective from the Northern Peten, Guatemala. Unpublished Ph.D. dissertation, Department of Geography, University of California, Berkeley.

Wahl, David B., Roger Byrne, Thomas Schreiner, and Richard Hansen. 2006. Holocene Vegetation Change in the Northern Peten and Its Implications for Maya Prehistory. *Quaternary Research* (University of Washington) 65:380–389.

———. 2007. Palaeolimnological Evidence of Late-Holocene Settlement and Abandonment in the Mirador Basin, Peten, Guatemala. *Holocene* 17(6):813–820.

Wahl, David B., and Thomas Schreiner. 2004. La secuencia paleo-ambiental de la Cuenca Mirador. In *Abstractos del XVIII Simposio de Investigaciones Arqueológicas en Guatemala*, 61. Ministerio de Cultura y Deportes, Dirección General del Patrimonio Cultural y Natural, Instituto de Antropología e Historia, Museo Nacional de Arqueología y Etnología, Asociación Tikal, Guatemala City.

Wahl, David, Thomas Schreiner, and Roger Byrne. 2000. A Stratigraphic Record of Environmental Change from a Maya Reservoir in the Northern Peten, Guatemala. *Program Abstracts from Archaeometry: 32nd International Symposium* (May 15–19, 2000), 64. Conaculta-INAH, Universidad Nacional Autónoma de México, Mexico City.

———. 2001. La secuencia ecológica de la Cuenca Mirador: La evidencia de polen. In *Abstractos del XV Simposio de Investigaciones Arqueológicas en Guatemala*, 28. Ministerio de Cultura y Deportes, Dirección General del Patrimonio Cultural y Natural, Instituto de Antropología e Historia, Museo Nacional de Arqueología y Etnología, Guatemala City.

———. 2005. La secuencia paleo-ambiental de la Cuenca Mirador en Peten. In *XVIII Simposio de Investigaciones Arqueológicas en Guatemala, 2004*, ed. Juan Pedro Laporte, Bárbara Arroyo, and Héctor E. Mejía, 53–58. Ministerio de Cultura y Deportes, Instituto de Antropología e Historia, Asociación Tikal, FAMSI, Guatemala City.

Wahl, David, Thomas Schreiner, Roger Byrne, and Richard Hansen. 2007. A Paleoecological Record from a Maya Reservoir in the North Peten. *Latin American Antiquity* 18:212–222.

Walker, Debra S., editor. 2016. *Perspectives on the Ancient Maya of Chetumal Bay.* University Press of Florida, Gainesville.

Warburton, David. 1998. Economic Thinking in Egyptology. *Studien zur altägyptischen Kultur* 26: 143–170.

———. 2000. State and Economy in Ancient Egypt. In *World System History: The Social Science of Long-Term Change*, ed. R. A. Denmark, 169–184. Routledge, London.

Watanabe, John M. 2007. Ritual Economy and the Negotiation of Autarky and Interdependence in a Ritual Mode of Production. In *Mesoamerican Ritual Economy: Archaeological and Ethnological Perspectives*, ed. E. Christian Wells and Karla L. Davis-Salazar, 301–322. University Press of Colorado, Boulder.

Watts, Joshua, and Alanna Ossa. 2016. Exchange Network Topologies and Agent-Based Modeling: Economies of the Sedentary-Period Hohokam. *American Antiquity* 81:623–644.

Weber, Max. 1958. *The City* (1921). Translated by Don Martindale and Gertrud Neuwirth. Free Press, Glencoe, NY.

Webster, David. 1985. Surplus, Labor, and Stress in Late Classic Maya Society. *Journal of Anthropological Research* 41(4):375–399.

Webster, David L., Tim Murtha, Kirk D. Straight, Jay Silverstein, Horacio Martínez, Richard Terry, and Richard Burnett. 2007. The Great Tikal Earthwork Revisited. *Journal of Field Archaeology* 32(1):41–64.

Webster, David, and William T. Sanders. 2001. La antigua ciudad mesoamericana: Teoría y concepto. In *Reconstruyendo la ciudad maya: El urbanismo en las sociedades antiguas*, ed. M. Josefa Iglesias Ponce de León and M. Carmen Martínez Martínez, 34–64. Publication 6. Sociedad de Estudios Mayas, Madrid.

Weddepohl, Claus. 1990. Overlapping Generations Models: An Introduction. *Advanced Lectures in Quantitative Economics* (1990):249–313.

Weiner, Annette B. 1985. Inalienable Wealth. *American Ethnologist* 12:210–227.

———. 1992. *Inalienable Possessions: The Paradox of Keeping-While-Giving.* University of California Press, Berkeley.

Weiss-Krejci, Estella. 2006. Identifying Ethnic Affiliation in the Maya Mortuary Record. In *Maya Ethnicity: The Construction of Ethnic Identity from the Preclassic to Modern Times: Proceedings of the 9th European Maya Conference, Bonn, December 2004*, ed. F. Sachse, 47–60. Verlag Anton Saurwein, Markt Schwaben, Germany.

Wells, E. Christian. 2006. Recent Trends in Theorizing Prehispanic Mesoamerican Economies. *Journal of Archaeological Research* 14:265–312.

Wells, E. Christian, and Karla L. Davis-Salazar. 2007. *Mesoamerican Ritual Economy: Archaeological and Ethnological Perspectives.* University Press of Colorado, Boulder.

Wells, E. Christian, and Patricia A. McAnany, editors. 2008. *Dimensions of Ritual Economy.* Research in Economic Anthropology, Vol. 27. Emerald Press, Bingley, UK.

Wells, E. Christian, Richard E. Terry, Jacob Parnell, Perry J. Hardin, Mark W. Jackson, and Steven D. Houston. 2000. Chemical Analyses of Ancient Anthrosols in Residential Areas at Piedras Negras, Guatemala. *Journal of Archaeological Science* 27(5):449–462.

Welsh, Bruce M. 1988. *An Analysis of Classic Lowland Maya Burials.* BAR International Series No. 409, British Archaeological Reports, London.

West, Georgia. 2002. Ceramic Exchange in the Late Classic and Postclassic Maya Lowlands: A Diachronic Approach. In *Ancient Maya Political Economies*, ed. Marilyn A. Masson and David A. Freidel, 140–196. Altamira Press, Walnut Creek, CA.

Wheat, Joe Ben, James C. Gifford, and William W. Wasley. 1958. Ceramic Variety, Type Cluster, and Ceramic System in Southwestern Pottery Analysis. *American Antiquity* 24(1):34–47.

Wheatley, Paul. 1971. *The Pivot of the Four Quarters: A Preliminary Enquiry into the Origins and Character of the Ancient Chinese City.* Aldine, Chicago.

White, Devin A., and Sarah L. Surface-Evans, editors. 2012. *Least Cost Analysis of Social Landscapes: Archaeological Case Studies.* University of Utah Press, Salt Lake City.

Whittaker, John C., Kathryn A. Kamp, Anabel Ford, Rafael Guerra, Peter Brands, Jose Guerra, Kim McLean, Alex Woods, Melissa Badillo, Jennifer Thornton, and Zerifeh Eiley. 2009. Lithic Industry in a Maya Center: An Axe Workshop at El Pilar, Belize. *Latin American Antiquity* 20(1):134–156.

Whittington, Kjersten, Jason Owen-Smith, and Walter W. Powell. 2009. Networks, Propinquity, and Innovation in Knowledge-Intensive Industries. *Administrative Science Quarterly* 54(1):90–122.

Wiersum, K. F. 2006. Diversity and Change in Homegarden Cultivation in Indonesia. In *Tropical Homegardens: A Time-Tested Example of Sustainable Agroforestry*, ed. B. M. Kumar and P.K.R. Nair, 13–24. Springer, New York.

Wilk, Richard R. 1983. Little House in the Jungle: The Cause of Variation in House Size among Modern Maya. *Journal of Anthropological Archaeology* 2:99–116.

———. 1988. Maya Household Organization: Evidence and Analogies. In *Household and Community in the Mesoamerican Past*, ed. Richard R. Wilk and Wendy Ashmore, 135–151. University of New Mexico Press, Albuquerque.

———. 1989. *The Household Economy: Reconsidering the Domestic Mode of Production.* Westview Press, Boulder, CO.

———. 1991. *Household Ecology: Economic Change and Domestic Life among the Kekchi Maya in Belize.* Arizona Studies in Ecology. University of Arizona Press, Tucson.

Wilk, Richard R., and Wendy Ashmore, editors. 1988. *Household and Community in the Mesoamerican Past.* University of New Mexico Press, Albuquerque.

Wilken, Gene C. 1971. Food-Producing Systems Available to the Ancient Maya. *American Antiquity* 36:432–448.

———. 1987. *Good Farmers: Traditional Agricultural Resource Management in Mexico and Central America.* University of California Press, Berkeley.

Wilkinson, Toby C. 2014. *Tying the Threads of Eurasia: Trans-Regional Routes and Material Flows in Transcaucasia, Eastern Anatolia and Western Central Asia, c. 3000–1500 BC.* Sidestone Press, Leiden, the Netherlands.

Wilkinson, Toby C., Susan Sherratt, and John Bennet, editors. 2011. *Interweaving Worlds: Systemic Interactions in Eurasia, 7th to 1st Millennia BC.* Papers from a Conference in Memory of Professor Andrew Sherratt: What Would a Bronze Age World System Look Like? World Systems Approaches to Europe and Western Asia 4th to 1st Millennium BC. Oxbow Press, Oxford.

Willey, Gordon R. 1972. *The Artifact of Altar de Sacrificios.* Papers of the Peabody Museum of Archaeology and Ethnology, Harvard University, Vol. 64. Peabody Museum, Cambridge, MA.

———. 2004. Retrospective. In *Ancient Maya of the Belize Valley: Half a Century of Archaeological Research*, ed. James F. Garber, 15–24. University Press of Florida, Gainesville.

Willey, Gordon R., William R. Bullard Jr., John B. Glass, and James C. Gifford. 1965. *Prehistoric Maya Settlements in the Belize Valley.* Paper 54. Peabody Museum, Harvard University, Cambridge, MA.

Willey, Gordon R., T. Patrick Culbert, and Richard E. W. Adams. 1967. Maya Lowland Ceramics: Report from the 1965 Guatemala City Conference. *American Antiquity* 32(3):289–315.

Williams, Louis O. 1981. The Useful Plants of Central America. *Ceiba* 24(1–4):1–381.

Wills, David M., and John M. Burke. 2006. Chloroplast DNA Variation Confirms a Single Origin of Domesticated Sunflower (*Helianthus annuus* L.). *Journal of Heredity* 97(4):403–408.

Wisdom, Charles. 1950. *Materials on the Chorti Language*. University of Chicago Library, Chicago.

Wittfogel, Karl. 1957. *Oriental Despotism: A Comparative Study of Total Power*. Yale University Press, New Haven, CT.

Wolf, Eric R. 1982. *Europe and the People without History*. University of California Press, Berkeley.

Woodfill, Brent K. S. 2010. *Ritual and Trade in the Pasión-Verapaz Region, Guatemala*. Vanderbilt Institute of Mesoamerican Archaeology Monograph Series, Vol. 6. Vanderbilt University Press, Nashville, TN.

Woodfill, Brent K. S., and Chloé Andrieu. 2012. Tikal's Early Classic Domination of the Great Western Trade Route: Ceramics, Lithic, and Iconographic Evidence. *Ancient Mesoamerica* 23 (2):189–209.

Woodfill, Brent K. S., Brian Dervin Dillon, Marc Wolf, Carlos Avendaño, and Ronald Canter. 2015. Salinas de los Nueve Cerros, Guatemala: A Major Economic Center in the Southern Maya Lowlands. *Latin American Antiquity* 26(2):162–179.

Woodfill, Brent K. S., Alex Rivas, Judith Valle, and Carlos Efraín Tox Tiul. 2017. Investigaciones regionales, espeleología y trabajo comunitario de Salinas de los Nueve Cerros: La importancia de acercamientos comunitarios en la arqueología guatemalteca. In *XXX Simposio de Investigaciones Arqueológicas en Guatemala, 2016*, ed. Bárbara Arroyo, Luis Méndez Salinas, and Gloria Ajú Álvarez, 393–400. Museo Nacional de Arqueología y Etnología, Guatemala City.

Woods, James C., and Gene L. Titmus. 1996. Stone on Stone: Perspectives on Maya Civilization from Lithic Studies. In *Eighth Palenque Round Table, 1993*, ed. Merle Green Robertson, Martha J. Marci, and Jan McHargue, 479–489. Palenque Round Table Series, Vol. 10. Pre-Columbian Art Research Institute, San Francisco.

Wooten, Stephen. 2003. Women, Men, and Market Gardens: Gender Relations and Income Generation in Rural Mali. *Human Organization* 62(2):166–177.

Wootson, Cleve R. 2018. Maya Civilization Was Vaster Than Known: Thousands of Newly Discovered Structures Reveal. *Washington Post*, February 3.

Wright, Rita P. 2013. Commodities and Things: The Kulli in Context. In *Connections and Complexities: New Approaches to the Archaeology of South Asia*, ed. Shinu Anna Abraham, Praveena Gullapalli, Teresa P. Raczek, and Uzma Z. Rizvi, 47–62. Left Coast Press, Walnut Creek, CA.

Wu, Shubiao, Tao Lyu, Yaqian Zhao, Jan Vymazal, Carlos A. Arias, and Hans Brix. 2018. Rethinking Intensification of Constructed Wetlands as a Green Eco-Technology for Wastewater Treatment, *Environmental Science Technology* 52:1693-1694 (February 2018): https://www.researchgate.net/publication/322879260_Rethinking_Intensification_of_Constructed_Wetlands_as_a_Green_Eco-Technology_for_Wastewater_Treatment.

Wunsch, Cornelia. 2010. Neo-Babylonian Entrepreneurs. In *The Invention of Enterprise: Entrepreneurship from Ancient Mesopotamia to Modern Times*, ed. David Larsen, Joel Mokyr, and William J. Baumol, 40–61. Princeton University Press, Princeton, NJ.

Wurtzburg, Susan J. 1991. Sayil: Investigations of Urbanism and Economic Organization at an Ancient Maya City. Unpublished Ph.D. dissertation, Dept. of Anthropology, State University of New York.

———. 2015. Contemporary Maya Marketplaces: Gender, Social Change, and Implications for the Past. In *The Ancient Maya Marketplace: The Archaeology of Transient Space*, ed. Eleanor M. King, 251–271. University of Arizona Press, Tucson.

Wyatt, Andrew R. 2004. Operation 4. In The Chan Project: 2004 Season, ed. Cynthia Robin. Report Submitted to the Institute of Archaeology, Belmopan, Belize.

———. 2008a. Gardens on Hills: The Archaeology of Ancient Maya Terrace Agriculture at Chan, Belize. Unpublished Ph.D. dissertation, Dept. of Anthropology, University of Illinois at Chicago.

———. 2008b. Pine as an Element of Household Refuse in the Fertilization of Ancient Maya Agricultural Fields. *Journal of Ethnobiology* 28(2):244–258.

Ximénez, Francisco. 1666–1772. *Historia de la Provincia de San Vincente de Chiapas y Guatemala de la Orden de Predicadores*. Vol. 1. Sociedad de Geografía e Historia, Guatemala City (from the 1929–1931 edition).

Yaeger, Jason. 2000. Changing Patterns of Social Organization: The Late and Terminal Classic Communities at San Lorenzo, Cayo District, Belize. Unpublished Ph.D. dissertation, Dept. of Anthropology, University of Pennsylvania, Philadelphia.

———. 2010. Commodities, Brands, and Village Economies in the Classic Maya Lowlands. In *Cultures of Commodity Branding*, ed. Andrew Bevan and David Wengrow, 167–195. Left Coast Press, Walnut Creek, CA.

Yaeger, Jason, M. Kathryn Brown, and Bernadette Cap. 2016. Locating and Dating Sites Using LiDAR Survey in a Mosaic Vegetative Environment in Western Belize. *Advances In Archaeological Practice* 4:339–356.

Yaeger, Jason, M. Kathryn Brown, Christophe Helmke, Marc Zender, Bernadette Cap, Christie Kokel Rodríguez, and Sylvia Batty. 2015. Two Early Classic Elite Burials from Buenavista del Cayo, Belize. In *Research Reports in Belizean Archaeology: Papers of the 2014 Belize Archaeology Symposium*, ed. John Morris, Melissa Badillo, Sylvia Batty, and George Thompson, 181–192. NICH, Belize.

Yaeger, Jason, and Cynthia Robin. 2004. Heterogenous Hinterlands: The Social and Political Organization of Commoner Settlements near Xunantunich, Belize. In *Ancient Maya Commoners*, ed. Jon Lohse and Fred Valdez Jr., 148–173. University of Texas Press, Austin.

Yanagisako, Sylvia Junko. 1979. Family and Household: The Analysis of Domestic Groups. *Annual Review of Anthropology* 8:161–206.

Yang, Xiaokai, and Jeffery D. Sachs. 2003. *Economic Development and the Division of Labor*. Wiley-Blackwell, Hoboken, NJ.

Yoffee, Norman. 1991. Maya Elite Interaction: Through a Glass, Darkly. In *Classic Maya Political History*, ed. T. Patrick Culbert, 285–310. Cambridge University Press, Cambridge.

———. 2005. *Myths of the Archaic State: Evolution of the Earliest Cities, States, and Civilizations*. Cambridge University Press, Cambridge.

Yoffee, Norman, and Gojko Barjamovic. 2018. Old Assyrian Trade and Economic History. In *Hans Neumann Festschrift anlässlich seines 65. Geburtstages am 9. Mai 2018*, ed. S. Paulus, K. Kleber, and G. Neumann, 815–824. Grenzüberschreitungen: Studien zur Kulturgeschichte des Alten Orients, Münster, Germany.

Zaheer, Akbar, Bill McEvily, and Vincenzo Perrone. 1998. Does Trust Matter? Exploring the Effects of Interorganizational and Interpersonal Trust on Performance. *Organization Science* 9:141–159.

Zender, Marc. 2004. A Study of Classic Maya Priesthood. Unpublished Ph.D. dissertation, Dept. of Anthropology, University of Calgary, Calgary, 2004.

Zender, Marc, Ricardo Armijo Torres, and Miriam Judith Gallegos Gómora. 2001. Vida y obra de Ah Pakal Tahn, un sacerdote del siglo VIII en Comalcalco, Tabasco, México. *Los Investigadores de la Cultura Maya* 9(1):118–123.

Zetina Gutiérrez, María de Guadalupe. 2004. La cuestión demográfica en la Región Puuc: Perspectiva desde los sectores rurales del Distrito de Santa Elena durante el Clásico Terminal. *Las Investigadores de la Cultura Maya* 12(2):481–491.

Żrałka, Jarosław. 2014. *Pre-Columbian Maya Graffiti: Context, Dating and Function*. Wydawnictwo Alter, Krakow, Poland.

Żrałka, Jaroslaw, Wieslaw Koszkul, Bernard Hermes, Juan Luis Velásquez, Varinia Matute, and Bogumil Pilarski. 2017. From E-Group to Funerary Pyramid: Mortuary Cults and Ancestor Veneration in the Maya Centre of Nakum, Petén, Guatemala. *Cambridge Archaeological Journal* 27(2):1–26.

Zucker, Lynne G. 1986. Production of Trust: Institutional Sources of Economic Structure, 1840–1920. In *Research in Organizational Behavior*, ed. Barry M. Staw and Larry L. Cummings, 53–111. JAI Press, Greenwich, CT.

Contributors

Anthony P. Andrews, New College of Florida, Sarasota

Chloé Andrieu, CNRS Université Paris I, La Sorbonne, Archéologie des Amériques, Paris, France

Beatriz Balcárcel, Universidad de San Carlos, Guatemala City

Adolfo Iván Batún Alpuche, Universidad de Oriente, Valladolid, Yucatán, Mexico

George Bey, Millsaps College, Jackson, MI

Ronald L. Bishop, Smithsonian Institution, Washington, DC

Geoffrey E. Braswell, Department of Anthropology, University of California San Diego, CA

Marcello Canuto, Tulane University, New Orleans, LA

Bernadette Cap, Department of Anthropology, University of Texas, San Antonio

Arlen F. Chase, Department of Anthropology, Pomona College, Claremont, CA

Diane Z. Chase, Vice President for Academic Innovation, Student Success, and Strategic Initiatives, Claremont Graduate University, CA

Rubén Chuc Aguilar, Facultad de Ciencias Antropológicas, Universidad Autónoma de Yucatán, Mérida

Maia Dedrick, University of North Carolina, Chapel Hill

Pedro Delgado Kú, Centro INAH–Yucatán, Mérida, Mexico

Arthur A. Demarest, Department of Anthropology, Vanderbilt University, Nashville, TN

Keith Eppich, TJC (Texas Junior College), Tyler, TX

Bárbara Escamilla Ojeda, Centro INAH–Yucatán, Mérida, Mexico

Scott L. Fedick, University of California–Riverside, Riverside, CA

Luis Flores Cobá, Proyecto Mayapán, Telchaquillo, Mexico

Lynda Florey Folan, Universidad Autónoma de Campeche, Mexico

William J. Folan, Universidad Autónoma de Campeche, Mexico

David A. Freidel, Washington University, St. Louis, MO

Tomás Gallareta Negrón, Centro INAH–Yucatán, Mérida, Mexico

Charles Golden, Department of Anthropology, Brandeis University, Waltham, MA

Stanley P. Guenter, FARES Foundation/Mirador Basin Project, Salt Lake City, Utah

Joel D. Gunn, University of North Carolina, Greensboro

Richard D. Hansen, University of Utah FARES Foundation, Salt Lake City, Utah

Timothy S. Hare, Morehead State University, Morehead, KY

Enrique Hernández, Universidad de San Carlos, Guatemala

Rachel A. Horowitz, Appalachian State University, Boone, NC

Scott R. Hutson, Department of Anthropology, University of Kentucky, Lexington

Takeshi Inomata, Department of Anthropology, University of Arizona, Tucson

Eleanor M. King, Howard University, Washington, DC

Marilyn A. Masson, Department of Anthropology, University at Albany, SUNY, Albany, NY

Patricia A. McAnany, University of North Carolina, Chapel Hill

Carlos Morales-Aguilar, Université Paris 1, Panthéon Sorbonne, France

Carlos Peraza Lope, Centro INAH–Yucatán, Mérida, Mexico

Dorie Reents-Budet, Museum of Fine Arts, Boston

Prudence M. Rice, Department of Anthropology, Southern Illinois University, Carbondale

William Ringle, Davidson College, Davidson, NC

Fernando Robles Castellanos, Centro INAH–Yucatán, Mérida, Mexico

Alejandra Roche Recinos, Department of Anthropology, Brown University, Providence, RI

Bradley W. Russell, Hartgen and Associates, Renssalaer, NY

Andrew Scherer, Department of Anthropology, Brown University, Providence, RI

Whittaker Schroder, Department of Anthropology, University of Pennsylvania, Philadelphia

Payson Sheets, Department of Anthropology, University of Colorado, Boulder

Edgar Suyuc, FARES Foundation/Mirador Basin Project, Salt Lake City, Utah

Alexandre Tokovinine, Department of Anthropology, University of Alabama, Tuscaloosa

Paola Torres, Universidad de San Carlos de Guatemala, Guatemala City

Daniela Triadan, Department of Anthropology, University of Arizona, Tucson

Kenichiro Tsukamoto, Department of Anthropology, University of California, Riverside

Clive Vella, Department of Anthropology, Brown University, Providence, RI

Bart Victor, Owen Graduate School of Management, Vanderbilt University, Nashville, TN

Beniamino Volta, Department of Anthropology, University of California, San Diego

Brent K. S. Woodfill, Department of Sociology and Anthropology, Winthrop University, Rock Hill, SC

Andrew R. Wyatt, Department of Sociology, Middle Tennessee State University, Murfreesboro

Norman Yoffee, University of Michigan, Ann Arbor

Index

Page numbers followed by *f* and *t* refer to figures and tables.

Amaranth (*Amaranthus caudatus, A. dubius, A. hybridus, A. retroflexus, A. spinosus, A. viridis*), 232, 233, 234, 490

Amatenango ceramics, 155

Anacardium occidentale. See Cashew

Ancient Maya Civilization (Hammond), 451

Anderson, David, 376

Andrews, Anthony P., 9, 179, 371, 373, 374, 482

Andrieu, Chloé, 4, 9, 11, 360–61, 366

Angiosperm Phylogeny Group (APG), 230

Annona (*Annona sp.*), 202, 203t, 233, 491

Annona cherimola. See Cherimoya tree

Annona muricata. See Soursop tree

Aoyama, Kazuo, 300, 422

Appadurai, Arjun, 5, 31, 52

Architectural art, 334–35, 351

Architecture: *bajareque,* 245; distribution of benefits and, 39; elites and, 44, 46, 177; labor demands and, 218–19; marketplace exchange and, 35, 41, 58, 61; Preclassic period, 334; triadic-style, 334–35; wealth and, 71–72, 74. *See also* Monumental architecture

Arnaya Hernández, Armando, 318

Arrowroot (*Maranta arundinacea*), 232, 506

Arroyón, 332

Artifact distribution: Caracol (Belize), 4–5, 134–35, 137, 147; market economy and, 135, 153; Mayapán, 4, 8, 40–41, 96–97; systems for, 135; Tikal (Guatemala), 4, 40–42, 62, 64, 72

Atlas arqueológico del Estado de Yucatán, 374

Atzam Red bowls, 174, 176

Autarky, 152, 154f, 156, 167–69

Autonomy, 465, 467

Avocado (*Persea americana*), 202, 205t, 234, 504

Azcorra Ivory ceramics, 350

Azote Naranja ceramics, 161

Aztecs: cotton textile exchange and, 345, 347; dendritic system for, 318, 328; markets and, 16, 35, 473, 487; *pochteca,* 20; political and economic systems, 318, 328, 339; *xiuhmolpilli,* 287. *See also* Tenochtitlán

Bactris gasipaes. See Peach palm

Balakbal (Mexico), 332

Ball, Joseph W., 260, 394, 424

Barkbeaters, 273

Baron, Joanne, 487

Barter: ceramics and, 166, 168–69; defining, 156; exchange and, 152, 154f, 156–57; market transactions and, 18, 157, 485; reciprocity

and, 18, 157; small-scale collectives and, 417; social relations and, 157; terminology and, 32, 36–37

Basin of Mexico, 321f

Bat Head (Suutz) polity, 356, 359, 365, 367

Batún Alpuche, Adolfo Iván, 7, 219–20, 419, 467, 468

Bean, common (*Phaseolus vulgaris*), 205t, 232, 234, 503

Bean, lima (*Phaseolus lunatus*), 232, 233, 503

Beans, 224–25, 231–32

Beaudry-Corbett, Marilyn, 245

Becán, 336, 350

Beekeeping, 220

Beliaev, Dmitri, 452, 471

Belize: agriculture and, 168, 219; Callar Creek Quarry (CCQ), 124–25, 128; ceramic trade networks in, 348; chert in, 118, 120, 123–24, 128–29; economic activity in, 123; lithic production in, 120, 122, 125, 128, 130; nonlocal chert in, 129; obsidian trade and, 130; red-slipped pottery in, 135; settlement in, 123; Three Rivers area, 190; Tikal-Copán network and, 349; upper Belize River valley (UBRV), 123–26. *See also* Caracol (Belize); Colhá (Belize)

Belize Red footed dishes, 140

Belize River Valley, 191, 193

Berdan, Frances F., 473

Bernal Romero, Guillermo, 293

Bey, George J., 11, 107t, 112–13, 468

Bilbao, 348

Bishop, Ronald, 10, 137, 300, 334, 415, 467, 472, 480, 481, 483

Blackmore, Chelsea, 197

Black sapote tree (*Diospyros nigra*), 233, 500

Blanton, Richard, 341, 345, 473, 478, 486–87

Blom, Frans, 277

Bocas de Dzilám, 368, 370, 373–74, 380

Body painting, 250

Bolonchén District, 99–101

Bolonchén Regional Archaeological Project (BRAP), 107t

Bone tool production, 413–14

Boucher, Sylviane, 214, 364

Bounded networks, 318, 320f, 321–22

Bové, Frederick J., 346

Bozarth, Steven, 335

Braswell, Geoffrey E., 7, 27, 359, 363–64, 366

Bronson, Bennet, 227

Brosimum alicastrum. See Ramón tree

Caracol (Belize)—*continued*

148; Early Classic period, 146; economy of, 44, 134–35, 137, 144–48; food exchange and, 33, 144; imported goods in, 140, 145–47; institutional economy of, 138–40, 148; intervention in Tikal by, 143; items in markets, 136*f*; jadeite distribution in, 142*f*, 145–46; Late Classic period, 143–44; lithic debitage in, 422; lithic production in, 139, 145; map of, 133*f*; marine shell in, 145; marketplace exchange in, 138–40, 141*f*, 145–47, 389–90; metropolitan area of, 133; monkey motif on ceramics in, 445; monumental architecture and, 133; obsidian production in, 145; political economy of, 8, 138, 142–43, 148; pottery imports in, 146; prosperity in, 137, 143; shared identity in, 142; status-linked ceramics, 147; subsistence agriculture in, 138; symbolic egalitarianism in, 143; textile production in, 139; transportation routes in, 144

Caribbean coast, 357

Carica papaya. See Papaya

Carmean, Kelli, 100

Carmelita Incised ceramics, 438, 440, 443

Carpio, Edgar, 177

Carr, Christopher, 5

Carrillo y Ancona, Crescencio, 373, 381

Cashew tree (*Anacardium occidentale*), 232, 490

Cattail (*Typha domingensis*), 232, 515

Cauich, 371

Causeway systems: Aguateca (Petén, Guatemala), 297–98; Buenavista del Cayo (Belize), 393; Caracol (Belize), 44, 133, 133*f*, 139–40, 144–45, 147; Cozumel Island, 213; Elevated Interior Region (EIR), 354; El Mirador, 7, 323*f*, 327–28, 332; Great Western Trade Route, 172; Mirador-Calakmul Basin, 318, 322, 323*f*, 326–28, 331–32, 334–35, 339; Nakbé, 327–29, 332; Petén, 339; Tenochtitlán, 320; transportation and, 139–40, 144; Yucatán, 371–72

Ceballos, Teresa, 376

Ceibal, 336, 389–90, 437–38, 440, 446

Celestún, 368, 370–71, 374

Celestún River, 376

Cenotes, 212, 215. *See also* Sinkholes

Central Karstic Uplands, 7, 261, 353

Central Mexico: green obsidian and, 359, 362, 365, 367, 381; marketplace exchange in, 35, 419, 487; trade and, 18, 350, 372, 380

Ceramics: *ajaw* sign on, 441; autarky and, 156, 167–69; Calakmul-Tabasco lowland network

and, 349–51; chronologies of, 39, 42–43; commoners and, 165*f*; consumption of, 71–72; decorated types, 442*t*; distributional approach to, 153; elites and, 155, 165, 165*f*, 166–67, 298, 300–301; food serving vessels, 308–9, 309*f*–10*f*; food storage and, 302, 304, 304*f*, 305, 305*f*, 306; gift-giving and, 260–61, 263; glyphic texts and, 269, 269*f*, 270–71, 273; iconographic images, 271; *ik*ˣsign on, 440–41, 443–44, 450; innovation in, 449–50; Kaminaljuyú-Pacific coast network and, 347–48, 350–51; marketing activity and, 153, 164, 166, 168; marketplace exchange in, 42, 147, 150, 153, 155; microtraditions in, 153, 155; minimum number of vessels (MNV) and, 92–93, 93*t*, 96; modes of exchange, 150–51; monkey motif on, 439–40, 441*f*, 442–43, 445–46, 450; monochrome, 150, 153, 161, 163–64, 166–67, 299*f*; mortuary offerings and, 270; occupational longevity and, 92; Pacific coast-produced, 346; palace-school, 260, 270; pictorial record of cotton and, 342–43, 343*f*; producers of, 137; regionalization of, 169; rural households and, 88, 92–93, 93*t*, 95*t*, 96; salt molds, 174, 176, 179–81; social affiliations and, 481; southern lowland systems of, 446–49; status-linked, 147; Tikal-Copán network and, 348, 350–51; tobacco containers, 10, 270; trade networks and, 346–49, 349*f*, 350, 378, 380, 449; uniformity in, 332–33; workshops for, 88, 155; Xolalpan phase, 380. *See also* Fancy pottery

Ceramic systems, 446–49, 481–82

Ceramic types: Achotes Negro, 163, 165*f*, 166–67, 438, 440–41, 442*t*, 443, 446; Altar group, 415; Altar Naranjo, 153; Amatenango, 155; Atzam Red bowls, 174, 176; Azcorra Ivory, 350; Azote Naranja, 161; Cambio/Encanto, 298, 299*f*, 302, 305; Campo Composite, 443, 444*f*; Carmelita Incised, 438, 440, 443; Chablekal Gray, 299*f*, 300, 301*f*, 302, 437, 441–42, 442*t*, 443, 446, 448; Chablekal group, 414–15; Chanal, 155; Chaquiste Red, 309*f*–10*f*; Chicanel sphere, 332–33; Chimbote Cream, 350; Cotebal Red molds, 174, 181; Cubeta Incised, 440, 441*f*, 442; Danta group, 162*f*, 441; Fine Gray paste wares, 436; Fine Orange, 436, 438; Guzmán Group, 268, 268*f*, 269–71; Infierno Negro, 153, 161, 162*f*, 164, 165*f*, 167, 438, 441, 442*t*, 443, 446; Mama Red, 383; Maquina Café, 161, 164, 165*f*, 166; Matillas Fine Orange,

Clark, John E., 409–10, 424

Classic period: ceramics in, 49, 169; community networks in, 52–53; cotton textile exchange and, 340–41; economic data from, 38; economic system in, 117–18, 149, 168, 170–71, 260; exchange and, 149; feasting and, 345; food storage and, 407; lithic production in, 418–21; loans and, 277–78; marketplace exchange in, 6, 150, 260, 387; merchant agency in, 34; politics and economy in, 259–60, 273; *sacbe*s and, 38; salt production and distribution in, 181–82; shared identity in, 142; stoneworking in, 107; symbolic control of elites in, 177; tallies and, 276–78, 283, 285–94; textile trade and, 10; war captives in, 289; writing skill and, 268; Yucatán settlement in, 372, 375

Cnidoscolus aconitifolius. See Chaya

Cobá, 389

Codex Madrid, 217, 217*f*, 220

Coe, Michael D., 421

Coe, William, 60

Colhá (Belize): agricultural landscape of, 219; chert production in, 11, 129, 135, 331; collapse of, 336; Late Classic period, 23; lithic production in, 14, 23, 25; market model, 23, 25–27; trade and, 23, 24*f*, 25–26

Columbus, Christopher, 221

Comalcalco (Mexico), 283–85

Commerce, 152–53, 154*f*, 155, 157. *See also* Marketplace exchange

Community (*cah*), 212–14, 218, 221

Community networks, 38, 48, 51–53

CONANP (Comisión Nacional de Áreas Naturales Protegidas), 198, 200, 207

Connell, Samuel V., 267

Contact period: food plants and, 230–31, 234; land ownership in, 7, 211; loans and, 277; marketplace exchange in, 477, 486; material exchange and, 340, 478; socioeconomic impacts and, 225; stick tallies and, 290, 293

Contreras, Diego de, 221

Copal, 239

Copán: Ajpach' Waal and, 265; ceramic trade networks, 10, 348; construction in, 100; obsidian debitage in, 422; polychrome pottery vessels and, 279; trade networks and, 348–49

Cortés, Carlos, 376

Cortés de Brasdefer, Fernando, 263

Cosmology, 334

Cotebal Red salt molds, 174, 181

Cotton: growing regions for, 341, 345, 347–48;

350–51; production of, 351, 480; seed storage, 253

Cotton textiles: Campeche-Petén network and, 349–50; as commodities, 340–41, 344; economic value of, 342, 345, 351; exchange and, 10, 253, 340–42, 345–48, 351; feasting system and, 345; as gifts or tribute, 342–43, 343*f*, 344, 344*f*, 347*f*; pictorial record of, 342–43, 343*f*; as prestige good, 341–45; as tax payments, 350; Tikal-Copán network and, 349; as tribute commodity, 221, 340, 344–45; Yucatán production of, 220–21, 341, 345

Covarrubias, Miguel, 377

Cowgill, George, 31

Coyol (*Acrocomia aculeata*), 233, 493

Cozumel Island, 170, 213, 217

Crescentia cujete. See Calabash tree

Cubeta Incised ceramics, 440, 441*f*, 442

Cucurbita argyrosperma. See Cushaw squash; Squash

Cucurbita lundelliana. See Squash

Cucurbita moschata. See Moschata squash

Cucurbita pepo. See Pepo squash; Squash

Cuenca Mirador, 322. *See also* Mirador-Calakmul Basin

Culbert, T. Patrick, 60, 453, 472, 474

Cultural Resource Management (CRM), 368, 376

Cushaw squash (*Cucurbita argyrosperma*), 234, 499

Cycads (*Dioon mejiae* and *D. spinulosum*), 232, 516

Cyphers, Ann, 471

Dahlin, Bruce H., 3, 6, 471, 478

Dalton, George, 460

Danta ceramic group, 162*f*, 441

Deal, Michael, 153

Dedrick, Maia, 7, 220, 419

Demarest, Arthur A., 4–5, 9, 361, 366, 451, 452, 464, 466, 474, 475, 476, 485

Demarest, David, 451

Dendritic networks, 318, 320*f*, 322, 328, 337, 339

Díaz del Castillo, Bernal, 487

Dillon, Brian, 174, 179, 181

Dioon. *See* Cycads

Dioscorea. See Yams

Diospyros nigra. See Black sapote tree

Distribution: in archaeology, 38–43; blurred patterns in, 40–41; causeway systems in, 318; ceramic chronology in, 43; chert and,

El Juilín, 425, 426*t*

El Mirador: abandonment of, 336, 356; causeway systems in, 323*f,* 328, 332; centralized rulership in, 356; ceramic exchange and, 334; location of, 353; monumental architecture and, 332; monuments in, 338*f,* 339; terraced cultivation in, 7; trade routes and, 358, 365, 367; triadic-style architecture in, 335; walking and canoeing routes, 7; wealth in, 350. *See also* Mirador-Calakmul Basin

El Muc, 377, 381

El Palmar (Mexico): Guzmán Group, 261, 263, 264*f,* 266–75; interregional networks of dynasties in, 275, 301–2; K'aanul dynasty, 261, 265–66; *lakam* in, 259, 265–66, 269–71, 273–75; location of, 261, 262*f;* political dynamics in, 261–62; polychrome vessels, 263, 263*f,* 268; royal title at, 262

El Pedernal, 430

El Perú-Waka' (Guatemala): abandonment of, 159; bone tallies in, 285; Calakmul and, 158; ceramic distribution in, 150–51, 153, 161, 162*f,* 163–65, 165*f,* 166–71; ceramic trade networks, 350; Chakah Cluster, 161, 164–65, 165*f;* Chok Group, 164–65, 165*f,* 166–67; Classic period, 157–59, 170–71; Early Classic period, 158; economic system in, 170–71; household ceramics in, 150–51, 153; Late Classic period, 158–59, 163–65, 167–68; Late Preclassic period, 158; map of, 160*f;* marketplace exchange in, 8, 150; Mirador Complex, 158–59; monkey motif on ceramics in, 443; monumental architecture and, 158–59; Northwest Palace Group, 164, 165*f,* 166–67; Paal Group, 165, 165*f,* 166; residential groups in, 159; settlement patterns in, 159, 161; shaman-king rulers of, 158–59; Terminal Classic period, 159, 161, 163, 165–68, 170–71; Tolok Group, 165, 165*f,* 166–67; Tres Hermanas Cluster, 161, 165, 165*f,* 166–67

El Pesquero, 332, 336

El Pilar, 124, 399

El Porvenir, 415

El Remate, 374, 377

El Salvador, 239–42, 357. *See also* Cerén (El Salvador)

El Señor del Petén, 263, 270

El Tigre/Itzamkanak, 358, 361

Emal (Yucatán), 219–20

Emch, Michael, 212

Emery, Kitty F., 300, 311, 413

Enterolobium cyclocarpum. See Guanacaste

Environment: instability in, 241; seasonal flooding and, 120; supposed agricultural limitations, 224–25; tropical forest, 32–34; value of microenvironments in, 212, 216

Environmental diversity, 32–33

Epiclassic period, 434, 436, 440, 448–50

Eppich, Keith, 8, 161, 169, 474, 476, 480, 485

Escalera al Cielo, 106, 113

Escamilla, Bárbara, 90

Esparza Olguín, Octavio Q., 262, 301

Espinosa, Antonio, 371

Estado Mayor (Mexico), 371

Exchange: anthropology of, 14–15; autarky and, 152, 154*f,* 156; barter and, 152, 154*f,* 156–57; commerce and, 152–53, 154*f;* cotton textiles and, 340–42, 345; even distribution and, 57–58; gift-giving and, 134, 149, 168, 260–61, 263; long-distance trade and, 152; markets and, 18; multiple modes of, 150–52, 154*f,* 157; political control of, 365; prestige goods and, 341–42, 474; redistribution in, 152, 154*f,* 155–56; role of trust in, 50; as social interaction, 15; social relations and, 151–52; Venetian systems, 49. *See also* Marketplace exchange; Trade

Fancy pottery: Chunchucmil consumption of, 58, 59*t,* 65*t*–66*t,* 72, 74; as indicator of wealth, 72; producers of, 60; rural households and, 95*t*

Feasting, 132–34, 271, 274, 345

Fedick, Scott L., 235–36, 466–67

Feeley-Harnik, Gillian, 219

Fine Gray paste wares, 436

Fine Orange ceramics, 436, 438

Finley, M. I., 455–56

Firewood, 180–82

Flores, 440, 442, 443, 446

Foias, Antonia E., 300

Gallareta Cervera, Tomás, 112, 218

Gallareta Negrón, Tomás, 11, 99, 99*f,* 106, 110, 373, 468

Garraty, Christopher P., 156

General Utility Bifaces (GUBs), 126

Geografía de Yucatán (Lope), 371

Geografía novísima de Yucatán (Vega), 371

Germplasm Resources Information Network (GRIN), 230

Gift, The (Mauss), 405

Gift exchange: Classic Maya and, 149, 260; economic systems and, 134; polychrome pottery vessels and, 260–61, 263; prestige goods and, 168

Glascock, Michael D., 363, 366

Globalization, 133

Gluckman, Max, 98

Golden, Charles, 12, 407, 414, 460

Golitko, Mark, 363, 365

Góngora, Ángel, 376, 377

Góngora, Pedro, 104

González, Juan de Dios, 371

González Aparicio, Luis, 320

Graeber, David, 10, 485

Great Western Trade Route, 172, 360

Grube, Nikolai, 318, 365

Grupo Chulul, 105

Grupo Kuché, 105–6

Guanacaste (*Enterolobium cyclocarpum*), 232, 502

Guatemala: ceramic trade networks, 346–48; chert in, 120; cotton-growing regions in, 345; obsidian production in, 140; salt production in, 177, 179. *See also* El Perú-Waka' (Guatemala); Mirador-Calakmul Basin; Tikal (Guatemala)

Guava tree (*Psidium guajava*), 205t, 233, 508

Guenter, Stanley P., 318

Gulf Coast: Cancuén and, 49; Chablekal Gray vessels, 437; cotton-growing regions in, 347; Fine Orange ceramics and, 436; Matillas Fine Orange pottery, 93; Mixe-Zoquean words, 435; monochrome pottery from, 436–37; trade goods from, 364, 380; trade routes and, 121, 170, 350, 361, 372, 435; Zaragoza obsidian from, 90

Gunn, Joel, 7

Guzmán Group: barkbeaters, 273; ceramic assemblage at, 268, 268f, 269, 269f, 270–71; differential access to resources in, 275; elite competition in, 274; El Palmar (Mexico), 263, 265–75; hieroglyphic stairway of, 265–66, 268; lithic assemblages and, 271–72, 272t, 273–74; map of, 264f; occupation at, 266; structures at, 266–67, 274; termination ritual, 271, 273

Haley, Bryan, 394

Hammond, Norman, 451–52

Hansen, Richard D., 7, 356, 467, 479

Hare, Timothy S., 81

Haviland, William A., 41, 60, 72, 74

Helianthus annuus. *See* Sunflowers

Helms, Mary, 455

Hematite, 413

Henequen (*Agave fourcroydes*), 234, 384, 495

Hester, Thomas, 23, 25

Hill, Robert M., II, 300

Hirth, Kenneth, 5, 8, 14, 36, 38, 57, 75, 80, 135, 153, 155, 387, 471, 485–87

Hixson, David, 73

Hog plum. *See* Jocote/hog plum tree

Hohmann, Bobbi, 329

Holley, George, 415

Holmes, William H., 373

Holmul, 279, 424

Homegardens: archaeology of, 190–91; Caracol (Belize), 465; Chan (Belize), 12, 194, 196–97, 465; common plants in, 201–2, 202f, 203t–6t, 206; defining, 188; displays of wealth through, 207–8, 466; diversity in, 202, 207; economic value of, 190; El Mirador, 465; households and, 188–91, 196–97, 200–202, 207–9; indigenous food plants in, 237; intensive labor requirements of, 188–89, 191, 194; maize in, 189; Mensabak (Chiapas, Mexico), 197–202, 206–9, 466; political economy of, 207–8; soil management for, 190, 196; space requirements for, 190–91; supplementary crops in, 189–90; water management for, 194–95, 195f, 196; women and, 190

Honduras, 345, 365

Horowitz, Rachel, 11, 400

Households: adaptation and, 209; agricultural terracing and, 194; basic artifact types in, 62, 64; bone tool production in, 413–14; commoners and, 154f, 155–56, 165, 165f; craftspeople in, 73–74, 83, 101, 139; defining, 187; domestic ceramics in, 150, 154f, 155–57, 165, 165f; domestic economies in, 79, 81–82, 138–40, 146, 148, 401; elites and, 122, 154f, 155–56, 165, 165f, 413–14; fancy pottery in, 58; homegardens in, 188–91, 196–97, 200–202, 207–9; jade artifacts and, 129, 253; lithic artifacts in, 72, 249, 253; lithic production in, 124–25, 145; market-obtained goods, 239, 246, 248–50, 253–54; market-obtained goods in, 134, 387, 401, 407; obsidian consumption in, 57–58, 74–78; political economy of, 473; production and distribution of, 451; residential structures in, 187; self-provisioning and, 465; service relationships and, 238–40, 242–55; settlement agriculture in, 188, 191; stoneworking in, 103, 108; textile production in, 414; wealth disparities in, 62

Kofyar (Nigeria), 191

Kohl, Philip, 455–56

Komchén, 337, 378

Komkom, 391

Kopytoff, Igor, 31, 52

Kovacevich, Brigitte, 362

Kowalewski, Stephen A., 473, 476

Kuhn, Thomas, 3

Kunselman, Ray, 330

Kurjack, Edward B., 107t

Kurnick, Sarah, 219

Kusimba, C., 27

Labná, 100, 103, 106, 112

Labor: agriculture and, 196, 218, 238, 335, 466–67; authority and, 222–23; captive, 218–21; children and, 238; cloth-making and, 341, 344–45, 351; colonial demands, 210, 218–21; corvée and, 218; cotton production and, 220–21; demands of indigenous lords, 218; homegardens and, 188–89, 191, 194, 197; honey production and, 220; landscape and, 210, 213, 217–23; lithic production and, 400, 432; masonry construction and, 103, 106, 108, 111, 114, 468; monumental architecture and, 218–19, 332, 334; *mulmenyah* (work party) organization, 218; northern/southern governance and, 219; precolonial perceptions of, 210; prestige goods and, 341; salt production and, 219; shrine construction and, 218; surplus production demands, 219–21; tallies and, 281f, 282–83, 294, 467–68; transportation and, 454; tribute-related, 218, 221; value and, 210; voluntary, 218, 221, 468. *See also* Service relationships

Lacadena García-Gallo, Alfonso, 266

Lacandón Maya: culture of, 198; homegardens of, 200–202, 202f, 203t–6t, 206, 207–8; Mensabak (Chiapas, Mexico), 197–201, 206–8; socioeconomic impacts and, 198, 202, 207–8; tourism and, 198, 200

La Ceibita, 332

La Corona: ceramic trade networks, 350; chert and, 11, 121–22, 125, 127–29; debitage at, 126, 127t, 128, 422; Early Classic period, 121; lithic economies in, 126, 128, 130; nonlocal chert in, 128–31; obsidian trade and, 362; political importance of, 121; stone tool production in, 122, 126–27, 127t, 128; Terminal Classic period, 121; topography of, 120–21; trade and, 361, 363

La Florida, 331, 334, 350

Laguna de Términos, 358, 435

La Isla, 332

La Joyanca, 350

Lakam: ambassadorial duties, 10, 259, 265–66, 275; economic activities of, 259, 274–75; feasting and, 271, 274; hieroglyphic stairway inscriptions and, 265–66, 270–71, 273; political status of, 266, 273; tribute collection and, 274; writing skill and, 268–70, 273

Lake Macanché, 443, 444f

Lake Mensabak, 199

Lake Mensabak Homegarden Project (LM-HGP), 197, 200–201

Lake Petén Itzá, 435–38

Lake Tzibaná, 199

La Libertad Arch, 353

Lamanai, 422

La Mar, 412

Lamberg-Karlovsky, C. C., 460

La Muerta, 332

La Muñeca, 361

Land: authority and, 213, 217, 222–23; cah (community) held, 212–13, 222; colonial period, 210–12, 215, 217, 222; contact period concepts, 7, 211; cultural identity and, 222; labor demands and, 216–20, 223; precolonial perceptions of, 210; proprietary claims to, 212–17; tree crops and, 212; wall demarcations in, 212–13; water retention features and, 212, 216; Yucatec ownership of, 210–12

Landa, Diego de, 211, 289

La Selva, 415

Late Aak phase, 76

Late Classic period: Calakmul control of trade in, 366; ceramics and, 161, 162f, 163–65, 165f, 166–69, 436, 449; community networks in, 48; cross-peninsular trade in, 7; economic systems in, 134, 137; exchange systems in, 361–63; interdependent economies in, 147–48; lithic production in, 126t; marketplace exchange in, 4, 8, 139, 146–47; obsidian trade and, 359; political economy in, 142–43; population growth in, 383; population increase in, 98; pottery imports in, 146; Q'eq' Complex ceramics, 161; transformation in, 434; Yucatán ports in, 381f; Yucatán settlement in, 375, 377, 380, 382f

Late Postclassic period, 35, 219–20

Late Preclassic period: banded chert imports in, 331; ceramics in, 332–33, 333*f,* 334; cosmology in, 334; economic system in, 318, 320; intracoastal waterway in, 385; Mirador Basin occupation, 327, 335–36; monuments in, 336; prestige and power of rulers in, 335–36; sculpture in, 335; triadic-style architecture in, 334–35; use of lime in, 331; Yucatán ports in, 379*f;* Yucatán settlement in, 372, 377–78

La Venta, 378

Lawton, Crorey, 376

Lentz, David L., 180

Lesure, Richard, 473

Leventhal, Richard M., 222

Lévi-Strauss, Claude, 106

LiDAR imagery: agricultural terracing in, 407; *cal* (lime) production and, 101, 102*f;* in Campeche, 5; Classic period sacbes and, 38; community networks and, 53; economic structures and, 339; Mayan landscapes and, xv, xvi; settlement patterns and, 81–82

Lime, 331. *See also Cal* (lime) production

Limestone bifaces, 391, 397–400

Literacy: Classic period, 268, 278–79; craftspeople and, 279; elites and, 278; Lakam and, 268–70, 273; low levels of, 278–79; record-keeping and, 278–79; use of tallies and, 280

Lithic analysis, 418, 421

Lithic debitage: bifacial thinning flakes, 424, 426–30; Budsilhá (Chiapas), 411; Buenavista del Cayo (Belize), 394–97; in caches and burials, 77, 420–22, 423*t,* 424, 424*t,* 427–28, 428*t,* 432; Callar Creek Quarry (CCQ), 125, 126*t,* 128; Cancuén, 427, 429, 429*t,* 430, 432; chert microdebitage, 395–96; core reduction and, 397; economic control and, 421; El Achiote, 428–29, 429*t;* El Juilín, 425, 426*t;* Guzmán Group, 272; hard percussion techniques, 422; Huntichmul, 103; jade and, 360; La Corona, 126, 127*t,* 128; Mirador Basin, 331; Naachtún, 425–26, 426*t,* 427, 430; obsidian microdebitage, 412; Piedras Negras, 412–13; prismatic blade production, 425, 427, 429–30; production stages of, 424–30; reuse and relocation of, 420, 425; in ritual contexts, 420–21, 430–31; symbolic meaning of, 421; Tikal, 360

Lithic production: Buenavista del Cayo (Belize), 397–400; Caracol (Belize), 139; centralist/decentralist debate on, 418–19, 432; chaine opératoire in, 421–22; Colhá (Belize), 14, 23, 25; elite control of, 430; Guzmán Group,

271–72, 272*t,* 273; informal economy and, 23, 25; itinerant craftspeople and, 420; lack of Maya workshops for, 418–20; organization of, 418–19, 421–22, 424–27, 432–33; Piedras Negras, 409; ritualization and, 431; tributes and, 431–32. *See also* Stone tool-making

Loans, 277–78, 295, 485

Lope, Albino, 371

López Medel, Tomás, 226

Lycopersicum esculentum. See Tomato

Ma'ax Na, 12, 390

Maize (*Zea mays*): as commodity, 225, 231; as dominant food plant, 224–27, 231, 409; ethnographic emphasis on Maya subsistence through, 224–25, 236; food exchange and, 407–8; in homegardens, 189; marketplace exchange in, 407–8; overproduction and, 407; overrepresentation in archaeological record, 227–28, 235–36; photosynthetic pathways used by, 236; plant alternatives to, 227; preparation of, 243–45; processed for market, 407–8; Spanish uses of, 225; storage vessels for, 305–6, 307*f;* surplus production and, 416–17; as survival crop during revolt and warfare, 225–26; as tribute commodity, 225

Makal. *See* Malanga

Malanga or makal (*Xanthosoma violaceum* and *X. yucatanense*), 232, 234, 493

Maler, Teobert, 106, 109*f*

Mama Red ceramics, 383

Mamey tree (*Pouteria sapota*), 205*t,* 233, 498, 513

Management network models, 48

Maní, 345

Manihot esculenta. See Manioc/yuca

Manilkara zapota. See Chico sapote

Manioc/yuca (*Manihot esculenta*), 228, 232, 234, 501

Manos. *See* Metates and manos

Maquina Café ceramics, 161, 164, 165*f,* 166

Maranta arundinacea. See Arrowroot

Marcus, Joyce, 318

Marine shell: Caracol (Belize), 145; as currency, 329–30; Pacific tusk shell (Scaphopoda), 329; *Prunum apicinum* (Marginelladae), 329; rural households and, 88, 89*t,* 90–91, 95*t; Spondylus* shells, 330; *Strombus* shells, 329, 330*f*

Market economy: artifact distribution and, 135, 153; Cancuén and, 42, 45–46; defining, 16; distributional patterns in, 39; marketplace exchange and, 35; polythetic traits and, 32, 34, 36–37; relative scale of elements in, 32–38

Marketplace exchange: *ah k'iwik yah* and, 21; barter and, 18, 157; Buenavista del Cayo (Belize), 12, 391–94, 398–402; Calakmul, 22, 406; Cancuén, 42; Caracol (Belize), 138–40, 141*f*, 145–47, 389–90; Central Mexico and, 35, 487; ceramics and, 42, 147, 150, 155; Chunchucmil, 6, 12, 57–58, 60–61, 73, 76–78, 390; Classic Maya and, 35, 77–78, 150, 387–91, 399, 402; Colhá (Belize), 25; distributional approach to, 38–43; El Perú–Waka' (Guatemala), 8, 171; food production and, 407; household provisioning and, 134, 387, 401, 407; identification of, 35, 388–89; limestone bifaces and, 391, 397–400; market economy and, 35–37, 76; Mayapán, 2, 4; negotiations in, 38; obsidian in, 76, 249; peddlers in, 21–22; Piedras Negras, 12, 403–8, 408*f*, 414–17; plazas for, 389–90, 393–94; Preclassic period, 452; reciprocal exchange and, 22; regulation of, 22; resellers in, 25; service relationships and, 248; special exchange of the lords and, 22, 26; surplus production and, 238–39, 246; Tikal, 4–6, 8, 22, 41, 57, 60–61, 73–74, 77–78, 389; tributes and, 21; trust and, 405–6, 417; upper Belize River valley (UBRV), 123; urban exchange in, 35; women and, 21

Marketplaces: activities in, 389, 390*t*; central location of, 41, 73, 77; distributional approach to, 4, 40; elite administration of, 401–2, 477–78; goods exchanged in, 248, 253, 387–88, 398–99; identification of, 5, 12, 35, 389–90; infrastructure for, 389; lithic production in, 124, 396–98, 400; local, 41–42; negotiations in, 38; perishable goods in, 21, 389; permanent, 57, 61; plazas for, 389–90, 393–94; as ritual places, 452; socializing in, 6, 401; specialization of, 473

Markets: ancient societies and, 132–33; creative destruction in, 153; defining, 36; exchange and, 18; merchants and, 471–78; modeling, 14, 20; multiple aspects of, 134; pre-capitalist, 15–16; prehispanic, 16, 22, 27; scales of, 17–18; as social constructions, 462

Martin, Simon, 109, 263, 292, 318

Masonry stone houses: employment and, 111; façades in, 108, 109*f*; patronage and, 108–9, 111–12; preservation and, 115n7; Puuc region, 11, 100, 106–7, 107*t*, 108–9, 111–13; unfinished sides in, 108, 109*f*

Masson, Marilyn A., 4–6, 27, 41, 81, 416, 451, 452, 462, 471, 475

Mateyá: artifact distribution in, 94; chert/chalcedony in, 95*t*; marine shell in, 95*t*; obsidian density in, 89, 95*t*; pottery in, 92–93, 95*t*; Terminal period dwellings in, 84, 85*f*, 86–87, 89*t*

Mathews, Peter, 454

Matillas Fine Orange pottery, 80, 93, 97

Matrícula de tributos, 344

Matsumoto, Mallory, 412

Mauss, Marcel, 15, 405

May, Ciau, Rossana, 112

Maya area: ceramic exchange in, 150; ceramic systems in, 447; ceramic uniformity in, 333; chert trade in, 118, 331; cultural collapse in, 372; dispersed settlement patterns, 16–17; domestic economies in, 120, 138, 187; dwellings in, 79–81; gift exchange in, 260; introduction of plants to, 230, 234; lithic production in, 418, 432; long-distance trade in, 16, 20; maize consumption in, 409; marketplaces in, 20, 26; producer/consumer assemblages in, 97; record-keeping in, 276, 280, 294

Maya Biosphere Reserve (MBR), 120

Maya Ceramics Project, 346, 350

Maya city-states, 452–53, 459, 461–62

Maya collapse: abandonment of coastal settlements, 372; breakdown in trust and, 295; competition for control of trade routes and, 172–73; deforestation and, 337; disruptions to interconnected economies and, 147–48; trade and, 461–62

Maya economies: agricultural productivity and, 318; autonomy and, 465–70; boundedness and, 478–80; comparison with Mesopotamia, 452–53; complexity of, 484–87; conceptual approaches to, 31–35; cotton textile exchange and, 345; distributional approach to, 14; distribution of goods in, 3, 134–35, 137, 480–82; elite involvement in, 419, 461; exchange networks in, 9–10, 12, 149–50, 345, 481; household production and distribution in, 451; interdependence and, 13, 466–67, 470; labor specialization and, 467–71; market exchange in, 276–77, 403, 419; merchants in, 451–52, 471–78; Mirador-Calakmul Basin, 328–29; monies and, 484–85, 487; multiple aspects of, 134–35; *pars pro toto* logic in, 43–44; prestige goods and, 296, 486; regional, 478–80; sociopolitics and, 317, 339; strategic management studies and, 28–38, 47–54; subsistence, 130,

Maya economies—*continued*
228, 231, 233, 235; systems for, 318, 320, 320*f*;
trade routes and, 482–83; tributes and, 10,
351, 431–32

Maya lowlands: agricultural terracing in, 193;
architecture and, 334; ceramic system in, 169,
332–33, 434–37, 446–50; chert distribution in,
117–18, 120–24, 129*t*, 130–31; drought in, 337,
383; economic system in, 5, 43–44, 47, 117–18,
120; exchange networks in, 22, 35, 48–49,
51–54, 120–21, 348–50, 357, 364; homegardens
in, 189, 191; household economies and, 97;
indigenous food plants of, 224–36; lithic
economies in, 120, 130–31; lithic production
in, 419–22, 424–27; map of, 119*f*; market
economy and, 38, 117, 400, 402–3; northern/
southern governance, 219; obsidian trade
and, 118, 357, 359, 362–64, 398; political landscape of, 121, 361; population estimates for,
226–27; ritual settings in, 49; salt trade and,
9–10, 172; trade routes and, 170, 172–73, 350

Maya Mountains, 193

Mayapán: artifact distribution in, 4, 40–41,
88, 96–97; ceramic exchange in, 93, 479;
chert/chalcedony in, 91–92; craft economies
in, 80–83; domestic economies in, 79–82;
marketplace exchange in, 4, 6; monumental
architecture and, 469; obsidian in, 90; rural
households in, 79–83, 83*f*, 84–94, 96–97; social
benefits and, 41; urban households and, 80

Mazeau, Daniel, 73

McAnany, Patricia A., 7, 81, 341, 351, 419, 452,
471, 484

McCracken, John, 180

McKillop, Heather, 486

Medina, Edgar, 376

Medrano, 346

Meggers, Betty, 484

Mensabak (Chiapas, Mexico): homegardens
in, 197, 199f, 200–202, 202*f*, 203*t*–6*t*, 206,
207–9; households in, 209; Lacandón Maya
in, 197–202, 206–8; location of, 198, 199*f*;
occupation at, 200

Merchants: agency in food exchange, 32–34;
elite portrayal of, 475; enhanced role of, 34;
markets and, 471–78; Maya economies and,
451–52; as sociopolitical entity, 451–52. *See
also* Traders

Mérida, 373, 376

Merk, Stephan, 112

Mesoamerican societies: concept of time in,
287; cotton-growing regions, 345; economic
models for, 317–18; households in, 187–88;
settlement agriculture in, 188, 191; sociopolitical structure of, 317; tallies and, 279–80

Mesopotamia: elites and, 461; household economy of, 453; markets and, 460; merchants
and, 452; Old Assyrian trade in, 452, 456–59;
political systems in, 459, 462; royal inscriptions in, 454; trade and, 451, 453, 460

Metates and manos: Aguateca (Petén, Guatemala), 303*f*, 306–7, 308*f*; Caracol (Belize) resources for, 144–45; Chunchucmil, 65*t*; cotton
seed grinding and, 253; food processing and,
306; Guzmán Group, 272*t*; imports to Mirador Basin, 331; overhang, 177–78, 178*f*; salt
production and, 177–78; service households
and, 243–45, 250; Tikal (Guatemala), 62, 72

Microtraditions, 153, 155

Middle Preclassic period: architectural art and,
334; causeway systems in, 332; cosmology in,
334; economic system in, 318, 320; hierarchical
societies in, 356; imported goods in, 329–31;
long-distance trade in, 378; marine shell in,
329–30; monumental architecture and, 331–32;
monuments in, 336; Xcambó occupation in,
375; Yucatán settlement in, 375–78

Migration: ceramic systems and, 481–82; to
Cerén, 241, 254; to Chichén Itzá, 435; environmental risk and, 9; Epiclassic period and, 434,
449; to Petén Lakes region, 435, 448; rural to
urban in Yucatán, 378; travel routes and, 482

Mijangos, Blanca, 177

Miksicek, Charles H., 306

Milpa agriculture: alternative cropping systems,
227; distance from households, 189; misconceptions about, 224–27; reevaluation as
high-performance system, 236–37; Spanish
colonial administrator forced emphasis on,
225–26

Mina de Oro, 376–77

Mirador Basin Project, 331

Mirador-Calakmul Basin: agricultural systems
in, 326–27, 335; architectural development of,
327; *bajo* systems in, 322, 324–25, 337; causeway systems in, 318, 323*f*, 327–28, 332, 339;
central authority and, 332, 335–36; ceramic
exchange in, 334, 350; ceramic uniformity in,
332–33; chert production in, 331; *civales*, 325–
26, 326*f*, 327; collapse of, 336–37; demographics of, 335–37; dendritic system for, 7, 318, 320,
328, 337, 339; economic and sociopolitical

structures of, 339; geographic setting of, 322, 324–25; imported goods in, 329–31; LiDAR imagery of, 318, 324, 327; lime production in, 331; map of, 319f; Middle Preclassic period, 325, 329–32; monkey motif on ceramics in, 440, 443, 446; monumental architecture and, 322, 324, 328, 331–32, 334; obsidian imports to, 330–31; Preclassic occupation, 318, 320, 324–25, 327–37; religious ideologies and, 334; shell repertoire of, 329–30; sociopolitical complexity of, 328; stratified society in, 335; triadic-style architecture in, 334–35. *See also* El Mirador

Miramar, 376

Missouri Botanical Garden, 230

Moholy-Nagy, Hattula, 41–42, 77, 420, 422

Molcajetes (pottery grater bowls), 437, 443, 446

Monies, 277, 484–85, 487

Monkey motif: death symbolism and, 445–46; El Perú–Waka' ceramics and, 443; Jato Black-on-Gray ware, 439, 439f, 440, 442–43, 445–46, 450; Late Classic period, 445; Mirador Basin ceramics and, 440, 443, 446; in mortuary contexts, 443, 445–46, 450; Petén Lakes region ceramics and, 448; Piedras Negras ceramics and, 440

Monumental architecture: Caracol (Belize), 133; Classic period, 351; community investment in, 218–19; El Palmar (Mexico), 262; El Perú–Waka' (Guatemala), 158–59; labor networks and, 218; Late Classic period, 461; Late Preclassic period, 332; marketplace exchange in, 477; Mayapán, 469; Middle Preclassic period, 331–32; Mirador-Calakmul Basin, 322, 324, 328, 331–32, 334; nonlocal influences on, 435; Nueve Cerros, 176, 181, 183; person-centric rulership and, 348; religious ideologies and, 334; Tzikul, 380; Yucatán, 375

Mopan-Macal Triangle Project, 394

Mopán River valley, 391, 392f, 397, 399–400

Morai Complex ceramics, 163

Moral-Reforma, 350

Morley, Sylvanus, 150

Moro Cream ceramics, 350

Morris, Earl H., 104–5

Mortuary offerings, 260, 270, 274

Moschata squash (*Cucurbita moschata*), 232, 234, 499

Motaguá jade, 348–49

Motaguá Valley, 129, 348, 357

Motul de San José: chert production in, 121;

literate artists in, 278; marketplace exchange in, 390; rulers in, 293; tally scenes on vessels in, 276, 278, 290–91, 291f, 294–95; Yaxchilán and, 435

Munro-Stasiuk, Mandy J., 214

Naachtún: Bat Head (Suutz) polity in, 356, 359; ceramic imports in, 364; Early Classic period, 359, 425–27; El Chayal obsidian in, 363; elite exchange networks in, 359–60; green obsidian and, 359; Kaan polity in, 362, 366; lithic debitage in, 425–26, 426t, 427, 430; Maax complex in, 362; polyadic exchange in, 365; population growth in, 337; ritual debitage deposits and, 430

Naah Uti' K'ab, 391

Nabanché pottery, 378

Nakbé: *bajo* systems in, 322, 324; causeway systems in, 327–29, 332; ceramic exchange in, 334; civic-ceremonial centers at, 356; collapse of, 336; food exchange and, 34; jade imports to, 331; marine shell in, 357; obsidian consumption in, 330, 357; Preceramic occupation at, 325; trade routes and, 358, 365–66

Namon Cupul, 221

Nance (*Byrsonima crassifolia*), 233, 505

Naranjo (Guatemala), 123, 143, 279, 391

Nigra de San Martín, Santiago, 371

Nim Li Punit (Belize), 348

Nixtamalization, 102, 115n4

Nixtún-Ch'ich', 7, 437–38, 441

Nohmul, 25

Norman, William M., 286

Northeast Group, 197

Nueve Cerros. *See* Salinas de los Nueve Cerros

Obsidian: Budsilhá workshop, 409–10, 410f, 411–12, 415; Calakmul trade in, 361–62; Cancuén trade in, 9, 34, 51; Caracol consumption of, 140; Chunchucmil consumption of, 6, 57–58, 59t, 60–61, 70–78; craft specialization correlation, 73–74; debitage and, 424; distance to market correlation, 73; distribution of, 129; Early Classic period, 359; El Chayal, 61, 76, 90, 330, 357, 359, 362–63, 398–99, 409, 411; elite oversight of, 412; gift-giving and, 362; green Central Mexican, 359, 362, 365, 367, 381; Guatemalan trade routes for, 357; Ixtepeque, 398–99; Late Classic period, 359, 399; Late Preclassic period, 330–31; marketplace blade production, 397–99; Maya lowlands trade in,

Obsidian—*continued*

118, 357, 359, 364; prismatic blade production, 409–11, 430; rural households and, 88–89, 89*t*, 90, 95*t*; San Martín Jilotepeque, 398–99, 409; sources of, 61, 75–76, 90; Terminal Classic period, 363; Tikal consumption of, 6, 57, 60–61, 70–75, 77–78; trade partnerships and, 76; trade routes and, 357; transportation and, 454; urban households and, 89*t*; wealth correlation, 71–72, 74, 76–77, 89–90

Ochoa, Lorenzo, 358

Oka, R., 27

Okoshi Harada, Tsubasa, 318, 337, 339

Old Assyrian trade, 452, 456–59, 462

Overhang mano and metates, 177–78, 178*f*

Oxkintok, 378

Oxpemul, 366

Pacbitún (Belize), 329

Pachira aquatica. See Provision tree

Pachuca (Mexico), 359, 365, 411

Pachyrhizus erosus. See Jícama

Pacific tusk shell (Scaphopoda), 329

Padilla, Ana María, 376

Palaces: accounting practices, 279, 291; Cancuén, 50; elite consumption and, 110; El Perú–Waka' (Guatemala), 158–59, 164, 166–67; patronage and, 111–12, 114; redistribution of goods and, 456; stoneworking and, 103, 108; as storehouses, 112, 413

Palenque, 300, 415–16, 435

Palm (*Chamaedorea tepejilote*), 203*t*, 233, 494

Papaya (*Carica papaya*), 203*t*, 233, 498

Paradigm shifts, 3–4

Parry, William J., 424

Pasión River Valley, 33–34, 61, 357, 361–62, 435

Pasión-Usumacinta trade route, 173, 357, 360, 362

Paso Holuntún, 374, 377

Patronage, 108–14

Peach palm (*Bactris gasipaes*), 234, 494

Pearsall, Deborah M., 220

Pendergast, David M., 348

Peniche, Nancy, 376

Pepo squash (*Cucurbita pepo*), 232, 234, 499

Peraza Lope, Carlos, 81, 416, 479

Pérez, Andrés Aznar, 371

Petén (Guatemala): causeway systems in, 328, 339; chert distribution in, 118, 121–22, 124, 128; chert production in, 120, 122–24; community networks in, 38, 51; cotton textile exchange and, 349; environmental diversity in, 33; lithic economies in, 130; obsidian trade and, 130; salt trade and, 378; trade and, 50, 347, 380; transportation routes and, 144. *See also* La Corona

Petenes de Xlabarco, 374, 377, 380–81

Petén Gloss ware, 441

Petén Lakes region: Achotes Negro ceramics, 438; Carmelita Incised ceramics, 438; ceramic production in, 436; ceramic system in, 448–49; demographics of, 434–35; Late Classic period, 438, 448; location of, 434; in-migration to, 448–49; political/economic interactions in, 435–36; Tayasal-Paxcamá region, 436; Terminal Classic period, 434–38, 448; trade and, 435; Tres Naciones Fine Gray ceramics, 437–38. *See also* Jato Black-on-Gray ware

Petexbatún Kingdom, 45*f*, 173, 190, 193, 435

Petkanché Orange ceramics, 350

Physalis pubescens. See Tomatillo

Physic nut (*Jatropha curcas*), 232, 233, 501

Piedras Negras: agricultural core of, 408*f*; bone tool production, 413–14; ceramic assemblages at, 414–16; chert production in, 412–13; Classic period, 337, 403; Early Classic period, 406, 416–17; hematite production, 413; jade adornments and, 412; Late Classic period, 406, 409, 411, 413–14, 416–17, 435; lithic production in, 409, 424; maize and, 407–9, 416–17; map of, 404*f*, 406*f*; marketplace exchange in, 12, 403–8, 408*f*, 414–17; monkey motif on ceramics in, 440; obsidian consumption in, 409, 411–12, 416; polities in, 350; royal patronage of sculptors in, 109; settlement in, 406; tallies and, 288*f*, 289; Terminal Classic period, 413

Pillsbury, Joanne, 486–87

Piña Chan, Román, 466

Piperno, Dolores R., 220

Pitahaya (*Hylocereus undatus*), 204*t*, 234, 497

Plants (as food): archaeological identification of, 227–29; beans and, 224–25, 231–32; biases in archaeological recovery of, 228, 235; biases in pollen data interpretation, 228, 235–36; botanical diversity in, 466; cacao beans and, 232; chilis and, 233, 252; as commodities, 231–33; cultivation methods for, 224–27, 236; destruction of orchards and, 226; diversity in, 231; domesticated species of, 233–34; drought adaptations of, 236; economic significance

Tzaquib Unslipped salt molds, 174, 181
Tzeme, 378, 380, 384
Tzikul, 374, 377, 378, 379*f*, 380
Tzotzil Maya, 280
Tzuc Pool: artifact distribution in, 94; chert/chalcedony in, 92, 95*t*; marine shell in, 90, 95*t*; obsidian density in, 95*t*; pottery in, 92, 95*t*; Terminal period dwellings in, 84, 85*f*, 87, 89*t*

Uaxactún, 336, 438, 440–41
Ucareo (Mexico), 411
Uci, 378
United States National Plant Germplasm System, 230
University of Pennsylvania Tikal project, 60
Upper Belize River valley (UBRV), 123–26, 392*f*
Urban households: affluence in, 80, 90; artifact distribution in, 135; chert/chalcedony in, 91–92; dependence on rural provisioning, 81; marine shell in, 90; obsidian density in, 88–89, 89*t*, 90; pottery in, 93; surplus crafting in, 80, 82, 97; wealth disparities in, 97
Urbanism, 133
Urrutia, Juan de, 211
Usulután ceramics, 357
Usumacinta region, 12–13, 416, 435
Usumacinta River, 347, 349–50, 357, 435–36
Utilitarian goods, 296, 298
Uxul, 109, 337, 359–60, 362–64, 366

Valdez, Fred, Jr., 219
Valeri, Valerio, 98
Valley of Mexico, 347
Vance, J. E., 328
Vanilla (*Vanilla planifolia*), 34, 172, 234, 509
Vargas Pacheco, Ernesto, 358
Vega C., Juan Ramón, 371
Velásquez García, Erik, 292
Vella, Clive, 409
Venezia, 376
Veracruz, 345, 347, 350, 372, 378
Victor, Bart, 4
Volta, Beniamino, 7, 480, 483

Wakná, 332, 336, 356
Walker, Debra S., 7, 358
Warburton, David, 98, 110–11, 113
Waxaklajuun Ubah K'awiil, 10, 265
Wealth: architecture and, 72; artifact distribution and, 41, 88; Cancuén and, 48, 51; Chunchucmil households and, 62; craft special-

ization and, 74; fancy pottery as indication of, 72; household goods diversity and, 72; imported goods and, 331; market economy and, 35; obsidian consumption and, 71–72, 74, 76–77, 89–90; Puuc region, 110; rulership strategies and, 114; rural households and, 94; through tributes, 110–11; urban households and, 80, 90
Weber, Max, 455–56
Weiner, Annette B., 114
Westfall, Erin, 376
Wilk, Richard R., 187, 208–9
Wilken, Gene C., 227
Willey, Gordon R., 169
Women, 21, 190
Woodfill, Brent K. S., 9, 360
Workshops: bifacial tool production and, 124, 399–400, 425, 428–30; elite polychrome ceramic, 164, 167, 171, 278–79; hematite production, 413; jade preforms and, 362; lack of Mayan, 418–20; lithic production in, 11, 91–92, 94, 397, 399, 409, 410*f*, 412–13, 415, 431; marine shell in, 90, 329; pottery in, 88, 153, 155, 470; prismatic blade production, 425, 430; reuse of debitage and, 420, 425, 430–33; ritualization and, 431; salt production and, 174, 176–78, 181; stoneworking in, 101, 104; surplus production and, 419; tributes and, 431–32
Wright, Frank Lloyd, 11
Wright, Lori, 6
Wyatt, Andrew, 12

Xanthosoma. See Malanga
Xcambó: abandonment of, 376, 381; archaeological exploration of, 374; ceramics and, 372, 375; growth of, 380; location of, 374; long-distance trade in, 375, 377, 380; monumental architecture and, 375; occupation at, 375; port in, 378, 380–81, 382*f*; Postclassic shrines in, 376, 383; *sacbes* and, 375; salt production at, 375–76, 378
Xkipché, 106, 107*t*
Xkopté, 371, 374, 377, 381, 382*f*
Xochicalco, 5, 40, 471
Xolalpan phase, 380
Xtampú, 375–76, 384
Xtul, 376
Xuenkal (Yucatán), 214
Xulnal, 332, 336, 356
Xunantunich, 123–24, 190, 209, 390, 399

Maya Studies

EDITED BY DIANE Z. CHASE AND ARLEN F. CHASE